CH01067187

Small Press
Yearbook 1993

compiled and published by the

Small Press Group
of Britain Ltd

Published in Great Britain by
THE SMALL PRESS GROUP OF BRITAIN LIMITED
© The Small Press Group of Britain Limited 1992
ISBN: 0 9513630 6 9
Printed in Great Britain by The Book Factory, 35/37
Queensland Road, London N7 7AH

Trade Distribution by Turnaround Distribution, 27 Horsell Road, London N5 1XL.

Cover design by Ed Baxter. Cover photograph of the 1992 Small Press Fair by Mike Dash. Book design by Boggis and Baxter.

Contents

Part 1

Part 2

Part 3

An Introduction to this Yearbook

Welcome to the 1993 **Small Press Group of Britain**'s *Yearbook*, the essential guide and directory for small, independent publishers.

This fifth edition of the *Yearbook* reinforces our claim that Small Presses are booming. More and more people realise the value of their home word processors. It isn't necessary to have a DTP machine - the different sytems are learning to talk to each other ("interface"). making computers easy to understand ("user-friendly"). People seek information on how to do it, to get into print for themselves. We predicted a boom in bedsit publishers because the equipment was in the home. Next, they would emerge, hungry for information on how to sell!

The **SPG** with around 300 members and its contacts provides that starting point.

In this edition the *Directory* has double the number of entries - which means twice the number of pages! We are therefore not including last year's selection of essays on Small Press topics, instead **Part Two** is made up entirely of over 4,000 listings of Small Presses which have been inputted into the *Small Press Group of Britain*'s database during the last twelve months.

Part Three - the legendary *Rudimentary Guide To Doing It Yourself*, has been revised and updated for this year's edition. The Guide's co-ordinator, Dr Abel Snoddy, will be presenting short courses at the newly-opened **Small Press Centre** so you will soon be able to benefit from his knowledge and experience *in the flesh*!

Part One is, as usual, a mixture of general information and features. (Suggestions and contributions for future editions are always welcome.) Mike Kidson speaks for many aspects of small presses when he describes the position of small press comics; Clare Baker shares her expertise with advice on selling your product.

Once more, we believe the *Yearbook* lives up to its reputation as the 'writer's and artist's handbook' for the small press world. And this 1993 edition has more listings, more information, more advice and is bigger and better than ever before.

1

At the end of July 1992 a half page column about the DTP phenomenon appeared in *The Financial Times*. It gave the **Small Press Group** as the referral. The *FT* is hardly the obvious place to find bedsit publishers, but the story brought more than 250 enquiries to the **SPG** in two weeks!

This abstract community, or network, is growing. From January 1988, when the **SPG** was formed, to around 300 members by Autumn 1992 - shows the need. The *Yearbook*'s directory grew from 200 listings to 2,000 between 1988 and 1991. This year these have doubled to 4,000.

But the biggest leap is the physical meeting place for this enormous amount of activity: the new **Small Press Centre**.

For three years the **SPG**'s membership has put it alongside the other two organisations catering for independent publishing, the *Independent Publishers Guild* and *Association of Little Presses*. While there is a tiny overlap between groups, it is safe to say that together we speak for 900 independent publishers. What has been remarkable about the **SPG** has been the rate of growth. In less than 5 years it has created the **Small Press Centre** to take its place alongside the other **SPG** institutions: the *Yearbook* and the *Annual Small Press Fair*.

The **Small Press Centre** will take the phenomenon onto a new level. It will grow with the phenomenon of Small Presses. It will be a mutual exploration. The adventure now moves into new areas.

It has been exciting and rewarding to serve as Chair of the **SPG** during this period of expansion and innovation.

Cecilia Boggis

Chair, the Small Press Group of Britain Ltd.

The Birth of the Small Press Centre

The **Small Press Centre** at Middlesex University is more than an office and base - it is an organising agency and focal point for a range of activities.

The Centre's Director, John Nicholson, was the founding Chairman of the **Small Press Group** of Britain and is still active in the group.

The **Centre** will concentrate on establishing itself and getting known, both in the university and the local community. A publicity campaign will spread the word not only to the Small Press world and other countries but also to the general public and relevant specialist bodies.

Like the *Small Press Group* the **Centre** will be a clearing-house for information on all aspects of small press activity, not just in Britain but around the world. As the only **Small Press Centre** in Britain it will provide an international focal point, linking to other Small Press Centres, organisations and Archives.

The **Small Press Centre** can offer Small Presses a wide range of activities at all levels: short courses, meetings, exhibitions, launch parties, workshops, demonstrations, press receptions, Small Press showcases, specials and seminars, events, readings, performances, conferences...

With the University's assistance the **Small Press Centre** offers access to the University's Print Room which will give free estimates for printing. Also the Centre is actively seeking 'placements' for students to gain work experience with Small Presses.

Do visit and make use of the Centre. Our prospectus is now available - ask to be placed on our mailing list.

The Small Press Centre is at Room T202, All Saints Site, Middlesex University, White Hart Lane, London N17 8 HR. Telephone: 081 362 5000 Ext. 6058.

Exhibitions

The **Small Press Centre** will host exhibitions and arrange exhibitions. It will also be a focus for touring exhibitions as well as sending its own exhibitions on tour. In conjunction with overseas **Small Press Centres** the Small Press centre at Middlesex University will host and supply exhibitions internationally.

The **Small Press Centre** is actively seeking Small Press related exhibitons. These can by by subject, format or genre. The **Small Press Centre** of New York has toured exhibitions on the themes of Small Presses and cookery, children, green issues. The SPG hosted an exhibition from the Archive of Eeklo, Belgium: "Fanzine as Art Object." It will invite other Small Press archives (such as the archive of football 'zines at Manchester Poly and the archive at University College, London, to bring exhibitions to the **Small Press Centre**.

We are already in discussion with a wide range of Small Press genres from artists books and fine presses to small press comics and art networkers. An exhibition of comics art held in March is being revived, relevant exhibitions at the Poetry Library and the new National Museum of Cartoons are being invited to transfer to the **Small Press Centre** at Middlesex University.

Events

The **Small Press Centre** fills a gap long experienced by Small Presses: where to hold meetings, discussions, readings, performances and launch parties. The **Small Press Centre** can provide premises for events of all sizes from regular intimate poetry readings to international conferences!

All these activities can be part of multiple events. For example a Press may wish to hold a showcase exhibition and have a launch party. It could also give a reading, a performance or hold a press reception. An entire programme can be compiled with the expertise and experience of the **Small Press Centre**'s staff.

The associations of so many events with the Centre will in turn have cross-fertilising effect as the Centre builds up its audience of regulars and media contacts.

Printing

The Small Press Centre cannot print but Middlesex University has its own Print Room. This provides a comprehensive service at competitive rates.

The Centre is in touch with the Print Room so we can refer you. Please contact us to discuss your requirements and for a free estimate.

How to get there

RAIL

British Rail from Liverpool Street station. There are three services to White Hart Lane station. This means there is a train approximately every 10 minutes. The journey averages 15 minutes. The station is in All Saints Road. Turn left and follow the road round. Five minutes walk brings you to the University's gate and gatehouse. NB Travelcards are valid on these trains.

CAR

All Saints Road is a turning off the A10. Two minutes drive along the road brings you to the gate of the campus. Please note that All Saints Road loops round to pass the campus. The site is sign posted. There is parking inside the site or in the road outside the gate.

Tube: Wood Green (Piccadilly Line), then W3 bus.
Rail: White Hart Lane BR, then 5 minutes walk.
Bus: To White Hart Lane: W3; along Tottenham High Road:
149, 259, 279, 279a; along Great Cambridge Road: 144, 144a, 217, 231.

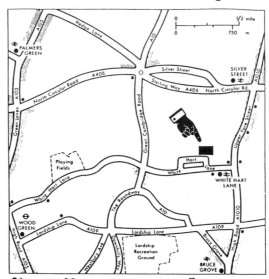

Sell – Sell – Sell
Read all about it!

As one of the minority of *Women in Publishing* members who work in sales I am often asked by women publishing maybe their first feminist title, how to go about selling and distributing books in this country. Having always worked for very large publishers (Routledge and Cambridge University Press), who have their own sales forces and substantial promotion backup, I have a very partial view of the book trade. But the system of selling books in the UK is the same for large and small publishers and often the small publisher can use that system to make up for her lack of cash for full colour ads in the Sunday Times.

My first piece of advice is to go into a bookshop and have a really good look round! Have a look at books on similar subjects to yours, their format, price, publisher etc and then ask the bookseller where they obtained the book - direct from the publisher; through a wholesaler; via a freelance rep?

Booksellers are very busy people and they don't always have time to answer questions, but they have a vested interest in getting good books onto their shelves and they are the most underutilised resource available for learning how to market books. If you want to sell the book in to bookshops yourself, it is these people you must convince to buy it before your eager feminist audience ever gets to see the book. If you decide to get someone else to sell and distribute on your behalf, a good bookseller will know who specialises in distributing books like yours, who delivers on time, comes round regularly and whom they trust to sell them saleable books. That is the distributor you must get to sell your book!

I would certainly recommend a good distribution agency as the best way to sell books through bookshops in the UK; the days when you could wander into a high street shop and get them to take a few copies of a single title are gone. This is mainly because the big bookshop chains - WH Smith, (who own Waterstones), Dillons,

(who own Hatchards and Claude Gill) and the Blackwells Group;
dominate the market and increasingly operate centrally. Distributers
will already have accounts set up and selling arrangements in place
with all of these people, and if you choose a politically sympathetic
agent they will also have good relationships with the specialist
independent shops - feminist and radical bookshops.

Checkpoints

* Pricing and terms - remember that most bookshops will
demand at least 35% discount calculated on the final selling price.
The distributor is likely to require another 25%, which means you
will be left with 40% of the cover price to pay the author, yourself
and all production costs. And this 40% will not be paid until the
money has been received from the bookseller who will expect at least
30 days credit from delivery.

* Agree in advance with your agent who will pay for damaged
copies, what happens to returns (few bookshops buy books on 'firm
sale' but can return them if unsold from between around 6 -12
months after delivery and who will be responsible for bookseller bad
debts. Also agree on whether they have a monopoly on sales in a
particular area or if you will be free to sell at special exhibitions. Find
out when their sales conferences are held and whether you can attend
to tell the reps about your book. If you plan to go round the bookshops
after the book is published, it's best to let your agent know.

* Prepare an Advance Book Information sheet on each title, 4-
6 months before publication. This should list the contents, author/
contributers and who they are, page extent, price and ISBN (International Standard Book Number which you can obtain from
Whitakers). Include marketing details - adverts, relevant conferences, leaflets and author availability. Always ask your authors for
sales leads, for a non-fiction title, they will probably know a large
part of the possible audience. And it should have a contact name -
both the publisher and distributer. This will go out to the reps,library
suppliers, wholesalers and will form the basis of the press release.
Together with the jacket which should be ready at least 3 months
before publication, this will form the primary selling tool for your

book. Most decisions on whether to stock a particular title are made before anyone sees the finished copy.

Hopefully this should help to ensure that the next time you go into a bookshop you'll be able to see your book displayed and ready to be sold in huge quantities.

Clare Baker

Useful Addresses

Turnaround Distribution, 27 Horsell Road, London N5 1XL Tel 071 609 7836

Central Books, 99 Wallis Road, London E9 5LN Tel 081 986 2946

Silver Moon Women's Bookshop, 68 Charing Cross Rd, London WC2H OBB Tel 071 836 7906

Sisterwrite Bookshop, A Women's Co-operative Bookshop, 190 Upper Street, London N1 1RQ Tel 071 226 9782

DISTRIBUTORS OF SMALL PRESSES AND SMALL PUBLISHERS IN BRITAIN

A DISTRIBUTION London 071 558 7782

AIRLIFT London 071607 5792

AK 3 Balmoral Place, Stirling, Scotland FK8 2RD

ART DATA London NW10 081 961 3642

ASHGROVE PRESS, Bath 0225 425 539

BEBC (Bournemouth English Book Centre) Poole, Dorset 0202 715 555

BMS (Best Mailing Services Ltd) Epping 0378 824 343

BOOKSPEED Edinburgh 031 225 4950

BRAD (Book Representation & Distribution Ltd) Hadleigh, Essex 0702 552 912

CENTRAL BOOKS London E9 081 986 4854

COUNTER DISTRIBUTION London 071 274 9009

ELEMENT Dorset 0747 51339

GAZELLE BOOK SERVICES Lancaster 0524 68765 & 071 242 3298

NEWNAME, Marlow 0628 481 810

PASSWORD 23 New Mount, Street, Manchester M4 4DE

TURNAROUND London 071 609 7836/7

VINE HOUSE Sussex 0825 723 398

This list is not conclusive and it omits mail-order dealers such as Delectus (081 963 0979), Spacelink 115 Hollybush Lane, Hampton, Middlesex TW12 2QY, Specialist Knowledge Services (0373 451 777), Spectacular Diseases 838 London Rd, Peterborough PE2 9BS, or Zardoz (0373 865 371). Then there are reps such as Terry Fruin (081 886 4609), Unlimited Dream Company (071 482 0090).

Please tell us of anybody who should be included. Also any experiences.

What price the recession?

While the recession has forced mainstream publishers to sack staff and prune lists, the ranks of independent publishers have continued to grow.

At its inception in 1988, the SPG knew of some 50 small presses dotted around the country; the 1992 Yearbook lists over 2,000. The group's annual Small Press Fair, held in London each September, has grown from a group of 20 tables and 700 visitors to 130 and 3,500 visitors. Small Presses have plugged into the international network of independents that flourishes from New York to Mainz.

All human life is here - from news-stand titles such as **Fortean Times,** the journal of strange phenomena, to one-man or woman outfits too small even to support a dog. Yet many of these fanatical specialists dominate their chosen fields.

Take Mark Pawson, for example - author of Mark's Little Book About Kinder Eggs, the standard reference work for collectors of small plastic toys - or A K Ashe of Aard Press, Britain's only author of transvestite pulp detective thrillers. Others, less prominent, pester friends, neighbours and local bookshops. Last Ditch Press writes: "Tiny since 1978. I found an electric duplicator in a junk shop for £20. Out poured trash teen mags and postcards with poems. Familiar story of addiction."

Addiction, yes, but also originality and excellence by the lorryload. Small presses may not be in it for the money, but nothing else is amateur about the output of the majority of SPG members.

Onwards and upwards! The Small Press Group has yet to realise more than a tiny fraction of its potential. Next comes the Small Press Centre, where the output of a thousand demented wordprocessors can be stored, catalogued and marketed. A bigger, better annual fair. Stronger links with our colleagues overseas through SPINE, the recently-established Small Press Information Network Exchange. An improved **Small Press World**, the impressive quarterly magazine. And, who knows, a few more entries for the directory in the next yearbook too.

Help! - all this has become obsolete as I type! What differences will happen now there is a Small Press Centre?

Mike Dash

The Invisible Made Visible

When wanting to introduce a creative scene to readers who may know little, if anything, about it, where do you start? With history? It's impossible to trace the origins of small press comics in the pre-Twentieth century tradition of broadsides and chapbooks. The likes of *Nasty Tales, OZ* and Sixties "underground" publications are more recent ancestors. The current wave of comics self-publishing derived considerable impetus from the "punk" DIY ethos of the late Seventies. But while history may convey an impression of established tradition, it fails to address the really important questions Which are, why do ever-increasing numbers of British comics creators self-publish their work? And in what ways are small press comics different from mainstream comics?

Some of the answers to both questions are familiar ones. Freedom to produce what you want, when you want, to standards - of execution and production - which satisfy you; freedom from interference by editors whose capacity for creative input is too often hampered by having to satisfy commercial interests and schedules: these are advantages indubitably common to self-publishers everywhere. But small press comics perhaps constitute an unusual case, because many of them are produced not only through a desire to circumvent commercial pressures; they also afford a unique opportunity for creative experimentation with a traditionally limited medium.

In Britain and America, the majority of mass produced comics are turned out by production-line methods to meet strict weekly or monthly deadlines. Given such circumstances, it's hardly surprising that they are formulaic and repetitive; but the narrowness of their content and aspirations remains astonishing. British weeklies offer a range of adventure tales, sports stories and humorous, mildly iconoclastic, caricatures to male readers; to girls they offer "realistic" fables which are individually intriguing but dulled by constant recycling. They are intended exclusively for pre-teen readers; older readers turn to imported American comicbooks. There they encounter an even narrower vision, a combative mythos in which good and evil are placed in constant, violent opposition. Despite attempts at characterization and touches of "realism", comicbooks remain populated by masculinist ciphers, "heroes" whose heroism is defined by their use of physical force against "villains" from whom they are distinguishable only by virtue of their affiliation with law and order. What these genre productions lack, as a direct result of corporate ownership which effectively stifles any possibility of consistent, creative development, is humanity.

During the last decade, small press comics creators on both sides of the Atlantic have been working to broaden the scope of the medium. To be sure, there are many small pressers who emulate the mainstream genres and art styles in the hope of gaining eventual employment. But there are many who are not content to work within such exhaustively mined areas, who are using the creative freedom of self-publishing to develop and disseminate new ideas, to experiment with story-telling and drawing techniques, to examine motive and motivation rather than adventure and action. While major publishers stick to the tried and tested, self-publishers are excitedly discovering the myriad expressive possibilities of a largely unexplored medium.

In American and Canada, this spate of exploration has spawned a number of small publishing houses which print creator-owned and controlled comics and distribute them through specialist comics shops. In Britain a similar development met with failure, perhaps because of the absence of a national readership over junior school age. Whatever the reason, the result was a collapse of small press comics activity during the late Eighties.

However, activity and interest have picked up again in the last year or two. The Fast Fiction distribution service, established in 1981, has been superceded by ZUM!, a critical review and listings magazine which provides a focal point for exchange of information about activities and publications. Small press comics are being regularly reviewed in the mainstream trade magazines. Self-publishers are now taking tables at the Autumn Small Press Fairs, and updates on their activities appear in each issue of *Small Press World*.

Annual conventions and conferences are being established, and new methods of distribution are being discussed and planned.

Which is all to the good, not just of the creators involved, but because it is within the confines of small press activity that the creative future of this powerful communicative medium is being nurtured. In France, comics are regarded as "the ninth art"; if they are even to achieve a similar status in this country, it will be because of the work and mutual support of the small press community.

Mike Kidson

Sex and the single press
The Small Press Group and Women

Fact: the **Small Press Yearbook** lists more publishers of science fiction than it does women's presses. Also more poets, sexologists, local historians and black magicians than women in publishing.

Not because the *Small Press Group of Great Britain,* which represents several hundred of the country's most committed, eccentric and determinedly-enthusiastic publishers has failed in its research, nor (so far as we can tell) because women's presses have failed to make themselves known. The *'92 Yearbook*'s curt listing of a dozen oddly-assorted groups - from **Bristol Radical Lesbians** to the **Working Mothers Association** - simply obscures the frenetic activity of hundreds of women working for, or more often running, many of the two thousand independent presses listed alongside "Feminism/Women's Issues" in its directory.

Former **SPG** chair Roberta McKeown, for example, resigned the post at the turn of the year to devote more time to **Indelible Inc.,** the Yorkshire-based children's book publisher responsible for *Derek the Dust Particle* and many other fine works. Her successor, current chair Cecilia B**oggis, a long-time stalwart of Women In Publishing, is owner of Pythia Press,** which specialises in "reprints of rare writing by remarkable women".

Other names leap from the *Yearbook*'s pages: Clare Bolton of **Alembic,** the private press specialising in limited editions printed by traditional letterpress methods; Susan Howard, co-owner of a leading local history magazine; Narissa Brough of **Urgent Magazine,** whose rhyming couplets grace the poetry section of the directory.

Margaret Lord's **Black Swan Press,** or Frances McDowall's **Old Stile**, produce books far superior in quality to those of run-of-the-mill publishers such as Faber and Faber. And Miss Tuppy Owens, publisher of the *Sex Maniacs' Bible,* speaks for an entire sub-culture of fetishists, nymphomaniacs, doggers and other perverts.

Jan Roberts, wife of the great earth mysteries writer Anthony, helped him run **Zodiac Books** for years - and after his death took over the operation, reissued her husband's works and continues to run the company in his memory.

These women make the small press scene perhaps the most vibrant in British publishing.

Mike Dash

Will of the Wisp

"Fact, the 1992 directory lists more publishers of Science Fiction that Womens Presses" It depends what you mean by "womens presses". Certainly the *1993 Yearbook* Directory lists many small presses *run* by women.

Sylvia Hartmann Kent of **Doghouse** and Heather Haig of **AwRa** publish books about dogs. Mrs Jill Groves of **Northern Writers Advisory Services** is a stalwart of the directory and indispensable to hosts of small presses. Oddly women are strongly represented in Fine and Private Presses: Shirley Jones **Red Hen**, Penny Berry **Pullet** and Kate Duncan **Silent** while Jane Rolo **Bookworks, Denise Hawrysio,** Jane Colling **X-Press** and Natalie d'Arbeloff **NdA** are amongst the leaders in the Artists Book world. Poetry and literature has been championed for years by, inter alia, Brenda Walker **Forest Books,** Sarah Hopkin **Tears in the Fence,** Dinah Livingstone **Katabasis,** Ann Bagnall **Southover,** Pat Khan **Unibird** and **Nancy Wybrow** who organised a national convention of Presses and small presses. Suzanne Riley's **Quartos** magazine is the trade magazine for creative writers. Rosemary Pardoe **Ghosts and Scholars** is a mini-industry for ghost stories while Sabine McNeill **Turning Points** runs networker conferences. Josephine Bacon **Pholiota** provides a translation service. Margaret Timms **Brentham** has an enviable list of minor classics. **Joan Gale** publishes booklets on Nothumbria which become standard works as Cheryl Straffon's **Meyn Mamvro** is *the* magazine of Cornish antiquities. Christine Rhone is business manager and contributor to the **Cerealogist.** Ruth at **Mandrake** and Cathy at **TV International Repartee** are indispensable. The **Friendly Press** is run by Irish Quaker grandmother Anne Hodgkinson. Refusing to grow old and shut up are the sister of real life Just William, Margaret Disher whose **Outlaws** published her memories of her brother and aunt; Charlotte Clarke **Potpourri** became a publisher at 80 with her autobiographical anthology reaching back to Germany in the 1920's. Traditional women's subjects are treated in different ways by Gladys Archer **Warnes** with titles on nursing, cats and psychic experiences. Brenda Fuller **Cakebreads** has an historical study of nursing. Cookery from Sue Mellis **Food and Futures.** Fun can be had from Erika Smith **Girl Frenzy** a zine with comic strips or **Owl** which produces cartoon books for the services.

And that's far from comprehensive, check some more: Josephine Austin **First Time,** Wendy Ashby **Glosa**, Pat Earnshaw **Gorse,** Fern Flyn **Froglets**, Judi Benson **Foolscap, North and South, Feminist Arts News...**

There is an organisation *Women in Publishing* (WiP). How about *Women in Small Presses* (WISP)?

Cecilia Boggis

The Small Press Group of Britain Limited

Membership as of August 28th 1992

4 U

Aard Press

Danielle Agni

Aireings Publications

AK Press

The Alembic Press

All Saints Centre

Association of Little Presses (ALP)

A-Mail

Animals

Aporia Press

Assocation Lilim

Atma Enterprises

AUX

Avert

Ballinakella Press

Richard Alan Barnes Publications

Mr G P Bartlett

Barton House Publishing

Beihireyo Books

Bellerophon

Black Ace Enterprises

Black Sheep Press

Bookworks London Limited

Ms Anne Boyd

Mr Philip Boys

Bozo

Mr Martin Brazil

Brentham Press

The Brynmill Press

The Bunyan Press, Ampthill

Mr D J Burke

Cactus Graphic Design

The Cerealogist

Cervera Press

Challenge

Chapman

Circle Press

Common Ground

Consider

Mr Chris de Coulon Berthoud

Counter Productions

Creation Press

Critique

Dark Diamonds Publications

John Dawes Publications

Deerhurst Publications

Deprovent Publishers

Derby TV/TS Group

Destronic

Detonator

Mr Karl L Dunkerley

The Edgeley Press Limited

Editorial Matters

Education Now Publishing Co-operative

Ellenbank Press

Elliot Manley Associates

Empress

English Companions

Identification of English Pressed

Enram Press

Equinox Press

Feasible Products

Feltham Press

Feminist Art News

First Time Magazine

First Time Press

Fitzgerald Publishing

Flaunden Press

Mr Bill Fleming

Flying Sugar Press

Flyleaf Press

Fortean Times

Mr Anthony Peers Fothergill

Friendly Press

Mr K Fulcher

Mr Alan Fulton, City of Aberdeen

Gateway Books

G C S

Geiser Productions

GGA International Publishers

GK Books

Mr D Gobell

Gorse Publications

Gothic Garden Press

Robert Greene Publishing

Mr Colin A Hammond

Mr Neil A Harvey

Hauteville Press

Headpress

Heart Action

Heart of Albion Press

Heindesign Stempelspass

Heritage Press

Hermitage Publishing

Highland Printmakers Workshop

Ms Greta Hill

Mr H E Hill

Miss K J Holme

Mr J E Holmes

Ms K G Holroyd

Home Base Holidays

Homer, The Slut

Jonathan Horne Publications

Housmans

Mr P W Hunter

Image Direct

Indelible Inc

The Ingvi Press

Inkling

Innovative Publishing Co

Insight Publications

Interface

Iolo

Jac Publications

Jane Publishing

Janus Publishing Company

Jardine Press

Mr Anthony Jenkinson

Ms Sandra Johnstone

Joint Publications

Ms Yvonne Jones

18

Mr Sydney A Josephs

Juma

Ms Flora Kerrigan

Mr Peter A Kerr

Simon King Press

Kittiwake

Knust

Krax Magazine

The Lamp Publishing House

R J Leach & Co

Dr Clive Leatherdale

Mr Bruce Lindsay

Liver & Lights

Living Archive Publishing

Local History Press

London Cartoon Centre

Mr Arthur Luke

The Lymes Press

Mandrake

Marine Day Publishers

Mast Publications

Maypole

Mr Patrick McEvoy

The McGuffin Press

Meanwhile...

Mr Edmund Mercer

Mr Par Middleton

Millers Dale Publications

Minx Prints

Montag Publications

John Morin Graphics

Morning Star Publications

Mortain Books Limited

Mulberry Press

Nan Elmoth Publications

Natural Friends Update

NdA Press

New Arcadian Press

New Departures

New Hope International

New Name Distribution

New River Project

No Rent Publicatons

North and South

Northern Writers Advisory Services

NPR Publications

Off Pink Publishing

Old Ferry Press

Old Stile Press

The Oleander Press

O'Media

Mr Chris Orr

Oscars Press

Otherwise Press

Outlaws Publishing Company

Owl Press

Owlet Books

Palliser Press

Paper Safe

Partizan Press

Passport Magazine

Mark Pawson

Pericles Publications

Personal Rights Association

Peyrere Indent

Phaedra Books

Phoenix Press

Pholiota Press Limited

Pickpockets

Pintsize Press

Polygon Explorer Guides

Portia Publishing

Power Publications

Powercut

Praxis Books

Previous Parrot Press

Providence Press

Psychopoetica Publications

The Putney Press

Mr Ian Pyper

Pythia Press

QED Books

In Type Book Reproduction

The Quarter-Day Press

Quartos Magazine

The Quilliam Press

Mrs J S Rajab

Reality Studios

Reaper Books

Red Hen Press

Redstone Press

Redwords

Right Now Books

Ring o'Bells Publishing

Mr David Robinson

Romer Publications

Mr Don Rout

Ryder Publishing

Salmon Publications

Mr Chris Sanders

Mr Richard L Saunders

Seven Islands Press

Severnside Press

Mr John Sharland

Sherlock Publications

Silconas Publications

Silent Books

Ms Janice Simons

Simple Logic

Ms Jane A Skerrett

Mr Slim Smith

Snake River Press

Sorcerer's Apprentice

South Yorkshire Writers

Spacelink Books

Specialist Knowledge Services

Spel Publications

Spiral Ascent

Steppenmole

Ms Janet Stevenson

Stop Messin About!

Sunk Island Review

Sun Tavern Fields

Svecia Antiqua Limited

Swan Books & Educational Services

Tak Tak Tak

Taprobane Limited

Temple Press

The Press

Thresholdworks

Ti Parks Artists Books

Tradition

Mr Anthony Mann

The Tufnell Press

Turning Points

Tyrannosaurus Rex Press

UK Consultancy Services Limited

Ultima Thule Limited

Ungawa

Unlimited Dream Company

Variant

Vennel Press

Mr Martin Wagner

Weavers Press Publishing

Wellsweep Press

Mrs Jane White

Wild Caret Press

Wild Swan Publishing Ltd

Mr T W Wilkin

Mr Alisdair Willis

Witan Books

Ms Maria J Wood

The Word Factory

Words Magazine

Dr R L Worrall

X-Press

Zeon Publications

Zodiac House

Why do we bother?
An introduction and tips for the
1993 directory

"I suspect the Yearbook was ill-considered and not thoroughly pre-pared which was proved when I saw it at the Fair and my entry bore no resemblance to the one I submitted or previous years. Not only was my home address supplied rather than my postal address BUT it was incorrect. How can I trust the rest of the Yearbook?"

In fact a disproportionate amount of discussion was spent on the '92 *Yearbook*. (It had an entire meeting in April and dominated another in May. One in June went astray through error. It had three other subsequent meetings.) The 92 edition was a turning point as the team which made the previous three gave notice they would not continue, so it was re-thought from top to bottom. There was even much discussion of changing its date, i.e. not launching it at the Annual Small Press Fair. (Sales of 120 copies at the Fair proved the wisdom of retaining this free launch party. Also, we were able to get the printer to deliver and distributors to collect copies from the Fair - so saving large delivery costs.)

Your entry? In fact *no* entry was supplied by you. Hence an abbreviated version of your previous entry was done - out of the goodness of my heart. As to wrong address - it was taken from your letterhead.

Can you trust the rest of the *Yearbook*? Absolutely not. Never could. What a silly remark. The introduction warned you shouldn't rely on *anything*. You aren't buying *The Bible*. Nor *Whittakers*. Nor the *A-to-Z of London* (who's first compiler lost all the "Ts" when they blew out of her window onto the top of a double-decker bus), but a hit-and-miss epic by a few loonies. I know I speak for them when I say how we spend ludicrous amounts of time on the work so we really have no patience. Do you think we include wrong details for fun?

"I had a listing ... which was totally unsatisfactory and (along with other listings) almost unreadable (type too small, poor design, minimal information)."

What would be satisfactory? The 92 edition was a breakthrough. It contained four times as many listings and about 200 more profiles. The choice was simple. Either we exclude 75%, we make the book three times as big, or we rethink and redesign. We solved it three ways. We omitted the Index. We kept every listing but limited their entry to 40 words description and three main titles. We made the type smaller. In other words, we turned it into a Directory, not a vague review section.

These changes laid a foundation for growth - which is lucky because in this year's edition we have doubled the entries! From 2,000 to 4,000! (We have had to sacrifice other features to squeeze them in! We believe the directory is the most valuable asset for all Small Presses.) And we know there are hundreds, no thousands, more out there! How to cope with all this info? The other huge innovation for the 92 edition was the introduction of a database. This is why we can bring you an extra 2,000 in one year. Naturally, the usual provisos apply. It will contain junk. There is no way the *Small Press Group* can guarantee anything. Besides, part of the fun is finding out. Have you no curiosity? Plus, we don't incorporate other directories, so this is not comprehensive. We do take out when requested (less than six), but more importantly we add the flavour when we are sent details.

We believe it **is** possible to get a flavour from 40 words and three titles. Quite simply, this Directory is NOT a catalogue. Nor is it a shop. The connection must be between the Press and the punter. That is where catalogues come in. You must understand some of these presses have over 100 titles so it would be silly to list all of them - we can't do their job for them and won't try with our resources to do a *Titles in Print*. For 4,000 imprints?? However, the Presses can get

21

more exposure by taking display advertisements. Our rates are silly they are so cheap - because they are designed to be affordable by tiny outfits. In this edition we have concentrated more on the presses than the Services.

Another lesson is noteworthy. The technical production of this Directory is an object lesson in what can be done. We began with a database of 2,000. Over the last year more has been added from all sources. Our Recruiting Secretary, Calum Selkirk, gutted weird 'zines. Eamar O'Keefe scoured everywhere are used her home computer. Her disk was then incorporated. So was *SPG* member Northern Writers Advisory Services's list and disk - another 1,000! Many were gleaned from Whittakers by checking their code for Small Publishers and Presses. Then there were the 250+ replies to our massive send out. The processing of replies was done by volunteers, as in previous years. The majority this work was done by a 14-year old girl. She struggled with idiosyncratic handwriting, spelling and bloody-mindedness. The *Small Press Group* and Small Presses in Britain and elsewhere owe a big 'thank you' to Wendy Groves, the daughter of Northern Writers Advisory Services.

Last minute entries were input by Andy Hopton who could ill afford the time, while Celia, who had less, dealt with the awkward squad. If you didn't make the deadline for this year's edition try harder next time. Besides there is an all-year-round free listings service in the 'Out Of The Woodwork' in *Small Press World*. This links up to the *SPG*'s database too.

The editing - i.e. cutting out duplicates, unsuitables and unlikelies and restoring omissions - was done in four hellish days by myself and then proof read by... It wasn't. There wasn't time. The final version was formatted by Cecilia Boggis and pasted up by Ed Baxter. Or it may be sent to the printer direct from the computer...

What of next year?

How To Use This Directory

If any private individuals who deny they publish have been included, we naturally apologise and ask them to tell us so that we delete their entries from our database.

A few non-British presses contacted us. It seemed churlish to refuse to include them. Obviously there will be a limit at some point to what we can include, but until then - welcome. They want to communicate, don't ignore them...

Foreign member of the *Small Press Group*, Betty Silconas, (see her advertisement) used the Yearbook. She got more of her poems published in Britain than America!

This *Directory* is meant to be used, so is your common sense. Don't do a mailing to all of them if you are promoting something specialist. (People happily turning out monographs on railways, walking sticks or stained glass really may not welcome invitations to subscribe to your red hot offering of sex and satanism. And vica versa.) Still - market forces... You could get a better, quicker result by shortlisting a dozen certainties and writing each a letter. (Letters - remember them? Handwritten? Not junk circulars. Personal. Not spewed out of a machine, but an individual human being.)

This edition of the directory is doubly remarkable. Why? Because there are double the number of names. That means you have to read it before you can use it.

A forgotten pleasure is revived by this *Directory*. Browsing. Like an old fashioned bookshop you can spend hours finding extraordinary treats and surprises.

As last year, we have included lots of names and addresses which give no idea of what they publish. (Or if they publish.) We must have been given their details for some reason. Ask them -it's part of the adventure. Have you no curiosity? Perhaps they will fill in a free entry next year. (Plenty who were only names and addresses last year have sent in their descriptions this time.)

I offer this selection as *A Boot Up the Arse of the Arrogant Culturists and Righteous Causists* who really behave as though Small Press means them.
ABCADO - academic history, geography, religion; ABLE - school text books; ACADEMY - history of cars; ACTIVITY DIGEST - adults working with kids; AGRICOLA TRAINING - stockbreeding; AIRE - guide to Leeds; ALAN BARNES - organs; APOSTLE - walking sticks; AVERT - Aids; ANN BABER - food and drink; BAROT BOOKS - barometers; BEECH PUBLISHING HOUSE - poetry; stockbreeding; pets; BERSWELL - royal year; fishing; Wessex.
And that's only the 'As' and the start of the 'Bs'! Off you go...

The principle of diversity is established. What about size? Do we reject *big* Small Publishers? Not unless it is silly. If they seriously think it sensible to masquerade as a Small Press they will be found out soon enough. Why bother?

Mistakes? We don't even have time to proof read, it is so frantic! (609 pages to check before the next session on the word-processor!) If *you* have the time, skill, inclination... Besides if you don't tell us how can we know it's wrong? We want it correct too.

What is the use of lists of names and addresses without any indication of what they do? As you can tell from the names, many of then *are* publishers. As far as we are concerned their details were referred to us for some reason. Next year we shall invite them to tell us about themselves. In the meantime you can ask them yourself.

Note down the names of others near you. Check them out with a pc or call. Do they offer any services? Can they share? Do they have full

24

details in the directory? Tell us! (Editing the 609 pages I found 5 in my town. I thought this was the deadest hole. Now we can check each other out.) As I check I spot at least three specialising in haiku. Do you all know each other? Or two having a go at British Telecom (Sherwood Forest, Topical).

This list is not all. It isn't comprehensive. It makes no claim to be authorative let alone reliable. But it is a start. It changes everything. It mobilises the inhabitants of a neglected continent. Who didn't even know there was anybody else!

Rather than chop out swathes (which takes time and choices) we put it all in. Choose for yourself.

Last year we dreamed it will all be different this year. It is and it isn't. It wasn't nearly as improved as we hoped. There is so much we could do, given the time, help and resources! The only consolation is that we can see that these will come before next year. The foundations laid last year are being built on and the results will really show next year because they will be combined with the new *Small Press Centre*. Instead of a last month panic we will be able to polish the Database continually. I am actually looking forward to the next *Yearbook*!

These thousands of entries are the answer to that bugbear *What is a Small Press?* Here they are. You decide.
Is it because they cover obscure subjects? Partly. Here be spiders, the weather, swimming pools, mines, ferries, meccano - apart from the predictable oddities: flying saucers and drag queens.

Are they identifiable by format? Partly. There are hosts of tiny magazines ('zines) or comix. But there are lavish beauties, starting price £500. Or absolutely 'straight' books.
Perhaps it comes down to motive? All these publications are special. They are labours of love. Somebody wanted to see them in print and took enormous trouble to realise that dream. So these people are practical. Hard headed even.

25

You won't find here the dross of 'proper' publishing which finishes up as Remainders. Small Press titles last. The definitive study about a school, a parish church, a local antiquity, buisness or industry ... all parts of our life which would otherwise vanish. Small Presses enrich us all.

Perhaps we may adapt Whitman to say *"Who touchs this book is touched"*.

John Nicholson

A & J PARTNERSHIP
Plum Tree Cottage
Royston Place
Barton-on-Sea
BH25 7AJ

A & L PUBLICATIONS
c/o 25 Poplar Road
Herne Hill
London
SE24 0BN.
Subjects: Poetry.

A & M PUBLISHERS
7 Flax Close
Helemshall
Rossendale
BB4 4JL

A-2 PUBLICATIONS
7 Hart Street
Edinburgh
EH1 3RN

AARD PRESS
D. Jarvis
31 Mounteral Gardens
London
SW16 2NL
Experimental and Visual concrete Poetry; Artists'
Bookworks; Mail-art documentation; Ephemera;
(artistamps badges cards); Zines. Handmade prod-
ucts in small print-runs: 'Jade'-thrillers and 'zines:
'PunKomik' (M-a)
'Eos'-- the Arts & Letters of Transkind (work by
eonists: TV/TSs and others).'I Jade Green' by A.K.
Ashe. 96pp 1990m 0 906307 05 8. 'Pulp'-thrillerwith
transvestite as heroine-narrator; set in London and
Brazil of the near future.
'Jade's Ladies' by A.K. Ashe. 96pp; 1990 0 906307
06 6 £5. 'Pulp'-thriller with transvestite as heroine-
narrator; set in London and Yorkshire of the near
future.
'Jade AntiJade' by A.K. Ashe. 96pp 1990 0 906307
07 4 £5. 'Pulp'-thriller with transvestite as heroine-
narrator: set in London Afghanistan and Siberia of
the near future.

AARDVARK PUBLISHING
11 Cobbins Way
Harlow
CM17 0LU

ABBEY BOOKS
P.O. Box 29
Uttoxeter
Staffordshire.
Subjects: Poetry.
Books July to December 1991 - 1

MS DENISE ABBOTT
3 King William Walk
Greenwich
LONDON
SE10 9KH

RICK ABBOT
58 South Street

Braunton
Devon
EX33 2AN.
Subjects: Travel. Books July to December 1991 - 1

ABCADO PUBLISHERS
Wayne Browne
20 St. Mary's Meadow Wingham
Canterbury
Kent
CT3 IDF. Tel 0227 722391
Book Publishers - of academic books on History
Geography Religion Art Poetry Medicine and Aus-
tralian History.
A History and Geography of English Religion by
Frank Hansford-Miller Volumes 1-8 100pp 20 figs
£22.95 pbk each net ISBN 1 873093 13 6 Poems of
Two Feminine Minds by Angela Beryl Clayton and
Phyllis Hansford-Miller. ISBN 1 873093 09 8 £7.95
pbk net.
A History of Medicine in Western Australia 1820-
1870 by Frank Hansford-Miller ISBN 1 86284 003
2 Volumes 1-6 £22.95 pbk each net.

ABC BOOKS
P.O. Box 189
Leigh-on-Sea
SS9 1NF.
Subjects: Occult.
Books July to December 1991 - 1 (reprint)

ABDL ALE
476 Cheetham Hill Road
MANCHESTER
M8 7JW 061 740 1758

ABERYSTWYTH ARTS CENTRE PUBLICA-
TIONS
University College of Wales
Penglas
Aberystwyth
SY23 3DE.
Subjects: Art.

ABLE CHILDREN (Pullen Publications)
9 Station Road
Knebworth
SG3 6AP.
Subjects: School Textbooks.
Books July to December 1991 - 1

MR JOHN ABRAHAMS
9 Hillway
WESTCLIFFE-ON-SEA
Essex
SS0 8QA

ABSOLUTE PRESS
14 Widcombe Crescent
Bath
BA2 6AH.
Subjects: Food and Drink. Plays. Books January to
June 1991 - 4 Books July to December 1991 - 7

ABSTRACT
1A Elm Row
London
NW3 1AA

ABYSS
34 Cottage Street
PO Box 69, Easthampton
MA 01027
United States of America

ACAB Press
BM 8884
LONDON
WC1N 3XX
Publisher of a series of anonymous accounts of the
Polltax riot of 31st March 1990 prsenting "the other
side of the story."

ACADEMY BOOKS
35 Pretoria Avenue
London
E17 7DR.
Subjects: Cars. Classic Cars. History of Cars. Welsh
History. Books January to June 1991 - 7 Books July
to December 1991 - 3

ACCENT EDUCATIONAL PUBLISHERS
17 Isbourne Way
Winchcombe
Cheltenham
GL54 5NS.
Subjects: School textbooks. Literature.
Books July to December 1991 - 4 original 123 new
editions.

ACCESS COMMITTEE FOR ENGLAND
35 Great Smith St
London
SW1P 3BJ

ACCORDIA RESEARCH CENTRE
Queen Mary and Westfield College
Mile End Road
London
E1 4NS

ACE OF RODS
BCM Akademia
LONDON
WC1N 3XX

MR ARCHIE ACHEAMPONG
University of Portsmouth
Milton Site, Locksway Road
SOUTHSEA
Hampshire
PO4 8JF

ACL COLOUR PRINT AND POLAR
Publishing (UK)
2 Uxbridge Road
Belgrave
Leicester
LE4 7ST.
Subjects: Sport.
Books January to June 1991 - 1 Books July to
December 1991 - 3

ACORN PUBLISHING
Spindlewood, Watery Lane

Lower Westholme, Pilton
SHEPTON MALLET
Somerset
BA4 4EL 057 284 200

ACORNTYPE
Acorn House
28 Honey Hill Road
Kingswood
BRISTOL
BS15 4HJ

ACTIVE DISTRIBUTION
B M Active
LONDON
WC1N 3XX

ACTIVITY DIGEST/PRINTFORCE
David Saint
Westmead House
123 Westmead Road
Sutton Surrey
SM1 45H. Tel 081 7701100
Activity Digest publishes books for adults working
with children particularly on games activities and
things to do.Printforce publishes books for adults
working with children particularly in youth group
and schools.
Really Wet Games by Dave Wood (printforce)
Wide Games and Incidenthines by David Saint
(Printforce)
Fun For All Seasons by Jean Barrow (Activity
Digest)

ACUMEN PUBLICATIONS
Patricia Oxley
6 The Mount, Higher Furzeham
Brixham
South Devon
TQ5 8QY. Tel 0803 851098
Press developed out of magazine; devoted to producing good poetry in an aesthetic setting. Each
fully illustrated book is printed on high-quality
paper with wrap-round cover. Acumen magazine
(bi-annual; £5.50pa) publishes best poem available
plus reviews articles and the Acumen Interview.
Patient reconstruction of Paradise (poems of South
Devon) William Oxley ISBN 1 873161 00 X pbk
1.8.91 £2.95
An Average Revenge - John Gurney - 1 873161 03
4 pbk 36pp 1.9.92 £4.95. Sonnets on past poets
Between Dark Dreams - Rupert Loydell - 1 873161
02 6 pbk 36pp 1.9.92 £4.95. Poems.

MR DENIS ADAMS
Flat 12, The Croft
Sutton Park Road
KIDDERMINSTER
Worcestershire
DY11 6LJ

GARY ADAMS
31a St Georges Road
Leyton
LONDON
E10

JOHN ADAMS

8730 Edmonston Road
BERWYN HEIGHTS
MD 20740
United States of America

ADARE PRESS
White Gables
Ballymoney Hill
Banbridge
BT32 4DR.
Subjects: Local History.
Books July to December 1991 - 2

ADCO Associates
Richard Adams
2 Blenheim Crescent
LONDON
W11 1NN 071 221 7680
Graphics stuido which grew out of Open Head
Press, commercial work undertaken.

ADDISCOMBE CRICKET CLUB
C Williams
113 Falconwood Road
Addlington
CR0 9BF

MR J R ADDISON
5 Merton Road
Highfield
WIGAN
WN3 6AQ

AD HOC PUBLICATIONS
PO Box 850
London
W14 8EW

A DISTRIBUTION
84b Whitechapel High Street
LONDON
E1 1EW
Distributor of small presses, especially anarchist.

MS NANCY ADLER
Garpg 5
S-724 62 VAESTERAES
SWEDEN

ADOLPHUS PUBLICATIONS
Sharnden Old Manor Farm
Mayfield
TN20 6QA.
Subjects: Children's Fiction.
Books July to December 1991 - 1

ADULT LITERARY AND BASIC SKILLS UNIT
Kingsbourne House
229-231 High Holborn
London
WC1V 7DA.
Subjects: Education. Mathematics. Books January
to June 1991 - 10 Books July to December 1991 -
4

ADZINE
Jane Ellicott

43 Brooksbank House
Retreat Place, Hackney
LONDON
E9
Quarterly listing of fanzines, conventions, fan clubs,
ads - sale or wanted.

AFTER THE BATTLE MAGAZINE
Church House
Church Street
London
E15 3JA

AFRICA BOOKS
3 Galena Road
London
W6 0LT.
Subjects: Biography. History of Africa. Books January to June 1991 - 3 Books July to December 1991
- 1 (new editn)

AFRICA ARTS COLLECTIVE
(Source books)
3 Myrtle Parade
Myrtle St
Liverpool
L7 7EL

AGE EXCHANGE
11 Blackheath Village
LONDON
SE3 9LA

AGE CONCERN GREATER LONDON
54 Knatchbull Road
London
SE5 9QY.
Subjects: Social Welfare.
Books July to December 1991 - 1

AGE EXCHANGE
11 Blackheath Village
London
SE3 9LA

ORIOL AGELL
St Francesc Xavier
5-D
08190 St Cugat del Valles
Spain

AGENDA
William Cookson
5 Cranbourne Court
Albert Bridge Road
LONDON
SW11 4PE
Four p.a. arts council support.

DANIELLE AGNI
384 Barks Drive
Norton
STOKE-ON-TRENT
ST6 8EU

AGOG
Mr Ed Jewansinski

116 Eswyn Road
LONDON
SW17 8TN
Poetry-based mag. Available on disc.

AGRICOLA TRAINING
Ryelands
Stouw
Lincoln
LN1 2DE.
Subjects: Stockbreeding.
Books January to June 1991 - 2

A S AHMAD
3 Ambleside Avenue
BRADFORD
West Yorkshire
BP9 5HX

AIM HIGH PRODUCTIONS
280 Liverpool Road
Eccles
Manchester
M30 0RZ

BEULAGH AINLEY
1 Vicarage Road
STRATFORD
E15 4HD

A I P E
Via Cernaia 3
I-10121 TORINO
ITALY

AIRE PRESS AND PUBLISHING
Roger Ratcliffe
Po Box HP 36
LEEDS
LS6 3RN. Tel 0532-789618
Former Sunday Times Northern Correspondent
Roger Ratcliffe publishes the only guides to Leeds
and Bradford praised for their design and described
by the Guardian as Encyclopedic free of advertis-
ing. Libraries/ Bookshops without stock titles on
these cities can order direct. Leeds Fax: The First-
Ever Handbook/Survival Guide to Leeds Roger
Ratcliffe. 192pp 23.5.89 ISBN 1 871774 00 4
£4.95.
The Bradford Book: The First-Ever Handbook/
Survival Guide to Bradford Roger Ratcliffe. 192pp
25.3.90 ISBN 1 871774 01 2 £4.95. Leeds Fax: The
Complete Handbook to Life in Leeds (totally new
edition) Roger Ratcliffe. 192pp 16.7.92 ISBN 1
871774 02 0 £4.99.

AIREINGS PUBLICATIONS
20 Lee Lane East
Horsforth
LEEDS
LS18 5RE

AIREINGS
Jean Barker
3/24 Brudenell Road
Leeds
LS6 IBW Tel 0532-785893
Poetry Magazine illustrated with live drawings. 40

pages. Some short reviews. Occasional Competitions. Twice yearly. Editorial deadlines 1st January
and 1st July. Sub 4.50 p.a. (£1.50 p+p) from above.
Submissions /Subs etc. to above address

AIRFIELD PUBLICATIONS
18 Ridge Way
Wargrave
Reading
RG10 8AS.
Subjects: Military Airfields.
Books July to December 1991 - 1

AIR RESEARCH PUBLICATIONS
34 Elm Road
New Malden
KT3 3HD.
Subjects: Second World War.
Books July to December 1991 - 1

AIRTIME PUBLISHING
13 The Hollows
Long Eaton
Nottingham
NG10 2ES.
Subjects: Railways.
Books July to December 1991 - 1

A.J.F. DESK TOP PUBLISHING:
Tudor Mint
Vulcan Road
Solihull
B91 2JY.
Subjects: Fiction General.
Books July to December 1991 - 1

AK PRESS
Ramsay Kanaan
3 Balmoral Place
Stirling
Scotland
FK8 2RD. Tel 031 667 1507
AK Press is the publishing wing of the ever-expand-
ing AK Empire. We publish everything from poetry
to parapolitics and most in between. Other active
service units include AK Distribution which
wholesales to the trade; and a massive mail order
catalogue of several thousand titles.
Sabotage In The American Workplace: Anecdotes
of Dissatisfaction Mischief and Revenge. edited by
Martin Sprouse and illustrated by Tracy Cox. 184pp
ISBN 1 873176 65 1 9.95. A series of interviews
with employees - from garbagemen to paralegals
soldiers to sex trade workers - on how they fuck up
their work.
Ecstatic Incisions: The Collages of Freddie Baer. By
Freddie Baer with a preface by Peter Lamborn
Wilson. 80pp 72 illustrations ISBN 1 873176 60 8
£7.95. The first anthology of the graphic art of this
prolific genius. Poll Tax Rebellion by Danny Burns.
ISBN 1 873176 50 3 208pp £4.95. The inside story
of the anti-poll tax movement from registration to
poll tax riots. Profusely illustrated with photographs and graphics from those heady days. Forthcoming books include new work by James Kelman
Noam Chomsky and a 'best of' the graphic artist
Winston Smith.

30

AKLO
50 St John Street
OXFORD
OX1 2LQ

AKROS PUBLICATIONS
18 Warrender Park Terrace
Edinburgh
EH9 1EF.
Subjects: Poetry.
Books July to December 1991 - 2

ALBA PUBLISHING
78 Weensland Road
Hawick
TD9 9NX.
Subjects: Family History.
Books January to June 1991. - 1

ALBION HOUSE
Parkend Walk
Coalway
Coleford
GL16 7JS

MR ROBERT ALBURY
47 Dalmeny Road
LONDON
N7 0DY

MR D G ALCOCK
18 Wray Common Road
REIGATE
Surrey
RH2 0RW

ALDA PUBLISHERS
3A Beaufort Close
Reigate
SY
Books January to June 1991 - 1

ALDEN PRESS
Mr T S Steptoe
Osney Mead
OXFORD
OX2 0EF

GEOFFREY ALDERMAN (self-publisher)
Department of History
Royal Holloway and Bedford New College
Egham Hill
TW20 0EX

G.L.D. ALDERSON
Canny Hill
Pool Lane
Brocton
Stafford
ST17 0TY.
Subjects: Military History.
Books January to June 1991 - 1

P ALDWORTH
79 Dalberg Road
Brixton
LONDON

SW2 1AL

ALECTO HISTORICAL EDITIONS
46 Kelso Place
London
W8 5QG.
Subjects: History of Art.
Books January to June 1991 - 1

THE ALEMBIC PRESS
Claire Bolton
139 Upper Road
Kennington
Oxford
OX1 5LR. Tel 0865 730381
A private press printing limited edition books by
traditional letterpress methods. Books bound by
hand-mainly at the press. also run letterpress work-
shops. Send for hand printed prospectus as current
titles.
A Winchester Book Shop & Bindery. C. Bolton.
80pp 1991 ISBN 0907482 45 5 £68.00.
Awa Gami. C. Bolton 60pp 1992 ISBN 0907482 52
X £63.00. Japanese handmade papers from Fuji
Mill Tokushima
Compton Marbling Port Folio of Patterns. C. Bol-
ton. 19 folios ISBN 0907482 49 X £54.00. Text 1
samples of compton marbling.

J ALEXANDER
Chapter
Market Road
CARDIFF
CF5 1QE

ALF SUPPORTERS GROUP
BCM 1160
London
WC1N 3XX
The ALF Supporters Group helps with the expenses
incurred when people are arrested fined and imprisoned for ALF activities; helping towards defend-
ant's expenses solicitors' fees fines and compensa-
tion orders and also towards animal rights prisoners
needs while imprisoned.
The SG Newsletter. Reports from Britain and around
the world on the welfare of those arrested on trial or
imprisoned for animal rescue or ALF-type activities such as criminal damage (within the ALF policy
of non-violence).

ALICE PUBLICATIONS
Richard Hull
2 Co-op Buildings, Pecket Well, Hebden Bridge,
West Yorkshire HX7 8QP
Dedicated to the memory of Radio Alice, Bologna
, Italy, 1974-77. One person business, part time
using Acorn Archimedes DTP facilities. I am at-
tempting to provide greater access to publishing
resources.
My New Glasses: Anthology of Poetry by Children
with Learning Difficulties. Milsom & Gadd (Editors). Now out of print.
In Praise of Wimps: A Social History of Computer
Programming - some work in progress. Forthcoming, October 1992.

ALICE IN WONDERLAND

31

Rikki Hollywood
62 Stanhope Road
Greenford
Middlesex
UB6 9EA. Tel. 081 578 7114
Alice in Wonderland comic - Hippy/Gothic version!! Double issue Pt 1+2 collectors (includes Postage + packing) payable to Rikki Hollywood. Alice in Wonderland. 48pp. Out now! £2.00 per copy

MR RAJIT ALI
31 Denmark Road
NOTHAMPTON
NN1 5QR

MR GORDON ALLAN
18 Carshalton Park Road
CARSHALTON
Surrey
SM5 3SS

KEITH ALLARDYCE
Ingledene
Wansbeck Road
Ashington
NE63 8JE.
Subjects: Photography.
Books July to December 1991 - 1

ALLARDYCE BARNETT PUBLISHERS
14 Mount Street
LEWES
East Sussex
BN7 1HL
Literature, Art and Music.
Veronica Forrest-Thompson Collected Poems and Translations. 2818pp Cloth 1990 28.00 ISBN 0 90795408 1 Poetry.
Stuff Smith (ed A Barnet & E Logager) 64pp, 8 photo's, checklist and recordings Index 1991 £6.95 ISBN 0 907954 15 4 Fair Music Biography. Anthony Barnet & Natalie Cohen Would You Tread on a Quadruped? An animal alphabet of Questionable Rhymes 60pp, 1992, £4.99 ISBN 0 907954 17 0. Childrens Poetry & Paintings in colour.

ALLBOROUGH PRESS
15A Vinery Road
Cambridge
CB1 3DN

ALLEN & TODD
9 Square Street
Ramsbottom
Bury
BL0 9BE

BENJAMIN ALLEN PUBLICATIONS
1 Carnhill Avenue
NEWTONABBEY
Co Antrim
BT36 6LE
Artists Books, postcards, badges, ephemera.

D C ALLEN
17 Rutland Avenue
Aylestone Road

LEICESTER
LE2 7QF

ALLENHOLME PRESS
10 Woodcroft Road
Wylam
NE41 8DJ.
Subjects: Bibliographies. Books January to June 1991 - 1. Books July to December 1991 - 1

ALLIED CONTINENTAL HOLDINGS
PO Box 129
Manchester
M60 1HN

ALLIED DUNBAR ASSURANCE
1st Floor, Clockhouse Court
5-7 London Road
ST ALBANS
Hertfordshire
AL1 1LA 0727 836511

ANNE ALLINSON
33 Cranemoor Avenue
Highcliffe
Christchurch
BH23 5AN.
Subjects: Poetry.
Books January to June 1991 - 1

ALMA PUBLISHERS
18 Evelyn Road
Ham
Richmond
TW10 7HU.
Subjects: History of Education.
Books July to December 1991 - 1

ALMERIA PRESS
127 High Street
Teddington
Middlesex

ALOES BOOKS
69 Lancaster Road
London
N4 4PL.
Subjects: Poetry.
Books January to June 1991 - 2

ALO-WA
c/o Southwark Women's Centre
2-8 Peckham High Street
London
SE15 5DY.
Subjects: Biography.
Books January to June 1991 - 1

ASSOCIATION OF LITTLE PRESSES (ALP)
89a Petherton Road
London
N5 2QT 071 226 2654
ALP was formed in 1966 to bring together and assist small presses of all types and persuasions. Subscription is £10.00; which brings the bi-monthly newsletter; three issues of Poetry and Little Press Information (PALPI) and the current catalogue.

Our 25th year.
'Catalogue of Little Press Books in Print'. £3.00.
ISBN 0 902478 20 6 'Poetry and Little Press
Information' (PALPI) thrice-yearly (£1.50 subscription £4.50) ISSN 0260 9339
'Publishing Yourself - Not Too Difficult After All'
by Peter Finch. £0.50 ISBN 0 902478 24 1

ALPHA BEAT PRESS
68 Winter Avenue
SCARBOROUGH
Ontario
CANADA M1K 4M3

ALPHA BEAT SOUP
Dave Christy
31 Waterloo Street, New Hope, PA 18938 USA
(215) 862 0299
Journal of Beat Generation and post-beat independent writings since 1987. Bi-annual, $15 subscription. Past contributors include Allen Ginsberg,
Jeann Conn, Carolyn Cassady and Clapton
Eschelman. Also Alpha Beat Press poetry books.
Flowers of Consciousness - Kaviraj George Dowden
Pip, Beat, Cool & Antic - John Montgomery
Mary Magdalen - Joy Walsh
Alphachart Ltd
6a High Street
Aldreth
ELY
Cambridgeshire
CB6 3PQ

ALPINE FINE ARTS COLLECTION (UK)
5 Grosvenor Cottages
Eaton Terrace
SW1

J ALSOP
Lawrences Close
High Street
Pavenham
MK43 7NU.

ALSRATH PUBLICATIONS
263 Station Road
Balsall Common
Coventry
CV7 7EG

ALTERNATIVE ARTS
49-51 Carnaby Street
London
W1V 1PF.
Subjects: Art.
Books July to December 1991 - 1

JOURNAL OF ALTERNATIVE &
COMPLEMENTARY MEDICINE
53A High Street
Bagshot
Surrey
GU19 5AH

MS ELAINE MCINTOSH
Alternative Tentacles
61-71 Collier Street
LONDON

N1 9BE

ALICK ALTMAN
118 Bilton Lane
Harrogate
HG1 3DG.
Subjects: General Fiction.
Books July to December 1991 - 1 new edition.

ALUN BOOKS:
Goldleaf Publishing
2nd Floor Royal Buildings
Port Talbot
West Glamorgan.
Subjects: Poetry.
Books July to December 1991 - 1

ALWYN PRESS
14 Alwyn Avenue
London
W4 4PB

ALZHEIMER'S DISEASE SOCIETY
158/160 Balham High Road
London
SW12 9BN.
Subjects: Social Welfare. Food and drink.
Books July to December 1991 - 3

A-MAIL
John Wraight
23 New High Street
Headington
OXFORD
OX3 7AJ 0865 741261
Providing academic mailing lists for publishers of
any size.

AMANUENSIS
12 Station Road
Didcot
OX11 7LL

AMAR PUBLICATIONS
31 Watling Street
Bury
BL8 2JD

THE AMATE PRESS
Robin Waterfield
St. John's Lodge
14A Magdalen Road
Oxford
OX4 1RW.
Tel 0865-722091
Founded in 1973 we have published over 60 volumes of biography poetry and religious with contributions by Iris Murdoch Graham Greene Anne
Ridler and AM Allchin & Bishop John Taylor
Aldwinckle
(Stella) Christ's Shadow in Plato's Cave foreword
by Iris Murdoch 1990 ISBN 0 947561 20 X £7.50.
Allchin (AM)ed Profitable Wonders Aspects of
Thomas Traherne 1989 £6.50 ISBN 0 94756117X.

AMAZING AMAZING AMAZING
BCM Amazing

London
WC1N 3XX
Amazing stuff from whatever comes off the top of my head when I do a multi -media thing. Any girls out there into multi-media: poetry kite-flying PsuChi (healing through gentle poking with a stick) film Cobbing nose picking with rice paper etc. 'Amazing Things: The Final Thingy'. Magazine published when we've got enough stuff and we can use the copier at the Poly. Send your stuff and things and let's interlock in a global networkthingy. Anyone want an Ian Curtiss autographed picture disc of Love will Tear us Apart ?

AMAZING COLOSSAL PRESS
18 Hind Street
Retford
DN22 7EN

AMAZON
Merton College
Oxford
OX1 4JD

AMBER VALLEY PRINT CENTRE
388 Boldmere Road
Sutton Coldfield
B73 5Ez

AMBIT
17 Priory Gardens
Highgate
LONDON
N6 5QY

REUTH AMBRE
7 York Terrace
Woodfield Grove
SALE
Cheshire
M33 1LW

AMCD PUBLISHERS LTD
PO Box 102
Purley
Surrey
CR8 3YX 081 668 4535
Chinese Japanese Russian - as well as French German & Spanish. More eclectically it publishes material on Croydon's history as well as that of Surrey.
English - Japanese Dictionary of Finance (1992).
'Lords of Croydon Palace 871-1780' by Yvonne Walker 100 pp 10 illust. £5.00
'Surrey Ghosts Olde & New' by Frances D. Stewart 10pp 10 illust £5.00

THE AMERICAN DOWSER
American Society of Dowsers
DANVILLE
Vermont 05828
United States of America

AMETHYST SUPPLIES
Unit 3
Avonmead House
40-48 Stokes Croft
BRISTOL

BS1 3DQ

TORR A'MHULLAICH BOOKS
5 Kirkton Muir
Bunchren
Inverness
IV3 6RH

AMMONITE BOOKS
58 Coopers Rise
Goldalming
GU7 2NJ.
Subjects: Health and Hygiene.
Books July to December 1991 - 1

AMOEBA PUBLICATIONS
Lakeside Manor Farm
Crowland Road
Eye Green
Peterborough
PE6 7TT.
Subjects: Education.
Books January to June 1991 - 1

AMPERSAND PRESS
Firedog Mothers
c/o #8
89 Lancaster Road
Ladbroke Grove
LONDON
W11 1QQ 071 792 0341
A visual arts magazine intended to embody the best of, respectively, artists books and poetry/literature magazines. A bi-yearly publication in limited edition, featuring artists prints and exploiting the particularity of experience anything that lies flat concidered, no poems about Woodpeckers! Multiples prefered.
Ampersand 1 (soft cover) August 1991, 40pp, A3 photocopy £2.50 (£2.00 concs) Poetry, prose, copy art. Edition of 100 (few left)
Ampersand 2 (stiff cover) May 1992. 24pp, A screenprint 5.00 (£3.00 concs) Poetry, prose, prosepoetry, mixed media, screen prints. Edition of 200 Ampersand 3. Oct 1992, ?pp, A3 Screenprint 5.00 (£3.00 concs)

AMPLEFORTH ABBEY TRUSTEES
Ampleforth Abbey
Ampleforth
York
YO6 4EN.
Subjects: Historical Biographies.
Books July to December 1991 - 1

AMRA IMPRINT
21 Alfred Street
SEAHAM
Co Durham
SR7 7LH
Amra Imprint is the successor to Bill's 'Pirate Press' of the 1970s. It publishes booklets on Anglo-Saxon culture, local history and some modern poetry.
A USER FRIENDLY DICTIONARY OF OLD ENGLISH edited by Bill Griffiths, 40pp B5, 1989 [0 905194 11 X] £2.80
THE PATRICK POEMS by Ian Davidson. 16pp, A5, 1991 [0 905194 18 7] £1.50 A SEAHAM

READER 5: THE MINES edited by Bill Griffiths, 48pp, A5, 1992 [0 905194 24 1] £1.50

Amskaya
25 Albert Road
Addlestone
WEYBRIDGE
Surrey
KT15 2PX

A.N. PUBLICATIONS
PO BOX 23
Sunderland
SR4 6DG.
Subjects: Economics for Artists. Law for artists. Organising Exhibitions. Books January to June 1991 - 2 Books July to December 1991 - 1 new edition

BULLETIN OF ANARCHIST RESEARCH
Department of Politics
University of Lancaaster
LANCASTER
LA1 4YF

ANARCHO PRESS
30 Greenhill
Hampstead High Street
LONDON
NW3
Aimed to extend consciousness to bring about a rational society. Method - publishing poetry etc.

A N C
P O Box 38
28 Penton Street
London
N1 9PR

ANDERSON FRASER PUBLISHING
230-232 Holloway Road
London
N7 8DA.
Subjects: Recycled Papers.
Books July to December 1991 - 7

J.D ANDERSON
29 The Fairway
Blaby
Leicester
LE8 3EN

MR P ANDERSON
26 Davits Drive
LITTLEHAMPTON
BN17 6RU

ANDIUM PRESS
Haut du Mont
La Haule
Jersey
Channel Islands

ANDRED PUBLISHING
Pennies
Church Lane
Sheering

Bishop's Stortford

MR DAN R ANDREW
16 Ravenswood Court
Hill View Road
WOKING
Surrey
GU22 7NR

CHRIS ANDREWS
1 North Hinksey Village
Oxford
OX2 ONA

CHRIS ANDREWS PHOTOGRAPHIC ART
1 North Hinksey Village
Oxford
OX2 0NA.
Subjects: Local Travel Guides.
Books July to December 1991 - 1

MISS SUZANNE ANDRISSON
Lawn Farm House
Mill Road, Mutford
BECCLES
Suffolk
NR34 7UP

AND WHAT OF TOMORROW
(edit Jay Woodman)
14 Hillfield
Selby
N Yorks
YO8 0ND
(also see Woodmans Press)

ANGEL ROW GALLERY
9 Angel Row
Nottingham.
Subjects: Art.

ANGLICA PRESS
18A lake Road
Hamworthy
Poole
BH15 4LH.
Subjects: Poetry.
Books July to December 1991 - 1

ANGLO-SAXON BOOKS
Tony and Pearl Linsell
25 Malpas Drive
Pinner
Middlesex
HA5 1DQ. Tel. 081-868 1564.
We specialise in Old English Texts and things Anglo-saxon from monastic sign language through Old English verse to runes. Future publications are planned on Anglo-Saxon Herbs and Anglo-Saxon Plants and Food. Catalogue available.
Monasteriales Indicia (The Anglo-Saxon Monastic Sign Language) edited by Debby Banham 90pp published 1991 ISBN 0-9516209-4-0 £6.95 paperback. The Battle of Maldon: Text and Translation. Anglo-Saxon text translated and edited by Bill Griffiths 90pp first published 1991 reprinted 1992 ISBN 0-9516209-0-8 £6.95 paperback.
Anglo-Saxon Runes written by Tony Linsell and

35

illustrated Brian Partridge 106pp Sept. 1992 ISBN 0-9516209-6-7 £14.95 hardback.

ANIMALS
Selborne Agencies Limited
25 Selborne Road
SIDCUP
Kent
DA14 4QP 081 302 1629
Publish bi-monthly colour conservation magazine reporting on captive breeding programmes, information on events at zoological gardens, reviewing activities of the Zoo world.

ANOMALOUS PHENOMENON REVIEW
Nottingham UFO Investigation Society
443 Meadow Lane
NOTTINGHAM
NG2 3LF

ANPAR BOOKS
11 South Park Gardens
Berkhamsted
HP4 1JA.
Subjects: Animals.
Books January to June 1991 - 1

AN POST
General Post Office
Dublin 1
Republic of Ireland.
Subjects: Stamps.

MARY ANTHONY
Deepdene
Amacre Drive
Plymouth
PL9 9RJ

ANTI ANTI INFORMATION NETWORK
37 Pamplins
Basildon
Essex
SS15 5RN
In the run up to Armageddon we will be concentrating on publishing experimental writing and poetry. We will be specifically trying to push the boundaries of the written word to its limits and beyond. We will use any means available to us in this quest. Mind Crash. Sheet double sided monthly testing ground for future long term projects typeset with computer graphs. Accidentally humorous too. Send s.a.e.
All Night Long. Bi-Monthly. A4 Photocopied zine features on new technology house music smart drugs cyberpunk positive attitudes. love of life articles - Price T.B.A. We will also concentrate on short news of works by acclaimed new authors such as 'The Glass Harmonica' by Nikkie Davies. Price T.B.A.

ANTI COPYRIGHT
PO Box 368
Cardiff, CF2 1SQ
Worldwide distribution for agit/scuril. fly-posters/ art. Subversion and supercessionist.

THE ANTI-PROHIBITIONIST REVIEW

97 rue Belliard, Rcm 512
1040 Brussels
Belgium

ANTIQUE ATLAS PUBLICATIONS
31A High Street
East Grinsted
RH19 3AF.
Subjects: Antique Maps.
Books July to December 1991 - 1 new edition.

ANVIL BOOKS LTD
45 Palmerston Road
Dublin 6
Ireland

APEX CENTRE
Kingston Polytechnic
Penrhyn Road
Kingston-upon-Thames
KT1 2EE

APEX MAGAZINES
John Nicholson
Editorial: 11 Ashburnham Road, Bedford MK40 1DX
Subscriptions: 20 Paul Street, Frome, Somerset BA11 1DX
Publisher of the quarterly Small Press World. The only newstand outlet in Britain with news, information, articles, files and ideas. Also an international section.
Small Press World; Spring 1992; A4 36pp; £3.00 ISSN 0954-9110.
Small Press World; Summer 1992; A4 36pp; £3.00 ISSN 0954-9110.
Small Press World; Autumn 1992; A4 36pp; £3.00 ISSN 0954-9110.

APORIA PRESS
308 Camberwell New Road
London
SE5 0RW
Aporia Press publishes a variety of titles, ranging from 17th century TRACTS to contemporary polemic. MSS NOT solicited. Distributed by Counter Productions (qv). Write for our full list of numinous wonders. Tyranipocrit Discovered. Anon. Ed. Andrew Hopton. 80 pages. 1991. hardback ISBN 0 948518 50 2. £30.00 paperback. 0 948518 55 3 £5.00 DIGGER TRACTS 1649-50. Ed Andrew Hopton. 36 pages. 1990. ISBN 0 948518 35 9. £2.50
Selected Writings. Gerrard Winstanley. 120 pages. 1990. Ed A Hopton. hardback ISBN 0 948518 40 S. £21.00 paperback ISBN 0948518 45 6. £6.00

APOSTLE PRESS
Mr Theo Fossel
119 Station Road, Beaconsfield, Buckinghamshire, HP9 1LG
Book on walking-sticks has sold thousands. Sticks available too.

APOSTROPHE
41 Canute Road
Faversham
Kent

36

ME13 8SH

APPLES AND SNAKES
Room 2
Peter Pan Block
23 Ladywell Lodge,Slagrove
LONDON
SE1 37HT

APPROACH POETS
28 Grosvenor Wharf Road
London
E14 3EF.
Subjects: Poetry.
Books July to December 1991 - 1

APRA BOOKS
443 Meadow Lane
Nottingham
NG2 3GB

APRA PRESS
S.W. Honley
443 Meadow Lane
Nottingham
NG2 3GB. Tel 0602 874615
Local History and Folklore Publishing research
into both. Short run publications for groups indi-
viduals and societies. Typesetting Graphic design
etc.
Nottingham's Onigmatic Homelock. Stone. R.W.
Morrell. 22pp illustrations 1991 ISBN 1 872957 20
X £1.25
Nottinghamshire's Holy Wells and Springs. R.W.
Morrell. 43pp illustrations 1990 ISBN 1872957 05
6 £1.50
Hidden History. Approx 34pp illustrations. 1992
(latest) - our periodic periodical. £1.50 per issue. 4
issues comprise one volume

A.P.T. Books
Bryntirion
Llanfair Caereinion
Welshpool
SY21 0BZ.
Subjects: Air Transport.
Books July to December 1991 - 1

AQUARIAN ARROW
BCM Opal
LONDON
WC1N 3XX

AQUARIUS
6th Floor
The White House
111 New Street
Birmingham

ARC PUBLICATIONS
Nanholme Mill
Shaw Wood Road
TODMORDEN
Lancashire
OL14 6DA

ARCADIAN
(Gothic Garden Press)

Mike Boland
30 Byron Court
Harrow Middx
HA1 1JT

ARCANUM
15 Oxford Street
MEXBOROUGH
South Yorkshire
S64 9RL
Magazine of weird fiction; surreal, outre, decadent.
Influenced by Lovecraft, Machen, Hodgeson, Ligotti,
Nyctalops etc. One issue published July 1990. No. 2
available August 1991. Published annually. £3.50
(including post and packing) U K: $£10.00 USA.
A4. 50 pages approximately.

ARCHANGEL PRESS
6 Sluvad Road
Panteg
Pontypool
NP4 0SX

MR BARRY ARCHER
56 Carlton Avenue
GILLINGHAM
Kent
ME7 2JX

D. ARCHER
The Pentre
Kerry
Newtown
SY16 4PD.
Subjects: Maps. Bibliography. Books July to De-
cember 1991 - 1 new book 1 new edition.

MS JUDITH ARCHER
92 Mount Street
CLECKHEATON
West Yorkshire
BD19 3QL 0274 862155

ARCHETYPE PUBLICATIONS
31-34 GORDON SQUARE
London
WC1H 0PY

THOMAS W ARCHIBALD
PO Box 912
South East PO
Edinburgh
EH16 5SB

Architectural Publications
182 Ralenhill Road
Belfast
BT6 8EE.
Subjects: Local History.
Books July to December 1991 - 1

ARCTURUS BOOKS
I. Hayes
The New House, East Grafton
Malborough
Wiltshire
SN8 3DB.

Mail-order service for esoteric and occult. Same address for the Blue Angel imprint.

ARDO PUBLISHING COMPANY
Methlick
Ellon
AB41 0HR.
Subjects: Fiction General.
Books July to December 1991 - 1

MR GREGORY ARENA
Via San Giornni Bosco 28
24100 Bergamo
Italy

ARESTOS PUBLICATIONS
11 Redhill Crescent
Wollaston
Wellingborough
NN9 7SX.
Subjects: Literature.
Books January to June 1991 - 2

ARIADNE PUBLICATIONS
56 Whiting Road
Glastonbury
BA6 8HR.
Subjects: British Mythology.
Books July to December 1991 - 1

ARK PUBLICATIONS
PO Box 150
Plymouth
PL1 1AX

ARKEN BOOKS
108 Aviemore Way
Beckenham
BR3 3RT

ARLEN HOUSE
1 Middle Street
Galway
Ireland

ARMA PUBLICATIONS
PO Box 2299
Barnet
EN5 5PN.
Subjects: Education.
Books January to June 1991 - 1

MS AMANDA ARMSTRONG
Writers Monthly
29 Turnpike Lane
LONDON
W8 0EP

ARNCLIFFE PUBLISHING
Roseville Business Park
Roseville Road
Leeds
LS8 5DR.
Subjects:
Books January to June 1991 - 36 Books
July to December 1991 - 5 books 3 new editions.

ARNISTON RANGERS F.C.
73 Hunterfield Road
Gorebridge
EH23 4TS.
Subjects: Football History. Books July to December 1991 - 2

A ARNOLD
9 Goldhill
Saffron Lane Estate
LEICESTER
LE2 6TQ

CHRISTOPHER J ARNOLD (self-publisher)
Bronawel
Green Lane
Abermule
SY15 6LB

MR MALCOLM ARNOLD
7 Primrose Road
Halton
LEEDS
LS15 7RS

ARTENN MAAT
Dr B J Cocksey
PO Box 197
Epson
Surrey KT17 1YJ
Books and booklets on psychic research, coincidence, inspiration and evidence of intelligence beyond current ideas of space and time. The emphasis is on rigorous genuinly open-minded scientific enquiry. Artenn Maat would like to hear from anyone with relevant experience.

ARTIQUE PRESS
Edwards Centre
Regents Street
Hinckley
LE10 0BB.
Subjects: Customs and Folklore.
Books July to December 1991 - 1 new edition.

ARTISAN
45 Kew Road
Failsworth
Manchester
M35 9LB.
Subjects: Historical Biography.
Books January to June 1991 - 1

ARTISTS' COLLECTIVE GALLERY
166 High Street
Edinburgh
EH1 1QS.
Subjects: Art.
Books January to June 1991 - 1

ARTMUSIQUE PUBLISHING COMPANY
31 Perry Hill
London
SE6 4LF

ARTRAGE
28 Shacklewell Lane

38

London
E8 2EZ

ART SALES INDEX
1 Thames Street
Weybridge
KT13 8JG.
Subjects: Art.

ARTSCAPE
Orrel
Fish Street
Shrewsbury
Shropshire.
Subjects: Folklore. Books July to December 1991 -
1

ARTS COUNCIL
(Access Unit)
14 Great Peter Street
London
SW1P 3NQ

ARTS IN MEDWAY
Marlborough Road
GILLINGHAM
ME7 5HB

ARTSREACH
Dorchester Arts Centre
School Lane
The Grove
Dorchester
DT1 1XR.
Subjects: Poetry.
Books July to December 1991 - 1

ASHBRAKEN
14 Cropwell Road
Radcliffe-on-Trent
Nottingham
NG12 2FS.
Subjects: Geography.
Books July to December 1991 - 1

ASHBY LANE PRESS
Mr B K Foster
Ashby Lane
BITTESWELL
Leicestershire
LE17 4SQ

MS NINA ASHBY
20 Bank Street
INVERNESS
IV1 1QE

WENDY ASHBY
PO Box 18
RICHMOND
Surrey
TW9 2AU

ASHDOWN PUBLISHING
104 High Street
Steyning
BN4 3RD.

Subjects: Art. Handicrafts. Books January to June
1991 - 1 Books July to December 1991 - 1 new
edition

ELIZABETH ASHFORD
Trelaske House
Lewannick
Launceston
PL15 7QQ

MR TOM ASHTON
A-2344 Maria Enzersdorf
Thurnbergstr 43-14
Austria

ASH TREE PUBLICATIONS
Ash Tree Close
Baghill Road
West Ardsley Tingley
Wakefield
WF3 1DF
Subjects: School Textbook.

ASHWATER PUBLISHING
68 Tranmere Road
Twickenham
TW2 7JB

(The) ASIAN WEEKLY
Cross Lances Road
Hounslow
Middx
TW3 2AD

ASIAN WOMEN'S WRITING FORUM MAGA-
ZINE
(AWWF)
c/o 1 Ferndown Street
Bradford
BD5 9QT

ASIA PUBLISHING HOUSE
45 Museum Street
London
W 1

ASIAN WOMEN'S NETWORK
c/o London Women's Centre
Wesley House
4 Wild Court
London
WC2B 5AU

ASLAN PUBLISHING
P O Box 887
Boulder Creek
CA 95006
United States of America

ASPECT
33a High Street
Thatcham
NEWBURY
Berkshire
RG13 4JG

ASPEX GALLERY

Art Space Portsmouth
27 Brougham Road
Southsea
PO5 4PA.
Subjects: Art. Books July to December 1991 - 1

ASSOCATION LILIM
5 Rue St Jean
11000 Carcassonne
FRANCE
High Quality, small edition runs of mythological - occult books. No unsolicited mailings.

ASTON PRESS
Joan Selby-Lowndes
22 Church Lane
Aston Rowant
Oxford
OX9 5SS

ASTRA PRESS
20 Candleby Lane
Cotgrave
Nottingham
NG12 3JG

ASTRAPOST
7 The Towers
Stevenage
SG1 1HE

ASYLUM MAGAZINE
Mr Bob Haynes
7 Walmersley Road, New Moston, Manchester,
M10 0RS
Magazine 'Chimera' uses strips and short stories.

ATD PUBLICATIONS
10 WYKELEY ROAD
Wyken
Coventry
CV2 3DW

ATELIER BOOKS
4 Dundas Street
Edinburgh
EH3 6HZ.
Subjects: Biography.
Books July to December 1991 - 1

ATHOL BOOKS
10 Athol Street
Belfast
BT12 4GX.
Subjects: Local History. Education. Irish History
Books July to December 1991 - 4

MR SAM ATKINSON
The Bell Tower
Little London
OAKHILL
Somerset
BA3 5AU

ATLANTIC EUROPE PUBLISHING COMPANY
86 Peppard Road
Sonning Common

Reading
RG4 9RP

ATLANTIC SALMON TRUST
Moulin
Pitlochry
PH16 5JQ.
Subjects: Fish.
Books July to December 1991 - 2

ATLANTIS PRESS
Michael Dainiell
1 Wolvercote Court
Wolvercote Green
Oxford
OX2 8AB

ATLAS PRESS
BCM Atlas Press,
London WC1N 3XX
Emissions of the anti-tradition. Specialists in surrealism, 'pataphysics and logorrhoetics of surprising virulence. Trade editions (distributed by Airlift) and the limited edition series 'The Printed Head'.
The Castle of Communion by Bernard Noel; 140pp; Mar 93. 0 947757 29 5. £7.99. Fiction.
The Autobiography of Albert Einstein by Gerhard Roth; 96pp; Feb 93. 0 947757 47 3. £7.99.
College of 'Pataphysics: The True, The Beautiful, The Good; 96pp; Dec 92 (Printed Head). 0 947757 48 1. £8.00.

ATMA ENTERPRISE
Christopher Gilmore
13 Bull Pitch
Dursley
Gloucestershire
GLU 4NG. Tel. 0582 405354
Talking books of family fables four illustrated by gifted teenagers stories written and read by Christopher Gilmore. At once funny fantastic exciting andenchanting...filled with light and laughter - Artswest. books and/or tapes: telling tales Snow Ghosts. Horace Hedgehog etc.
Telling Tales bbok/tape of family fables written and read by Christopher Gilmore. Illustrated 81pp ISBN 0 9512769 0 5
Snow Ghosts Fable appealing to adults and children alike spoken English. Coloured illustrations 7pp £1.99; £3.95 with tape (2 stories) by Christopher Gilmore. ISBN 0 9512769 1
Dovetales Maths Science Technology 3 books for Holistice Education by Christopher Gilmore. £9.95 100+pp ISBN 0 9519609 0 3

ATTIC BOOKS
The Folly
Rhosgoch
Builth Wells
LD2 3JY.
Subjects: Biography.
Books July to December 1991 - 1

AUGURIES
(edit N Norton)
48 Anglesey Road
Alverstoke
Gosport

40

Hants
PO12 2EQ

A.U.L. Publishing
Queen Mother Library
Meston walk
Aberdeen
AB9 2UE.
Subjects: Photography.

AULTON PRESS
Aulton Croft
Ardallie
Peterhead
AB4 8BP.
Subjects: Poetry.
Books January to June 1991 - 1

AUROBINDO ASHRAM:
Batstone Books
12 Gloucester Street
MALMESBURY
Wiltshire
SN16 0AA
Subject: Philosophy
Books July to Dec 1991 - 2 new eds.

MR BEN AUSELL
55 Palace Road
Homsey
LONDON
N8

AUSSTEIGER PUBLICATIONS
8 Back Skipton Road
Barnoldswick
Lancashire
BB8 5NE. 0282 812741
Through the medium of an enjoyable day's walking
we aim to bring to the fore the economic and social
history of the Pennine and Dales region that all can
gain from - truly journeys of exploration.
'Historic Walks Around the Pendle Way' by John
Dixon Bob Mann July 1990. 116pp. illustrated
paperback. £4.50. ISBN 1 872764 002
'Journeys Through Brigantia Vol. 1' by John Dixon
Philip Dixon. July 1990 . 132pp. illustrated paper-
back. £4.50. ISBN 1 872764 010. Walking guide.
'Journeys Through Brigantia Vol.2' by John Dixon
Philip Dixon. Nov. 1990. 120pp. paperback. £4.50.
ISBN 1 872764 029. Walking guide.

MR M G AUSTEN
4 Gayton walk
Old Catton
NORWICH
NR6 7EP

MATTHEW D. AUSTIN
22A Chief's Street
Ely
CB6 1AT.
Subjects: Photographic Record Local History.
Books July to December 1991- 1

AUX
64 Beechgrove
Brecon

POWYS
Wales
LD3 9ET 0874 625725
AUX serves as a clearing house for flyers, maverick
information, incendiary artwork, eclectic
paraphernazia and specializing in autonomous publishing. Many items are not intended for sale and are
only avaliable on an exchange basis or for a substantial cash incentive.
DATAKILL-I-III, 20pages, 25p + irregular magazine. Music, rants,cartoons, strange art, interviews,
contact address, etc, etc, etc.... HOAX!, A periodacal
of pranks, mischief, and meyhem! (debut issue
avaliable 1/4/92 - further details to be announced...)
The Shocking Truth. Robert Anton Wilson inspired
magazine containg far-out conspiracy theories,
anomalous data, forbidden knowledge and assorted
weird shit!

AVEC DESIGNS
PO Box 709
Bristol
BS99 1GE.
Subjects: Education for the Deaf. Education for the
Disabled. Books January to June 1991 - 2. Books
July to December 1991 - 1

AVENUES PRESS
117 Park Avenue
Hull
HU5 3EX.
Subjects: Local History.
Books July to December 1991 - 1

AVERNUS
35 Fishers Lane
London
W4 1RX

AVERT
PO Box 91
HORSHAM
West Sussex
RH13 7YR
Avert is an Aids charity producing publications on
Aids and HIV infection. Curre nt titles include:-
Prisons, HIV & Aids; A Survey of Aids Education in
Secondary Schools; Positively Primary (a book for
primary school teachers) Prisons, HIV & Aids: Risk
and Experience in Custodial Care. By Paul J
Turnbull, Kate A Dolan & Gerry V Stimpson. 54
pages. June 1991. ISBN 0 9515351 3 7. £8.00 A
Survey of Aids Education in Secondary Schools. By
David Stears & Stephen Clift . 56 pages. Nov 1990.
ISBN 0 9515351 1 0. £6.95
Positively Primary: Strategies for Approaching HIV/
Aids with primary school chil dren. By Pete Sanders
& Clare Farquhar. 40 pages. Feb 1991. ISBN 0
9515351 2 9. £8.95.

AVES PUBLICATIONS
5 Athol Street
Douglas
Isle of Man.
Subjects: Art.
Books July to December 1991 - 1

AVON POETRY NEWS

(see Pennyfields Press)

aw-Ra BOOKs
Ms Heather Haig
BCM aw-Ra, London WC1N 3XX
Reporting the cause and effect of growing irresponsibility towards domestic animals. "Action for animals" series has eight titles including 'Chasing Shadows.'

AXLETREE COMMUNICATIONS
10 Merebank Lane
CROYDON
CR0 4NP

D P AYKROYD
The Priory
Nun Monkton
York
YO5 8ES

AYLESFORD PRESS
158 Moreton Road
Upton
Wirral
L49 4NZ.
Subjects: Poetry. Books January to June 1991 - 3.
Books July to December 1991 - 2

DAVID AYRES
11A Batford Road
Harpenden
AL5 5AX.
Subjects: Poetry.
Books July to December 1991 - 1

[B]

B4 PUBLISHING
3 Tyers Gate
London
SE1 3HX

B & B PUBLISHERS
31 St Martin's Road
Caerphilly
CF8 1EF

B & W Publications
7 Sciennes
Edinburgh
EH9 1NH

ANN BABER
22 Lawrence Close
Weston-super-Mare
BS22 9EX.
Subjects: Food and Drink.
Books July to December 1991 - 1

BACK BRAIN RECLUSE MAGAZINE
16 Somersall Lane
Chesterfield
Derbyshire
S40 3LA
A Magazine that aims to expand the literary taste of readers by publishing the more expermental forms

of speculative fiction; by moulding an outlet for new writers and artists and by reviewing/publicising other magazines in this field.
Back Brain Recluse Magazine. ISSN 0269-9990.
Published quarterly. 4 issue subscription £6.30.
Writers' guidelines available for sae.

BACKGAMMON
61 Dunsmure Road
London
N16 5PT

D.H. BACON
3 The Glade
Crapstone
Yelverton
PL20 7PR.
Subjects: Industry.
Books January to June 1991 - 1.

BACSA
76.5 Chartfield Avenue
London
SW15 6

Badger Publishing
Unit 1
Parsons Green Estate
Boulton Road
Stevenage
SG1 4QG.
Subjects: School Textbooks.
Books January to June 1991 - 10 Books July to December 1991 - 2

Bad Taste Publications
24 Hartham Road
LONDON
N7 9JG
Specialists in contemporary adult and not so adult humour that hasn't been hijacked by cartoon-strip merchants, at the expence of scribblers.
The Tittler. Satirical/humourous/scatalogical/philisophical monthly magazine now in it's fourth year of publication. Something like Private Eye meets Viz. 5 for a yearly subscription (at least 12 issues)
Plays Yourself. Great fun at office parties or down the pub for budding Richard Burtons and Elizabeth Taylors. Everyone takes a part reading from short (15-20 minute) scripts, and acting out their fantasies. Kits available at just 3 each, send for details.

BAD WRITER'S PRESS
c/o Artworks
Barrow Borough Council
Piel View House Abbey Road
Barrow-in-Furness
LA13 9BD.
Subjects: Poetry.
Books January to June 1991 - 1

MR PETER BAGWAT
7 Vincent Road
NEW MILTON
Hampshire
BH25 6SN

MR DAVID BAILEY
Bell Lodge
Bell Vale
HASLEMERE
Surrey
GU27 3DH

MR D J BAILLIE
112 Stewarton Drive
Cambuslang
GLASGOW
G12 8DJ

MARTIN BAIRSTOW
Fountain Chambers
Halifax
HX1 1LR

MR J BAKER
The Willows
3 Pine Chase
HIGH WYCOMBE
Buckinghamshire
HP12 4UG

KIM BAKER
Beauville, Red House Farm Lane
Bawdsey
WOODBRIDGE
Suffolk
IP12 3AN

MR MICHAEL BAKER
Apartment 5
42 Clarenden Square
LEMINGTON SPA
Warwickshire
CU32 5QZ

MISS C BAKER-PEARCE
9 Beauepaire Crescent
Belper
DERBY
DE5 1HR

RAY BAKER
15 Lambeth Road
Linthorpe
Middlesbrough
TS5 6ED

BALANOSTER PRESS
P.O Box 67
Carlisle
CA4 9DE

BALCOMBE BOOKS
PO Box 101
Epsom
KT19 9GY

MR G H BALCOMBE
58 Argyle Road
West Ealing
LONDON
W13 8AA

BALDER
60 Elmhurst Road
READING
Berkshire
RG15 5HY

JIM BALDWIN PUBLISHING
Graham Pooley
11 Smith Lane
Fakenham
NR21 8LQ.
Subjects: Local History.
Books January to June 1991 - 1

MARK BALDWIN
24 High Street
Cleobury Mortimer
Kidderminster
Worcester
DY14 8BY. Tel 0299 270110.
Transport; particularly inland waterways and local
history and topography. Hold on a Minute by Tim
Wilkinson 1990. 8vo 188pp 16 photos; index map
endpp h/b £12.00 ISBN 0 947712 14 3. Recollec-
tions of working on canals in the 1940s
By Lock and by Pound by Vivian Bird 1988. 8vo
208pp 27 photos; 9 maps; index ISBN 0 947712 06
2 h/b. £12.95. Journalist's recollection of lengthy
journeys on working canal boats in the 1950s
West Midlands Wanderings by Bill Elliot 1990. 8vo
72pp 16 photos ISBN 0 947712 16 X p/b. £3.95.
Nine local walks (Ludlow to Bewdley) with historical backgrounds.

BALLINAKELLA PRESS
Whitegate
County Clare
Republic of Ireland
Small publishing house producing mainly Irish and
European historical and topographical books. Three
main series: People & Places (of Irish clans), Houses
of Irish Counties, Biographies. Also Ballinakella
paperbacks of International interest and Bell'acards,
post and greeting cards of high quality.

BAM Books
159 Warwick Road
Solihull
B92 7AR

MR FRANK BAMFORD
9 Malvern Drive
ALTRINCHAM
Cheshire
WA14 4NQ

FRANK BAMFORD
9 Malvern Drive
Altrincham
WA14 4NQ.
Subjects: Local History.
Books January to June 1991 - 1. Books July to
December 1991 - 1

HELEN H BANEY
Orchy Bheag
Dalmally
Argyll

43

PA33 1AX

BANK PRESS
8 Bank House
Grains Road
Oldham
OL2 8JG

BANNATYNE BOOKS
R. Court
6 Bedford Road
LONDON
N8 8HL

BANNERWORKS
1st Floor, Kings Head Buildings
Cloth Hall Street
HUDDERSFIELD
West Yorkshire
HD1 2EF
Yorkshire based community arts group. Banners, murals, photography, fabrics and graphics.

MR DAVID BANNISTER
26 Kings Road
CHELTENHAM
Gloucestershire
GL52 6BG

BANTON PRESS
75 Nelson Street
Largs
KA30 9AB.
Subjects: (all facsimile editions) Customs and Folklore.
Occult. History of Religion. Archaeology. Place Names. Philosophy.

MR JOHN BARBER
The Wall Cottage
Manor Road
OVING
Buckinghamshire
HP22 4HW

BARE BONES
16 Wren Close
FROME
Somerset
BA11 2UZ
The bare bones press is devoted to Haiku and other forms of poetry in miniature. A quarterly magazine and occasional chapbooks are published. A mail order booklist of haiku titles from the USA and Japan is available.

DAVID AND JOCELYN BARKER
47 Sayes Court
Addlestone
KT15 1NA.
Subjects: Local History.
Books July to December 1991 - 1

CJ BARNES
50 St Helen's Park Road
Hastings
TN34 2DN

RICHARD ALAN BARNES PUBLICATIONS
118 Watling Street
Grendon
Atherstone
Warwickshire
CV9 2PE 0827 713360
Publisher of scholarly books on historic organs and historic instruments in historic places. Also: other interests include music of a general nat ure and music in education.
Historic Organs in Historic Places: The 18th Century Chamber Organ in Kedleston Hall Derbys by Dr Alan Barnes. 68pp. 29b/w photos. 15 illust rations. A4. full colour b&f. 0 948653 01 5. £5.00 + £1.00 post. 1990.

BARN OWL BOOKS
WESTOWE FARMHOUSE
Lydeard St Lawrence
TAWNTON
TA4 3SH
Reference book for collectors of detective fiction.

BARNS PUBLICATIONS
14 High Elm Road
Hale Barns
Altrincham
WA15 0HS

BARNY BOOKS
The Cottage
Hough-on-the-Hill
Grantham
NG32 2BB

BAROS BOOKS
5 Victoria Road
Trowbridge
BA14 7LH

BAROS BOOKS
Edwin Banfield
5 Victoria Road
Trowbridge
Wiltshire
BA14 7LH. Tel 0225 752915
Publisher of books on antiques but mainly on all aspects of Barometers and Barographs which includes cistern wheel and aneroid antique instruments.
Barometer Makers and Retailers 1660-1900 by Edwin Banfield. 256pp 1991 0 948382 06 6 £7.95.
Care and Restoration of Barometers by Philip Collins. 128pp 1990 0 948382 05 8 175 illustrations £5.95
Anique Barometers: An Illustrated Survey by Edwin Banfield. 128pp 1989 0 948382 04 X 118 illustrations £4.95

MR D A BARRETT
5 Blenheim Crescent
BATH
BA1 6NL

MR J BARRETT
9 The Village
LONDON

44

SE7 8UG

MR RUSSELL BARRETT
55 North Street
SKIBBEREEN
West Cork
IRISH REPUBLIC

BARRINGTON BOOKS
Bartle Hall, Liverpool Road
Hutton
PRESTON
Lancashire
PR4 5HB 0772 616816
We aim to promote the new movement of experi-
mental, sociopolitical Science Fiction, by publish-
ing an annual collection of original short stories by
new and established writers. High standards of
writing and production. Writers please send S.A.E.
for our manifesto.

LOUIS BARROW
184B Wisbech Road
March
PE15 8EZ.
Subjects: General Fiction.
Books July to December 1991 - 1

MR G P BARTLETT
Adams Farm, The Street
North Warnborough
BASINGSTOKE
Hampshire
RG25 1BL
Publishers of 'How to...' advice books and educa-
tional cassettes.

BARTLETTS PRESS
39a Kildare Terrace
LONDON
W 2

THE BARTON PRESS
30 Broomy Hill
HEREFORD
HR4 0LH

DAVID BARTON
45 Wellmeadow Road
Hither Green
London
SE13 6SY. Tel 081 698 3392
Self-publisher collections or drawings in related
sequences. Artists Books. Mainly line drawings
with occasional texts. Also a number of books in
collaborationwith poets comprising line drawings
and poems/prose all relating to thehuman figure
Drawing a Blank: Page on Page by David Barton.
A5 160pp June 1992 line drawings £9.00. ISBN 0
90755949 2
Making Room by David Barton. A5 56pp line
drawings £4.50. ISBN 0 907559 43 3. June 1992
Brooding by David Barton. A5 112pp line drawings
£7.50. ISBN 0 907559 45 X.

BARTON HOUSE PUBLISHING ANd
Datacraft Publications
9 Barton Orchard

BRADFORD-ON-AVON
Wiltshire
BA15 1LU
We publish new age (Barton House) and new age
titles, selling them through the book trade and
direct mail. We are now moving into audio and
combined print/audio .

MR JEFF BARTON
5 Avebury Close
WESTBURY
Wiltshire
BA13 3TE

R D BARTON
Postbus 75027
1117 ZN SCHIPOL-OOST
The Netherlands

BASEMENT WRITERS
Sally Flood
23 Mount Terrace, Turner St.,
Tower Hamlets,
London E1 2BB
071 247 1854
We publish new writers. have been meeting &
publishing since 1973, & are a non profit making
group.
In My World; Sally Flood; 40pp; 1989; £2.95.
Phases of one womans life - poems.
Take It From Me; Sean Taylor; 70pp; 1992; £3.00.
Poems on life.
Wiggerly Words; Joan Vincente; 40pp; 1992; £1.99.
Poems for children.

Ms Julia Baslar
1 Grafton House
The Farmlands
NORTHOLT
Middlesex
UB5 5ER

BASSET PUBLICATIONS
60 North Hill
Plymouth
PL4 8HF

MR A J F BATES
365 Sandycoombe Road
Kew Gardens
RICHMOND
Surrey
TW9 3PR

LADY HENRIETTA BATHURST
42 Elm Park Road
Chelsea
London
SW3 6AX

BATSTONE BOOKS
12 Gloucester Street
Malmesbury
SN16 0AA.
Subjects: Biography.

BATTLE OF BRITAIN PRINTS INTERNA-
TIONAL

Church House
Church Street
London
SE15 3JA

BAULKING TOWERS PUBLICATIONS
David Caldwell
Baulking Towers
UFFINGTON
Oxfordshire
SN7 7QE
Local sports, local authors, rural satirical magazine.

BAVERSTOCK BOOKS
50 Westbury Leigh
Westbury
Wiltshire

C. BAXTER PHOTOGRAPHY
Unit 2/3 Block 6
Caldwellside Industrial Estate
Lanark
ML11 6SR.
Subjects: Biography. Mammals. Birds. Books January to June 1991 - 2 Books July to December 1991 - 5 1 new edition.

MR R N BAXTER
45 Chudleigh Crescent
ILFORD
Essex

BAY FOREIGN LANGUAGE BOOKS
19 Dymchurch Road
St. Mary's Bay
Romney Marsh
TN29 0ET.
Subjects: Language.
Books July to December 1991 - 1

MR PETER BAYLISS
Lea Cottage
Withybrook Road, Street Ashton
RUGBY
Warwickshire
CV23 0PJ

BAZAAR
South Asian Arts Forum
237 Bon Marche Building
444 Brixton Road
London
SW9 8EJ

BB Books
1 Spring Bank
Longsight Road
Copster Green
BLACKBURN
BB1 9EU 0254 249128
An attempt to bypass traditional publishing and distribution networks. Setting, platemaking, printing and sales are in-house. The press mainly publishes short-run poetry pamphlets. Post-Beat counter-culture emphasis. Anarchic and untrendy in production and content.
LOVEJUICE. Bill Wyatt. Transformations from Ikky's Chinese poetry. 14 pages. 14 illustrations.

June 1991. Poetry, calligraphy and paintings. TERRIBLE GARDEN WORLD. By Arthur Moyse. A folio of drawings, cartoons and colla ges. 22 illustrations. Re-issued. Juyly 1991. £2.00
HERE WE GO. A poetry celebration of soccer. Edited by Dave Cunliffe. 84 pages 22poets. 102illustrations. Re-issued August 1991. £2.00

BBNO
Tapping Well Farm
Burrowbridge
BRIDGWATER
TA7 0RY
Subjects: Food & Drink
Books July to December 1991 - 2

BBR Design
Chris Reed
16 Somersall Lane
CHESTERFIELD
Derbyshire
S40 3LA

BCM-CANIMPEX
London
WC1N 3XX

BUSINESS DEVELOPMENT CENTRE
21 Temple Street
WOLVERHAMPTON
West Midlands
WV2 4AN

A BEACHAM
8 Fletcher Crescent
Plymstock
PLYMOUTH
PL9 8LQ

BEACON BOOKS
Malvern
23 Worcester Road
Malvern
WR14 4QY.
Subjects: Walks Books.
Books January to June 1991 - 1

BEAMSCAN
20 Vaughan Avenue
London
NW4 4HU

BEAN PRESS
5 Vauxhall Crescent
Castle Bromwich
Birmingham
B36 9JP

R. BEAN
Victoria Farmhouse
Carlton
MK43 7LP.
Subjects: Lace-making.
Books July to December 1991 - 1

MR M R BEASLEY
Stables Cottage

46

Saling Hill, Great Saling
BRAINTREE
Essex
CM7 5DT

BEATRIX POTTER SOCIETY:
W.G. Fawkes
White House
Ugthorpe
Whitby
YO21 2BQ.
Subjects: Literature.

MRS BEATTIE
Manchester House
Church Hill
Slindon
ARUNDEL
BN18 0RD

BEAUCLERK PUBLISHING
29 The Gilberts
Sea Road
Rustington
West Sussex

BEAUFORT PUBLISHING LTD
PO Box 22
Liphook
Hampshire
GU30 7PJ 042 876 588
A specialist publisher of reference books in the field
of military architecture - hillforts castles fortifications - from architectural archaeo logical historical
and military points of view.
'Fortress' - The Castles and Fortifications Quarterly
edited hy Andrew Saunders. 64pp. 70 illustrations.
£18.00 per annum. Leading journal with profes-
sional and lay enthusiast readership.
'Military Architecture' by Quentin Hughes. 256pp.
400 illustrations. £25.00. A broad survey of the art
of defence from earliest times to the second World
War.
'Fortress Britain' by Andrew Saunders. 256pp
255 illustrations. £20.00.
A history of fortification in the British Isles and
Ireland since the in troduction of artillery.

BECCON PUBLICATIONS
75 Rosslyn Avenue
Harold Wood
Romford
RM3 0RG

BECK BOOKS
29 St. Mary's Mount
Station Road
Cottingham
HU16 4LQ.
Subjects: Hull Jazz.
Books July to December 1991 - 1

V BECKER, KEIP
Hamerweg 46
Postfach 700563
6000 FRANKFURT 70
GERMANY

RICHARD BECK
49 Curzon Avenue
Stanmore
HA7 2AL.
Subjects: Mathematics.
Books July to December 1991 - 2

OLIVER A BECKERLEGGE
74 Grange Garth
Fulford Road
York
YO1 4BS

STAN BECKINSALE
4 Leazes Crescent
Hexham
NE46 3JX.
Subjects: Archaeology.
Books July to December 1991 - 2

BECKSIDE DESIGN
18 Willowfield Avenue
Nettleham
Lincoln
LN2 2TH

BEDFORD TO BLETCHLEY RAIL USERS
ASSOC.
23 Hatfield Crescent
Bedford
MK41 9RA
Newsletter for members, outings on old trains to
nationwide destinations, exhibitions.

BEDLAM PRESS
Church Green House
Old Church Lane
Pateley Bridge
Harrogate
HG3 5LZ
Publishes only long poems or sequences of poems
informed by some political consc 'At the Antipodes:
homage to Paul Valery' by David Moody. 16pp
1982. £1.20 ISBN 1 870260 02 3 (long poem)
'News Odes: the El Salvador Sequence' by David
Moody. 46pp 1984 . £2.20 ISBN 1 870260 03 1
(poem sequence)
'Night Flight to Santiago' by Richard Drain. 26pp
1986. £2.20 ISBN 1 870260 00 7 (poem sequence)

BEDS AND BUCKS INFORMATION SERVICE
Science and Technology Library
Cranfield Institute of Technology
Cranfield
MK43 0AL.
Subjects: Library Science.
Books July to December 1991 - 1

BEECH PUBLISHING HOUSE
15 The Maltings
Turk Street
Alton
GU34 1DL.
Subjects: Poetry. Stockbreeding. Pets.
Books July to December 1991 - 3 new books 4 new
editions

BEECHES PRESS

John Pitt
44 Marsala Road
London SE13 7AD
Fine Printer

ROBERT BEECH
11 Springwood View Close
Sutton-in-Ashfield
NG17 2HR.
Subjects: Family History.
Books July to December 1991 - 1

J. BEE
Computer Bureau
Carlton House
Whassett
Milnthorpe
LA7 7DN.
Subjects: Short Stories.

BEESTON & DISTRICT CIVIC SOCIETY
10 Winchester Avenue
Beeston
Nottingham
NG9 1AU

BEESWAX SCORPION PRESS
154 Blake Road
West Bridgford
Nottingham
NG2 5JZ

BEIHIREYO BOOKS
Mrs AK Turya
60 St. Fabians Drive
Chelmsford
Essex
CM1 2PR. Tel 0245 261079
Publishing medical, nursing and heath care books
and manuals; and handbooks for secondary school
level subjects on heath issues; and communication
skills.
What is Primary Health Care? EB Turya 108pp
1990. ISBN 0 9515819 0 2; £5.00. Discusses health
care provision.
Essential Mother and Child Health. EB Turya.
302pp 1990
ISBN 0 9515819 1 0 £10.00
Write them Right - how to write effective letters job
applications curriculum vitae & take interviews. EB
Turya. 84pp 1992 ISBN 0 9515819 4 5 £4.50.

BELAIR PUBLICATIONS
PO BOX 12
Twickenham
TW1 2QL

BEL-AIR PRESS
7E Sharp Street
Gourock
PA19 1UL.
Subjects: Sport.
Books July to December 1991 - 1

BELFRY BOOKS
118 St. Pancras
Chichester
PO19 4LH.

Subjects: short Stories.
Books July to December 1991 - 1

BELHAVEN PUBLISHERS
8 King's Saltern Road
Lymington
SO41 9QF

MR ADRIAN BELL
Victoria Cottage
Constitution Opening
NORWICH
NR3 4BD

MR GERRARD BELLART
Old Coach House
Langham Place
Rode
BATH

BELLCODE BOOKS
10 Ridge Bank
Todmorden
OL14 7BA

BELLEROPHON
Manchester House
Church Hill, Slindon
ARUNDER
West Sussex
BM18 0RD
Fiction, aviation history, psychology and paranor-
mal investigation

BELLEVIRE PUBLISHING TRUST
8/5 Ehrickdale Place
EDINBURGH
EH3 5JN

PETER BELL (BOOKSELLER)
4 Brandon Street
Edinburgh
EH3 5DX.
Subjects: Bibliographies.
Books January to June 1991 - 1

BELLY-LAUGH BOOKS
18 Sefton Press
Leigh
WN7 1LX.
Subjects: Children's Fiction.
Books July to December 1991 - 1

BELTANE FIRE
Kevin & Ingrid Carlyon
16 Cross Street
St Leonards on Sea
E Sussex

BELVOIR BOOKS
The Chapel
Redmile
Nottingham
NG13 0GA

BEMERTON PRESS
9 Hamilton Gardens

London
NW8 9PO

MR DOUGLAS BENCE
Byways
Bodmin Hill
Lostwithiel
Cornwall
PL22 0HA

BENET BOOKS
Sunnyside
Derrythorpe
SCUNTHORPE
South Humberside
DN17 8EY

BENEVENAGH BOOKS
89 Springfield Road
New Elgin
Elgin
IV30 3BZ.
Subjects: History of Local Aviation. Books July to
December 1991 - 1

BENJAMIN PRESS
69 Hillcrest Drive
Bath
BA2 1HD.
Subjects: Poetry.
Books July to December 1991 - 1

MR K N BENNETT
13 Skaife Road
SALE
Cheshire
M33 2HA

MR T W BENSON
13 Yew Road
Bitterne
SOUTHAMPTON
Hampshire
SO2 5AW

MR DARREN BENTLEY
74 Monteith Crescent
BOSTON
Lincolnshire
PE21 9AY

BENTOS PUBLISHING COMPANY
52 Melville Road
Stillorgan
Blackrock
County Dublin
Republic o
Subjects: Historical Biography.
Books July to December 1991 - 1

JACOB J BERGER
174 Plum Lane
London
SE18 3HF.
Subjects: Philosophy. Russian Literature. Books
January to June 1991 - 2. Books July to December
1991 - 1

BERKS BUCKS & OXON NATURALISTS'
TRUST
3 Church Cowley Road
Rose Hill
Oxford
OX4 3JR.
Subjects: Wild Life.
Books July to December 1991 - 1

PROVINCIAL GRAND LODGE OF BERKSHIRE
Berkshire Free Masonic Centre
Mole Road, Sindlesham
Wokingham
RG11 5DR

BERKSWELL PUBLISHING COMPANY
P.O Box 420
Warminster
BA12 9XB

BERKSWELL PUBLISHING Co LTD
J. ST. Dolph Managing Director
PO Box 420
Warminster
Wiltshire
BA12 9XB. Tel 0985 40189
Berkswell's annual publication the Royal Year now
in its nineteenth consecutive edition is established
as the best selling annual authoritative record of the
activities of the Royal Family. In addition to Royal
publications Berkswell also publishes books of interest to readers in Wessex.
The Royal Year 1992-93 ISBN 0 904631 09 5
Twice Hooked by David Barr. A fishing Autobiography ISBN 0 904631 07 09 Three Hundred Years
of Foxhunting in South and West Wiltshire ISBN
0904631 08 7.

MR HUGH BERNAYS
74 Dale Street
YORK
YO2 1AE

BERNICA BOOKS
11 The Ridge
Ryton
NE40 3LN.
Subjects: Local History.
Books July to December 1991 - 1

MISS TINA BERNSTIEN
3 Carpenter Court
37-41 Pratt Street
LONDON
NW1 0BJ

ALLAN W BERRY
10 Blackneath
Colchester
CO2 0AA

BERRYDALES BOOKS
5 Lawn Road
London
NW3 2XS.
Subjects: Food.
Books July to December 1991 - 1

49

MR J BERRY
34 Faracre Court
Bellinge
NORTHAMPTON
NN3 4BJ

BERTRAND RUSSELL PEACE FOUNDATION
Bertrand Russell House
Gamble St
Nottingham
NG7 4ET

BERWICK PUBLISHERS
Argosy Libraries
96 Haddington Road
Dublin
Republic of Ireland

BESSACARR PRINTS
Historic Scotland
20 Brandon Street
Edinburgh
EH3 5RA

BEST PUBLISHING COMPANY
High Gillerthwaite
Ennerdale
Cleator
CA23 3AX

BETE NOIRE
(edit John Osborne)
American Studies Dept
The University
Cottingham Road
Hull
HU6 7RI

BETJEMANIAN
c/o Mr E Griffin
Manor Farm House
Queen Catherine Road
Steeple Cleydon Bucks
MK18 2QF

BETTER PUBS
Old Chapel
Bottreaux Mill
South Molton
Devon

ERIC RAYMOND BEVINGTON
Holmans Cottage
Bisterne Close
Burley
BH24 4AZ

TREVOR ALLEN BEVIS
28 St Peter's Road
March
PE15 9NA

BEWICK PRESS
132 Claremont Road
Whitley Bay
NE6 3TX

MR J R BEWSHER
68 Watermint Quay
Craven Walk
LONDON
N16 6DD

BEYOND THE RISING SUN
530 Great Western Road
Kelvinbridge
Glasgow
G12 8EL.
Subjects: Art.
Books January to June 1991 - 18

BEYOND THE PALE PUBLICATIONS
7 Winetavern Street
Belfast
N Ireland
BT1 1JQ

BHASVIC Resources
c/o Brighton Hove and Sussex
Sixth Form College
Dyke Road
Hove
BN3 6EG.
Subjects: Social Sciences. Books January to June
1991 - 1

MR SUTAPAS BHATTACHARYA
31 William Street
LONDON
E10 6BD

MR LES BICKNELL
18 Fleets Road
Sturton By Stow
LINCOLN
LN1 2BU
Minimal environmental bookworks looking at the
form from a sculptural perspective.

MR SIMON BIDDELL
833 Alum Rock Road
Ward End
BIRMINGHAM
B8 2AC

MR JOE BIDDER
33 Queensdown Road
Hackney
LONDON
E5 8NN

LAWRENCE BIDDLE
The Woods
Leigh
Tonbridge
TN11 8NA.
Subjects: Local History.
Books July to December 1991 - 1

(THE) BIG ISSUE
4 Albion Place
Galena Road
Hammersmith

50

London
W6 0LT
(tel: 081-741-8090)
(fax: 081-741-2951)

MS KAREN BILLING
Bindells Bookshop, 20a North Street
SKIBBEREEN
West Cork
IRISH REPUBLIC

BILLIONTH PRESS
45 Handforth Road
London
SW9 0LL

Mr John Binns
14 Silver Royd Close
Wortley
LEEDS
LS12 4QZ

BIOPRESS
The Orchard
Clanage Road
Bristol
BS3 2JX.
Subjects: Botany. Historical Biography Books January to June 1991 - 1. Books July to December 1991 - 1

MR R BIRCH
44 Fletcher Road
Cowley
OXFORD
OX4 2UF

MR SID BIRCHBY
40 Parrs Wood Avenue
Didsbury
MANCHESTER
M20 0ND

A P M BIRD
Upper Billesley
Stratford-on-Avon
CV37 9RH

HINTON BIRD
Rushen Vicarage
Port St. Mary
Isle of Man.
Subjects: History of Education.
Books January to June 1991 - 1

MR JOHN BIRD
13 Priory Road
LONDON
W4 5JB

BIRDWORLD
Holt pound
Farnham
GU10 4LD.
Subjects: Birds.
Books January to June 1991 - 1

MR ANDY BIRKET
5 Courtside Mews
Redlands
BRISTOL
BS6 6PS

BIRMINGHAM & MIDLAND INSTITUTE
9 Margaret Street
Birmingham
B3 3BS

BIRMINGHAM POLYTECHNIC
Department of English
Franchise Street
Perry Barr
BIRMINGHAM
Anthology by the writer in residence.

BIRMINGHAM PUBLISHING COMPANY
PO Box 1779
Quinton
BIRMINGHAM
B32 3AZ
Looking for business books - using USA marketing methods to promote titles.

UNIVERSITY OF BIRMINGHAM
Faculty of Education
P.O Box 363
Birmingham
B15 2TT

BISHOPSGATE INSTITUTE
230 Bishopsgate
London
EC2M 4QH.
Subjects: History of Education.
Books January to June 1991 - 1

ALLAN BLACK
70 Oakshaw Street
Paisley
PA1 2DR

BLACK ACE ENTERPRISES
Mr Hunter Steele
Ellemford Farmhouse
DUNS
Berwickshire
TD11 3SG
Publishing modest print runs of high quality editions.

BLACK ARTS IN LONDON
28 Shackewell Lane
London
E8 2EZ

BLACKBOARD REVIEW
Unit 25 Devonshire House
High St
Deritend
Birmingham
B12 0LP

BLACKCURRENT STAIN
Burdett Cottage

4 Burdett Place
Hastings
TN34 3ED

BLACK FROG PRESS
14 Ramsey Close
Manton Heights
Bedford
MK41 7NE.
Subjects: Occult.
Books July to December 1991 - 1

BLACKHEATH PUBLISHING
14 Greenwich Church Street
London
SE10 9BJ.
Subjects: Plays.
Books January to June 1991 - 1.

MATT BLACK PUBLICATIONS
51 Pearson Place
Sheffield
S8 9DE

MR R H BLACKMAN
3 Buckenham Court
Mill Lane
SOUTHWOLD
Suffolk
IP18 6JT

BLACKOUT
c/o Jason Cobley
47 Borough Meadows
Catterick Village
North Yorkshire
DL10 7NX

BLACK PENNELL PRESS
THOMAS RAE
36 Margaret Street
GREENOCK
Scotland
PA16 8EA

BLACK SHEEP PRESS
Alan Henson
Coast Cottage Donna Nook
Louth
Lincolnshire
LN11 7PA. Tel 0507 358 669
A recently formed press specialising in publications
to assist children's speech and language develop-
ment. Practising speech therapists are involved in
design and production ensuring practical material
with appropriate illustrations and content.
Consonant Word Book. G.I.S.T. 54pp illustrated
October 1992 £3.90 2300+ most useful words for
phonology work.
Phonology and Articulation Work Sheets. Suitable
children 3+. on card for Photocopying. November
1992.

THE BLACKSMITH
Swords into Ploughshares
7 Plum Lane
LONDON
SE18 3AF

THE BLACK SWAN PRESS
28 Bosleys Orchard Grove
Oxfordshire
OX12 7JP

BLACKWATER BOOKS
45 Approach Road
London
E2

BLACK WOMANTALK
Box 32
190 Upper Street
London
N1 1RQ

MR A M BLAIR
13 Leurel Avenue
EDINBURGH
EH12 6DW

BRIAN BLAIR-GILES
Norbury Hall
Norbury Hall Park
55 Craignish Avenue
London
SW16 4RW.
Subjects: Biography. Poetry.

LEWIS BLAKE
Gordon Dennington
62 Park Hill Road
Shortlands Bromley
Kent
BR2 0LF. Tel 081 464 9260
Detailed factual accounts of south east London
under air attack in World War II. Original research
of unpublished material. Illustrated with original
photos. Absorbing reading.
Red Alert - Lewis Blake. Paperback 192pp revised
1992 £7.50 (including postage).
Bolts from the Blue - Lewis Blake. 94pp 1990 £4.00
(including postage). Covers V2 rock campaign.

R. BLAKE
Regent Cottage
13A Regent Parade
Harrogate
HG1 5AW.
Subjects: Historical Biography.
Books July to December 1991 - 1

TRUDY BLAKE
25 Aked Close
Longsight
Manchester
M12 4AN.
Subjects: Poetry.
Books July to December 1991 - 1

MR MICHAEL J BLAND
Caldew Beck
Welton
Dalston
CARLISLE
CA5 7ET

BLANK PAGE
B4 Westminmster Business Square
Durham Street
LONDON
SE11 5JH
Limited editions of artists books. Signed prints.

ROB BLANN PUBLISHING
349 Tarring Road
Worthing
West Sussex
BN11 5JL. Tel 0903 246587
Carefully researched and written by Rob Blann two
fascinating books expose the joys and traumas of
Victorian and Edwardian fishermen in a seaside
resort - action-packed with daring lifeboat rescues
colourful town parades civic events and some curi-
ous occurrences.
A Town's Pride: Victorian Lifeboatmen and Their
Community. £9.95. ISBN 0 9516277 0 8. A4 soft
cover 174pp 110 authentic photos.
Edwardian Worthing: Eventful Era in a Lifeboat
Town. ISBN 0 9516277 1 6. A4 hardback 194pp
210 period photos.

MR STEVE BLINCO (Fat Knite)
46 Labernham Way
LITTLEBOROUGH
Lancashire
OL15 8LS

ROYAL NATIONAL INSTITUTION FOR THE
BLIND
224 Great Portland Street
London
W1N 6AA

BLIND SEPENT PRESS
Brenda Shaw & John Glenday
65 Magdalen Yard Road
DUNDEE
DD2 1AL

BLORENGE BOOKS
3 Holywell Road
Abergavenny
NP7 5LP

BLUE WINDOW BOOKS
53 Elderfield Road
London
E5 0LF

BLUNTISHAM BOOKS
23 Priory Road
Newcastle
ST5 2EL.
Subjects: Walks in the Falkland Islands.
Books July to December 1991 - 1

BLUNT SLUG COMIC
62 Stanhope Road
GREENFORD
Middlesex
UB6 9EA 081 578 7114
'If David Lynch wrote a comic - this would be it!'
Sublime! (Speakeasy). When y ou were sperm you
beat the rest of your batch to the egg - with that
same enthus iasm. Send cheque/po £1.50 payable
to R J Hollywood for double issue (1 and 2)

BLYTH SPIRIT
11 The Ridgway
Flitwick
Beds
MK45 18H

MS CLAIRE BOARMAN
79 Danson Way
RAINHAM
Kent
ME8 7EN

BOB
3 Maidstone Street
Victoria Park
Bedminster
BRISTOL

MR PHILIP BOBER
15 Lane End Road
Middleton-on Sea
BOGNOR REGIS
West Sussex
PO22 6LL

BODY SHOP INTERNATIONAL
Hawthorn Road
Wick
Littlehampton
BN17 7LR.
Subjects: Art.
Books January to June 1991 - 1

BOGG (U K address)
George Cairncross
31 Belle Vue St
Filey N Yorks
YO14 9HU

BOGGART'S PRESS
3 Sutton Street
Blackburn
BB2 5ES

BOGLE L'OUVERTURE
52 Chignell Place
London
W13 0TJ

BOJANGLES PRESS
J Bigotto
The Cosmic Centre
25 Acacia Avenue
Romford
IG25 4GH
The truth is you can only be what you are and it can
only be what it is. 'The It'. Quarterly Writings - Ed.
Swami Nythanis (formerly Frank Nulty) £3.00 on
rice pape; handwritten in the Psu Cha style.

BERGEN BOKKAFE
Postboks 2725 Mohlenpris
N-5026 Bergen

Norway

BOLAND PUBLISHING
Bondway Business Centre
71 Bondway
London
SW8 1SQ

THE BOLD PRESS
Kelvin Smith
7 Minster Road
Oxford
OX4 1LX. Tel 0865 243095
The Bold Press was established in 1992 to bring to
Europe writings from the Western States of America
particularly works by Native American and His-
panic American writers.
Send for details of first titles to be published early in
1993.

J & C BOLDERO
Hall Cottage
Thurning
Dereham
NR20 5QT

THE BOLO PRESS
7 Mister Road
OXFORD
OX4 1LX

BOOK ART PROJECT
30 Queenstown Road
MANCHESTER
M20 8NX
Book Art Project
Mr Paul Johnson
30 Queenstown Road, Manchester, M20 8NX
Paul Johnson is director of the Gulbenkian founda-
tion-funded BOOK ART PROJECT based at Manchester Polytechnic which aims to develop children's literacy through the book arts. He is also a
successful book artist exhibiting widely.

THE BOOK CASTLE
Paul Bowes
12 Church Street
Dunstable
Bedfordshire.
 Tel 0582 605670
Local interest titles primarily on Bedfordshire Herefordshire and Buckinghamshire walks autobiography History photographic country-side folklore
childrens also retail bookseller.
Changes in our Landscapes: Aspects of Bedfordshire Buckinghamshire and the Chilterns: Eric
Meadows: 176pp 29.10.92 ISBN 1 871199 31 X
£19.95 Leafing Through Literature: A4 hb colour/
b-w photographs. Writers Lives in Herts and Bedfordshire: David Carroll: 208pp 3.9.92 £7.95 A5
p.b ISBN 1 871199 01 8
Swans in My Kitchen: The Story of a Swan Sanctuary: Lis Dorer: 88pp 29.9.92 £4.95 A5 pbk ISBN
1871199 16 6

BOOKMARQUE PUBLISHING
John Rose
26 Cotswold Close

Minster Lovell
Oxford
OX8 55X. Tel 0993 775179
Bookmarque Publishing was started in 1987 - it's
intention to fill gaps in motoring history and gen-
eral/transport. 3-6 titles year. Husband/wife team
only. Alldesign phototypesetting in-house.
Uphill Racers - History of British Speed Hill climbing Chris Mason. 448pp ISBN 1870519086. 1991.
280mm x 220mm £39.95 net
Lawrence Laurie Bond - The Man - The Marque'
Nick Wotherspoon. 176pp ISBN 1870519167 10/
92 £18.95 net provis Hdbk
David and Peter Henshaw Travel the A5 and take
a journey through British History Series (no.1)
'Britains Roads' pbk 10/92 £9.95 net provis ISBN
1870519159.

BOOKS FOR KEEPS
6 Brightfield Road
Lee
London
SE12 8QF.
Subjects: Bibliography.
Books July to December 1991 - 1

BOOK HOUSE
Kirkby Stephen
Grey Garth, Ravenstonedale
Kirkby Stephen
CA17 4NQ

BOOKMARQUE PUBLISHING
26 Costwold Close
Minster Lovell
OX8 5SX

BOOK TRUST
Scotland
15a Lynedock Street
Glasgow
G3 6EF

BOOK SHOP (Home Counties)
20 High Street
Princes Risborough
Aylesbury
HP17 0AX.
Subjects: Local History.
Books July to December 1991 - 1 new edition.

BOOKS UNLIMITED
Leslie Waller
69 Onslow Square
LONDON
SW7 3LS

BOOK WORKS
Jane Rolo
No.1 Arch
Green Dragon Court
Borough Market
London
SE1 9AH. Tel 071 407 1692.
The Prince of Words Places to Remember 1-26 by
Lily R. Markiewiez. 60pp 1992 £15.50 artist's bk
Coloured People. Adrian Piper. 292pp 1991 £27
Reading the Glass Management of the Eyes Mod-

54

eration of the Gaze. C. Barber S. Kichard and C. Leyser. 1991 144pp £16

MR CHRISTOPHER BOON
Bowsey Hill House
Bowsey Hill, Wargrave
READING
Berkshire
RG10 8QJ

MR J BOOTH
28 Criccieth Road
Cheadle Heath
STOCKPORT
Cheshire
SK3 0ND

BOOTH-CLIBBORN EDITIONS
18 Colville Road
London
W3 8BL

MS JO BOOTY
The Old Hall House
Westwell
ASHFORD
Kent
TN25 4LQ

BORDER PRESS
The Outdoorsman's Bookstore
Llangorse
Brecon
LD3 7UE.
Subjects: Sport.
Books July to December 1991 - 1

BORDERLINE PRODUCTIONS
P.O. 93
Telford
TF1 1VE.
Subjects: Music.
Books July to December 1991 - 1

MS ANNE BORN
Oversteps
Froude Road
SALCOMBE
South Devon
TQ8 8LH

HENRY BOSANQUET
22 Stanhope Road
DARLINGTON
DL3 7AR
Mr Henry Bosanquet
22 Stanhope Road, Darlington, DL3 7AR
Author of the legendary 'Walks Round Vanished Cambridge' series, which can't now be got for love nor money. His magnus opus is still in the card-index.

JOHN BOSWORTH PUBLICATIONS
8 Folly Field
Bishop's Waltham
SO3 1EB

BOTANICAL SOCIETY OF THE BRITISH ISLES
B.S.B.I. Publications
24 Glapthorn Road
Oundle
Peterborough
PE8 4JQ.
Subjects: Botany.
Books July to December 1991 - 1

BOTTON BOOKSHOP
Botton
Whitby
YO21 2NJ
Canimpex Publishing

J. BOUDRICOT PUBLICATIONS
Ashley Lodge
Rotherfield
Crowborough
TN6 3QX.
Subjects (mostly translated from the French): Industrial History. Military Ships History. Books January to June 1991 - 4.

JOHN HENRY BOUGHTON
69 Amersham Road
Little Chalfont
Amersham
HP6 6SP

BOUNDARY MAGAZINE
The King's Road Writers
23 Kingsley Road
Runcorn
Cheshire
WA7 5PL

BOURNEMOUTH LOCAL STUDIES PUBLICATION
40 Lowther Road
Bournemouth
BH8 8NR.
Subjects: Historical Biography.
Books January to June 1991 - 1. Books July to December 1991 - 2

BOUSSIAS BUSINESS INFORMATION
7 Solonos Street
106 71 ATHENS
Greece

MR SIMON BOWLANDS
SJB Publishing
78 Park Lane
SANDBACH
Cheshire
CW11 9EF

THE BOX PUBLISHING
318 Corn Exchange
Hanging Ditch
MANCHESTER
M4 3BG

Ms Anne Boyd
144 Peperharow Road
GODALMING

Surrey
GU7 2PW

MISS JEANETTE BOYD
54 Firisbury House
Partridge Way
Bounds Green Road, Wood Green
LONDON
N22 4DU

MEGAN BOYES
49 Evans Avenue
Allestree
Derby
DE3 2EP.
Subjects: Biographies of the Byron family.
Books July to December 1991 -1

BOYS AND GIRLS' WELFARE SOCIETY
57A Schools Hill
Cheadle
SK8 1JE.
Subjects: Social Welfare.
Books January to June 1991 - 2 Books July to
December 1991 - 1

MR PHILIP BOYS
9 Calbourne Road
Balham
LONDON
SW12 8LW

BOZO
John Nicholson
BM BOZO,
London WC1N 3XX
Ethnically cleansed? Virally purged? The human
infestation is being cured! What's going on? Get
your news from the Front. Smuggled despatches
and lies. BOZO NEWS is coming. True. The dead
send their regards. IT'S ALIVE!!
Women Who Go Bump In The Night - a topogra-
phy of murder, lies and sex; John Nicholson; £4.99;
Autumn 1992; 0904063 28 3.
Scared Shitless - the sex of horror; John Nicholson;
Winter 92/93; Price t.b.a.; 0904063 27 5.
An Elizabethan Lady's Missal of Shrunken Head
Arrangements; author t.b.a.; Spring 1993.

Cambridge House Boys' Grammar School
Cambridge Avenue
Ballymena
BT42 2EN

MR RICHARD G BOYTON
The Rockery
Poole Street
Great Yeldham, Halstead
Essex
CO9 4HS

BOYZ
77 City Garden Row
London
N1 8EZ

BRACKEN PRESS
Byways

Low Street, Scalby
SCARBOROUGH
North Yorkshire
YO13 0QS
Limited editions. Intaglio, silk screen and wood-
engravings.

A.G BRADBURY
3 Link Road
Stoneygate
Leicester
LE2 3RA

MR D E BRADBURY
High Pines
Pyrford Woods
WOKING
GU22 8QL

BRADFORD & ILKLEY COMMUNITY COL-
LEGE
Great Horton Road
Bradford
BD7 1AY

BRADFORD POETRY
(edit Clare Chapman)
9 Woodvale Way
Bradford
W Yorks

UNIVERSITY OF BRADFORD
Disaster Planning and Limitation Unit
Department of Industrial Technology
Bradford
BD7 1DP

BRADLEY PRESS
7 Durham Road
Wolviston
Billingham
TS22 5LP.
Subjects: Handicrafts.
Books January to June 1991 - 2. Books July to
December 1991 - 1

MR NIGEL BRADLEY
91 Hawksley Avenue
CHESTERFIELD
Derbyshire
S40 2TJ

MR NIGEL BRADLEY
Research Services Ltd
Station House, Harrow Road
WEMBLEY
Middlesex
HA9 6DE

BRADPEAK INTERNATIONAL
110 Bellingham Road
Catford
LONDON
SE6 2PR 01 697 3864

MR JAMES BRADSHAW
Natural Friends

56

15 Benyon Gardens
Culford
BURY ST EDMONDS
IP28 6EA

E.F. BRADFORD
Orchard House
Castleton
Whitby
YO21 2HA.
Subjects: Historical Biography.
Books July to December 1991 - 1

MR R J BRAGGINS
Windy Chase, 23 Stanthorpe Road
Bowden
ALTRINCHAM
Cheshire
WA14 3JZ

BRAID BOOKS
c/o 69 Galgorm Road
Ballymena
BT42 1AA

BRAINWAVE
33 Lorn Road
LONDON
SW9 0AB

Dean Braithwaite
Strange Matter
The Ruby Book Review, Dept DB
Rhyd-Dderwen, Hebron
WHITLAND, Dyfed
SA34 0XX

BRAMCOTE PRESS
27 Seven Oaks Crescent
Bramcote Hills
Nottingham
NG9 3FW.
Subjects: General Fiction.
Books July to December 1991 - 1

BRAMPTON PUBLICATIONS/S.B PUBLICA-
TIONS
5 Queen Margaret's Road
Loggerheads
Market Drayton
TF9 4EP

LEONARD BRAND
Woodside Junior School
Morland Road
Croydon
CR0 6NF.
Subjects: History of Education.
Books July to December 1991 - 1

BRANDON BOOK PUBLISHERS
Cooleen
Dingle
Co Kerry
Ireland

MR C BRANIGAN

Garden Cottage
Ingoe
NORTHUMBERLAND
NE20 0SP

CHARLES BRAVOS
H S Gibbons
35 Lamont Road
LONDON
SW10 0HS

MR MARTIN BRAZIL
The Printing Centre
30 Store Street
LONDON
WC1E 7BS

BREAD 'N ROSES
Tenants Corner
46a Oval Mansions
Vauxhall Street
London
SE11 5SH

BREAKAWAY PUBLICATIONS
The Old Vicarage
Newchapel
STOKE-ON-TRENT
ST7 4QT
Publish Rouge, a lesbian and gay socialist quarterly.
Some books, pamphlets and packs.

Tony Breeze
70 Nottingham Road
Burton Joyce
Nottingham
NG14 5AL

ALAN H BREMNER
Bendigo
St Ola
Kirkwall
KW15 1SX

BRENTHAM PRESS
40 Oswald Road
St Albans
Hertfordshire
AL1 0727 835731
Small publications of literary and social value outside the commercial market: poetry local history
essays occasional criticism and reprints. 'Strawberries in the Salad' by May Ivimy. New title (December 1991). Poetry. ISBN 0 905772 31 8. 56pp.
£4.50, paperback.
'A Poem is Mad' by M.A.B. Jones. More prize-
winning poems from a writer of distinction 40pp.
£3.00 ISBN 0 905772 30 X (1991)
'Ruskin and Sienna' by Anthony Harris (Nov 1991)
- illustrated lecture by the Master of the Guild of St
George. ISBN 0 905772 32 6. 24pp illustrated. £3.0
0, paperback

BREWIN BOOKS:
Alton Douglas
371 Rednal Road
Kings Norton
Birmingham

57

B38 8EE.
Subjects: Local History. Books July to December
1991 - 4 new books 1 new edition.

BREWERS QUAY
Hope Square
Weymouth
DT4 8TA.
Subjects: Historic Local Walks.
Books July to December 1991 - 1

BRIDGE PUBLICATIONS
2 Bridge Street
Penistone
Sheffield
S30 6AJ

(THE) BRIDGE
(James Mawer)
112 Rutland Street
Grimsby
S Humberside
DN32 7NF

BRIDGE BOOKS
61 Park Avenue
Wrexham
LL12 7AW

BRIDGE HOUSE PUBLISHERS
Burdett Cottage
4 Burdett Place
George Street Old Town
Hastings
TN34 3ED.
Subjects: Literature.
Books July to December 1991 - 1

BRIDGE STUDIOS
Kirklands
Scremerston
Berwick-on-Tweed
TD15 2RB

BRIDGEWATER BOOKS
Bridgewater House
Langford
Lechlade
Gl7 3LN.
Subjects: Fiction General.
Books January to June 1991 - 1

(THE BRIEF & BLYTH SPIRIT)
British Haiku Society
Sinodun
Braintree
Essex
CM7 5HN

MR RON BRIEFEL
26 Springfield Road
LONDON
NW8 0QN

BRIGHT BOOKS
Carpenters
Moor End

Great Sampford
Saffron Walden
CB10 2RQ.
Subjects: Children's Fiction.
Books July to December 1991 - 1

WIN BRINLOW
Gneiss House
Invershin
Laing
IV27 4ET

BRISTOL BROADSIDES
108c Stokes Croft
BRISTOL
BS1 3RU
A publishing co-op running writers workshops.
Books by local people including autobiography,
peotry, history.

BRISTOL JUNIOR CHAMBER
16 Clifton Park
Bristol
BS8 3BY.
Subjects: Secret Underground Bristol.
Books January to June 1991 - 1

BRISTOL PRESS
226 North Street
Bedminster
BS3 1JD

BRISTOL RADICAL LESBIAN
Feminist Magazine
c/o The Women's Centre
44 The Grove
BRISTOL
BS1 4RB
Collective of lesbian feminists publishing a maga-
zine welcoming articles and letters.

BRISTOL TEMPLAR
Julian Lea-Jones
33 Springfield Grove,
Henleaze, Bristol,
BS6 7XL

UNIVERSITY OF BRISTOL
Department of Politics
12 Priory Road
Bristol
BS8 1TU

BRITISH NATIONAL CARNATION SOCIETY
3 Canberra Close
Hornchurch
RM12 5TR

BRITISH BIKE MAGAZINE
48 Union Lane
CAMBRIDGE
CB4 1QTS

BRITISH COPYRIGHT COUNCIL
29-33 Berners Street
London
W1P 4AA

58

BRITISH EARTH MYSTERIES SOCIETY
David Barclay
40 Stubbing Way
SHIPLEY
West Yorkshire
BD18 2EZ
Magazine for flying saucers and similar. Cups.

BRITISH FANTASY SOCIETY
15 Stanley Road
MORDEN
Surrey
SM4 5DE
Began 1971. Newsletter for members. Magazines, conference and awards.

BRITISH HUMANIST ASSOCIATION
14 Lamb's Conduit Passage
London
WC1R 4RH.
Subjects: Customs. Philiosophy.
Books July to December 1991 - 1 new book 1 new edition.

BRITISH INSTITUTE IN PARIS
Senate House
Mallet Street
London
WC1E 7HU.
Subjects: Poetry.

BRITISH INSTITUTE OF MENTAL HANDICAP
Wolverhampton Road
Kidderminster
DY10 3PP.
Subjects: Education.
Books January to June 1991 - 1

BRITISH LEISURE PUBLICATIONS
Windsor Court
East Grinstead
RH19 1XA

BRITISH MAHABODHI SOCIETY
London Buddhist Vihara
5 Heathfield Gardens
London
W4 4JU

BRITISH ORGANIC FARMERS AND
THE ORGANIC GROWERS ASSOCIATION
Lowsonford Farm
Henley-in-Arden
Solihull
B95 5HJ.
Subjects: Agriculture.
Books July to December 1991 - 1

BRITISH PRINTING SOCIETY
BM/ISPA
LONDON
WC1N 3XX

BRITISH PRINTING SOCIETY PUBLISHING
GROUP
c/o Alfred Jones,

14 Penrose Arc Aest
Liverpool L14 6UT

BRITISH RECORD SOCIETY
Subjects: List of Wills and Inventories at Lincoln.
Books July to December 1991 - 1

BRITISH ROMANI UNION
The Reservation
Hever Road
Edenbridge
TN8 5DJ.
Subjects: Children Fiction. Poetry. Social Sciences.
Books January to June 1991 - 4

BRITISH ROMANY UNION
The Reservation
Hever Road
EDENBRIDGE
Kent
TN8 5DJ

BRITISH SCIENCE FICTION ASSOCIATION
114 Guildhall Street
FOLKESTONE
Kent
CT20 1ES

BRITISH SHINGON BUDDHIST ASSOCIATION
58 Mansfield Road
London
N W 8

BRITISH SMALL ANIMAL VETERINARY
Association
Kingsley House
Church Lane Shurdington
Cheltenham
GL51 5TQ.
Subjects: Pets. Beekeeping. Books Jul to December
1991 - 1

BRITISH SOCIETY OF
MASTER GLASS PAINTERS
The Ridings
Singleborough
Buckingham
MK17 0RF.
Subjects: Stained Glass.
Books January to June 1991 - 1

BRITISH TRUST FOR ORNITHOLOGY
Beech Grove
Station Road
Tring
HP23 5NR

BRIXTON POETS
2 Lorn Court
Lorn Road
Brixton
London
S W 9

THE BRIXTON SOCIETY
Ken Dixon
139 Herne Hill Road

London
SE24 OAD
The Brixton Society is the amenity group covering the whole Brixton area from Stockwell to the South Circular active in environmental and community issues acting as Planning Watch-dog and a focal point for local history research.
'Brixton Town Trails - six walks around Brixton Stockwell' 84pp A4 reprinted 1992 ISBN 1 873052 00 6 £3.99
'Brixton the Story of a Name' by Ken Dixon 20pp A4 1991 ISBN 1 873052 01 4 £1.00 + 25p postage.

BROOKSIDE PRESS: KETTERING BOOKS
14 Horsemarket
Kettering
NN16 0DO

BROADCAST BOOKS
Pitt House
Chudleigh
Newton Abbot
TQ13 0EL

BROADHEAD PUBLISHING
Broadhead
Castleshaw
Delph
Oldham
OK3 5LZ

BROAD LEYS PUBLISHING CO.
Buriton House
Station Road
Newport
CB11 3PL

BROAD MAGAZINE
Suite 7G Agate Chambers
69 Upper Duvell St
Ipswich
Suffolk
IP4 1HP

BROADSIDE
Peter Johnson
68 Limes Road
Tettenhall
Wolverhampton
WV6 8RB. Tel 0902 753047
Birmingham and Black Country History Folklore Photographs EZ and English folklore and folksong books.
The Book of the Black Country Jon Rauen. 64pp 1989 ISBN 0 946 757 04 6 £5.99 Black Country Towns and Villages Michael Raufn. 96pp 1991 ISBN 0 946 757 10 0 £7.99 (A4)
Black Country Jokes and Humour Doug Parker. 64pp 1991
ISBN 0946 757 127 £2.50 (A5)

MR GEOFF BROADY
18 Haslemere Court
Grange Street
DERBY
DE3 8JJ

BROCH BOOKS

c/o N James
0/1, 31 Willowbank Crescent
Glasgow
G3 6NA

BROCKWELL BOOKS
64 Selsdon Road
London
SE27 0PG

MS CRIOSE BROGAN
Tara
Kinsale
Co Cork
Ireland

BROMPTON PUBLICATIONS
16 Trebovoir Road
London
SW5 9NH.
Subjects: Library Science.
Books July to December 1991 - 2

J. BROOKE
Guildford
53 Chantry View Road
Guildford
GU1 3XT.
Subjects: Poetry.
Books July to December 1991 - 1

BROOKS BOOKS
23 Sylvan Avenue
Bitterne
Southampton
SO2 5JW.
Subjects: Biography.
Books July to December 1991 - 2

Ms Elizabeth Brooks
12 Molyneux House
Molyneux Street
LONDON
W1H 5HU

HENRY C G BOOTHROYD BROOKS
Harroway Edge
Keppel Road
DORKING
RH4 1NG

BROOKSIDE BOOKS
28 Colesbourne Road
Bloxham
Banbury
OX15 4TB

MR MARK A BROTHWELL
51c Linton Road
Eastmoor
WAKEFIELD
West Yorkshire
WF1 4HH

M SERGE VAN DEN BROUCKE
83 Rue Philippe Fabia
69008 LYON

France
BROWN & BROWN
Keeper's Cottage
Westward
Wigton
CA7 8NQ

MR ANGUS BROWN
c/o New River Project, Unit P8
Metropolitan College of Craftsmen
Enfield Road
LONDON
N1 5AZ

C.E. BROWN
Jackson's Drive
Charlecote
Warwick
CV35 9EW.
Subjects: Biography.
Books July to December 1991 - 1

D BROWN
TPAS
48 The Crescent
SALFORD
M5 4NY

MR LIAM BROWNE
17 Selkirk House
Bingfield Street
LONDON
N1 0AG

BROWNES PUBLISHERS
17 Gainsboro Road
Bognor Regis
PO21 2HT

JO BROWN
Portsmouth
48 Dunbar Road
Portsmouth
PO4 8ET

MR LAURIE BROWN
H W Wilson Co
950 University Avenue, Bronx
NY 10452
United States of America

MS MAUREEN BROWN
25 Rothschild Road
Linslade
LEIGHTON BUZZARD
Bedfordshire
LU7 7SY

R. & S. BROWN
13 Goppa Road
Pontarddulais
Swansea
SA4 1JN.
Subjects: Customs and Folklore.
Books July to December 1991 - 1

MR T E BROWN
1 Angel Cottages
Mile Spit Hill
LONDON
NW7 1RD

BROWN WELLS AND JACOBS
2 Vermont Road
London
SE19 3SR.
Subjects: Children's non-fiction.
Books July to December 1991 - 4

BROWSE PRESS
10 Highcroft
STEVENAGE
Hertfordshire

BRUNDALL BOOKS
12 Belgrave Mount
Wakefield
WF1 3SB.
Subjects: Short Stories.
Books July to December 1991 - 1

ALAN BRYAN
c/o 36 Tower Road North
Warmley
Bristol
BS15 2YR.
Subjects: Historic Guide.
Books January to June 1991 -1

MR C BRYAN
PO Box 6, Ripley Sorting Office
Market Place
RIPLEY
Derbyshire
DE5 3XD

MR R BRYANT
24 Ash Way
BIRMINGHAM
B23 5DN

MARGARET E BRYANT ROSIER
71 Grenfeld Crescent
Cowplain
Portsmouth
PO8 9EL

MR T BRYANT
75 Ravenmill Road
Knowle
BRISTOL
BS3 5BS

BRYNGLAS PUBLICATIONS
23 Durham Avenue
Bromley
BR2 0QH.
Subjects: Autobiography.
Books July to December 1991 - 1

BRYNMILL PRESS (Professor John Pick)
Willow Cottage 20 High Street
Sutton-on-Trent

Newark
Nottinghamshire
NG23 6QA.
'Twenty years of ... works of literary criticism,
philosophy and theology -always of the first quality'
- Salisbury Review. Poetry and novels as well.
Subjects: Poetry. Literature. Philosophy. Theology.

BSDR & D
13A The Bull Ring
Wakefield
WF1 1HB.
Subjects: Education.
Books January to June 1991 - 1

B.S.M.W. Books
50 Ceres Road
London
SE18 1HL.
Subjects: Biography.

BUCEPHALUS PRODUCTIONS
Flat 4 3 Hornsey Lane Gardens
London
N6 5NY.
Subjects: Poetry.
Books July to December 1991 - 1

BUCHAIR UK
Wellingtonia 8
Raglan Road
Reigate
RH2 0DP.
Subjects: Air Transport. Books January to June
1991 - 1.
Books July to December 1991 - 2

BUCHU BOOKS
PO Box 2580
Capetown
SOUTH AFRICA

BUCKINGHAM PRESS
25 Manor Park
Maids Moreton
MK18 1QX

Mr Des Buckley
1 Cartile House
Hunter Close
LONDON
SW1 4UT

MR PAUL BUCK
4 Bower Street
MAIDSTONE
Kent

BU-COMP PUBLISHERS LIMITED
Andrew Fairclough
25 Durmford House
LONDON
SE6 2TA
Mnemonics, lateral thinking, jazz, Japanese culture, organice farming, history of radical movements, body-building - just a few of our subjects -
not in the same book.

(THE) BUDDHAPADIPA TEMPLE
14 Calonne Road
Wimbledon Parkside
London
SW19 5JH

(THE) BUDDHIST PUBLICATION SOCIETY
58 Eccleston Square
London S W 1

BUDDY BOOKS
Tomkin-Hill
543 Victoria Road
South Ruislip
Middlesex.
Subjects: Poetry.
Books July to December 1991 - 1

MR GARY BUDGEN
60 Burgoyne Road
Haringey
LONDON
N4 1AE

BUFO
3 Elim Grove
Bowness-on-Windermere
LA23 2JN

BRITISH UFO RESEARCH ASSOCIATION
16 Southway
BURGESS HILL
West Sussex
RH15 9ST

THE BUG
The Editor
88 Foster Road
Trumpington
Cambridge
CB2 2JR
The Bug is describable as a single-sheet periodical
(about twice a year). Area of interest: paradox
wisdom anonymity and good-naturedness; mainly
in the part of sentences supplied as spare parts for
recycling. Ideal: totally our own language and be
widely understood.
The Bug. Nos 1-5 2pp illustrated £0.02 (or exchange).

MR G BULGER
35 Mayfair Avenue
SALFORD
M6 8AF

BULLFINCH PUBLICATIONS
245 Hunts Cross Avenue
Woolton
Liverpool
L25 9ND.
Subjects: Fiction General.
Books July to December 1991 - 2

WALTER HENRY BULLOCK
35 Forest Road
Burton-on-Trent

DE13 9TW.
Subjects: Historic Architecture.
Books January to June 1991 - 1

MR M BULLOUGH
15 Meadowsweet Road
STRATFORD-UPON-AVON
Warwickshire
CV37 0TH

MR BULSTRODE
September
42 High Street
IRCHESTER
Wellingborough

MR ANDERW BUNDY
328 Rue des Pyrenees
75020 PARIS
France

BASIL BUNTING POETRY ARCHIVE
Durham University Library
Palace green
DURHAM
DH1 3RN
Pretty self-explanatory.

THE BUNYAN PRESS
Brian Maunders
34 Park Hill
AMPTHILL
Bedfordshire
MK45 2LP
Subjects: Poetry
I have a Vandercook press which allows me to print
letterpress as well as a variety of relief printing
methods. I concentrate on producing limited edi-
tion works (poetry, broadsheets and books). These
I illustrate mainly with wood-engravings.

BUNYAN STUDIES
Faculty of Arts
The Open University
Walton Hall
Milton Keynes
MK7 6AA 0908 653674
Journal of mainly academic interest: Articles on
Bunyan and the history and literature of the seven-
teenth century. Bi-annual. Subscription £10 p.a.
single copies £6 each. Cheques payable to Bunyan
Studies. Editorial enquiries to Dr. W.K. Owens The
Open University (London) 527 Finchley Road Lon-
don NW3 7BG.
Bunyan Studies: John Bunyan and his Times. W.R.
Owens and S. Sim (eds) Volume 1 Number 1 88pp.
Autumn 1988. ISSN 0954 0970. Five articles eight
notes. Five book reviews.
Bunyan Studies: John Bunyan and his times. W.R.
Owens and S. Sim (eds) Volume 1 Number 2 88pp.
Spring 1989. ISSN 0954 0970. Five articles two
notes six book reviews.
Bunyan Studies: John Bunyan and his times. W.R.
Owens and S. Sim (eds) Volume 2 Number 1 96pp.
Spring 1990. ISSN 0954-0970. Six articles three
notes seven book reviews.

BURBURY CREATIVE WRITERS CIRCLE

Burbury Park Complex
Wheeler Street
Newtown
BIRMINGHAM
B19 2UP

BURDA
Mr Fred Schulenburg
Swan House
37/39 High Holborn
LONDON
WC1V 6AA

BURDEN AND CHOLIJ
Faculty of Music
12 Nicholson Square
Edinburgh
EH8 9DF

BURDETT COTTAGE
4 Burdett Place
Hastings
TN34 3ED
Blackwater Books

DR JOHN BURGESS
41 Millcroft
CARLISLE
CA3 0HZ

JOHN BURGESS PUBLICATIONS
41 Millcroft
Carlisle.
Subjects: Local History (anybody's).
Books January to June 1991 - 10

MR ROBERT BURGESS
1 Middlefield Road
ROTHERHAM
South Yorkshire
S60 3JH

MR D J BURKE
Kenelm
St Edwards Drive
STOW ON THE WOLD
Gloucestershire
GL54 1AW

MR N BURKE
15 Sherdley Road
Crumnsall Green
MANCHESTER
M8 6GE

PHILIP L. BURKINSHAW
Davis Brothers
The Courtyard
School Lane
Leominster
WR6 8AA.
Subjects: Biography.
Books July to December 1991 - 1

MR E D BURNELL
13 Bawimead
HENLEY-ON-THEMES

Oxfordshire
RG9 2DL

MR MAX BURNELL
Rose Cottage
New Street
OCKBROOK
Derbyshire
DE7 3RA

MR MARK BURNS
15 Grosvenor Gardens
Jesmond
NEWCASTLE-UPON-TYNE
NE2 1HQ

THE BURRELL PRESS
P.O. BOX 168
IPSWICH
Suffolk
IP2 8AQ
We hope to publish travel writing, fiction, poetry.
Not deliberately revolutionary or avant-garde; some
empasis on attractive printing & good book
productin, also on ilustration.
A LULL BETWEEN MONSOONS (An Experi-
ence of Malaysia) by Peter Gauld. Published Sept
91 cloth 208pp 14 b&w illustrations linocut cover
design. Travel. This is our pilot edition. Other titles
planned.

FRED H. BURTON
17 Davenport Fold Road
Harwood
Bolton
BL2 4HA.
Subjects: Historical Biography.
Books July to December 1991 - 1

MR G BURTON
21 Churchfield Road
Oxley
WOLVERHAMPTON
WV10 6TL

BURY LIVE LINES
The Derby Hall
Market Street
BURY
Lancashire
BL9 0BN
Writers workshops in the arts and crafts centre. Into
computers. Performance group available.

DONALD WILLIAM BUSFIELD
2 Purley Knoll
Purley
CR8 3AE.
Subjects: Local History.
Books July to December 1991 - 1 new edition

BUSINESS ARCHIVES COUNCIL
185 Tower Bridge Road
London
SE1 2UF.
Subjects: Biography.

BUSINESS EDUCATION PUBLISHING

Leighton House
10 Grange Crescent
Stockton Road
SUNDERLAND Tyne & Wear
SR2 7BN

BUSY BEEVER
Mark Beevers
Glenside Cottage
Saltburn
Cleveland
   Contact: Mark Beevers
One man and his demon press - photocopied book-
lets of own works poetry epigrams humorous &
serious (26 to date)
'Both Barrels Blazing' by Mark Beever 12pp. £0.50
(poetry) 'Double Edge Sword' by Mark Beevers
20pp playlet. 0.50
'Jesteryears II' by Mark Beevers 20pp £1.00 (po-
etry) P&P free

CHRIS BUTCHER
96 Dovecroft
New Ollerton
Newark
NG22 9RQ.
Subjects: History.
Books July to December 1991 - 1

BUTLER SIMS
55 Merrion Square
Dublin 2
Republic of Ireland.
Subjects: Travel in Ireland.
Books January to June 1991 - 1 Books July to
December 1991 - 1

BUTTERBUR & SAGE LTD
B J Hepburn
99/101 St Leonards Road
WINDSOR
Berkshire
SL4 3BZ
Proper recipes for proper living. Catalogues.

RALPH BUTTLE
28A Church Fields
Wellington
TA21 8SE.
Subjects: Historical Biography.
Books July to December 1991 - 1.

BYRGISEY
Tanzy Cottage
Rimpton
Yeovil
BA22 8AQ.
Subjects: Second World War History.
Books July to December 1991 - 1

MR GARY M BYRNE
76 Whistler Street
LONDON
N5

MR KEVIN BYRNE
The Hotel

64

ISLE OF COLONSAY
Argyll
PA61 7YP

[C]

CACTUS GRAPHIC DESIGN
PO Box 587
LONDON
SW2 4HA

CADENZA PRESS
Gilbert Beale
4 James Close
Blandford Forum
Dorset
DT11 7PQ
Fine Press

CAERDROIA
53 Thunderdsley Grove
Thundersley
BENFLEET
Essex
SS7 3EB

CAERMAEN BOOKS
109 Oak Tree Road
SOUTHAMPTON
SO2 4PJ
All sorts of wonders. Fantastic and decadent
(Machen). Journal AKLO. Has been known to
publish The Source a mag on wells. Networks with
weirder people.
Mr Michael Caine
12 rue Marie et Louise
F 75010 PARIS
FRANCE

MR ANDREW CAINES
Flat 1, 2 Fronheulog Terrace
Glenarfon Hill
BANGOR
N Wales

CAKEBREADS
Brenda Fuller
Ford End
Clavering
SAFFRON WALDEN
Essex
Currently publishing 'Quiet Heroines' by Brenda
McBryde, the story of the nurses of the Second
World War.
Paperback 246 pages. Retail £6.95 UK (hardback
Chatto, 1985)CB11 4PU

CALABRIA PRESS
15 Calabria Road
LONDON
N5 1JB

C A L C R E
Mr Roger Gaillard
Boite Postale 17
F-94404 VITRY-SUR-SEINE CEDEX
FRANCE

CALEDONIAN BOOKS
Slains House
Collieston
AB4 9RT

MR PAUL CALLAGHAN
Business Education Publishing
Leighton House, 10 Grange Crescent
Stockton Road
SUNDERLAND, Tyne & Wear
SR2 7BN

CALM DOWN PUPPY
332 Commercial Way
LONDON
SE15 1QN
A small independent Silk Screen Service printing t-
shirts for Artists, Poets and Musicians. Because we
run a smaller operation than most we charge com-
petitive prices for smaller runs. Our smallest edition
is 20 t-shirts.
Calton Promotions
PO Box 9
Exeter
EX1 2AQ

CALUMET PRODUCTIONS
6A Fairbourne Road
London
N17 6TP.
Subjects: Poetry.
Books July to December 1991 - 1

CAMBERWELL PRESS
Camberwell College of Arts
Peckham Road
LONDON
SE16 6RR

CAMBRIDGE CONTEMPORARY CLASSICS
Bridge House
Hildersham
Cambridge
CB1 6BU.
Subjects: Romantic Fiction.
Books July to December 1991 - 1

CAMBRIDGE HOUSE BOYS' GRAMMAR
SCHOOL
Cambridge Avenue
Ballymena
BT42 2EN.
Subjects: Local History.
Books July to December 1991 - 1 new book 1 new
edition.

CAMBRIDGE INSTITUTE OF EDUCATION
Shaftesbury Road
Cambridge
CB2 2BX.
Subjects: Bibliography.
Books July to December 1991 - 2

CAMBRIDGE POETRY WORKSHOP
10 Fulbrooke Road
Cambridge

CB3 9EE.
Subjects: Poetry. Books July to December 1991 - 1

CAMBRIDGE RESOURCE PACKS
38 Cambridge Place
Cambridge
CB2 1NS.
Subjects: Education. School Textbooks.
Books January to June 1991 - 6

CAMBRIDGE SCIENCE BOOKS
Cambridge Place
CAMBRIDGE
CB2 1NS
High quality eductional books, material for secondary eduction.

Camden Training Centre
57 Pratt Street
London
NW1 0DP

CAMELOT BOOKS
3 Grange Road
Bishopsworth
Bristol
BS13 8LE

CAMERON AND HOLLIS
P.O. Box 1
Moffat
DG10 9SU.
Subjects: Second World War History. Books July to December 1991 -1 new edition.

CAMPAIGN FOR REAL EDUCATION
18 Westlands Grove
Stockton Lane
York
YO3 0EF

CAMPAIGN LITERATURE
Adelaide College
3 Nineyard Street
Saltcoats
KA21 5HS.
Subjects: Biography.
Books July to December 1991 - 1

DR J L CAMPBELL
Canna House
Isle of Canna
Scotland
PH44 4RS

KEN CAMPBELL
3 Gibraltar Walk
LONDON
E2 7LH

CAMPHILL ARCHITECTS: CAMPHILL PRESS
Botton Bookshop
Botton
Whitby
YO21 2NJ

PETER J. CAMPION

Myrtle Cottage
Gretton
Cheltenham
GL54 5EP.
Subjects: Local Industrial History.
Books January to June 1991 - 1

MR R CANDAPPA
c/o Tilby & Leeves
King House
5-11 Westbourne Grove
LONDON
W2

CANDELABRUM
9 Milner Road
WISBECH
Cambridgeshire
PE13 2LR

CANIMPEX PUBLISHING
BCM-Canimpex
London
WC1N 3XX

(NATIONAL) CANINE DEFENCE LEAGUE
1 Pratt Mews
London
NW1 0AD

CANTO PRESS
2 Cricklewood Park
Belfast
BT9 5GW

CAPABILITY BOOKS
Stowe Bookshop
Stowe
Buckingham
MK18 5EH

CAPITAL GAY
38 Mount Pleasant
London
WC1X 0AP

CAPPRICCIO PRESS
Barry Turner
28 Beaulieu Place
Rothschild Road
Chiswick
LONDON
W4 5SY

CAPRICORN PUBLISHER
1 Hill House
38 Park Street
OLD HATFIELD
Hertfordshire
AL9 5AZ

CARA
c/o London Lighthouse
178 Lancaster Road
London
W 11

M CARBERRY
97 Park Winding
Park Mains
Erskine
PA8 7AT

CARCANET
208 Corn Exchange Buildings
MANCHESTER
M4 3BQ

CARDEN PUBLICATIONS
174 Eastgate Square
Chichester
PO19 1JL

CARDIGAN AND TIVY-SIDE ADVERTISER:
Welsh Books Centre.
Subjects: Local History.
Books July to December 1991 - 1

CARDOZO KINDERSLEY EDITIONS
152 Victoria Road
Cambridge
CB2 3DZ.
Subjects: Art.
Books January to June 1991 - 2

CAREER CONCERN
PO Box 75
Chesterfield
S40 1NZ.
Subjects: Career. Books January to June 1991 - 3

CARGO PRESS
34 St Pauls Road
BEDFORD
MK40

CARIAD BOOKS
28 Oaten Hill
Canterbury
CT1 3HZ.
Short Stories.
Books January to June 1991 - 1

CARING & SHARING
Lana Davies
Cotton's Farmhouse, Whiston Road
Cogenhoe
Northamptonshire

LORNA R CARLETON
.The Paddocks
Ladbrooke
Leamington Spa
CV33 0BU

MR A J CARLTON
195 Harley Shute Road
ST LEONARDS ON SEA
East Sussex
TN38 9JJ

CARMINA PUBLISHING
Flat 1
33 Knowle Road

Totterdown
BRISTOL
BS4 2EB 0272 715144

CARMINE PINK
4 Dashwood Road
OXFORD
OX4 4SJ
Non-profit making venture for creative women.
Make notepaper, cards and posters. Newsletter.
Contact lists.

MR R B CARNAGHAM
22 Wentworth Close
WATFORD
Hertfordshire
WD1 3LW

R B CARNAGHAN
22 Wentworth Close
WATFORD
WD1 3LW

CARNEGIE PRESS
18 Maynard Street
Ashton
Preston
PR2 2AL

CARNEGIE DUNFERMLINE TRUST
Abbey Park House
Dunfermline
KY12 7PB.
Subjects: History of Manufacturing.

CAREL PRESS
18 Chertsey Bank
Carlisle
CA1 2QF

MR PAUL CARNEY
21 Kelvington Road
Peckham
LONDON
SE15 3EQ

CARNIVOROUS ARPEGGIO
329 Beverley Road
Hull
HU5 1LD

CARNTYNE HOUSE PUBLICATIONS
14 Graystane Road
Invergowrie
DUNDEE
DD2 5JQ 0382 562471

CAR NUMBERS GALAXY
Noel Woodall
16 Boston Avenue
Blackpool
FY2 9BZ. Tel 0253 55159
Listing 67500 Historical car number registrations
many with owners. Plus all D.V.L.A. auction prices
from December 1991 Hundreds of photographs
Car Numbers 1992. 704pp June 1992. ISBN
9502537/6/6 £24 Compilation of Personalised

Registration
Car Numbers 1990 600pp June 1990. ISBN
9502537/5/8 £21. Compilation of Personalised
Registrations
Car Numbers 1988 200pp June 1988 ISBN
9502537/4/X £10 Compilation of Personalised
Registrations.

THE CARPATHIAN PRESS
Richard & Andrew Dolinski Peter Nagy
46 Campell Road
Woodley
Berkshire
RG5 3NB. Tel 0734 505641
Founded 1977. Specialise in fine limited edition
letterpress printing and publishing. Books are both
hand and machine type set and printed on high
quality mould papers. On average two major titles
each year. Temptation Stephen Zeromski 75 copies
(26 cloth bound in slip case 49 copies soft bound)
11pp (195 x 270mm) 1989. Cloth bound £35.00
ISBN 1 8725 38 02 9. Soft bound £15.00 ISBN 1
872538 01 0
P.P.C.A Lady's Narrative Mme Rygier-Nalkowska
125 copies (26 copies quarter bound in cloth 99
copies soft bound) 16pp (195 x 270mm) 1990 cloth
bound £35.00 ISBN 1 872538 05 3 soft bound
£15.00 ISBN 1 872538 04 5

CARPHOLOGY COLLECTIVE
16 Wiverton Road
Forest Fields
Nottingham
NG7 6NP.
Subjects: Poetry.
Books July to December 1991 - 1

MS LYNNE CARR-JONES
9 Waterford Close
Lilliput
POOLE
Dorset
BH14 8EX 0202 739369

MR BRIAN CARRUTHERS
5 Counom Grove
LONDON
SE5 9LG

CARTERPRINT ENTERPRISES
26 Crinton Road
Hartburn
Stockton-on-Tees
TS18 5HE

MR B CARTWRIGHT
51 New Road
Armitage
RUGELEY
Staffordshire
WS15 4AA

MRS E A J CARTWRIGHT
Hignett
Iford Manor
BRADFORD-UPON-AVON
Wltshire

CARTY/LYNCH
Dunsany
Navan
Co. Meath
Republic of Ireland.
Subjects: Castles.
Books January to June 1991 - 1

CASDEC
22 Harraton Terrace
Birtley
Chester-le-Street
DH3 2QG

CAST PUBLICATIONS
18 Haverbearks Place
Lancaster
LA1 5BH

CASTLE BOOKS AND PUBLISHERS
6 Bank Street
Castletown
Isle of Man.
Subjects: European History.
Books July to December 1991 - 2

CASTLE BAILEY PRESS
West Dean
Salisbury
SP5 1JL.
Subjects: Local History.
Books July to December 1991 - 1

CASTLEBERG
18 Yealand Avenue
Giggleswick
Settle
BD24 0AY

CASTLEDEN PUBLICATIONS
11 Castlegate
Pickering
North Yorkshire
YO18 7AX 0751 76227
Publisher of local history and guide books. Printing
done 'in house'. Page origination: Letterpress. Lat-
est books litho printed.
'Pickering Through the Ages' by Keith Snowden.
38pp. 8 pages of photo graphs. ISBN 0 9514657 1
6.
'Malton and Norton Through the Ages' by Keith
Snowden. 48pp. 7 pages of photographs. ISBN 0
9514657 3 2.
'Helmsley and Kirkby Through the Ages' by Keith
Snowden. 56pp. 18 photo raphs and 5 drawings.
ISBN 0 9514657 4 0.

CATCHROSE
Brampton Bridge House
12 Queen Street
Newcastle-under-Lyme
ST5 1ED.
Subjects: Biography.
Books July to December 1991 - 1

CATHAIR BOOKS
1 Essex Gate
Dublin 8

Republic of Ireland.
Subjects: Historical Biography.
Books July to December 1991 - 2

CATH TATE CARDS
39 Kingswood Road
London
SW2 4JE

CATHOLIC INSTITUTE FOR
INTERNATIONAL RELATIONS
22 Coleman Fields
London
N1 7AF

CATS Trust
3 Alexandra Road
Heaton
Newcastle-upon-Tyne
NE6 5QS.
Subjects: Education.
Books July to December 1991 - 1

J. CATT
Great Glemham
Saxmundham
IP17 2DH.
Subjects: Education.
Books July to December 1991 - 3 new books 2 new
editions

CAUSEWAY PRESS
Bangor: John Menzies
Boucher Road
Belfast
BT12

CAVALIER HOUSE
35 Sandiway
Knutsford
WA16 8BU

MR W J CAVE
36 Park Road
Gressenhall
EAST DEREHAM
Norfolk
NR20 4LP

CAXTON AND HOLMESDALE PRESS LTD
c/o 31 Braeside Avenue
Sevenoaks
Kent
TN13 2JJ.
Subjects: Literature.

C.B PUBLISHING
18 Lochlann Terrace
Culloden
Inverness
IV1 2DU

C BOOKS
PO Box 11
Redcar
Cleveland
TS10 1PY

CELCAKES
Springfield House
Gate Helmsley
York
YO4 1NF

THE CELTIC CROSS PRESS
Rosemary Roberts
The Old Vicarage
Collingham
WETHERBY
West Yorkshire
LS22 5AU
Fine Printer

CELTIC DAWN
(Prebendel Press Ltd)
P O Box 30
Thame
Oxon
OX9 3AD

CENCRASTUS
Unit 1 Abbeymount Techbase
8 Easter Road
Edinburgh
Scotland
EH8 8EJ

CENTAUR PRESS
J Kingsley Cook
72a Marquis Road
LONDON
NW1 9UB

CENTERPRISE
136 Kingsland High Street
LONDON
E8 2NS

CENTRAL BRISTOL ADULT EDUCATION
CENTRE
189C Newfoundland Road
Bristol
BS2 9NY.
Subjects: Biography
Books January to June 1991 - 1. Books July to
December 1991 - 1

Centre Publishing
Cuilleann
Wester Galcantray
Cawdor
Nairn
IV22 5XX.
Subjects: Literature.
Books January to June 1991 - 1

Centre for Accessible Environments
35 Great Smith Street
London
SW1P 3BJ

Century Press and Publishing
Century Newspapers
51-67 Donegall Street

Belfast
BT1 0NX.
Subjects: Travel in Britain.
Books July to December 1991 - 1 new edition.

Century House
Erdington
Birmingham
B23 5XN
Canto Press

Century Press (Sussex)
2 East Meadway
Shoreham-by-Sea
BN43 5RF.
Subjects: Asian History. Biography. Short Stories
Books January to June 1991 - 1. Books July to
December 1991 - 2

Cerberus Press
24 Fairmount Drive
Loughborough
LE11 3JR

The Cerealogist
11 Powys Gardens
LONDON
W11 1JG
The journal for crop circle studies, published three
times a year. Annual sub £7.50.

Ceres Trading Company
Mr Arnold Drenthy
South Bank Technopark
90 London Road
LONDON
SE1 6LN

Certain Gestures
55 Perowne Street
ALDERSHOT
Hampshire
GU11 3JR
The 'zine that turned into music. Tapes availble.

CERTAINTY MAGAZINE
85 West Ealing Broadway
LONDON
W13 9BP
Adult fetishism. Magazine.

CERVERA PRESS
Language of Dance Centre
Flat 4
17 Holland Park
LONDON
W11 3TD
The Cervera Press publishes dance materials on
specialized dance styles; Historical, Classical and
Contempory. These are made more explicit and
educationally valuable through use of Labanotion
(the universally based dance notation system) Together with background history and study/per-
formance notes.

CERVERA PRESS
Labanotation Institute
University of Surrey

Guildford
GU2 5XH.
Subjects: Operatic dances.
Books July to December 1991 - 1

CETOS PUBLISHING
75 Beattyville Gardens
Ilford
IG6 1JY.
Subjects: Geology.
Books July to December 1991 - 1

C G H Services
Cwm Gwen Hall
PENCADER
Dyfed
SA39 9HA

CHAPTER TWO
199 Plumstead Common Road
London
SE18 2UJ

Jill Chadbom
143 Chapel Road
West Bergholt
Colchester
CO6 3EZ

CHALCOMBE PUBLICATIONS
Honey Lane
Hurley
Maidenhead
SL6 5LR

CHALICE
(New Age Networking South Wales) magazine
16 Blenheim Rd Beechwood
Newport
Gwent
NP9 8JL

CHALLENGE
Mr Chris F Atton
14 Logan Street
Langley Park
DURHAM
DH7 9YN
Following the death of our eponymous magazine,
we are concentrating on THE PACKAGE and
diversifying into improvised music with our SERF
MUSIC cassette series. Other proposals always
welcome. Our best unsolicited testimonial still stands.
Discover why: send SAE for catalogue.
REBARBATIVE AMBIGUITY.The Zen Architrave
Collective. 28pp. £2.50. Anthology of rabid writ-
ings from CHALLENGE.
THE PACKAGE No 3. Various hands, December
1992. £7.00. Comics, artworks, cassette.
FROM THE MAD LAB. cERTAIN ANTS. £5.00.
C60 cassette.

MR C J CHAMBERLAIN
95 North Street
Stilton
PETERBOROUGH
Cambridge
PE7 3RR

70

JILL CHAMBERS
24 Rockery Walk
Clifton
Shefford
SG17 5HW

CHAMELEON PRESS
EIP House
PO Box 117
Huntingdon
PE18 6PF

CHAMELIUS BOOKS
1 Merewood Cottages
Ecclerigg
Windermere
LA23 1LH

CHANGE
P O Box 824
London
SE24 9JS

CHANGING PERSPECTIVES LIMITED
Riverside House
Winnington House
NORTHWICH
Cheshire
CW8 1AD

CHANGING PERSPECTIVES:
PROTECTION THROUGH PREVENTION
Ashfield Nursery School
Elswick Road
Newcastle-upon-Tyne.
Subjects: Child Protection.
Books January to June 1991 - 1.

CHANGING PLACES PUBLICATIONS
23 Crossvale Road
Huyton
Liverpool
L36 0UY.
Subjects: Biography.
Books July to December 1991 - 1

CHANNEL PUBLICATIONS
No 1 Hope Bay Studio
Kingsdown
Deal
CT14 8ER

CHANNEL TUNNEL ASSOCIATION
44 Westbourne Terrace
London
W2 3UH.
Subjects: Bibliography.
Books January to June 1991 - 1

CHANSITOR
St. Mary's Works
St. Mary's Plain
Norwich
NR3 3BH.
Subjects: School Textbooks. Books July to December 1991 - 2 new books 1 new edition

CHANTRY PRESS
Rose Cottage
The Street
Eastcombe
Stroud
GL7 7DN.
Subjects: Local History.
Books July to December 1991 - 1

C.H.A.O.S. INCORPORATED
Edd A Hillier Pizza Research Centre
148 Humber Road South
Beeston
Nottingham
NG9 2EX
Another member of a network of incoherence.
Sometime publisher of Lobster Telephone and exchange of ideas and information and the number II.
Dedicated to confusion. Interested and interesting.
Truth is no obstacle. Write...The means is the end.
Trickster: Now - Barry Powell Dominic Morris 32 pages pub 1990 70p + SAE Lobster Telephone - Various - 24 pages sporadic appearance 10p + SAE

CHAOS INTERNATIONAL
BCM Sol
London
WC1N 3XX

CHAPMAN MAGAZINE
80 Moray Street
BLACKFORD
Perthshire
PH4 1QF 031 557 2207
Promotes Scottish writers. Magazine and books.
Chapman
4 Broughton Place
EDINBURGH
EH1 3RX
Literary publisher specialising in poetry and in promoting new writers and experimental work. The central commitment is to Scottish lierature and culture in Scots as well as English.

MR PETER CHAPMAN
11 Armstrong Avenue
COVENTRY
CV3 1BL

CHAPTER TWO
95 Genesta Road
London
SE18 3EX 081 316 5389.
Chapter Two concentrates on publishing Christian literature of a conservative Evangelical nature. Dispensational and fundamental books are stocked and a catalogue listing all the books is available on request. Chapter Two operate a very efficient mail order department.
The Rock & the Sand (pb) by Geoffrey T. Bull. 186 pp. Nov. '90 0-85307-002 -5. £5.95. Spiritual reflections of a missionary formerly held captive in Communist China 1951-53.
The Prospect by William Kelly. 380 pp (hb). Nov '89. 085307-001-7 £45. Facsimile of magazine a tool for biblical theological & historical study. The Revelation of Jesus Christ by W.R. Hartridge. 92 pp

(hb). Facsimile commentary of a biding use & value to Bible students & teachers. ISBN 185307. 003 2 £10.

CHAPTER & VERSE
Granta House
96 High Street
Linton
Cambridge
CB1 6JT

CHRIS CHARLES
137 Parklands
Coopersale
EPPING
Essex
CM16 7RQ

CHARLEWOOD PRESS
Middle Burgate House
Fordingbridge
Hampshire
SP6 1LX. Tel 0425 653393
Charlewood was an ancient open field in the parish of Breamore on the edge of The New Forest. The Press publishes carefully researches leaflets on the Historyof Breamore and the nearby small town of Fordingbridge. A. Light & G. Pointing. A walk to Breamore Miz-Maze; ISBN 0 95 12310 4 4PP 35P
Light and Pointing: A Walk Through Old Fordingbridge; ISBN 0 951231022 6pp. 35P
Light and Pointing The Tragedies of the Dodingtons ISBN 0 95 12310 3 0 20pp 95p

MR DAVID CHARNLEY
Plockton High School
PLOCKTON
Rosshire
IV52 8TU

CHASE PUBLICATIONS
The Chase
Hinton Martell
Wimbourne
BH21 7HE.
Subjects: Sport.
Books July to December 1991 - 1 new edition.

MR MARTIN CHATFIELD
31 Towngate
Heptonstall
HEBDEN BRIDGE
West Yorkshire
HX7 7NB
Illustrator, designer, photographer, small publisher, animator and computer graphics person.

CHAUCER WRITERS
51 Blayton Road
SHEFFIELD
S4 7DH

CHB PUBLISHING
123 Pemros Road
Plymouth
Devon
PL51LU
Publications of Railway and Bus books, and also poem and general interest books. Torbay Railway Delights at £3.95, covering the Railways of the Torquay, Paignton and Brixham lines in South Devon including The Tourist Steam Line between Paignton and Kingswear.
Modelling the Lynton and Barnstaple Railway at £2.90, A delightful look at a model layout of the famous narrow gauge Lynton and Barnstaple line by Brian Taylor.
The Sedton Branch, at £3.40 by Colin Henry Bustin, covering in text & pictures the former steam branch line of the Southern rail, and the present day electronic tramway which runs on its old route.

V P CHEEK
12 Greenholme Road
Eltham
LONDON
SE19 1UH

CHRIS CHEETHAM
10 Galloway Drive
Teignmouth
TQ14 9UX

CHELTENHAM AND GLOUCESTER COLLEGE
OF HIGHER EDUCATION
Centre for the Study of Religion
The Park Campus
Cheltenham
GL50 2QF.
Subjects: Trade Union History.
Books January to June 1991 - 1

CHENARA PUBLICATIONS
PO Box 267
Cheltenham
GL51 0UY.
Subjects: Occult.
Books July to December 1991 - 1

Ms Tania C Chen
2 Rocombe Crescent
LONDON
SE23 3BL

CHERRY GARDENS PUBLICATIONS
Cherry Gardens
Groombridge
Tunbridge Wells
TN3 9NY.
Subjects: Countryside. Books January to June 1991 - 1

MS ANDREA CHERSI
Via Cipro 96
I-25125 BRESCIA
ITALY

CHERUB PUBLICATIONS
19 South Quay
Great Yarmouth
NR30 2RG

CHERUB PRESS
David and Kim Butcher
18 Hargrave Road

Shirley
SOLIHULL, West Midlands
B90 1HX
Fine Printers

THE CHEVERELL PRESS
Hamilton House
66 Upper Richmond Road
LONDON
SW15 5PQ
Theatre books. Fiction - no.
How to become a working actor
Writing and Managing your own One Man Show.

CHEVINGTON PRESS
D R Wakefield
Triangle
Saltmarshe
Near Howden,North Humberside
DN14 7RX

CHIAROSCURA
(also Curious Press)
88 Laurence Court
Northampton
NN1 3HD

CHILD POVERTY ACTION GROUP (CPAG)
1-5 Bath Street
London
EC1V 9PY

NORTHERN CHILDREN'S BOOK FESTIVAL
Broad Lane
Moldgreen
Huddersfield
HS5 8DD

CHILDREN'S SOCIETY
Edward Rudolf House
Margery Street
LONDON
W1X 0IL
Subjects: Childrens' Fiction
Books July to December 1991 - 6

CHILDWALL WRITERS
Leybourne Close
Gateacre
LIVERPOOL
L28 4SP

CHILFORD HALL PRESS
Chilford Hall
Linton
CAMBRIDGE
CB2 6LE

CHIMAERA PRESS
Michael and Helen Hutchins
16 Oakhill Road
BECKENHAM
Kent
BR3 2NQ

CHINA CAT
20 Perry Road

Great Barr
BIRMINGHAM
B42 2BQ

P.A CHORLEY
10 Sycamore Close
Sixpenny Handley
Salisbury
SP5 5QQ

ALFRED TANG CHOW
100 Idmiston Road
LONDON
SE27 9HL 081 670 9969

Mr Charles Christian
Ferndale House
North Lopham
DISS
Norfolk
PE22 2NQ

CHRISTIAN FOCUS PUBLICATIONS
Geanies House
Fearn
Tain
IV20 1TW.
Subjects: Children non-fiction. Religion.
Books July to December 1991 - 7 new books 3 new
editions.

MR ANTHONY CHRISTIE
Hermafrodux Limited
14b Elsworthy Terrace
LONDON
NW3 3DR

D D CHRISTIE
18 St John's Road
POOLE
Dorset
BH15 2NB 0202 679891
An octogenarian hobby publisher of self-produced
books.
A Bumpy Wicket by Donald Chrisie ISBN 0 9507176
4 9. The Horace cricket sagas illustrated by the
author. Verse, 31 A5 pages. Paperback. £2.95 inc
p+p The Evolution of Horace ISBN 0 9507176 5 7.
His story told in rhyme by Donald D Christie, with
marginal vignettes. 38 A5 pages, paperback, £2.95
inc p+p The Colleger & The Oppidan. A Story of
two boys at Eton in 1755 tooled hardback in
illustrated slip-case. 209 pages. Originally published by Geo.Mann Books, now by the author,
Donald D Christie at revised price £7.15 inc p+p
ISBN 0 7041 0200 5

PAX CHRISTI
9 Henry Road
London
N4 2LH

DAVID CHRISTOPHER
8 Reed Court
Longwell Green
Bristol
BS15 7DX

CHTHONIOS BOOKS
7 Tamarisk Steps
HASTINGS
East Sussex
TN34 3DN

D CHUDASAMA
29 Durnton Road
Stirchley
BIRMINGHAM
B30 2TE

CHUDLEIGH PUBLISHING
45 Chudleigh Crescent
ILFORD
Essex
IG

CHURCH ACTION ON POVERTY
Central Buildings
Oldham Street
Manchester
M1 1JT.
Subjects: Social Welfare.
Books July to December 1991 - 1

CHURCH PASTORAL AID SOCIETY
Athena Drive
Tachbrook Park
Warwick
CV34 6NG.
Subjects: children's Religious Books.
Books January to June 1991 - 4. Books July to
December 1991 - 2

CHURCH OF ST AIDAN
Little Chalfont
Finch Lane
Little Chalfont
Amersham

C I A NOTTINGHAM COMMUNITY ARTS
39 Gregory Boulevard
Hyson Green
NOTTINGHAM
NG7 6BE

CICADA PRESS
Monolog Poems
20 King's Road
LONDON
NW5 2SA

CICATRIX
Eamer O'Keeffe
BM/Cicatrix
London
WC1N 3XX

CICERONE
2 Police Square
MILNTHORPE
Cumbria
LH7 7QE 05395 62069
A leading guidebook company specialising in out-
door activities and in general bo oks about the
North. Approach with a synopsis in first instance.

No fiction or poetry.
THE SHROPSHIRE HILLS. By David Hunter.
ISBN 0 85284 064 1. 168 pages. Laminat ed cover
paperback. 8 pages coloured, numerous black and
white plus maps. £5.95 March 1991.
LOST RESORT? By roger Bingham. ISBN 0 85284
071 4. 320 pages. 155 photographs . The story of
Morecambe. £14.95. December 1990.
LIMESTONE (100 Best Climbs). By Chris Craggs.
ISBN 0 85284 087 0. 160 pages. L arge format
hardbound. 100-plus pictures in full colour. £19.95.
September 199 1.

CINNABAR
38 St Pauls Road
Bedford MK40 4NT

CIRCLE PRESS
Ronald King
26 St Lukes Mews
Notting Hill
London
W11 1DF Tel: 071 792 9298
First formed in 1967 by a group of printmakers
interested in publishing limited edition artist's books.
Since then the press has produced more than 150
classic and contemnporary titles; letter press; litho;
intaglio and silk screen; ranging in price from £5-£1
000.
'Alphabeta Concertina'. designer Ronald King.
1983. 165 x 110mm; cut and creased; no text in
PVC Box. £25.00. ISBN 0 901308 46 6. Pop out
alphabet book.
'Turn Over Darling'. designer Ronald King. 200 x
150mm. £21.00. No ISBN. Intaglio printed from
wire drawings - series of six drawing which join to
make twelve poses.
'London Series'. 200 x 300m. A box of eight new
poems each by a different poet and artist limited to
25 signed sets and 75 single copies. ISBNs on
application.

CIRUS ASSOCIATES (S.W.)
Little Hintock
Kington Magna
Gillingham
SP8 5EW

C.I.S.S. Publishing
63 Ravensbourne Gardens
Clayhall
Ilford
IG5 0XH.
Subjects: Stamps. Postal History.
Books January to June 1991 - 1. Books July to
December 1991 - 1

CITY PUBLISHING
Regent House
291 Kirkdale
London
SE26 4QE.
Subjects: Local Travel Guides.
Books January to June 1991 - 1. Books July to
December 1991 - 1

CITY TECHNOLOGY COLLEGES TRUST
15 Young Street

London
W8 5EH.
Subjects: Education.
Books July to December 1991 - 3

CITY WOMEN'S NETWORK
30 Essex Street
London
WC2R 3AL

CIVIL-COMP PRESS
10 Saxe-Coburg Place
Edinburgh
EH3 5HR.
Subjects: Engineering.
Books July to December 1991 - 2

CIVIL SERVICE AUTHOR
c/o Iain R McIntyre
Burnside
Station Road, Beauly
Invernesshire
IV4 7EQ

C.K.D. PUBLICATIONS
61 Highfield Road (South)
Chorley
PR7 1RH.
Subjects: Local History.
Books July to December 1991 - 1

CLAIBORNE PUBLICATIONS (UK)
36 High Street
Saxmundham
IP17 1AB

CLAIRE PUBLICATIONS
Tey book Craft Centre
Brook Road
Great Tey
Colchester
CO6 1JE.
Subjects: School Textbooks.
Books July to December 1991 - 2

CLAM PUBLICATIONS
13 Pound Place
Shalford
Guildford
GU4 8HH

MR D A CLARE
37 Cardy Road
Boxmoor
HEMEL HEMPSTEAD
Hertfordshire
HP1 1RL

MR ROLAND CLARE
Cambridge Silent Artists
5 Churchways Avenue
Horfield
BRISTOL
BS7 8SN

CLARK AND HOWARD BOOKS
4 Merridale Garden

Wolverhampton
WV3 OH4. 0902 22715
Small publisher run as a hobby. Books typed by
Hilary Clark commercially printed (offset litho or
similar) paperbacks.
'Horse and Cart Days. Memories of a farm boy' by
A.B. Tinsley. 1990. 68pp 24 drawings. paperback.
£2.00. ISBN 0 9509555 8 2.
'The Greens of Grasmere. A Narrative by Dorothy
Wordsworth 1808'. publish ed 1987. 60pp. 8 illus-
trations and map; paperback. £1.50. ISBN 0 9509555
3 1.
'A Night in the Snow. A Struggle for Life on the
Long Mynd' by the Revd. E. Donald Carr 1865.
1985. 32pp. 1 photograph. paperback. £1.35. ISBN
0 9509555 1 5.

MS ALEX CLARKE
30b Lady Margaret Road
Kentish Town
LONDON
NW5 2XL

B.R. CLARKE
11 Penn Gardens
Bath
BA1 3RZ.
Subjects: Railways.
Books July to December 1991 - 1

MS EILEEN M CLARKE
24 Manor House Way
Brightlingsea
COLCHESTER
Essex
CO7 0QN

J CLARKE
37 Grafton Way
London
W1P 5LA

Nigel J Clarke Publications
Unit 2 Russell House
Lym Close
Lyme Regis
Dorset
DT7 3DE 02974 3669
We publish Walking Guides/Historical Town
Guides/Booklets on Local West Country attrac-
tions/Fossil booklets/Local speciality Maps/Tide
Tables. We wholesale postcards and touring maps.
Our market is mainly the West Country and we sell
25 000 titles annually.
The Illustrated Map and Guide to Avebury. Pub-
lished 20.3.91. ISBN 0 907683 35 5. Full colour 25
illustrations. Two maps of Avebury £2.35. A map
guide to Avebury and area. 907683 12 6. 10 line
drawings £1.50. 35 pages. Published 18.2.90. by J.
Chadwick.
The Rude man of Cerne Abbas and other Wessex
Landscape Oddities by Leslie Cooper. ISBN 0
107683 07 X. 21 line drawings £1.50. Published
21.7.91.

PAT CLARKE
Oriel-y-Ddraig
Unit 2, Diffwys Square

BLAENAU FFESTINIOG
Gwynedd
LL41

S N CLARKE
75 St Thomas Road
LONDON
N4 2QJ

MS ROSEMARY CLARK
Old School
Worms Hill
SITTINGBOURNE
Kent
ME9 0TR

CLAUDIA PRESS
Claudia
BM Claudia
London
WC1N 3XX
Political essays in pamphlet form. I Claudia and
Love lies bleeding currently out of print but will be
included in a book of essays coming out this year.
Read (her) or remain a fool- 'maximum rock and
roll' review.
I Claudia by Claudia 32pp 1988 feminism unveiled
Love Lies Bleeding by Claudia 32pp 1990 domestic
violence - the consequence of romantic love
The Rebels' New Clothes 40pp 1992 A critical look
at rebellion

CLAYHANGER BOOKS
The Old Rectory
Clayhanger
Tiveton
EX16 7NY.
Subjects: Anthropology. Books January to June
1991 - 1.
Books July to December 1991 - 1

MR CHRISTOPHER CLAYTON
The Print Business Limited
91 Church Road
LONDON
SE19 2TA

CLEARWATER COMMUNICATIONS
77a Fountainhill Road
ABERDEEN
AB2 4EA

CLEARWELL CAVES
Clearwell
Coleford
Forest of Dean
Gloucestershire
GL16 8JR.
Subjects: Children's Fiction.
Books July to December 1991 - 1

PETER V CLEGG
Squirrel's Leap
9 Park Close
Godalming
GU7 1TL

MRS MARGARET CLERESI
37 Leckford Road
OXFORD
OX2 6HY

CLEVELAND KEY
8 Worcester Close
Stanford-le-Hope
SS17 8AL

CLOCKTOWER PRESS
Duncan McLean
17 West Terrace
South Queensferry
West Lothian
EH30 9LL 031 331 4117
Our aim is to produce small cheap booklets of new
writing mostly Scottish and almost all short stories.
All feature high quality illustrations. 3 or 4 pro-
duced per year. Order direct from the above ad-
dress. 'Safe/Lurch' by James Meek and Duncan
McLean December 1990. 16pp 5 illust rations by
Olivia Irvine £1.00. Short stories.
'The Druids Shite It Fail To Show' by Duncan
McLean May 1991. 20pp. 5 illustrations by Jane
Hyslop £1.00. ISBN 1 873767 00 5. Fiction.
'Zoomers: Short Sharp Fiction' by Jim Ferguson
Gordon Legge Sandy Watson and others July 1991.
20pp 4 illustrations by Eddie Farrell £1.00. Very
short stories.

CLOUD
48 Biddlestone Road
Heaton
Newcastle-upon-Tyne
NE6 5SL

CLUANIE DEER FARM PARK
Beauly
IV4 7AE.
Subjects: Scottish Red Deer.
Books July to December 1991 - 1

HILARY ANNE CLUTTEN
Rose Farm
North Green
Pulham St. Mary
Diss
IP21 4XX.
Subjects: Local Food.
Books July to December 1991 - 1

C.M.R (Constance Rover) Publications
Flat 1
4 Clifton Crescent
FOLKESTONE
Kent
CT20 2EW

CND PUBLICATIONS
162 Holloway Road
London
N7 8DG.
Subjects: Law.
Books July to December 1991 - 1 new book 1 new
edition.

C N P PUBLICATIONS

Dr James Whetter
Roseland
Gorran
ST AUSTELL
Cornwall
0726 843501
Publishes a quarterly Cornish magazine, The Cornish Banner/An Banir Kernowck, and occasional booklets that develop from that: viz. political essays, poetry, celtic design, history etc. ISSN 0306 9079.
Dr James Whetter CORNISH ESSAYS 1971-76. 1977 ISBN 0 906009 0 6. Paperback 156 pages. £4.75. Historical and political essays.
Pieter Huisman LYVER GWYN NA DU 1984 Paperback. 36 pages. £2.75. Celtic desig ns ISBN 0 9060090 3 0.
Jaclk Carno BANNER POEMS 1989 Paperback 48 pages £4.75 ISBN 0 906009 06 5

COALVILLE PUBLISHING COMPANY
Springboard Centre
Mantle Lane
Coalville
LEICESTER
LE6 4DR

D J COBB
Sinodun
Shalford
BRAINTREE
Essex
CM7 5HT

COBDEN OF CAMBRIDGE PRESS
47 Newnham Road
Cambridge
CB3 9EY.
Subjects: Historic Rivers.
Books July to December 1991 - 1

COBTREE PRESS
Anthony Smith
Little Preston Lodge
Coldharbour Lane,Aylesford
MAIDSTONE,Kent
ME20 7NS
Fine Printer

COBWEB
57 William Morris House
Margravine Road
LONDON
W6 8LR

COCKBIRD PRESS LIMITED
PO Box 356
HEATHFIELD
East Sussex
TN21 9QW

MRS M COE
2 Dentwood Street
LIVERPOOL
L8 9SR

MR R M COLCLOUGH
Elm Cottage, The Old Farmhouse

South Newingtonse
BANBURY
Oxfordshire
OX15 4JW

BEEWOOD COLDELL
43 Birchall Avenue
Culcheth
Warrington
WA3 4DD

COLLECTORS' BOOKS
Bradley Lodge
Kemble
Cirencester
Gl7 6AD

COLLINDIST PUBLICATIONS
Robert Corfe
6 Southgate Green
Bury St. Edmunds
Suffolk
IP33 2BL Tel 0284 754123
Publishing arm of the Campaign For Industry and The Collindist Association. The CFI is the only U.K. organisation promoting the productive economy within the constraints of social and environmental responsibility. The CA is the philosophical think-tank for the CFI. New Life For British Industry Robert Corfe 68pp. September 1985 ISBN 0 948571 00 4 £2.50 industry/economics.
Swindling Of The Unemployed Guy Tallice 70pp. November 1991 ISBN 0 948571 10 1 £3.50 exploitation by the financial institutions Righteousness Triumphant Robert Corfe 70pp. March 1992 ISBN 0 948571 11 X £3.50 failure of the Churches to maintain ethical standards.

COLLINS AND BROWN
MERCURY HOUSE
195 Knightsbridge
London
SW7 1RE

MR ANTHONY COLLINS
80 Pasture Lane
LEEDS
LS7 4QN

John Hugh Collins
15 Oakenbrow Sway
Lymington
SO41 6OY.
Subjects: Family History.
Books January to June 1991 - 1

S COLL
94 Offord road
Islington
LONDON
N1 1PF

MS BETTY COLMAN
59 Strand on the Green
Chiswick
LONDON
W4 3PE

MR CORRADO COLOMBINI
St Brelades
4 Parrys Lane
Stoke Bishop
BRISTOL
BS9 1AA

COLOPHON PRESS
18A Prentis Road
London
SW16 1QD.
Subjects: Bibliography.
Books July to December 1991 - 2

COLORIFIC IDEAS
Doug Rees
Hall Place
Penshurst Road, Leigh
TONBRIDGE
Kent
TN11 8HH 0732 833619

COLOUR GROUP (G.B.)
17 Castlebar Road
London
W5 2DL.
Subjects: History of technology. Books July to December 1991 - 1

COLT BOOKS
9 Clarendon Road
Cambridge
CB2 2BH

KIM COMBE
Bayfield Hall
Holt
NR25 7JN

COMPOSERLINK
Mr Richard Lauder
18 Ashwyn Street
Hackney
LONDON
E8 3DL

COMMON GROUND
45 Shelton Street
Covent Garden
LONDON
WC2H 9HJ

COMMON SENSE
16 Keir Street
EDINBURGH
EH3 9EU
A journal of new ideas.

COMMONWORD
21 Newton Street
MANCHESTER
M1 1FZ

COMMUNITY DEVELOPMENT FOUNDATION
60 Highbury Grove
London
N5 2AG.

Subjects:

CENTRE FOR COMMUNITY STUDIES
210/212 Borough High Street
London
SE1 1JA.
Subjects: Law. Social Sciences.
Books July to December 1991 - 8

COMMON GROUND: WORLDLY GOODS
Unit G. Arnos Castle Estate
Junction Road
Brislington
Bristol
BS4 3JP.
Subjects: 'Apple Source Book'.
Books July to December 1991 - 1

COMMON SENSE
Richard Gunn or Brian McGrail
PO Box 311
SDO
Edinburgh
EH9 15F
Common sense journal of Edinburgh Conference of Socialist Economics publishes political analysis philosophy fiction poetry and reviews. Recent issues have debated the anti-poll tax struggle fascism in Germany Italian Autonomia and Scottish culture. Subscribe and help change the world.
Issue 10(May 1991) includes articles on the Gulf War Student Debt Nazism and Poll Tax. ISBN 0 957204X
Issue 11(winter1991) includes articles on Italian workers and Scottish common sense philosophy.
Issue 12(summer 1992) contains material on the General Election Scotland and Germany.

COMPACT SERVICES
29 St Helen's Road
Sandford
Wareham
BH20 7AX

COMPASS PUBLICATIONS
191 Field Avenue
Canterbury
CT1 1TS

COMPOSITIONS BY CARN
10 Laburnam Grove
Eastleigh
Hants
S05 4DJ

COMPUPRINT PUBLISHING
1 Sands Road
Swalwell
Newcastle-upon-Tyne
NE16 3DJ.
Subjects: Political Science.
Books January to June 1991 - 1

COMUNN NA CLARAICH
(The Clarsach Society)
65 Mount Vernon Road
Edinburgh
EH16 6JH.

Subjects: Poetry.
Books July to December 1991 - 1

CONCATENTION
44 Brook Street
ERITH
Kent
DA8 1JQ

A.T CONDIE PUBLICATIONS
Merrivale
Main Street
Carlton
CV13 0BZ

CONFRATERNITY OF ST JAMES
57 Leopold Road
London
N2 8BG

CONNECTIONS
c/o Jeanne Conn
165 Dominic Drive
New Eltham
London
SE9 3LE

MRS R CONNELLY
132a Sturton Street
CAMBRIDGE
CB1 2QF

CONNOLLY ASSOCIATION
c/o Four Provinces Bookshop
244-246 Grays Inn Road
London
WC1X 8JR

CONSIDER
Dr Charles Harvey
58 Keyford
FROME
Somerset
BA11 1JT
(Business: 20 Paul Street, Frome, Somerset, BA11
1DX. Tel: 0373 451777).
Etymology: L. considerare, (sidus -eris, a star)
originlly, and still amongst those who know, 'to
examine the stars'. CONSIDER has been set us to
publish consid ered works on all aspects of astology,
especially in relation to psychology, philosophy,
and world affairs.
ASTROLOGY: A Model for Chart Interpretation.
By Charles Harvey (1992). £7.99 paperback. ISBN
1 873948 00 X.
SUN AND MOON IN ASTROLOGY. By Charles
Harvey (1992). £9.99 paperback. ISBN 1 873 948
01 8.

ROBERT CONSTANT
17 Droxford Crescent
Tadley
Basingstoke
RG26 6BA.
Subjects: Children's Fiction.
Books July to December 1991 - 1

CONSUMERS' ASSOCIATION

Castlemead
Gascoyne Way
Hertford
SG14 1LH

CONTOUR SCHOOL SUPPLIES
46 High Street
Emsworth
PO10 7AW

SUSAN M CONWAY
8 Ferryman's Quay
Sands Wharf
William Morris Way
London SW6

SUZETTE M COOKE AND PHILIP CROME
16 Park Lane
Alford
LN13 9DN

F COOK TRAVEL GUIDES
8 Wykeham Court
Old Perry Street
Chislehurst
BR7 6PN

MRS J COOK
97 Passingham Avenue
BILLERICAY
Essex
CM11 2TB

MR W R COOK
Stronemill
Hartfield Court
COVE
Helensborough
G84 0PW

MR ROBERT COON
20 Selwood Road
GLASTONBURY
Somerset
BA6 8HN

COOPER PUBLICATIONS
24 Pelham Road
Clavering
Saffron Walden
CB11 4PQ.
Subjects: Local Walks Books. Books July to December 1991 - 1

COPPER BEECH PUBLISHING
11 Martyns Place
East Grinstead
RH19 4HF

MS DIANE COOPER
69 Kensington Court
LONDON
W8 5DS

DAVE COOPER
5 Kingsgate Drive
Blackpool

79

FY3 8HB.
Subjects: Biography.
Books January to June 1991 - 1

MRS J COOPER
2 The Anvil
Bugbrooke
NORTHAMPTON
NN7 3PX

MR JOHN S T COOPER
40 Malden Court
NEW MALDEN
Surrey
KT3 4PP

MISS N M COOPER
3 Hythe Road
POOLE
Dorset
BH15 3NN

R.A.COOPER
Butterhill House
49 Old North Road
Wansford
Peterborough
PE8 6LB.
Subjects: Family History.
Books July to December 1991 - 1

COORLEA PUBLISHING
West Lodge
Taverham Hall
Norwich
NR8 6HU

I.S. COPINGER:
J.W. Dickenson
44 St. Monica Grove
Durham
DH1 4AT.
Subjects: Local History. Books July to December
1991 - 1

COQUELICOTS PRESS
Fovant Elm
Tisbury Road
Salisbury
SP3 5JY

CORBIE PRESS
11 River Street
Ferryden
Montrose
DD10 9RT.
Subjects: Art. Poetry.
Books July to December 1991 - 3

CORDEN OF CAMBRIDGE PRESS
47 Newham Road
CAMBRIDGE
CB3 9EY
Little Press
The Historic River by S M Haslam. 324pp, 700 figs,
mostly new line drawings. 1991. ISBN 0951796305
£15.50. Rivers and culture down the ages. Wide-

ranging. East style.
Outdoor Games for Brownies in Built-Up Areas by
S M Haslam. 20pp, 1992. ISBN 0951796305 £2.50.
As title - for Brownie Guide section of the Girl
Guides Association.
Guiding Brownies, 165pp, 17 illustrations, 1988.
No ISBN Available through Corden of Cambridge.
£4.95. Brownies (junior Girl Guides) and the devel-
opment of innate potential and of character

CORK WORKERS CLUB
9 St Nicholas Church Place
Cove Street
Cork City
Ireland

CORNER HOUSE PUBLISHING
70 Oxford Street
MANCHESTER
M1 5NH

THE CORNUCOPIA PRESS
10 Curzon Street
LONDON
W1Y 7FJ

CORNWALLIS PRESS
24 Linton Crescent
Hastings
TN34 1TJ.
Subjects: Literature.
Books January to June 1991 - 1

CORPORATE LINK
Swale View
Low Row
Richmond
DL11 6NE

CORRIB CONSERVATION CENTRE
Ardnasillagh
Oughterard
County Galway
Republic of Ireland.
Subjects: Archaeology.
Books January to June 1991 - 1 Books July to
December 1991 - 1

CORYLUS PRESS
Hazel Harvey
53 Thornton Hill
Exeter
EX4 4NR. Tel 0392 54068
Exeter local guides to parks and gardens
Secrets of a Garden City by G. Levine 40 pages 4.50
ISBN 0 951571508
Exeter Park Leaflets by G. Levine 50p each.

THE COSMIC ELK
Heather Hobden
13 Swallowbeck Avenue
Lincoln
LN6 7EZ. Tel 0522 691146
The Cosmic Elk publishes readable and affordable
works on Science History and the History of Sci-
ence.
John Harrison and the Problem of Longitude 1990
ISBN 1 871443 04 0 £5 inc. p+p.

Law of War? The Legal Aspects of the Cuban Missile Crisis £7 inc. p+p. 1992 ISBN 1 871443 06 7.
A Series of Booklets on the History of Astronomy £1 + 50p p+p. each. includes First Scientific Ideas on the Universe ISBN 1 871443 05 9 The Telescopes revolution ISBN 1 871443 07 5.

MS CATHERINE COT
c/o L'Autre Journal
2 rue du Colonel Drint
F-75001 PARIS
France

COTHILL HOUSE SCHOOL:
Niche Marketing and Publishing Srrvic
The Dovecote
6 Turville Barns Eastleach
Cirencester
GL7 3QB.
Subjects: History of Education.
Books July to December 1991 - 1

COTHU
The Business Council for the Arts
Irish Management Institute
Sandyford Road
Dublin 16
Republic o
Subjects: Art.
Books July to December 1991 - 1

COTSWOLD MUSIC
Bridge Cottage
Beckford
Tewkesbury
GL20 7AN.
Subjects: Music.
Books July to December 1991 - 2

COTTAGE BOOKS
1 Higher Hill Lane
Cullompton
EX15 1AG.
Subjects: Poetry.
Books July to December 1991 - 1

COTTAGE GALLERY PUBLICATIONS
Husilar Cottage Studio/Gallery
South Yorkshire Buildings
Moorend Lane Silkstone Common
Barnsley
S75 4RJ.
Subjects: Art.
Books July to December 1991 - 1

COTTAGE LOAF: THE COPPERS
Scothern Lane
Sudbrooke
Lincoln

COTTAGE PUBLISHING
Norton Cottage
Station Road
Letterston
Haverfordswest
SA62 5RZ.

Subjects: Food.
Books January to June 1991 - 1

MR PETER COTTERELL
N E A
29a Market Square
BRIGGLESWADE
Bedfordshire
SG18 8AQ

CHRIS DE COULON
73 Fitzgerald House
East India Dock Road
LONDON
E14 0HH

MR JACK COUNSELL
21 Carrick Court
Kennington Park Road
LONDON
SE11 4EE

COUNTER INFORMATION
p/h CI
11 Forth Street
EDINBURGH
EH1
Broadsheet reporting resistance activity worldwide.

COUNTER PRODUCTIONS
PO Box 556
LONDON
SE5 ORW 071 274 9009
Mail Order sales of UK and overseas small press publications. Specialising in radical, dissident, surreal, outre, anarchic, visionary, fortean, anti-authoritarian books, magazines and pamphlets. Descriptive catalogue avaliable. Also trade distribution.

COUNTYVISE/MERSEYSIDE PORT FOLIOS/
Birkenhead Press
John Emmerson
1-3 Grove Road
Rock Ferry
Birkenhead
L42 3XS.
Subjects: Local biography. Local History. Historical Biography. History of History of the Port of Liverpool and its Docks.

MS YVONNE COURTNEY
9 Carnaby Street
LONDON
W1V 1PG

MR DEM A COUTARELLI
Av Kifisias 118
B 11526 ATHENS
GREECE

MARY E COVE
3 Springfield Drive
Kingsbridge
TQ7 1HG

COVENTRY CHURCH CHARITIES

c/o Godfrey-Peyton and Co.
Hill Street
Coventry.
Subjects: Local History.
Books July to December 1991 - 1

COVEROPEN: A.G. (NORTHERN)
138 Albert Road
Farnworth
Bolton
BL4 9NE.
Subjects: Humour.
Books July to December 1991 - 1

MR WILLIAM COWAN
82 Leonard Close
Donnington
TELFORD
Shropshire
TF2 8BQ

R & E COWARD
16 Sturgess Avenue
London
NW4 3TS

MISS BRENDA COWBURN
4 Clement View
NELSON
Lancashire
BB9 7AB

JOHN COWELL
52 Lon-y-bryn
Menai Bridge
LL59 5LL.
Subjects: Local History.
Books July to December 1991 - 1

C.P.I. Press
Science House
Winchcombe Road
Newbury
RG14 5QX.
Subjects: Agriculture.

C.R Publishing
35 Thorn Grove
Cheadle Hulme
Cheshire
SK8 7LP

CRABFLOWER PAMPHLETS
The Frogmore Press
42 Morehall Avenue
Folkstone
Kent
CT19 4EF
Crabflower Pamphlets which are distributed by the
Frogmore Press publish anthologies and individual
collections by new and established poets. Crabflower
Pamphlets are always limited editions of one hun-
dred copies.
New Pastorals by Robert Etty. 18pp June 1992
ISBN 0 9515063 5 8 £2.75 (INCL. P+P) Poetry.
The Frogmore Poetry Prize Anthology by Ed. Jeremy
Page. 30pp January 1992 ISBN 0 9515063 4 X.

£3.00 Poetry
Blush Klaxon Has A body Like A Trio Sonata by
Bob Mitchell. 24pp October 1991 ISBN 0 9515063
3 1 £2.75. Poetry

CRABTREE PRESS
4 Portland Avenue
Hove
BN3 5NP.
Subjects: Historical Biography.
Books July to December 1991 - 1

CRABWELL PUBLICATIONS
2 The Ridgeway
River
Dover
CT17 0NX

CRACKED BELL PRESS
51 York Avenue
Great Crosby
LIVERPOOL
L23 5RN

CRAFTS MAGAZINE
44a Pentonville Road
Islington
London
N1 9BY

CRAKEHILL PRESS
5-7 Sowerby Road
Thirsk
YO7 1HR

CRANBOURN PRESS
7 Cecil Street
London
WC2N 4EZ.
Subjects: Art.
Books July to December 1991 - 1

CRANE PRESS
30 South Street
Ashby-de-la-Zouch
LE6 5BT.
Subjects: Local History. Books January to June
1991 - 1

A M CRANE
37a Nile Street
KIRKCALDY
Fife
KY2 5AX

NICO CRAVEN
The Coach House
Ponsonby
Seascale
CA20 1BX. Tel Beckermet 841256
A book on cricket published each spring by the
author - mostly about the character and characters
of county and village cricket.
A Tale of Two Counties by Nico Craven. 72pp
March 1992 £5.95 There's Life after Cheltenham
by Nico Craven. 48pp March 1991 £4.95. Summer
Pudding by Nico Craven. 62pp March 1990 £4.35.

82

CREATION PRESS
83 Clerkenwell Road
London
EC1
Contemporary horror titles and new edition of
Poe's poems. Bridal Gown Shroud Adele Olivia
Gladwell ISBN 1 871592 13 5 PUB: September
24th 1992 208pp £6.95 Post Feminist Fiction Es-
says. Blood and Roses (Edited Gladwell and Havoc)
ISBN 1 871592 14 3 PUB: October 31st 1992
320pp £8.95 19th Century Vampire Literature
Rapid Eye 2 Simon Dwyer (Ed) ISBN 1 871592 23
2 PUB: November 5th 1992 400£pp £9.95 Non-
fiction:'Occulture'

CREATION RESOURCES TRUST
Mead Farm, Downhead
West Camel
Yeovil
BA22 7RQ

CREATIVE MIND
Lark Lane Community Centre
80 Lark Lane
LIVERPOOL
L17 8UU

CREATIVE MONOCHROME
20 St Peters Road
CROYDON
CR1 1HD

CREEK PUBLISHERS
Tarn Hows
Wyre Road Skippool
Thornton-Cleverleys
Blackpool
FY5 5LF.
Subjects: Local History.
Books July to December 1991 - 1

CRESCENT MOON
Mr J Robinson
18 Chaddesley Road
KIDDERMINSTER
DY10 3AD
We publish poetry, fiction, literary crticism and art
books. PAGAN AMERICA. An anthology of New
American Poetry edited by Jeremy Robinson.70
pages. Early 1991. £9.95. (poetry anthology).
BLINDED BY HER LIGHT. The lost poetry of
Robert Graves. By Jeremy Robinson. 7 5 pages.
£14.95. ISBN 1 871846 11 0.
THOMAS HARDY AND JOHN COWPER
POWYS. Wessex Revisited. By Jeremy Robinson.
153 pages. £21.95. ISBN 1 851846 16 1.

CYNTHIA CRESSWELL
22 Michael's Way
Sling
Coleford
GL16 8LZ

MR ERIC CREW
26 St David's Drive
BROXBOURNE
Hertfordshire
EN10 7LS

ASSOCIATION OF CRICKET STATISTICIANS
3 Radcliffe Road
West Bridgford
Nottingham
NG2 5FF.
Subjects: Cricket.
Books July to December 1991 - 11

CRITICAL WAVE PUBLICATIONS
Steve Green Martin Tudor
33 Scott Road
Olton
Solihull.
Tel 021 706 0108
Critical Wave The European Science Fiction and
Fantasy Review is the Genre's leading showcase for
news reviews features and art portfolios. Founded
in 1987 Michael Moorcock has called it The most
consistently interesting and intelligent review on
the SF scene.
Critical Wave #26 (June 1992; 32pp) Contributors
incl. Brian Aldiss Dan Simmons David Wingrove
Critical Wave #25 (March 1992; 32pp) Contribu-
tors incl. Robert Holdstock Nicholas Royle
Critical Wave #24 (November 1991; 32pp) Contributors incl. Ramsey Campbell Paul J McAuley

CRITIQUE
Deau Braithwaite
Rhyd-Dderwen
Hebron
WHITLAND
Dyfed
SA34 0XX
Critique is a new, independent review, supplying to
the printed and broadcast media in general, with
special emphasis on 'alternative' and small press
publications. All submissions and publicity mate-
rial welcome.

CROCHET DESIGN
17 Poulton Square
Morecambe
LA4 5PZ.
Subjects: Handicrafts.
Books July to December 1991 - 2

MR ALAN CROCKER
22 Gastans Road
CHIPPENHAM
Wiltshire
SN14 0NT

CROCUS
Cathy Bolton
Commonword
Cheetwood House
21 Newton Street
M1 1F2. Tel 061 236 2773
We are a community publisher. We publish a vari-
ety of work by North West Writers. In particular we
seek to give a voice to people who traditionally have
been denied or lacked access to publication. A
Matter of Fat. 158 pages by Sherry Ashworth
publication date 1/11/91 ISBN 0 94 6745 95 1
Price £4.95
Rainbows in the Ice. poetry by disabled writers 94

pages. Publication date March 1992 ISBN 0 946745
90 0 Price 4.50
The Delicious Lie Poetry by Georgina Blake Publication date August 24th see form for more details.

CROFTSPUN PUBLICATIONS
Catherine Gill
Drakemyre Croft
Cairnorrie
Methlick
Ellon Aberdeenshire
AB41 OJN. Tel 0651 4252
Pocket sized booklets with card cover desk-top
published for individuality and up to the minute
accuracy. The Birthday Book is specially written for
the client's birth date and the Cottage Guide is
being continually updated.
The Esoteric Birthday Book Catherine Gill 12-16
pages £2.25 post free Astrology (birth date re-
quired)
The Cottage Guide to Writer's Postal Workshops
Compiled by Catherine Gill 14 plus pages £1.00
post free Writer's directory.

CROLKERNE BOOKS
95 Westward Drive
Pill
Bristol
BS20 0JS

CROMWELL EDITIONS
43 Manchester Street
London
W1M 5PE.
Subjects: Art. Biography.
Books July to December 1991 - 5

CROSBY'S BOOK PROMOTION
14 Highmead
Fareham
PO15 6BM.
Subjects: Romantic Fiction.
Books January to June 1991 - 1.

PHYLLIS CROSSLAND
Trunce Farm
Greenmoor
Wortley
Sheffield
S30 7DQ.
Subjects: Second World War.
Books January to June 1991 - 1

MAGGIE CROSS
China-graphic
91 Village Road
Gosport
PO12 2LE.
Subjects: Art.
Books January to June 1991 - 1

MR J CROSTHWAITE
Birchwood
Dixshott Road
LEATHERHEAD
Surrey
KT22 0BZ

G.L CROWTHER
224 South Meadow Lane
Preston
PR1 8JP

CROW'S ROCK PRESS
c/o A McHugh
The G.A.A Centre
Caherlistrane, Galway
Republic of Ireland

CROYDON DANCE THEATRE
53A Croham Road
South Croydon
CR2 7HE

C.R.S. RECORDS
26 Crosland Road North
Lytham St. Annes
FY8 3EP.
Subjects: Children's Fun Books.
Books January to June 1991 - 1

Diana Cruikshank
Hunter's Moon
Orcheston
Salisbury
SP3 4RP.
Subjects: Entertainment.
Books July to December 1991 - 1

CRUITHNE PRESS A.P.G.
10 The Square
Glasgow
G12 8QQ.
Subjects: European History.
Books January to June 1991 - 1

CRUSE
Cruse House
126 Sheen Road
Richmond
Surrey
TW9 1UR

CRYPTOZOOLOGY NEWSLETTER
Huntshieldford
St Johns Chapel
BISHOP AUKLAND
Co Durham
DL13 1RQ

CRYSTAL PALACE FOUNDATION
84 Anerley Road
London
SE19 2AH

C S PUBLISHING
PO Box 8186
Nicosia
Cyprus
357 2 333069

C.T.A PUBLICATIONS OFFICE
Generation Centre
Dame Street
Rochdale

OL12 6XB

C.T.W PUBLICATIONS
75 High Street
Spennymoor
DL16 6BB

CUBE PUBLISHING
Croydon College Company
College Road Croydon
CR9 1DX.
Subjects: Poetry.
Books January to June 1991 - 2

CUBE PUBLICATIONS
Local Heritage Books
6 Pound Street
Newbury
RG14 6AB

CUCKOO PUBLISHING
40 Hayward Avenue
Loughborough
Leicestershire.
Subjects: Children's non-fiction.
Books July to December 1991 - 1

CUCKOO HILL PRESS
David Chambers
Ravelston
South View Road
PINNER, Middlesex
HA5 3YD
'Lettice Sandford: Wood Engravings'. 23 engravings printed on I.M. Imprint 115 copies (100 for sale). £92.50 - morocco 1988

CULLABINE BOOKS
11 Pound Close
Ringwood
BH24 1LR

CULVA HOUSE PUBLISHERS
A. Whitworth
Linden The Carrs
Briggswath
Whitby
YO21 1RR.
Subjects: Local History.
Books July to December 1991 - 1

MR C S CUMBERBEACH
25 St Patrick's Hill
CORK
IRISH REPUBLIC

MR M W CUNLIFFE1
53 Carrington Road
CHORLEY
Lancashire
PR7 2DQ

MR DARRYL CUNNINGHAM
63 Whin Knoll Avenue
Black Hill
KEIGHLEY
West Yorkshire

BD21 2HY

MR MARLON CURDY
144 Colney Hatch Lane
LONDON
N10 1EA

CURIOUSLY STRONG
Bateman Street
Cambridge
CB2 1NB

MR DAVID CURL
43 Ashley Close
Edgbaston
BIRMINGHAM
B15 2JL

M CURTIS
Olcote
Callanith
Isle of Lewis

CURVED AIR
8 Sherard Road
LONDON
SE9 6EP
Model yachts

MR P CUTHBERT
44 Folly Lane
HOCKLEY
Essex
SS5 4SJ

G. CUTRESS
34 Park Hill
London
SW4 9PB.
Subjects:
Books January to June 1991 - 5 Books July to December 1991 - 4 new editions

(THE) CUTTING ROOM
(edit Wendy Richmond)
51 Blayton Road
Sheffield
S4 7DH

CYGNUS MEDIA SERVICE
45 Woodlands Road
REDHILL
Surrey
RH1 6HB

CYPHERS
3 Selskar Terrace
Ranelagh
Dublin 6
Ireland

[D]

D.A.C PUBLICATIONS
12 South Bank
Staplehurst
Tonbridge

TN12 0BD

DADA DANCE MAGAZINE
47 Forrest Road (3FR)
Edinburgh
EH1 2QP

DAEMON PRESS
35 Kinnard Way
Cambridge
CB1 4SN.
Subjects: Biography.
Books July to December 1991 - 1

HENRY DAGNALL
30 Turner Road
Queensbury
Edgware
HA8 6AY.
Subjects: Astronomy. Books July to December 1991
- 1

DAGON MAGAZINE
11 Warwick Road
TWICKENHAM
Middlesex
TW2 6SW
Journal of eldritch lore and fantasy fiction inspired
by Lovecraft.

DAINICHI(ACADEMIC)PUBLICATIONS
c/o PO BOX 556
London
SE5 0RL
Independent Academic publisher specialising in
philosophy. Titles include primers and speculative
works.

ALAN DAKERS
RAGDON
Church Stretton
SY6 7EY.
Subjects: Local History.
Books July to December 1991 - 1

MR MATTHEW DALBY
The Vicarage
Austwick
LANCASTER
LA2 8BE

DALPHINIS PUBLICATIONS
7 Birling House
Graveney Grove
London
SE20 8XA.
Subjects: Poetry.
Books July to December 1991 - 1

DALRIADA
2 Brathwic Place
Brodick
Isle of Arran
KA26 8BN

DALTON WATSON FINE BOOKS
14 Highfield Road

Birmingham
B15 3DU.
Subjects: Military History.
Books July to December 1991 - 1

DAMIER BOOKS
5 Waterloo Street East
Tipton
DY4 8NG

DANDELION ARTS/MAGAZINE
(Fern Publ's)
24 Frosty Hollow
East Hunsbury
Northamptonshire
NN4 0SY
(ed J Gonzales-Marina)

DANIELS PUBLISHING
Barton
Cambridge
CB3 7BB.
Subjects: Health. Medicine. School Textbooks. So-
cial Welfare. Books July to December 1991 - 10

MR LEO DANZIGER
38 Woodcroft Avenue
Mill Hill
LONDON2
NW7 2AG

CLARKE DARGAVEL
26 St Leonards Road
East Sheen
London
SW14 7LX

DARK DIAMONDS PUBLICATIONS
Andrew Cocker
1 St. John's View Boston Spa
Wetherby
West Yorkshire
LS23 6NQ.
Autonomous Publishing outfit established 1988
publishes Dark Diamonds Magazine- articles mainly
of Third World/Environment subjects. A Riot of
Emotions; Poetry/Prose/Art Anthology. Also home
of twisted vision graffix - surreal/political since
1985.
A Riot of Emotions 1 28 pages illustrations PUB
January 1990 ISBN 1 873290 15 2 30p & SAE UK
$1 Europe $2 USA
Dark Diamonds 3/4 72 pages illustrations essays on
Third World issues PUB July 1990. ISBN 1 873290
00 4 £1.32 UK $3/$4
A Riot of Emotions 2 40 pages illustrations PUB
April 1992 ISBN 1 873290 05 5 50p & SAE UK $2
Europe $3 USA

DARK LILY
BCM Box 3406
LONDON
WC1N 3XX

DARK PEAK DESKTOP PUBLISHING
63 Warley Town Lane
Warley
HALIFAX

West Yorkshire
HX2 7SA 0422 839899

MR S P DARRELL
Forge Cottage
7 Castle Road
Wooton
WOODSTOCK
OX7 1EG

MR COLIN DARROCH
Windward
Peninver
Campbeltown
ARGYLL
PA28 6QP

DART
13 Prince of Wales Terrace
LONDON
W8 5PG

PER PRO DATNOW LIMITED
Thames Vieew Business Centre
ABINGDON
Oxfordshire
OX14 3LF 0235 555506

DAUPHIN PUBLISHING
118A Holland Park Avenue
London
W11 4PA.
Subjects: Art. Books July to December 1991 - 1

KAY DAVENPORT
1 Cannon Flynn Court
Minrow Road
Rochdale
OL16 5DP.
Subjects: Local History.
Books July to December 1991 - 1

MRS ANNE DAVEY ORR
182 Ravenhill Road
BELFAST

MR BERNARD DAVID
Ridgemount House
1 Totteridge Lane
LONDON
N20

DAVID ESSELMONT
6 Tan Yr Eglwys
Tregynon
NEWTOWN,
Powys,Wales
SY16 3EZ

DAVID'S B S HOLS
Sandra Grimes
14 Eastcheap
LETCHWORTH
Hertfordshire

MR ANDREW DAVIDSON
26 Firgrove Court

Bournmouth Road, Parkstone
POOLE
Dorset
BH14 0EP 0202 735696

MR B DAVIDSON
Wright Robinson Hall
Altrincham Street
MANCHESTER
M1 7JA

MR A DAVIES
21 Terndale Road
Lodmoor Hill
WEYMOUTH
Dorset
DT4 7QZ

MR E GLYN DAVIES
Cartref
21 Claremont Avenue
Bishopston
BRISTOL
BS7 8JD

ELIZABETH W DAVIES
5 FFORDD-GWENLLIAN
Llanfair Pwllgwyngyll
LL61 5SU

MISS JANE C DAVIES
Lower Toothill House
Toothill
ROMSEY
Hampshire
SO51 9LN

L. DAVIES
14 Larkhill Lane
Freshfield
Liverpool
L37 1LX.
Subjects: Poetry.
Books July to December 1991 - 2 new editions

MR LESLIE PAUL DAVIES
2096 S W 27 Terr
FORT LAUDERDALE
FL 33312
United States of America

M.D DAVIES
13 Baronsmead
Henley-on-Thames
RG9 2DL

ROGER W DAVIES
42 High Street
Tarring
Worthing
BN14 7NR

MR ALAN DAVIS
37 Sunningdale Park
Queen Victoria Road
CHESTERFIELD
Derbyshire

S42 6DZ

LEONARD DAVIS
82 Brightfield Road
London
SE12 8QF.
Subjects: Music.
Books January to June 1991 - 1

MR M I DAVIS
The Manor Farmhouse
Winson
CIRENCESTER
Gloucestershire
GL7 5ER

MR PETER DAVIS
109 Meeting Street
Quorn
LOUGHBOROUGH
Leicestershire
LE12 8AQ

MR TOM DAVIS
31 Southlands Road
Moseley
BIRMINGHAM
B13 9RL

DAWES PUBLISHING
Oaklands
Elm Grove
Worthing
BN11 5LH

JOHN DAWES PUBLICATIONS
12 Mercers
HAWKHURST
Kent
TN18 4LH
Swimming pool and energy efficiency technologies
and aplications, handbooks and directories to in-
form the specifiers and the user.

DAWN PUBLICATIONS (BAR HILL)
84 The Spinney
Bar Hill
Cambridge
CB3 8SU.
Subjects: Sport (Soccer).
Books July to December 1991 - 1

G. DAWSON
7 Rockland Road
London
SW15 2LN.
Subjects: Careers.
Books July to December 1991 - 4

DAY DREAM PRESS
39 EXMOUTH STREET
SWINDON
SN1 3PU

N. DAY PUBLISHING
Clematis Cottage
Church Walk

Thames Ditton
KT7 0NN.
Subjects: Travel.
Books January to June 1991 - 1

DAYTON'S PUBLISHING
Homend House
15 The Homend
Ledbury
HR8 1BN.
Subjects: Fishing Vessels.
Books January to June 1991 - 1

MR A J DAYTON
5 Halsmere Road
Camberwell
LONDON
SE5 9LN

D.B ENTERPRISE
72 Brenton Road
Penn
Wolverhampton
WV4 5NX

BERNARD DEACON
51 Plain an Gwarry
Redruth
Cornwall
TR15 1JE

DEAD PAN
Richard Lanyon
Polcrebo Moors
Nancegollon
HELSTON
Cornwall

MR B M DEAN
85 Oldfield Crescent
CHESTER
CH4 7PF

MR T DEAN-SMITH
15 Saint Dionis Road
LONDON
SW6 4UQ

DEAR SIR
(edit John Johnson)
54 Frant Road
Tunbridge Wells
Kent
TN2 5LJ

DEBORAH CHARLES PUBLICATIONS
173 Mather Avenue
LIVERPOOL
L18 6JZ 051 724 2500
Specialist press for academic lagal publications.
Journals include international journal for the semi-
otics of law, law and critique, feminist legal studies.
Monograph series in legal semiotics. Also custom
typesetting including Hebrew and Greek.
LAW, FACT AND NARRATIVE COHERENCE
by Bernard S Jackson. 214pp, 1988. Cloth: ISBN 0
9513793 05 £18.00 Paper: ISBN 0 9513793 13

£12.00. Scholarly monograph.
NARRATIVE AND LEGAL DISCOURSE edited
by David Ray Papke. 368pp, 1990. Cloth: ISBN 0
9513793 21 36.00
POSTMODERN LAW AND DISORDER by
Draean Milovanovic. 280pp 1992. Cloth: ISBN 0
9513793 3X £29.95

DECADE
26 The Meadway
Buckhurst Hill
IG9 5PG.
Subjects: Local History.

DEDALMS
Langford Lodge
St Judiths Lane
SAWTOY
Cambridgeshire
PE17 5XE 0487 832382

THE DEDALUS PRESS
John F. Donne
24 The Heath
Cypress Downs
Dublin 6W.
Irish Republic
 Dublin 902582
New poetry by Irish poets and poetry in translation;
the emphasis is on widening the horizons of Irish
poetry producing work that stimulates challenges
and delights.
'The Hanged Man Was Not Surrendering' by
Macdara Woods. 84pp. £4.95. ISBN 0 948268 64
6. Poetry.
'The Stylized City' by John F. Deane. 120pp. £5.95.
ISBN 0 948268 89 1. New and selected poems.
'Dostoevsky's Grave' by Leland Bardwell. 72pp.
£4.95. ISBN 0 948268 91 3. Poetry.

MR FRANK DEEMING
16 Locarno Road
TIPTON
West Midlands
DY4 9SH

DEERHURST PUBLICATIONS
Kevin Law
17 Frenchgate Road
Eastbourn
Sussex BN22 9EU
We publish low cost consumer guides. We special-
ise in medicine and health.

DEFECTIVE COMICS
Ravensbourne Road
East Twickenham
Middlesex
TW1 2DG

DEFIANT PUBLICATIONS
190 Yoxall Road
Shirley
Solihull
B90 3RN

DELAINE COACHES
D.P.R Marketing and Sales

37 Heath Road
Twickenham
TW1 4AW

DELECTUS BOOKS
27 Old Gloucester Street
LONDON
WC1N 3XX
Books on Sadeian interest. Deal in decadent litera-
ture as a mail order bookseller.

DELHI LONDON POETRY QUARTERLY
50 Penywern Road
London
SW5 9SX

MR EDMUND DELL
4 Reynolds Close
LONDON
NW11 7EA

DELOS PRESS
11 School Road
Moseley
Birmingham
B13 9ET

DEMI ARTS
The Business Village
Broomhill Road
LONDON
SW18 4JQ

DEMI-GRIFFIN PRESS
74 Victoria Road
OXFORD
OX2 7QE

MR BRIAN DEMPSTER
33 Florence Avenue
HOVE
Sussex
BN3 7GT

MR C DENNIS
12 Wolfingham Place
TRURO
Cornwall
TR1 2RP

R DENNIS
Old Chapel
Middle Street
Shepton Beauchamp
TA19 0LE

DENVIL PRESS
1 Marlborough Road
Exeter
EX2 4TJ

DEORWENTA PUBLICATIONS
Westgarth
Edmundbyers
Consett
DH8 9NQ

DEOSIL DANCE PROJECTS
14 Littlemoor Lane
Balby
DONCASTER
South Yorkshire
DN4 0JZ Contact: Keith Morgan
Publishers of unique pagan/new age & occult literature works on witchcraft runes spells & other magickalities. Publishers of modern grimoires & much much more!

DEPROVENT PUBLISHERS
71 Havelock Close
Commonwealth Avenue
White City
LONDON
W12 7NQ 081 740 5160
Publisher of academic computer books and manuals. Accept contract jobs from self-publishers. Provide general printing services, runs self-publishing training workshops to aid interested writers from start to finish.

DERBY TV/TS GROUP
c/o Derby CVS Self Help Team
Temple House
Mill Hill Lane
DERBY
DE3 6RY

DERG HOUSE
St. Conlan's Road
Nenagh
Co. Tipperary
Republic of Ireland.
Subjects: Poetry.
Books July to December 1991 - 1

DERWENTSIDE CULTURAL ASSOCIATION
Old Miners Hall
Delves lane
Consett
DH8 7EY

DESKHAT
(Seema Jena)
90 Dunstable Road
Luton
Beds
LU1 1EH

DESKTOP PUBLICATIONS
6 Silver Street
Winteringham
Scunthorpe
DN15 9ND

DESTRONIC
57 Tyndale Street
West End
LEICESTER
LE3 0QQ
Electronic publishing, graphic design, psyklops.

DETONATOR OF DETONATOR PUBLISHING
Steve Ainger
33 Damask Way

Warminster
Wiltshire
BA12 9PX. Tel 0985 212871
Detonator is a sporadically published fanzine concentrating on new strips by upcoming writers and artists. Features and reviews on the British and American comics scene and a desire to inform and entertain. Upcoming projects planned for Detonator publishing in 1992.
Detonator #1 Various 24 pages £1.00 PUB July 1991. Comics and reviews etc.
Detonator #2 Various 32 pages £1.00 PUB October 1991 Comics and reviews etc.
Detonator #3 Various £1.25 PUB September/October 1992 Comics and reviews etc.

THE DEUCALION PRESS
D S Savage
67 Church Street
Mevagissey
ST AUSTELL
Cornwall
PL26 6SR
Publishers of works on religious philosophy by the late Revd E F F Hill (1896 - 1954)
Apocalypse and Other Essays by E F F Hill, introduction by D S Savage. Nine essaysin mystical philosophy, 116pp. 1989 ISBN 0 95142 760 1 Price 6.95 The Church and Unity by E F F Hill. Pamphlet on the true nature of the church. 8pp. No ISBN number. Price 50p 1991
A Theory of Sex by E F F HIll. 48pp 1992. Price 4.50. Exposition of human sexuality in the light of man's eternal destiny. ISBN 0 9514276 1 X

DEVELOPMENT EDUCATION CENTRE
Selly Oak Colleges
Bristol Road
Birmingham
B29 6LE.
Subjects: Education.
Books July to December 1991 - 1

DEVIZES BOOKS PRESS
Handel House
Sidmouth Street
Devizes
SN10 1LD

DEVON BOOKS
Wheaton Publisher
Hennock Road
EXETER
EX2 8RP

Ms J Devons
4 Tasso Road
LONDON
W6 8LZ

DEWDNEY PUBLISHING
Cairngorm Cottage
Treluswell
Penryn
TR10 9AN.
Subjects: Hunting.
Books July to December 1991 - 1

MR A DE WIT
c/o 58 Burnfoot Avenue
Fulham
LONDON
SW6 5EA

DEXTRAL BOOKS
P.O. Box 52 South D.O.
Manchester
M20 8PJ.
Subjects: Education.
Books July to December 1991 - 1

D.F.G PUBLISHING
15 Park Lane
Duston
Northampton
NN5 6QD

DIAL 174 MAGAZINE
14 Hall Close
Fakenham
Norfolk
NR21 8HG

THE DIAMOND PRESS
5 Berners Mansions
34/36 Berners Street
LONDON
W1P 3DA

DIAMOND PUBLISHING GROUP
73 Princes Gardens
London
W3 0LR

DICKENS PUBLISHING
Stoneleigh
North Cadbury
Yeovil
BA22 7DJ.
Subjects: Fiction General.
Books July to December 1991 - 1

DIDSBURY PRESS
7 Darley Avenue
Didsbury
M20

DIEHARD LETTERPRESS
3 Spittal Street
Edinburgh
EH3 9DY.
Subjects: Theatre History.
Books July to December 1991 - 1

MR TIM DIGBY
53 Fane Park Road
Putney
LONDON
SW15 2EE

MR P R DIGGENS
The Shieling
Bromley Road
Elmstead
COLCHESTER

CO7 7AE

DIGITHURST
Newark Close
Royston
SG8 5HL.
Subjects: General Fiction.
Books July to December 1991 - 1

DIHEDRAL PUBLISHING
PO Box 3
Havershill
CB9 8DJ.
Subjects: Mathematics.
Books January to June 1991 - 1

DILETTANTE PUBLICATIONS
44 St David's Hill
Exeter
EX4 4DT

JOHN DILLEY
84 Barton Avenue
Paignton
Devon
Mr Wolston's Little Line: The Story of the Torbay
and Brixham Railway. £3.40

JOHN DILNOT BOOKS
11 Harrowby Road
Liverpool
L21 1DP.
Subjects: Art. Handicrafts.
Books July to December 1991 - 2

MR JOHN DINGLE
The Flat
Orchard Lea
Boars Hill
OXFORD
OX1 5DF

DINGO PRESS
150 Hardy Crescent
Wimborne
Dorset
BH21 2AS

DINING TABLE PUBLICATIONS
22 Warleigh Road
Brighton
BN1 4NT

DIONYSIA PRESS
(see Understanding)

DIRECTCLAIM
86 Freston Road
London
W11 4BH

DIRECT EXPERIENCE
18 Anglesea Road
IPSWICH
IP1 3PP
Lectures and workshops for primary schools based
on our book.

A Tool for Learning, ISBN 0 9514026 09.

DIRECTOR'S GUILD PUBLISHING
13284 Rices Crossing Road
Suite #3, PO Box 369
RENAISSANCE CA 95962
United States of America

DISABILITY ALLIANCE EDUCATION
and Research Association
Universal House
88-94 Wentworth Street
London
E1 7SA.
Books July to December 1991 - 1 new edition

DISABILITY ARTS IN LONDON (DAIL)
c/o Artsline
5 Crowndale Road
London
NW1 1TU
(071-388-2227)

DISABILITY ARTS MAGAZINE (DAM)
10 Woad Lane
Great Coates
Grimsby
DN37 9NH

DISABILITY EQUALITY IN EDUCATION
78 Mildmay Grove
London
N1 4PJ

DISABILITY INFORMATION TRUST
Mary Marlborough Lodge
Nuffield Orthopaedic Centre
Windmill Road
Headington
OX3 7LD.
Subjects: Medicine.
Books July to December 1991 - 1 new book 1 new
edition

DISABILITY WRITES
2 Temple Square
Manchester
M8 8UP

DISCUSS
c/o DISC
Trinity Community Centre
Middle St
Lancaster

MR M DIVIANI
217 Clevedon Road
Tickenham
CLEVEDON
Avon
BS21 6RX

F.G-DIXON GALLERY
17-18 Great Sutton Street
London
EC1V 0DN

PETER DIXON BOOKS
30 Cheriton Road
Winchester
SO22 5AX

MR JOHN DODDS
Garrald PO
Garrald
HADDINGTON
East Lothian
EH41 4LN

DODMAN PRESS
Roger Burford Mason
26 West Hill
HITCHIN
Hertfordshire
SG5 2MZ

DODONA RESEARCH
Dalkeith House
8 Central Avenue
Leicester
LE2 1TB.
Subjects: Economics.
Books January to June 1991 - 1

DOG
(ed David Crystal)
99 Wallis Road
London
E9 5LN

DOG HOUSE PUBLICATIONS
18 Marlow Avenue
Eastbourne
East Sussex
BN22 8SJ 0323 29214
State of the art How To publications for companion
dog owners. 'Your Dog and Your Baby. A Practical
Guide' by S. Hartmann-Kent. 120pp. illustrated.
£5.95. ISBN 1 873483 00 7.
'Dominance. Boa Behaviour Booklet'. 26pp. 2.30.

DOG SITTERS
Charnborough Cottage
Fradswell
Stafford
ST18 0EZ

MR COLIN JAMES DONALD
c/o Penman & Partners
1 West garden Place
Kendal Street
LONDON
W2 2AQ

MS GABRIEL D DONLEARY
Business School
Hong Kong University
Hong Kong

MR S DONOVAN
94 Wedhey
HARLOW
Essex
CM19 4RF

92

T DONOVAN PUBLISHING
52 Willow Road
London
NW3 1TP

DOORS IN AND OUT OF DORSET
(Words & Action Dorset Ltd)
43 Avenue Road Dorset
BH21 1BS

DORCHESTER PRESS
69 Strathalmond Road
Edinburgh
E14 8HP

DORSET WISE/GLOSA
Wendy Ashby
PO Box 18
Richmond
Surrey
TW9 2AU
'Dorset Wise' A5 magazine: Peace; Environment;
3rd World. 60p plus 20p postage with more to come
in the future when computerised. ALSO: Glosa;
international auxiliary language based on
'Interglossa' 'Plu Glosa Nota' 60p; 'Eduka Glosa'
Qtrly for teachers. £1.50. (contact Glosa; 17 Wel-
lington Ave Christchurch Dorset BH23 4HJ. Tel.
081 948 8683)

DOT PRESS LIMITED
54 Sandford Industrial Estate
Kennington
OXFORD
OX1 5RP

DOUDLE WAND
JLTD c/o 15 Collier Street
GLOSSOP
SK13 8L3

DOUGLAS BARRY PUBLICATIONS
21 Laud Street
CROYDON
CR0 1SU

MR STEPHEN DOUGLAS
Rohoku Haitsu 106
Iwazomo-Cho 32-4
Ashuja-Shi, Hyogo-Ken T659
Japan

DOVECOTE HOUSE PRESS
Dovecote House
Wadenhoe
Peterborough
PE8 5SU.
Subjects: Poetry.
Books January to June 1991 - 1. Books July to
December 1991 - 7

C J DOVEY
173 Chaldon Way
Coulsdon
Surrey
CR5 1DP. Tel 0737 555157
Educational Books

Accounting for Beginners James Dovey 132pp
ISBN 0 9517472 1 5 £16.95

DOWER HOUSE PUBLICATIONS
7A Westminster Street
Yeovil
BA20 1AF

DOROTHY DOWLING
18 Blackstock Drive
Gleadless Valley
Sheffield
S14 1AG

DOWNHOLLAND PUBLICATIONS
2 Southern Heys Cottage
Moss Side
Formby
Liverpool
L37 9BE.
Subjects: Poetry.
Books July to December 1991 - 1

MR R A DOWNIE
195 High Street
Alsagers Bank
STOKE-ON-TRENT
Staffordshire
ST7 8BA

UNA DOWDING
P.O Box 43
Gloucester
GL3 3JP

J L DOWNS
5 Jordan Street
BUCKFASTLEIGH
South Devon
TQ1 0AU

MR DAVID P DOYLE
33 Rue Du Mont Valerien
92210 St Cloud
France

DRAGONBY PRESS
Richard Williams
15 High Street
Dragonby
SCUNTHORPE
South Humberside
DN15 0BE 0724 840645
Bibliography (crime fiction and mass market pa-
perbacks)
WILLIAMS, RICHARD (Ed). Pan Books 1945-
1966 72 pages. Jan 1990. 1 871122 06 6. Paper-
back. £6.00.
GIBBS, ROWAN (Ed). Ngaio Marsh: A Bibliogra-
phy. 51 pages. October 1990. 1 871122 07 4. £6.00
paperback.
GREENSLADE & LESSER. Boardman Crime and
Science Fiction. 43 pages. Mey 1991. 1 8 71122 08
4. £6.00 paperback.

DRAGONFLAIR
PO Box 5
Church Stretton

93

SY6 6ZZ.
Subjects: Computers.
Books January to June 1991 - 1

DRAGONFLY PRESS
2 Charlton Cottages
Barden Road
Speldhurst
TUNBRIDGE WELLS
TN3 OLM 0892 862395
Small press with a literary bias. Sporadic output. We do not welcome unsolicite d manuscripts. Apart from titles listed, we also have books about Clemence Dane THEREFORE IMAGINE and doctors who were writers THIS IDLE TRADE and a history of the village of Knockholt in Kent.
THE WRITERS' GUIDE TO SELF PUBLISHING. Charlie Bell. 24 page booklet, four bla ck and white illustrations. ISBN 0 9513503 3 X £1.95 plus 30p post and packing ASK A SILLY QUESTION About Your IBM PC. Charlie Bell. 20 page booklet. Eleven b lack and white illustrations ISBN 0 9513500 v5 6 £1.50 plus 30p post and packi ng.
FE FI FO FUM: Poems to Fight Giants. Madeline Munro. Protests about modern inten sive farming methods. 24 page booklet. Illustrated. ISBN 0 9513500 6 4. £1.95 plus 30p post and packing.

DRAGONHEART PRESS
Mr. S. Woodward
11 Menin Road
Allestree
Derby
DE22 2NL
Dragonheart Press harbours the voice of artists able to transform their perception into powerful new poetry. Using DTP and high definition copiers it is able to produce affordable new works. Past collections include zemgeist by Sunday Times story winner Paul Heapy.
The Kite Maker's Dream by John S. Rowe £3.00 ISBN 1 871058 10 4 winner 1991 Poetry Competition.
Derbyshire Poets Ed Sean Woodward ISBN 1 871058 066 £3.95 Zeitgeist by Paul Heapy 3.50 ISBN 1 871058 015

DRAGONS BREW
50 Hookland Road
Porthcawl
Mid Glam
CF36 5SG

DRAGONWHEEL BOOKS
Sandcott
Rectory Lane
Pulborough
RH20 2AD

LAURENCE & PAMELA DRAPER
Laurence & Pamela Draper
Cnocnigan Culbokie
Dingwall
Ross-Shire
IV7 8JH. Tel 034 987 559
(of Title 1 - the only product)
Social and Technical story of the Mine worked in World War I mainly by German Prisoners of War.

Recipient of the prestigious Lloyds Bank Award for Independent Archeologist
The Raasay Iron Mine - Where Enemies Became Friends Laurence and Pamela Draper 78pp PUB 1990 Reprint 1992 8.00 ISBN 0 9514870 0 0.
Dreadful Work Press
Cora Greenhill
9 The Windses, Upper Padley
Grindleford
South Yorkshire
S30 1HY

DREAM PUBLICATIONS
4 Bradstock House
Harrowgate Road
London
E9 7BS.
Subjects: Pyschology.
Books July to December 1991 - 2

DREAMTIME BOOKS
21 Portland Road
Oxford
OX2 7EZ

DREWFERN
83 St Helen's Road
Leamington Spa
CV31 3QG

DRIFFIELD
41 North Road
London
N7 9DP.
Subjects: Driff's Guide to All the Second-hand and Antiquarian Bookshops in Britain. Books July to December 1991 - 1 new edition

P DRINKWATER
56 Church Street
Shipton-on-Stour
CV36 4AS

DRUM FROAICH
Garrie View
Conon Bridge
Dingwall
IV7 8HB.
Subjects: Children's Fiction (in Gaelic).
Books July to December 1991- 3

DRUMLIN PUBLICATIONS
Nure
Manorhamilton
Co. Leitrim
Republic of Ireland.
Subjects: Biography.
Books January to June 1991 - 1. Books July to December 1991 - 1

DRUNKEN DRAGON PRESS
84 Suffolk Street
Birmingham
B1 1TA

D SQUIRREL PRESS
12 WILLOW CORNER

94

Bayford
Hertfordshire
SG13 8PN
Children's puppet show/story, verses sessions.
Worshop for puppetry. Magazine of unpublished
authors.

DULWICH PICTURE GALLERY
Gallery Road
London
SE12 7AD

ALAN DUMAYNE
55 Chandos Avenue
London
N14 7ES

MR GEORGE W DUNCAN
33 FRIARS STILE ROAD
RICHMOND
Surrey
TW10 6NH

DUNCEITHERN PUBLISHING
111 Mussenden Road
Castlerock
Coleraine
BT51 4TU

MR KARL L DUNKERLEY
16 Dovecourt Road
SHEFFIELD
South Yorkshire
S2 1UA 0742 766653

Mr P C Dunkley
69 High Cross Lane
Rogerstare
NEWPORT
Surrey
NP1 9DJ

MS TRISH DUNLEARY
139 Woolley Lane
Hollingworth
HYDE
Cheshire
SK14 8NN

MR ALAN DUNNETT
8 Bowers Avenue
NOTTINGHAM
NG3 4JA 0602 624960

J DUNNING PUBLICATIONS
20 Riverside Gardens
Romsey
SO51 8HN

DUNSCAITH PUBLISHING LIMITED
28 West Lodge Avenue
LONDON
W3 9SF
Well written and imaginative fiction. Hostile to
authoritarian values and bureaucratic instituions.
Censorship of any sort we oppose.

RUTH DUNSTAN
102 Redlands Road
Solihull
B91 2LU.
Subjects: Poetry.
Books July to December 1991 - 1

DEAN & CHAPTER OF DURHAM
Chapter Office
The College
Durham
DH1 3EH

MARLOW DURNDELL
18-20 Chapel Street
Titchmarsh
Kettering
NN14 3DA

MRS DUTSCHAK
12 Orton Crescent
West Denton
NEWCATLE-UPON-TYNE
091 264 9448

DYKE PUBLICATIONS
38 Bankside
Westdene
Brighton
BN1 5GN

DYKE PUBLICATIONS
Ernest Ryman
38 Bankside
Brighton
East Sussex
BN1 5GN. Tel 0273 552241 (answ
Since 1984 this one-man band has concentrated on
producing booklets and Cards of local interest and
usually of nostalgic flavour. The main area featured
has been the Devil's Dyke near Brighton But
Rottingdean and Edmonton have also been cov-
ered.
Glimpses of Old Edmonton by Ernest Ryman 30
pages ISBN 0 9509756 4 8 Published March 92
2.00
Views and Legend of the Devil's Dyke by Harrison
Ainsworth 28 pages ISBN 0 9509756 1 3 £1.50
Devil's Dyke in Old Picture Postcards by Ernest
Ryman 30 pages ISBN 0 9509756 0 3 £2.50

DYLLANSOW PENGWELLA
2 Chapel Terrace
Trispen
Truro
TR4 9BA

[E]

EAGLETRIM PUBLISHERS
16 Kingsmill House
Kingsmill Terrace
London
NW8 6AA

E.A.H.
1 Thompson Drive
Thatcham

95

RG13 4FJ.
Subjects: Civil Aircraft.
Books July to December 1991 - 3

EARTH
Paul Bennett
20 Stonegate Road
BRADFORD
West Yorkshire
BD10 0HF
Magazine dedicated to Jonathan Seagull's magical
mystery tours, Forteana, UFOs.

EARTH FIRST
Box 152a Info Shop
56 Crampton Street
LONDON
SE17

EARTHGIANT
35a West Street
Abbotsbury
WEYMOUTH
Dorset

EARTHLINES
7 Brookfield
Strichley
TELFORD
Shropshire
TF3 1EB

EARTHQUEST NEWS
19 St Davids Way
Wickford
Essex
SS11 8EX

EARTHRIGHT MAGAZINE
Burnfoot Lodge
Barskinning
MAUCHLINE
Ayrshire
KA5 5TB
Scotland's only journal of radical economics/
geonomics.

EARTHSCAN PUBLICATIONS.
Subjects: Health and Hygiene. Books January to
June 1991 - 16. Books July to December 1991 - 16

EARTH SCIENCE TEACHERS' ASSOCIATION:
Geo Supplies
16 Station Road
Chapeltown
S30 4XH.
Subjects: School Textbooks. Books January to June
1991
- 3 Books July to December 1991 - 2

EARTHWISE
498 Bristol Road
Selly Oak
Birmingham

M. Earwicker
34 Marisfield Place

Selsey
Chichester
PO20 0PD.
Subjects: Biography.
Books January to June 1991 - 1

MR J EASTAFF
Bismarck allee 4
5200 Bonn 2
Germany

EAST ANGLIA TOURIST BOARD
Toppesfield Hall
Hadleigh
Ipswich
IP7 5DN

UNIVERSITY OF EAST ANGLIA
Centre for Creative and Performing Arts
University of East Anglia
Norwich
NR4 7TJ

EAST END PUBLISHING
44 Oxted Road
Sheffield
S9 1BP

MR B EASTER
88 Colworth Road
LONDON
E11 1JD

EASTERN RAINBOW
17 Farrow Road
Whaplode Drive
Spalding
Lincs
PE1 0TS

EASTFIELD PRESS
140 Boundary Road
Newbury
RG14 7NX.
Subjects: Local Travel Guide.
Books July to December 1991 - 1

H EASTHOPE
17-18 Newport Street
SWINDON
SN1 2DX

EATON PUBLISHING COMPANY
5 Hatfield Road
Westbrook
Margate
CT9 5BL

EAVESDROPPER
Mr Philip Woodrow
15 Mount Pleasant Crescent
LONDON
N4 4HP
Monthly poetry broadsheet.

(THE) ECHO ROOM
c/o 45 Bewick Court

Princess Square
Newcastle-upon-Tyne
NE1 8EG

Association for European Economic Education
Computers in Economics Unit
Staffordshire Polytechnic
Stoke-on-Trent
ST4 2DF

ROSS EDWARDS
Flat 17
Annaty Upper Springland
Isla Road
Perth
PH2 7HQ.
Subjects: Poetry.
Books July to December 1991 - 1

MR ANDREW EDGAR
23 Glanvill Road
STREET
Somerset
BA16 0TN

THE EDGE
Magazine/Distribution for Savoy Comics
The Edge
PO Box 1106
Chelmsford
CM1 2SF.
Magazine of imaginative past-SF writing (mostly).
Writers of fiction include Shirley Moorcoct Bertheht
Dr. Filippo Kilworth etc. Also use interviews; Shirley
Cabaret Voltaire Mr. John Harrison. Articles; on
Dnli William Carboon Sux Rohmer and reviews:
book/film/comic/music We don't publish poetry.
Prices £1.50 including postage cheques/POs payable to The Edge.

BRIAN EDGE
48 Woodside Avenue
Wistaston
Crewe
CW2 8AN.
Subjects: Numismatics.
Books January to June 1991 - 1

EDGE CREATIONS
PO Box 7
South Delivery Office
Manchester
M20 0BR.
Subjects: General Fiction.
Books January to June 1991 - 1

THE EDGELEY PRESS LIMITED
Molys House
39 Moscow Road, Edgeley
STOCKPORT
Cheshire
SK3 9QB 061 477 0744
Takes a look at and comments on the Arts, consumer affairs, and where to dine in the North-West
of England. Titles in print: John's Journal, The
Manchester Chari vari - monthly 50p per issue.
Subscription 6.00 per annum post paid.

EDINBURGH PICTORIAL
Smiths Place House
Edinburgh
EH6 8NU

EDINBURGH SOCIETY OF ORGANISTS
44 Bonaly Avenue
Edinburgh
EH13 0ET.
Subjects: Music.
Books July to December 1991 - 1 new edition

EDIT
22 Moorway Lane
Littleover
DERBY
DE3 7FR

EDITIONS
Bluecoat Chambers
School Lane
Liverpool
L1 3BX

EDITORIAL MATTERS
Mr Peter Muir
PO Box 61
LONDON
SE21 7HS
Produces business magazines, books and newsletters. Also included in specialist music publications.

EDLINGTON PRESS
163 Walton Road
Walton-on-the-Naze
CO14 8NE.
Subjects: Second World War History.
Books July to December 1991 - 1

MR C F EDMONDSON
96 Cambourne Court
Shelley road
WORTHING
Sussex
BN11 4BQ

EDUCATIONAL HERETICS PRESS
113 Arundel Drive
Bramcote
Beeston
Nottingham
NG7 3FQ.
Subjects: Education.
Books July to December 1991 - 1

EDUCATIONAL PUBLISHING SOCIETY
Dr George West
27 Cavendish Road
Hazel Grove
STOCKPORT
Cheshire
SK7 6HY 0625 878604

EDUCATION FOR DEVELOPMENT
7 Westwood Row
Tilehurst
Reading

RG3 6LT.
Subjects: Education.
Books July to December 1991 - 1

EDUCATION NOW PUBLISHING CO-OPERA-TIVE
113 Arundel Drive
Bramcote Hills
NOTTINGHAM
NG9 3FQ 0602 257261
The group is a non-profit making research, writing and publishing co-operative devoted to developingthe mainstream press. It reports posit more flexible forms of education and educational diversity through such initiatives as flexischooling, minischooling and democratic learning. Flexischooling by R. Meighan. 68pp. 1988. ISBN 1 871526 000. 6.00. Learning all the Time by John Holt. 168pp. 1991. ISBN 1 871526 04 3. £5.95 The Democratic School by C. Harber and R. Meighan. 204pp. 1989. ISBN 1 8715126 01 9. £12.00

EDUCATION SERVICES
364 Woodstock Road
Oxford
OX2 8AE

MR BIB EDWARDS
88 High Street
Bildeston
IPSWICH
IP7 7EA

MR JOHN EDWARDS
7 Allison Gardens
Purley-on-Thames
READING
Bershire
RG8 8DF

MR R EDWARDS
21 Camerow Close
BEXLEY
Kent
DA5 2JL

EGERTON PRESS
5 Windsor Court
Avenue Road
London
N15 5JQ.
Subjects: Short Stories.
Books July to December 1991 - 1

EGOTIST PRESS
BM Egotist
London
WC1N 3XX. 081 556 2293
Egotist Press publishes avant-garde literature and intellectual theory. 'Mad' by Jonathan Bowden. 1989. 108pp. paperback. £3.95 (plus £1.00 p&p). ISBN 1 872181 00 7. Literature/philosophy. 'Aryan' by Jonathan Bowden. 1990. 128pp. paperback £3.95 (plus £1.00 p&p). ISBN 1 872181 01 5. Literature/philosophy. 'Sade' by Jonathan Bowden. 1991. 134pp paperback. £3.95 (plus £1.00 p&p) ISBN 1 872181 02 3. Literature/philosophy.

EIGHTEENTH CENTURY BRITISH BIOGRA-PHY
Park House
Ashow
Kenilworth
CV82LE

EIGHTFOLD PRESS
Fiona Beckett
c/o 1 Cage Lane
Great Stoughton
HUNTINGDON
Cambridgeshire
PE19 4DB

ELANOR & HEREMOND LIMITED
Nantissa House
69 Leaside Road
ABERDEEN
AB2 4RX 0224 625574

ELDORADO COMMUNICATIONS
17 Condor Close
Garston
Liverpool
L19 5NU.
Subjects: Soccer.
Books July to December 1991 - 1

MS MICHAELA ELDRIDGE
267 Hillbury Road
WARLINGHAM
Surrey
CR6 9TL 0883 622121

ELECTRIC FIREFLIES
41 Oxford Road
SOUTHPORT
PR8 2EG

ELECTRONIC MEDIUM
126 Cleveland Street
LONDON
W1P 5DN

ELEPHANT EDITIONS
BM Elephant
LONDON
WC1N 3XX
Anarchist pocket books.

G ELIOT FELLOWSHIP
71 Stepping Stones Road
Coventry
CV5 9JT

ELITE Words & Images
P.O. Box 24
Sherborne
Dorset.
Subjects: Humour.
Books July to December 1991 - 1

EL KHOUARIKI
15 Ada Road
Hay Mills

98

BIRMINGHAM
B25 8DD

ELLENBANK PRESS
The Lathes
Selby Terrace
Maryport
Cumbria
CA15 6LX 0900 817773
Ellenbank Press - based in Cumbria - specialises in high quality hard backs and paperbacks on the Lake District walking climbing conservation and natural history.
Coleridge Walks the Fells: A Lakeland Journey Retraced by Alan Hankinson 216pp. 8pp b&w photographs. 27 Sept 1991. ISBN 1 873551 00 2. £14.95. hardback
The Bliss of Solitude: A Conservationist's Tour of the Lakes by John Wyatt. 224pp. 13 b&w drawings. 27 Sept 1991. ISBN 1 873551 0 1. £14.95. hardback
The Lakeland Museum Guide by Bruce Bennison. 160pp. b&w illus throughout. 27 Sept 1991. ISBN 1 873551 02 9. £5.95. paperback

ELLERTON PRESS
Michael Brown
20 Ferndown Drive
Clayton
Newcastle-under-Lyme
ST5 4NH.
Subjects: Poetry.
Books July to December 1991 - 1

ELLIOT MANLEY ASSOCIATES
Tilford Reeds House
FARNHAM
Surrey
GU10 2DJ 025 125 2555
Software Quality Management, published five times a year. ISSN 0960-2518. Annual sub: £24.00, sae for free sample.

GEORGE EDWARD ELLIOTT
L W.N Hall
Darling Street
Enniskillen
County Fermanagh

MR BRYAN M ELLIS
20 Woodland Avenue
Weston Zoyland
BRIDGWATER
Somerset
TA7 0LQ

ELLISONS' EDITIONS 4
1 High Street
Orwell
Royston
SG8 5QN.
Subjects: Biography. Australian History.
Books July to December 1991 - 2

ELM BOOKS
Flat 4
4 Elm Park Gardens
London

SW10 9NY

THE ELMETE PRESS
22 Beck Lane
Collingham
WETHERBY
West Yorkshire
LS22 5BW

ELTHAM SOCIETY: P BENNETT
2 Imber Court
North Park
London
SE9 5AX

PROFESSOR W R ELTON
Ph.D Program in English / Box 510
Graduate Center, 33 West 42nd Street
New York 10036-8099
United States of America

ELVENDON PRESS
The Old Surgery
High St
Goring-on-Thames
Reading
RG8 9AW

ELVET PRESS
9 Crofters Green
Wilmslow
SK9 6AY.
Subjects: Biography. Poetry.
Books January to June 1991 - 1. Books July to December 1991 - 1

ELVISLY YOURS
107 Shoreditch High Street
London
E1 6JN

MR GARRY ELY
26 Farnell Road
STAINES
Middlesex
TW18 4HT

EMBERS HANDPRESS
Roy and Eve Watkins
16 St Leonard's Road
NORWICH
Norfolk
NR1 4BL

EMERGENCY BOOKS
c/o Central Books
14 The Leathermarket
LONDON
SE1 3ER
Magazine featuring work by names.
Gordon Emery
27 Gladstone Road
Chester
CH1 4BZ

MR JOHN EMERY
66 MARLOW HOUSE

99

Hallfield Estate
Bayswater
LONDON
W2

EMJAY
17 Langbank Rise
Rise Park
NOTTINGHAM
NG5 5BU

Mr Andrew Emmerson
71 Falcutt Way
NORTHAMPTON
NN2 8PH

EMPRESS
PO Box 92
PENZANCE
Cornwall
TR18 2XL 0736 65790
Publishes The Ley Hunter. Runs its own specialist
book service. The Ley Hunter Journal. Editor Paul
Devereux. average pages per issue: 28 nominally
quarterly. £7.00 for UK subscription. £8.00 Europe;
US$20 over seas.
The Ley Guide 1987. By Paul Devereux and Ian
Thomson. 78pp. 70 photo and line illus. 1 871343
00 3. £3.95. Perennial classic on ley lines and
geomancy.
Earth Lights Revelation. By Paul Devereux. 239pp.
40 colour plates. 22 line illus. 0 7137 2209 6. £4.95.
leading highly acclaimed world-wide study of ex-
otic national light phenomena.

ENCOUNTERS PRESS
Box 1
5 Freemount Street
London
E9 7NQ

ENDEAVOUR PUBLISHING
Doreen Farrand
42 Stoke Road
Ashton
Northampton
NN7 2JN. Tel 0604 864 346
We publish work which support our philosophy:
'Life should be simple improvable practical and
above all enjoyable'. - Childrens books Alternative
energy Small businesses Self improvement Anything that feels right - Send S.A.E.for catalogue -
New titles to be published
shortly:-The Searcher - A.Bede - a life's didication
to meaning. One Step - A.Bede - What to do when
life gets stuck!
Unknown Wisdom - M.K.Cobb - Wisdom from a
surprising source.

ENGLANG BOOKS
PO Box 240
Southampton
SO9 7RJ.
Subjects: Languages.
Books January to June 1991 - 1

MR ANDY ENGLISH
10 Matthew Wren Close

Little Downham
ELY
Cambridgeshire
CB6 2UL

ENGLISH COMPANIONS
BM Box 4336
London
WC1N 3XX.
Subjects: Plays.
Books July to December 1991 - 1

English in Wales /
Saesneg yng Nghymru
(see National Language Unit of Wales)

THE ENGLISH LANGUAGE SOCIETY
46 Great Russell Street
LONDON
WC1B 3PE

PETER ENGLISH
2 Cheltenham Villas
Bath Road
Devizes
SN10 1PW

IDENTIFICATION OF ENGLISH PRESSED
GLASS
Nunwick Hall
PENRITH
Cumbria
CA11 9LN
The Identification of English Pressed Glass 1842 -
1908, provides a concise, clear and comprehensive
guide to identification of pressed glass objects, with
an analysis of the characteristic designs of indi-
vidual firms as well as details of the actual registra-
tions.

ENITHARMON
40 Rushes Road
PETERSFIELD
Hampshire
GU32 3BW

ENNISFIELD PRINT AND DESIGN
Telfords Yard
6-8 The Highway
Wapping
LONDON
E1 9BQ

ENRAM PRESS
35 Bank Street
HERNE BAY
Kent
Fine colour printers from conceptual artwork to
complete limited edition books and prints, including specialist bookbinding and picture-framing.

ENSIGN PUBLICATIONS
226 Portswood Road
Southampton
SO9 4XS

ENSLOW PUBLISHERS

US PO Box 38
Aldershot
GU12 6BP.
Subjects: Children's non-fiction.
Books January to June 1991 - 25. Books July to
December 1991 - 19

ENTERPRISE PUBLICATIONS
2A Southmoor, Buckleigh Road
Westward Ho!
Bideford
EX39 3PU

ENTERPRISE AVIATION
42 Claygate Road
London
W13 9XG.
Subjects: Aviation.
Books January to June 1991 - 1

ENTERPRISE FIRST
FOA Jim Prettyman
47 Queen Charlotte Street
EDINBURGH
EHJ6 7EY

AMATEUR ENTOMOLOGY
The Hawthorns
Frating Road
Great Bromley
CO7 7JN

ENVOI POETS PUBLICATIONS
Anne Lewis-Smith
Pen Ffordd
Newport
Dyfed
SA42 0QT. Tel 0239 820 285
An important stage in a poet's development is the
step from individual poems in magazines to a small
collection. We aim to provide this step hoping that
the poet will go on upwards. EPP are non-profit
making publishing 12 books a year.
Opening the Stone Heart by James Deahl 40 pages
April 1992 ISBN 0948478 926 Price £3.50 $8.00
Poetry
The Greening of the Rose by Michael Mariscotti 40
pages June 1992 ISBN 0948478 95 0 Price £3.50
$8.00 Poetry
Colours by Fay Green 40 pages November 1991
ISBN 0948478 85 3 Price £3.00 $6.00 Poetry

EON PUBLICATIONS
(see Issue One/The Bridge)

EONTA
27 Alexandra Road
Wimbledon
London
SW19 7JZ

FOTHEN PRESS
7 Bridge Street
Wistow
Huntingdon
PE17 2QA

E.P.A.

Blythburgh House
Wendens Ambo
Saffron Walden
CB11 4JU.
Subjects: Historical biography.
Books January to June 1991 - 1. Books July to
December 1991 - 1

EPSOM
KT18 5JD
Mel Hulme
PO Box 7
Garforth

EQUINOX PRESS
Sinodun House
Shalford
Braintree
Essex
CM7 5HN 0371 851097
For the present; minimalist poetry (such as haiku)
only; in English or another language with English
translation.
'A Leap in the Light' by David Cobb. 64pp 8
drawings 1991 p/b. £2.95 ISBN 0 9517103 0 3

ESCARGOT PRESS
Old Park Cottage
Woodbury Lane
AXMINSTER
Devon
EX13 5TL
Formed in 1991, self publishing poetry and later, it's
hoped, stories. Texts are lettered by hand, then
photocopied or printed on fine paper; binding was
also hand done until orders increased. Our name
indicates slowness, succulence and determined sil-
very track.
Letter To John Keats by David Grant. 30 pages -
500 line poem pub. date: Hardback Nov 9th 1991
ISBN 0 951 7261 0 2 Price £11.50
Paperback May 1st 1992 ISBN 0 951 726110 Price
£4.95
Letter To W H Auden by David Grant. 30 pages -
150 stanzas. Pub date Nov 1992 Paperback.

ESCREET PUBLICATIONS
Garthend House
Millington
YORK
YO4 2TX
Small press set to establish a name in the field of
writing tuition and advice Write a Succesful Novel
by Frederick E Smith and Moe Sherrard-Smith
ISBN 09517623 0 3 (second printing). Definative
book on writing and marketing a novel.

ESSENCE OF MAN CHURCH
Postlagernd
A-9535 SChiefling
Austria

ESTAMP
204 St. Albans Avenue
London
W4 5JU
Reflects interest in professional involvement in
printmaking and papermaking. The books are about

101

the making of books and their materials.

ESTUARY PRESS
11 CLARE CLOSE
Waterbeach
Cambridge
CB5 9PS.
Subjects: Poetry.
Books July to December 1991 - 1

MS V R ETCHELLS
21 Chadwick Road
SUTTON COLDFIELD
West Midlands
B75 7RA

ETHNIC COMMUNITIES ORAL HISTORY
GROUP
2 Royal Parade
Dawes Road
Fulham
LONDON
SW6 7RE

ETHNIQUE
42 Mackay House
Australia Road
London
W12 7PB

ETHNOGRAPHICA
19 Westbourne Road
London
N7 8AN.
Subjects: Nigerian Traditional Architecture. Vegetarian Cooking. Art. Photography. Books July to December 1991 - 7

ASSOCIATION OF EUROPEAN ECONOMICS
Computers in Economics Unit
Staffordshire Polytechnic
Stoke-on-Trent
ST4 2DF.
Subjects: Education.
Books July to December 1991 - 1

NORTH EAST CENTRE FOR EDUCATION
c/o Prof G R Batho
University of Durham
Durham
DH1 1TA

MR D EVANS
39 Hampton Towers
International Way
Weston
SOUTHAMPTON
S02 9PB

EILEEN EVANS
c/o Social Services
The Grove Rax Lane
Bridport
DT6 3JL.
Subjects: Children's Fiction.
Books July to December 1991 - 1

K. JANE EVANS
7 Seafield Court
51 South Road
Weston-super-Mare
BS23 2LU.
Subjects: Biography.

LEONARD EVANS
6-21 Lymington Road
London
NW6 1HZ

MISS M EVANS
St Brides
BURTONPORT
Co Donegal
IRISH REPUBLIC

ROGER D.C. EVANS
Brook House
Kirklands Road
Nailidon
Shipley
BD17 6NS.
Subjects: Military History.
Books July to December 1991 - 1

EVENSFORD PRODUCTIONS
Evensford
Little Chart
Ashford
Kent.

EVERY CHANCE AT THE LAST
PUBLICATIONS
18 Owthorpe Grove
Sherwood
Nottingham
NG5 2LX.
Subjects: National Hunt (Sport).
Books July to December 1991 - 1

EVERYWOMAN
34 Islington Green
London
N1 8DU

EXCALIBUR PUBLICATIONS
13 Knightsbridge Green
LONDON
SW1X 7QL

EXECUTIVE PUBLICATIONS
Spring Valley Industrial Estate
Braddan
Douglas
Isle of Man

EXILE PUBLICATIONS
38 Emerald Street
SALTBURN-BY-THE-SEA
Cleveland
TS12 1ED
Poetry magazine, accepting poems from the North East and other regions In Search of Judah. By Ann Elliott. 20 pages. April 1991. £0.75. A 5 format. EXILE. Edited by Herbert Marr & Ann Elliott. 20

102

pages quarterly. £0.75. A 5 form at.

EX LIBRIS PRESS
1 The Shambles
Bradford-on-Avon
BA15 1JS

EXPERT BOOKS
18 Rawlins Close
Woodhouse Eves
LOUGHBOROUGH
Leicestershire
LE12 8SD

EXPRESSIONS
10 Turfpits Lane
Erdington
Birmingham
B23 5DP

EXTRA PUBLICATIONS
82 Trinity Road
London
SW17 7RJ

EXTRANCE
33 Meredith Street
Great Lever
BOLTON
BL3 2DD
Providing a platform for prose and polemic, visual...
concerned with surrealism.

EXUBERANCE
c/o Jason Smith
34 Croft Close
Chipperfield
Hertfordshire
WD4 9PA

EYEBROW EDITIONS
82 Sinclair Road
London
W14 0NJ

[F]

(THE) FABIAN SOCIETY
11 Dartmouth Street
London
SW1H 9BN

MR J FADGEAN
PO Box 479
GERRARDS CROSS
Buckinghamshire
SL9 7EX

DOUGLAS V FAGAN
3 Chestnut Corner
Stow-on-the-Wold
Cheltenham
Gl5 1AZ

FAILTE
Mr David McCann
93 High Street

INNERLEITHEN
Peeblesshire
EH44 6HD

MR ANDREW T FAIRIE
7 Tiffany Lane
Pendeford
WOLVERHAMPTON
WV9 5QU

FAIR WAY PUBLICATIONS
1 Fairway
Tiverton
EX16 4NF.
Subjects: Education.
Books July to December 1991 - 2

MS VAL FALLON
P O BOX 335
LONDON
NW1 7TD

MR T MATTHEW FALL
The Tilehouse
Bakehouse Lane
Ockbrook
DERBY
DE7 3RH

FAMEDRAM PUBLISHERS
School Road
Gartocham
Alexandria
G83 8RT

FAMILY TREE MAGAZINE
Michael Armstrong
15/16 Highlode, Stocking Fen Road
Ramsey
HUNTINGDON
Cambridgeshire
PE17 1RB
Monthly magazine for genealogists, family and
local historians. TRACING YOUR FAMILY HIS-
TORY. By Jean A Cole. 84 pages. ISBN 0 9511465
2 1. Third Edition 1988. £3.95. Beginners book for
those wishing to trace their family history.
IN AND AROUND THE RECORD REPOSITOR-
IES in Great Britain and Ireland. 102 pages. I SBN
0 9511465 4 8. Compiled by Jean A Cole and
Rosemary Church. 2nd Edition 199 0. Editor Avril
Cross. Listings of record offices and holdings. IN-
DEX TO PARISHES IN PHILLIMORES MAR-
RIAGES. 18 pages. M. E. Briant-Rosier. ISBN 0
9511465 6 4. 2nd Edition 1991. £1.60. Lists of
parishes catalogued in Phill imores Marriages re-
cording marriages up to 1812.

FAMILY WELFARE ASSOCIATION
501-505 Kingsland Road
London
E8 4AU.
Subjects: Education.
Books July to December 1991 - 1

FANCLUB & FANZINE DIRECTORIES
c/o Simon Wade
236 Kingsway

Huyton
LIVERPOOL
L36 9UF

FANNAG PRESS
PO Box Box 100
Port Erin
Isle of Man

FANTASY ASSOCIATION
15 Stanley Road
MORDEN
Surrey
SM4 4DE

FAR COMMUNICATIONS
5 Harcourt Estate
Kibworth
Leicester
LE8 0NE
Subjects: Pyschology.
Books January to June 1991 - 3

MR PASCALE FARGES
APEPE
56 rue des Fecleries
F-74400 CHAMONIX
FRANCE

MCKINNON FARMAR PUBLISHING
33 Abbey Road
Grimsby
DN32 0HQ

JACK FARMER
65 Theydon Park Road
Theydon Bois
CM16 7LR

MR D FARRAND
20 Hartwell Road
Ashton
NORTHAMPTON
NN7 2JR

T.C. FARRIES
IRONGRAY ROAD
Lochside
Dumfries
DG2 0LH.
Subjects: Animals.
Books July to December 1991 - 1

MICHAEL FARR
40 Lillywhite Crescent
Andover
SP10 5NA
Subjects: Railway History.
Books July to December 1991 - 1

THE FARTHING PRESS
THREE COTTAGES
Short Green
Winfathing, DISS
Norfolk

FAST....HARD

15 Bellegrove Close
WELLING
Kent
DA16 3RG

FATCHANCE
c/o Mary Maher
Pippins Hillhead
Chittlehampton Umerleigh
Devon
EX37 9RG

INSTITUTE OF FATUOUS RESEARCH
27 Whitmore Street
Shelton
STOKE ON TRENT
ST1 4JS

FAULKNER PUBLISHING
28 Fairhaven Close
Lode
Cambridge
CB5 9HG.
Subjects: Literature. Ancient History.
Books July to December 1991 - 2

MR IAN FAULKNER
347 Cherry Hinton Road
CAMBRIDGE
CB1 4DJ

FAUST PUBLISHING COMPANY
Thorneyholme Hall
Roughlee
Burnley
BB12 9LH

FAX-PAX
Bowling Green Studio
Norfolk Road
Falmouth
TR11 3NT

FEASIBLE PRODUCTS
Alasdair Johnson
1/8 Dunbar's Close
Canongate
Edinburgh
EH8 8BW. Tel 031 557 1863
A mantelpiece press for writers and readers - send
for catalogue! Spring Tide by Ernest Syme 18 pages
August 1992 ISBN 1 874199 00 0 £1.00 Fin de
siecle.
Delitiage by Evelyn Stalker 8 pages November
1992 ISBN 1 874199 05 1 £1.00 Humorous
Whiskey by Moonlight by Ernest Syme 10 pages
December 1992 ISBN 1 874199 10 8 £1.00 Writers
Block!

FEATHER BOOKS
Revd John Waddington-Feather
Fairview, Old Coppice
Lyth Bank
Shrewsbury
SY3 0BW. Tel 0743 872177
Publishes children's quality fiction and poetry. Books
of verse must have a religious/environmental slant
also publishes the Quill Hedgehog Clubs booklets

newsletter and poems written by members of Quill Hedgehog novels' fans.
(Details from Feather Books)
Quill's Adventures in Grozzieland by John Weddington-Feather 100pp ISBN 0 947718 12 5 £4.99 (children's environmental fantasy) The World About Us by Marjery Lea 20pp 0 947718 17 6 1992 environmental poetry.
The Oceanic Response by Bruce James 20pp ISBN 0 947718 16 8 1992 religious poetry.

JENNIFER FELL
Haseldene
The Green, Hellidon
Daventry
NN11 6LC

FELPHAM PRESS: KATHY KIDD
6 Crescenta Walk
Bognor Regis
PO21 2YA

FELTHAM PRESS
111 Station Road
NEW MILTON
Hampshire
BH25 6JP

FEMINIST ARTS NEWS
PO Box CR8
Leeds
LS7 4TD
0532 629023
Radical arts magazine for the 90s relevant to womens lives.

FEMINIST AUDIO BOOKS
52-54 Featherstone Street
London
EC1Y 8RT

FEMINIST REVIEW
11 Carleton Gardens
Brecknock Road
London
N19 5AQ

MS JILL FENNER
45 Islington Park Street
LONDON
N1 1QB 071 226 7450

ROBERT FERGUSON-GRANDE
17 Kingsbury Road
London
NW9 7HY.
Subjects: Poetry.
Books July to December 1991 - 1

FERN PRESS
2 Charlton Cottages
Barden Road, Speldhurst
TUNBRIDGE WELLS
Kent
TN3 0LH 0892 862395
See 'Words and Images'
SPELDHURST SKETCHES. No 1. The Heart of the Village. By Charlie Bell. 32 page pa perback.

145 x 150 mm, b&w illust. ISBN 0 9513500 2 1. £2.95 inc post & packing. (£3.25 overseas).

FERARD-REEVE PUBLISHING
Greenfields Farmhouse
Kings Barn Lane
Steyning
BN44 3YG.
Subjects: Plays.
Books July to December 1991 -

FERRY PUBLICATIONS
Miles Cowsill
12 Millfields Close
Pentlepoir
Kilgetty
Dyfed
SA68 0SA 0834 813991
Ferry Publications produces specialist books on the history of ferries and ferry companies. Ferry Publications also produces a quarterly ferry maga zine on the British ferry scene.
By Road Across the Sea. Cowsill. 72 pages. over 150 illustrations. January 1991. 1 871947 07 3 £6.95 Ferrybooks.
Winston Churchill. By Hendry and Cowsill. 32 pages; over 60 photographs. May 1991. 1 871947 08 1. £2.50. Ferrybooks.
Dover-Ostend. Hendry. 56 pages; over 100 illustrations. May 1991. 0 951350 6 5X. £5.95. Ferrybook.

FESTIVAL EYE
38 STANMER STREET
LONDON
SW11 3EG
For the new-age traveller and Stonehenge fan.

FICEDULA BOOKS
PO Box 10
Llandrindod Wells
LD1 5ZZ.
Subjects: Birds.
Books January to June 1991 - 1. Books July to December 1991 - 1

FIELDER GREEN ASSOCIATES
294 Tadcaster Road
York
YO2 2ET

Fields & Frames Productions
Corshellach
Bridgend
Dunning
PH52 0RS

FIELD STUDIES COUNCIL
Preston Montford
Shrewsbury
SY14 1HW

FILM WORDS
London House
243 Lower Mortlake Road
RICHMOND
Surrey
TW9 2LS

Fine Publishing
Priory Lane
Toft Monks
Beccles
NR34 O62

FINGER PRESS
27b Daventry Street
LONDON
NW1 6TE
Four of seven poetry titles in print and six postcards.

MR S A FINSLEY
Grooms Cottage
Betton House, Betton
MARKET DRAYTON
Shropshire
TF9 4AD

FIREFLY PUBLICATIONS: J HART
7 Millward Road
Ryde
Isle of Wight

FIRE RAISERS
Alistair Fitchett
64 Lugar Place
Troon
Strathclyde
KA10 7EA. Tel 0292 314057
Boredom of Fire Raisers You can't have both!
Blending media and music fiction and the politics of
dissent Fire Raisers is a magazine of contemptible
writingof the '90s. The intention; to engender hope
through action...take a risk!
Fire Raisers 1; 20 pages A4 Summer '90 85p
Fire Raisers 2; 24 pages A4 Winter '90 85p
Fire Raisers 3; 24 pages A4 Summer '91 95p

FIRST CLASS PUBLICATIONS
P O Box 1799
London
W9 2BZ

FIRST RESOURCE
43 Vyner Street
York
YO3 7HR

1ST RESOURCE
Paul Cowell
43 Vyner St
York
YO3 7HR. Tel 0904 638721
Religious publishers with a special interest in: Mys-
ticism music worship Dionysius' Mysticism Anon
trans T. Timothy 16pp 1990 ISBN 0 9515137 29
£2.75 - Modern version of Middle English transla-
tion. A Ladder of Four Rungs Guigo trans T.
Timothy 28pp 1990 ISBN 0951513737 £2.95 -
Modern Version of Middle English translation.
Copyright - A Basic Guide For Church Leaders
Paul Cowell 20pp 1990 ISBN 1 873291 00 0 £1.50

FIRST TIME MAGAZINE
Burdett Cottage
4 Burdett Place, George Street
HASTINGS

East Sussex
TN34 3ED

FIRST TIME PRESS
4 Penswick Grove
Coddington
NEWARK-ON-TRENT
Nottinghamshire
NG24 2QL
Interested in one act playscripts only, that may or
may not have been performed, but have never
previously appeared in print. No playscripts
concidered without a preliminary letter (S.A.E.)
Royalties paid (50/50 basis) once initial expences
have been met.

FIRST WORLD PUBLISHING
Richard House
30-32 Mortimer Street
London
W1N 7RA.
Subjects: Holidays. European Travel.
Books July to December 1991 - 2

FIR TREE PRESS (CONNIE STRANKS)
FIR TREE HOUSE
Warmington
Banbury
OX17 1BU

FISHER PRESS
P.O. Box 41
Sevenoaks
TN15 6YN.
Subjects: Biography.
Books July to December 1991 - 2

Ms Anne-Louise Fisher
46 Lexington Street
LONDON
W1R 3LH 071 494 4609

MS BETH FISHER
68 High Street
Old Aberdeen
ABERDEEN
AB2 3EY

MRS R FISHER
29 Ham View
Upton-upon-Severn
WORCESTER
WR8 0QE

ALISTAIR FITCHETT
64 Lugar Place
Troon
Strathclyde
KA10 7EA
Publisher of 'Fire Raisers' a means of inspiration; a
magazine of new writing for the '90s aimed at
inciting a new agitation. A collision of geography
and intimacy or the hell fire sermons of future David
Ickes without the dubious media training turquoise
shell suits and the claim to Truth...TAKE A RISK.
Fire Raisers; issues 1 & 2 85p or £1.45 for both.
Fire Raisers; issue 3. 95p all three together: £2.05.
All prices inc p & p

106

FITZGERALD PUBLISHING
89 Ermine Road
LONDON
SE13 5JJ
Tim Fitzgerald
Fitzgerald Publishing is a specialist entomological and arachnological company producing books about spiders and stick insects for the university and hobbyist market.
Baboon Spiders - Tarantula of Africa by Andrew M Smith. 143pp. A4. 1000 illus. 1990. ISBN 0 9510939 7 5. £25.00
Stick Insects of Europe and the Mediterranean by Paul Brock. 50pp. A4. 200 illus. 1991. ISBN 0 9510939 8 3 .£15.00
How to Keep Tarantula by Andrew M Smith. 20pp. 60 illus. 1991. 3rd Edition. ISBN 0 9510939. £2.00

FIVE LEAVES LEFT
Flat 7
4 Chestnut Avenue
LEEDS
LS6 1BA

FIVE SEASONS PRESS
The Butts
Shenmore
Madley
HEREFORD
HR2 9NZ

FLAIR
5 Delavall Walk
Eastbourne
Sussex
BN23 6ER

FLAMBARD PRESS
4 Mitchell Avenue
Jesmond
Newcastle-upon-Tyne
NE2 3LA
Time's Fly-Past by Michael Standen 60pp May 1991 ISBN 1 873226 01 2 £6 poetry
Moving Towards Light by Cynthia Fuller 72pp October 1992 ISBN 1 873226 02 0 £6 Poetry
Foreign Bodies by Christopher Pilling 72pp October 1992 ISBN 1 873226 03 9 £6 Poetry.

MRS A FLANDERS
Industrial Relations Research Unit
University of Warwick
COVENTRY
CV4 7AL

FLAUNDEN PRESS
Old Town Books
94 High Street
STEVENAGE
Hertfordshire
SG1 3DW
Set up 1991. Co-Operative venture drawing on profesional skills of a small group of colleagues with high standards. Initially to publish FORSTER COUNTRY, other titles may follow.
FORSTER COUNTRY by Margaret Ashby, 176pp. 251 x 190 mm. 56 illustrations, line drawings, black

& white photos, full-colour print, full colour jacket, hardback £14.95 - Mail Order £16.50. Tade terms.

SIMON LAWRENCE: FLEECE PRESS
1 Grey Gables
Blacker Lane
Netherton
Wakefield
WF4 4SS.
Fine Printer
Subjects: Historical Biography. Book Binding.
Books July to December 1991- 3

FLEETING MONOLITH
62 Langdon Park Road
LONDON
N6 5QE

FLEMING PRESS
PO Box 662
Sheffield
S10 1DU.
Subjects: Humour.
Books January to June 1991 - 1

MR BILL FLEMING
The Gables
4 St Andrews Avenue
Bothwell
GLASGOW
G71 8DL

MR PAUL FLETCHER
104 Main Street
Dreghorn
IRVINE
Ayreshire
KA11 4AB

FLEXIBLE LEARNING PROJECT
Yorkshire and Humberside
York Education Centre
Park Grove York
YO3 7ED.
Subjects: Education.
Books July to December 1991 - 2

FLICKS BOOKS
29 Bradford Road
Trowbridge
BA14 9AN.
Subjects: History of Cinema. World Cinema.
Books January to June 1991 - 2. Books July to December 1991 - 3

MS A G FLOOD
Arle Mill
The Weir
ALRESFORD
Hampshire
SO24 9DG

Mr Steve Flood
35 Ilchester Close
HULL
HU7 6AT

FLORENCE NIGHTINGALE MUSEUM
Gassiot House
2 Lambeth Palace Road
LONDON
SE1 7EW

MR ALLEN W FLORES
1 Market Place
Linton
CAMBRIDGE
CB1 6HJ

THE FLORIN PRESS
Weavers Cottage, Cot Lane
Biddenden
ASHFORD
Kent
TN27 8JB

FLOWERS EAST
199-205 Richmond Road
London
E8 3NN.
Subjects: Art.
Books July to December 1991 - 5

FLYING SAUCER REVIEW
PO Box 12
SNODLAND
Kent
ME6 5JZ

FLYING SUGAR PRESS
18 Beaumont Court
38/40 Beaumont Street
LONDON
W1N 1FA
Flying Sugar Press fulfils a childhood dream of self-publishing, and brings tog-ether my skills in drawing and writing. Last year I discovered the techniques of etching, and the dream crystallised into Flying Sugar - my misnomer for the suga r lift process. Finely-crafted artists' books in small hand-printed editions, il lusrations with my own etchings and text.

FLYLEAF PRESS
James Ryan
4 Spencer Villas
Glenagearcy
Co Dublin
Republic of Ireland.
(01) 280 6228
Specialises in Family and local history of Ireland.
IRISH RECORDS - Sources for Family & Local History. By James G Ryan. 363pp & illusrations. Published 1988. ISBN 0 9164489 22 1. IR£24.50 Irish Family History Guide.
TRACING YOUR KERRY ANCESTORS By Michael O'Connor. 96pp & illustrations. Published 1990. ISBN 0 9508466 3 5. IR£6.50 Family History of Co Kerry LONGFORD & ITS PEOPLE By David Leahy. 220pp. Published 1990 ISBN 0 9508466 2 7. IR£18.50. Index to the 1901 Cencus of Co Longford

FOCAL POINT PUBLICATIONS
81 Duke Street

London
W1M 5DJ.
Subjects: Second World War.
Books July to December 1991 - 1

FOCUS PUBLICATIONS
9 Priors Road
WINDSOR
Berkshire
SL4 4PD

FOLENS
Albert House, Apex Business Centre
Boscombe Road
Dunstable
LU5 4RL

FOLK DANCE ENTERPRISES
Lambert's Hall
Kirkby Malham
Skipton
BD23 4BT

FOLKLORE FRONTIERS
Paul Screeton
5 Egton Drive
Seaton Carew
HARTLEPOOL
Cleveland
TS25 2AT

THE FOLKLORE SOCIETY
c/o University College
Gower Street
LONDON
WC1E 6BT

FOLLOW, FOLLOW
PO Box 539
GLASGOW
G11 7LT

FOLLY PUBLICATIONS
Folly Cottage
151 West Malvern Road
Malvern
WR14 4AY

FOOD & FUTURES
SUE MELLIS
49 Halifax Road
LONDON
NW3 2HX

FOOD MATTERS WORLDWIDE
38-40 Exchange Street
Norwich
NR2 1AX

FOOLSCAP
Judi Benson
78 Friars Road
East Ham
London
E6 1LL. Tel 081 470 7680
Quarterly (Jan/June/Sept) magazine of poetry and prose as well as art work. 66 pages on A4 with seam

binding. Began in 1987 and has just published issue 13 which includes poets: Ken Smith Rhona McAdam Jonathan Davidson Frances Wilson and many more. Foolscap - issue 13 66 pages June 1993 0952 3979 £2 single Poetry and Prose

FOOTBALL SUPPORTERS ASSOCIATION
P.O. Box 11
Liverpool
L26 1XP.
Subjects: Football.
Books July to December 1991 - 1

FOOTMARK PUBLICATIONS
Robert Rose
12 The Bourne
FLEET
Hampshire
GU13 9TL 0252 621431
A series of local walks books, giving directions and maps, suitable for families Walsks between two to seven miles. Most take about two hours to walk.
FAMILY WALKS AROUND FLEET AND CHURCH CROOKHAM. By Bob Rose. 24 pages. Maps. F ebruary 1991. ISBN 0 9515738 1 0. £1.35. Local Walks Book.

Mr P FORBES
34c Overcliffe
GRAVESEND
Kent
WA11 0EN

MR CARL T FORD
11 Warwick Road
TWICKENHAM
Middlesex
TW2 6SW

Foreland Publishers
Foreland Fields Road
Bembridge
PO35 5TP

FOREST (FREEDOM ORGANIZATION FOR THE RIGHT TO ENJOY SMOKING TOBACCO)
Chris Tame
2 Grosvenor Gardens,
London SW1W ODH
071 823 6550
Publishes a wide range of leaflets, pamphlets and monographs relating to the general case for individual liberty and free choice and against social authoritarianism and medical paternalism.
Terry Liddle 'The Right to Smoke: A Socialist View'; 12pp; 1989; ISBN 1 871833 03 5; £1.00.
Stephen Davies 'The Historical Origins of Health Fascism'; 10pp; 1991; ISBN 1 871833 15 9; £1.00
Chris R. Tame/Nick Elliott 'Up in Smoke: The Economics, Ethics, and Politics of Tobacco Advertising Bans'; 38pp; ISBN 1 871833 19 1; £2.00
Forest Books
20 Forest View
Chingford
London
E4 7AY

FOREST 2

Grosvenor Gardens
London
SW1W ODH.
Subjects: Health (Smoking).
Books January to June 1991 - 1. Books July to December 1991 - 4

FOREST ARTWORKS
Forest Youth & Community Centre
College Campus, College Road
CINDERFORD
Gloucestershire

FOREST PUBLISHING
Woodstock
Liverton
Newton Abbot
TQ12S 6JJ.
Subjects: Railways.
Books July to December 1991 - 1

FORMIL MODEL ENGINEERING
12 Oak Tree Close
Bedale
DL8 1UG

JOHN H. FORREST
64 Belsize Park
London
NW3 4EH.
Subjects: Travel (South America).
Books January to June 1991 - 1

Forster Davies: J White
'Jenkin'
Loweswater
Cockermouth
CA13 0RU

S FORSYTH
10 Gladstone Street
London
SE1 6EY

FORTEAN TOMES
127 Windsor Road
LONDON
E7 0RA

FORTH NATURALIST & HISTORIAN
L Corbett
University of Stirling
Stirling
FK9 4LA
Charitable volunteer-run publisher/promoter of local studies - naturalist environmental historical Central Scotland area. Est 1975. 13 vols of annual 6 books; annual symposia on Man & The Landscape
'Forth Naturalist & Historian Vol 13'. 118pp ISBN 0 9514147 4 7. £3.50 plus p&p 80p Climate & Scottish Lochs; Moorland Birds; Early Gravestones; Dickens at Bridge of Allan.
'The Stirling Region - standard B Association type survey 1974 P Reduced to £2.00 (p&p £1.40)
'Doune - Historical Notes - MacKay inc Kilmadock parish'. 126pp ISBN 0 950692 5 0. £3.50 (plus 70p p&p)

E.L. FORTY
22 Annesley Road
Iffley
Oxford
OX4 4JQ.
Subjects: Poetry.
Books July to December 1991 - 1

FORUM BOOKS
Little Heath Road
Chobham
Woking
GU24 8RL

FORUM FOR SOCIAL STUDIES
53 Kinlet Road
London
SE18 3BZ

MS L FOSTER
83a St Marks Road
Bush Hill Park
ENFIELD
Middlesex
EN1 1BJ

MR ANTHONY PEERS FOTHERGILL
Pilgrims Bell
7 Janice Drive, Fulwood
PRESTON
Lancashire
PR2 4YE
No Unsolicited Peoms/ Prose

EDITIONS DU FOURNEAU
21 Rue de l'Evangile
F-75018 PARIS
FRANCE

FOUR OAKS PUBLICATIONS
4 Oaks Road
Shiplake
Henley-on-Thames
RG9 3JH.
Subjects: General Fiction.
Books July to December 1991 - 1

FOURTH WORLD REVIEW
John Papworth
24 Abercorn Place
St Johns Wood
LONDON
NW8

MR C R FOWLES
155 Round Road
BIRMINGHAM
B24 9SN

THE FOX PRESS
Oak Tree
Main Road, Colden Common
WINCHESTER
Hampshire
SO21 1JL
Poetry, animal welfare, natural history, local publi-

cations, magazine and booklets.

FOXLINE PUBLISHING
32 Urwick Road
Romiley
Stockport
SK6 3JS.
Subjects: Railways. Buses.
Books July to December 1991 - 6

FOX PUBLICATIONS
31 St Andrewgate
York
YO1 2BR

DEREK FOXTON
15A Commercial Street
Hereford
HR1 2DE.
Subjects: Local History.
Books July to December 1991 - 1

FRACTAL REPORT
West Towen House
Porttowan
Cornwall
TR4 8AX
Details of the production of Fractal images on
home computers. Most makes covered. Free sam-
ple. Authors get free subscription to following vol-
ume. 20 pages. A4. Bi-monthly. Subs. £10 UK; £12
Europe; £13 USA.

FRAGMENTE
(magazine of contemporary poetics)
8 Hertford Street
Oxford
OX4 3AJ

FRANCHISE PUBLICATIONS
32 Sutton Road
Bournemouth
BH9 1RN

KEVIN FRANCIS PUBLISHING COMPANY
85 Landcroft Road
London
SE22 9JS

MERVYN E. FRANKLIN
61 Chelsworth Avenue
Ipswich
IP4 3BB.
Subjects: Handicrafts.
Books July to December 1991 - 1

FRASER PRESS
203 Bath Street
Glasgow
G2 4HZ.
Subjects: Architecture.
Books July to December 1991 - 1

MR D G FRASER
Windmill Farm
Beckwithshaw
HARROGATE

HG3 1QL 0423 503930

MR JOHN FRASER
via I Jacometti 2
Anguillara Sabazia
I-00061 ROMA
ITALY

(THE) FRED
711D Park Hall
Martell Road
London
S E 21

FREELANCE FOCUS
7 King Edward Terrace
BROUGH
North Humberside
HU15 1EE

MS A L FREEMAN
Flat 11b Glen Bank
WELLINGBOROUGH
Northamptonshire
NN8 1HQ

MR ROLAND FREEMAN
14 North Ridge
Northian
RYE
East Sussex
TN31 6PG

MS URSULA FREEMAN
The unidentified flying Printer
Brook House, Clun
CRAVEN ARMS
Shropshire
SY7 8LY

FREE RADICAL
Mr Steve Green
33 Scott Road, Olton
SOLIHULL
West Midlands
B92 7LQ
Topics as diverse as religious fanaticism and the
author's experience as a newspaper jounalist.

FREE RANGE PUBLISHING
Bilton Road
Chelmsford
CM1 2UJ

FREE SUN PUBLICATIONS
16 Viewbank
Hastings
TN35 5HB

MS ANNE FRENCH
Crafts Council - Information Section
12 Waterloo Place
LONDON
SW1Y 4AU

J E FRENCH
Caerleon

Wareham Road, Sandford
Wareham
BH20 7AF

FRESHWATER
Ferry House
Far Sawrey
Ambleside
LA22 0LP

MR ANTHONY E FREWIN
P O Box 123
BOREHAMWOOD
Hertfordshire
WD6 1AF

FRIAR'S BUSH PRESS
24 College Park Avenue
Belfast
BT7 1LR

MR PAUL FRIDAY
81 Meadway Drive
Horsell
WOKING
Surrey
GU21 4TF 0483 761963

FRIENDLY PRESS
Anne Hodgkinson
300 Gloucester Road,
Horfield,
BRISTOL
0272 429142
We work with primary children and teachers. Our
courses offer complete training kits, tapes, books
aids. Send for catalogue of many items including
Friendly Press, Quaker imprint.

FRIENDS FELLOWSHIP OF HEALING: CUR-
LEW
Thirlestane House, Yetholm
Kelso
TD5 8PD

FRIENDS OF THE CROYDON ENGLISH LAN-
GUAGE
South Norwood Adult Education Centre
Sandown Road
London
SE25 4XE

FRIENDS OF THE WESTERN BUDDHIST OR-
DER
c/o The London Buddhist Centre
51 Roman Road
London
E 1

FRIEZE
21 Denmark St
London
WC2H 8NE

MR TIM FRITH
Beech Hurst, Warwick Road
Southam

LEAMINGTON SPA
Warwickshire
CV33 0HN

FROGLETS PUBLICATIONS
Mrs Fern FlynnFroglets
Brasted Chart
Westerham
Kent
TN16 1LY 0959 562972
Specialising in environmental historical and weather books mainly pictorial; donations to environmental charities to date exceed £60 000 'In the wake of the Hurricane' by Bob Ogley. A pictorial account of the great storm of October 1987. 140pp. £9.95. ISBN 0 9513019 0 X 'Biggin on the Bump' by Bob Ogley. A pictorial history of the RAF at Bigg in Hill. 160pp. £9.50 pb. £14.95 hb. ISBN 1 872337 05 8 Series of Historical Pictorial Weather books coming Autumn 1991; focusing on Kent & Sussex.

FROGMORE PAPERS
42 Morehall Ave
Folkestone
Kent
CT19 4EF

FROGMORE PAPERS
131 North View Road
Hornsey
London
N 8

FRONTIER PUBLISHING
Windetts
Kirkstead
NORWICH
NR15 1BR 0508 58174
Titles from unusal travel to photographic studies.

FRONT PAGE SYSTEMS
18 Ashwin Street
LONDON
E8 3DL

FROSTED EARTH
77 Rickman Hill
Coulsdon
CR5 3DT

FROSTED EARTH
Ian Currie
77 Rickman Hill
Coulsdon
Surrey
CR5 3DT. Tel 0737 554869.
Frosted Earth initiated the Country Weather Book Series documentary in a pictorial record the main events to affect the South East back to Caesar's invasion. Everybody talks about the weather. This is a unique way to read about it.
The Surrey Weather Book ISBN 0 9516710 1 4 Second Revised Edition Price 7.50 by M. Davidson and I. Currie
In Conjunction with Froglets Publications - The Kent Weather Book ISBN 1 872337 35 X by Bob Ogley Ian Currie and Mark Davidson £9.95 In Conjunction with Froglets Publications - The Sus-

sex Weather Book ISBN 1 872337 30 9 Price £9.95 by Bob Ogley Ian Currie and Mark Davidson

MR D FRYER
8 Catherton Close
Burberry Grange
TIPTON
West Midlands
DY4 0DQ

FTT
Joseph Nicholas
5a Frinton Road
Stamford Hill
LONDON
N15 6NH
"Dear People, We don't know how FTT came to be added to your mailing list, but for the past couple of years or so we've received invitations from you to advertise in your yearbook, appear at Small Press Fairs, and so on. I'm writing to suggest that it might not be worth your while to continue sending us such invitations, since our aims would appear to be somewhat different from those of the majority of small press publishers. We publish two or three issues of FTT a year, in a print run of 150-180 copies, for an active response from those prepared to write us letters of comment, provide contributions for future issues, or send us their own publications in exchange, and we aren't particularly interested in expanding our readership base much beyond this. We may indeed be missing out on a great deal by not doing so, but we publish FTT principally for its own sake, and if it were to involve us in any more work than at present it would rapidly cease to be a hobby and become instead a deadly chore. So I think it might perhaps be best if we didn't advertise in your yearbook, appear at small press fairs, or indeed remain on your mailing list!"

MR K FULCHER
141 Rosary Road
NORWICH
NR1 4DA

MR MATTHEW FULLER
30 Piercefield Place
CARDIFF
CF2 1LD

MR ALAN FULTON,
City of Aberdeen
Arts & Recreation Division
Libraries Section, Central Library
Rosemont Viaduct
ABERDEEN
AB9 1GU 0224 634622
A Printing and recording section which mainly concentrates on the heritage of North East Scotland.

FUN AND LEARNING PUBLISHERS
24 North Road
Leadenham
LN5 0PG.
Subjects: Children's Fiction.
Books July to December 1991 - 1

MR RICHARD FUNGE
58 Belmont Street
WORCESTER
WR3 8NN 0905 612898

FUCHSIAPRINT
122 Northumberland Avenue
Stamford
PE9 1EA

F.W.H. TRANSPORT MONOGRAPHS
Bishop's Castle
High Heaton
Newcastle-upon-Tyne
NE7 7QF.
Subjects: Railways.

[G]

MS H GADDING
20 Old Nazeing Road
Lower Nazeing
Essex
EN10 6RW

GAIRFISH
9 Pankhurst Court
Caradon Close
LONDON
E11 4TB
Publishing anthologies on all aspects of Scottish
culture. Literary criticism, polemic, shorter fiction
and cutting edge poetry. Edited by poets Richard
Price and W N Herbert.
Scotland and the Avent-Garde. An Avent-Garde
reader. New work from Edwin Morgan, Tom
Leonard, Kathleen Jamie, Robert Crawford. The
unpublished MacDiarmond. 150 pages. 1992. £3.50.
Dundee: an anthology of Dundee. Essays from
Douglas Dunn, Tracy Herd. Poems from Val Warner,
Ann Stevenson, John Glenday, A D Foote, Sean
O'Brian. 96 pages. 1991. £3.50
The Anarchy of Light. Essays on the 20th century
novelist Neil M Gunn. New work from Stewart
Conn, David Kinloch, Meg Bateman. 80 pages.
1991. £3.50

GALACTIC CENTRAL PUBLICATIONS
'Imladris'
25a Copgrove Road
Leeds
LS8 2SP
Publisher of SF and SF-related reference works
specialising in author bibliographies.
'Philip K. Dick: Metaphysical Conjuror' edited by
Phil Stephensen-Payne and Gordon Benson jr. Feb.
1990. 102pp. 4.00. ISBN 1 871133 20 3. Biblio
graphy.
'Frederick Pohl: Merchant of Excellence' edited by
Phil Stephensen-Payne and Gordon Benson jr. March
1989. 109pp. £3.95. ISBN 1 871133 09 2. Biblio
graphy.
'Clifford D. Simak: Pastoral Space Farer' edited by
Phil Stephensen-Payne June 1991. 64pp. £3.00.
ISBN 1 871133 28 9. Bibliography.

THE GALDRAGON PRESS
136 Byres Road

GLASGOW
Scotland
G12 8TD
Small poetry publisher, established 1991. Also
typesetting + printing services. On Orkney by Pam
Beasant, June 1991, 6 pages, 1 illustration on cover.
ISBN 1 873932 00 6, £1.50, 100 limited edition.
Printed on 100 gms laid/hamd sewn. Sold Out.
Knockariddera by Jerry Loose, November 1991, 12
pages, 1 illustration on cover £1.95, ISBN 1 873932
01, 200 limited edition, 50 copies signed by author.
Printed on 100gms laid/hand sewn cover.
Exile's Journey by Hayden Murphy, 12pp. 1 illus-
tration cover. £1.95 100 limited edition. ISBN 1
873932 03 0, ISBN 1 873932 02 2 (27-100) Printed
on 100gms/hand sewn cover. Lettered + signed by
author + artist. June 1992

GALE CENTRE PUBLICATIONS
Whitakers Way
Loughton
IG10 1SQ
Subjects: Social Welfare.
Books January to June 1991 - 2. Books July to
December 1991 - 2

MR F GALE
32 Drayson Mews
LONDON
W8 4LY

JOAN GALE
Brackenrigg Cottage
Rothbury
Morpeth
Northumberland

H J GALLACHER
School House
North Douglas Street
Clydebank
GLASGOW Scotland
G81 1NQ

MR IAN GALLACHER
2 Glebelands
Churchtowne
CALSTOCK
Cornwall
PL18 9SG 0822 833256

GALLERY PRESS
70-71 High Street
LAVENHAM
Suffolk
CO10 9PT
Gamehawk by Ray Turner 20.00

GALLIARD PUBLISHERS
21 Hillside Crescent
Edinburgh
EH7 5EB

H. GALLOWAY
39 Nutwell Road
Worle
Weston-super-Mare
BS22 0EW

Subjects: Family History.
Books July to December 1991 - 1

THE GAMECOCK PRESS
11 Park Road
RUGBY
Warwickshire
CV21 2QU

MR DAVID GAMESON
11 Ffordd Mon
Rhosddu
WREXHAM
Clwyd
LL11 2LL

MR DAVID GAMMON
11 West Town Grove
BRISTOL
BS4 5EQ

MR JOHN GAMMONS
10 Christchurch Road
LONDON
N8 9QL 081 340 2454

RICHARD GANDER
20 MSB House
The Mall
Bromley
BR1 1TT.
Subjects: Local History.
Books July to December 1991 - 1

GANYMEDE
PO Box 421
SWINDON
SN1 5AU

GARBONZA BEANPRESS
128 Centenary Road
Goole
DN1Y 6PE.
Subjects: Poetry.
Books July to December 1991 - 1

MR B GARDNER
The Manse
Baptist Street
CALSTOCK
Cornwall

JOHN MITCHELL GARDNER
2 North Campbell Avenue
Milngavie
GLASGOW
Subjects: Biography
Books July to December 1991 - 1

GARGOYLE'S HEAD PRESS
Chatham House
Gosshill Road
CHISLEHURST
Kent
BR7 5NS
Subjects: Historical Biography
Books July to December 1991 - 2

GARNETT (SUSAN GARNETT)
Holme Lee
Longsight Road
Copster Green
Blackburn
BB1 9EU.
Subjects: Education.
Books July to December 1991 - 1

GARRARD AND CO.
112 Regent Street
London
W1A 2JJ.
Subjects: Garrard and Co. history of.
Books January to June 1991 - 1

S GASCOIGNE
12a Newcomen Road
DARTMOUTH
Devon

GATEHOUSE BOOKS
St Lukes
Sawley Road
Manchester
M10 8D 061 9522
Gatehouse is unique in that its writers are adults who are developing their reading and writing skills. Gatehouse books are especially popular in Adult Basic Education; schools and the prison service. Titles range from 'Adult Beginner Readers' to 'Reminiscence' collections by women black writers and writers with disabilities.
'A Guide to the Monsters of the Mind' by Victor Grenko. 32pp A4 Dec 1990 45 colour illustr ISBN 0 906253 32 2. £4.95. Comic/art therapy/literacy
'Opening Time' various Ed G Frost & C Hoy 341pp 14 sections; illustrations & photos A4 writing resource pack for Adult Basic Education & schools ISBN 0 906253 13 6. 25.00
'Bagels with Babushka' by Hilda Cohen 63pp 1989 photos ISBN 0 906253 31 4. 2.95 Autobiography of Jewish poet pensioner & feminist from Salford (gen readership/literacy/social history/Jewish/women's issues)

GATES OF ANNWN
Mr C E Bradwood
395 Broxburn Drive
SOUTH OCKENDON
Essex
RM15 5PJ
'Gates of Annwn' is a Pagan contact magazine dedicated to the Old Religion.

GATEWAY BOOKS
The Hollies
Wellow
BATH
BA2 8QJ 0225 835 127

GATEWAY GUIDES
235 Queens Road
Penkridge
STOKE-ON-TRENT

MR JOHN GATRELL

114

Campions, Le Petit Val
Alderney
GUERNSEY
Channel Islands

MR MIKE GAUNT
John Blackburn Ltd
Old Run Road
LEEDS
LS10 2AA

GAY AUTHORS W/S NEWSLETTER
c/o Kathryn Byrd
Gemma
BM Box 5700
London
WC1N 3XX

GAY MEN'S PRESS
PO Box 247
LONDON
N17 9QR

GAY TIMES
Millivres Ltd
Ground Floor Worldwide House
116-134 Bayham St
London
NW1 0BA

GAYWRITES! (R.I.P.)
Andrew Gatheridge
11 Whitchurch Place
Cathays
Cardiff
CF2 4HD
Gay Writes! was a one-off and after a third edition
of 'Bedsitter Boys' decided to jack it all in. I encourage everyone to produce at least one book. You've
got nothing to lose and may learn a few new things
about your life. 'Bedsitter Boys' is photocopy Gay-
Art.
Bedsitter Boys and Mr PO Box 599. By A. Authori-
zation (me the editor) it consists of 8 pages; 4 poetry;
6 story pages; 3 stories. Available free while stocks
last with s.a.e. Not many left. Be prepared to be
shocked.

G.C BOOK PUBLISHERS
10 Bank Street
Wigtown
DG8 9HP

GCCR
1 Robin Close
Ingleby Barwick
Stockton-on-Tees
TS17 0TD

G C S
Dave GilbertWaterdene House
Water Lane
Leighton Buzzard
Bedfordshire
LU7 7AW
GCS publish guide books and offer a typesetting
service to publishers. Our guaranteed 'delivery on
time' has proved invaluable to some of the country's

foremost publishers. Special rates for members of
SPG. Tel 0525 371324.

BARBARA GEERE
15 Stamford Drive
Bromley
BR2 0XF
Subjects: Education.
Books July to December 1991 - 1

GEERINGS OF ASHFORD
Cobbs Wood House
Chart Road
Ashford
TN23 1EP.
Subjects: Historical Biography.
Books July to December 1991 - 1

GEFN PRESS
Flat b
7 Elmwood Road
LONDON
SE24 6AQ

GEISER PRODUCTIONS
Sidney Du Broff
7 The Corner
Grange Road
London
W5 3PQ. Tel 081 579 4653
Geiser Productions are producers of sponsored and
commissioned works creators of books on the out-
doors and fiction. We will do an article or an
encyclopedia or anything else in between. Work
emanating from Geiser Productions has appeared
in twenty-three countries.
Black Fuse (fiction). A black man in the USA tells
his own story. Rights available.
Still Water Fly for Young People created especially
to meet the needs of young anglers. Rights available.
Fly Fishing on Still Water A daily amount of what
worked and what didn't. Rights available.

MR CHRISTOPHER GEMMELL
36 Salisbury Avenue
St Albans
Hertfordshire
AL1 4TV

JOURNAL OF GENDER STUDIES
Humberside Poly
Inglemire Ave
Hull
HU6 7LU

GENERATION X
1 South View
Mexborough
South Yorkshire
S64 9NE 0709 890116
Covers the worldwide fanzine scene (100s reviews/
contacts every issue). music strange films and per-
sonalities and associated subjects like comics .
Heavily into promoting DIY projects (music press
and film etc). All the following edited by Adrian F.
'Neighbourhood Watch'. A5 music newsletter; ran
for 4 issues - available for 1.00 in stamps. Now

renamed and expanded 12-24 pp; review£s news contax 'Generation X'. ISSN 0962 2381. Follow-on from N.W. Now A4 24pp. gloss cover and free 7" EP by Little Brother. No 1 £1.00 inc p&p. 'Information Overload' ISBN tba. Music fanzine small press contacts book 10 000 contacts worldwide (forthcoming). SAE for details

GEOLOGICAL SOCIETY
Publishing House
Unit 7
Brassmill Enterprise Centre
Bath
BA1 3JN 0225 475046
Two scientific journals and ten books per annum on all aspects of earth sciences. The Geoscientist; a bimonthly magazine with a circulation of 7 000 is also published by the Society as is the Geologist's Directory. 'Geology of Scotland - 3rd Edn.' Ed. G Y Craig. 628pp 200+ illus. Sept 1991 ISBN 0 903317 64 8 p/b: £29.00 h/b: £65.00
'The United Kingdom Oil & Gas Fields' Ed. I.L. Abbotts. 464pp 400 illus. 57 colour plates July 1991 ISBN 0 903317 62 1. £80.00
'Atlas of Palaeogeography & Lithofacies' Ed. J.C.W. Cope. 164pp A3. 106 colour maps Sept 1991 ISBN 0 903317 65 6. £295.00

MISS J GEORGE
28 Arberry Road
LONDON
E3 5DD

MR MIKEY GEORGESON
45 Stafford Road
BRIGHTON
BN1 5PE

MR MIKE GERRARD
5 Parsonage Street
Wistow
Huntingdon
Cambridgeshire
PE17 2QD

GERSHOM PUBLICATIONS
1 Daisy Road
London
E18 1EA.
Subjects: Poetry.
Books January to June 1991 - 1

G.G. PUBLISHING
26A Park Road
Cheveley
Newmarket
CB8 9DF.
Subjects: Poetry.
Books July to December 1991 - 1

G.G.A. INTERNATIONAL PUBLISHERS
Mr. Gavin Green
Casa Mimosa, Santa Eugenia,
Mallorca, Baleares,
Spain 07412
Mallorca 62 04 88

Publishes children's books, action/adventure/romance novels, non- fiction. Trade terms, enquire. Licenses special editions to other publishers, royalty against agreed print-run. Licensed 30 books world-wide in over 80 editions since established 1967. Seeks distributors 1992. U.K. . - U.S.A.
The Adventures of Hugglemush; by Katie Kent. Dec. 1991. ISBN 0 948776 05 6. £3.50. Children's.
Adventures of Hugglemush - Two; by Katie Kent. Oct. 1992. ISBN 0 948776 15 3. £3.95. Children's.
The Tiddley-Wink Man; by Katie Kent. Sept. 1992. ISBN 0 948776 10 2. £4.50. Children 7 - 12.

GHOST PUBLISHING
12 Seager Road
Sheerness
ME12 2BG

GHOSTS & SCHOLARS
Rosemary Pardoe
Flat One
36 Hamilton Street
Hoole
CHESTER
CH2 3JQ

MR JOHN W GIBBONS
37b St Stephens Road
SALTASH
Cornwall
PL12 4BQ

J.P.GIBSON & CO, ART PRODUCTIONS
80 Hillcrest Rise
Cookridge
Leeds
LS16 7DL

MR ROBERT GIDDINGS
Flat 1, 12 St Peters Road
Parkstone
POOLE
Dorset
BH14 0PA

MS CATHE GIFFINN
240 E 27th Street, #20k
NEW YORK
NY 10016
United States of America

C GILBERT
5 The Grove
Forest Hall
Newcastle-upon-Tyne
NE12 9PE

MR MARK GILBERT
83 Honeybourne
BISHOPS STORTFORD
Hertfordshire
CM23 4ED

GUILD OF ST GEORGE
Rose Cottage, 17 Hadassah Grove
Lark Lane
Liverpool
L17 8XH

ANN GILLANDERS
The Holistic Healing Centre
92 Sheering Road
Old Harlow
CM17 0JT

MARSHALL GILLESPIE PUBLICATIONS
92 Belvoir Close
Fareham
PO16 0PR

SU GILLES
5 The Links
Welwyn Garden City
AL8 7DS

CORNELIUS A. GILLICK
Moderne Shoppe
6 Hulme Hall Lane
Manchester
M10 8AZ.
Subjects: Education.
Books July to December 1991 - 1

MR JASBIR GILL
209 Station Road
HAYES
Middlesex
UB3 4JB

MR C N GILMORE
54 Frederick Crescent
PORT ELLEN
Isle of Islay
Scotland
PA42 7AY

SORCHA GILROY
56 Palmerston Road
Dublin 6
Republic of Ireland

GIMELL RECORDS
4 Newtec Place
Magdalen Road
Oxford
OX4 1RE.
Subjects: History of Music.
Books July to December 1991 - 1

MR CHRISTOPHER GINGELL
21 Selborne Road
Horfield
BRISTOL
BS7 9PH

GIRLFRENZY
BM Senior
LONDON
WC1N 3XX
A Comic/fanzine produced by women for people -
a divine mix of articles, strips and no make up tips.
Created because of the vacuum in provision of
comics by women and few outlets for views outside
mainstream feminist thought. Girlfrenzy 1. A4,
28pp, 90p. (sold out) b&w, 2 colour cover. Comic

strips and articles. Editor: Erica Smith.
Girlfrenzy 2. A4, 32pp, £1.50. B&W, 2 colour
cover. Comic strips & articles. Editor: Erica Smith

ARTHUR NORMAN GIRLING
13 Gleneagle Road
Streatham
London
SW16 6AY

ANNE GITTINS
14 Victoria Road
Fleet
Aldershot
GU13 8DN.
Subjects: Biography.
Books July to December 1991 - 1

GK Books
George Lawson
74 Goldstone Road
HOVE
East Sussex
BN3 3FH
0273 208049
Publishers of books on Travel, Humour, True Crime,
and Childrens Books. Appreciate hearing from
people who have researched their market and have
a sound sales base. Synopses rather than MSS. S.A.E
for reply. 'The Kerkennah Islands'. By George
lawson. 76pp. 12 Illustrations. Travel ISBN 0
9518061 0 6. Sept 1991. £3.50 + 50p P&P.
'Alexander, Dobbin and Captain Cuttlefish'. By
George Lawson. 16pp. 10 Full colour illustrations.
Childrens. ISBN 0 9518061 1 4. Nov 1991. £3.50 +
50p P&P. 'See you in the Pub' By Simon Lee. 20pp.
14 Illustrations. Humour. ISBN 0 9518061 2 2. Apr
1992. £2.50 + 50p P&P.

THE GLADE
62 Hook Rise
North Tolworth
KT6 7JY.
Subjects: Archaeology.
Books July to December 1991 - 1

MR P GLANFIELD
Gwella Chons
76a Melvill Road
FALMOUTH
Cornwall
TR11 4DB

GLASGOW COLLECTION
34 Loanbank Quadrant
Glasgow
G51 3HZ

UNIVERSITY OF GLASGOW LIBRARY
Millhead Street
Glasgow
GL2 8QE

GLASGOW PRESS
6 Doune Quad
Glasgow
G20 6DL

GLASGOW PUBLISHING COMPANY
Graham Yuill
6 Doune Quad
Glasgow
G20 6DL. Tel 041 946 5552
Glasgow Publishing Company specialise in driving books for learners and all instructors. Behind the wheel contains sections for the disabled the deaf and theunable to speak. No other driving book has this unique feature.
Behind the Wheel Driving For Learners And Their Instructors By Graham Yuill 1 July 1992 ISBN 09516519 1 9.

GLASGOW SCHOOL OF ART
167 Renfrew Street
Glasgow

UNIVERSITY OF GLASGOW
French & German Publications
Modern Languages Building
Glasgow
G12 8QL

GLENIFFER PRESS
PO Box 56
Paisley
PA2 6AT

GLENVIL GROUP
Salisbury Hall
Park Road
Hull
HU3 1TD.
Subjects: Russian History.

GLEVUM PRESS
2 Honyatt Road
Gloucester
GL1 3EB

GLIDDON BOOKS
Skeetshill Farmhouse
Sotesham St Mary
Norwich
NR15 1UR

GLOBAL ACADEMIC PUBLISHERS
PO Box 22167
NL-1100 KD AMSTERDAM
The Netherlands

GLOBAL EGO NETWORK
Ego 1
Global HQ
New Street
Birdsall
BM31 4RG
The self-zine ! Happening thingies spurting outa your mind in a mega med ia sort of way with film video rantings scribblings poetic sequences or just anything you like... All contributions considered. Anything legal or not; so long as it's easy and never has to actually get done. 'All About Me' Ed. Ego 1 1pp 'zine of myself; quarterly; £1.00 inc p&p 'All About my Friend Ron' Ed Ego 1. 2pp 'zine of Ron's desperate hero wor ship of his friend Ego; 1st issue £1.00.

'Dark Thoughts from Hell to Eternity' Eds. Ego & Sally 1. Nasty things we think of when we're drunk - 12pp with doodles and horoscope. £1.50

GLOBAL TAPESTRY JOURNAL
Spring Bank
Longsight Road
Copster Green
Blackburn
BB1 9EU 0254 249128
A post-underground magazine with varied and wide ranging content. mainly Beat, Bohemian and High-energy. Creativity which represents an entire dissident or li berated spectrum across age gaps and surface cult image.
Typeset, offset litho. Last issue was sponsored by North West Arts. A supplemen t was funded by Oracle Books. 80 pages. ISSN 0141 1241. Incorporates PN Newsle tter 40 was 26 pages of book, magazine, video and poetry reading reviews. £1.90 postpaid. 4 issue post-subsidised subscription for £7.00.

GLOSA
Ron Clark and Wendy Ashby
PO Box 18
Richmond
Surrey TW9 2AU.
Tel 081 948 8417.
Glosa 6000 - 6000 Greek and Latin words and roots which occur in the Euro - Languages and Internation of Scientific Terminology April 1992. English - Glosa 1000 Dictionary April 1992 Introducing Euro-Glosa 1990
Also in October 1992 French - Glosa German - Glosa and Spanish -Glosa Dictionaries. Also revised 3rd edition of '18 Steps to Fluency in Euro - Glosa'

G.M.S. ENTERPRISES
67 Pyhill Bretton
Peterborough
PE3 8QQ.
Subjects: Air Transport. Military Aircraft. Air Force History. Books July to December 1991 - 4

MR D GOBELL
50b Seaforth Grove
SOUTHEND-ON-SEA
Essex
SS2 4EW

G O C (Gay Outdoor Club)
P O Box 1
Newton St Cyres
Exeter
EX5 5QN

W D GODDARD
9 Pine Walk
UCKFIELD
East Sussex
TN22 1TK

MR J GODSELL
7 Upton Road
BEXLEY
Kent

MR JAMES GOLBEY
1 Penerley Road
Catford
LONDON
SE6 2LQ

GOLDEN APPLE PRODUCTIONS
Hinton House
Hinton
Christchurch
BH23 7EA

GOLDEN BELL PRESS
1 Hungate Lane
Aylsham
Norwich
NR11 6UD.
Subjects: Local History.
Books January to June 1991 - 1

GOLDEN-EYE MAPS
The Cottage
Mill Street
Prestbury
Cheltenham
GL52 3BG.
Subjects: Travel Guides.
Books January to June 1991 - 8

GOLDEN FLEECE PRESS
63 Barshaw Road
Penilee
GLASGOW
G52 4EE
Golden Fleece Press a new imprint specialising in
poetry was established in June 1991 by Charles E
Stuart the sole proprietor. Golden Fleece Poets are
either previously published or, in many cases, pre-
viously unpublished the press acting as a stepping
stone for new poets.
Charles Edward Stuart, Selected Poems, 40 pages,
cover illustration. Date of publication 30th June
1991. ISBN 0 9517642 0 9. Price £3.50. Poetry.
Three Poets Made in Scotland, Edited by C E
Stuart. 25 pages, cover design. Date of publication,
4th June 1992. ISBN 0 9517642 1 7. Price £2.50.
Poetry.

GOLDFINCH BOOKS
P.O. Box 2414
London
N12 0NG.
Subjects: Art.
Books July to December 1991 - 1

MS DIANA GOLDMAN
6 Talmadge Hill Road
Darien
CT 06820
United States of America

GOLDMARK
Orange House
14 Orange Street
Uppingham
LE15 9SQ

MR DAVID GOLDSMITH
12 Holyoake Walk
LONDON
N2 0JX

MR I M GOLDSMITH
14 Oakworth Close
Redbrook
BARNSLEY
South Yorkshire
S75 2PP

GOLDSMITHS' GALLERY
Lewisham Way
London
SE14 6NW.
Subjects: Art.
Books January to June 1991 - 1. Books July to
December 1991 - 1

GOODALL PUBLICATIONS
Larchwood House
274 London Road
St Albans
AL1 1HY

MR M C GOODALL
3 Robson Terrace
Shincliffe Village
DURHAM
DH1 2NL

GOODAY PUBLISHERS
PO Box 60
Chichester
PO 20 8RA

MR DARREN GOODEN
18 Stirling Avenue
LEIGH-ON-SEA
Essex
SS9 3PP

JOHN M. GOODIER
15 Rectory Lane
Lymm
WA13 0AJ.
Subjects: Walks Books.
Books July to December 1991 - 1

SINCLAIR GOODLAD
Petersham Hollow
226 Petersham Road
Richmond
TW10 7AL

GOOD-READ BOOKS
30 Spen Valley Road
Dewsbury
WF13 3EZ.
Subjects: Children's Fiction.

GOOD STORIES MAGAZINE
(see Oakwood Publications)

TIMOTHY GOOD
4 Vancouver Close

Lower Wick
Worcester
WR2 4XS

GOOD TIMES
The Elephant House
Hawley Crescent
London
NW1 8NP

GOODWINS BOOKSELLERS
28E High Street
Leighton Buzzard
LU7 7EA.
Subjects: Local History.
Books July to December 1991 - 1

GOON SHOW PRESERVATION SOCIETY
3 Flotterton Gardens
Fenham
NEWCASTLE-UPON-TYNE
NE5 2DS

MR DAVID GORMAN
Burleigh
8 Grove House
316 Oxford Road
MANCHESTER
M13 9NG

MR BARRY GORNALL
9 Hendre Close
Llandaff
CARDIFF
CF5 2HT

GORSE PUBLICATIONS
Pat Earnshaw
PO Box 214
Shamley Green
Guildford
GU5 0SW. Tel and fax 0483 2743
Gorse Publications specialise in books on all aspects of lace from History and fashion through the story of lace threads to practical manuals with fully illustrated instructions for making the Youghal Laces of Ireland and the Halas Laces of Hungary. Outlines and Stitches Pat Earnshaw 1992 ISBN 0 951389149 £12.50 Halas Laces of Hungary a guide to shapes and stitches.
Lace in Fashion Pat Earnshaw 168pp 1991 ISBN 0 9513891 3 0 £11.50 Types designs and centres of manufactures of fashion laces Threads of Lace Pat Earnshaw 108pp 1989 ISBN 0 9513891 1 4 £10.00 Origins spinning of fibres of lace threads and their use.

GOSTOURS
29 Marchwood Road
Sheffield
S6 5LB.
Subjects: Birds.
Books July to December 1991 - 1

GOTHIC PRESS
PO Box 542
Highgate
London

N6 6BG
History biography supernatural and occult nonfiction is the essence of material published by Gothic Press to date. Poetry and gothic romantic fiction are planned. Unsolicited manuscripts are not welcome at present. 'The Highgate Vampire' by Sean Manchester. July 1991. 192pp 30 illustrations. Hardback £19.99. ISBN 1 872486 01 0. Completely revised and updat ed. Second edition.

GOTHIC GARDEN PRESS
Mr Mike Boland
30 Byron Court
HARROW
Middlesex
HA1 1JT

GOTHIC IMAGE
7 High Street
GLASTONBURY
Somerset
BA6 9DP
Bookshop

GOTHIC SOCIETY
Chantham House
Gosshill Road
CHISLEHURST
Kent
BR7 5NS

MISS M GOUGH
2 Cross Cottages
Stogursey
BRIDGEWATER
Somerset
TA5 1HA

V GOULD
The Coach House
Monkshatch, Compton
Guildford
GU3 1DG

MS CAROLINE GOURLAY
Hill House Farm
Knighton
Powys
LD7 1NA

GOVERNMENT ART COLLECTION
St Christopher House
Annexe, Sumner Street
London
SE7 9LA

GOWER PRESS
G Daniel
19 Gwynant Place
Lakeside
CARDIFF
CF2 6LT

GOWLAND & CO
93 Bedford Road
Birkdale
Southport

120

PR8 4HT

F. GRAHAM
10 Blythswood
North Osborne Road
Jesmond
Newcastle-upon-Tyne
NE2 2AZ.
Subjects: History Atlases.
Books July to December 1991 - 1

GRAHAM-CAMERON ILLUSTRATION
10 Church Street
Willingham
CAMBRIDGE
CB4 5HT

MR STEVEN GRAINGER
Pan 2000
LONDON
WC1N 3XX

GRAINLOFT BOOKS
Grainloft
Ansty
Haywards Heath
RH17 5AG.
Subjects: Poetry.
Books January to June 1991 - 1

GRAND PRIX SPORTIQUE
Upton
Tetbury
GL8 8LP

MR ASHLEY GRANGER
4-6 Althorpe Road
LONDON
SW17 7ED

GRANT BOOKS
Victoria Square
Droitwich
Worcestershire
WR9 8DE 0905 778155
Limited edion golf books with the emphasis on
history, architecture and the early players. Also
bibliographies of golf books.
The Murdoch Golf Library. By Joseph S F Murdoch.
233 pages Illustrated with dr awings and photo-
graphs. Limited edition and also subscribers. £25
and £35. July 1991. ISBN 0 907186 12 2.
Golf Course Architecture. 78 Pages. Illustrated
with photographs. Limited edit ion. Cloth and
Leather. ISBN 0 907186 10 6. September 1990.
GOLF AT HOYLAKE by Behrend and Graham.
171 pages. Illustrated in colour and mon ochrome.
Limited edition. Cloth and Leather. April 1990.
ISBN 0 907186 12 2.

MS SALLY R F GRANT
Cherry Tree Cottage
High Common, Swardeston
NORWICH
Norfolk
NR14 8DL

GRAPHICOM EXPRESS

2A Comeragh Road
West Kensington
LONDON
W14 9HP

GRAVE ORC INCORPORATED
George N. Houston
The Cottage Smithy Brae
Kilmacolm
Renfrewshire Scotland
PA13 4EN
Grave Orc publishes one publication only at the
moment - George Houston is the founder of Grave
Orc and the Editor of Midnight in Hell. Both were
established in 1990! Possible future publications:
Pulp magazine (all fiction fan magazine) and Ulti-
mate Cult Video Collector's Price Guide
Midnight in Hell (Weirdest Tales of Fandom) - Fan
Magazine - Short stories articles etc. printed -
covers Horror Sci-Fi Fantasy Genres! Accepts sub-
missions and correspondence from Genre fans #9
available in September at £1.50 (exclusive of postage). Cheques/POs payable to G. N. Houston

MR E D GRAVES
9 Earlsthorpe Road
Sydenham
LONDON
SE26 4PD

MS JENNIE GRAY
Chatham House
Gosshill Road
Chislehurst
Kent
BR7 5NS

MR R GRAY
36 Princes Street
Tunbridge Wells
Kent
TN2 4SL

GREATER LONDON ASSN FOR DISABLED
PEOPLE
(GLAD)
336 Brixton Road
London
SW9 7AA
(071-274-0107)

GREAT WEN PUBLICATIONS
P.O. Box 1500
London
SW5 0DA.
Subjects: Travel Accommodation.
Books July to December 1991 - 1

GREEN ANARCHIST
Box H
34 Cowlcy Road
OXFORD
OX4 1HZ
Magazine

GREEN BAY PUBLICATIONS
72 Water Lane
Histon

Cambridge
CB4 4LR

GREEN BOOK LTD
2 Sydney Place
Bath Avon
BA2 6NF

GREEN CIRCULAR
c/o Quest
BCM-SCL-QUEST
London
WC1N 3XX

GREENCROFT BOOKS
Trefelin
Cilgwyn
Newport
SA42 0QN.
Subjects: Local Folk Tales.
Books July to December 1991 - 1

MR DAVID GREEN
14 Polstead Road
OXFORD
OX2 6TN

ROBERT GREENE PUBLISHING
John Coutts
1 Cirrus Crescent
GRAVESEND
Kent
DA12 4QS

GEOFF GREEN
37 Underhill Road
Charfield
Wotton-under-Edge
GL12 8TQ

GREEN INK PUBLICATIONS
c/o Green Ink Bookshop
8 Archway Mall
London
N19 5RG

MR LAWRIE GREEN
Westwood, Down Barton Road
St Nicholas at Wade
BIRCHINGTON
Kent
CT7 0PZ

GREEN LEAF BOOKSHOP
82 Colston Street
BRISTOL
BS1 5BB

GREENLEAF
96 Church Road
Redfield
Bristol
BS5

GREENLIGHT PUBLICATIONS
Ty Bryn Coomb Gardens
Llangynog

Carmarthen
SA33 5AY.
Subjects: School Textbooks.
Books January to June 1991 - 1. Books July to
December 1991 - 1

MR MICHAEL T GREEN
Enfield House
7 Old Durham Road
Annfield Plain
Co Durham
DH9 7UF

GREEN PRINT
10 Malden Road
London
NW5 3HR

MR S GREEN
1 Cross End
Kirk Lane, Embsay
SKIPTON
North Yorkshire
BD23 6RG

GREENSWARD PUBLICATIONS
Charles Westaway
116 Wessex Oval
Wareham
Dorset
BH20 4BS TEL: 0929 554838
Guide books: particularly walking guide on county
basis
'Pub Walks in Wiltshire and Avon' by Charles
Westaway. May 1990. 96pp. £4.95. ISBN 1 872888
00 3.

GREEN WATER PRESS
Hazelwood
Waters Green
Brockenhurst
Hampshire
SO42 7RG 0590 23915
Cottage industry making of books. Personal expe-
riences philosophy psycho logy in essays prose
poetry or visual imagery. Ideas welcome for consid
eration.
'Artist by the wayside' by Yvonne Jones. Selection
of poems. ISBN 1 872901 00 X 1990 75pp. 4.50.

GREENWAY WOMEN'S PRESS
Greenway Women's Centre
19 Greenway
Cregagh
Belfast
BT6 0DT.
Subjects: Poetry.
Books January to June 1991 - 1

GREENWICH EXCHANGE
161 Charlton Church lane
London
SE7 7AA.
Subjects: Literature. Education.
Books July to December 1991 - 2

GREENWICH GUIDE-BOOKS
72 Kidbrooke Grove

London
SE3 0LG

R.E. GREENWOOD
Copy Right
7 New Street
Uppermill
Oldham
OL3 6AU.
Subjects: Local History

MR NICHOLAS GREET
6 Sylvan Way
Belair 5052
South Australia

MR J GREGORY
37 Kylemilne Way
Stourport
Worcestershire
DY13 9NA

MR PATRICK GREGORY
93 Vernon Road
Kirkby-in-Ashfield
Nottinghamshire
NH17 8EE

D S GREMBLE
34 Lower Cliff Avenue
Northridge
Sydney
Australia 2063

GREVATT & GREVATT
9 Rectory Drive
Newcastle-upon-Tyne
NE3 1XT
Established in 1981 to make available academic, educational and literary works not normally viable commercially. Up to three titles a year with limited print runs. No royalties on first 500 copies; no unsolicited mss; proposals with SAE on language and linguistics, religion and philosophy.
WATERSON, N: Prosodic Phonology: The Theory and its Application to Language Acquisition and Speech Processing. 0 9472202 5. £14 net in UK, xii + 162 pages, 28 plates.
KILLINGLEY, D (Ed) et al. A Handbook of Hinduism for Teachers. 0 95079186 5. 8.50 net in UK. 1984. x + 139 pages; 2 maps, 21 line drawings.
KILLINGLEY, D M (1900-1980). Farewell the Plumed Troop: A Memoir of the Indian Cavalry 1919-1945. 0 947722 04 1. £12.95 in UK, 1990. x + 134 pages; 1 map, 8 photographs; photograph on cover.

GRH PUBLICATIONS
2 Wayne Close
Gunton
Lowestoft
NR32 4SX

Grierson Memorial Trust
21 Stephen Street
London
W1P 1PL

MR CLIVE GRIFFIN
46 Brownberrie Avenue
Harsforth
Leeds
LS18 5PN

G.M GRIFFIN: D BAMFORD
34 Windsor Drive
Sleaford
NG34 7NL

MR GRAHAM T GRIFFITHS
125 Wildwood
Woodside
Telford
TF7 5PR

JOHN GRIFFITHS
1 Denholm Close
Ringwood
BH24 1TF

MEC GRIFFITHS
I Pentrefelin Street
Carmarthen
SA31 1RJ

MR V L GRIFFITHS
See Pericles Publications

MR W D GRIFFITHS
5 Skipwith House
Portpool Lane
London
EC1N 7UH

GRILLE
c/o Simon Smith
53 Ormonde Court
Upper Richmond Road Putney
London
SW15 5TU

GRIM HUMOUR (magazine)
Richard Johnson (editor)
PO Box 63
Herne Bay
Kent
CT6 6YU
Magazine devoted to the innovative experimental and provocative end of our counter-culture whether music film or literature/graphics. Also open to intelligent inspired and thought-provoking fiction besides as much related review material as it can possible get.
Grim Humour (volume 2) #1: Published Mid-1991 64pp £1.50 features include John Waters Richard Kern Tom Vague and Lydia Lunch. Grim Humour: Nick Zedd Pigface Jon Savage and Peter Greenway £1.75

GROCER'S HALL PRESS
33 Glenrandel
Eglinton
Londonderry

GRUFFYGROUND PRESS

123

Anthony Baker
Ladram Sidcot
Winscombe
Somerset
BS25 1PW. Tel Winscombe 2285.
Publisher from 1976 of signed limited editions of (mostly new of uncollected) poetry. Announced early in 1992 that there will be no further titles but ten remain in print.
Aquamarine by Lawrence Sail. Wood engraving by Christopher Wormwell 1988 20p 130 copies £32.
Cynics and Romantics by Robert Graves. Wood engraving by Robert Tilleard. 1989 16p 125 copies £228.

MR DAVID GRUNDY
Dept of Systems & Inf Mangmnt
University House
Bailrigg
Lancaster
LA1 4YW

JOHN GRUNDY
59 Finglaswood Road
Finglas
Dublin 11
Republic of Ireland.
Subjects: History of Irish Republic.
Books January to June 1991 - 1

TOM GRUNDY
233 Liverpool Road
Haydock
St Helens
WA11 9RT

GRYFFON PUBLICATIONS
The Close
Barnsley
Cirencester
GL7 5EE

GRYPHON PRESS
4 Orchard Road
St Margarets
TWICKENHAM
Middlesex
TW1 1LY

GSSE
11 Malford Grove
Gilwern
ABERGAVENNY
Gwent
NP7 0RN
Applications of psychology to education especially small businesses.

JAN GUICE
12 Whitehall Mansions
121 Elderfield Road
London
E5 0LD.
Subjects: Poetry.
Books July to December 1991 - 1

GUILDHALL PRESS

Paul Hippsley
41 Great James Street
Londonderry
Northern Ireland
BT48 7DF. Tel 0504 264413
Community Book Publisher Specialising in Local History publications associated with Derry Donegal and the North West of Ireland. Typesetting and design Facilities available for external clients using In-House Desktop publishing system. Third party Publshing considered. Derry Walls - Paul Hippsley - 32pp - July 1988 ISBN 0946451 03 6 -£1.50 - History of Derry's Walls.
Parade of Phantoms - Peter McCarthney - 48pp ISBN 0 946451 16 8 -£1.75 - Ghost Stories.
Talk of the Town - Seamus McConnell - Nov. 1989 ISBN 0 946451 09 5 -£1.50 - Phrasebook of Derry Sayings.

NORMAN GUNBY
31 Falmouth Gardens
Redbridge
Ilford
IG4 5JU.
Subjects: Local History.
Books July to December 1991 - 2

GUNGARDEN BOOKS
Gungarden Lodge
Rye
TN31 7HH.
Subjects: Children's Fiction.
Books January to June 1991 - 1. Books July to December 1991 - 1

PETER B GUNN
Riberslaw
Back Street, Gayton
King's Lynn
PE32 1QR

MR RICHARD GUNN
16 Keir Street
Edinburgh
EH3 9EU

MR ANDREW J GUNZ
Badgers
71 Wolsey Road, Moor Park
Northwood
Middlesex
HA6 2ER

MR RAM GUPTA
Beechwood Recruitment
221 High Street
London
W3 9BY

MR ARNOLD GUTBUCKET
10 Eastney Road
Eastney
Portsmouth
PO4 9HY

GWASG GREGYNOG
David Esslemont
Newtown

Powys
SY16 3PW
Fine printer

GWASG GWALIA
Gorwelion
Y Groeslon
Caernarfon
Gwynedd

GWASG PRIFYSGOL CYMRU
Gwennyth Street
Cathays
Cardiff
CF2 4YD.
Subjects: Welsh Customs and Folkore (in Welsh).
Books July to December 1991 - 2

GWELFRYN PUBLISHERS
Llandiloes Road
Newton
SY16 4HX.
Subjects: School Textbooks.
Books July to December 1991 - 2

GWYDYR MINES PUBLICATIONS
78 Oakenshaw Lane
Walton
Wakefield
WF2 6NH

[H]

S HADLINGTON
Derwent House
Thorganby
York
YO4 6DB

HAGGERSTON PRESS
38 Kensington Place
London
W8 7PR

MR MATTHEW HAGGIS
Instant Muscle Scotland Limited
67 McDonald Road
Edinburgh
EH7 4NW

(THE) HAIKU QUARTERLY
Day Dream Press
39 Exmouth Street
Swindon
Wilts
SN1 3PU

HALFSHIRE BOOKS
6 High Street
Bromsgrove
B61 8HQ

MS ANNA HALL
25 Morpeth Mansions
Morpeth Terrace
London
SW1P 1WT

MR G S HALLETT
61 Bowyer Crescent
Wokingham
Berkshire
RG11 1TF

J.H HALL
Siddals Road
Derby
DE1 2PZ

LINDEN HALL
223 Preston Road
Yeovil
BA20 2EW

HALLMARK BOOKS
42 Tennyson Road
Penarth
CF6 1RZ.
Subjects: Mystery Fiction.
Books July to December 1991 - 2

ROBERT HALL
140 Sutherland Avenue
London

HALSTEAD PUBLICATIONS
13 Queens Road
Harrogate
HG2 0HA

HAMBLEDON PRESS
102 Gloucester Avenue
London
NW1 8HX
Used to publish cricket books, now we publish
academic history books.

M J HAMER
Icon Graphics
PO Box 69
Aberystwyth
Dyfed
SY23 2EU

MR ALAN F HARRISON
54 Kemsing Gardens
Canterbury
Kent
CT2 7RF

MR COLIN A HAMMOND
1 Ryarsh Lane
West Malling
Kent
ME19 6QP 0732 844398

JACK HAMNER
4 Cowbrook Avenue
Glossop
SK13 8QT

MR G HAMPSHIRE
6 Teall Court
Ossett

West Yorkshire
WF5 0PG

HANBOROUGH BOOKS
The Foundry
Church Hanborough
Oxford
OX7 2AB
Now Previous Parrot.

KATHLEEN AND JOHN HANCOCK
28 Pump Mead Close
Southminster
CM0 7AE

HANDPOST BOOKS
84 Llanthewy Road
Newport
NP9 4LA.
Subjects: Travel.
Books July to December 1991 - 1

HANDSAW
Mr Felix Prior
20a Maclise Road
LONDON
W14 0PR

HANDY PRESS
Box 79
Woodford Green
Essex
IG8 0QZ

HANGMAN BOOKS
32 May Road
ROCHESTER
Kent
ME1 2HY
Have published poetry, prose and artists books. The
work of Billy Childish, Celine, Sexton Ming and
others.

HAPPY LEARNING
Una Dowding
18 Trevor Road
Hucclecote
Gloucester
GL3 3JL. Tel 0452 618828
Happy Learning Series:- 36 Educational Games (3
sets) 20 + 5 p+p per set. Teach essential reading
skills to all ages used by classroom special needs
teachers and parents. Book supports and advises on
basic learning problems. £4.99 + 50p. p+p.
Games - as above - Happy Learning Educational
Games (reading). Can I Read To You Mummy?
(Current) ISBN 0 9516878 0 8

HARD F
Jonathan Meggit
3 Long Road
Cambridge
CB2 2PP

HARDIE PRESS
35 Mountcastle Terrace
Edinburgh
EH8 7SF.

Subjects: Music.
Books January to June 1991 - 1.

PETER HARDING
Mossgiel
Bagshot Road Knaphill
Woking
Surrey
GU21 2SG
Railway publisher.
New Romney Branch Line. 2.00
Hellingly Hospital Railway. 2.00

MR B HARDMAN
The Chase
Brent Street
BRENT KNOLL
Somerset
TA9 4EH

HARDWARE I M O
P O Box 114
Sevenoaks
Kent
TN13 1BS

HARDY PLANT SOCIETY
Rosefield House
Tatsfield
Westerham
TN16 2NJ

HARE'S EAR PRODUCTIONS
9 St Paul's Gate
Wokingham
RG11 2YP

HARMONY PUBLISHING LIMITED
Elaine R Abraham
14 Silverston Way
Stanmore
Middlesex
HA7 4HR

HARMOR BOOKS
Foxwell
Wendlebury
Bicester
OX16 8PW.
Subjects: Education.
Books January to June 1991 - 1

MR MIKE HARNER
10 Tyrells CFlose
Springfield
Chelmsford
CM2 6BT

HARPIES & QUINES
P O Box 543
Glasgow
G20

MR JOHN HARRIS
4 South Road
Puckeridge
Ware

126

Hertfordshire
SG11 1TH 0727 59100

MISS J A HARRIS
8 Jersey Close
Westlands
Newcastle-under-Lyme
Staffordshire
ST5 3LP

MR HARRISON11
High View
Moorland Way
Gunnislake
Cornwall
PL18 9EX

MR B HARRISON
516 Otley Road
Adel
Leeds
LS16 8DL

MR JOHN HARRISON-BANFIELD
118a Holland Park Avenue
London
W11 4PA 10 727 0715

MR JOHN HARRISON
9 Baggrave End
Barsby
Leicester
LE7 8RB

MRS J HARRISON
35 Herald Close
Beeston
Nottingham
NG9 2DW

MR LESLIE HARRISON
5 California Road
Longwell Green
Bristol
BS15 5AZ

MRS WENDY HARRIS
21 Curzon Street
Basford
Newcatle-under-Lyme
Staffordshire
ST5 0PD

MR C S HART
Morva
32 Tredova Crescent
Falmouth
Cornwall
TR11 8LQ

MR DEREK F HART
Crossways
Newdigate
Dorking
Surrey
RH5 5AH

HART, MACLAGAN AND WILL
2D Churchill Way
Bishopbriggs
Glasgow
G64 2RH

HARVENNA BOOKS
Leo Alison
Barton Lane
Fraddon
St Columb
Cornwall
0726 860413
Cornish local history
Newquay to Chacewater Railway: Part 1. £2.50;
Part 2 £2.85 History of Gwennap Pit Newlyn Pit
and the Indian Queens Pit. £1.95 Newquay and Its
Railway. £2.50

HARVEY PRESS
Ward 23/20
Royal Hospital
Chelsea
London
SW3 4SR.
Subjects: Biography.
Books July to December 1991 - 1

MRS E H B HARVEY
Sea View Farm
Black Rock, Praze
Cambourne
Cornwall
TR14 9NG

ELIZABETH HARVEY-LEE
1 Belton Road
London
NW2 5PA.
Subjects: Printmaking.

MR M J HARVEY
20 Cascade Road
Buckhurst Hill
Essex
IG9 6DX

MR NEIL A HARVEY
1 Lamerton Street
Deptford
London
SE8 3PL

MR NEIL HARVEY
46 Honor Oak Road
Forest Hill
London
SE23 3RZ

MR DAG HASLEMO
Skogstua
1560 Larkollen
Norway

MR K HASSALL
22 Park Road

South Harrow
Harrow
Middlesex
HA2 8NQ

MR ZAKI HASSAN
Flat 42
46 Budiya Road 303
Naim, Manama
Bahrain

MS MARION HASSLEDINE
The Quay
East End
Whitney
Oxford
OX8 6OA

JOHN HASTED
1 Eton Court
Pemberley Avenue
Bedford
MK40 2LH.
Subjects: Biography.
Books July to December 1991 - 1

SCOTT HASTIE
24 Coniston Road
Kings Langley
WD4 8DU.
Subjects: Poetry.
Books July to December 1991 - 1

HASTINGS ARTS POCKET PRESS
25 St Mary's Terrace
Hastings
East Sussex
TN34 3LS

HASTINGS TRUST
Small Business Press
58a High Street
Hastings
TN34 3EN

C JANE HATCHER
22B Bridge Street
Richmond
DL10 4RW

PETER B. HATTON
27 Church Road
Hale
Liverpool
L24 4AY.
Subjects: Local History.
Books July to December 1991 - 1

HATTYLAND ENTERPRISES
9 Sedgmoor Road
Flackwell Heath
High Wycombe
HP10 9AU

HAUNTED LIBRARY
Rosemary Pardoe
Flat 1 36 Hamilton Street

Hoole
Chester
CH2 3JQ. Tel 0244 313685.
The twice-yearly Ghosts and Scholars is devoted to the ghost story tradition of M. R. James with new and reprint fiction and articles. The Haunted Library also publishes single-author booklets of Jamesian or off-beat ghost stories.
Ghosts and Scholars 14 48pp March 1992 £2.50
Spirits of Another Sort by Alan W. Lear 40pp July 1992 ISBN 0 906153 23 9 £2.50
Popes and Phantoms by John Whitbourn November 1992 ISBN 0 906153 24 7.

HAUTEVILLE PRESS
1 Hauteville Court Gardens
Stamford Brook Avenue
London W6
Translations and commentaries of classical texts; English literary comment, unusual incidents in history.

HAVERS' DIRECTORIES:
Elsdon Mailing Unit
16 Nonsuch Industrial Estate
Kiln Lane
Epsom
KT17 1EG.
Subjects: Bibliography.

HAWKER PUBLICATIONS
13 Park House
140 Battersea Park Road
London SW11 4NB.
Subjects: Social Welfare.
Books July to December 1991 - 2

MR RODERICK M HAWKEY
The Lodge
Bullbrooke Farm, Barns Green
Horsham
West Sussex

MR GORDON HAWKINS
Spanners
North Lane, Marschapel
Grimsby
South Humberside
DN36 5TA

T.D HAWKINS
Greyfriars
Little Wilbraham
Cambridge
CB1 5LE

DENISE HAWRYSIO
108 Crampton Street
London SE17 3AE
Artists books of a truly remarkable quality.

HAWTHORN PRESS
Bankfield House
13 Wallbridge
Stroud GL5 3JA.
Subjects: Music. Occult.
Books January to June 1991 - 2

MS B M HAWTHORNE
9 Stowe House
Emmott Close
London NW1 6QA

HAWTHORNE EDUCATION
17 Guillemot Close
Hythe
Southampton
SO4 6GJ

C. HAYES
2 Undercliff Gardens
Ventnor
Isle of Wight
PO38 1UB.
Subjects: Music.
Books January to June 1991 - 1

HAYLOFT PRESS
99 Oakfield Road
Selly Oak
Birmingham
B29 7HW

HAY THREE
29/30 Warwick Street
London W1R 5RD

J.B HAYWARD
The Old Rectory
Polstead
Colchester
CO6 5AE

HAZELWOOD
122 Sunningfields Road
London NW4 4RE
Books January to June 1991 - 1

HAZLEWOOD PUBLISHING
Staverton Court, Staverton
Dartington
Totnes
TQ9 6NU

HEAD PRESS
David Slater
PO Box 160
Stockport
Cheshire
SK1 4ET. Tel 061 476 0592.
Sex Religion Death is the mastiff for Headpress
Magazine a Quarterly exploration of bizarre cul-
ture deviant conceptions and cinematic extremes.
Each issue kind of a psychotic dip a platform for
criticism, interviews, reviews and anecdotes.
Headpress encourage correspondence from writers
and groups.
Killer Komix Various artists 40 pages PUB late
1992 £3.00 true crime comic book.

HEADLAND POETRY PUBLICATIONS
Wirrall, 38 York Avenue
West Kirkby
Wirrall
L48 3JF

HEADSTART HISTORY
PO Box 41
Bangor
LL57 1SB

MR ANDREW HEALD
7 Rustic Avenue
Stouhowram
HALIFAX
HX3 9QW

HEARING EYE
Box 1
22 Torriano Avenue
London NW5 2RX

HEART ACTION
P.O. Box 2055, Moseley, Birmingham B14 7LS
Mail order suppliers of radical, occultural, esoterical
and essential books for the discerning reader. Over
400 titles listed in our catalogue. Any book currently in print also supplied. Send an SAE for
catalogue.

HEART OF ALBION PRESS
2 Cross Hill Close
Wymeswold
Loughborough
Leicestershire
LE12 6UJ 0509 880725.
Earth mysteries, Midlands local history, neo-pa-
ganism and Northern mythology. Plus much more!
Send for a current catalogue.
Good Gargoyle Guide by Rob Trubshaw. 48pp. 23
illus. July 1991. 1 8728830 5 2. £1.95 + 25p p&p.
Medieval Church carvings in Leics.
Holy Wells. by Cuming Walters. 39pp. 4 illus. June
1991. 1872883 087. £1.95 + 25p p&p. Reprint of
folklore from 1898.
23 Cantos for the Goddess by Kati-Ma. 26pp with
illus.March 1991. 1 872883 06 0. £1.95 + 25p p&p.
Poetry.

MR G HEATH
14 Cheyne Walk
London NW4 3QJ

MR MIKE HEDDLES
51 Anchor Road
Barrow island
Barrow in Furness
Cumbria
LA14 2QP

HEDGEHOG PRESS
Alan Brignall
33 Heath Road
Wivenhoe
Colchester
CO7 9PU
Fine Printer

THE HEDGEHOG PRESS
23 Gladstone Avenue
Loughborough
Leicestershire
LE11 1NP

129

HEDGEROW PUBLISHING LIMITED
Mr T M Hale
325 Abbeydale Road
Sheffield
S7 1FS 0742 554873
Photographers and publishers of high quality photographic greeting cards and po st cards. Other books currently under consideration.
Rhosneigr then and now. A Pictorial History of the Village. By T T M Hale. Forew ord by Glenys Kinnock. ISBN 1 872740 00 6. £7.85 post paid. 21 000 words, 164 il lustrations. 'A delightful study' - Country Quest Magazine. 'A treasure trove of pictures and text.' - The Star newspaper. 1990.

HEELEY WRITERS GROUP
60 Upper Valley Road
Sheffield

HEINDESIGN STEMPELSPASS
Diana Arseneau
Eiper Str. 76,
5800 Hagen 1,
Germany
0049 2331 72211. Fax. 0049 2331 72292
With a rubber stamp in your hand, you're a one-person print shop! Create works of art, statements of love. Amaze your friends, confuse your enemies. Over 700 designs, write for free catalogue. Artists/designers: always seeking new ideas. Write us!

HELM INFORMATION
The Bank
Mountfield
Robertsbridge
TN32 5JY.
Subjects: Literature.
Books July to December 1991 - 1

HELSFELL PRESS
235 Windermere Road
Kendall
LA9 5EY

MR P C A HEMELRYK
1 Homers House
51 Church Street
Rugby
Warwickshire
CV21 3PT

MR P F HENDERSON
10 Solon Road
Brixton
London
SW2 5UY

MS RUTH HENDERSON
Ceterach
Wigpool
Mitcheldean
Gloucestershire
GL17 0JW

HENDERSON-ROBERTSON PUBLISHING
Struan
Toberonochy

Oban
PA34 4UG.
Subjects: Children's Fiction.
Books July to December 1991 - 1

HENDON PUBLISHING
Hendon Mill
Colne
Nelson
Lancashire

T HENEAGE
1 Stewart's Court
220 Stewart's Road
London
SW8 4UD

MR CRAIG HENRY
2 Tewit Green
Illingworth
Halifax
West Yorkshire
HX2 9SH

R J HEPWOTH
Loyne Garth
Stanmore Drive
Haverbreaks
Lancaster
LA1 5BL

CLIVE HERBERT WILDLIFE PUBLISHING
Clive Herbert
67A Ridgeway Avenue
East Barnet
Herts
EN4 8TL. Tel 081 440 9314
Publisher of wildlife and natural history booklets/leaflets relating directly to the North London area only. Specifically local material and topics which would not find publication elsewhere.
Checklist of the Birds of Barnet J. Colmans and C. Herbert 8 pages 1989 30p = SAE.
Mammals of Barnet ISBN 0 9515608 0 8 C. Herbert 44 pages 1990 £2.95 incl. postage.
The Naturalist in Barnet a focus on Barnets Wildlife. Edited by M. Melling ISBN 0 9515608 16 66 pages 1990 £1.95 incl. postage.

MR T R HERBERT
Hillmount
Butts lane
Eastbourne
East Sussex
BN20 9EN

HERCULANEUM PRESS
Joel Biroco
BM Utopia
London
WC1N 3XX

HERCULES FISHERMAN
75 Lambeth Road
London
SE11

130

HERE AND NOW
c/o Transmission Gallery
28 King Street
GLASGOW
G1 5QP

HERE AND NOW
West Yorkshire or Scotland based
collectives
PO Box 109
Leeds
LS5 3AA and
c/o Transmission Gallery 28 King St. Glasgow G1
5QP.
Magazine from collectives in Scotland and West
Yorkshire. Emerging from the barricades of the left
to view the wreckage and the wasteland sold to us
as paradise. Is the choice between Pepsi and Coke?

HERGA PRESS
7 High Street
Harrow-on-the-Hill
HA5 2EH.
Subjects: Historical Biography.
Books July to December 1991 -.1

A HERIOT
PO Box 1
Northleach
Cheltenham
GL54 3NX

HERITAGE MAGAZINE
2 The Courtyard
Wokingham
RG11 2LW

HERITAGE PRESS
1 St James Drive
Malvern
Worcestershire
WR14 2UD 0684 561755
The first of Heritage's Art Travel Guides on Burne-
Jones and William Morris appeared in 1991 with 50
illustrations, 16 in colour. Other titles on these
artists and on other topics including Armour,
Hereldry and Costume will follow, some in Limited
Editions.

HERMAFRODUX LIMITED
Anthony Christie
14b Elsworthy Terrace
London
NW3 3DR

HERMETIC JOURNAL
PO Box 375
Headington
Oxford
OX3 8PW

HERMIT PRESS
Anthony CHristmas
15 Robertson Road
Buxton
Derbyshire
SK17 9DY
Fine Printer

HERMITAGE PUBLISHING
Chris Street
PO Box 1383
London
N14 6LP 081 886 1414
Publisher of 'Earthstars' a book which suggests
there's nothing straight -forward about ley-lines. It
reveals that London's ancient sacred sites form
precise geometric patterns - a vast landscape temple groundplan. Earthstars. A4. ISBN 095159967 0
5. 80 maps and other illustrations. 134 pages. Price
£12.50. Published Aug.1990. No others yet in print.

MR JOHN HERON
89 Highfield Avenue
London
NW11 9TJ

HERTIS
Hatfield Polytechnic Library
College Lane
Hatfield
AL10 9AD

CHRIS D. HEWITT
1 Coleswood Road
Harpenden
AL5 1EF.
Subjects: Cycling History.
Books January to June 1991 - 1

BERNADETTE HEY
63 Summerbridge Crescent
Eccleshill
Bradford
BD10 8BA

HEYFORD PRESS: R DENNIS
The Old Chapel
Shepton Beauchamp
Illminster
TA19 0LE

MR B J HEYWOOD
54 Cambridge Road
ST Albans
AL1 5LD

H.G.B. SERVICES
32 Dudley Street
Grimsby
DN31 2AB.
Subjects: European Travel.

H HIBBS
Hilltop Cottage
Little Ouseburn
York
YO5 9TD

MR GARY HICKS
Freelance Focus
7 King Edward Terrace
BROUGH
North Humberside
HU15 1EE

MR W J HICKS
100 Compit Hills
CROMER
Norfolk
NR27 9LP 0263 512457

HIDCOTE PRESS
33 Hidcote Road
Oadby
Leicester
LE2 5PG.
Subjects: Geography.
Books January to June 1991 - 1

MR BRIAN HIGGINS
83 Withens Lane
WALLASEY
Wirral
L45 7NF

ANDY & SUE HIGGS
27 Oaktree Park
Sticklepath
OKEHAMPTON
Devon
EX20 2NB

HIGHFIELD PRESS
224 Coast Road
Ballygally
Larne
BT40 2QQ

HIGHFIELD PUBLICATIONS
Vue Pointe
Spinney Hill
Sprotborough
Doncaster
DN5 7LY.
Subjects: Hygiene.
Books January to June 1991 - 3

HIGH FORCE PUBLICATIONS
12 Edinburgh Drive
Darlington
Co. Durham
DL3 8AW 0325 468390
Booklets of local history and geographical and
architectural interest. RURAL DARLINGTON. By
Vera Chapman. 64 pages. 19 line drawings. 1975.
New edit ion 1989. ISBN 0 9510991 3 2. A4
paperback. £3.00.
Darlington historic town centre walkabout. By Vera
Chapman. 16 pages. 17 line drawings 1990. ISBN
0 9510991 4 0. A5 paperback. 80p.
Cotherstone village, past and present. By Vera
Chapman. 20 pages. 13 line draw ings. 1986 ISBN
0 9510991 2 4.

HIGHGATE PUBLICATIONS
24 Wylies Road
Beverley
HU17 7AP

HIGHLAND PRINTMAKERS WORKSHOP &
GALLERY
Ms Nina Ashby

20 Bank Street
Inverness
IV1 1QE
We generally edition original prints but have just
produced our first loose-leaf book: 'The Sea', a
collection of six Haiku poems by Irene Irvine, set in
Albertu s 18 pt and illustrated by six wood engrav-
ings by Ross-shire artists; calico bou nd slip cover -
sponsored by Ross & Cromarty District Council.
Edition size of book - 12 copies.

BRIAN MERRIKIN HILL
Ingmanthorp
Hall Farm Cottage
Wetherby
West Yorkshire
LS22 5EQ. 0937 584674.
Poetry magazine with reviews. 2.00 single issues.
7.00 for three issues.

MS GRETA HILL
12 Moorfields
Whalley
Blackburn
Lancashire
BB6 9SA

MR H E HILL
4 Manor Road
Sole Street, Cobham
Gravesend
Kent
DA13 9BN

HILLINGDON MIND NEWSLETTER
c/o MIND
Sterling House 276A High St
Uxbridge
Middx
UB8 1LQ
(0895-271559)

MR MARK HILL
Pacific I R
1st Floor
109 Kingsway
London
WC2B 6PP 071 430 0292

PETER HILL PUBLICATIONS
2 Lovap Way
Great Oakley
Corby
NN18 8JL.
Subjects: Local History.
Books July to December 1991 - 1

HILLSIDE PUBLICATIONS
11 Nessfield Grove
Keighley
BD22 6NU

HILLTOP PRESS
Steve Sneyd
4 Nowell Place Almondbury
Huddersfield
West Yorkshire

HD5 8PB
Founded 1965. Since 1988 concentrating on aspects of science fiction poetry. Available publications list (including limited quantities of some earlier items) for SAE Cheques/POs payable S. Sneyd. No unsolicited mss; relevant project suggestions (with SAE) gladly considered. The Fantastic Muse by Arthur C. Clarke 12pp June 1992 ISBN 0 905262 05 0 £1.00/$£2.50. Reprints 1938 article and poem to mark author's 75th Birthday. War of the Words edited Steve Sneyd 20pp 1991 ISBN 0 905262 03 4 £1.25/ $£3.00. Anthology of Humorous SF verse; 30s to 80s; John Brunner Sam Youd etc. Icons of Starchasm edited Steve Sneyd 60pp 1990 60p/$2.00 Anthology of SF poetry read at iconoclasm; Andrew Darlington; John F. Haines etc.

P.HINGSTON
Westlands House
Tullibardine
Auchterarder
PH3 1NJ

HINGTON ASSOCIATES
Westlands House
Tullibardine
Auchterarder
PH3 1NJ.
Subjects: Travel.
Books January to June 1991 - 1

MISS S HINSULL
118 Brays Road
Sheldon
Birmingham
B26 1NS

HIPPOPOTAMUS PRESS
R. John
22 Whitewell Road
Frome
Somerset
BA11 4EL. Tel 0373 466653
Publisher of full poetry collections. Publisher of Outposts Poetry Quarterly
Peter Dale Earthlight 72pp 12.95. C 6.95 P.
Debjani Chatteriee I Was That Women 59pp £10.00. C £5.95.P.

HI RESOLUTION
4 Smallbridge Cottages
Horsmonden
Tonbridge
Kent
TN12 8EP

HISTORIANS' PRESS
9 Daisy Road
London
E18 1EA.
Subjects: Historical Biography.
Books July to December 1991 - 1

HISTORICAL PUBLICATIONS:
Highgate Literary and Scientific Inst
11 South Grove
London

N6 6BS.
Subjects: Local History.
Books July to December 1991 - 4

HISTORIC ROYAL PALACES
Marketing Department
Hampton Court Palace
East Molesey
KT8 9AU.
Subjects: Historic Palaces.
Books July to December 1991 - 2

HISTORY ON YOUR DOORSTEP
15 Welbeck House
Ashton-under-Lyne
PL6 7TB.
Subjects: Local History.
Books July to December 1991 - 1

ROY WILLIAM HOBB
8 Bacon Avenue
Normanton
WF6 2HR.
Subjects: Railways.
Books January to June 1991 - 1

HOBBY PUBLICATIONS
11 Walton Heath Road
Walton
Warrington
WA4 6HZ

HOBLINK NEWSLETTER
Morrigan
Box 1
13 Merrivale Road
Stafford
ST1 79GB
The Hoblink Newsletter is for lesbian gay and bisexual Pagans Witches and Occultists. It is produced 6 or 8 times a year and includes articles opinion news and contacts.
The Newsletter averages 6-8 sides of A4 published on the Festivals. Membership of Hoblink is £5 (waged) £2 (unwaged) per annum.

MR DAVID HOCKLEY
127 Boundry Street
Southport
Merseyside
PR8 5EJ

(Alison)
HODGE PBRS & BOOK DISTRIBUTORS
Bosulval Newmill
Penzance
Cornwall
TR20 8XA

MR ADRIAN HODGES
3 Ashfield Close
Bishops Cleeve
Cheltenham
Gloucestershire
GL52 4LG

MISS ELIZABETH M HOGG

Selby Cottage
Denholm
Hawick
TD9 8NF

HOLCOMBE PUBLISHING
1 Raylees
Ramsbottom
Bury
BL0 9HW.
Subjects: Coastal Shipping.
Books January to June 1991 - 1

MARGARET HOLDERNESS
10 Holwick Court
Off Summer Lane
Barnsley
S70 2PE.
Subjects: Short Stories.
Books July to December 1991 - 1

HOLDSOME PRESS
Barnwood
West Hill Park
Titchfield
Fareham
PO14 4BT.
Subjects: Poetry.
Books July to December 1991 - 1

HOLIDAY CARE SERVICE
2 Old Bank Chambers
Station Road
Horley
Surrey
RH6 9HW

MS MARGARET HOLLAND
136 Hinton Way
Great Shelford
Cambridgeshire
CB2 5AL

HOLLIES PUBLICATIONS
69 Hawes Lane
West Wickham
BR4 0DA

MS SHEILA HOLLIGAN
Brookside Farm
Leatholme
WHITBY
North Yorkshire
YO21 2AP

FRANK G HOLMES: DJ ELLIS
Fernwood, Nightingales
West Chiltingdon
Pulborough
RH20 2QT

MR J E HOLMES
33a Blurton Road
London
E5 0NJ 081 986 5105

MR K F HOLMES

Tigh-a-Gharaidh
Ballachulish
Argyll
PA39 4SE

PETER HOLMES
37 Longdown Road
Little Sandhurst
Camberley
GU17 8QG

HOLOCAUST EDUCATIONAL TRUST
BCM Box 7892
London
WC1N 3XX

Ms K G Holroyd
GRINDLE PRESS
PO Box 222
Ipswich
Suffolk
IP9 1HE
Publishes 'Arthritis at your age? Late teens to early 50's: A friendly handbook for young and youngish adults with a rhumatic disorder.'

HOLY GRAIL
PO Box 542
London
N6 6BG
Illustrated exposure of present day witchcraft and satanism.
Highgate Vampire; from Satan to Christ.

HOME BASE HOLIDAYS
Lois Sealey
7 Park Avenue,
London N13 5PG
081 886 8752
Publishes annual bed & breakfast directories for visitors to the USA and Canada. Also distributes unique personalised American bed & breakfast and route planning guides.
Bed & Breakfast in the United States & Canada; by Lois Sealey. 82pp; 22 line drawings. Pub. 5.1.92. ISBN 0 9510866. £6.00.
The Vacation Home Exchange and Hospitality Guide; by Jim Kimbrough; 172pp. Pub. 1.8.91. ISBN 0 9628199 0 5. £12.00
Vactation Route Planning Service - complete driving itinerary for your visit to the USA. Printed to order.

HOMEFRONT BELLES
PO Box 64
Civic Square
Canberra 2608
Australia

HOMEMADE BOOKS
Broadacres
Southwood
Glastonbury
BA6 8PG
Subjects: Historical Biography
Books July to December 1991 - 1

134

HOMER, THE SLUT
24a Inglethorpe Street
Fulham
London
SW6 6NT
"Homer, the slut": Quarterly Bob Dylan fanzine
with a yearly bonus issue for subscribers. A mixture
of news from around the world and serious analysis
of work from his entire career. "Analytical but
understandable" for even the most in-depth cri-
tiques.

(THE) HONEST ULSTERMAN
(edit Ruth Hooley)
159 Lower Braniel Road
Belfast
N Ireland
BT5 1NN

DEPARTMENT OF MANAGEMENT STUDIES
K K Leung Building
University of Hong Kong
Hong Kong

HONNO
Ailsa Craig
Heol-y-Cawl
Dinas Powys
South Glamorgan
CF6 4AH
Books by women living in Wales or with a Welsh
connection in English and Welsh.

DAVID HOOK
125 Folly Lane
ST Albans
AL3 5JQ
Subjects: Literature

P HOPE-EVANS
14 Eastbank Road
Hampton Hill
Middlesex
TW12 1RP

HOPE VALLEY PRESS
Unit 15
Vincent Works
Brough Bradwell
Sheffield
S30 2HG
Subject: Sporting History.
Books July to December 1991 - 1

MR PETER HOPKINS
32 Quarendon Street
LONDON
SW6 3SU

MR MIKEL HORL
97 Resthall Avenue
Chiswick
London
W4 1BN

HORNBY WRITERS

c/o 104 Scargreen Avenue
Noris Green
Liverpool

JONATHAN HORNE PUBLICATIONS
66c Kensington Church Street
London
W8 4BY 071 221 5658
Jonathan Horne Publications is a small press, pub-
lishing specialist monographs o n antique ceramics.

HORSEHOE PRESS, C/O D HEATHER
Eight Ash House
Eight Ash Green
Colchester
CO6 3PX

Barbara Horsfall
87 Brookhouse Road
Farnborough
Hampshire
GU12 0BU
Now running Concordat poetry folio.

HORUS COMMUNICATIONS
67 Duesbury Street
Princess Avenue
Hull
HU5 3QE

HOTHERSALL & TRAVERS
P.O. Box 149
Sittingbourne
ME9 8AW

MR MAX HOTOPF
Church House
High Street
Nayland
Colchester
CO6 4JF

HOUSE OF THE GODDESS
33 Oldridge Road
London
SW12 8PN

HOUSE OF MOONLIGHT
Mr John Howard
15 Oakwood Road, Bulbrook
Bracknell
Berkshire
RG12 2SP
Poetry leaflets.

HOUSE OF RAINBOWS
14 Post Horn Place
Fords Farm
Reading
RG3 5QE

RICHMOND HOUSE PUBLISHING
1 Richmond News
London
W1V 5AG

HOUSMANS

5 Caledonian Road
Kings Cross
London
N1 9DX

HOVERCLUB
12 Mount Pleasant
Bishops Itchington
Lemington Spa
CV33 0QE

HOWARD PUBLICATIONS
Keenans Mill
Lord Street
Lytham St Annes
FY8 2DF

CHRISTIE HOWARD
Flints Farm
Knatts Valley, Woodlands
Sevenoaks
Kent
TN15 6XY

M HOWARD
Caemorgan Cottage
Caemorgan Road
Cardigan
Dyfed
SA43 1QU

MR ROGER HOWARD
Department of Literature
University of Essex
Wivenhoe Park
Colchester, Essex
CO4 3SQ

MR D HOWE
Arow Lodge
Maynard Avenue
Warwick
CV34 4PU

D HOWELLS BOOKS
57 The Dene
Warminster
BA12 9ER

HOW-TO-BOOKS LTD
Plymbridge House
Estover Road
Plymouth
PL6 7PZ

H S B PUBLICATIONS
68 Lincoln Road
Leasingham
Sleaford
Lincolnshire
NG34 8JT 0529 305787
Publisher. Books on life in a Lincolnshire village in the early part of this century.
Sold. By Henry Brown. 92 pages, 16 illustrations, published 1986. ISBN 0 902662 71. Price £2.95. Reminiscences of a Lincolnshire auctioneer. THEM DAYS IS GONE. 143 pages, 28 illustrations. Pub-

lished 1988. ISBN 0 9513450 1 . By Henry Brown. £5.95. Recounts the author's boyhood in rural Lincolnshire up to 1932.
More of them days by Henry Brown. 165 pages, 28 illustrations. 1990. ISBN 0 9513 450 1 X. £7.95. Continues the author's life from 1932 to 1945, encompassing peace and war time.

J.C.E HUBBARD
2A Hillcrest Park
Exeter
EX4 4SH

DR J HUDDLESTON
16 Woodcote Green
Fleet
Hampshire
GU13 8EY

HUDSON
Ryecroft House
46 Downs Road
Epsom
KT18 5JD

MS P J HUDSON
5 Roseacre
Newcastle-under-Lyme
Staffordshire
ST5 2LS

MR RICK HUDSON
5 Holly Road
Wilmslow
Cheshire
SK9 1LX

MS GERALDINE HUGHES
Coldwell Farm
Oughtibridge
Sheffield
S30 3FY

MR JOHN HUGHES
15 Shelbourne Court
Shelbourne Road
High Wycombe
Buckinghamshire
HP12 3NH

K. HUGHES
Royal Crescent Road
Southampton
SO9 1WB.
Subjects: Astronomy.
Books January to June 1991 - 1. Books July to December 1991 - 1

MR D HULME
Room 2
18 Queensland Road
Boscombe
Bournemouth
B45 2AB

MEL HULME
PO Box 7

136

Garforth
Leeds
LS6 8XA

HULME VIEWS
9 Otterburn Close
Hulme
Manchester
M15 5HB

HUMAN POTENTIAL
3 Netherby Road
London
SE23 3AL
Magazine

HUMAN RIGHTS FORUM
2 Eaton Gate
London
S W 1

W. HUNT
Stourton View
East Stour
Gillingham
SP8 5JZ.
Subjects: Printing and Printers.
Books July to December 1991 - 1

DAVID HUNT
54 Priory Road
Richmond
TW9 3DH.
Subjects: Historic Gardens.
Books January to June 1991 - 1

C HUNTER
Shore House
Lerags
Oban
PA34 4SE
Subjects: Zoology
Books Jan to Jun 1991 - 1

HUNTER HOUSE
4 Thiepval Avenue
Belfast
BT6

MR P W HUNTER
9 Kendal Steps
St Georges Fields
Hyde Park
London
W2 2YE

MR MARK S HUNT
56a Santley Street
London
SW4 7QD

MR NORMAN H G HURST
25 Byron Avenue
Coulsdon
Surrey
CR3 2JS

MR STANLEY HURWITZ
8 Bowly Road
Cirencester
Gloucestershire
GL7 1FE

GEOFFREY GEORGE HUTCHINSON
Mill Cottage
Crackle Street, Brede
Rye
TN11 6EA

MR KEITH HUTCHINSON
60 Norfolk Road
Maldon
Essex
CM9 6AT

MR PETER HUTCHINSON
44 Craighouse Avenue
Edinburgh
EH10 5LN

HUTTON PRESS LTD
130 Canada Drive, Cherry Burton
Beverley
North Humberside
HU17 7SB

MR ERIC HUTTON
60 Fulmer Drive
Gerrards Cross
Buckinghamshire
SL9 7HL

MR R G HUXTABLE
Rowan House
105 Gunville Road, Corisbrooke
Newport22
Isle of Wight
PO30 5LD

HYBRID
42 Christchurch Place
Peterlee
Co Durham
SR8 2NR

HYBRID WRITERS
42 Christchurch Place
Peterlee
Durham
SR8 2NR

HYDATUM
PO Box 4
Ross-on-Wye
HR9 6EB

MRS ALICE HYDE
Walburton House
Cricket Green
Hartley Wintney
Hampshire
RG27 8PH

ICELAND INFORMATION CENTRE

PO Box 434
Harrow
HA1 3JE

ICON PRESS
Philip Brown
71 Northbourne Road
Eastbourne
BN22 8QP. Tel 0323 645081.
Produce art handbooks for full and part-time students by international artist and tutor Philip Brown who has exhibited widely in France England Spain and recently Japan. His paintings are in private collection in many countries.
Pen Drawing and The Art of Hatching with Philip Brown A4 1989 22 pages £4.50 + £1.50 p+p
Picture Making with Philip Brown A4 1991 72 pages £7.00 + £1.50 p+p ISBN 1 873812 00 0
Colour - Beyond The Ostwald Colour Solid with Philip Brown September 1992 A5 22 pages (14 in colour) Hand prints £19.95 + £1 p+p

ICONOCLAST PRESS
c/o Fulbeck Cottage
Sudthorpe Hill, Fulbeck
Grantham
Lincolnshire

ICPA
11 Dale Close
Thames Street
OXFORD
OX1 1TU

IDAF PUBLICATIONS LTD
Canon Collins Hse
64 Essex Road
London
N1 8LR

IDEAS UNLIMITED
PO Box 125
Portsmouth
PO1 4PP

IDENTITY MAGAZINE
Cheetwood House
21 Newton Street
Manchester
M1 1FZ

IGNATOR
20 Livingstone Road
Derby
DE3 6PR

IJATI PRESS
19 Chantry Road
Moseley
Birmingham
B13 8DL
Subjects: Poetry.

MISS PAULA M ILEY
The Old Silk Mill
Draycott Road
Blockley

Gloucester
GL5 9DY

ILLUMINATI PUBLISHING
119 Wellesley Road
Clacton-on-Sea
CO15 3PT.
Subjects: Children's Fiction.

ILLUMINATIONS
(Rathasker Press)
c/o Ryde School
Queens Road
Ryde IOW
PO33 3BE
(Ed Simon Lewis)
(East & S African writing)

IMAGE
Suite 310 Blackfriars Foundry
156 Blackfriars Road
London
SE1 8EN

IMAGE DIRECT
PO Box 4011
London
W9 3XW
This informative new book packed with over 65 superb rare previously unpublished B/W photographs documents the rise of Joe Strummer - from his early days fronting the legendary 101'ers through to the birth of the clash and the explosion of punk. Essential reading!
Joe Strummer with the 101'ers X The Clash 1974-1976 photographs by Julian Leonard Yewdall PUB date: 1st September 1992 ISBN 0 9519216 0 6 Price £7.99 + £1.00 p+p. UK + £2.00 p+p Europe.

IMAGES
Peter and Anne Stockham,
The Staffs Bookshop,
4/6 Dam Street, Lichfield,
Staffordshire, WS13 6AA
The reprint of 'Joyful Newes' a 17th century chapbook celbrates our move to Lichfield and our purchase of a very large Staffs bookshop. (We have closed our shop in Cecil Court.) We still specialise in illustrated children's books and dolls books but now include other subjects. We plan some local studies and have a long list of chapbooks in print which we can send you.

IMAGES PUBLICATIONS
Wood Lane
Barley Green
Woolpit
IP30 9RP.
Subjects:
Books January to June 1991 - 1

IMAGE THREE DESIGN
37 Pamplins
Basildon
Essex
SS15 5BN
We have a list of audio and visual material.

IMAGING SERVICES
Gable End
Hall Street
Long Melford
Sudbury
CO10 9JT
Subjects: Local History.

MR MARC IMBERECHT
Tetras Lyre
37 rue de la Brasserie
B-4630 Ayeneux
Belgium

I M IMPRIMIT
219a Victoria Park Road
London
E9 7DH

I.M.O. PUBLICATIONS
82 Woodhall Drive
Batley
WF17 7TE.
Subjects: Poetry.
Books July to December 1991 - 1

IMPERIAL PUBLICATIONS
PO Box 5
Lancaster
LA1 1BQ.
Subjects: Military Science. Manufacture of Guns.
First World War History. Second World War History. Books July to December 1991 - 5.

IMPRESS
7 Burghley Road
Bristol
BS6 5BL.
Subjects: Poetry.
Books July to December 1991 - 1

IMPRINT PUBLISHING
117 Waterside
Pear Tree Bridge
Milton Keynes
MK6 3DF

IMPRINTS
53 Aragon Tower
Longshore
Pepys Estate
London
SE8 3AH

INDELIBLE INC
Roberta McKeown
BCM 1698,
London WC1N 3XX
Defying categorisation Indelible Inc. continues to hurl charming and fascinating books at the uncaring public. Words which have never been used to describe the imprint include: chinless, flouncy, gelatinous and marsupial. Please write for a catalogue, enclosing an SAE and bubble gum.
Monstrous Births; Simon McKeown (ed); 72pp; 1991; £4.50; ISBN 1 871427 17 7. Illustrated introduction to teratology in early modern Eng-

land.
Massacre 3; Roberta McKeown (ed); 128pp; 1992; ISBN 1 872427 14 2; ISSN 0958-1154; £5.95.
Annual anthology of anti-naturalistic fiction & marginal writing.
Derek The Dust-Particle; Perry Natal & Frank Key; 32pp; 1989; £2.00; ISBN 1 871427 06 1. Metaphysical children's classic.

INDEPENDENT BOOKS
3 Leaves Green Crescent
Bromley
BR2 6DN 0959 73360
'Spitfire on my Tail' by Ulrich Steinhilder. 335pp 82 illus 1990. £14.95 ISBN 1 872836 00 3. A war biography from the Luftwaffe
'Ten Minutes to Buffalo' by Ulrich Steinhilder. 432pp 53 photos 1991. £14.95 ISBN 1 872836 10 1. Prisoner of war escape story from the German side

INDEPENDENT PUBLISHING CO
c/o Soma Books Ltd
38 Kennington Lane
London
SE11 4LS

CENTRE FOR INDEPENDENT TRANSPORT RESEARCH IN LONDON (CILT)
3rd Floor Universal House
88-94 Wentworth Street
London
E1 7SA.
Subject: Women and Transport; Town Planning.
Books July to December 1991 - 4 new books 1 new edition.

INDIA STUDY CIRCLE FOR PHILATELY
11 Boston Court, Brownhill Road
Chandler's Ford
Eastleigh
SO5 2EH

INDIGO PUBLICATIONS
72 Anmore Road
Denmead
PO7 6NT.
Subjects: Poetry.
Books January to June 1991 - 1. Books July to December 1991 - 1

INFORMATION
North Quaker Meeting House
1 Archobold Terrace
Newcastle-upon-Tyne
NE2 1DB.
Subjects: Bibliography.
Books July to December 1991 - 1

INFORMATION ON IRELAND
P O Box 958
London
W14 0JF

INFORMATION SOUGHT
Paul Todd
36-42 Southern Row
London

W10 5AN

MR M J INGHAM
Beechville
Canterbury Road
Wirksworth
Derbyshire
DE4 4DY

INGLETON PUBLICATIONS
8 Halifax Road
Briercliffe
Burnley
BB10 3QH

INGRAM PUBLISHING
The Lodge
Wardle Old Hall
Wardle
CW5 6BE

THE INGVI PRESS
BM Jed
London WC1N 3XX
Calum Selkirk
Mail Art, Copy Art, Networkery. Items on exchange
or gift basis. Sun shine, slug slime.
Sniffing glue - Me,You and a Park Bench; by
Charles Xmush.
'Clean This Fucking Mess Up You Fuckn' Punks!';
Anon.; broadsheet.
'IFA' Magazine. Sporadic M.A. compilations.

INIS GLEOIRE PUBLICATIONS
14 Fitzwilliam Avenue
Belfast
BT7 2HJ

INK INCLUSIVE
2 Hinge Farm Cottages
Long Drive
Waterbeach
CAMBRIDGE
CB5 9LW

INKLING
45 Enfield Cloisters
Fanshaw Street
London
N1 6LD 071 729 5569

INKSHED
387 Beverley Road
Hull
North Humberside
HU5 1LS

INLAND BOOK CO.
140 Commerce Street
East Haven
CT 06512
United States of America

INNER BOOKSHOP
34 Cowley Road
Oxford

INNOVATIVE PUBLISHING CO
19 Forest Street
Shepshed
Loughborough
Leicestershire
LE12 9BZ
Adventurous publishers - Modern Day pamphlet-
eers - Information should be broadcast - If it's
written, it should be read.

INSIDER PUBLICATIONS
43 Queens Ferry Street Lane
Edinburgh
EH2 4PF.
Subjects: Accommodation.
Books January to June 1991 - 3

INSIGHT PUBLICATIONS
Kevin D. Harper
P.O. Box 49
Camberley GU16 5FZ.
Publisher of poetry and lyric booklets paperbacks
and other books by young people. Part of the
EMKH Arts business involved with music and art
among students. Humour poetry music novels short
stories Christian interests write for a catalogue.
Hearsay Magazine £5 subscription £1.50 individual
copy small-label music releases and reviews.
A Book (I Never Thought that) 160pp £4.95 incl
p+p. Humour collection by Ewen Moore and Nick
Walker ISBN 1 874074 06 2.

INSTANT LIBRARY
PO Box 15
Loughborough
LE11 2RR.
Subjects: Libraries.
Books July to December 1991 - 3

INSTITUTE OF THIRD WORLD ART
& LITERATURE
16 Windemere Road
London
W5 4TO

J P R INSTONE
7 Winkley Street
Bethnall Green
London
E2 6PY

INTEGRATION NEWS
c/o Integration Alliance
132 Wimbledon Park Road
London
SW18 5UG

INTEGRITY WORKS
47 Marloes Road
London
W8 6LA

INTELLECT
Suite 2
108/110 London Road
Oxford
OX3 9AW Fax: 0865-865115.
intellect publishes books for people who work with

words. New technologies of computing artificial intelligence hypertext and multi-media offer novel ways of working with language. We cover these and more radical as pects of language and its use by people and computers.
Gethin A: Antilinguistics: A critical assessment of modern linguistic theory and practice. 'Amorey Gethin certainly does not pull his punches in this book which seeks to demolish a whole scaffolding of linguistic theory ..International. October 1990. £14.95. ISBN 1-871516-00-5. Williams N: Computer Assisted Composition. A selection of important papers on Computers and Writing. For writers teachers and learners of language related subject AI researchers developers of hypermedia those who communicate through networks. November 1990. £14.95. ISBN 1-871516-21-8.
Mealing S: The Art and Science of Computer Animation. This book provides a comprehensive primer to basic principles current applications in comm ercial scientific and creative environment. Winter 1991. 2£4.95. ISBN 1 -871516-16-1.

INTER-ARTS
62 Broughton Street
Edinburgh
EH1 3SA

INTERFACE
Larry Watson
Newtown Community House
117 Cumberland Road
Reading
RG1 3JY 0734 351116
Not a press Interface help community publishers with advice training but most of all support and encouragement. We work with all kinds of community groups in response to their needs and requirements aiming to make publishing accessible to everyone.
Newtown Diamond Community magazine. Published in Urdu Punjabi and English for and by the community of New Town.
St Stephens quarterly put together by elderly people for the sheltered housing project - St Stephens Court.
GO: Girls Only. A comic made by and for girls in Reading.

INTERFERENCE
Michael Gardiner
Wadham College
Parks Road
Oxford
OX1 3PN

INTERLINK DESIGN GROUP
Unit 2, Hartshorn House
Neath Road, Maesteg
Bridgend
CF34 9PG

INTERMEDIA GRAPHIC SYSTEMS LTD
Lewes Business Centre
North Street
Lewes
East Sussex
BN7 2PE

INTERNATIONAL PUBLISHERS
Casa Mimosa, Santa Eugene
Mallorca
Baleares 07142
Spain 62 04 88

INTERNATIONAL SEISMOLOGICAL CENTRE
Pipers Lane
Thatcham
Newbury
Berkshire
RG13 4NS

INTERPERSONAL
Martin J.S Briercliffe
BM Interpersonal
London
WC1N 3XX. Tel 0733 314758
Ever thought you'd like some help to deal with your personal problems but haven't been able to ask then this book is for you. A straight forward guide to help you identify and deal with the problems in your life. How To Deal With Your Inner Personal Problems Martin J.S. Briercliffe 128 16/9/92 ISBN 1 874769 00 1 £5.99 Psychology Self help.

INTERZONE & MILLION
David Pringle
217 Preston Drove,
Brighton, BN1 6FL
0273 504710
No longer small our circulation is thousands but we began as a small press. Britain's premier sf mag. Same team branched out with another newstand magazine. Send for details.
Interzone - £2.25; £26 per annum.
Million - £2.25; £13 per annum.

INTYPE
Input Typesetting Limited
See Quadrant House
Low cost short run book service. Books book proofs reprints manuals on-demand publishing in house magazines fanzines programmes slow sellers. Runs of 25 up to 1000 copies. Fast delivery competitive pricing help and advice. Price scale available on request.

IOLO
Mr Dedwydd Jones
Mr Dedwydd Jones, 38 Chaucer Road, Bedford, MK40 2AL
The mythic status 'Black Books On The Welsh Theatre' series reaches No. 5! Performed in the West End by Kenneth Griffith and to star in Cardiff this Autumn. Shit hits the fan forever. Couldn't care less about the topic? Buy them for a bloody good laugh then.

ION PRESS 23
56 Mulben Crescent
Crookston
GLASGOW
G53 7EH
New poetry with a major emphasis on good design. Desirable limited editions. Sand writings by David Rushmer. Due September 1991. Book of poetry/

design. £6.00 Limited first edition of 23 copies.
The road to Tarascon by Lyn Wilson. 20 pages.
Book of poetry. 10 illustrations. Second edition.

IOTA
David Holliday
67 Hady Crescent
Chesterfield
Derbyshire
S41 0EB

IPS Publishinh
8 Woodland Avenue
Hagley
Stourbridge
DY8 2XQ
Subjects: Food & Drink
Books July to December 1991 - 1

ALASTAIR IRELAND
23 Pinnnaclehill Park
Kelso
Roxburghshire
TD5 8HA
The Leadhills and Wanlockhead Light Railway.
£3.95

TONY IRESON
Beech Cottage
Tanners Lane
Kettering
NN16 8DP

(THE) IRISH IN BRITAIN HISTORY CENTRE
76 Salisbury Road
London
NW6 6NY

IRISH PEATLAND CONSERVATION COUN-
CIL
3 Lower Mount Street
Dublin Republic of Ireland.
Subjects: Local Travel Guides.
Books January to June 1991 - 2

IRISH WOMEN'S PERSPECTIVES
c/o 123 Lavender Sweep
London
SW11 1EA

IRON PRESS
Peter Mortimer
5 Marden Terrace
Cullercoats
NorthShields
Tyne & Wear
NE30 4PD
091 2531901
Veteran poetry mag with spin-off books.

WORSHIPFUL COMPANY OF IRONMONGERS
Ironmongers' Hall
Barbican
London
EC2Y 8AA.
Subjects: History of the Ironmongers' Company.

Books January to June 1991 - 1

IRWELL PRESS
3 Durley Avenue
Pinner
HA5 1JQ

C.J. ISAACSON
7 Golds Pightle
Ringstead
Hunstanton
PF36 5LD.
Subjects: Biography.
Books July to December 1991 - 1

I.S ENTERPRISES
PO Box 379
Clarkston
Glasgow
G76 8AD

ISIAN NEWS
F O I
Huntingdon Castle Clonegal
Enniscorthy Wexford
Ireland

MR STEVE ISKOVITZ
PO Box 1531
Cambridge
MA 02238
United States of America

ISLE OF WIGHT COUNTY PRESS
29 High Street
Newport
Isle of Wight
PO30 1ST

THE ISLINGTON POETRY WORKSHOP
Bruce Barnes
19a Marriott Road
London
N4 3QN 071 281 2369
A Writing workshop that produces occasional an-
thologies.
The Nagging Heads. Editor Bruce Barnes. 40 pages
(illustrated) 1985 £1.35 inc P+P. Poetry Anthol-
ogy.
Above the Neck. Editor by Martyn Crucetix. 36 pp,
1988, £1.35 inc P+P. Poetry Anthology.
Out of Our Heads. Editor Bruce Barnes. 44pp,
1983, ISBN 0 9518212 02 £1.85 inc P+P. Poetry
Anthology.

ISLINGTON WRITING FORUM
c/o Bruce Barbes
19a Marriott Road
LONDON
N4 3QN

I.S.O. PUBLICATIONS
137 Westminster Bridge Road
London
SE1 7HR.
Subjects: Humour. European Naval History.
Books July to December 1991 - 2

142

ISSUE
Jeremy Nuttall
24 Eastwood Road
Balsall Heath
Birmingham
B12 9NB 021 440 1739
Issue magazine is a magazine devoted to discussion
of all types on all subjects; especially morality faith
religion politics and music. The Victory point Ga-
zette is devoted to interactive fiction and postal
games. Issue. Editor: Jeremy Nuttall. A5. 28pp. bi-
monthly. £0.75. Number 11. The Victorypoint Ga-
zette. Editor: Jeremy Nuttal. A5. 16pp. bi-monthly.
£0.50. Number 7.

ISSUE ONE
(Eon Publications)
2 Tewkesbury Drive
Grimsby
S Humberside
DN34 4TL

ITEC LIMITED
Convent Garden Itec Ltd
99-103 Long Acre
London
WC2E 9NR

ITINERANT PUBLICATIONS
Ronald McNeil
13 Albert Road
Gourock
Renfrewshire Scotland
PA19 1NH Tel 0475 34999
Publish writers from West Central Scotland, also
public performances.

I.T.M.A. - INFOTEXT MANUSCRIPTS
A Baron/T.D. Man
c/o 93c Venner Road
Sydenham
London
SE26 5HY. Tel 081 659 7713
The Ballad of Captain by The ITMA Team - 25th
June 1992 2.99 Satire on Robert Maxwell ISBN 1
87147 08 X.
The Story of Ronnie and Llyde ISBN 1 871473 55
1 £1.50 by Ronnie Barker (edited Baron)
United Europe/Divided Britain ISBN 1 871473 50
0 1990 £1.50

IT'S A SMALL WORLD
92 Hornsey Lane
London
N6 5LT

IVANHOE PRESS
Kings Meadow
Ferry Hinksey Road
Oxford
OX2 0DP

MR R J A IVESON
Woodcroft
1 Ferriby High Road
North Ferriby
North Humberside

HU14 3LD

MRS A IVEY
Home Farm
Abington Pigotts
Royston
Hertfordshire
SG8 0SN

IVORY TOWER PUBLICATIONS
Masters Office
Darwin College
University of Kent
Canterbury
CT2 7NY
Subjects: Education
Books: Jan to Jun 1991 - 1

I-WAS
BCM Utopia
London
WC1N 3XX

[J]

JAC PUBLICATIONS
Mr John Vasco
28 Bellomonte Crescent
Drayton
Norwich
NR8 6EJ 0603 861339
Publication of books relating to the activities of the
Luftwaffe in World War 2. BOMBSIGHTS OVER
ENGLAND. The history of the Erprobungsgruppe
210, Luftwaffe figh ter-bomber unit in the Battle of
Britain. By John J Vasco. 104 pages, 144 photos ,
£17.95. ISBN 0 9515737 0 5.

MR D E JACKSON
105 Regent Street
St Thomas
Exeter
Devon
EX2 9EJ

JACKSONS ARM
PO Box 74
Lincoln
LN1 1QG
The small press with a spiky, subversive feel,
Jackson's Arm specialises in short-run, high quality
productions - mainly first collections or work by
new poets. Unsolicited MS are not required. Founded
1985
The Prospect and the River by Rutger Kopland;
Poetry, translated by James Brockanay; 20pp; 1987.
First British edition of poems by one of Holland's
leading poets. £3.00 ISBN 0948282 04 5
The Smallest Arts Festival in the World: ed. Michael
Blackburn: Cassette of readings, etc from Festival
held in Lincoln 1991: 5.00: includes Robert Edrik,
Brendan Cleary, Martin Stannard, Sue Dymoke,
etc, etc. 40 mins Chrome The Prophecy of Christos
by Michael Blackburn. Poetry; 70pp; 1992: 6.95
ISBN 0948282 09 6

JADE PUBLISHERS
10 Madeville Road

Aylesbury
HP21 8PA

JAMES & JAMES
75 Carleton Road
London
N7 0ET

GOVERNORS OF JAMES ALLEN'S
Girls' School
East Dulwich Grove
London
SE22 8TE
Subjects: History of James Allen's Girls' School.

ELIZABETH JAMES
61 Crofton Park Road
London
SE4 1AF.
Subjects: General Fiction.
Books July to December 1991 - 1

MR K JAMES
2 Brecon Rise
Pant
Merthyr Tydfill
Mid Glamorgan
CF48 2BW

JANE PUBLISHING
23 Bright Street
York
YO2 4XS 0904 647086
As a performance poet Adrian is commited to this
early medium. Looking always for oppertunities to
share with writers and listeners particularly in the
field of vocal and drama poetry. LET IT LIFT UP
FROM THE PAGE! Send s.a.e. for reply. Pomes.
Ed. Adrian Spendlow. 24 pp. A5 quarterly. ISBN
1872 994 00. £1.50. or A3 issue sub. for £3.75.
Postal performance poetry platform - partic ipation
by purchasers is positively pushed.
Kid's Pomes, young peoples poetry edited by Adrian
Spendlow. 24 pages as quarterly £1.50 inc p+p or
£3.75 for a 3 issue sub. A poetry newspaper by post.
Cushdie for Dossin. Great vocal poetry by Adrian
Spendlow 32 pages. A5 £2 inc p+p

JENNIE JANES
29 Pynchon Paddocks
Little Hallingbury
Bishops Stortford
CM22 7RJ.
Subjects: Crosswords.
Books January to June 1991 - 1.

MR JACK JANICEN
18 Davies Avenue
Leeds
LS8 1JY

JANET JANKOVSKIS
9 Chartersfield Lane
Stonnall
Walsall
WS9 9EF

JANUARY BOOKS

18 Amberley Grove
Croydon
CR0 6ND

JANUS PUBLISHING COMPANY
Duke House
37 Duke Street
London
W1M 5DF
Co-partnership publishers

JARDINE PRESS
James Dodds
2 Clipt Bush Cottage
Polstead Street, Stoke-by-Nayland
Colchester
Essex
CO6 4SD

MR NEIL G JARMAN
26 Grovsner Square
Sheffield
S2 4NS

MR O M JARREAU
1 The Granary
West Mills
Newbury
Berkshire
RG14 5HR

MRS L JARRETT
Eden Lodge
54 Melville Road
Falmouth
Cornwall
TR11 4DQ

JAY BOOKS
30 The Boundary
Langton Green
Tunbridge Wells
TN3 0YB.
Subjects: Etiquette.
Books January to June 1991 - 2. Books July to
December 1991 - 2

MRS JEAN
PO Box 2111
London
E3 5UA

JOHN W.T. JEFFERIES
57 Weston Crescent
Aldridge
Walsall
WS9 0HA.
Subjects:
Books January to June 1991 - 1

JEMA PUBLICATIONS
40 Ashley Lane
Moulton
NN3 1TJ

JENKINS MAIL ORDER
121 Lent Rise Road

Burnham
Slough
SL1 7BN.
Subjects: Photocopiers and How to Win.
Books January to June 1991 - 1

MS BRYONY JENKINS
38 Muswell Hill Road
London
N10 3JD

MR M JENKINS
3 Clare Gardens
Riverside
Cardiff
South Glamorgan

MR ANTHONY JENKINSON
88 Brookdene Avenue
Oxley
Watford
Hertfordshire
WD1 4LF

MR STEPHEN JENKINS
Flat 6, Richard Fox House
Queen's Drive
London
N4 2TA

MR E A JENNINGS
244 Soothill Lane
Batley
West Yorkshire
WF17 6EZ

JERSEY ARTISTS
P.O Box 75
Normandy House, St Helier
Jersey
Channel Islands

JERSEY WILDLIFE PRESERVATION TRUST
Les Augres
Manor Trinity
Jersey
Channel Islands.
Subjects: Zoology.
Books July to December 1991 - 1

JESUS LA PRODUCTS
Christopher
c/o 15 Belegrove Close
Welling
Kent
DA16 3RG
Approaching our tenth year we deal in low-tech ephemera. Our literary magazine 'Fast...Hard' is now at its sixth issue. We encourage postal exchange of genuine reality - proving publications and printed items. Such is life.
Fast...Hard No.4 - Theme - Bad Mood Free September 1991. Fast...Hard No.5 - Theme - Ceavsesiv Free January 1992. Fast...Hard No.6 - Theme - Control Free forthcoming summer 1992.

JEWISH BOOK NEWS AND REVIEWS

138 Middle Lane
Crouch End
London
N8 7JP

CENTRE FOR JEWISH EDUCATION
80 East End Road
London
N3 2SY.
Subjects: Children's Fiction.
Books January to June 1991 - 6

JIGLAG PRODUCTION COMPANY
2nd Floor
70 Ashley Street
Glasgow
G3 6HW

J K SOFTWARE LTD
13 Yarrow Close
Horsham
West Sussex
RH12 4FP

J.M.F. BOOKS
Llanerch
Felinfach
Lampeter
SA48 8PS.
Subjects: Local History.
Books July to December 1991 - 1

JMK CONSULTANCY
39 Balgreen Road
Edinburgh
EH12 5TY.
Subjects: Customs and Folklore.
Books July to December 1991 - 1

JOAN GALE
Brackenrigg Cottage,
Rothbury,
Northumberland
0669 20946
Northumbrian background all three books, also small local history book about the Coquet Valley, Northumberland.
'My Pit Pony' by Joan Gale; published 1985.
'The Blaydon Races' by Joan Gale; published 1990.
'Before the Forest' by Joan Gale; published 1991.

JOE SOAP'S CANOE
Mr Martin Stannard
30 Quilter Road
Felixtowe
Suffolk
IP11 7JJ

H & A JOHN LIMITED
28 Carlton Street
Normanton
Wakefield
West Yorkshire
WF6 2HY

MR ALAN JOHNSON
66 Newhouse Road

Heywood
Lancashire
OL10 2NU

MISS ASTRID E JOHNSON B.D
Kerloch
Strachan
Banchory
Kincardineshire
AB31 3NL

MR B C JOHNSON
39a Kildare Terrace
London
W2

MR I K JOHNSON
11 Church Hill
Loughton
Essex
IG10 1QP

MARION JOHNSON
199 Victoria Avenue
Borrowash
Derby
DE7 3HG

MR MICHAEL JOHNSON
4 Wellington Avenue
Hounslow
Middlesex
TW3 3sx

MRS MARGARET JOHNSON
Garden Cottage
Youngsbury
Ware
Hertfordshire
SG12 0TZ

JOHNSONS PUBLISHING
James Street West
Bath
BA1 2BU

JOHNSTON AND BACON
PO Box 1
Stirling.
Subjects: Loch Ness Monster.
Books July to December 1991 - 1

MS SANDRA JOHNSTONE
82 Fernbank Hill
Sudbury Hill
Wembley
Middlesex
HA0 2TR

MR H JOHNSTON
31 Devonshire Road
Penbroke Dock
Dyfed
SA72 6EE

JOINT CENTRE FOR SURVEY METHODS
35 Northampton Square

London
EC1V 0AX.
Books January to June 1991 - 2

MR RICHARD JOLLY
117 Monteith Row
Glasgow
G40 1AX

NORMAN F JOLY
28 Oakington Avenue
Harrow
HA2 7JJ

JONATHON PRESS
16 Poplar Grove
Flint Hill
Stanley
Co Durham
DH9 9BE
Poetry magazine

JONES-SANDS PUBLISHING
10 Startin Close
Exhall
Coventry
CV7 9NA

BOB JONES
67 Cecil Road
Hertford
SG13 8HR

JONES-BLAKEY
4 Penswick Grove
Coddington
Newark-on-Trent
Nottinghamshire
NG24 2QL

D JONES
The Flat, The Cottage
Weston
Shrewsbury
SY4 5OX

DORIS JONES
89 Linwood Drive
Coventry
CV2 2LZ.
Subjects: Short Stories.
Books July to December 1991 - 1

DAVID BRYAN JAMES
Dolhuan
Llandre
Bow Street
Dyfed
SY24 5AB.
Subjects: Local History.
Books July to December 1991 - 1

MR HUGH JONES
c/o Taylor Joynson Garrett
10 Maltravers Street
London
WC2R 3BS 071 836 8456

146

JOHN JONES
Oxford
Balliol College
Oxford
OX1 3BJ

MS J JONES
Brynteg
North Road
Whitland
Dyfed
SA34 0BH

MR PHIL JONES
Lorien, Lee Lane
Millhouse Green
Penistone
Sheffield
S30 6NN

R JONES
London
36 Granville Square
London
WC1X 9PD

MR RHYS GRUFFYDD JONES
149 Fairfax Road
London
N8 0NJ

S J JONES
30 Vale Road
Parkestone
Poole
Dorset
BH14 9AU

MS YVONNE JONES
Hazelwood
Waters Green
Brockenhurst
Hampshire
SO42 7RG

JORDAN PUBLICATIONS
1 Ashfolds
Horsham Road
Rusper
Horsham
RH12 4QX.
Subjects: Children's Fiction.
Books July to December 1991 - 1

MR WALTER JORTS
Lange Winkelhaak Straat
B-2008 Antwerpen
Belgium

MR G JOSEPH
97b Willow Vale
London
W12 0PA

MR SYDNEY A JOSEPHS

The British Council, Rainbow Street
First Circle, Jebel Amman
PO Box 634, Amman
Jordan

(THE) JOURNAL
18-20 Dean Street
Newcastle-upon-Tyne
NE1 1PG

JOURNAL OF THE AUSTRALIAN CENTRE OF
UFO STUDIES
Box 229
Prospect SA 5082
Australia

JOURNAL OF METEOROLOGY
54 Frome Road
Bradford-on-Avon
Wiltshire
BA15 1LD

JOY HIBBERT
11 Rutland Street
Hanley
Stoke on Trent
ST1 5JG

JPA SUBSCRIPTION SERVICES
PO Box 415
Colwyn Bay
Clwyd
LL29 8HX

J.S.B PUBLICATIONS
14 Moorfield Place
Shepshed
Loughborough
LE12 9AW

JUDD STREET GALLERY
99 Judd Street
London
SE8 3AH

JUMA
Martin Lacey
44 Wellington Street,
Sheffield S1 4HD
0742 720915. Fax 0742 786550
Litho printers specialising in small press work:
books, magazines, publicity material &c. Low prices.
Book publishers - principal subject football. Book
and fanzine mail order.
El Tel Was a Space Alien; ed M. Lacey; 1989 ISBN
1 872204 00 7; 210pp A4; £5.95.Compilation of
Fanzine Writing.
Get Your Writs Out! ed M. Lacey; 1992 ISBN 1
872204 02 3; 210pp A4; £6.95. Compilation of
Fanzines.
Where's the Bar; 91/92; ed. M. Lacey 1991 ISBN 1
872204 03 1; 98pp A4; £3.95. Non-league Football
Yearbook.

MS CAROLINE JUPP
27 Muspole Street
Norwich
NR3 1DJ

JUST WOMEN
3 Holway Hill
Taunton
Somerset

J.W.B. PUBLICATIONS
(John White Brown)
5 Hambledon Close
Ladybridge
Bolton
BL3 4ND.
Subjects: Poetry.
Books July to December 1991 - 1

[K]

KABET PRESS
John Hort
239 Bramcote Lane,
Wollaton,
Nottingham NG8 2QL
0602 283001
Shakespeare for children

KADATH
6 Boulevard St Michel
B-1150 Bruxelles
Belgium

KADATH PRESS
The Hermatage
East Morton
Keighley
BD20 5UJ

KADU BOOKS
6 Ivy Avenue
Blackpool
PY4 3QG.
Subjects: European Travel.
Books January to June 1991 - 1

K.A.M PUBLICITY
11 Soutbank Road
Kenilworth
CV8 1LA

R.M. KAMARYC
43 Broomfield
Harlow
CM20 2JZ.
Subjects: Military Science.
Books July to December 1991 - 2

MS ROSE KAMEL
78b Great Percy Street
London
WC1X 9QU

KAMPO GANGRA BUDDHIST CENTRES
(Admin office) c/o 1A Reynard Road
Chorlton
Manchester
M21 2DB

MR MICHAEL KANTEY

Watercourse, 41 Alma Road
Rosebank
Cape Town 7700
South Africa

KARRERA
Foxworthy Lotton
Ivybridge
PL21 9SS

MS PEARL KARRER
570 Kingsley Avenue
Palo Alto
CA 94301
United States of America

KATABASIS
10 St Martins Close
London
NW1 0HR 071 485 3830
Publishes English poetry and bi-lingual editions of
poetry in translation mainly Latin American.
The Peasant Poets of Solentiname. Bi-lingual ed.
translated and introd uced by Peter Wright; illustrated by Anna Mieke Lumsden. 118 pages (1991)
0 904872 15 7. £5.95.
Keeping Heart. poems 1967-1989 by Dinah
Livingstone. 240 pages. 1989. 0 904872 11 4.
£6.50.
The Nicaraguan Epic by C and L.E. Mejia Godoy
and Julio Valle-Castill. songs and poems telling the
story of the Revolution. Translated by Dinah
Livingstone with numerous notes and archive photos. 158 pages. 1989. 0 904872 12 2. £5.95.

KAWABATA PRESS
Knill Cross
Millbrook
Torpoint
PL10 1DX

MR GERALD KAYE
3a Durham Terrace
Bayswater
London
W2 5PB

RICHARD KAY PUBLICATIONS
Richard Allday
80 Sleaford Road
Boston
Lincolnshire
PE21 8EU. Tel 0 205 353231
Publishes only from 4-8 titles per year. Principally
Lincolnshire material (dialect. Biographical. Hu-
mour): Local History. Lincs. - USA interest. some
Politico-economic. Locality and range expanding.
William Brewster - The Father of New England
Revd. Dr. H. Kirk-Smith Pp. 372+xii: PUB. 12/9/
92: ISBN 0902662 937 cased £25. Hist. Biog. of the
principal Pilgrim Father.
The Stars Anthology of Poems for Burma Star Assn.
Ed 'Sandy' Wiiliams. Pp.159. PUB May 1990
0902662 998 £4.95 (and cased 10.95). Poetry of
the Burma Campaign.
Lincolnshire Dialects Edward Campion. Pp. 61 0
902662 31 7: 2.95 (now in 3rd printing). Scholarly
but also easy reading and at time quite humorous.

148

DR RONALD W KAY
13 Grange Loan
Edinburgh
EH9 2NP

UNIVERSITY OF KEELE
Centre for Local History
Department of History
Keele
ST5 5BG

DENNIS KEEN
51 Warren Road
Rugby
CV22 5LG.
Subjects: Sport.
Books July to December 1991 - 1

KEEPSAKE PRESS
2 Park House Gardens
Twickenham
Middlesex
TW1 2DE

KELLY'S DIRECTORIES
Windsor Court
East Grinstead House
East Grinstead
West Sussex
RH19 1XA

KELSEY PUBLISHING
Kelsey House
77 High Street
Beckenham
BR3 1AN.
Subjects: Cars. Car restoring.
Books January to June 1991 - 11. Books July to
December 1991 - 2

KELTIA PUBLICATIONS
Kaledon Naddair
PO Box 307
Edinburgh
Alban
EH9 1XA Tel 031 666 2822
Keltia Publications produce books monographs
and Journals by Kaledon Naddair and other writers
on all aspects of Keltic Culture e.g. Art-Symbolism
Poetry Language Megalithic Sites Nature-Reser-
voirs Mythology and Pagan-Spiritually. We pro-
duce the Real McCoy - pioneering research is our
speciality.
Keltic Folk and Faerie Tales (Their Shamanism
Explored) Kaledon Naddair 269pps 1987 ISBN
0712616799 8.95.
Keltic Animal Lore and Shamanism (companion
Vols to Tree a Bird Lore) Kaledon Naddair 164pps
1987 ISBN 090 6590760 6
Awen No3 (Keltic. Pagan a Nature-poetry) Various
Authors ISBN 0268 5736 80pps

MS LAURIE KEMP
1 Wreay Court
Wreay
Carlisle
Cumbria

CA4 0RJ 069 7473720

MR J A KENCHINGTON
The Old Stables
Ravenswood House
Farnham
GU9 9RP

H.M. KENDALL
20 Mortimer Close
Orelton
Ludlow
SY8 4PG.
Subjects: Historical Biography.
Books January to June 1991 - 1

MR JOHN KENDALL
5 Starrs Close
Axbridge
Somerset
BS26 2BZ

KENRIC
BM Kenric
London
WC1N 3XX

KENSINGTON WEST PRODUCTIONS
338 Old York Road
London
SW18 1SS.
Subjects: Sport.
Books July to December 1991 - 2

UNIVERSITY OF KENT
Personal Social Services Research Uni
Canterbury
CT2 7NF

MR R DONALD KEPPOCH
Lady Watson Gardens
Hamilton
Lanarkshire
ML3 8RD

KEROUAC CONNECTION
76 Calderwood Square
East Kilbride
GLASGOW
G74 3BQ

MR PETER A KERR
37 Foxlease
Bedford
MK41 8AP

TOM KERR
1 Winsor Avenue
Holywood
Belfast
BT18 9DG.
Subjects: Poetry.
Books July to December 1991 - 1

A.S KERSWILL
113 High Street
Berkhamsted

HP4 2DJ

JOHN R KETTERINGHAM
27 Bunkers Hill
Lincoln
LN42 4QS

PAMELA KETTLE
Sutton Court
Sutton Scarsdale
Chesterfield
S44 5UT.
Subjects: History of Hardwick Inn.
Books July to December 1991 - 1

KETTLE'S YARD GALLERY
Castle Street
Cambridge
CB3 0AQ.
Subjects: Art.
Books January to June 1991 - 2. Books July to
December - 2.

KEYHOLE PUBLICATIONS
BCM Keyhole
London
WC1 3XX

MR LAURENCE KEYNES
c/o Astounding Comics
61 Pyle Street
Newport
Isle of White

KHABS
Bos TR 24
Leeds
LS12 3QU

KIBLAH PUBLISHING
Park House
Cerne Abbas
Dorset
DT2 7BG
Equinox magazine

MS SUSAN C KIMBER
60 Catherine Street
Cambridge
CB1 3AW

KINDRED SPIRIT
Room T
Foxhole
Dartington
Devon
TQ9 6EB

A R KING
15 Cinder Hall
Matfield
Tonbridge
Kent
TN12 7ED

MR G P KING
Kingstone Court

Kingston
Canterbury
Kent
CT4 6HY

SIMON KING PRESS
Ashton House
Beetham
Milnthorpe
Cumbria
LA77 7AL. Tel 05395 62194.
Letterpress rules OK! And I'm expanding in more
sense than one. The single poems series continues
illustrated with my own wood engravings. A vol-
ume of Saki short stories is planned for next year.
Put your name on my mailing list.
Ode To The West Wind Shelley 9 pages January
1992 ISBN 0 946497 07 9 £14 illustrated poem.
Ten Poems Robert Bridges 19 pages July 1992
ISBN 0 946497 08 7 £17 unillustrated poems.

THE KING'S ENGLAND PRESS
Steve Rudd
37 Crookes Lane Carlton
Barnsley
South Yorkshire
S71 3JR. Tel 0226 722529
The Press is reprinting the entire 'King's England'
series of guidebooks to each of the English coun-
tries first published in the 1930s. In addition we also
do distribution for other small Local History Pub-
lishers and run Local History bookshop.
Facsimile Reprint of the Entire King's England
Series by Arthur Mee [41 volumes in progress
please send for free catalogue]

KINGSLEA PRESS
137 Newhall Street
Birmingham
B3 1SF
Subjects: General knowledge.

MR C M KINGSLEY
63 Fitzjohn Avenue
Barnet
Hertfordshire
EN5 2HN

KINGSTON SCHOOL
Pickering Road
Hull
HU4 7AE

KINMEL PUBLISHING
Kinmel Hall
St George
Abergele
LL2 9DA

KIRKBY WRITERS
18 Pershore Road
Southdene
Kirkby
L32 3XA

CONGREGATIONAL BOARD
Kirkliston Parish Church
c/o J.W. Henderson 4

150

1 Maitland Road
Kirkliston
EH29 9DD.
Subjects: Local History. Books July to December
1991 - 1

RJ KIRKPATRICK
244 Latimer Road
London
W10 6QY

KISSING THE SKY
Miss Sharon Elton
23 Southwark Close
Lichfield
Staffs
WS13 7SH

THE KIT-CAT PRESS
Kenneth Hardacre
10 Fosseway Drive
Moreton-in-Marsh
Gloucestershire
GL56 0DU
Fine printer

KITES
The Highgate Society
10A South Grove
London
N 6

KITHEAD
De Salis Drive
Hampton Lovett
Droitwich
WR9 0QE

KITTIWAKE
David Parrott
Darowen
Machynlleth
Montgomeryshire
SY20 8NS 0650 511314 (fax 5116
Truly helpful pocket-sized guide books based on
personal research; carefully designed and fully
mapped and illustrated.
'Guide to the Western Isles of Scotland' by David
Perrott. 96pp ISBN 0 9511003 2 7 (NO PRICE
GIVEN). All islands fully described and mapped.
'Outer Hebrides Handbook and Guide' Ed. David
Perrott. 96pp ISBN 0 9511003 3 5 Authentic intro-
duction to the Outer Hebrides written by locals
'Guide to the Dyfi Valley Way' by Lawrence Main.
96pp. illustrated prac tical guide to a 108 mile walk
around a beautiful Welsh valley (1988)

KLICK MAGAZINE
Polytechnic of Huddersfield
Writing Society

K.M.S BOOKS
Market Place
Boston
PE21 6LY

KIM KNEE
WP Secretarial Service

72 Lauriston Road
Hackney
London
E9 7HA

MRS P J KNEEN
Christina Baixa 8
El Vendrell
43700 Tarragona
Spain

F. KNIGHT
11 Church Cottages
Stopham
Pullborough
RH20 1EG.
Subjects: Local History.
Books January to June 1991 - 1

KNIGHTSBRIDGE PUBLICATIONS
Newcastle Road
Newsham
Blyth
NE24 4AG

(LIZ) KNOX BOOK DESIGN
20 High Street
Coton
Cambridge
CB3 7PL

KORVET PUBLISHING AND DISTRIBUTION
Sarah Garrett
PO Box 115, Old Post Office Gallery, Royal Leam-
ington Sp, Warwickshire, CV31 1GH
0926 315262/Fax 0926 450973
'British Forces in the Korean War'; Eds Ashley
CUnningham-Boothe and Peter Farrar; 200pp; 0
9512622 0 3; £14.50 (p&p incl); 1989.
'Marks of Courage'; ed Ashley Cunningham-Boothe;
328pp; 0 9517750 6; £20 (p&p incl); the definitive
record of Honours, Decorations and Awards for
Gallantry for the Korean Theatre of War 1950-53,
Great Britain, Northern Ireland and The Common-
wealth.

MS JANET R KOVACIK
24 Marlow Road
Cambridge
CB3 9JW

THE KOVAC LETTERS
Toad House Books
Mole Cottage
Durham
DH7 7EJ 0913 732893
Humour travel arts sociology.
The Kovac Letters. 0 9510807 1. 7 wittily enter-
taining letters between an American photographer
and British composer. Music and Life; autobiogra-
phy etc by Antony Elton.

KOZMIK PRESS LTD
David Ryan
134 Elsenham St.
London
SW18 5NP. Tel 071 935 5913
Kozmik publishes two travel guides - India and

America. Fiction poetry and biography. No unsolicited manuscripts. Write for full catalogue for details of new publications ask to go on our mailing list.
John Lennon's Secret 256pp. £9.95 updated definitive Lennon Biography with songs ISBN 0 905116 208
The Lost Journel of Robyn Hood - Outlaw ISBN 0 905116 18 6 10.95. A look at the man behind the myth based on research.
The Cream of the Troubadour Coffee House £10.95 0 905116 19 4 40 poets from around the world.

THE KQBX PRESS
James Sale
16 Scotter Road
Pokestown
Bournemouth
BH7 6LY. Tel 0202 42155
Committed to promoting poetry in the south and to publishing high-quality collections from any region we are proud to announce Sean Street's and David Orme's latest volumes and to introduce Anthony Watts a big hit at Bournemouth International Festival. Submission welcome.
This True Making by Sean Street. 48pp 1 June 1992 ISBN 0 946541 17 5 6.95
The Gravedigger's Sandwich by David Orme. 20pp 1 March 1992 ISBN 0 946541 16 7 £2.50.
Strange Gold by Anthony Watts. 24pp 4 Jan 1992 ISBN 0 946541 15 9 2.95.

THE KRAX MACHINE
Andy Robson
c/o 63 Dixon Lane
Leeds
Yorkshire
LS12 4RR.
A nine-monthly light-hearted poetry mag with the odd story interview illustration thrown in. Snap up the excesses of our twenty-first birthday edition - not just full of old codgers. Also produces mini-books and occasional special editions.
Jackets Poems of Young Romance by Maura gage. 32pp plus dust-jacket 1991 £1.95
Ecstasy (or just a drug?) Passionate poems from Geoff Stevens. A6 mini-book 16pp 1992 10p.
Which way to the Castle? Village-life portrayals by Jocelyne Precious. A6 mini-book 16pp 1992 10p.

KRINO
The Paddocks
Glenrevagh
Corrandulla
Co Galway
Ireland

KRISTALL PRODUCTIONS
71B Maple Road
Surbiton
KT6 4AG

KK KRISTO PRODUCTIONS
31 Thistle Grove
Welwyn Garden City
AL7 4AD

KROPOTKIN'S LIGHTHOUSE PUBLICATIONS
Jim Huggon

Box KLP, Housemans Bookshop
5 Caledonian Road
London
N1
Kropotkins Lighthouse Publications is an anarchist-pacifist press specialising in poetry, posters, pamphlets from within that tradition. William Morris and Walter Crane: An earthly Paradise Calender (dateless) 14pp, A3. Including extracts from William Morris' 'Earthly Paradise' and Walter Crane's complete illustrated poem 'The Sirens Three@. 26 plates. £1.50 ($£2.50) plus 40p postage.
Arther Moyse: More in Sorrow: Six short stories. (illustrated bt thr author) (26pp ppr) £0.75 (19p) [1.25 + 0.50 dollars post]
Carl Slienger: A Checklist of Freedom Press Publications 1886-1927. (16pp ppr) £0.60 (12p) [1.25 + 0.25 dollars post]

K.T PUBLICATIONS
Editor: Kevin Troop
16 Fane Close
Stamford
Lincolnshire
PE9 1HG
Magazine

KUDOS
(Graham Sykes)
78 Easterly Road
Leeds
W Yorks
LS8 3AN

KUMA COMPUTERS LTD
12 Horseshore Park
Pangbourne
READING
RG8 7JW 0734 844335
Kuma specialise in publishing quality computing books. Topics include DTP programming an usage of microcomputers portable computers and their soft ware.
'Pagemaker 4.0 For Windows' by W. Saunders. 350pp. 19.95. ISBN 0 7457 003 1 4.
'Desktop Publishing Sourcebook - Font and Clip Art for the IBM PC' by Jan i Lynne Borman. 350pp. fully illustrated. £24.95. ISBN 0 7457 0030 6. 'The Psion Organiser Deciphered' by Gill Gerhardi. 240pp. 12.95. ISBN 0 7457 0139 6

Z KWINTNER BOOKS
6 Warren Mews
London
W1P 5DJ

[L]

LAAM
PO Box 249A
Surbiton
KT6 5AX

LABOUR RESEARCH DEPT (LRD)
78 Blackfriars Road
London
SE1 8HF

Paul Lacey
17 Sparrow Close
Wooshill
Wokingham
RG11 2UL

L.A DESIGN BOOKS
Flat 2, The Courtyard
Woolverstone Hall, Woolverstone
Ipswich
IP9 1AZ

LAECE BOOKS
T.R. Leach
3 Merleswen
Dunholme
Lincoln
LN2 3SN. Tel 0673 860637
Publishes a series of books on Lincolnshire country houses and other material relating to local history in Lincolnshire.
Lincolnshire Country House and Their Families Part 1 by T.R. Leach. 84pp 1990 0 9500803 5 7 £6.50.
Lincolnshire Country House and Their Families Part 2 by T.R. Leach. 124pp 1991 0 9500803 6 5 9.00.
'A Swinethorpe and Harby Miscellany' by Terence R. Leach. 40pp £2.25.

LAGAN PRESS: ANNA LIVIA PRESS
21 Cross Avenue
Dun Laoghaire
County Dublin
Republic Ireland.
Subjects: Literature.
Books January to June 1991 - 1

MARY LAKER
Chantry
Church Road
Kennington
Ashford
TN24 9QD.
Subjects: Poetry.
Books January to June 1991 - 1

MR A C LAMB
10 Camilla Court
Ossett Lane
Dewsey
West Yorkshire

MR DAVID LAMBERT
Central Library
Harper Street
Bedford

LAMBETH LANGUAGE CENTRE
Effra School Effra Parade
London
SW2 1PL.
Subjects: Education. Bibliographies.
Books January to June 1991 - 3

LAMBETH WOMEN AND CHILDREN'S HEALTH
Brixton Enterprise Centre

444 Brixton Road
London
SW9 8EJ.
Subjects: Children's Non-fiction.
Books July to December 1991 - 1

LAMBOURN PRESS
The Old Forge
7 Caledonian Road
London
N1 9DX

Lambourn Publications
12-14 High Road
London
N2 9JP.
Subjects: Biography.
Books January to June 1991 - 2

LAME DUCK PUBLISHING
71 South Road
Portishead
Bristol
BS20 9DY.
Subjects: Education.
Books July to December 1991 - 6

THE LAMP PUBLISHING HOUSE
BM Follower
London
WC1N 3XX
Dedicated to publishing works which present a moderate, non fundamentalist approach to religion and human spirtuality. More specifically, publishes literature based on philosophy of first Galilean followers of Jesus of Nazareth, emphasising his humanity, and his teachings on Kingdom of God.
'The Ketaba'; editor: Tchr R A Ferreira; published: June 92; ISBN 1 874193 01 0; £19.50; The religious scriptures of modern darqayism.
'Background Notes to the Ketaba'; author: Tchr R A Ferreira; Published: June 92; £3.50; Contains helpful notes which assist in understanding the text of the Ketaba.

LAM RIM BUDDHIST CENTRE
Pentwyn Manor
Penrhos
Raglan
Gwent
NP5 2LE

THE FIRST BOOK OF THE LANCASHIRE HEELER
Miss K. B. Kidd
Bay House 6 Crescent Walk
Bognor Regis
Sussex
PO21 2YA Tel 0243 863796.
The first book about the rare breed of dog Lancashire Heeler. Containing characteristics of dog its history uses life as a show dog whelping section. Information about Lancashire Heeler Club. About 70 photographs of dogs.
The First Book of The Lancashire Heeler by Kathie Kidd published 1990 243 pages ISBN 1 870690 060 Price £9 plus £1.60 p&p.

153

MARGARET LANCASTER
Wood End Farm
Salterforth
Colne
BB8 5SN

LANCASTRIAN TRANSPORT PUBLICATION
5 Rossall Road
Blackpool
FY5 1AP

LANDFALL PUBLICATIONS
Bob Acton
Landfall
Penpol, Devoran
Truro
TR3 6NW

LANDY PUBLISHING COMPANY
3 Staining Rise
Staining
Blackpool
FY3 0BU

LANDY PUBLISHING
Bob Dobson
3 Staining Rise
Staining
Blackpool
FY3 0BU. Tel 0253 886103
Publishes Lancashire local history and dialect books.
Also operates as a second-hand bookseller and
book fair organiser. I.P.G. member. In Lancashire
Language Dobson. 64pp Nov 1991 ISBN 1 872895
08 5 4.00. Poetry.
Blackpool and Fleetwood A Century Ago Dobson.
64pp May 1991 ISBN 1 872895 07 7 3.90. Local
History.
Southport A Century Ago Wright. 72pp June 1992
ISBN 1 872895 10 7 5.00. Local History.

LANGDON PUBLISHING
Acorn Workshops
250 Carmarthen Road
Swansea
SA1 1HG

DR E R LANGLEY
P O Box 1000
St Albans
Hertfordshire
AL3 5NY

LANGTRY PRESS
23 St Marks Road
Henley-on-Thames
Oxfordshire
RG9 1LP

LAPIN BLANC
Elizabeth Rudd
55 Warwick Square
London
SW1C 2AJ

LARK PUBLICATIONS
68 Lamble Close

Beck Row
Bury St. Edmunds
IP28 8DB.
Subjects: Botany.

MR HUGH LARKIN
51 Weatherill Street
GOOLE
North Humberside

LARKS PRESS
Ordnance Farm House
Guist Bottom
DEREHAM
Norfolk
NR20 5PF
Original material about the history of Norfolk.

LAST DITCH PRESS
22 Evesham Road
Stratford-upon-Avon
Warwickshire
CV37 9AA
Trash teen-mags and postcards with poems.

LATHAM PRESS
9 Latham Avenue
Runcorn
WA7 5DS.
Subjects: Betting Shops.
Books January to June 1991 - 2

MR ROBERT LATHAM
Svecia Autique Ltd
Dowding Way
Tunbridge Wells
Kent
TN22 3UX

MR DAVID LATIMER
1 Ruby Street
South Bank
York
YO2 1EE

LATIN AMERICA BUREAU
(Research & Action) Ltd
1 Amwell Street
London
EC1R 1UL

LATIN AMERICAN WRITERS PUBLICATION
107 Gorefield House
Gorefield Place
London
NW6 5TB 071 328 2895

LAUNDRY PRESS
41 Bryony Road
London
W12 0LS.
Subjects: Poetry.
Books July to December 1991 - 1

MS CAROL LAWRENCE
1 Rose Farm Cottage
Rose Farm

154

Shotley
Suffolk
IP9 1PH

DENYS LAWRENCE
Hambledon Place
Henley-on-Thames
RG9 3BL

D.H. LAWRENCE SOCIETY
7 Bromley Road
West Bridgford
Nottingham
NG2 7AP.
Subjects: D.H. Lawrence.
Books January to June 1991 - 1

MR D LAWRENCE
40 Holkham Avenue
Chilwell
Beeston
Nottingham
NG9 5EQ

MR A J G LAWRIE
16 Ravenscroft Gardens
London
W6 0TU

BARBARA LAWSON
1 Elverlands Close
Ferring
Worthing
BN12 5PL.
Subjects: Poetry.
Books July to December 1991 - 1

THELMA LAYCOCK
34 Jacques Close
Queenswood Drive
Leeds
LS6 3NQ.
Subjects: Poetry.
Books January to June 1991 - 1

MR JOHN LAYFIELD
1 Walker Street
Bowburn
Durham
DH6 5BG

R J LEACH & CO
38 Inglemere Road
Forest Hill
London
SE23 2BE
Mainly military publishing producing up to six titles
per year, both reprints an d new books. Those
published so far are Napoloeonic and Colonial
India.

LEADER BOOKS
MFPA 9
Inverness Place
London
W2 3JF.
Subjects: Art.

Books July to December 1991 - 1

LEADING EDGE PRESS
The Old Chapel
Burtesett
Hawes
North Yorkshire
DL8 3PB

Leaf Publishing
9 Lock Road
Richmond
TW10 7LQ.
Subjects: Travel.
Books January to June 1991 - 1

LEARNING MATERIALS DESIGN
Ms Carole Joslin
Lovat Bank, Silver Street
Newport Pagnell
Buckinghamshire
MK16 0EJ

LEARNING STYLES
P.O. Box 1071
Andover
SP10 1YN.
Subjects: Careers. British History. School Text-
books.
Books July to December 1991 - 12.

LEARNING TOGETHER ABC
Dorothy Dowling
18 Blackstock Drive
Gleadless Valley
Sheffield
S14 1AG Sheffield 642912
A fingerspelling ABC book for Deaf and Hearing
children. Full colour and fully illustrated through-
out. Educational but fun to learn. For age group 1
to 8 years. Wipe clean cover.
'Learning Together' by Dorothy and Jacqui Dowling.
May 1990 1st edition. October 1990 2nd edition.
A4. 32pp. full colour illustrations on 28 pages
paperback. 3.99. ISBN 0 9516851 0 4. Discounts
available on request. Orders over 6 copies or Trade.

MR RONALD LEARY
58 Domville Road
Liverpool
L13 4AS

DR CLIVE LEATHERDALE
38 Essex Close
Rayleigh
Essex
SS6 8SX

LEAVES/SCALES
14 Ropery Street
London
E3 4QF
Poetry
The Fabulist - (Selected poems 1984 - 1991) by
Paul Holman. 52pp, cover + title page image by
Alison Marchant. Published 1991. ISBN 0 9518081
0 9 £4.50

155

LEAVESISCALES
P. Holman
14 Ropery Street
London
E3 4QF.
Poetry
The Fabulist Paul Holman (cover and title page artwork by Alison Marchant) 52pp 1991 ISBN 0 9518081 0 9 £4.50.

LECHLADE PRESS
89A Allport Lane
Bromborough
Wirral
L62 7HL.
Subjects: Sport.
Books January to June 1991 - 1

LEECHWELL PRESS
Leechwell Cottage
Totnes
TQ9 5SY

LEE DONALDSON ASSOCIATES
14 Pall Mall
London
SW1Y 5LU.
Subjects: Town Planning.
Books January to June 1991 - 1

LEEDS PHILOSOPHICAL AND LITERARY SOCIETY
Central Museum
Calverley Street
Leeds
LS1 3AA.
Subjects: Literature.
Books July to December 1991 - 2

LEEDS POSTCARDS
P O Box 84
Leeds
LS1 4HU

KITTY LEE
13A New Street
Cromer
NR27 9HP.
Subjects: Social Welfare.
Books July to December 1991 - 1

MR MATTHEW LEE
Industrigation 14
S-153 00 Jaerna
Sweden

LEEMAN PRESS
227A High Street
Northallerton
DI7 8LU

B LEESON
5 St Agnell's Lane Cottages
Hemel Hempstead
HP2 7HJ

MS SARAH LEES

Independent Illustration & Design
Clare Chambers, 33 Inkerman Street
Llanelli
Dyfed
SA15 1AS

LEEWAY PUBLICATIONS
185 Baring Road
London
SE12 0LD.
Subjects: School Textbooks.

LEICESTERSHIRE GOLF CLUB1
Evington Lane
Leicester
LE5 6DJ

LEICESTERSHIRE ADULT BASIC EDUCA-TION
Room 409
County Hall
Glenfield
Leicester
LE3 8RF.
Subjects: Political Science.
Books January to June 1991 -2

LEIGHTON PARK SCHOOL
Shinfield Road
Reading
RG2 7DH

LEINSTER EXPRESS NEWSPAPERS
Dublin Road
Portlaoise
County Laois
Republic of Ireland.
Subjects: Local History.
Books July to December 1991 - 1

LEISURE
PO Box 368
Cardiff
CF2 1SQ
Magazine promoting cultural subversion.

JOHN LE MESURIER
Radipole
Les Hibits
St. Martin's
Guernsey
Channel Is
Subjects: Short Stories.
Books January to June 1991 - 1

MR D J LEMMON
8 Wood Green
Salthouse
Holt
Norfolk
NR13 6NS

LEO PUBLISHING
31 Callis Street
Clare
Sudbury
CO10 8PX

LEOMANSLEY PRESS
16 Leomansley Road
Lichfield
WS13 8AW.
Subjects: General Fiction.
Books January to June 1991 - 1. Books July to
December 1991 - 1

LEONARDO PUBLISHING
22-26 Paul Street
London
EC24 4JH

S LEON
16 Sandringham House
Courtlands, Sheen Road
Richmond
Surrey
TW10 5BG

LEO'S PUBLISHING SERVICE
29 Fardale Road
Stretham
London
SW16 6DA

LESBIAN & GAY CHRISTIAN MOVEMENT
Journal, LCGM
Oxford House
Derbyshire Street
LONDON
E2 6HG

LESBIAN & GAY FREEDOM MOVEMENT
NEWSLETTER
BM Box 207
London
WC1N 3XX

LESBIAN INFORMATION SERVICE
PO Box 8
Todmorden
Lancashhire
OL14 5TZ
Newsletter

MR MICHAEL LEVER
16 Goldsmith Avenue
West Hendon
London
NW9 7HB

MARY LEWIS
Periwick Cottage
The Street, Plaxtol
Sevenoaks
TN15 0QF

MS JENNIFER LEWIS-SMITH
Chaucers, Oare
Hermitage
Newbury
Berkshire
RG16 9SD

LEX SERVICE

Lex House
17 Connaught Place
London
W2 2EL

LIBANUS PRESS LTD
Rose Tree House
Silverless Street
Marlborough
Wiltshire
SN8 1JQ

LIBERTARIAN ALLIANCE
Chris Thame
1 Russell Chambers,
The Piazza,
Covent Garden,
London WC2E 8AA
071 821 5502
Publishes a wide range of leaflets pamphlets and
monographs on all aspects of economic, political,
social, moral and sexual freedom from classic lib-
eral, libertarian, free market and anarcho-capitalist
perspectives.
Tuppy Owens; 'What is Pornography?': My Career
and How I've Been Censored'; 2pp; ISBN 1 856370
88 7; June 1992; 20p.
B. Micklethwait; 'Why I Call Myself a Free Market
Anarchist and Why I am one"; 4pp; ISBN 1 856370
82 8; June 1992; 40p.
Sean Gabb; 'The Full Coercive Approach of a
Police State: Thoughts on the Dark Side of the
Thatcher Decade'; 4pp; ISBN 1 870614 39 9; July
1989; 40p.

LIBRA
Miss Norton & Mr Day
3 Hall Terrace
Crook
Co Durham
DL15 0QN

MR ERIC LIGGETT
High Dam Barn
Arkholme
Carnforth
LA6 1BE 05242 21895

LIGHT'S LIST OF LITERARY MAGAZINES
Dr John Light
The Light House, 29 Longfield Road
Tring
Hertfordshire
HP23 4DG

LILBOURNE PRESS
Nicholas Reed
26 Hichisson Road
Peckham Rye
London
SE15 3AL. Tel 071 732 7778
We specialise in books on Local History and Art
History.
Pissaro in West London by N. Reed. 28pp 13 colour
illustrations 3rd ed. 1990 ISBN 0 9515258 2 4
£3.95
Sisley and the Thames by N. Reed. 50pp 20 colour
illustrations 1990 ISBN 0 9515258 3 2 £4.95.

LILBURNE PRESS
26 Hitchisson Road
London
SE15 3AL

LILLIPUT PRESS LTD
4 Rosemount Terrace
Arbour Hill
Dublin 7
Ireland

LIMITCODE
Tatton Buildings
6 Old Hall Road
Gatley
Cheadle
SK8 4BE.
Subjects: Languages in Business.
Books July to December 1991 - 2.

LINDEN HALL: H. MCNICHOL
Liberten Park Court
1-4 Lasswade Road
Edinburgh
E16 6JH.
Subjects: Biography.
Books July to December 1991 - 1

LINDEN PUBLICATIONS
Old School Wormhill
Sittingbourne
ME9 0TR.
Subjects: Trees.
Books January to June 1991 - 1

MR BRUCE LINDSAY
522 Felsham Way
Thorpe Marriott
Norwich
NR8 2QX 0603 261936

LINES REVIEW
(MacDonald Publishers)
Edgefield Road
Loanhead
Midlothian Scotland
EH20 9SY

LINGUASIA
45 Museum Street
London
WC1A 1LR.
Subjects: Language.
Books July to December 1991 - 4

LINGUAVIVA CENTRE
Eason and Son
Brickfield Drive
Crumlin
Dublin 12
Republic o
Subjects: General Fiction.
Books July to December 1991 - 1

LINK PRESS
35 Elizabeth Walk

Reading
RG2 0AW.
Subjects: Asian History.
Books July to December 1991 - 2

LINK UP
51 Northwick B Centre
Blockley
Moreton-in-Marsh
Gloucestershire
GL56 9RF
Magazine for those who care about the future of the planet

W J LINSKEY
25 Ballater Road
London
SW2 5QS

LISEK PUBLICATIONS
58a Comerford Road
London
SE4 2AX.
Subjects: Historic Biography. Second World War.
Books July to December 1991 - 2

LISIEUX HALL
Whittle-le-Woods
Chorley
PR6 7DX.
Subjects: Social Welfare.
Books July to December 1991 - 1

LITTLE big BOOKS
Mikel Horl
The Drawing Room,
38 Mount Pleasant,
London WC1X OAP
071 833 1335
Hand-made books, written, illustrated, designed
and published in London by Mikel Horl. Editions of
25 to 1,000 books. Ranging from pocket sized
picture stories to collections of words and images in
boxes and bags, and sets of original prints.
'Unlikely Hero number 00327'; Mikel Horl. 32pp;
1991; £3.00. Tragic Optimism.
'A Nook of Bon Sense'; Various Authors (ed. Mikel
Horl) 48pp (Gatefold Format) 1990. £9.00 Nonsense.
'Outlandish and Endangered Species'; Mikel Horl.
16 Loose leaves (etchings) in box. 1992. £180.00.
Hybrid animals, hand-coloured, from around the
world.

LITTLE CHERUB PUBLICATIONS
19 South Quay
Great Yarmouth
Norfolk
NR30 2RG. 0493 842637
'Guess the Question!' An original quiz book compiled by quiz wizard Valerie Jordan. You are given
the answers and have to supply the Question. The
questions are printed in the back of the book. The
only reversible Quiz Book!
'Guess the Question!' by Valerie Johnson. December 1990. 24pp. £1.50. ISBN 0 951 6791 0 4. Quiz
book.

LITTLE PRESSES (ASSOCIATION OF)
89a Petherton Road
LONDON
N5 2QT

E.R. LITTLER
St. Andrew's Vicarage
65 Electric Avenue
Westcliff-on-Sea
SS0 9NN.
Subjects: Architecture.
Books July to December 1991 - 1

LITTLEWOOD PRESS
Nanholme Centre
Shaw Wood Road
Todmorden
Lancashire
OL14 6DA
Littlewood Arc publishes 10-12 titles per year
including prizewinners of the Annual Northern
Short Stories Competition. Poetry predominates,
although occasionally prose concidered. Unsolicited MSS. not encouraged. The Dream of Intelligence by Sebastian Barker. 220pp long poem based
on life and philosophy of F Neitzche. HBK 0 946407
80 0 £15.95. PBK 0 946407 72 X 9.95. Pubdate 10-
05-1992
A Certain Koslowsk by Michael Augustin translated from the German by Hartmut Eing 0 946407
83 5 PBK £5.95 64 pages. Pub July 1992. Biographical prose pieces based on the fictional life of
a radical humanitarin thinker. Black literary humour.
The Fire in the Tree by Donald Atkinson. 0 946407
84 3 PBK £5.95. 64 pages. 1990 Aldeburgh Prize-
winner. Poetry.

LITTLEWOOD ARC
The Nanholme Centre
Shaw Wood Road
Todmorden
Lancashire
OL14 6DA

LIVER AND LIGHTS
John Bentley
120 Goodrich Road
London
SE22 0ER. Tel 081 693 0952
Liver and Lights is the collective title for series of
books made by John Bentley since 1984. Since
1987 the series has increasingly concentrated on
depicting an invented parallel world inhabited by
vivid eccentric characters.
Liver and Lights No.10 'The Ginge'. 30pp 15 x 11
x 11cm 1990 handcoloured boxed (contains childs
toys and Berlin Wall fragments) ed 100 £30.00
Liver and Lights No.11 'The Beastmaster' (a
bestiary). 40pp carved wood covers letterpress hand
coloured ed 100 1992 £150.00
Liver and Lights No.12 'An Opera for Dog' (dog
turd and poem in box) 1992 ed 30 £20.

LIVERPOOL UNIVERSITY LIBRARY
Sydney Jones Library
PO Box 123
Liverpool

L69 3DA

LIVERPOOL & WRITERS
Edge Hill Library
Lodge Lane
Liverpool 8

LIVING ARCHIVE PUBLISHING
3 Stratford Road
Wolverton
Milton Keynes
MK12 5LJ
Individual and collectives of reminisences from the
Milton Keynes area; documentary arts hour-to-do-
it manuals; documentary play scripts; teachers' packs
based on local archive material.

MR A LI WAN PO
2 Cleaver Avenue
BELFAST
BT9 5JA

LIZZIE BOOKS
Rutland Road
Twickenham
TW2 5ER

LLANELLI WRITERS CIRCLE
c/o Carole Ann Smith
20 Rectory Close
Loughor
SWANSEA
SA4 2JU

LLANERCH PUBLISHERS
Derek Bryce
Llanerch Felinfach
Lampeter
Dyfed
SA48 8PJ. Tel. 0570 470567.
New books and facsimile reprints ancient/mediae-
val history legend literature esoteric/ancient wis-
dom.
Tao Te Ching Lao-Tzu translated by L. Wieger.
120pp Jan 1992 £4.95. Oriental wisdom.
Taliesin Poems translated by M. Pennak. 120pp
1989 1992 reprint £4.95. Ancient poetry.
Two Lives of Gilda translated by H. Williams.
120pp facsimile 1990/1992 reprint £4.95. History.

LLANGEITHO TIMES
Derlwyn Fach
Langeitho
Tregaron
SY25 6QU.
Subjects: Community Journalism. Children's Fic-
tion.
Books January to June 1991 - 1. Books July to
December 1991 - 2

LLANGORDA PRESS
40B Jessop Road
Walsall
WS1 3AS.
Subjects: Local History. Historical Biography.
Books January to June 1991 - 1

MR PETER M LLEWELYN

27 Eddison Road
AYLESBURY
Buckinghamshire
HP19 3TE

LOBSTER TELEPHONE
148 Humber Road South
Beeston
NOTTINGHAM
NG9 2EX
'Zine

LOCAL HISTORY PRESS
3 Devonshire Promenade
Lenton
NOTTINGHAM
NG7 2DS 0602 700369.
Publish Local History Magazine six times per annum - A national review & listings periodical with news, articles & free 50 word noticeboard for all subscribers. Also run a mail order bookshop & history-into-print service for self-publishing authors.

LOCAL HISTORY PUBLICATIONS/REPRINTS
316 Green Lane
London
SW16 3AS.
Subjects: Reprints and original books on London's local history. 15 books were published in one great rush in June 1991 all at £1.00 each.

LOCHAR PUBLISHING
8 The Holm
Moffat
DG10 9JU

LOCHINVAR WINDOWS LTD
Units 10 & 11 Albyn Ind. Est
Greendykes Road
BROXBURN
West Lothian
EH52 6PG 0506 854216

T. LOCKE MEMORIAL FUND:
Great Glen Foods
PO Box 10 Old Ferry Road
North Ballachulish
Fort William
PH33 6RZ.
Subjects: Health.
Books July to December 1991 -1

MR WALTER LOCKHART
16 Bristol Road
IPSWICH
IP4 4LP

LODDEN VALLEY BOOKS
Rex Hora
108 Chilcombe Way
Lower Earley
READING
RG6 3DB

K.R. LODGE SCHOOL OF MODERN LANGUAGES
AND EUROPEAN HISTORY

University of East Anglia
Norwich
NR4 7TJ.
Subjects: Indoor Games.

LOGASTON PRESS
Andy Johnson
Little Logaston
Woonton Almeley
Herefordshire
HR3 6QH. Tel 0544 6344
Started with books on Herefordshire and surrounding area covering walking history local people folklore etc. now encompassing natural history cookery South Wales photography. Essence is to take on books with people with whom we enjoy working.
Is It Still Raining In Aberfan? A Pit and its People by Melanie Doeland Martin Dunkenton ISBN 0 951024 9 9 9.95 history (ed) photography biography. 100 new photos (50 full page) 160pp.
Folklore of Hereford and Worcester by Roy Palmer. 288pp July 1992. ISBN 1 873827 02 4 8.95.
Coastal and Valley Walks in South Wales by Andrew Johnson. 80pp March 1992. ISBN 1 873827 01 6 £4.95.

MR PAUL SAMUEL LOMAX
108 Taplow
LONDON
NW3 3NX

THE LOMOND PRESS
R L Cook
4 Whitecraigs
Kinneswood
KINROSS
Scotland
KY13 7JI
Poetry

LONDON ARCHITECTURAL PRESS
37 Alfred Place
London
WC1E 7DP.
Subjects: Architecture.
Books July to December 1991 - 1

LONDON CALLING
(edit Daphne Ayles)
19 Chelsham Road
Clapham
London
SW4 6NR

LONDON CARTOON CENTRE
14 Conlan Street
LONDON
W10 5AR
Set up in the 1980s, the Centre offers womens' groups juniors, master classes etc in a 10 week vocational qualification (the only in Europe). Courses in all aspects of cartooning skills (finished art, life drawing, scripting, colouring, humour, comic book, comic strip, editorial cartoons and marketing self-publishing projects.

LONDON CYCLIST

London Cyclist Campaign
3 Stamford Street
LONDON
SE1 9NT

LONDON EARTH MYSTERIES CIRCLE
15 Freshwater Court
59a Crawford Street
LONDON
W1H 1HS

LONDON ICOM
18 Ashwin Street
London
E8 3DL

LONDON IRISH WOMEN'S CENTRE
59 Stoke Newington Church Street
London
N 16

J. LONDON
Coomless
Broughton-in-Tweeddale
Biggar
ML12 6QH.
Subjects: History of Education.
Books January to June 1991 - 1

LONDON LIGHTHOUSE
178 Lancaster Road
London
W11 1QT

LONDON MAGAZINE
30 Thurloe Place
London
S W 7

LONDON STAMP EXCHANGE
5 Buckingham Street
London
WC2N 6BS

UNIVERSITY OF LONDON
Institute of Commonwealth Studies
27-28 Russell Square
London
WC1B 5DS

LONDON VOICES
70 Holden Road
LONDON
N12 7DY

LONDON VOLUNTARY SERVICE COUNCIL
68 Chalton Street
London
NW1 1JR.
Subjects: History of Voluntary Service in London.
Books January to June 1991 - 4. Books July to
December 1991 - 4

LONDON WOMEN'S CENTRE
Wesley House
4 Wild Court
London

WC2B 5AU

F.W LONGBOTTOM
38 New Road
Childer Thornton
South Wirral
L66 5PX

MR PETER LONGBOTTOM
80 Campbell Crescent
EAST GRINSTEAD
West Sussex
RH19 1JS

LONGCROFT SCHOOL
Burton Road
Beverley
HU17 8EJ

LONGDALE PRESS
23/23 Ward, Royal Hospital
Chelsea
London
SW3 4SR

LONG DISTANCE WALKERS ASSOCIATION:
10 Park Side
Buckhurst Hill
IG9 5TB

LONGEVITY REPORT
West Towan House
Porthtowan
TRURO
Cornwall
TR4 8AX
J de Rivaz
Debates the use of science to extend human lifespan.
Free sample. Authors get free subscription to fol-
lowing volume. 20 pages A4, bimonthly. Subscrip-
tions 10.0 0 UK, 12.00 Europe, £13.00 USA.

MR G EDGELEY LONG
31 Hunt Road
Somerfield
CHRISTCHURCH
Dorset
BH23 3BW

MS JEAN LONG
Christ Church
OXFORD
OX1 1DP

PADRAIG LONG
Dun Mhuire
Dromcollogher
County Limerick
Republic of Ireland

(THE) LONGSTONE
37 Lowtherville Road
Ventnor
Isle of Wight
PO38 1AR

MR JAMES LONGWILL

608 Farm Road
Eaglescliffe
STOCKTON-ON-TEES
Cleveland
TS16 0DQ

LORACLE ENTERPRISES
BCM Loracle
LONDON
WC1N 3XX
Spreading knowledge of occult traditions

D P LORNE
33 Robert Road
SHEFFIELD
S8 7TL

LORN HOUSE PUBLICATIONS
80 Jane Street
Edinburgh
EH6 5HG

LOST DREAMS
Box 184
52 Call Lane
Leeds
W Yorks
LS1 6DT

Loughborough University
Transport Technology Department
Loughborough
LE11 3TU

BILLIE LOVE COLLECTION
3 Winton Street
Ryde
PO33 2BX.
Subjects: Poetry.
Books July to December 1991 - 1

LOVELY JOBLY (L J)
75 Lambeth Walk
London
SE11 6DX

SIR JOHN LOVERIDGE
The White House
82 Fitzjohn's Avenue
Hampstead
LONDON
NW3 6NP

MR ROLF LOVSTROM
Skovveien 22
N-0257 OSLO 2
NORWAY

CHRISTOPHER J LOWE
4 Brick Kiln Cottages
Boxford
Colchester
CO6 6NT

MR GEOFF LOWE
75 Newland Road
HULL

HU5 2DR

LOWLANDER PUBLICATIONS
592A Chatsworth Road
Chesterfield
S40 3JX

LOWNDES PUBLICATIONS
17 Lowndes Park
Driffield
YO25 7BE.
Subjects: Local History.
Books July to December 1991 - 1

MRS CLAIRE M LOWREY
22 South Street
Southsea
PORTSMOUTH
Hampshire
PO5 4DP

LRO BOOKS
The Hollies
Botesdale
Diss
IP22 1BZ.
Subjects: Military Road Vehicles. Humour. Civil
Road Vehicles. Books January to June 1991 - 3.

LUATH PRESS
Barr
Ayrshire
KA26 9TN Barr (046 586) 636
Publishers of Scottish books of all types in the three
languages of Scot land.
'Seven Steps in the Dark' by Bob Smith. 314pp.
original black and white illustrations. paperback.
8.95. ISBN 0 946487 21 9. Autobiography of a
Scottish miner.
'Barefeet and Tackety Boots' by Archie Cameron.
Black and white illustra tions paperback. £5.95.
ISBN 0 946487 17 0. A boyhood on Rhum. 'The
Crofting Years' by Francis Thompson. Original
black and white illust rations. £4.95. ISBN 0 946487
06 5. A history of crofting and the Crofting Wars of
1866.

MS JACKIE LUBEN
The Glade
Bullswater Common
Pirbright, WOKING
Surrey
GU24 0LY

MR ARTHUR LUKE
46 Whistler Street
Highbury
LONDON
N5 1NT

HYLDA LUMSDEN
St John's House
Heron's Ghyll
Uckfield
TN22 4BY

LUNDIN LADIES GOLF CLUB

162

Woodielea Road
Lundin Links
Leven
KY8 6AR.
Subjects: Lundin Ladies Golf Club 1891.
Books January to June 1991 - 1

MR W W LUND
14a Wissett Way
LOWESTOFT
Suffolk
NR32 4DL

MR BRIAN LUNN
Aircraft Down, Hardwick Publications
36 Darrington Road, East Hardwick
PONTEFRACT
West Yorkshire
WF8 3DS

MR MIKE LUNN
24 Howburgh Court
Cheshunt
Hertfordshire
EN8 0UL

THE LUTE SOCIETY
103 London Road
OLDHAM
OL1 4BW

MR MARTIN LUTZE
Am Weidenkamp 17
4920-LEGMO/ENTRAP
GERMANY

LYFROW TRELYSPEN
Roseland
Gorran
ST AUSTELL
Cornwall
Historical work about Cornwall, biographies, local
history, etc Anthony Harrison-Barber. 'Thomas
Holloway: Victorian Philanthropist'. 1990. ISBN 0
9514510 1 4. Paperback. 66 pages. £4.75. Biogra-
phy.
Dr James Whetter. 'The History of Gorran Haven.
Part 1. 0 to 1800 AD'. 1990 IS BN 0 9514510 2 2.
Paperback, 140 pages. £7.75. Local history. Dr
James Whetter. 'The History of Gorran Haven: Part
2. 1800 to present day'. 19 91. ISBN 0 9514510 3
0. Paperback, 164 pages. £9.50. Local history.

LY-IF PRODUCTIONS
15 Tennyson Avenue
Motspur Park
New Malden
KT3 6LY.
Subjects: Legends.
Books July to December 1991 - '1

THE LYMES PRESS
'Greenfields'
Agger Hill Finney Green
Newcastle under Lyme
Staffordshire
ST5 6AA 0782 750387
Poetry written in Europe between 1590 to date.

The Life and Selected works of Richard Barnfield,
1574 - 1627. F. Clitheroe, editor. 47 pp. 1992. 5.00.
Life, bibliography and selections from the Eliza-
bethan poet and acquaintance of Shakespeare.
'Valentines'. Germain Nouveau. 22p. 1991. £2.
Life, bibliography and translations from French
poet contemporary and friend of Rimbaud and
Verlaine. 'For an anniversary'. Laura Pavia. 22pp.
1990. £2. Life and translations from contemporary
Italian poetess, winner of Prix Minerva.

MR BRYAN LYNAS
Cami de Sarria 72a
07010 Palmade Mallorca
Spain

MR C A LYNCH
17 Glendor Gardens
Mill Hill
LONDON
NW7 3JY

KEVIN LYNCH
P.O. Box 7
Barnstaple
Devon
EX31 1UN.
Publisher of money-making and spare-time busi-
ness opportunity guides. Prices include postage and
packing.
The Small Businessman's Advertising Guide to
Greater Profits £7.95. Start and Build a Successful
Business by James Carr £7.95 How to be a Travel
Writer 2.00

STANLEY LYONS
4 the Rise
Shipton Oliffe
Cheltenham
GL54 4JQ.
Subjects: Literature.
Books January to June 1991 - 1

MR PETER LYSSIOTIS
33 Lorraine Drive
East Burwood
MELBOURNE
AUSTRALIA Vic 3151

[M]

M PRESS
45 Stafford Road
Brighton
BN1 5PE.
Subjects: Art.
Books July to December 1991 - 1

M5 PRESS (THE LOOKER)
Winscombe Farm Studio
WINSCOMBE
Avon
BS25 1BT
Magazine

MR MAATS
27 Barclay Square
Metric Optic Publishing

LONDON
W1X 5HA

MR MACDONALD
BIDDLES
Walnut Tree House
Woodbridge Park Estate
GU1 1DA

MAGONIA
Mr John Rimmer
John Dee Cottage, 5 James Terrace
Mortlake Churchyard
LONDON
SW14 8HB

MS MARIANNE MACDONALD
47 Tetherdown
Muswell Hill
LONDON
N10 1NH

MR RONALD MACDONELL
Right Angle Print
Easter Kinkell
DINGWALL
Ross-shire
IV7 8HY

PROFESSOR R MACGREGOR-HASTIE
Osaka Gakuin University
Kishibe Suita
OSAKA
JAPAN

MR W MACGREGOR
145 Lower Granton Road
EDINBURGH
EH5 1EX

MACH II PLUS
51A Sutton Court Road
Hillingdon
Uxbridge
UB10 9HR

MR A E MACINNES
135 Old Greenock Road
BISHOPTON
Renfrewshire
PA7 5DL

MR EDWARD MACKENZIE
AB Consultants
120 Wooton Street
LONDON
SE1 8LY

GILLIAN F MACKENZIE
Nether Kingshill
Kingswells
Aberdeen
AB1 8QB

NOELA M MACKENZIE
29 Lyndhurst
Ashurst

Skelmersdale
WN8 6UH

MACLAIN PRESS
BCM Box 6732
London
WC1N 3XX.
Subjects: Biography.
Books July to December 1991 - 1

MACLEAN PRESS
60 Aird Bhearnadail
Portree
Isle of Skye

MRS H D MACLEAN
Tigh-an-Duin
Ellenabeich, Easdale
OBAN
Argyll
PA34 4RF

J W MADGIN
110 GAston Way
SHEPPERTON
Middlesex
TW17 8EY

MAGMA
Caeu Gwynion
Llansadwrn
Porthaethwy
LL59 5SR

MAGPIES NEST
Bal Saini
176 Stoney Lane
Sparkhill
Birmingham
B12 8AN

MAJOR BOOK PUBLICATIONS
The Homestead, Burrator Road
Dousland
Yelverton
PL20 6NE

MAKE YOUR MARK
71 Goodram Gate
YORK

MAKING WAVES/BULLS HEAD GATE
Anthony Selbourne
PO Box 226
Guildford
GU3 1EW.
Poetry imprint which also organises and publishes
art/poetry exhibitions/portfolios. Exhibition for
1993 features eight Scandinavian Poets illustrated
by way of etchings by John Tatchell Freeman.
Ahab's Dead - Michael Paul Hogan. 30pp ISBN 0
9511290 9 0 2.00. Poetry.
Song Abroad -English version of German and
Chinese song cycles translated by Lawrence James.
40pp ISBN 0 873918 01 1 £3.00. Alum Rock -
Michael Croshaw. ISBN 0 873918 02 X £3.00.
Poetry.

164

THE MALAPROP PRESS
30 Wiberforce Road
LONDON
N4 2SW

MALCOLM PRESS
18 Princess Way
Swansea
SA1 3LW

MR LEONARD MALCOLM
Royal College of G Ps
14 Princes Gate
Hyde Park
LONDON
SW7 1PU

MALDON GOLF CLUB
Beeleigh
Maldon
CM9 6LL.
Subjects: Sport.
Books July to December 1991 - 1

MALICE AFORETHOUGHT PRESS
328 Brettenham Road
LONDON
E17 5AU

MALLETT AND BELL
3 College Close
Coltishall
NR12 7DT

MRS MOLLY MALLON
PO Box 1332
SWINDON
SN4 0TE

H. MALTRAVER AND T. KAY
PO Box 1295
Bath
BA1 6TJ.
Subjects: Architectural salvage.
Books July to December 1991 - 1

MAM
21 Avenue Ch de Tollenaere
B-1070 BRUXELLES
BELGIUM

MAMMAL SOCIETY
Dexter House
2 Royal Mint Court
London
EC3N 4XX

T D MAN & A BARON
c/o 93a Venner Road
Sydenham
London
SE26 5HY 081 659 7713
Small Press; poetry and non-fiction. Pro-Forma orders only accepted for single copies. Trade terms for 10 copies or more only.

The Wickedest Woman in the World. A Baron. September 1991. 20 pages non-fiction. £1.50 1 871473 90 X. study in sexual perversion. Pirates on the Airwaves. N. Grant and others. biography of the first pirate radio station in London. 28 pages; non-fiction. £2.00. A4. 1 871473 60 8
Bonnie and Clyde (Poems). Bonnie Parker. the original poems by the gangster's moll. December 1990. £1.50. 16 pages B5. 1 871473 55 1.

MANAGEMENT UPDATE
99A Underdale Road
Shrewsbury
SY2 5EE.
Subjects: Canals. Local Walks.
Books January to June 1991 - 1. Books July to December 1991 - 1

MANCHESTER F P
Mr Andrew Caesar
Paragon Mill
Jersey Street
MANCHESTER
M4 6FP

MANCHESTER POETS
122 Petersburg Road
Edgeley Park
STOCKPORT
Cheshire
SK3 9RB
Tours, performances, workshops, competitions and anthologies.

UNIVERSITY OF MANCHESTER
Department of Sociology
Manchester
M13 9PL

MANDEVILLE PRESS
Peter Scupham
2 Taylor's Hill
Hitchin
SG4 9AD
Fine printer

MANDRAKE
Mogg Morgan
P.O. Box 250
Oxford
OX1 1AP. Tel 0865 243671
Specialists in Magick and new writing which is radical and subversive. One of the leading publishers of material which includes Crowley Tantrism Sexology Magical art and the Occult.
Shadow Matter and PSI-phenomena by G.D. Wasserman. ISBN 1 869928 32 6 £7.95.
Pan's Daughter - The Magical World of Rosaleen Norton by Nevill Drury. ISBN 1 869928 31 8 £7.95.
Visual Magick - Manual of Freestyle Shamanism by Jan Fries. ISBN 1 869928 18 0 £6.99.

MANDRAKE PRESS LTD
Essex House, Thame, Oxon, OX9 3LS
084 421 7567/Fax: 084 421 6420
'Now for Reality; Austin Osman Spare and Aleister Crowley; edition of 1000; hardback; 1 872736 01 7; £25. A fusion of the artistry and occult vision of

two of the twentieth century's greatest magicians. 'The Forbidden Lecture'; Gilles de Rais by Aleister Crowley; edition of 1000 copies; hardback; £12.95; 1 872736; this volume contains Crowley's revised text for his 'Banned Lecture' which he was to have delivered to the Oxford University Poetry Society. 'The Rites of Eleusis'; Aleister Crowley; edition of 1000 copies; hardback; £35; 1 872736 02 5; "Ceremonial Magic as the gateway to Ecstasy" (The Sketch, 1910).

W.S. MANEY
Hudson Road
Leeds
LS9 7DL.
Subjects: Mediaeval Art.
Books January to June 1991 - 2

MANNA PUBLISHING
4 Short Lane
Ingham
Lincoln.
Subjects: Poetry.
Books July to December 1991 - 2

MANNAMEDIA
Geoff Hollans
77A Mannamead Road
Plymouth
PL3 4SX.
Subjects: Philosophy.
Books July to December 1991 - 1

MR P MANNION
23 Parkfield Crescent
Kimpton
HITCHIN
Hertfordshire
SG4 8EQ

MANX EXPERIENCE
10 Tromode Close
Douglas
Isle of Man

THE MANY PRESS
15 Norcott Road
London
N16 7BJ Tel: 081 806 5723
Established in 1975, The Many Press publishes books and pamphlets of new poetry; around seventy items have appeared to date.
The Gifted Child by W G Shepherd. Collection of poems. 36 pages, ISBN 0 907326 19 6, Price 3.50
The Metro Poems by Peter Hughes. Collection of poems. 42 pages. Cover an original print by Peter Tingey. ISBN 0 907326 21 8. Pricee 3.50 The Book, The Bay, The Breakfat Table by Jeremy Harding. Poems sequence. Cover an original print by Peter Tingey. ISBN 0 907326 22 6. Price 3.50

MAPLETREE PRIVATE PRESS
Wisteria, The List
Wickhambreaux
CANTERBURY
Kent
CT3 1RX

MAR MAGAZINE
Flat 1
81 Back Road East
St Ives
Cornwall
TR26
Eclectic poetry prose and graphics; the editors will publish only what surprises them and contributors remain anonymous. 40pp Issues 1 & 2 £1.00; Issues 3 & 4 - £1.50. Distributed by New River Project.

MARABY
10 Eastcote Lane
Hampton in Arden
Solihull
B92 0AS.
Subjects: Local Education History.
Books January to June 1991 - 1.

THE MARCAN CATAPHYSICAL JIHAD
The Occam Suite
The Marcan Building
28 Standard Avenue
Jaywick
Essex

PETER MARCAN PUBLICATIONS
31 Rowliff Road
High Wycombe
HP12 3LD.
Subjects: Religion. London History
Books July to December 1991 - 1

MR R A MARCHANT
69 Vale Road
ST LEONARDS-ON-SEA
East Sussex
TN37 6PT

THE MARCHANTS PRESS
Whispers
Great Oakley
HARWICH
Essex
CO12 5AH

MARGIN
The Square Inch
Lower Granco Street
Dunning
PERTH
PH2 0SQ

MARIDIAN PUBLICATIONS
9 Old Pier Street
Walton-on-the Naze
Children's Fiction

MARINA PRESS
11 Heol Tre Dwr
Waterton
Bridgend
CF31 3AJ.
Subjects: Poetry.
Books January to June 1991 - 1

MARINE DAY PUBLISHERS

Mr Tony Durrant
64 Cotterill Road
SURBITON
Surrey
KT6 7UN
Publishers of local history books; book production
managers; typographical desig ners.
Malden - Old and New. By S Day. 80 pages paper-
back. 1990. £7.50 Malden - Old and New Revisited.
By S Day. 80 pages paperback 1991. £7.50.

MARINE TECHNOLOGY DIRECTORATE
19 Buckingham Street
London
WC2N 6EF

MARISCAT PRESS
3 Mariscat Road
Glasgow
G41 4ND.
Subjects: Poetry.
Books January to June 1991 - 1

MARITIME INFORMATION PUBLICATIONS
147 St. Pancras
Chichester
PO19 1SH.
Subjects: Civil Ships.
Books July to December 1991 - 1

A. MARK PUBLISHING COMPANY
Olsover House
43 Sackville Road
Newcastle-upon-Tyne
NE6 5TA.
Subjects: Music.
Books July to December 1991 - 2

STRATEGIC MARKETING SERVICES
15 Millers Yard
Mill Lane
Cambridge
CB2 1RQ

MARKET MONITOR LTD
Monkton House
Speen
Princes Risborough
Bucks

MARLBOROUGH BOOKS:
Marlborough Books Wholesalers
6 Milton Road
Swindon
SN1 5JG.
Subjects: Sport.
Books July to December 1991 - 3

MARLON PUBLICATIONS
P.O. Box 3
Beccles
NR34 0DF.
Subjects: Literature.
Books July to December 1991 - 1

MARLOW DURNDELL
18-20 Chapel Street

Titchmarsh
Kettering
NN14 3DA.
Subjects: Biography.
Books July to December 1991 - 1

MARREB
64 Ambler Thorn
Bradford
BD13 2DJ.
Subjects: Biography.
Books January to June 1991 - 1

MR BERNARD MARRIOTT
47 Western Park Road
LEICESTER
LE3 6HQ

BOB MARSDEN
108 Bankes Road
Small Heath
Birmingham
B10 9PS

MARTELLO BOOKSHOP
26 High Street
Rye
TN31 7JJ.
Subjects: Literary Biography.
Books July to December 1991 - 1

MR ANTHONY MARTIN
28 Nestor Road
LEICESTER
LE2 6RD

MR D MARTIN
32 Maidstone Road
RAINHAM
Kent
ME8 0DQ

J MARTIN
64 Warley Road
HAYES
Middlesex
UB4 0QN

MS JANET MARTIN
Laugton Villa Green
TUNBRIDGE WELLS
TN3 0BB

MS ROSEMARY MARTIN
98 Doyle Gardens
Willesden
LONDON
NW10 3JR 081 961 2478

MR T MARTIN
The Pastures
Crow Lane, Reed
ROYSTON
Hertfordshire
SG8 8AE

MR D C MASSEY

167

31 New Street
UTTOXETER
Staffordshire
ST14 7QS

MASS-OBSERVATION ARCHIVE
T Harrison
The Library
University of Sussex
Brighton
BN1 9QL.
Subjects: The Mass-Observation Archive.
Books July to December 1991 - 1

MAST PUBLICATIONS
31 Beaufort Gardens
Knightsbridge
LONDON
SW3 1QH
Specialising in books about the gay community
with a persentage of profits going to AIDS charities.
Also Publishing poetry and short story anthologies.
Performance-Letting the Boys Speak out due for
publication June 1992

MASTER FINANCIAL SERVICES
404/406 Finchley Road
LONDON
NW2 2HR

RAYMOND MASTERS
129 Park Road
Chandler's Ford
Eastleigh
SO5 1HT.
Subjects: General Fiction.

EUGENE MATHEWS
17 Harbour Street
Girvan
KA26 9AJ

MATHEMATICAL ASSOCIATION
259 London Road
Leicester
LE2 3BE

MATRIX PRESS
2 Stafford Mansins
Albert Bridge Road
LONDON
SW11

MATRIX FEMINIST ARCHITECTURAL CO-
OP LTD
The Printhouse
18 Ashwin Street
London
E8 3DL

MATRIX MARKETING
Ravenscraig
Charles Hill
TILFORD
Surrey
GU10 2AU

A. MATTHEW PUBLICATIONS
44 Royal Avenue
Calcot
Reading
RG3 5UP.
Subjects: Historical Bibliographies. Bibliographies.
Books January to June 1991 - 7. Books July to
December 1991 - 10

MAWALANA CENTRE
34 Hollytree Close
Inner Park Road
London
SW19 6EA.
Subjects: Biography.
Books July to December 1991 - 1

MAWLANA CENTRE
34 Hollytree Close
Inner Park Road
Wimbledon
LONDON
SW19 6EA

MAX
c/o Jurgen Wolff
16 Huguenot House
19 Oxendon Street
London
SW1Y 4EH

MAXIPRINT
Kettlestring Lane
Clifton Moor
York
YO3 8XF.
Subjects: Snickelways of York.
Books July to December 1991 - 1

MRS JENNIFER MAY
2 Cherry Tree Walk
Sarratt Lane
RICKMANSWORTH
Hertfordshire
WD3 6AF

MAYFIELD PUBLISHING
68 Main Road
Wybunbury
Nantwich
CW5 7LS

MAYFLOWER ENTERPRISES
54 St. Margaret's Road
Horsforth
Leeds
LS18 5BG.
Subjects: Music.
Books January to June 1991 - 1. Books July to
December 1991 - 1

MISS J MAYNARD
Flat 3 Carfax
Undercliff Drive
St Lawrence, VENTOR

168

Isle of Wight
PO38 1XG

MR ROBERT MAYNE
3 Billing Bear Lane
BINFIELD
Berkshire
RG12 5PU

MAYPOLE
57 Cowley Road
ILFORD
Essex
081 554 7258
Fiction, poetry, history, satire, humour.

MAYSDALE BOOKS
63 Fford Glyn
Coed-y-Glyn
Wrexham
LL13 7QW

M.B.S. PUBLICATIONS
10 Summerbridge Crescent
Eccleshill
Bradford
BD10 8BB.
Subjects: Poetry.

MR MARK MCANDREW
24 Pennine Road
Hazle Grove
STOCKPORT
Cheshire
SK7 5BG

MR MCARDLE
5a Lulworth Road
Birkdale
SOUTHPORT
PR8 2AS

C MCATEER
Top Flat
15 Alexander Grove
Finsbury Park
LONDON
N4

SIMON MCBRIDE PRINTS
P.O Box 31
Newton Abbot
TQ12 5XH

BERNARD MCCALL
120 Pontypridd Road
Barry
CF6 8L

NICK MCCANN
49a Crossman Street
Sherwood
Nottingham
NG5 2HR

MCCLUSKEY & ASSOCIATES
c/o Irish Typesetting & Publishing Co

Galway
Ireland

MS ELLEN MCCORMICK
390 Main Street
Nashua
NH 03060
United States of America

ELIZABETH MCDOUGALL
New Inn Farm
West End Lane
Henfield
BN5 9RF.
(see E. Warneford) Subjects: Warneford Family
History.
Books July to December 1991 - 1

MR PATRICK MCEVOY
8 Clintons Park
Downpatrick
Co Down
BT30 6NS

DR DOUGLAS M C MACEWAN
Volturna Press
52 Ormonde Road
HYTHE
Kent
CT21 6DW

MAUREEN MCGAURAN
41 Hillhead Crescent
Belfast
BT11 9FS.
Subjects: Biography.
Books July to December 1991 - 1

MR BRIAN MCGEE
3F2, 35 West Preston Street
EDINBURGH
EH8 9PY

EDDIE MCGRORY PUBLICATIONS
41 Sythrum Crescent
Glenrothes
KY7 5DG

THE MCGUFFIN PRESS
100 Balls Pond Road
LONDON
N1 4AJ

MR CONNOR MCHALE
65 Brighton Road
Rarhgar
DUBLIN 6
Ireland

K.L. MCHUGH
81 Hall Avenue
Aveley
South Ockendon
RM15 4LD.
Subjects: Historical Biography.
Books July to December 1991 - 1

169

MR NEIL MCINTOSH
96 Earl Bank Avenue
GLASGOW
G14 9DY

MR RONALD C MCINTOSH
28 Waverly Road
ST ALBANS
Hertfordshire
AL3 5PE

MR KEITH MCKIBBIN
Coolbrae
52 Castlewellan Road
Banbridge
Co Down
BT32 4JF

D. MCLEAN
Forest Bookshop
8 St. John Street
Coleford
GL6 8AR.
Subjects: Historical Biography. Biography.
Books January to June 1991 - 2

MR GORDON MCLELLAN
1 Greyhound Lane
Heol Sticil-Y-Beddau
Llantrisant
Mid Glamorgan
CF7 8BU

MS FIONA MCNANEY
1 Woodland Drive, Molesworth Road
COOKSTOWN
Co Tyrone
Northern Ireland
BT80 8PL

MONA MCNEE
2 The Crescent
Toftwood
Dereham
NR19 1NR.
Subjects: Children's Non-fiction.
Books July to December 1991 - 1

MS PERI MCQUAY
Westport
ONTARIO
Canada
K0G 1X0

MR CHRIS MCSHANE
5a Alandale Drive
PINNER
Middlesex
HA5 3UP

MR G J MCWHIRTER
52 Graham Road
LONDON
E8 1BZ

M.D.E. PUBLICATIONS

16 Hardwick Crescent
Sheffield
S11 8WB.
Subjects: Children's Fiction.

MEADOW BOOKS
Cynthia O'Neill
22 Church Meadow
Milton-under-Wychwood
Oxford
OX7 6JG. Tel 0998 381338.
Excellent insight into nursing at the turn of the
century. Picture reproductions of superb quality of
interest to all especially social historians. First book
now sold over 5 000 copies - 'A Picture of Health'.
A Picture of Health by Cynthia O'Neill.
More Pictures of Health by Cynthia O'Neill. Both of
hospitals and nursing at the turn of the century. Well
illustrated.

MEADOW BOOKS
22 Church Meadow
Milton-under-Wychwood
Oxford
OX7 6JG

INTERNATIONAL MECCANOWOMAN
The Malt House
Church Lane
Streatley
Reading
RG8 9HT 0491 873001
Magazine for Meccano enthusiasts of all ages in 17
countries worldwide. Published annually since May
1988. Thrice yearly from Jan 1992. 'International
Meccanowoman' Ed John Westwood. 24pp (May
91) with line drawings of new Meccano models &
mechanisms. £3.00 plus P & P. Meccano is in
revival worldwide!

MEDIAIR MARKETING SERVICES
72 High Street
Poole
Dorset
BH15 1DA

THE MEDIA STORE
PO Box 73
West PDO
NOTTINGHAM
NG7 4DQ

MEDI THEME
Medical Philately Study Group
Tom Wilson Hon. Vice President
162 Canterbury Road
Ashford Kent
TN24 9QD. Tel. Ashford 0233 623
Medi Theme is the quarterly journal of the group
which promotes communication between collec-
tors of medical philately. It has 240 members in 24
countries. The annual subscription is 8.50.

MEDIUM PUBLISHING CO
1a Clumber Street
Hull
HU5 3RH

170

MEETING HOUSE PRESS
24 Pitreavie Road
Cosham
Portsmouth
PO6 2ST.
Subjects: Science Fiction.
Books July to December 1991 - 1

MR JOHN MEIER
61 Keys Park
Parnwell
PETERBOROUGH
PE1 4SN 0733 314758

MR ROLAND MEIGHAN
113 ASrundel Drive
Bramcore Hills
Beeston
NOTTINGHAM
NG9 3FQ

MR DAVID L MELL
5 Greenacre Close
Pocklington
YORK
YO4 2US

MELLEDGEN PRESS
71 Thornbury Road
Southbourne
Bournemouth
BH6 4HH. Tel 0233 623642.
Melledgen Press specialises in transport historical
economic technological and related topographical
works aimed at an academic and university reader-
ship but also accessible to the more general but
interested reader. Southern England's local and
regional history is the other main strand.
Contractors' Lines by L. Popplewell. 84pp 1988
ISBN 0 906637 18 X. Pirate Sea and Studland by L.
Popplewell. 60pp 1991 ISBN 0 906637 21 X.
Records of Slanage by N. Haysom. 42pp 1992 ISBN
0 906637 22 8.

MELLEDGEN PRESS
71 Thornbury Road
Southbourne
Bournemouth
BH6 4HH.
Subjects: Historical,
Criminology.

MEMES
Norman Joe
c/o 38 Molesworth Road
Plympton
Plymouth Devon
PL7 4NT.
Once described as 'the quintessence of the small
press counterculture' (BBR) Memes offers a chal-
lenging blend of contemporary literature graphics
reviews and comment. Smartly-produced and mus-
cle-packed with meaning costs just £2 for a sample
issue; £5 for a 3-issue subscription Memes #5 (52pp
May 1991)
Memes #6 (44pp December 1991)
Memes #7 (44pp June 1992)

MEN-AN-TOL STUDIO
Bosullow
Newbridge
Penzance
Cornwall

THE MENARD PRESS
8 The Oaks
Woodside Avenue
London
N12 8AR 081 446 5571
Menard may be returning to active publishing after
a phase of relative dormancy. 5-7 new titles to be
announced in Autumn

MR A J MENDES
Ashfield House
Sutton Road, Huttoft
ALFORD
Lincolnshire
LN13 9RH

MENDIP PUBLISHING
High Street
Castle Cary
BA7 7AN

MENTOR STUDIO
399-401 Strand
London
WC2R 0RB.
Subjects: Music.
Books January to June 1991 - 1

MR JULIAN MENZ
Top Flat
20 Homefield Road
Wimbledon
LONDON
SW19 4QF

MERCATOR LANGUAGE SERVICES
1 Tan Hinon
Old Hall
LLANIDLOES
Powys
SY18 6PR 05512 3845
Services offered include editing, proof-reading (BS
5261), ghost-writing, translation and rewriting from
French and German. Also includes training for
verbal pr esentations, interviews and meetings.

MR EDMUND MERCER
Cremer Press
26 Whalley Banks
BLACKBURN
Lancashire
BB2 1NV 0254 661208

MERCIA CINEMA SOCIETY
19 Pinders Grove
Wakefield
WF1 4AH.
Subjects: History of Cinema.
Books January to June 1991 - 1. Books July to
December 1991 - 2

MERCIAN MYSTERIES
2 Cross Hill Close
Wymeswold
Loughborough
LE12 6UJ

MERDON MARQUE
11 Swanton Gardens
Chandlers Ford
Eastleigh
SO5 1TP.
Subjects: Biography.
Books July to December 1991 - 1

MRS BRIDGET MEREDITH
The Old Quarry House
Nettlestead
MAIDSTONE
Kent
ME18 5HU

MERE PSEUD
Gareth Gordon
PO Box 148
BELFAST
BT1
Magazine providing a voice for alternative music
scene in Belfast and Ireland.

MERIDIAN BOOKS
Peter Groves
40 Hadzor Road
Oldbury
Warley
B68 9LA. Tel 0214 294397
A home-based business publishing 4-5 books a year
on walking local guides regional guides and local
history.
Streetwise: Street Names in and Around Birming-
ham by Vivien Bird. 104pp 44 b/w photos 1991
paperback ISBN 1 869922 11 5 £3.95 Exploring
Stratford-upon-Avon by Enid Colston. Paperback
48pp 37 b/w photos 1991 ISBN 1 869922 10 7
£2.25.
Blue Coat: A History of the Blue Coat School
Birmingham by John Myhill. Cased 152pp 31 photos (7 in colour) ISBN 1 869922 14 X £11.95.

MERIVALE EDITIONS
Peter Sampson
14 Merivale Road,
Putney,
London SW15 2NW
081 785 9034
Merivale Editions publish prints and portfolios by
contemporary British artists and illustrators. These
include: Edward Bawden, John Bellany, Elizabeth
Blackadder, Edgar Holloway, Alan Powers and
Robin Tanner.

MERRI-MIMES PRESS
21A St Johns Wood High Street
London
NW8 7NG

MERSEYSIDE ASSOCIATION OF WRITERS
12 Aspinall Street
Precot

Merseyside.
Subjects: Poetry
Books January to June 1991 - 2

MERTHYR TYDFIL HERITAGE TRUST
Ynsfach Engine House
Ynsfach Road
Merthyr Tydfil
CF48 1AG.
Subjects: Local Transport and Travel.
Books July to December 1991 -1

MESMERISM
c/o Mark McKay
341 Oldham Road
Middleton
MANCHESTER
M24 2DN

R.R. MESTER
2 Dolanog Villas
Machynlleth
SY20 8AS.
Subjects: Fiction General.
Books July to December 1991 - 1

METHOUDINGLE
9 Allard Gardens
Clapham
LONDON
SW4

METRO ENTERPRISES
48 Southcliffe Drive
Baildon
Shipley
WF17 0HS

MEVALYN DEFINITIONS
Vic Baxter
77a Fountain Road
ABERDEEN
Scotland
AB2 4EA

MEYN MAMRO
Cheryl Straffon
51 Cam Bosavern St. Just
Penzance
Cornwall
TR19 7QX. Tel. (0736) 787612
Specialises in books and booklets on the sacred sites
and ancient ways of Cornwall including earth ener-
gies ley paths Cornish prehistory and culture mega-
lithic mysteries and legends and folklore.
The Earth Mysteries Guide to Ancient Sites in West
Penwith by Cheryl Straffon. 52pp 1992 ISBN 0
9518859 0 1 2.95.
Cornwall - Land of the Goddess by Cheryl Straffon
(to be published early 1993).
Meyn Mamvro journal. 28pp published 3 x annu-
ally. ISSN 0966-5877 £1.50.

M.H PUBLICATIONS
17 West Heath Drive
London

172

NW11 7QG

MICAWBER PUBLICATIONS
64 St. Mary's Street
Bridgnorth
WV16 4DR.
Subjects: Art.
Books January to June 1991 - 1

TIMOTHY J. MICKLEBURGH
Stavelea
Birchcliffe Road
Hebden Bridge
HX7 8DB.
Subjects: Poetry.
Books July to December 1991 - 1

MICKLETON METHODIST CHURCH COUN-
CIL:
W.A. Warmington
Westington Corner
Chipping Camden
GL55 6DW.
Subjects: History of Mickleton Methodist Church.
Books January to June 1991 - 1.

MICROBRIGADE
74 Lodge Lane
LONDON
N12 8JJ

MICROPROC DESIGN & PRINT
71 Commercial Road
Kirkstall
LEEDS
LS5 3AT

MICROSYSTER
c/o Wesley House
4 Wild Court
London
WC2B 5AU

MIDDLE EAST LIBRARIES COMMITTEE
Diane Ring
Middle East Centre
St. Anthony' College
Oxford
OX2 6JF. Tel 0865 59651 Extn.
Research guides to the bibliography of the Middle
East
Introductory Guide to Middle Eastern and Islamic
Bibliography by Paul Auchterlonie. 1990 ISBN 0
94889 04 7 9.50.
Middle Eastern Photographic Collections in the
UK by Gillian Grant. Hardback 222pp 1989 ISBN
0 94889 04 7 £25.00.
Official Publications on the Middle East: A Selec-
tive guide to the Statistical Sources by C.H. Bleaney.
32pp 1985 no ISBN £5.25.

MIDDLESBOROUGH FREE WRITERS
30 Dinting Close
Peterlee
Co Durham
SR8 2NY

JUDY MIDDLETON
22 Mile Oak Gardens
Portslade
Brighton
BN41 2PH.
Subjects: History of Education.
Books January to June 1991 - 1

MR K MIDDLETON
50 Fairview Road
Penn
WOLVERHAMPTON
WV4 4TE

MR PAR MIDDLETON
80 Lansdowne Avenue
LEIGH-ON-SEA
Essex
SS9 1LL

MR S J MIDDLETON
43 Keats House
Churchill Gardens
LONDON
SW1V 3HZ

MIDDLESBOROUGH FREE WRITERS
30 Dinting Close
Peterlee
DURHAM
SR8 2NY

MID KIRK OF GREENOCK
Cathcart Square
Greenock
Renfrewshire.
Subjects: Local History.

MIDNIGHT IN HELL
The Cottage
Smithy Brae
Kilmacolm
Renfrewshire
PA13 4EN

MID-SOMERSET EARTH FIRST
PO Box 23
5 High Street
GLASTONBURY
Somerset
BA6 9DP

MIKE R.L PUBLICATIONS
28 Windermere Drive
Adlington
Chorley
PR6 9PD

MILEPOST PUBLICATIONS
39 Kilton Glade
Worksop
S81 0PX

MR SIMON MILES
282 Derby Road
Lenton
NOTTINGHAM

NG7 1PZ
Newsletter,
Archangel for the congregationalists of William
Blake, see also 'Dragonheart'.

(THE) MILITANT
c/o 47 The Cut
London
SE1 8LL

MILITANT PUBLICATIONS
3/13 Hepscott Road
London
E9 5HB

MILITARY HISTORY HERITAGE BOOKS
Robert Downie
95 Hassell Street
Newcastle
Staffs.
ST5 1AX. Tel. 0782 723329. Fax
Specialist history and military publications particularly history of Staffordshire Shropshire and Cheshire. New authors wanted. Help and advice available
to would be authors living in the region. The Pot-
teries Martyrs by Robert Anderson. Available now.
80pp illustrated ISBN 0 9519048 0 9 £3.95. History
general. Stafford Gaol by William Payne. Due 30-
9-92. 120pp illustrated £4.95. History true crime.

MR R MILLEN
6 Mumby Close
NEWARK
Nottinghamshire
NG24 1JE

DAVID T. MILLER
23 Main Street
Pathhead
EH37 5PZ.
Subjects: Art.
Books July to December 1991 - 1

MR JAMES MILLER
St Catherines College
OXFORD
OX1 3UJ

MILLERS DALE PUBLICATIONS
Gerald Ponting
7 Weaver's Place
Chandler's Ford
Eastleigh Hants
SO5 1TU. Tel 0703 261192
An imprint introduced by Gerald Ponting of
Charlewood Press to publish detailed How To...
manuals for sale by mail order.
How To Run A Successful Auction of Promises G.
Ponting. ISBN 0 9517423 0 2 64pp 15 inch p&p
How To Get It Into Print G. Ponting 80pp 10 inch
p&p.

MILLGATE PUBLISHING
48 Hill Carr Road
Rawtenstall
Rossendale
BB4 6AW.
Subjects: Humour.

Books July to December 1991 - 1

MILLINGTONS DIRECT MARKETING
25 Alexandra Road
KINGSTON-UPON-THAMES
Surrey
KT2 6SD 081 546 9779

MR DAVID MILLS
c/o Parkgate Ltd, Midmoor House
Parkshot
RICHMOND
Surrey
TW9 2RG

MILNER AND HILL
3 Duneden House
Somerville Street
Crewe
CW2 7NS.
Subjects: Art.
Books July to December 1991 - 1

MIND
Nat Assn for Mental Health
22 Harley Street
London
W1N 2ED

MINORITIES RESEARCH GROUP
Dr. E. Ross-Langley
PO Box 1000,
St. Albans,
Herts AL3 5NY
0727 52801
Publications in Minorities filed, e.g. single mother-
hood; female homosexuality; British expatriates in
Spain; high-IQ children.
Send for catalogue describing your particualr inter-
ests: full- length books; short stories; magazines &c.

MINORITY RIGHTS GROUP
29 Craven Street
LONDON
WC2N 5NT

MINORITY RIGHTS GROUP
Alan Phillips
379 Brixton Road
London
SW9 7DE. Tel 071 978 9498
Publishes books and reports on human right minor-
ity rights and international affairs. Also publish
education resources.
Armenis and Karabagh: The Struggle for Unity
edited Christopher J. Walker. Paperback 176pp
ISBN 1 873194 00 5.
The Balkans: Minorities and States in Conflict by
Hugh Poulton. Paperback 256pp ISBN 1 873194
05 6.

MINX PRINTS
Simon Bond
Flat 3
34 Tremadoc Road
LONDON
SW4 7LL

174

MIRANDA PRESS
28 Fire Station Square
Salford
M5 4NZ.
Subjects: Biography.
Books July to December 1991 - 1

CHRIS MITCHELL
1/L, 11 Woodlands Drive
GLASGOW
G4 9EQ
Distributor of tape books.

MR TIM MITCHELL
44 Newton Avenue
LONDON
W3 8AL

W MITCHELL
Whetherly House
52 Shirley Drive
Hove
BN3 6UF

MR MIKE MITSON
8 Deans Drive
EDGEWARE
Middlesex
HA8 9NU

MODERN RHINE SEA SHIPS - RIVER SEA
TRANSPORT
Chris Cheetham
10 Galloway Drive
Teignmouth
Devon
TQ14 9UX. Tel. 0626 779488.
Publication every two years concerning European
river sea vessels their trades cargoes and routes.
Vital to a more environmentally friendly atmos-
phere when road transport will come to a grinding
halt in the near future! Contains articles plans
photos drawings.
Modern Rhine Sea Ships
Modern Rhine Sea Ships 1990
Modern Rhine Sea Traders

MR JACQUES MOLLER
Ensslin
Reawick
BIXTER
Shetland Isles
ZE2 9NJ

MOMENTUM
c/o Christine Stace
31 Alexandra Road
WREXHASM
Clwyd
LL13
Magazine for poetry and short stories.

MOMENTUM MAGAZINE
Almere Farm
Rossett
Clywd
Wales

LL12 0BY

MONDO COMIX
Lee Davis
35 Manly Dixon Drive
Enfield
Middlesex
EN3 6BQ. Tel. 0992 651891
Mondo Comix ... comic book fanzines featuring a
mix of superheroes satire comedy action-adventure
horror sci-fi and drama. All writers and artists are
aspiring to a professional standard and are allowed
to tell whatever style of story they see fit. Mondo
doesn't censor its contributors and we consider all
comers for possible inclusion in the title.
Mondo Comix monthly. 20pp £1.00. 12 issues per
year (photocopied) starting Aug. 92. Comic fanzine.
Passive Dreaming monthly?. 20pp 1.00?. 12 issues
(photocopy) comic fanzine. Launches: Oct 92?
Alien Love Stories quarterly. 20pp £1.00. 4 issues
(photocopy). Starting Nov 92. Comic fanzine.

MONKEY PRESS
36 Richmond Road
CAMBRIDGE
CB4 3PU

MONKSVALE PRESS
14 Monksvale Grove
Barrow-in-Furness
LA13 9JQ

MONOLITH PUBLICATIONS
9 Baggrave End
Barsby
Leicster
LE78 8RB 0664 840018
Still small and independent despite the need for
wider distribution; covering earth mysteries and
travellers of today; the two being linked; the new
green religion starts in the fields not in the super-
market. 'Build Your Own Stone Circle' by John
Harrison. 20pp ISBN 1 87 2525 008 £1.00. DIY
Guide. Humorous but also serious
'The Stonehenge Conflict' by John Harrison. 20pp
ISBN 1 872525 01 6. £1.00 experiences & opinions;
free festivals & travellers 1984-89 'Cropwords' by
John Harrison 20pp ISBN 1 872525 03 2 . £1.00. A
not of this earth mystery ? Crop circles UFOs
hippies Gods & governments.

MONOLITH/FULL CIRCLE
119 Brassey Road
London
NW6 2BB

MONTAG PUBLICATIONS
6 Minster Avenue
BEVERLEY
North Humberside
HU17 0NL
Specialist history and modern literature including
English/German parallel text publications and art
catalogues. Translation work and European market access consultancy undertaken. We
assistGerman authors and small publishers put their
work onto the English speaking market.

GEORGE GALLERY MONTAGUE
128 Lower Baggot Street
Dublin 2
Republic of Ireland

MONTENAY COMMUNITY WORKSHOP
49 Morrall Road
Sheffield
S5 9AJ

MALCOLM BERESFORD MONTGOMERY
26 Cambridge Road
Southampton
SO2 0RD.
Subjects: Stamp Collecting.
Books July to December 1991 - 1

MR HAROLD MONTON
c/o 119 Ebury Street
LONDON
SW1

ROYAL COMMISSION ON THE HISTORICAL
MONUMENTS
Shelley House
Acomb Road
York
YO2 4HB

MOONDRAGON PRESS
20 Linden Road
Birmingham
B30 1JS.
Subjects: Poetry.
Books July to December 1991 - 1

MOONSHINE
498 Bristol Road
Selly Oak
BIRMINGHAM

MOONSTONE
SOS The Old Station Yard
Settle
BD24 9RP
(editors: Talitha Clare Robin Brooks)

CHRISTINE MOORE
Whitehorn
Back Lane
Waldron
Heathfield
TN21 0NH.
Subjects: Stockbreeding.
Books January to June 1991 - 3

MOORLAND PUBLISHING COMPANY
Moor Farm Road
Airfield Estate
Ashbourne
DE6 1HD

MOORLEY'S PRINT & PUBLISHING
23 Park Road
Ilkeston
DE7 5DA

MR A G MORAN
27 Waldair Court
Bargehouse Road
LONDON
E16 2NH

LAURIE MORAN
67 Red Courts
Brandon
Durham
DH7 8QN.
Subjects: Local History.
Books January to June 1991 - 1

MR A J MORANT
302 Whitchurch Lane
EDGEWARE
Middlesex
HA8 6QX

MR ROLAND W MORANT
7 The Pike
NANTWICH
Cheshire
CW5 7AP

MORAY HOUSE PUBLICATIONS
Moray House College
Holyrood Road
Edinburgh
EH8 8AQ.
Subjects: Biography. Education. Social Sciences.
Books July to December 1991 -4

MORETO PUBLISHERS
18 Plympton Road
London
NW6 7EG.
Subjects: Political Science.
Books July to December 1991 - 2

MR DAVID MORGAN
44 Brooklands Park
CRAVEN ARMS
Shropshire
SY7 9RL

MORGAN PUBLISHING LINCOLN
26 May Crescent
Lincoln
LN1 1LP.
Subjects: Political Science.
Books July to December 1991 - 1

MR ROBERT MORGAN
72 Anmore Road
Denmead
PORTSMOUTH
PO7 6NT

MORGANS
30,32 Cardiff Road
CAERPHILLY
Mid Glamorgan
883280

MORGAN TECHNICAL BOOKS:

R.C. Pickernell
232 Stroud Road
Gloucester
GL4 0AU.
Subjects: General Fiction.
Books January to June 1991 - 1. Books July to
December 1991 - 1

MMORIARTY
Mr P Allen
1 Cedar Close
Langley Green
CRAWLEY
RH11 7SB

JOHN MORIN GRAPHICS
82a Gaffer's Row
Victoria Street
CREWE
CW1 2JH
Typesetting and page make-up on Macintosh computer. Scanning and OCR available. Short-run printing (minimum 25) at reasonable rates. Help and advice freely given.

KENNETH C MORLEY
121 Winslow Road
Wingrave
Aylesbury
HP22 4QB

MORNING STAR PUBLICATIONS
Alec Finlay
14 Clark Street
EDINBURGH
Scotland
EH8 9HX 031 667 7560
Publishers of the Morning Star Folios: letterpress editions featuring one poet a nd artist in collaboration. Published in editions of 200-350 copies, signed and numbered by the artists. Subscritpions: First Series and Second Series (8 issue s) £27.50. Second series: 16.00. Individual issues 5.00. Second Series: 2/1 TRAVEL SONG. By Peter dent. Illustrated by Susan Paterson; with an accompanying excerpt from Peter Dent's Handling the flower; some working notes on poetry.
2/2 Kurt Schwitters, Merzfolio: Poems trans. Jerome Rothenburgh a nd Pierre Joris. With '15th Merzgedichte in Memoriam Kurt Schwitters' by Jackso n Mac Low: and a song setting Country Life by Christopher Fox. Special poster i ssue.
2/3 Robert Lax, Poems. Illustrated by Anbdrew Bick; with an acco mpanying essay by David Miller.

MORRELL WYLYE HEAD
Wylye Head
Kilmington
BA12 6RD.
Subjects: Photography.
Books January to June 1991 - 2. Books July to
December 1991 - 2

MORRIGAN BOOK COMPANY
Gore Street
Killala Ballina
Co. Mayo
Republic of Ireland.

Subjects; Irish Mythology.
Books July to December 1991 - 1

MR CLIFFORD MORRIS
Flat 1, Francome House
Brighton Road
LANCING
Sussex

MR M MORRIS
146 Clifton Road
South Norwood
LONDON
SE25 6QA

S M MORRIS
22 Forresters Drive
WELWYN GARDEN CITY
Hertfordshire
AL7 2HW

WILLIAM MORRIS SOCIETY
Kelmscott House
26 Upper Mall
London
W6 9TA

MORROW AND CO.
Wharton House
Bungay
NR35 1EL

MORTAIN BOOKS LIMITED
Mr G H Bransby
43 Sutton Park Road
SEAFORD
East Sussex
BN25 1SJ 0323 895112

MR CHRIS MORVAN
Le Touzel
Les Hautes Mielles, Vale
Guernsey
Channel Islands

MOSAIC C/O NOTTS CO COUNCIL
Leis Serv Arts/Libraries
Trent Bridge Hse Fox Rd
W Bridgford
NOTTINGHAM
NG2 6BJ

BRIAN S MOSELEY
21 Pennycross Park Road
Plymouth
PL2 3NP

MOSS ROSE PRESS
41 Hardwick Avenue
Chepstow
NP6 5DS

MOTE PRESS
The Courtyard, 1 Dinsdale Place
Sandyford
Newcastle-upon-Tyne
NE2 1BD

MOUBRAY HOUSE PRESS
Tweeddale Court
14 High Street
Edinburgh
EH1 1TE

MOUNT SANDFORD PRESS
22 Nutgrove Park
Dublin 14
Republic of Ireland.
Subjects: History of Scout Troops.
Books January to June 1991 - 1.

MOURNE OBSERVER PRESS
Castlewellan Road
Newcastle
BT33 0JX.
Subjects: Railway History.

THE MOUSE THAT SPINS
Wharf Mill
WINCHESTER
Hampshire
SO23 9NJ
Publish Thundersqueak - a new clear look at magic
and occultism in today's world.

MOVING FINGER
70 Poplar Road
Bearwood
Smethwick
Warley
B66 4AN.
Subjects: Literature. Short Stories.
Books January to June 1991 - 2. Books July to
December 1991 - 1

MOVING TARGET
Suite 194
Winifred Villa
68 Northman Avenue
LONDON
N22 5EP

MOWGLI BOOKS
Suite 309
Canalot Studios, 222 Kensal Road
London
W10 5BN

MR ALBERTO MOYANO
Embajada De Espana
Oficina Comercial
Kircicegi Sok 3/1 G O P
06700 Ankara

MOYLURG WRITERS
Boyle Mill Road
Boyle
County Roscommon
Republic of Ireland

MOYOLA BOOK
c/o Hill House
Owenreagh
Draperstown

Magherafelt
BT45 7BG.
Subjects: Biography.
Books January to June 1991 - 1. Books July to
December 1991 - 2

MOYTURA PRESS
3 The Dale, Stillorgan Grove
Stillorgan
County Dublin
Republic of Ireland

M.R.M. ASSOCIATES
322 Oxford Road
Reading
RG3 1AD.
Subjects: Poetry.
Books July to December 1991 - 1

M S PRESS
PO Box 464
BRADFORD
West Yorkshire
BD8 7SJ

MUILEACH PUBLICATIONS
fao F Langford, Glenleedle
Salen, Aros
ISLE OF MULL
Argyll
PA72 6JL

MS ANN MUIR
1 St Algar's Yard
West Woodlands
FROME
Somerset

MUIRALL PUBLICATIONS
Lane House
Higher Bockhampton
DORCHESTER
Dorset
DT2 8QH
Poetry, short stories, poem cards, children's poetry
and stories. Wet and Silly Willy Walking by John
Muir. 46 pages illustrated paperback. P.P.C £2.99.
Humorous story in poetry form.
Kid's Shiff (The Story of Brockly) by John Muir. 28
pages paperback.£2.10. A short story about a lonely
badger and childrens poems.
The Gifts of Wood by John Muir. 20 pages paper-
back. £2.50. Selection of poetry by Dorset poet John
Muir.

MULBERRY PRESS
Lionel Barnard
9 George Street
BRIGHTON
BN2 1RH
Dolls House; doll and teddy bear books for collec-
tors. Original works and reprints. Also specialist
booksellers in above subjects. Mail order and retail.
Book importers. Consultants to other publishers on
these subjects.

MR M MULLAN
7 Stable Walk

Strawberry Vale
East Finchley
LONDON
N2 9RD

MR JAMES MULLIGAN
25 Crummock Gardens
Colindale
LONDON
NW9 0DE

MULTISCOPE BOOKS
2 Mead Road
Torquay
TQ2 6TE.
Subjects: Health and Hygiene.
Books January to June 1991 - 1

MS SONDRA MUNDLE
4 Normansmead
Stonebridge
LONDON
NW10 0QH

MS PAT MUNGROO
18 Kings Road
CAMBRIDGE
CB3 9DY

D.W. MUNNINGS
2A Bedford Place
Southampton
SO1 2BY.
Subjects: Health and Hygiene.
Books January to June 1991 - 1

MUNROE BOOKS
1 Chapel Cottages
Kennington Road
Ashford
TN24 0TF.
Subjects: Children's non-fiction.
Books January to June 1991 - 1

MURRAY CARDS INTERNATIONAL
51 Watford Way
London
NW4 3JH

MUSEUM DEVELOPMENT COMPANY
Premier Suites
Exchange House
494 Midsummer Boulevard
Milton Keynes
MK9 2EA.
Subjects: Museum Development Company.
Books January to June 1991 - 1. Books July to
December 1991 - 1

MUSEUM OF MODERN ALIENATION
PO Box 175
Liverpool
L69 8DY Contact: Richard Turn
Produces post-situ zine anti clock wise and wrote In
your blood: football culture in the late '80s and early
'90s. Cultural anarchist set-up. Anti clock wise.
40p. Bi-monthly 12 page zine. Post-situ cultural

anarchy. In your Blood: Football culture in the late
'80s and early '90s. (Working Press). £4.95. 1990.
ISBN 1 870736 07 9. Blotter T-shirts. Range of
manic punk T-shirts screen-printed to order.

MUSIC IN MINIATURE
38 Northfield Road
Barnet
EN4 9DN.
Subjects: Military History.
Books July to December 1991 - 1

MUSLIM EDUCATION TRUST
130 Stroud Green Road
London
N4 3RZ.
Subjects: Education.
Books July to December 1991 - 1

MUSTAQIM
146 Whitlock Drive
London
SW19 6SN

WINIFRED JOYCE MUSTOE
63 Redhill Road
Northfield
Birmingham
B31 3JS

EDWARD MYCUE
PO Box 640543
SAN FRANCISCO
CA 94164-0543
United States of America

L ARTHUR MYERS
11 Manor Gardens
SAXMUNDHAM
Suffolk
IP17 1ET
Wild silk moths and how to rear them, 75p.

ELIZABEDTH MYHILL PUBLICATIONS
Farnborough, Sandy Lane
Belton
GREAT YARMOUTH
Norfolk
NR31 9LT

MYSTERIA PRESS
6 Wanderdown Way
Ovingdean
Brighton
BN2 7BX.
Subjects:
Books July to December 1991 - 1

MR ALERT ZUNGU MZILA
New Exchange Pharmacy
20 Pritchard Street
Johannesburg 2000
South Africa

[N]

NALGO

179

1 Mabledon Place
London
WC1H 9AJ
(NALGO News & Public Service)

NAN ELMOTH PUBLICATIONS
J J Morgan, Haberdasher
Shop 28, Chepstow Corner
Chepstow Place
LONDON
W2 4XA
Very short run small personal magazines and fanzines, mostly to do with Tolkien and related interest groups. Contact for the Tolkien Society. Other interests: Costume and textile technology; haberdashery, historical embroidery and design. Photocopy work a speciality.

NANHOLME/ARC PRESS
Nanholme Centre
Shaw Wood Road
Todmorden
OL14 6DA

NATIONAL ALLIANCE OF WOMEN'S ORGANISATIONS (NAWO)
279-281 Whitechapel Road
London
E1 1BY

NATIONAL CAMPAIGN FOR CIVIL LIBERTIES
(NCCL)
21 Tabard Street
London
SE1 4LA

NATIONAL COUNCIL FOR VOLUNTARY ORGANISATIONS
26 Bedford Square
London
WC1B 2HU

NATIONAL EDUCATIONAL RET COUNTY BRANCH
31 Trull Road
Taunton
TA1 4QG

NATIONAL ABORTION CAMPAIGN (NAC)
c/o Wesley House
4 Wild Court
London
WC2B 5AU

NATIONAL INSTITUTE OF ECONOMIC AND SOCIAL RESEARCH
2 Dean Trench Street
Smith Square
London
SW1P 3HE.
Subjects: Education.
Books July to December 1991 - 2

NATIONAL LIBRARY OF SCOTLAND
George IV Bridge
Edinburgh

EH1 1EW.
Subjects: Art.
Books January to June 1991 - 1

NATIONAL LIBRARY OF WALES
Aberystwyth
SY23 3BU.
Subjects: Welsh Legal History.
Books January to June 1991 - 1

NATIONAL ORGANISATION FOR PRACTICE TEACHERS
c/o 67 Hulme Hall Road
Cheadle Hulme
Cheadle
Cheshire.
Subjects: Education.
Books July to December 1991 - 1

NATIONAL PARENTS COUNCIL
Primary Hogan House
Hogan Place Grand Canal Street
Dublin 2
Republic of Ireland.
Subjects: Education. Books January to June 1991 - 1

NATIONAL PUBLICATIONS COMMITTEE
56 Grand Parade
Cork City
Ireland

NATIONAL RESOURCES INSTITUTE
Central Avenue
Chatham Maritime
ME4 4TB.
Subjects: Zoology.
Books January to June 1991 - 2

NATIONAL UNION OF RAILWAYMEN
London Transport District Council
Unity House
Euston
London
N W 1

NATIONAL LANGUAGE UNIV OF WALES
Brook St
Treforest
Pontypridd
Mid Glam
CF37 1UG
(see English in Wales)

NATIONAL POETRY FOUNDATION
27 Mill Road
Fareham
PO16 0TH

MR D NATRASS
47 Woodlands Road
BISHOP AUCKLAND
Co Durham
DL14 7LY

NATURAL FRIENDS UPDATE
15 Benyon Gardens

Culford
BURY ST EDMUNDS
Suffolk
IP28 6EA
Natural Friends is Britain's premier friendship service for vegetarians, and tho se who care about the world and each other. Updates produced bimonthly (2000 mem bers) containing about 25% text/classified, plus 75% members' ads. Scope for any green/ environmental ads.

NATURETREK EDUCATION BOOKS
4 Rhodfa Gwilym
St Asaph
LL17 0UU

JOURNAL OF THE ROYAL NAVAL MEDICAL SERVICE
Monckton House
Institute of Naval Medicine, Alversto
Gosport
PO12 2DL

MR C I NAYLOR
7 Cedar Close
BUCKHURST HILL
Essex
IG9 6EJ

MS KAREN NAZMI
8 Ashbourne Way
THATCHAM
Berkshire
RG13 4SH

NCVO PUBLISHING
National Council for
Voluntary Organisations
26 Bedford Square
London
WC1B 3HY 071 636 4066
NCVO publishes a range of practical information and policy books and dir ectories on issues related to the voluntary sector including the best selling 'Voluntary Agencies Directory'. Bedford Square Press series includ e 'Community Action'; 'Practical Guides'; 'Society Today' and 'Survival Handbooks'. 'Voluntary Agencies Directory 1991'. 238pp. 10.95. ISBN 0 7199128 6 5. Listing of some 1 800 national voluntary oganisations.
'Grants from Europe: How to Get Money and Influence Policy' by Ann Davison and Bill Seary. 1991. 131pp. 6th edition. £7.95. ISBN 0 7199 13047. How to get money from the European Community with information on contacts in Brussels and the UK.
'The Gentle Art of Listening: Counselling Skills for Volunteers' by J.K. Ford and P. Merriman. 1990. 113pp. ISBN 0 7199 12830. Covers practical and emotional questions for those working as or considering voluntary coun selling or befriending.

NdA PRESS
Natalie d'Arbeloff
6 Cliff Villas
London
NW1 9AL. Tel 071 267 1719
Hand-printed limited edition artist's books with NdA's etchings or mixed-media prints and mostly her own texts. Does not publish other people's work. Press established 1974. NdA books are in public and private collections internationally including the National Art Library of the Victoria and Albert Museum. From August-October 1992 a retrospective solo exhibition of her bookworks is being held at the Museum of the Book in The Hague. NdA is currently planning trade edition of some of her books. One paperback already published. Write for details of limited editions not listed here.
Augustine's True Confession by Natalie d'Arbeloff. 108pp 1989 ISBN 0 906487 11 0 £5.99. An illustrated journal/journey into a private world. Humorous and thoughtful.
The Augustine Adventures (in preparation for 1993) by Natalie d' Arbeloff. Trade edition full colour of 10 cartoon booklets. To be published as a boxed set.

NEBULOUS BOOKS
12 Raven Square
Alton
GU34 2LL.
Subjects: Railways.

A NELSON
PO Box 9
Oswestry
SY11 1BY

NEMETON PUBLISHING
PO Box 780
Bristol
BS99 5BB 0272 715144
Publishing poetry local history and the paranormal since 1985 (aka Carmina). X-CALIBRE is now a thematic series compiling on the theme of poets and poetry for next edition. S.a.e. for details of projects and publications please. Old stock going cheap.
X-Calibre 1991. vol 8 112 pages. 63 contributors; biographical notes; 40 illustrations; designed to delight entertain and inspire. £4.00 inc p&p. Poetry.
Oblivion's Signature by John Gonzalez. atributted to Federico Lorca. 20 pages perfect bound 1 869817 17 6.1990. £1.45 inc p&p. Poetry. Pebbles. By Novello Maynard. a collection of love poetry; a diary of subtle passions. 20 pages. 1 869817 16 8. 1989. £1.45 inc p&p. poetry.

NERUDA PRESS
51 Allison Street
Crosshill
Glasgow
G42 8NJ.
Subjects: Poetry.
Books July to December 1991 - 2

NETHER HALSE BOOKS
John Crisford
Nether Halse Winsford
Minehead
Somerset
TA24 7JE. Tel Winsford (064 385
A one-man firm founded in 1980 to publish a village guidebook now in its sixth edition. Publishes owner's poetry (three titles); local history (two titles) and local biography (one title).
Lot 201 - A box of assorted poems by John Crisford.

24pp 1984 ISBN 0 9507469 6 7 £2.00; 20 poems 1938-1983 and notes.
A Gloria for Special Occasions. Words and Melody by John Crisford arr. Braden Hunwick; std (A3 folded to A4) £1.00; small (A4 folded to A5) pkt of 10 £2.25; for any joyful occasion.
William Dicker - A Great Exmoor Schoolmaster by John Crisford. 44pp 1992 ISBN 1 870546 03 2; £2.95; illustrated biography 1862-1935.

R NETHERWOOD
Fulstone Barn
New Mill
Huddersfield
HD7 7DL

NETWORK EDUCATIONAL PRESS
PO Box 635
Stafford
ST18 0LJ.
Subjects: Education.
Books January to June 1991 - 2. Books July to December 1991 - 2

NEVER BURY POETRY
c/o The Derby Hall
Market Street
Bury
BL9 0BN

ADRIAN NEVILLE PRESTIGE
Abbots End
Amesbury
Salisbury
SP4 7BB

NEW ALBION PRESS
42 Overhill Road
LONDON
SE22 0PH
Collective of self-publishing poets.

NEW ANARCHIST REVIEW
846 Whitechapel High Street
London
E1
Quarterly(ish) 16pp A5 review newsheet with details of anarchist titles currently available in the UK. Available free to alternative bookshops or for a small donation to individuals. Very modest advertising rates.

ARTHUR ROY NEW
12 Vale Park
Blandford St Mary
Blandford Forum
DT11 9LT

NEW ARCADIAN PRESS
Patrick Eyres
13 Graham Grove,
Leeds LS4 2NF
0532 304608
Contemporary artist-writer collaborations on landscape and garden issues: poetry and prose with drawings, photographs and watercolours via small books, print portfolios, cards and an annual journal. The New Arcadian Journal, always contextual, comprises lyric celebration, polemic critique or iconographical analysis.
NAJ29/30 Castle Howard. Editor Patrick Eyres; £25.00. A5 pbk; 74 drawings; 2 maps,; 128pp. 3 writers; 5 artists.
NAJ 31/32 The Wentworths. Editor Patrick Eyres; £25.00. A5 pbk; 172pp; 107 drawings; 3 maps. 3 writers; 9 artists.
NAJ 33/34 A Cajun Chapbook. Editor Patrick Eyres; £30.00. In preparation; with accompanying cassette tape.

THE NEW ATLANTEAN
20 Ridge Avenue
HARPENDEN
Hertfordshire
contemporary artist-writer collaborations on landscape and garden issues. A regular journal, small books, print portfolios and cards: Poetry and prose with drawings, photographs and watercolours. The New Arcadian Journal, always contextual, comprises lyric celebration, polemic critique or iconographical analysis.
Castle Howard (NAJ 29/30) Editor: Patrick Eyres. 25.00, three writers and five artists explore the design of this 18th century landscape garden in the context of the sexual dynastic and party politics of the time. A5 paperback, 128 pp, 74 drawings, 2 maps.
The Wentworths (NAJ 31/32) Editor: Patrick Eyres. 25.00, A5 paperback, 172pp 107 drawings, 3 maps. Three writers and nine artists. Confrontational politics and family rivalry as delineated through the design of the Gothic landscape gardens at Wentworth Woodhouse and Wentworth Castle.
A Cajun Chapbook (NAJ 33/34) Editor: Patrick Eyres. In preparation sex, violence gardens, music, food. Artists, musicians, writers compile a gardenist compendium of things Arcadian from Britain, Canada, USA to illustrate the equation: Arcadian = Arcadian = Cajun. With cassette tape. 30.00

NEW BEACON
7b Stroud Green Road
LONDON
N4 3EN
Books from Africa, Carribean, black Britain and Afro America.

NEW BREED PUBLISHING
Hollywood House
100-102 Woodhouse Road
London
E11 3NA.
Subjects: Paintball Games Management.
Books January to June 1991 - 1

NEW BROOM PRIVATE PRESS
78 Cambridge Street
LEICESTER
LE3 0JP
Small booklets and broadsheets mainly poetry

NEWBY BOOKS
P.O Box 40
Scarborough
YO12 5TW

CITY OF NEWCASTLE GOLF CLUB
Three Mile Bridge
Gosforth
Newcastle-upon-Tyne
NE3 2DR.
Subjects: History of Newcastle Golf Club.
Books July to December 1991 - 1

NEW CAXTON PRESS
Flat Two
11 Clifton Park
Clifton
BRISTOL
BS8 3BX 0272 738997
Aims: to produce fiction in traditional and innovative formats, to explore the scope of desk-top publishing, for profit, to encourage and assist other self-
publishers.
In Black and White by Christopher Stevens. 32pp,
60 illustrations. Murder novel in Tabliod Newspaper format. ISBN 1 8738988 00 2. £1.95 Nov 1991
Get Into Ptint by Christopher Stevens. 192pp A5
comprehensive guide to D I Y publishing and
distribution. ISBN 1 873898 00 3 Sept 1992. The
Taleteller By Christopher Stevens. 254 pp A5 Comic
novel ISB 1 873898 00 4 Jan 1993

THE NEW CENTURY PRESS
1 Western Hill
DURHAM
Co Durham
Worthwhile books for literature.

NEW CENTURY FLYER
52 Wimbledon Park Road
London
SW18 5HS

NEW DEPARTURES
Michael Horovitz (editor)
Piedmont Bisley
Stroud
Gloucestershire
GL6 7BU
New Departures (organ of the Poetry Olympics) has
a few back issues available including multi-signed
collectors' items and also copies of Midsummer
Morning Jog Log Michael Horovitz's 700-line rural
rhapsody with drawings by Peter Blake. Lists sent
on request (please send sae or return postage)
Grandchildren of Albion: Voices and Vision of
Younger Poets in Britain (New Departures 17-20)
edited by Michael Horovitz 400pp 1992 ISBN 0
902689 14 2 9.99 and 1 p&p in UK £2.50 p&p
abroad. This is a lavishly produced and lavishly
bran-tub of poems poetics information and bio/
bibliographic data with a substantial selection from
40 energetic voices including John Agard Attila the
Stockbroker Sujata Bhatt Valerie Bloom Billy Bragg
Jean Binta Breeze Merle Collins John Cooper Clarke
Carol Ann Duffy Peter Gabriel Rob Galliano and
others. This book has been described by Q Magazine as a wonderful collection byturns bawdy el-
egant angry and extremely sexy and by Time Out as
exemplary in its endorsement of multi-racial work
... the essential buy for poetry lovers.

NEWDIGATE EDITIONS

8 Newdigate House
Kingsnymphton Park
KINGSTON-UPON-THAMES
Surrey
KT2 7TJ

NEW DIMENSIONS
1 Austin Close
Irchester
NN9 7AX

NEW ERA PUBLICATIONS
78 Holmethorpe Avenue
Redhill
RH1 2NL

NEW GALAXY PRODUCTIONS
Suite 78, Kent House
87 Regent Street
London
W1R 7HF

NEW HOPE INTERNATIONAL
20 Werneth Avenue
Gee Cross
HYDE
Cheshire
SK14 5NL 01 351 1878
NHI WRITING publishes poetry, prose and art-
work from traditional to avant-guarde NHI Review
covers books, magazines, tapes and PC software -
an essential guide. Singe issues £2($5) each, 6 issue
subscription (inc special edition chapbooks) 10($25)
ISSN 0260 7958.
The Art of Maiku - Excellent guide to this Japanese
poetry form with articles and original writing and
drawing. ISBN 0 903610 12 4 price £2($5) Brigflatts
Visited - A tribute to Basil Bunting. Poems and
articles by Christopher Pilling, Chris Challis, William
Oxley. ISBN 0 903610 08 06 price £1.50 ($3)
Steve Sneyd: A Mile Beyond the bus. Poetry exploring the unique character of the Southern Pennines.
Superbly illustrated by Ian M Emberson IBSN 0
903610 11 6 £2 ($5)

NEW IONA PRESS
Old Printing Press Building
Isle of Iona
PA76 6SL.
Subjects: Local Travel Guides.
Books July to December 1991 - 1

NEW LEAF
5425 Tulane Dr SW
Atlanta
Georgia 30336-2323
United States of America

NEW LEFT REVIEW
6 Meard Street
London
W1V 3HR

NEWMARK EDITIONS
34 Trenchard Close
Sutton Coldfield
B75 7QP

NEW NAME DISTRIBUTION
P O Box 1543
MARLOW
Buckinghamshire
SL7 2YB 0628 481810
Trade distribution of holistic, metaphysical and new age publications.

NEW NORTH PRESS
27-29 New North Road
Hoxton
Hackney
LONDON
N1 6JB

NEW POEMS FROM PORTSMOUTH
(Denise Bennett & Mike Merritt)
6 Algiers Road
Copnor
Portsmouth
PO3 6PJ

NEW PROJECTS
2nd Floor, Openshaw House
Birdshill
LETCHWORTH
Hertfordshire
SG6 1JB

NEW PROSPECTS POETRY
Prospect House
Snowshill
Broadway
Worcs
WR12 7JU

NEW PYRAMID PRESS
No 1 Arch
Green Dragon Court
Borough Market
LONDON
SE1 9AH

NEW RIVER PROJECT
89a Petherton Road
LONDON
N5 2PT Tel. 071 226 2657
Border blur of arts activity in movement sound & vision. Publications: Books, cassettes, records; distribution for other publishers; regular workshops for experimental and performance poetry mixed media performances, exhibitions, bookfairs, etc. Write or phone for details.
'Bob Jubilee. Selected Texts by Bob Cobbing 1944-1990' 120pp 6.00 ISBN 1 870750 01 2
'Old Angel Midnight' by Jack Kerouac 56pp £3.00.4th Ed. Midnight press -the only complete edition
'Southam Street' by Gavin Selerie. Inspiring poem about life in a London slum. 12pp 1991 £3.00 ISBN 1 870750 05 7

NEW SPOKES
45 Clophill Road
Upper Gravenhurst
Bedford
MK45 4JH

MR GUY NEWTON
39 Green Ridges
Headington
OXFORD
OX3 9PL

M. NEWTON
3 Brickfield Cottages
Roughton Road
Cromer
NR27 0HL.
Subjects: Biography.
Books July to December 1991 - 1

NEWTON PUBLISHERS
Hartfield Road
P.O. Box 36
Edenbridge
TN8 7JW.
Subjects: Mystery Fiction.
Books July to December 1991 - 2

(THE) NEW TRUTH
28 Collins Road
Pennsylvania
Exeter
Devon
EX4 5DY

NEW WAY PUBLISHING
Spearhead Unit 1
New Life Christian Centre
Cario New Road
Croydon.
Subjects: Children's Fiction.
Books January to June 1991 - 4. Books July to December 1991 - 4

NEW WELSH REVIEW
49 Pack Place
Cardiff
Wales
CF19 3AT

NEW WORLD PUBLISHING
The Fairpiece
Mill Road
Gringley-on-the-Hill
Doncaster
DN10 4QT.
Books July to December 1991 - 1

NICARAGUA SOLIDARITY CAMPAIGN
Red Rose Centre
129 Seven Sisters Road
London
N7 7QG

MS SYLVIE NICKELS
26 The Daedings
Deddington
Oxfordshire
OX15 0RT 0869 40284

NIGHTFALL PRESS

184

c/o Noel K Hannan
18 Lansdowne Road
Sydney, CREWE
Cheshire
CW1 1JY

DEREK NIGHTINGALE
12 Finches Rise
Merrow
Guildford
GU1 2UN.
Subjects: Local History.
Books January to June 1991 - 1

NIGHT WRITERS
Hackney Women's Centre
20 Dalston Lane
LONDON
E8

MR STUART M NISBET
15 Victoria Crescent
CLarkstgon
GLASGOW
G76 8BP

NNIDNID
Doc Shiels
3 Vale View
Ponsanooth
TRURO
Cornwall
TR3 7JB

NUMBER 9 BOOKS
47 St Georges Avenue West
Wolstanton
Newcastle-under-Lyme
ST5 8DF

D. AND M. NOBLE
Danar House
27 Longmoor Road
Ashton Gate
Bristol
BS3 2NZ.
Subjects: Family History.
Books July to December 1991 - 1

NOMADS PRESS
16 Beck Cottage
Digby
Lincoln
LN4 3NE.
Subjects: Poetry.
Books July to December 1991 - 1

NO RENT PUBLICATONS
11 Aldbourne Point
Trowbridge Road
Hackney Wick
LONDON
E9 5LA
Free speech: Fair comment: Unfair comment: Fair
game: Fair E-nuff.

NORFOLK ARCHAEOLOGICAL UNIT:

University of East Anglian Studies
Norwich
NR4 7TJ.
Subjects: Archaeology.
Books July to December 1991 - 2

NORHEIMSUND BOOKS & CARDS
1 Whitney Road
Burton Latimer
Kettering
NN15 5SL

NORLON PUBLISHING
63 Ermineside
Enfield
EN1 1DD

(THE) NORTH
(THE POETRY BUSINESS)
51 Bryan Arcade
Westgate
Huddersfield
HD1 1ND

NORTH AND SOUTH
23 Egerton Road
TWICKENHAM
Middlesex
TW2 7SL
North and South publishes poetry, prose and graphic
work by new and established writers and artists.

NORTH EASTERN EDUCATION AND LI-
BRARY
Area Resource Centre
28 Railway Street
Antrim
BT41 4AE

NOTTINGHAM WRITERS
18 Waterloo Road
Beeston
NOTTINGHAM
NG9 2BU

NORTHERN IRELAND ENVIRONMENT LINK
Armagh House
Ormreau Avenue
Belfast

NORTH OF SCOTLAND NEWSPAPERS
42 Union Street
Wick
KW1 5ED

NORTII-WEST BOOKS
23 Main Street
Limavady
BT49 0EP

NORTH YORK MOORS NATIONAL PARK IN-
FORM
The Old Vicarage
Bondgate, Helmsley
York
YO6 5BP

185

NORTH YORKSHIRE MARKETING
Lambert House
104 Station Parade
Harrogate
HG1 1HQ

NORTHDOWN PUBLICATIONS
50 Albert Road
NEW MALDEN
Surrey
KT3 6BS

J.W. NORTHEND
Clyde Road
Sheffield
S8 0TZ.
Subjects:
Books July to December 1991 - 1

NORTHERN ARTS PUBLISHING
Roper Lane
Thurgoland
SHEFFIELD
S30 7AA
Hobgoblin magazine.

NORTHERN EARTH MYSTERIES
Mr Rob Wilson
40b Welby Place
Meersbrook Park
SHEFFIELD
S8 9DB
Magazine investigating the ancient landscape of
the area.

NORTHERN ECHO
Promotions Department
Priestgate
Darlington
DL1 1NF

NORTHERN HERITAGE CONSULTANCY
Prince Building
7 Queen Street
Newcastle
NE1 3XL

NORTHERN HOUSE POETS
19 Haldane Terrace
Newcastle-upon-Tyne
NE2 3AN.
Subjects: Poetry.
Books July to December 1991 - 3

NORTHERN IRELAND CENTRE
for Learning Resources
Orchard Building
Stranmilus College
Belfast
BT9 5DY.
Subjects: School Textbook.
Books July to December 1991 -7

NORTHERN IRELAND COUNCIL
for Integrated Education
16 Mount Charles

Belfast
BT7 1NZ.
Subjects: Education.
Books July to December 1991 - 1

NORTHERN IRELAND HOUSING EXECUTIVE
The Housing Centre
2 Adelaide Centre
Belfast
BT2 8PB.
Subjects: Bibliography.
Books July to December 1991 - 10

NORTHERN LINE
London Underground
72 Euston Street
London
NW1 2HA

NORTHERN VOICES
Durham City Arts
Durham City Baths
Elver Waterside
DURHAM
DH1 3BW

NORTHERN WRITERS ADVISORY SERVICES
Jill Groves
77 Marford Crescent
Sale
Cheshire
M33 4DN. Tel 061 969 1573.
Local History biography.
Murder and Mystery in Derbyshire by Godfrey Cox.
A5 45pp 1991 £3.20. ISBN 0 9517782 0 X.
The Impact of Civil War on a Community: Two
Cheshire Manors Northenden and Etchells 1642-
1660 by Jill Groves. A4 40pp £2.70. ISBN 0 9517782
1 8. Publication: September 1992.

NORTH KENT BOOKS
162 Borstal Road
Rochester
ME1 3BB

NORTHLIGHT
136 Byres Road
Glasgow
Scotland
G12 8TD

NORTH OF SCOTLAND NEWSPAPERS
42 Union Street
Wick
KW1 5ED.
Subjects: Short Stories. Travel. Local Newspaper
history. Books July to December 1991 - 1

PAT NORTH
Northdale
Alford
LN13 9EY.
Subjects: Stockbreeding.
Books July to December 1991 - 4

NORTHSIDE WRITERS

186

134 Farranferris Avenue
Farranree
Cork
EIRE

NORTHUMBERLAND PIPERS' SOCIETY:
Matt Seattle Musical Services
44 Durban Street
Blyth
NE24 1PT.
Books January to June 1991 - 1.
Books July to December 1991 - 1

NORTH YORK MOORS
National Park Information Service
The Old Vicarage
Bardgate Helmsley
York
YO6 5BP.
Subjects: Children's non-fiction. Biology. Railways.
Town Planning. Books January to June 1991 - 2.
Books July to December 1991 - 4

NORTON
9 Woodlands Road
Cove
Farnborough
GU14 9QJ

MR T NORTON
116 High Street
Wingham
CANTERBURY
Kent
CT3 1DE

NORVIK PRESS
University of East Anglia
NORWICH
NR4 7TJ

NORWICH SCHOOL OF ART GALLERY
St. George Street
Norwich
NR3 1HH.
Subjects: Art.

NORWOOD PUBLISHERS
3 Chapel Street
Norwood Green
Halifax
HX3 8QU.
Subjects: School Textbooks.
Books July to December 1991 - 6

NOTTINGHAM COURT PRESS
44 Great Russell Street
LONDON
WC1B 3PA

UNIVERSITY OF NOTTINGHAM
Department of Art History
University Park
Nottingham
NG7 2RD

NOTTINGHAM WRITERS

18 Waterloo
Beeston
NOTTINGHAM
NG9 2BU

NOTTINGHAM SUBSCRIPTION LIBRARY
Bromley House
Angle Row
Nottingham
NG1 6HL.
Subjects: History of the Nottingham Subscription
Library. Books July to December 1991 - 1

NOVA PUBLISHING
29 Milber Industrial Estate
Newton Abbot
TQ12 4SG

Novata Press
3 The Leather House
72-76 St George's Street
Norwich
NR3 1DA

NOVA VISIONS INC
Indian Mountain Retreat Center
Hico
TX 76457
United States of America

GARY SCOTT NOWELL
Hydebeck House
51 Main Street, Carnaby
Bridlington
YO16 4UJ

NOX
15 Oxford Street
MEXBOROUGH
South Yorkshire

NPR PUBLICATIONS
8 Mendip Court
Avonley Village
Avonley Road
LONDON
SE14 5EU 071 639 5407
The Reid Review publishes short stories, poems and
short plays. The aim is to publish and promote the
very best of these forms, but the priority is the
encour agement of new poetry and fiction writing
all over the UK. The Reid Review. A monthly
review featuring the very best from new and established writers poetry plays short stories single issues
at £1.75 per copy including p & p or £18.00 sub for
12 issues (Europe 25.00; over seas £35.00).

NRB
N R Bradley
91 Hawksley Avenue
Chesterfield
Derbyshire
S40 4TJ 0246 208473
Specialist publisher of graphology hand-writing
psychology related texts .Founded 1987 to promote
research into character/ personality investigation.
Also buyer/seller used books.
'What Your Handwriting Shows' by Robert

187

Saunders. pp189 64 illutr 1991 p/b ISBN 0 9513207
3 4. £10.00. Popular book on experimental psychology of handwriting
'Oxford 1987 - Papers of the 1st British Symposium on Graphological Re search'. Ed N R Bradley
191pp. 56 illustr 1988 p/b ISBN 0 9513207 1 8. £12.00.
'100 Studies in Handwriting & Related Topics' by N R Bradley. 130pp 1989 p/b ISBN 0 9513207 2 6. £10.00.

NUIT ISIS
PO Box 250
OXFORD
OX1 1AP

NUTSHELL PUBLISHING CO.
12 Dene Way
Speldhurst
Tunbridge Wells
TN3 0NX

MR ALFRED N NWEZEH
P O Box 2816
Enugu
Enugu State
Nigeria

MR R J NYMAN
Indlun Kulu
22 The Haven
SOUTHSEA
Hampshire
PO4 8YQ

OXFORD SCRIBBLERS
c/o Bloomin' Arts
East Oxford Community Centre
Princess Street
OXFORD

OAKLANDS
Elm Grove
Worthing
BN11 5LH
D.B Enterprise

OAKLEIGH PUBLICATIONS: METRASTOCK LTD
Unit 7, Cobham Road
Cedar Industrial Park
Wimborne
Dorset

OAKLEY PUBLICATIONS
Oakley Printing Company
Bridge Street, Swinton
Mexborough
S64 8AP

M J OAKLEY
133 Boldmere Road
SUTTON COLDFIELD
West Midlands
B75 5UL

OAKWOOD PUBLICATIONS (WCC)

(see Good Stories Magazine)
23 Mill Crescent
Kingsbury
Worcs
B78 2LX

OASIS BOOKS - OASIS MAGAZINE
Ian Robinson
12 Stevenage Road
London
SW6 6ES. Tel. 071 736 5059
Oasis Books founded in 1969 specialises in editions of innovative poetry and fiction both in English and in translation.
And Working by Douglas Gunn (USA). 67pp January 1992
ISBN 0 903375 88 5 £5.95. 11 short stories.
The Bust of Minerva by Brian Louis Perace. 40pp November 1992 ISBN 0 903375 89 3 £4.95. Long short story.
Equinox by Peter Dent. 40pp November 1992 ISBN 0 903375 87 7 £4.95. Collection of poetry: 5 sequences.

OATMEAL PRESS
Alan Harrison
54 Kemsing Gdns
Canterbury
CT2 7RF 0227 760057
Committed to increasing public awareness of the numerous problem arising from the misuse of food in the home; and the manipulation of the public mind by government and the large food and drink manufacturers. 'Are we Really What We Eat ? - The thinkers book of food' by Alan Harrison Serious text on lack of Governmental food policy and the way food manufacturers influence the national diet. Numerous factors affecting personal food choice. 112pp. £5.50 ISBN 0 946017 08 5 (Orig. Pub. Weavers Press) 'Control and Starve: a Social History of Scottish food and Hospitality' Due Dec 1991 250pp. Deal with the control of food supply exerted by land owners in Scotland up to the 1st World War. Intended to explain the back ground to the poor modern diet in Scotland. Examines bogus gastronomic heritage eg haggis. Endorses Scots hospitality though.
Individual Papers on specifics food and drinks in society; send for de tails. £1.50 each

OBAIR
Conway Mill
Conway Street
Belfast
N Ireland

OBAN TIMES
PO Box 1
Oban
Argyll
PA34 5PY

OBELISK PUBLICATIONS
2 Church Hill
Pinhoe
Exeter
EX4 9ER

OBERON BOOKS
8 Richardson Mews
London
W1P 5DF.
Subjects: Plays. Theatre.
Books July to December 1991 - 4

MR BART O BRIEN
Breedveldsingel 98
3055 PL Rotterdam
The Netherlands
31 (10) 418 61 00

A J OBRIST
Denbigh House
Woodside
Aslpley Guise
MILTON KEYNES
MK17 8EB

OCCULTIQUE BOOKSHOP
73 Keltering Road
NORTHAMPTON
NN1 4DW 0604 27727

OCCULTURE
Topy, Station 23
PO Box 687
Halfway687
SHEFFIELD
S19 6UXZ

MR CHRIS O CONNELL
165 Gladstone Street
Forestfields
NOTTINGHAM
N67 6HX

ODIBOURNE PRESS
Richard Storey
32 High Street
Kenilworth
CV8 2EU. Tel 0926 57409 (Eves)
Publisher of all aspects of the history of Kenilworth
and its immediate locality. Also local reminiscences
and (to date) one booklet of poetry. Kenilworth at
School. Education and Charity 1700-1914 by J.
Powell. 64pp 1991 ISBN 0 9515147 3 3 £4.95.
Looking Back Again. People Places and Pastimes
in Kenilworth During the Past Hundred Years by E.
Tisdale. 56pp 1990 ISBN 0 9515147 2 5 2.95. A
Third Kenilworth Collection by H. Scott and R.
Storey. 28pp 1989 ISBN 0 9515147 1 7 32.00.
Postcard views and other pictorial matter.

ODINIC RITE
11 Philip House
Heneage Street
London
E1 5LW.
Subjects: Religious History.
Books July to December 1991 - 1

ODUN BOOKS
Odun Grange
Appledore
Bideford
EX39 1PT

ODYSSEY
(ed) Derrick Woolf)
Coleridge Cottage
Nether Stowey
Somerset

OFF PINK PUBLISHING
49a Adulphus Road
LONDON
N4 2AX 071 351 5952
Seeking to fill the gap in literature concerning
bisexuality and related subject s. The considerable
success of our first book has led to a second, well on
the way to publication.
Bisexual Lives. By Off Pink Collective. 114 pages.
1988. ISBN 0 9513103 0 5. £2.95 (plus post and
packing). Present day experiences of what it is like
to be bisexual.

O'FORTUNA
BCM Akademia
London
WC1N 3XX

M A OGILVIE
Glencairn
Bruichladdich
ISLE OF ISLAY
PA49 7UN

MISS MARGARET O'HARA
92 Bally Kelly Road
Finlagan
Limavady
Co Derry
BT49 9DS

O H B
Alan Johnson
Woodman Works
Durnsford Road
LONDON
SW19 8DR

OLD BELMONT PRESS
49 Moorside
Spennymoor
DL15 7DY

OLD BRIDGE MUSIC
P.O. Box 7
Ilkley
LS29 9RY.
Subjects: Music.
Books July to December 1991 - 1

OLD CHAPEL LANE BOOKS
8 Old Chapel Lane
Burgh Le Marsh
Skegness
PE24 5LQ

OLD FERRY PRESS
53 Vicarage Road
TYWARDRATH
Cornwall

189

PL24 2PH 0726 813709
A recently formed (1991) imprint with it's main
interest in maritime affairs, particularly naval -
historical. Viz: A Damned Cunning Fellow; the
eventful life of rear admiral Sir Home Popham

A. OLDHAM
Rhychydwr
Crymych
SA41 3RB.
Subjects: Biography. Caving.
Books January to June 1991 - 3. Books July to
December 1991 - 1

OLD ORCHARD PRESS
The Orchard
5 The Street
Gillingham
Beccles
NR34 0LH.
Subjects: Welsh History.
Books July to December 1991 - 1

OLD POLICE STATION MAGAZINE
80 Lark Lane
Liverpool
L17 8UU

OLD STILE PRESS
Catchmays Court
Llandogo
MONMOUTH
Gwent
NP5 4TN 0291 689 226
Limited editions of artists' books by letterpress and
relief printing. 'The More Angels Shall I Paint'.
Robin Tanner's sketchbook drawings; com
monplace books and letters. 72pp ISBN 0 907664
23 7. 65.00. 'A Wall in Wales' Images by Nicholas
Mc Dowall. 48pp ISBN 0 907664 27 X. 40.00
'In the Margins of a Shakespeare'. George Mackay
Brown wood engravings -Llewellyn Thomas (ready
autumn)

OLD SWAN WRITERS
Rose Cottage
35 High Street
Wavertree
LIVERPOOL 15
UK

OLD VICARAGE PUBLICATIONS
The Old Vicarage, Reades Lane
Dane-in-Shaw
Congleton
CW12 3LL

Old West Kirk
Campbell Street
Greenock
Renfrewshire.
Subjects: Local History.
Books January to June 1991 - 1.

THE OLEANDER PRESS
Philip Ward
17 Stansgate Avenue
Cambridge

CB2 2QZ.
0223 244688
Over 30 years as a small family publisher have
produced three best-sellers but the aim is to produce
a wide range of books not commercial enough for
the big publishers; such as minority travel books
innovative games books anda scholarly series devoted to 'Arabia past and present'. Philip Ward's
'Bulgaria' (£9.95) won the 1990 International Travel
Writers' Competition. Send for full list.
Bulgarian Voices: Letting the People Speak by
Philip Ward. 344pp July 1992 ISBN 0 906672 64 3
£10.95. Eastern European politics and society. Italian Key Words: the basic 2 000 word vocabulary
arranged by frequency with dictionaries by
Gianpaolo Intronati. 144pp 1992
ISBN 0 906672 25 2 £4.95. Italian language.
Western India: Bombay Maharashtra Karnataka by
Philip Ward. 287pp Dec 1991 ISBN 0 906672 32
7. India. Travel.

MR T OLIVER
37 Copse Road
Clevedon
BRISTOL
BS21 7QN

O'MEDIA
69 Festing Road
Putney
LONDON
SW15 1LW 081 788 6109

MR JON O'NEILL
12 Petersfield Close
MANSFIELD
Nottinghamshire
NG19 6UA

ONE-OFF PRESS:
K. Schubert
85 Charlotte Street
London
SW8 4UD.
Subjects: Art.

ONLYWOMEN PRESS
38 Mount Pleasant
London
WC1X 0AP

ONLY WOMEN
38 Mount Pleasant
LONDON
WC1X 0AP
Lesbian

OPEN CIRCLE
Hillhead Library
348 Byres Road
Glasgow
G12.
Subjects: Poetry.
Books July to December 1991 - 1

OPEN LETTERS
147 Northchurch Road
London

N1 3NT

(THE) OPEN PATH
5 Kingswood Place
Corby
NN18 9AF

OPEN TOWNSHIP
Michael Haslam
14 Foster Clough
Heights Bridge
HEBDEN BRIDGE
West Yorkshire
HX7 5QZ

OPTILEX INFORMATION SYSTEMS LTD
72C Twyford Avenue
Acton
LONDON
W3 9QB

ORACLE
82 Marine Parade
BRIGHTON
BN2 1AJ
Oracle was set up to, in the absence of enlightened response by the commercial publishing houses, publish a series of deluxe hardback books by the now 60 yr old American poet, writer, critic and reviewer. Because of no distribution, Oraclre folded after the one book listed here.
Great Love Desiderata by Kaviraj George Dowden with Anne Dowden 56pp - flower illustration. 1988 ISBN 0 9513263 hardback £5.95. The very last word on man-woman love at its greatest in 30 pure abstract prose aphorisms. The Moving I by Kaviraj George Downen. Inkblot - 235pp. - 1987 - ISBN 0 934301 15 8 - 8.95. Autobiographical novel featuring the author's spiritual seeking in India.
Flowers of Consciousness by Kaviraj George Dowden. Alpha Beat Press - 107pp -1991 - ISBIN 0 921720 04 1 - 5.00. Down-to-earth visionary poetry. Introduction by Sebastian Crevacoer, D.Litt.

ORANGE BOX
Simon Spain
59 Mildenhall Road
London
E5 0RT. Tel 081 985 0852
Orangebox works with artists to produce and publish editioned prints and books.Orange box also runs publishing workshops in schools where children can write illustrated layout and actually print their own edition of books.

ORANGE HERITAGE
c/o McCracken
5 Mansewood Crescent
Whitburn
Bathgate
EH47 8HA

ORBIS
199 The Long Shoot
Nuneaton
Warwickshire
CV11 6JQ

ORCHARD BOOKS
2B Wastie's Orchard
Long Hanborough
Oxford
OX7 2BA

ORCHID SUNDRIES
New Gate Farm, Scotchey Lane
Stour Provost
Gillingham
SP8 5LT

ORE
7 The Towers
STEVENAGE
Hertfordshire
SG1 1HE
Poetry and Prose magazine.

MR CARL OREND
Meisterlingerstrasse 110
8000 Munchen 81
Germany

ORIEL BOOKSHOP
Peter Finch
The Friary
CARDIFF
CF1 4AA

ORIFLAMME PUBLISHING LIMITED
Edward Marsh
125 Station Road
MICKLEOVER
Derby
DE3 5FN 0332 510230
Publisher. Mainly paperback books. Now chiefly education for mass market via W H Smith and direct to schools. Currently planning US editions. Some fiction in print: SF/Fantasy. In current market would only consider subsidised fiction deals. No unsolicitores MSS.
RULES OF MATHS. £3.95. ISBN 0 948093 06 4. 80 pages. Paperback, 278 x 210 mm. 1989 (2nd ed. 1990) By John Connors and Pat Soper. Basic maths handbook coveri ng ages 8-13 syllabus. Detailed explanations.
SPELLING. £3.95. ISBN 0 948093 05 6. 80 pages paperback. 278 x 210 mm. 1989 (2nd ed. 1990) Edited E Marsh. Basic handbook of spelling by phonetic system for schools, parents, revision, reference.
INVASION. 4.50. ISBN 0 948093 08 0. 512 pages. Standard paperback. 1990. By D A Slade. Fiction: alternative war story - succesful German invasion of Eng land in 1940.

ORINOCO PRESS
41 Oakthwaite Road
Windermere
Cumbria
LA23 2BD
Local history, folklore, legend, etc. dealing principally with the Windermere area.
Tales & Legends of Windermere by Peter Nock. 40 pages, 7 illustrations inc front cover. ISBN 0 9514778 1 1 Folklore. 2nd ed published May 1991

ORION PUBLISHING
6 Arcade Chambers
High Street
Brentwood
CM14 4AH.
Subjects: Travel Accommodation.
Books July to December 1991 - 1.

ORKNEY VIEW
3 Papdale Close
Kirkwall
Orkney
KW15 1QP

ORLANDO PUBLISHING
Chequers Cottage
Church Lane, Briston
Melton Constable
NR24 2LF

S ORME
West Mount
43 Williams Road
KENLEY
Surrey
CR8 5HA

CHRIS ORR PUBLICATIONS
Chris Orr
7 Bristle Hill, Buckingham, MK18 1EZ
0280 815255
Self employed artist occasionally publishing books
and catalogues on own work.
'Chris Orr's John Ruskin'; 32 pages; 1976; £5;
paperback; b/w illustraitons; colour cover.
'Arthur'; a story by Chris Orr; 50 pages; 1979; £5;
paperback; black and white illustrations; colour
cover.
'Many Mansions'; Chris Orr' 24 pages; 1990; £6;
paperback; colour and b/w. Contributions by
Michael Palin and Robert Hewisen. 09516616 0 4.

ORWELL PRESS
64 High Street
Southwold
IP18 6DN

OSCARS PRESS
BM Oscars
LONDON
WC1N 3XX
'The Vital and Vitalized Oscars Press' - Ian
McMillan, poetry review. Specialists in gay and
lesbian poetry anthologies, including Take Any
Train (ed Peter Daniels) and Whatever You Desire
(ed Mary Jo Bang)
Language of Water, Language of Fire: A celebra-
tion of lesbian and gay poetry, edited by Berta
Freistadt and Pat o'Brien. 80pp £5.99. June 1992.
ISBN 1 872668 01 1
Of Eros and of Dust: Poems from the city, edited by
Steve Anthony. 88pp, £5.99, June 1992. ISBN 1
872668 02 X

OSCO
Unit 3-4 Mars House
Calleva Park
Aldermaston

Reading
RG7 4QW.
Subjects: Biography.
Books January to June 1991 - 1

OSSIAN PUBLISHERS GLASGOW
268 Bath Street
Glasgow
G2 4JR.
Subjects: Mystery Fiction.
Books January to June 1991 - 2

OSTINATO
PO Box 522
LONDON
N8 7SZ

THE OTHER WAY PRESS
PO Box 130
London
W5 1DQ 081 998 1519
Self-help and practical books for the gay commu-
nity
'Making Gay Relationships Work' by Terry Sand-
erson. 164pp p/b. £4.95 ISBN 0 948982 02 0
'The Potts Correspondence & Other Gay Humour'
by Terry Sanderson. p/b. 3.50 ISBN 0 948982 01 2
'A Stranger in the Family: How to Cope if your
Child is Gay' by Terry Sanderson 200pp p/b. £5.95
(Nov 91)

OTHERWISE PUBLICATIONS
Forge Cottage, The Green
Abthorpe
Towcester
NN12 8QP

OTHERWISE PRESS
111 Blenheim Crescent
LONDON
W11 2JF
Publisher of ALTERNATIVE LONDON (now well-
extinct). Other unrelated projects pending, including book on absurd or anachroniistic laws.

OTTER
Chris Southgate
Parford Cottage
Chagford
Newton Abbot
Devon
TQ13 8JR

MR FREDERICK OUGHTON
Mansard Press
2 Holly Road
RETFORD
Nottinghamshire
DN22 6BE

OUR WONDERFUL CULTURE
75 Lambeth Walk
LONDON
SE11 6DX
Artist books and cards and magazines

OUTDOOR EVENTS PUBLICATIONS

30 Tudor Manor Gardens
Garston
Watford
WD2 7PP.
Subjects: Sport.
Books January to June 1991 - 1

OUTLAWS PUBLISHING COMPANY
40 Basildon Court
Devonshire Street
LONDON
W1N 1RH 071 935 3423

OUTLET
Mr Trev Faull
33 Aintree Crescent, Barkingside
ILFORD
Essex
IG6 2HD
Magazine

R OUZIA
Ketsstraat 25
B-2018 ANTWERPEN
BELGIUM

OVERCOAT PUBLICATIONS
143 Birchfield Road
Widnes
WA8 9EG.
Subjects: Biography.
Books January to June 1991 - 1

OVERDUE BOOKS
37 Melbourne Street
HEBDEN BRIDGE
West Yorkshire
HX7 6AS
Women writers from the North of England

OVERSPACE
25 Sheldon Road
CHIPPENHAM
Wiltshire
SN14 0BP

OVERTON PRESS
480 Moor Road
Beswtood
Nottingham
NG6 8UN

OWEN PUBLICATIONS
Bede House
28C Blakebrook
Kidderminster
DY11 6AP.
Subjects: Historical Biography.
Books July to December 1991 - 1.

MS ANN OWEN
Rivendale
Lower High Street, Tutbury
BURTON-ON-TRENT
Staffordshire
DE13 9LU

TUPPY OWENS
Box 42b
LONDON
W1A 42B
071 499 3527
Safer Sex Books

OWL BOOKS
27 Queensway
Wigan
WN1 2JA.
Subjects: Local History. Historical Biography. Sport.
Books January to June 1991 - 3

OWL PRESS
PO Box 315
Downton
SALISBURY
Wiltshire
SP5 3YE 0725 22553
Small independent book publisher specialising in
adult humour and books of interest to The Services.
'Gumboots and Pearls' by Annie Jones 129pp 30 b/
w cartoons Aug 1990. £3.95 ISBN 0 9515917 0 3
'The Backstabber's Guide' Ed Annie Jones
politics by Austin Mitchell MP
208pp 22b/w cartoons. £4.99 ISBN 0 9515917 2 X
(adult humour)

OWL PUBLISHING
7 Ludlow Drive
Ormskirk
L39 1LE.
Subjects: Customs and Folklore.
Books January to June 1991 - 1. Books July to
December 1991 - 1

OWLET BOOKS
'Ballochantuy'
Tunstall Road, Tunstall
SITTINGBOURNE
Kent
ME10 1YQ
New publishers of educational books for teachers
now moving into junior fiction. First educational
seeries - 'Using Information Technology Across the
National Curriculum' consists of 5 titles written by
an experienced teacher for other teachers. Direct
sales: seeking marketing arrangements.

OWNBASE ASSOCIATION
9 Salisbury Road
ANDOVER
Hampshire
SP10 2JJ
Newsletter for people who work at home

O WRITE
(admin editors)
FCHS Pathways Publications
New Street Rubery/Rednal
Birmingham
B45 0EU

OXFIN
Unit one
Paradise Street Business Centre

OXFORD
OX1

OXFORD GRAPEVINE
Box O
34 Cowley Road
OXFORD
OX4 1HZ
Alternative Yellow Pages for Oxford.

OXFORD PROJECT FOR PEACE STUDIES
Belsyre Court
57 Woodstock Road
Oxford
OX2 6HU

OXFORD POETRY
Magdalen College
Oxford
OX1 4AU

OXFORD PSYCHOLOGISTS PRESS
Lambourne House
311-321 Banbury Road
Oxford
OX2 7JH.
Subjects: Education.
Books July to December 1991 - 2.

OXFORD TRUST
STEP Centre
Osney Mead
Oxford
OX2 0ES.
Subjects: Architecture.
Books January to June 1991 - 1

OXFORD WOMEN'S HANDBOOK
Oxford Univ S U
New Barnett House
28 Little Clarendon St
Oxford
OX1 2HB

OXLEY DEVELOPMENTS COMPANY
Priory Park
Ulverston
LA12 9QG

[P]

P7S PUBLISHING
P.O Box 150
Ipswich
IP2 8PW

MS V PACE
65 Paddock Lane
DESBOROUGH
Northhamptonshire
NN14 2LZ

PACIFIC ISLANDS STUDY CIRCLE OF G.B.
c/o J.P. Deeny
32 Malvern Way
Croxley Green
Rickmansworth

WD3 3QG.
Subjects: Stamps.
Books July to December 1991 - 2

PACSEA
The Martin Centre
6 Chaucer Road
Cambridge
CB2 2EB

PADDA BOOKS
5 Tilgate Drive
Bexhill-on-Sea
TN39 3UH

PANDORA'S JAR
Blaenberem
Mynyddcerrig Pontyberem
Llanelli
Dyfed
SA15 5BL

PAGAN ANIMAL RIGHTS
Tina Foooox
23 Highfield South
Rock Ferry
Birkenhead
Wirral
L42 4NA 051 648 0485
Pagan Animal Rights advocates the treatment of
the earth and all her creat ures with respect. it works
on both physical and pychic levels using both
normal campaigning methods and meditation and
magical techniques. Par Magazine edited by T. Fox
and J. Boyd. Quarterly at fire festivals. 12pp. £2.50
p.a.

PAGAN FEDERATION
BM Box 7097
London
WC1N 3XX.
Subjects: Social Welfare.
Books July to December 1991 - 1

PAGAN FUNERAL TRUST NEWSLETTER
BM Box 3337
London
WC1N 3XX

PAGAN LIFE
Irish Pagan Movement
The Bridge House Clonegal
Enniscorthy
Co Wexford Ireland

PAGAN NEWS
Box 175
52 Call Lane
LEEDS
LS1 6DT

PAGAN PRATTLE
Box 333
52 Call Lane
LEEDS
LS1 6DT
Newsletter which covers the tabloid version of the

194

antics of the Christian right.

MR PHILIP PAGE
PO Box 123
MARGATE
Kent
CT9 1TX

MRS P A PAGE
104 Argyle Gardens
UPMINSTER
Essex
RM14 3EU

PAGES
Mr Robert Sheppard
239 Lessingham Avenue
LONDON
SW19 8NQ

PALACE THEATRE (LONDON)
Shaftesbury Avenue
London
W1V 8AY.
Subjects: Theatre History.
Books July to December 1991 - 1

PALAVER PUBLICATIONS
40 Langham Close
Sharples
Bolton
BL1 7RA.
Subjects: General Fiction.
Books January to June 1991 - 1

PALERMO PRESS
33 Burgage
Prestbury
Cheltenham
GL52 3DL.
Subjects: Literature.
Books July to December 1991 - 1

(THE) PALESTINE POST
P O Box 1EQ
London
W1A 1EQ

PALLAS PRESS
S. King
Brookdale Danyraig Road
Llanharan
Mid Glamorgan
CF7 0UX. Tel 0443 228490
We publish books of local interest. We also publishj
a local free monthly newspaper 'The Diary' circu-
lation 6 750.
Forgotten Years Vol 2 (history of Llanharan and
Bryna) by T.J. Witts. 292pp 1988 ISBN 1 871691
00 1 15.00.
Pencoed Past Vol 1 (history of Pencoed) by S.R.W.
King. 180pp 1990 ISBN 1 871691 03 6 £10.00.
Towards the Light (the story of Cardiff High School
for Boys) by W. King. pub. Autumn 1992.

PALLAS ARMATA
98 Priory Road

Tonbridge
TN9 2BP

PALLISER PRESS
William Taylor
69 West End Avenue
HARROGATE
North Yorkshire
HG2 9BX
Short runs of pamphlets, mainly on typographical
subjects, but occasionally re-prints of 'street litera-
ture', printed on hand presses, sometimes on hand-
made paper.

MR P PALMER
138 Kensington Park Road
LONDON
W11 2EP

PALMERS PRESS
5 Castle Street
Ludlow
SY8 1AS

PALTEN PRESS
66 Hayle Terrace
Hayle
TR20 4XN

PAM PRESS
PO Box 35
Hastings
TN34 2UX.
Subjects: General Fiction.

PAN CELTIC PUBLICATIONS
PO Box 2
Kyle
IV40 8AR.
Subjects: Travel (Scotland).
Books July to December 1991 - 2

PANDEMONIUM
c/o Matthew De Monti
42 Kings Lane, Little Harrowden
WELLINGBOROUGH
Northamptonshire
NN9 5BL

PANGBOURNE ENGLISH CENTRE
Shooters Hill
Pangbourne
RG8 7DZ

PANRUN COLLECTIVE
46a Trent Road
Brixton
LONDON
AW2 5BL

PAPER CASTLE
W Keene
Edco House, 10-12 High Street
Colliers Wood
LONDON
SW19 2AE

195

PAPER DRUM PUBLISHING
12 Sudbourne Road
LONDON
SW2 5AQ 071 326 0753

P.A. PUBLISHING COMPANY
Unit 3 Grand Union Centre
West Row
London
W10 5AS.
Subjects: The Knowledge.
Books January to June 1991 - 1

PARADINE DEVELOPMENTS
Audley House
9 North Audley Street
LONDON W1Y

PARANOIA PRESS
Richard Briddon/Kate More/
David Almond
35 Percy Street
Middlesbrough Cleveland
TS1 4DD. Tel (0642) 224617
A small press with local roots and international
interests emphasis is on quality production quality
of writing (several of our writers are award winning) though our material is not always mainstream. We are open to new writers.
Top sellers:
Of Many-Coloured Glass by Norah Hill. Paperback
128pp May 1992 ISBN 1 872687 17 2 4.50. Short
stories.
Snails by Mark Rutter. 40pp chapbook 1990 ISBN
1 872687 01 6 £2.50. Poetry.
Fear of Language by Brian Borr. 32pp chapbook
1990 ISBN 1 872687 04 0 £2.50. Poetry.

MR F E PARDOE
9m Crosbie Road
Harrogate
BIRMINGHAM
B17 9BG

MS ROSEMARY PARDOE
Flat 1
36 Hamilton Street
Hoole
CHESTER
CH2 3JQ

PARFORDWOOD
Parford Cottage
Chagford
Newton Abbot
TQ13 8JR.
Subjects: Poetry.
Books July to December 1991 - 1

J. PARKE
c/o Tim Howe (author)
Greenside
Little Kneton
Warwick
CV35 0DH.
Subjects: Children's Fiction.
Books July to December 1991 - 1

MR D PARKER
Salgate
St Jouin de Blavou
61360 Pervencheres
France

MRS NAOMI PARKER
31 Bassetts Way
Farborough
ORPINGTON
Kent
BR6 7AF

MR R N PARKER
11 Richmond Mount
Headingly
LEEDS
LS6 1DG

PARKE SUTTON PUBLISHING
Hitech House
10 Blackfriars Street
Norwich
NR3 1SF.
Subjects: Costume.
Books July to December 1991 - 1.

PARNASSUS PUBLISHING
Bowes Lyon House
St. Georges Way
Stevenage
SG1 1XY.
Subjects: Poetry.
Books July to December 1991 - 3

PARRALLEL
7 Rustic Avenue
Southowram
HALIFAX
HX3 9QW

VIC PARRY PUBLISHING
174 Edgwarebury Lane
Edgware
HA8 8NE

L. MICHAEL PARSONS
W. Tytherley
Salisbury
SP5 1NF.
Subjects: History.
Books July to December 1991 - 1

PARTICK PRESS
David Hamilton
18 Kirklee Circus
GLASGOW
G12
Fine printer

PARTIZAN PRESS
Dave Ryan
26 Cliffsea Grove
Leigh-on-Sea
Essex.
Tel. 0702 73986 and F
Military and local history publisher specialising in

196

C17th & C18th. Also dealing with political aspects of the Great Rebellion. We produce 4 magazines covering the period 1450-1820.
All Did Command: Political radicalism in the New Model Army by Paul Bemrose. 56pp illustrated 1987 ISBN 0 946525 2 8 £4.99. English Civil War Notes & Queries - 5 issues per year. £1.75 cover price. Officers and Regiments of Waller's Army volume II Regiments D-H by L. Spring. £3.99.

PARTIZANS/CAFCA
218 Liverpool Road
London
N1 1LE.
Subjects: Economics.
Books January to June 1991 - 1

BRENDA M.PASK
33 Bentwick Road
Newark
NG24 4HT

PASOLD RESEARCH FUND
London School of Economics
Houghton Street
London
WC2A 2AE

PASS PUBLICATIONS
11 Baring Road
London
SE12 0JP.
Subjects: School Textbooks.
Books January to June 1991 - 3. Books July to December 1991 - 10

PASSION PRESS
Sara Burlace/Munni Reddy
c/o 33 Trent Grove Clayton
Newcastle-under-Lyme
Staffs.
ST5 4EW.
Poetry
Crimes of Passion - Sara Burlace and Sue Redd. 20pp ISBN 1 872315 00 3 £1.50. Poetry.
Going Under - Sara Burlace and Sue Redd. 20pp ISBN 1 872315 01 1 £1.50. Poetry.

PASSPORT MAGAZINE
Mike Gerrard
5 Parsonage St
Wistow
Huntingdon
Cambridgeshire
PE17 2QD 0487 822100
Bi-annual literary magazine in A5 paperback format. Publishes new inter national prose. Published April and October. 208pp. £5.95 or 10 annual subscription. Has featured writing from UK USA Norway India Africa Yugoslavia Czechoslovakia Japan China Germany Argentina etc. etc.

PASSWORD BOOKS
Dedalus Press
23 New Mount Street
Manchester
M4 4DE

PASTEST SERVICE
Cranford Lodge
Bexton Road
Knutsford
WA16 0ED.
Subjects: Languages.
Books July to December 1991 - 2

PASTIME PUBLICATIONS
15 Dublin Street
Lane South
Edinburgh
EH1 3PX.
Subjects: Taste of Scotland Scheme. Fishing. Sport. Travel in Britain. Travel Accommodation. Books July to December 1991 - 6

PATCHWORK PUBLICATIONS
58 New Penkridge Road
Cannock
WS11 1HW.
Subjects: Poetry.
Books July to December 1991 - 1

PATHFINDER PRESS LTD
47 The Cut
London
S E 1

PATHWAYS
12 Southcote Road
LONDON
N19 5BJ

MR DAN PATRICK
10b Morrison House
Burns Road
CUMBERNAULD
G67 2AL 0236 736049

MR DAVID PATRICK
Hillside
Grampion Terrace
TORPHINS
Aberdeenshire
AB31 4JS

PATTEN PRESS
The Old Post Office
Newmill
Penzance
TR20 4XN.
Subjects: Health Care.
Books July to December 1991 - 1

PAULINUS PRESS
12 Blowhorn Street
MARLBOROUGH
Wiltshire
SN8 1BT

PAUPERS' PRESS
Colin Stanley
27 Melbourne Road
West Bridgford
Nottingham

197

NG2 5DJ. Tel 0602 815063
We publish mostly monographs on and by modern writers. Essays of 7 500-15 000 words considered for publication. We also distribute for 3 US publishers: Borgo Press Starmont House Leaves of Grass. Mozart's Journey to Prague: a playscript by Colin Wilson. 36pp Septe 1992 ISBN 0 946650 43 8 paper ISBN 0 946650 44 6 hard £6.95/£14.95. A Report on the Violent Male by A.E. van Vogt. 36pp July 1992 ISBN 0 946650 40 3 paper ISBN 0 946650 41 1 hard £5.95/£13.95. Sex America and Other Insights by Colin Wilson. 76pp Jan 1992 ISBN 0 946650 34 9 paper ISBN 0 946650 35 7 hard £7.95/£15.95.

PAVELIN
Alan Pavelin
172 Leesons Hill
Chislehurst
Kent
BR7 6QL. Tel 0689 835741.
'Fifty Religious Films' a self-explanatory title is a one-off self-publishing Venture. It has been reviewed in Time Out and in 3 religious weeklies. It covers many films by great directors like Bergman Bresson Rossellini and Tarkovsky
Fifty Religious Films by Alan Pavelin. 108pp 1990 ISBN 0 9516491 0 8 £4.95.

PAVIC PUBLICATIONS
Sheffield City Poly
36 Collegiate Crescent
Sheffield
S10 2BP

PAVILION PUBLISHING
42 Lansdowne Place
Hove
BN3 1HH.
Subjects: Social Welfare.
Books January to June 1991 - 10. Books July to December 1991 - 2

MARK PAWSON
P.O. Box 664
London
(new postcode)
E3 4QR
Last year I was seriously considering giving it all up and just concentrating full-time on collecting small plastic toys but for some reason I've been almost hyperactive this year making five books in the first 3 months and there's more on the way. Send sae for current list of books badges postcards T-shirts Artistamps etc.
Forthcoming: Mark's little book about Mark's little books. Eco-Frenzy recycling and ecology symbols M. Pawson. 32pp 1992 £1.30 (inc. p&p). A source book with an introductory essay and 150 symbols. Moustaches M. Pawson. 20pp 1992 £1.30 (inc. p&p). Surveys the field of toy and novelty 'tashes clip-on plastic ones hairy ones metal ones make-your-own etc.
Installation Book M. Pawson. 25pp 1992 edition of 65 numbered and handsewn £6.00 (inc. p&p). Documentation of and some of the photocopies that I used in a 2200 sq. ft wallpaper installation.

PAX CHRISTIE
9 Henry Road
LONDON
N4 2LH

PAYNE & SON (SILVERSMITHS)
Clock House
37 High Street
Tunbridge Wells
TN1 1XL

MS ROBERTA PAYNE
38 Jepson House
Pears Croft Road
Fulham
LONDON
SW6 2BG

PHIL PAYTER GRAPHICS
125 Highland Road
SOUTHSEA
Hampshire
PO4 9EY 0705 732160

PBB
57 Effingham Road
Lee Green
LONDON
SE12 8NT

PBN PUBLICATIONS
P. Webb or N. Weir
22 Abbey Road
Eastbourne
BN20 8TE. Tel (0323) 31206.
Original material transcribed and printed - of interest to genealogists and local historians. All genealogical books
Sussex Militia List - 1803 - Northern Division Pevensey Rape. 118pp 1988 ISBN 1 871384 03 6 £3.95
Withyham Inhabitants - 1838. 52pp 1991 ISBN 1 871384 18 4 £3.25 Hastings Gaol Records - 1832-41. 64pp 1990 ISBN 1 871384 15 X £3.50 Full list on application.

PDS
31 North Walls
WINCHESTER
SO23 8DB

P.E PUBLICATIONS
42 Dalkeith Road
Edinburgh
EH16 5BS

PEACE & FREEDOM
Pual Rance
17 Farrow Road
Whaplode Drive
Spalding
Lincolnshire
PE12 0TS 0406 330242
Established in 1985 as a vehicle for socially aware poets writers art ists and musician. Offset printed and mentioned on national radio encouraged by Brigitte-Bardot P & F is now circulated worldwide. In 6 months circulation has increased by a third.

'Peace & Freedom Magazine' Ed Paul Rance. 28pp (shortly A4) twice yearly; illustr poetry; stories; music reviews. £3.00 ($7) for 4 issues 'Peace & Freedom Tape Magazine' Ed Paul Rance. 90 mins quarterly version of the printed magazine. £2.50 ($6) and SAE
'Peace & Freedom Back Issues'
for full listing send SAE: Bruce; 187 Grange Rd Hartlepool TS26 8LX

PEACE NEWS
5 Caledonian Road
London
N 1

PEACE PLEDGE UNION
6 Endsleigh Street
London
WC1H 0DX

PEACEWORK PRESS
Bartle Hall, Liverpool Road
Hutton
PRESTON
PR4 5HB 0772 616816
We are an imprint of Barrington Books, publishing experimental poetry by new writers. Work often explores the affect of emotion on our perception of reality, and is less political than Barrington.
The Dreams Are Coming Back by Chris Kenworthy, 40 pages, paperback. Published 20th Febuary 1992, ISBN 0 9519021 0 5, 2.00. Poetry.

PEACOCK PRINTMATES
21 Castle Street
ABERDEEN
AB1 1AJ

PEACOCK VANE PUBLISHING
44 High Street
Ventnor
PO39 1LT.
Subjects: Food.
Books January to June 1991 - 2

PEAK BOOKS
18 St Anstell Drive
Wilford
NG11 7BP

PEAK PARK JOINT PLANNING BOARD
National Park Office
Baslow Road
Bakewell
DE4 1AE

ELLY PEARCE
45 Sir Isaacs Walk
COLCHESTER
CO1 1JJ

PEARL PRESS
69 Waldeck Road
LONDON
N15 3EL

PEATON PRESS
12 Birkhall Drive

Bearsden
Glasgow
G61 1DR

PECKETT WELL COLLEGE
35 Gibbet Street
HALIFAX
HX1 5BA

PECKHAM PUBLISHING PROJECT
The Bookplace
13 Peckham High Street
LONDON
SE15

PECO PUBLICATIONS & PUBLICITY
Underleys
Beer
Seaton
EX12 3NA

MR M D PEEL
12 Lindsey Close
Woodnewton
PETERBOROUGH
PE8 5EW

PEEPAL TREE PRESS
53 Grove Farm Crescent
LEEDS
LS16 6BZ
Radical Third World publishing house

PEEPING TOM
c/o David Bell
Yew Tree House
15 Nottingham Road
Ashby-le-Zough
Leics
LE6 5DJ

PEERS SCHOOL BOOKS
Michael O'Reagan
11 Warnborough Road
OXFORD
OXW 6HZ 0865 511518

PEMBERTON PUBLISHING
25 Hunters Rise
Barnsley
S75 2JX.
Subjects: Music.

PEN:UMBRA
Mr David Rushmere
1 Beeches Close
SAFFRON WALDEN
Essex
CB11 4BU
Magazine

PENDALAY
47 Water Street
Lavenham
Sudbury
CO70 9RN

PENDRAGON PRESS
Mr Paul Broadhurst
Trebeath, Egloskerry, Launceston, Cornwall, PL15
8RY
Publishing the work of Hamish Miller. But we were
suckered in by John Michell who said why not do it
yourself? We did with 'Sacred Shrines' - Holy Wells
in a de luxe limited edition. It worked, like the
second book so we caught the bug.

PENDULUM GALLERY PRESS:
Powerfresh
3 Gray Street
Northampton
or 56 Ackender Road Alton GU34 1JS.
Subjects: Art. Short Stories. Books July to December 1991 - 1

PENDYKE PUBLICATIONS
Goffeysfa, Methodist Hill
Froncysyllte
Llangollen
LL20 7SN

DR O C PENGE
The Moathouse
Drayton Beauchamp
AYLESBURY
Buckinghamshire
HP22 5LT

PENMARRAN PUBLISHING
60 Argyll Road
Pennsylvania
Exeter
Devon
EX4 4RY. Tel (0392) 71080
Publisher of local books colour notepaper and
colour bookmarks with ribbons
Down Dartmoor Way by Penny and Mary Housden.
273 x 216mm hardback 164pp 162 illus. 6 maps
and index ISBN 1 872852 00 9 £12.99 (plus £2.65
if buying by mail order). Collection of pen and ink
drawings of Dartmoor National park with decora-
tively scripted text and individual verses.

PENMIEL PRESS
Edward Burrett
Full Point
16 New Road
ESHER
Surrey
K10 9PG
Fine printer

PENNINE PENS
32 Windsor Road
Hebden Bridge
HX7 8LF.
Subjects: Cycling.

PENNINE PLATFORM
Brian Merrikin Hill
Ingmanthorpe Farm Cottage
WETHERBY
West Yorkshire
LS22 5EQ
Poetry

MR GRAHAM PENNINGTON
School House
School Lane, Westhead
ORMSKIRK
Lancashire
L40 6HL

PENNYFIELDS PRESS
32 Ashville Road
Ashton Gate
Bristol
BS3 2AP
(also see Avon Poetry News)

PEN PALS
43 Denbydale Way
Royton
Oldham
Lancs
OL2 5TN

JACQUIE PENROSE
2 Hallet Road
Havant
PO9 2PJ

PENROVE BOOKS
Christians Warehouses
23 Dockhead Wharf, 4 Shad Thames
London
SE1 2NW

PENTAMAN PRESS
Unit 1 Crossland Industrial Estate
Stockport Road
West Bredbury
Stockport
SK6 2BR.
Subjects: Sports.
Books July to December 1991 - 1

PEOPLE INTERNATIONAL
PO Box 26
Tunbridge Wells
TN2 5AZ

PEOPLE'S POETRY
(ed Peter Geoffrey Paul Thompson)
(Precious Pearl Press)
71 Harrow Crescent
Romford Essex
RM3 7BJ

PEOPLE'S PUBLICATIONS
50 Henslowe Road
London
SE22 0AR.
Subjects: Biography.
Books July to December 1991 - 1

PEOPLE TO PEOPLE
West Midlands Arts
82 Granville Street
Birmingham
B1 2LH

200

PEPAR PUBLICATIONS
Unit 26 Southside
249 Ladypool Road
Sparkbrook
Birmingham
B12 8LF.
Subjects: Poetry.
Books July to December 1991 - 1

PEPPERCORN BOOKS
Mrs Judith A White
24 Cromwell Road, ELY, Cambridgeshire, CB6
1AS
Very small publisher at present specialising in food-related books. We hope to expand in 1992, publishing general subject books including fiction for as yet unpublished authors. All enquiries welcome.
Bon Appetit. French/English menu dictionary. Compiler J A White. 148 x 105 mm. Paperback, 111 pages. 0 9516413 0 1. Retail price £4.80. Over 3500 menu items translated, together with a guide to eating out in France.

PERDIX PRESS
Walter Partridge
21 The Close
SALISBURY
SP1 2EB
Fine printer

PEREGINE PUBLISHING
7 Farnham Park
Bangor
BT20 3SR

PERFECT PUBLICATIONS
BM Perfect
London
WC1N 3XX

PERGAMON CHESS
Railway Road
Sutton Coldfield
B73 6AZ.
Subjects: Indoor Games. Biography
Books January to June 1991 - 3. Books July to December 1991 - 3

PERIAKTOS
6 Sandhurst Avenue
Ipswich
Suffolk
IP3 8DU

PERICLES PUBLICATIONS
48 Newton Road
Mumbles
SWANSEA
SA3 4BQ
Publisher of poetry, prose, historical texts etc. Plans to begin on nautical and Welsh subjects.

THE PERPETUA PRESS
14 Stanley Road
OXFORD
OX4 1QZ

BRYAN PERRETT

Matle Avenue
Burscough
Near Ormskirk
L40 5SL.
Subjects: Local History.
Books July to December 1991 - 1

PERROTT CARTOGRAPHICS
Darowen
MACHYNLLETH
Powys
SY20 8NS

PERRY AND PERRY PUBLISHING
16 Pickwick Road
Corsham
SN13 9BT.
Subjects: Music.
Books July to December 1991 - 1

DR W PERRY
69 Wimpole Street
LONDON
W1N 7DE

PERSEVERANCE WRITERS' CLUB
14 Drumbrae Avenue
Edinburgh
EH12 8TE

PERSIFLAGE PRESS
26 Clacton Road
LONDON
E17 8AR

PERSONAL RIGHTS ASSOCIATION
22 Wentworth Close
WATFORD
Hertfordshire
WD1 3LW
The Association was founded in 1871, and for many years published 'The Individualist'. Members included Josephine Butler and Auberon Herbert. Aims include repeal of the Bank Act of 1844, as advocated by Henry Meulen in 'Free Banking'.

PERSPECTIVE PRESS
92 Hertford Street
Cambridge
CB4 3AQ.
Subjects: Education.
Books July to December 1991 - 1

PETAL PRESS
2 Longford Wharf, Stephenson Road
Stretford
Manchester
M32 0JT

PETER PRESS
c/o M. Wilson-Smith
59 St. James' Street
London
SW1A 1LD.
Subjects: Poetry.
Books July to December 1991 - 1

PETERBOROUGH WILDLIFE GROUP
West Town School
Williamson Avenue
Peterborough
PE3 6BA.
Subjects: Wildlife.
Books July to December 1991 - 1

F. PETERS PUBLISHING
Gatebeck
Kendal
LA8 0HW.
Subjects: Travel Guide to Lake District.
Books July to December 1991 - 1

MS CATHERINE PETTS
1 Marlborough Avenue
READING
Berkshire
RG1 5JB

PEYRERE INDENT
Robin and Hilaire Rimbaud
5 Park Court
191A Battersea Park Road
London
SW11 4LD. Tel 071 498 3032
Embracing a joint devotion to art and books they
aim to create work which appeals to both the tactile
and intellectual senses. Designing and printing their
own unique books in extremely limited editions
other projects encompass graphics music and erotic
adventures
Spectacular incisions - An A5 glassine envelope
enshrines a dozen monochrome collages printed on
virginal acetate. Unlimited edition ever changing
[ZAHN 008] £5.00. August 1992.
A Reliquary - 10 full colour icongraphic images
counted on arches paper. Steel edition of 12. 59 x
33cms. 3 400 gms £78 [ZAHN 006] Jan 1991. A
book of Stretching - applied images - classical and
modern - physically stretched by technology. 15 x
10cms July 1991 [ZAHN 007] £2.00

PFC PUBLICATIONS
25 Totnes Close
Devon Park
Bedford
MK40 3AX.
Subjects: Poetry.
Books July to December 1991 - 1

PHAEDRA BOOKS
Doug Keating
23 Brougham Road,
Southsea,
Hampshire PO5 4PA
0705 812100
Phaedra (Fay-dra) was set up to help publish innovative writers , who might otherwise be overlooked
by the short-sighted publishing giants. We are una-
shamedly commercial in approach and proud of our
imaginative presentation of science fiction, and
other genre.
'The Eighth Colour'; Doug Keating; ISBN 0 951968
00 9; 300pp paperback; publication 1/9/92; price
£4.50.

PHAGPOS PRESS
34 Airlie House
Airlie Gardens
London
W8 7AN

DR J C PHEMISTER
Belaire
Chagford
NEWTON ABBOT
Devon
TQ13 8AT

PHILATELIC IMPRINT
12 Holyoake Walk
LONDON
N2 0JX
Publishers of books for stamp collectors.
THE CANCELLATIONS OF THE 1841 PENNY
RED. By David Goldsmith and Robert Danzig. I
llustrated guide and catalogue. 27.50. ISBN 0
9517063 0 6.

PHILERGON
57 Green Lane
Chesham Bois
Amersham
HP6 5LQ.
Subjects: Social Sciences.
Books July to December 1991 - 1

MR BRIAN PHILIPS
5 Chatsworth Road
TORQUAY
Devon
TQ1 3BJ

MR ALUN PHILLIPS
Bentinck Villa
Goat Street
NEWPORT
Dyfed
SA42 0PU

JOHN M PHILLIPS
138 Vicarage Road
Chelmsford
CM9 9BT

M PHILIPS
15 Kingswood Avenue
Bexhill-on-Sea
TN39 4EJ

PHILIPSON & SOB
Albany House
Blandford Square
Newcastle-upon-Tyne
NE1 4HZ

MRS C PHILPOTT
22 Essex Avenue
KINGSWINDORD
West Midlands
DY6 9RH

KATHLEEN M. PHILPOTT
3 King's Drive
Bishopston
Bristol
BS7 8JW.
Subjects: Local History.
Books July to December 1991 - 1

PHOENIX PRESS
John Fairfax
The Thatch
Eling Hermitage
Newbury
Berks
RG16 9XR 0635 200585
A poetry press, concerned with publishing both new
and established poets. The emphasis in publication
is not only an exciting poetry but on quality book
production.
Wild Children. By John Fairfax. 46pp. 1985. 0
900852 10 0. Poetry collection £4.00 (0.75p+p)
(Hbck signed limited edition £10.00)
Four Ways (collection). Sue Stewart Bruce Barnes
Louise Hudson Bart Keegan 61pp. 1985. 0
900852119. Poetry Anthology £4.50 (0.75p+p)
Snook. Michael Baldwin. 47pp, 1980. 0 905947878.
Poetry collection £3.00 (0.75p+p) (Published in
collaboration with Springwood Books)

PHOENIX PRESS
PO Box 824
LONDON
N1 9DL
Anarchist yearbook

PHOLIOTA PRESS LIMITED
82 Stonebridge Road
LONDON
N15 5PA 071 837 8300
Mainly books of Jewish interest
The Jews of Poland
The Jewish Cookery Book
The Citrus Cook Book
Life is a Dance: You Should Only Know the Steps.

PHOTON PRESS
Dr. John Light
The Light House,
29 Longfield Road,
Tring, Herts HP23 4DG
Publish only self-generated work.
Light's List of Literary Magazines; John Light;
12pp; 1/1/92 ISBN 0 951189 47 6; 50p.
Northumberland Ancestors: Short, Taylor and
Fawcus; John Light; 36pp; 1991 ISBN 0 951189 46
8; £2.00.

PHYSIOLOGY OF A FLY PUBLICATIONS
50 Clifford Road
Sheffield
S11 9AQ.
Subjects: Poetry.
Books July to December 1991 - 2

PIATKUS BOOKS
5 Windmill Street
London
W1P 1HF

PICKPOCKETS
M.E. Rose
25 St. Mary's Terrace
Hastings
East Sussex
TN34 3LS Tel 0424 714393
'Pickpockets' are finely produced pocket-sized
books illustrated by established artists on a variety
of unusual subjects. Especially suitable as gifts or
collectors' items at £1 they still cost less than many
greetings cards and have wide general appeal.
The Turning of the Year by Thomas Hardy illus-
trated by Graham Clarke. ISBN 1 873422 03 2.
Looking is a Marvellous Thing by Rainer Maria
Rilke on Cézanne. ISBN 1 873422 05 9.
Befriend a Bacterium text by Ivor Cutler cartoons
by Martin Honeysett. ISBN 1 873422 11 3.

PICKS PUBLISHING
83 Greenfields Crescent
Ashton-in-Makerfield
Wigan
WN4 8QY

PICTRE BOX PUBLICATIONS
New Exchange Buildings
Queens Square
MIDDLESBROUGH
Cleveland
TS2

PIG PRESS
7 Cross View Terrace
DURHAM
DH1 4JY
Poetry from the UK and USA

THE PIKERS' PAD
PO Box 97
Storrington
PULBOROUGH
West Sussex
RH20 3YZ
Cheap paperbacks and local history.

MR BERNIE PILCHER
6 Courtland Avenue
ILFORD
Essex
IG1 3DW

PILGRIM'S BELL
A.P. Fothergill
7 Janice Drive
Fulwood
Preston
PR2 4YE. Tel 0772 719469
Tony Fothergill is a retired insurance clerk and
currently the treasurer at Lune Street Chapel. He
writes to SPG: 'Herewith complimentary copy of
the one and only book I shall be publishing!' No
unsolicited material. Avowed Intent - A Brief Description of and Short History About Central Methodist Church Lune Street Preston by A.P. Fothergill.
A5 32pp illustrations 1992 ISBN 0 9517241 0 9
£3.00 (plus 25p p&p).

PILGRIM'S PUBLISHING
9 Lyon Street
Southampton
SO2 0LD.
Subjects: Second World War History.
Books July to December 1991 - 1

MR R A PINCKHEARD
24 Arnull Crescent
DAVENTRY
Northamptonshire
NN11 5AY

PINE TREE
The Street
Brundish
WOODBRIDGE
Suffolk
IP13 8BN

J PINEWOOD ENTERPRISES
37 Durham Road
London
W5 4JR

MR B T PINHEY
2 Old School House, Furzen Lane
Ellens Green, Rudgwick
HORSHAM
West Sussex
RH12 3AR

DEREK PINKERTON
522 Holly Lane
Erdington
Birmingham
B24 9LY.
Subjects: Cycling History.
Books July to December 1991 - 1

PINKFOOT PRESS
Balgavies
Forfar
DD8 2TH.
Subjects: Military Local History.
Books July to December 1991 - 1

PINK PAPER
77 City Garden Row
London
N1 8EZ

PINTSIZE PRESS
49 Essex Street
OXFORD
OX4 3AW 0865 516284

PIONEER PRESS
Station House
John Street Central
MERTHYR TYDFIL
Mid Glamorgan
CF47 0AW
Arthur Watkins has studied King Arthur for 24
years and is now issuing the results.

PIPKIN PRESS
19 Charnwood Avenue
Westone
Northampton
NN3 3DX

PIRA
Randalls Road
Leatherhead
KT22 7RU

MRS M PIRIE
Penyoke Cottage
Cargreen
SALTASH
Cornwall
PL12 6PA

PISCES PUBLICATIONS
Glamorgan Wildlife Trust
Wildlife Centre
Fountain Road
Tondu
CF12 0EH.
Subjects: Travel (Britain).
Books July to December 1991 - 1

PIT BULL TERRORIST
The Dollyhead International
c/o 73 Fitzgerald House
169 East India Dock Road
LONDON
E14 0HH

MR DAVID PITT
1265 La Cure
Switzerland

MR LEN PITTENDRIGH
5 The Oval
New Barb
LONGFIELD
Kent
DA3 7HD
Retirement hobby devoted to publishing unknown
but worthy poems, in hardback volumes at cost to
contributers, which can be recovered if they choose
to sell 4 books at the RRP for each 6 bought.
To Each Their Own 0 9510995 1 5 RRP 9.00
Hardback. Edited by Len Pittendrigh. 1986. An
anthology of verses by everyday people from the
Gravesham and Dartford area of North Kent. 147
pages. Intersection illustrations by Molly Sharpe.
Dust cover by Janet Reid. 1st volume of trilogy.
A Choise of Colours ISBN 0 9510995 2 3 RRP
£9.75 hardback. Edited by Len Pitten-drigh. 1988.
Anthology of verses, colour coded for each poet and
2nd book in trilogy, by everyday people of the area
of North Kent. 145 pages. Illustrations by Molly
Sharpe. Dust cover by Janet Reid.
Passing Clouds ISBN 0 9510995 3 1 RRP £9.00
Hardback. Edited by Len Pittendrigh. 1991. An
Anthologhy of verses, colour coded for each poet
and miscellanous collection. 3rd vol. of trilogy from
wider field of contributers. 147 pages. Illustrations
by Jane Chatworthy & Molly Sharpe. Dust cover by
Janet Reid.

MR D G PLAITER
13 St Edwards Road
PORTSMOUTH
PO5 3DH

ALICE PLANCTON
A J Willis
4 Trinity Street
BRIGHTON
BN2 3HN
I intended to publish a book of my own writing but
it turned into a four album set

PLANET - THE WELSH INTERNATIONALIST
John Barnie
P.O. Box 44
Aberystwyth
Dyfed.

TERRY PLANT
11 Lyndhurst Avenue
Kingskerswell
Newton Abbot
TQ12 5AJ

PLASTICS & RUBBER INSTITUTE
27 Cavendish Road
Hazel Grove
STOCKPORT
Cheshire
SK7 6HY
Developing software for the plastics industry.
Technology publications for schools.

PLATEWAY PRESS
Keith Taylorson
P.O. Box 973
Brighton
BN2 2TG
Plateway Press was formed in 1986 with the aim of
producing good quality books on neglected aspects
of the railway and transport scene without arbitrary
restriction on cover prices. The imprint was origi-
nally based on Church Road Croydon on the course
of the erstwhile Surrey Iron Railway an early
'Plateway' providing the inspiration for our name.
Lesser Railways of the Yorkshire Dales by Harold
D. Bowtell. ISBN 0 9511108 8 8 £12.95.
Narrow Gauge Railways - Two Feet and Under by
L.S. Roberston. ISBN 9511108 4 5 £9.95.
Locomotive Apprentice at North British by Nigel
Macmillan. ISBN 1 871980 10 0 £8.95.

PLATFORM
Folder 80
c/o Acorn Books
17 Chatham Street
READING
Magazine

PLATFORM 5 PUBLISHING
Lydgate House
Lydgate Lane
Sheffield
S10 5FH

PLATT CONTEMPORARY ART
The Gallery

The Street
Igtham
Sevenoaks
TN15 9HH.
Subjects: Art.

PLATYPUS PRESS
PO Box 209
SCARBOROUGH
WA 6019
AUSTRALIA

PLAYTIME FOREVER PRESS
BM Jed
London WC1N 3XX
Don't compete play. Genitality is a fetish. No more
dead time. Are you a happy shopper? New Age -
same old shite. Smile - there is no God. Demolish
serious buildings. Don't vote, don't work, don't
mind us. Down with fatuous slogans.
Fatuous Times Magazine; £1.50.
Away With All Cars - by Mr. Social Control.
Did the Rotary Club Kill J.F.K. - by Mr. Hiram J.
Kleenex III. Forthcoming.

PLAYWRIGHTS PUBLISHING COMPANY
Liz and Tony Breeze
70 Nottingham Road
Burton Joyce
Nottingham
NG14 5AL. Tel 0602 313356
A small family firm specialising in the publication
of new plays -authors are charge a small reading fee
and the best scripts are printed in book form and
sent out to libraries in the UK America and Australia. Birthmarks by Mark Jenkins - full length play
about the life of Karl Marx. ISBN 1 873130 5.00
Lifestyles by Sylvia Vaughan - one act play about
two women who have shared the same man. ISBN
1 873130 03 1 £2.50
Dominus Domina by Michael Hoyland - one act
play about the problems of a woman getting on
better than her partner. ISBN 1 873130 04 X £2.50.

PLEASURE BOOKS
Susan Brett
50 Lakeside Hightown
Ringwood
Hants
BH24 3DX. Tel 0425 477334
Non-fictional foccusing on areas of outstanding
beauty and interesting history. Profusely illustrated
with colour pictures and graphics. Easy reading -
highest quality production and design. Produced by
desk top publishing throughout ensures an extremely low retail price. A Dorset Wonderland by
Susan Brett. A5 100pp 112 colour pictures 2 edition
laminated sewn cover 1990 ISBN 0 951046 4 11
£3.95. Background history - walks and maps of
Purbeck in Dorset.

EDITIONS PLEINE PLUME
17 rue Pasteur
F-69520 GRIGNY
FRANCE

PLOUGH PRESS
2 Manor Way

Kidlington
OX5 2BD

PLUTO
345 Archway Road
London
N6 5AA. 081 348 2724
A radical independent press publishing academic books in the social sciences. We publish over a broad spectrum from the left; producing about 40 books per year.
'Citizenship and Social Class' by T.H. Monshall and T. Bottomore. Septem ber 1991. ISBN 0 74530 47 7 hardback £24.95. ISBN 0 74530 476 1 paperback £9.95. Sociology text.
'The Debt Boomerang' by Susan George. Nov. 1991. ISBN 0 74530 593 8 hard back £19.95. ISBN 0 74530 594 6 paperback. £7.95. Third World Debt. 'The Welfare State' by Dexter Whitfield. Sept 1991. ISBN 0 74530 080 4 paperback £15.50. ISBN 0 74530 608 X hardback £45.00. Political economics of privatisation

P.M.G. PUBLICATIONS
165 Jordanhill Drive
Glasgow
G13 1UQ.
Subjects: Law.
Books July to December 1991 - 1

PN REVIEW
208-212
Corn Exchange
Manchester
M4 3BQ

POET AND PRINTER
30 Grimsdyke Road
Hatch End
Pinner
HA5 4PW

POETICAL HISTORIES
27 Sturton Street
CAMBRIDGE
CB1 2QG
Small pamphlets handwritten, handprinted, hand-made paper.

THE POETRY BUSINESS
5 Byram Road, Westgate, Huddersfield, HD1 1ND
Poetry resource for Huddersfield and west Yorks. Books under the imprint Smith/Doorstep. Magazine 'North'. Run workshops and a poetry bookshop. Mial order and a library. Too good to be true?

POETRY & AUDIENCE
Leeds University Poetry Soc
School of English
The University
LEEDS
LS2

POETRY DIGEST
28 Stainsdale Green
Whitwick
LEICESTER

LE6 3PW

POETRY DURHAM
c/o School of English
Univ of Durham
Elvet Riverside New Elvet
Durham
DH1 3JT

POETRY IRELAND REVIEW
44 Upper Mount Street
Dublin 2
Ireland

POETRY LONDON NEWSLETTER
Leon Cych
26 Clacton Road
LONDON
E17 8AR
Listings of poetry events in the capital.

POETRY NOTTINGHAM
Summer Cottage
West Street
Shelford
Notts
NE12 1EG

POETRY NOTTINGHAM PUBLICATIONS
9 Charnwood Avenue
Keyworth
Nottingham
NG12 5JA.
Subjects: Poetry.
Books July to December 1991 - 1

POETRY NOW
4 Hythegate
Werrington
PE4 6ZP.
Subjects: Poetry.
Books July to December 1991 - 19

POETRY PROSE PICTURES
52 Wimbledon Park Road
London
SW18 5HS

POETRY REVIEW QUARTERLY
c/o The National Poetry Centre
22 Betterton St
London
WC2H 9BU

POETRY ROUND
c/o The National Poetry Centre
22 Betterton Street
LONDON
WC2H 9BU

POETRY WALES
26 Andrew's Close
Heolgerrig
Merthyr Tydfil
Mid Glam
CF48 1SS

CANNON POETS: PROF K MAHADVA
Century House
Erdington
Birmingham
B23 5XN

MR JOHN POINTER
14 Elizabeth Cottages
Kew
RICHMOND
Surrey
TW9 3NJ

MR MALCOLM POLLARD
42 East Park Parade
NORTHAMPTON
NN1 4LA

LAWRENCE POLLINGER LIMITED
18 Maddox Street
Mayfair
LONDON
W1R 0EU

POLYGON EXPLORER GUIDES
51 East Park Close
Ardwick
Manchester
M13 9SD 061 273 4995
Est 1988 to produce short runs of students' 'Map
Packs' as a low-cost record for those involved in
Don Lee's fieldwork in pioneering footpath routes
and urban safaris in and around the Manchester
region. 50 titles in print.
'Discover Hayfields Forgotten Footpaths' by Don
Lee. 17 Sheets of 6 walks (1990) £2.75
'Buxton's Forgotten Footpaths' by Don Lee. 23
sheets of 6 walks. £3.25 'The Footpaths of Kearsley'
by Don Lee. 14 sheets of 6 walks. £2.25

POLYGON
48 Pleasance
EDINBURGH
EH8 9TJ

POLYGON RESOURCES
P.O. Box 3
Hedge End
Southampton
SO3 4ZW.
Subjects: School Textbooks.
Books July to December 1991 - 4

POMA
'Ellan Beg Vannin'
17 Mendip Drive
Bolton
BL2 6LQ.
Subjects: Family History.
Books January to June 1991 - 2

POMES (ex Jane Publishing)
Adrian Spendlow
23 Bright Street
York
YO2 4XS.

Poetry societies were reeling with shock today that
poetry is for everyone! Questions are being asked in
the house 'What's for tea?'. Yes poetry is getting
vocal - ordinary people are reading it some of them
right out loud - join us.
Pomes editor Adrian Spendlow. A5 28pp quarterly
£1.50 or 3 issue sub £3.75 (inc. p&p). Postal performance poetry - participation by purchasers positively pushed.
Kid's Pomes - details as Pomes but younger stuff.
Cushdie For Dossin - Great Vocal Poetry by Adrian
Spendlow. 32pp A5 £2.00 (inc. p&p)

MR G PONTING
7 Weaver's Place
Chandler's Ford
EASTLEIGH
Hampshire
SO5 1TU

POOLBEG PRESS
Knocksedan House
Swords
Co Dublin
Ireland

MR MICK POPE
19 Campion Drive
Swinton
Mexborough
South Yorkshire
S64 8QZ

MR PETER POPHAM
145 Grosvenor Avenue
LONDON
N5 2NH

POPPYLAND PUBLISHING
13 Kings Arms Street
North Walsham
NR28 9JX

H PORDES
383 Cockfosters Road
Cockfosters
Hertfordshire
EN4 0JS 0814 492524
Reprints of Library Reference tools such as The
British Museum Subject Index 1881-1940;
Bibliografia Hispona-Americana; Canadian cata-
logue of books and historical basics such as
L.F.Saltzman's' English Industries of the Middle
Ages' &' English Industry of the Middle Ages';
Shakesperian dictionary; the complete works of
William Shakespeare in one volume; etc.

MR COLIN PORTER
Hill Cottage
Tollerton
YORK
YO6 2DS

M S PORTER
British S F Association
114 Guildhall Street
FOLKESTONE

Kent
CT20 1ES

MR STUART PORTE
138 Cranworth Gardens
LONDON
SW9 0NV

PORTFOLIO COMMUNICATIONS
c/o Ms Sheila Gimson
27 Emperor Gate
LONDON
SW7 4HX

PORTIA PUBLISHING
Beauchamp Cottage
Abbey Hill
KENILWORTH
Warwickshire
CV8 1LW 0926 58778

POTPOURRI PUBLICATIONS
Charlotte Boggis Clarke
12 Silver Street,
Newport Pagnell,
Buckinghamshire MK16 OEP
0908 614634
"'Perpetual Springtime' is a delicious mixture of stories about people and places, of poems and of thought-provoking pieces in a most attractive magazine of variety," (from the Foreword by Canon David Goldie).
Perpetual Springtime: an Autobiographical Anthology; ISBN 0 904063 26 7; 235pp, £4.99 includes contribution to Newport Pagnell Church Restoration Fund.

POWER PUBLICATIONS
Mike Power
Clayford Avenue
Ferndown
Dorset
BH22 9PQ Tel (0202) 875223
Local interest and pub walk series.
Pub Walks in Dorset - Mike Power. 96pp ISBN 0 9514502 0 4 £3.95. The Dorset Coast Path - Mike Power. 40pp ISBN 0 9514502 3 9 2.95. Famous Woman in Dorset - Elizabeth Edwards. 88pp ISBN 0 9514502 9 8 4.50.

POWERCUT
BM Powercut
LONDON
WC1N 3XX
Anti-sexist magazine for and by women and men, seeking to be as accessible as possible, with views, arguments,experiences of ordinary people, plus ace cartoons. Never academic or boring waffle. Sexual politics for now: sharp, realistic, close to home.

POWYSLAND CLUB
c/o Trewern Hall
Welshpool
SY21 8DT.
Subjects: Historic Local Photography.
Books January to June 1991 - 1

PRAXIS BOOKS

Rebecca Smith
'Sheridan' Broomers Hill Lane
Pulborough
West Sussex
RH20 2DU. Tel 0798 873504
New and reissued titles fiction and non-fiction. Small but growing. First title was ambitious but has been a big hit.
In Search of Life's Meaning by Matley and Smith. 288pp 7.50. An invaluable compendium.
Red Spider by S. Baring-Gould. (Due 1993). Old novel of Devon once very popular. Overdue for reissue.
William Penn. Pamphlet on his life and ministry with the Sussex connections emphasised.

PREBENDAL PRESS LIMITED
PO Box 30
THAME
Oxfordshire
OX9 3AD
Celtic Dawn magazine

PRECIOUS PEARL PRESS
71 Harrow Crescent
ROMFORD
Essex
RM3 7BJ
Founded in 1991, we publish 'The People's Poetry'. a quarterly poetry magazine. We are publishing poems and song lyrics from all over the U.K. shorter lyrical and romantic poems and song lyrics especially sought. Overseas submissions welcome.
The People's Poetry (Number one) Editor Peter Geoffrey/Paul Thompson. 24 pages. Published Winter 1991. Shorter poems and lyrics.
The People's Poetry (Number two) Editor Peter Geoffrey/Paul Thompson. 24 pages. Published Spring 1992. Shorter poems and lyrics of all kinds. The People's Poetry (Number three) Editor Peter Geoffrey/Paul Thompson. 24 pages Publication date Summer 1992, shorter poems and lyrics of all kinds. Increasingly lyrical/romantic, and not obscure.

PRELUDE
Darren Bentley
74 Monteith Crescent
Boston
Lincolnshire
PE21 9AY
Music art fashion publication. Mainly dealing with the extreme underground music underground art underground fashion. A publication for the deadly 90s.

PREPOSTEROUS PUBLICATIONS
PO Box 589
St John Street
Chester
CH1 1AA. 0244 831531 Ext 245
A small publishing company based in Chester dealing with a wide range of material.
'What a Load of Bails' by Chandra Senan. July 1990. 236pp. 10 cartoons. £4.95 plus £1.20 p&p. ISBN 0 9516045 0 3.

PRE-SCHOOL PLAYGROUPS ASSOCIATION

61-63 Kings Cross Road
London
WC1X 9LL.
Subjects: Education.
Books July to December 1991 - 2

PRESCOT & WHITSON WRITERS
12 Aspinall Street
Prescot
MERSEYSIDE
L35 5RU

JANET PRESHOUS
The Paddock
Lydham
Bishop's Castle
SY9 5HB

MR PRESTON
30 Russell Drive
Christchurch
Dorset
BH23 3PA

MIKE PRESTON MUSIC
The Glengarry
3 Thornton Grove
Morecambe
LA4 5PU

PRESTON OTHER PAPER
PO BOX 172
Preston
PR1 4BU

PREST ROOTS PRESS
P. Larkin
34 Alpine Court
Kenilworth
Warwickshire
CV8 2GP 0926 592778
Seeks to unite a distinctive contemporary poetry
with the best of trad itional fine printing at afford-
able prices.
'Sea Watches' by Peter Riley. 1991. 32pp. £7.50.
ISBN 1 871237 06 8. Poetry
'Airs and Ligatures' by D.S. Marriott. 1991. 32pp.
£7.50. ISBN 1 871237 07 6. Poetry.
'Word Order' by J.H. Prynne. 1990. 24pp. £6.00.
ISBN 1 871237 04 1.

PRETANI
638 Springfield Road
Belfast
BT12 7DY

PREVIOUS PARROT PRESS
Dennis Hall
The Foundry
Church Hanborough
WITNEY
Oxfordshire
OX8 8AB
Previously Hanborough Parrott, PPP seemed more
alluring alliteratively. Limited editions (100 to 180
copies) finely printed with a strong emphasis on
illustra-tion. Some copies hand coloured. Prose,
poetry, drawings and books on aspects of illustra-

tion.

PRIAPUS PRESS
John Cotton
37 Lombardy Drive
BERKHAMPSTEAD
Hertfordshire
Fine press

PRICE GUIDE PRODUCTIONS AND PUBLI-
CATIONS
125 East Barnet Road
New Barnet
EN4 8RF.
Subjects: Bibliography.
Books July to December 1991 - 1

MR R A PRICE
3 Westhill
Stantonbury
MILTON KEYNES
MK14 6BG

MR PHILLIP PRIESTLEY
15 Hawley Street
MARGATE
Kent
G9 1PU

GRAHAM PRIESTLEY
22 Cherry Tree Crescent
Balerno
EH14 5AL.
Subjects: Fishing.
Books January to June 1991 - 1.

PRINCELET EDITIONS
25 Princelet Street
LONDON
E7 6QH

PRINCIPIA
15 Hillcrest Drive, Slackhead
Milnthorpe
Lancashire
LA7 7BB

J L PRINGLE
Hayden Lodge
Gloucester Road, Staverton
CHELTENHAM
Gloucestershire
GL51 0SS

PRINTABILITY PUBLISHING
15 Moorland Close
Wolviston Village
TS22 5LX

THE PRINT BUSINESS LIMITED
91 Church Road
LONDON
SE19 2TA

PRINTED WORD BOOKSHOP
West Centre
St Hellans

Jersey
Channel Islands

PRINTERS DEVIL MAGAZINE OF NEW WRIT-
ING
South East Arts
10 Mount Ephraim
Tunbridge Wells
Kent
TN4 8AS

PRINTFORCE
6 Angel Hill Drive
Sutton
SM1 3BX

PRINT ORIGINATION
Stephenson Way
Formby Industrial Estate, Formby
Liverpool
L37 8EG

PRINTOUT PUBLISHING & PRINT
50 Beverley Road
IPSWICH
IP4 4BU

BCM PRINTS
LONDON
WC1N 3XX

PRINTWISE PUBLICATIONS
B68 Brunswick Business Park
Brunswick Enterprise
Liverpool

PRION
J Wilson (Booksales)
Lane End Road, Sands Industrial Estat
High Wycombe
HP12 4HG

PRIORY STUDIOS
Erik Russell
252 Belsize Road
LONDON
NW6 4BT

PRIORY BOOKS
28 Eccleshall Road
Walton
Stone
ST15 0HA

PRISM PRESS
2 South Street
BRIDPORT
Dorset
DT6 3NQ

PRIVATE LIBRARIES ASSOCATION
Ravelston
South View Road
Pinner
HA5 3YD

P R JENNER

16 Muswell Hill Road
LONDON
N6 5UG

PROCESSED TAPES
1st Floor
22 Lutton Place
EDINBURGH
EH8 9PE
Badges to order and Chasing Rainbows 'zine.

PROMISE PUBLICATIONS
2 Meon Walk
Riverdene
Basingstoke
RG21 2DX.
Subjects: Children's Non-fiction.

PROMOTIONAL REPRINT COMPANY
Harvey's Books
Magna Road
Wigston
Leicester
LE8 2ZH.
Subjects: Children's non-fiction.
Books January to June 1991 - 1

PROMOTION MAGAZINE
(see Purple Patch)

PROSPECT PUBLICATIONS
Buckley House
Manston
Sturminster Newton
DT10 1EZ

PROTEAN PUBLICATIONS
Flat 4
34 Summer Field Crescent
Edgbaston
Birmingham
B16 0ER.
Subjects: Poetry.
Books July to December 1991 - 1

PROUD
Suite 401
302 Regent St
London
W1R 5AL

N.D. PROUDLOCK
181 West Park Drive (West)
Leeds
LS8 2BE.
Subjects: History of Leeds Tramways.
Books January to June 1991 - 1

PROVIDENCE PRESS
Mr Martin Firrell
90 Victoria Road
LONDON
NW6 6QA

MRS DOROTHY L PRUSMANN
17 Seymour Road
Mile End

STOCKPORT
Cheshire
SK2 6ES

PRYOR PUBLICATIONS
75 Dargate Road
Yorkletts
Whitstable
CT5 3AE

PRYTANIA
126 Bevan Street
LOWESTOFT
Suffolk
NR32 2AQ

PSYCHIC NEWS
49A Museum Street
London
W C 1

PSYCHOPOETICA
Geoff Lowe
Dept. of Psychology,
University of Hull,
Hull HU6 7RX
0482 465581
A magazine of psychologically-based poetry. Two issues per year, plus special anthologies. Established 1980. International contributors and new writers.
Psychopoetica;ed Geoff Lowe; 40pp; twice yearly; £1.50.
Dream Poems; ed Geoff Lowe; (A4) 66pp; £1.50/$3.
Psychopoetica in Love; ed Geoff Lowe; (A4); 44pp; £1.50/$3.

PSYCHOLOGICAL LIBRARIES
Michael Carr-Jones
P.O. Box 1193
Poole
Dorset
BH14 8PT. Tel. 0202 739369
Distribution to hypnotherapy psychotherapy association health education units doctors interested in alternative medicine.
Love Sex and Hypnosis by Bryan Knight. 17.03.92
ISBN 0 919848 08 7. What makes successful therapy; who abuses clients?

P.T.L. PUBLICATIONS
10 Richmond Park
Wrexham
LL12 8AB.
Subjects: Biography.
Books January to June 1991 - 1

PUFFIT PUBLICATIONS
47 South Hill Park
London
NW3 2SS.
Subjects: Music.
Books July to December 1991 - 1

DORIS E PULLEN
155 Venner Road
London

SE26 5HX

PULLET PRESS
Penny Berry
Oak Cottage, Lower Road
Middleton
SUDBURYon
Suffolk
CO10 7NS
Fine printer

PULLINGERS
56 High Street
Epsom
KT19 8AP.
Subjects: Local History.
Books July to December 1991 - 2

PULSE PUBLICATIONS
26 Burnside Gardens
Clarkston
Glasgow
G75 7QS

F PULSFORD
8 Oakbank
Watling Street
RADLETT
Hertfordshire
WD7 7JG

PUMPKIN PIE PUBLICATIONS
PO Box 125
Sutton
SM1 2DT

MR BRYN PURDY
Head, Rowan House School
Holbrook Road
Belper
DERBY
DE5 1PB

ALICE KELLY PURNELL
3 Hartington Villas
Hove
BN3 6HF

PURPLE HEATHER PUBLICATIONS
Richard Mason
16 Rokeby Gardens
Headingly
Leeds
LS6 3JZ 0532 740325
Founded 1980. Publishers of small press magazines; individual collections and audio cassettes of poetry. Promoters of 'live' poetry/literature in performance on a regular basis via Leeds Alternative Cabaret. 'A major literary and cultural figure..'
THE NORTHERN STAR
'Voice of Playtime Verse' Eds. Wiley/Mason/McGill.
58pp 1990 (children's poetry anthology) ISBN 1 872363 00 8. 4.00 p/b.
'Style in Performance' Suandi 68pp 1991 ISBN 1 871426 30 8. 4.00 p/b. 'Leeds Festival Poets 1990'.
Adrian Henry Claude Raine Attila Lemn Sisay John Hegley Circus of Poets Debjani Chatterjee Henry Normal Jim Burns et al. ISBN 1 872363 05 9. 2.00

211

p/b

PURPLE PATCH
8 Beaconview House
Charlemont Farm
West Bromwich
W Midlands
B71 3PL

PURPOSE PRESS
159 Meadowview
Drogheda
County Louth
Republic of Ireland.
Subjects: Poetry.
Books July to December 1991 - 1

MR C A PUSHONG
4 Papworth Way
Cressingham Gardens Estate
Tulse Hill
LONDON
SW2 2NL

THE PUTNEY PRESS
Richard Nathanson
PO Box 515
London
SW15 6LQ 081 788 2718
Initially set up to publish and promote 'Walk to the
Moon' 'Walk to the Moon - the illustrated story of
the artist Albert Houthuesen. 1903. 79 128pp 169
illust 11 x 8 inches. £12.50 (£16.00 inc p & p)

IAN PYPER
Graphikon A.D.
4 Mirefield Street
Kensington
LIVERPOOL
L6 6BD
Since Early 1991 the main activity of Graphikon
A.D. has been to produce artists limited edition
bookworks by Ian Pyper. Inspired by contempory
surrealism, dream language and an interset in so
called Primative Cultures. A Garden for Paul Klee
Ten black and white xerox prints in a card folder.
Limited edition of 30 Price= £6.50 (incl P+P)
Procession - catalogue plus handmade extras - all in
a card folder Price= £5.50 (incl P+P)

MR SAUN PUSZLAC
35 Irene Avenue
LANCING
East Sussex
BN15 9NZ

PYTHIA PRESS
Cecilia Boggis
7 Silver Street
GLASTONBURY
Somerset
BA6 8BS
Reprints of Rare Writing by Remarkable Women.
"Womens Speaking Justified", ISBN 1 872134 00 9,
£1.95

QED BOOKS
1 Straylands Grove

YORK
YO3 0EB 0904 424381
Formerly John Bibby Books

QUADRANT HOUSE BUREAU
In Type Book Reproduction
Woodman Work
Durnsford Road, Wimbledon
LONDON
SW19 8DR
Low cost short run book service. Books, book
proofs, reprints, manuals on demand publishing in
house magazines, fanzines, programmes, slow sell-
ers. Runs of 25 up to 1000 copies. Fast delivery
competitive pricing help and advice. Price scale
available on request.

MR C J P QUAEDVLIEG
Benzenraderweg 256A
NL-6417 SZ Heerlen
The Netherlands

QUA IBOE FELLOWSHIP
7 Donegall Square
West Belfast
BT1 6JE.
Subjects: Biography.
Books July to December 1991 - 1

QUARRY PUBLICATIONS
64 Quarry Avenue
Bebington
Wirral
L63 3HF

THE QUARTER-DAY PRESS
18 Fitzwarren Gardens
London
N19 3TP
Original illustrated books in limited editions of
forty copies. The Bear Friend. By Rachel Swan.
20pp. 1991. £10.00

MR NIGEL GAUVIN, EDITEUR
Quartier Peroton
BP 17
F-26800 ETOILE-SUR-RHONE
FRANCE

QUARTOS MAGAZINE
Suzanne Riley
BCM Writer
27 Old Gloucester Street
LONDON
WC1N 3XX
A bimonthly creative writing publication for begin-
ners and established writers 28 pages of informa-
tion, gossip, news and competition details. Friendly
-informative - approachable. For a free sample
copy, send 28p to Quartos, BCM - Writer, London,
WC1N 3XX

QUARTZ
Dept of Literature & Languages
Nottingham Poly
Clifton Lane Clifton
Nottingham
NG11 8NS

QUAY BOOKS EXETER
Tuck Mill Cottage
Payhembury
Honiton
Devon
EX14 0HF 0404 34388
Small one-man publishing co set up in 1990 to
establish outlet for local West Country writers and
minority interest texts. Mss welcomed with s.a.e.
please.
BBC Radio Devon Vintage Profiles by Chris Smith.
Drawings by Robin Murray. 160 pp. 30 b/w draw-
ings 40+ photos. pub May 90 £4.95. 0 9515946 0
5.
The Fourth Wise Man by Chris Smith. 18b/w line
drawings by Bud Kennedy. Re-telling of traditional
nativity story to be pub Sept'91. £2.95. 0 9515946
1 3.
Musical script of The Fourth Wise Man by Chris
Smith with Keith Vaughan. details t.b.a. Contact
publishers.

QUEENSCOURT PUBLISHING
David Cox
1 Queens Court Kenton Lane
Harrow
Middx
HA3 8RN. Tel. 081 907 4548
Queenscourt Publishing a new imprint for poetry
and light fiction Publishers of:
Soundings Daphne Schiller's collection of 40 po-
ems. 32pp 1989 ISBN 0 9516949 0 1 £2.50 net.
But Mostly Laughter: Stories by Pauk Feakes. Cho-
sen and introduced by I. and S. payne. 110pp 1990
ISBN 0 9516949 1 X £5.50 net. Humour Poem
Cards of Shakespeare Daphne Schiller Deirdre
Barrie printed as keepsakes/correspondence cards.

QUEENSCOURT PUBLISHING: S PAYNE
47 Radcliffe Road
Winchmore Hill
London
N21 2SD

QUEEN SPARK BOOKS
Carmel Kelly
Lewis Cohen Urban Studies Centre, 68 Grand
Parade, Brighton, BN2 2JY
0273 571916
Queen Spark is a Community Writing and Publishing group based in Brighton. We believbe that
anyone who wannts to can be a writer and our aim
is to encourage publishing writing by people who
do not normally get into print.
'Backyard Brighton'; reprinted 1991; 0 904733
165; £4.95; 30 full page photos; 75 pages.
'Daring Hearts', 0 904733 319; published Spring
1992; Lesbian and Gay Brighton in the '50s and
'60s.
'Brighton Behind the Front'; photographs and memories of life in Brighton during the 2nd WW, 0
904733 40 8, £3.95; 65pp.

QUEST
BCM-SCL Quest
LONDON
WC1N 3XX

QUEST BOOKS
2 Slievenabrock Avenue
Newcastle
BT33 0HZ

QUEST
YUFOS, 106 Lady Anne Road
Soothill
BATELY
West Yorkshire
WF17 0PY

QUESTION PRESS
Maryanne Aytoun-Ellis
'Brookside',
Southover High Street,
Lewes, East Sussex BN7 1HU
0273 474893
Young printmaker/sculptor & designer/artist using
the intimate environment of books to more fully
express, transform & unfold ideas that appear in
other areas of their work.
Pith & Stone; Maryanne Aytoun-Ellis; 24pp; 1990;
11.5" X 15.5". Collection of Poems with Stone
Lithographs, Wood-Engravings & Silk Screen. £250
Lost in Translation; Maryanne Aytoun-Ellis; 10pp;
1992; 18.5" x 27". Collection of Etchings,
Woodblock & Stone Lithographs. £300
Prisoner of Conscience; Mike Gibson; 16pp; Photocopy edition £7.00; 126 x 102mm (A Version 277
x 325mm Card leaves slipcase edition £60).

THE QUILLIAM PRESS
80 Lamble Street
London
NWS 4AB 071 267 7567
The Quilliam Press publishes works on tradionalist
Islam for the British Muslim community. Its series
classics of Muslim Spirituality includes translations
into English of well-known works on Muslim devo-
tional and mystical themes.
'Islam: Religion of Life' by Abdul Wadod Shalabi.
1989. viii + 79pp. paper back. £3.95. ISBN 1
872038 02 6.
'Key to the Garden' by Habib Ahmad al-Haddad.
1990. ix + 153pp. £4.95 paperback. £10.95 hardback. ISBN 1 872038 06 9 paperback. ISBN 1
872038 05 0 hardback.
'The Lives of Man' by Imam abdallah al-Haddad.
1991. xiv + 97pp. paperback . £3.95 paperback.
£10.95 hardback. ISBN 1 872038 08 5 paperback.
ISBN 1 872038 07 7 hardback.

QUIM
BCM 82
LONDON
WC1N 3XX

QUINCETREE
J C Carr
27 Milldale Road
Kettering
The grandfather and grandmother of Small Presses.

QUINCY'S COOKERY BOOK
Ian Dowding
42 High Street

Seaford
East Sussex
 0323 95490
A book of recipes from this award winnng restaurant: unusual exciting easy to follow and illustrated with charming drawings. 93pp 24 illus May 1990 ISBN 0 9515727 0 9.

MR NIALL QUINN
8 Rochester Road
NEWPORT
Gwent
NP9 8PB

QUOIN PUBLISHING
The Barn, 36A North Road
Kirkburton
Huddersfield
HD8 0RH

R AND B PUBLISHING
PO Box 200
Harrogate
HG2 9RB

MS WENDY RADFORD
49 Salehill
Broomhill
SHEFFIELD
S10 5BX

RADIO SOCIETY OF GREAT BRITAIN
Lambdo House
Cranborne Road
Potters Bar
EN6 3JE.
Subjects: Electrionic Engineering.
Books July to December 1991 - 8

RAFFEEN PRESS
Union Place
Fowey
PL23 1BY

RA HOOR KUIT
14 Linden Close
EXMOUTH
EX8 4JW

RAILWAY CUTTINGS
Tony Hancock Appreciation Society
56 Raddlebarn Farm Drive
Bourneville
BIRMINGHAM
B29 6UW

RAIN PRESS
David Wells
6 Carmarthen Road
WWestbury on Trym
BRISTOL
BS9 4DU 071 794 3433
Publishing materials written by the editor/author, in the fields of education. Philosophy and cross-cultural psychology, etc.
Three essays on the teaching of mathematics. 48 pages. £1.00 sterling. By David Wells. 1982. ISBN

0 907944 00 0.
Russia and England, and the transformations of european culture. 192 pages £4.9 5. By David Wells. 1990. ISBN 0 907944 02 7.
Studies of meaning, language and change (Journal, published three times a year, but irregular recently). Editor, David Wells. £1.00 per issue. ISSN 0261 3212

RAINBOW
Mr David A Stringer
96 Redhall Crescent
LEEDS
LS11 8DY

J RAINES
Hazel Cottage
Thornton-le-Clay
York

RAISING HELL
Box 32
52 Call Lane
LEEDS
LS1 6DT

MRS J S RAJAB
5 Russell Gardens Mews
LONDON
W14

MR S A RAJI
52 Howard Raod
LONDON
NW2 6DR

MS MARGO RALPH
24 Elizabeth Street
Evandale 5069
South Australia

RAMBLERS' ASSOCIATION
London
1-5 Wandsworth Road
London
SW8 2XX

RAMBLERS' ASSOCIATION (KENDAL GROUP)
6 River Bank Road
Kendal
LA9 5JS

THE RAMPANT LIONS PRESS
12 Chesterton Road
CAMBRIDGE
CB4 3AB

MR S RANDALL
89 Rossmore Road
Parkstone
POOLE
Dorset
BH12 3HN

RANNOCH GILLAMOOR PRESS
51 Stepney Avenue
Scarborough

YO12 5BW.
Subjects: Short Stories.
Books July to December 1991 - 1

MR ADAM RAOOF
35 Orchard Grove
HARROW
HA3 9QR

RAP LTD
201 Spotland Road
Rochdale
Lancs
OL12 7AF

RAPID EYE
P O Box 23
BRIGHTON
BN2 3PG

VERNA RAPLEY
Garden Orchard
East Knowstone
South Molton
EX36 4DZ

RATS CAN READ BOOKS
10 Fox Road
Stevenage
SG1 1JD

RATTLER'S TALE
BCM Keyhole
LONDON
WC1N 3XX

RAVEN ARTS PRESS
PO Box 1430
Finglas
Dublin 11
Republic of Ireland

RAVENCROFT PUBLICATIONS
Haydn House
Castle Street
Llangollen
LL20 8NY

MR ANDREW RAVENSDALE
235 Soundwell Road
Kingswood
BRISTOL
BS15 1PW

MR S RAZA
58 Roebuck Road
Crookesmoor
SHEFFIELD
S6 3GQ

R.B. PUBLICATIONS
Westfield House
Coleshill Heath Road
Birmingham
B37 7HY.
Subjects: Art.
Books July to December 1991 - 1

MR PHILIP READ
21 Lower Hanger
HASLEMERE
Surry
GU27 1LU

READ THIS
70 Walstead Road
Delves
Walsall
WS5 4LX

READY RHINO PUBLICATIONS
Tim J. Latham
31 Braemore Close
Thatcham
RG13 4XP.
Subjects: Shipbuilding History in Barrow-in-Furness.
Books Julyto December 1991 - 1

REAL ART
Malcolm Gibson
'Gilesway'
How Mill
Carisle
Cumbria CA4 9JT
Tel 0228 70415
A bi-annual limited edition publication devoted entirely to visuals. Malcolm Gibson, Andrew Law and James Hall contribute to every issue. Artists are invited to print or make their own editions for inclusion. Other projects include limited edition books and boxes.
'Real Art' journal edition 300 28pp size A4 printed bi-annually. Original prints and collages. Postal price £8.
'Real Art Box' a limited edition of 250 prints and collages by 28 artists in an A6 box pub. 1991. Postal price £11.
'Real Art Print Box' an A6 box containing work by 16 artists using a new litho technique developed by Lowick House Workshop Edition 250 pub. 1992. Price on application.

REALITY STUDIOS
4 Howard Court
Peckham Rye
LONDON
SE15 3PH 071 639 7297
Modernist/experimental poetry press, publishing books of poetry in the tradition of The New British Poetry and A Various art. Forthcomming titles by John Seed, Kelvin Corcoran, Maggie O'Sullivan. No unsoliceted submissions -Sorry.
Cut Memories and False Commands By Andrew Duncan. 96pp, 1991, 0 9507018 6 6 £6.95 Poetry.
Blood and Dreams by John Welch. 88pp, 1991, 0 9507018 7 4. £6.95 Poetry The Bay of Naples by Wendy Mulford. 48pp, 1992. 0 9507018 8 2. £5.99 Poetry

REAPER BOOKS
11 Brickley Acres
Eastcombe
Stroud
Gloucestershire
GL6 7DU 0452 770 440

Reaper Books is the self-publishing imprint of artist/writer Leo Baxendale creator of Minnie the Minx The Bash Street Kids - and latterly The Guardian strip 'I Love You Baby Basil!' 'The Encroachment' by Leo Baxendale 1988. A4 48pp. paperback. £5.00. ISBN 0 9513277 0 4. The study of a process of accumulating power and the controlling ideologies of capitalism and patriarchy. 'On Comedy: The Beano and Ideology' by Leo Baxendale. A4. paperback. 64pp £5.00. ISBN 0 9513277 1 2. Cartoon frontispece. The inside dope on a bunch of endearing dopes. The ideology of bangers and mash and everything else. 'I Love You Baby Basil!' The Collected Cartoon Strips from The Guardian. March 1990-March 1991' by Leo Baxendale. Landscape. 64pp. hardback. sewn with a 5 000 word prologue. £9.95. ISBN 0 9513277 2 0.

REARDON PUBLISHING
N. Reardon
56 Upper Norwood Street
Leckhampton
Cheltenham
GL53 0DU.
Family publishing company covering the Cotswold area. Postcards prints driving guides and walking books. in fact mostly anything covering tourism in the Cotswold and nearby counties.
Cotswold Walkabout by N. Reardon. 32pp 1983 ISBN 0 9508674 0 3 £1.95. Walks in the Cotswolds.
Cotswold Driveabout by P. Reardon. 32pp 1990 ISBN 0 9508674 6 2 £1.95. Drives in the Cotswolds
The Donnington Way by C. Handy. 44pp 1992 ISBN 0 9508674 00 6 £2.50. 62 mile walk between real ale Donnington inns.

REARDON & SON
56 Upper Norwood Street
Leckhampton
Cheltenham
GL53 0DU

REBEL PRESS
846 Whitechapel High Street
London
E 1
Publishers of anarchist situationist and related books and pamphlets. 'The Revolution of Everyday Life' by Raoul Vaneigem. 1983. 216pp. ISBN 0 946061 01 7. Situationist.
'The Bonnot gang: The story of the French Illegalists' by Richard Parry. 1987. 189pp. ISBN 0 946061 04 1. Anarchist history.
'Dynamite: A Century of Class Violence in America 1830-1930' by Louis Adam ic. 1984. 224pp. ISBN 0 946061 03 3. History.

RECO-PRESS
22 Goldstone Crescent
HOVE
East Sussex
BN3 6BA

THE RED CANDLE PRESS
M.L. McCarthy or Helen
9 Milner Road
Wisbech

Cambridgeshrie
PE13 2LR
Candelabrium - Poetry magazine of the Traditionalist Revival - one double issue each June (2.00) Volume (3 issues) £5.50.

REDCLIFFE EDITION
68 Barrowgate Road
London
W4 4QU

RED EARTH PUBLICATIONS
Alan McFadzean
7 Silver Street
Marton
Ulverston
Cumbria
LA12 ONQ 0229 64172
Local history; local interest. Anything that falls loosely into this bracket and relates to the north of England - we will publish. Force Crag: The History of a Lakeland Mine (Tayler) 1990. The Iron Moor - The History of iron mining in Furness (McFadzean) 1989. The Lead Miners of Hevellyn (McFadzean) 1987.

RED GULL PRESS
St Bridgets
Radcliffe Road
Hitchin
Hertfordshire

RED HEN PRESS
Shirley Jones
2 Croham Park Avenue
South Croydon
Surrey
CR2 7HH 081 686 4178
Shirley Jones publishes her own artist books of etchings aquetints and mezzotints. The accompanying poems prose pieces and translations from Old English are written set and printed letterpress by her on hand-made paper in editions limited to 40 copies.
Two Moons. Shirley Jones. Artist book of 9 mezzotints and 8 poems. 20 page s; text in Gill Sans on Rives mould made paper size 15 x 14; edition size 40. £550
Five Flowers for My Father. Shirley Jones. artist book; seven folders printed with text in baskerville enclosing seven mezzotints 18 x 13; 40 copies £525
Soft Ground Hard Ground. Shirley Jones. Artist book. 12 poems and prise pieces in perpetua type and 12 colour etchings; Barcham Green hand made paper. 40 copies; size 12 x14. £555

THE REDLAKE PRESS
Ursula Freeman
Brook House, Clun, Shropshire, SY7 8LY
058 84524
Private press producing limited edition hand-made books. Also hand-printed stationery, ephemera.
'The Secret Garden'; anthology John Fuller, Laurie Lee, Peter Levi, David Scott, Pauline Stainer etc; illustrated Brotherhood of Ruralists; 32pp; 1989; 1 870019 06 7 pb; £10.
'The Gardener's Song'; Lewis Carroll; illus Brian Partridge; 32pp; 1990; 1 870019 07 5; £25hb.

'Calendar'; Simon Rae; illus Brian Partridge and Sue Cave; 44pp; 1990; 1 870019 08 3; hb £25. Private press limited editions. Handmade mostly poetry. Formerly The Unidentified Flying Printer.

GR (GEORGE REDMOND) BOOKS
Knotty Lane
Lepton
Huddersfield
HD8 0ND

MR ROBERT S REDMOND
194 Grove Park
KNUTSFORD
Cheshire
WA16 8QE 0565 632657

RED POST PRESS
Mr Chris Winter
39a Red Post Hill
LONDON
SE24 9JJ
A small press set up to publish independent writing by football supporters. CRYSTAL PALACE FC: 1969-1990. A biased commentary written and illustrated by Chr is Winter. 96 pages, 100 illustrations. 0 9516636 0 7. £5.95. Football history.

REDSTONE PRESS
7a St Lawrence Terrace
LONDON
W10 5SU 071 221 5219

REDWOOD PUBLISHING
20-26 Brunswick Place
London
N1 6DJ.
Subjects: Travel in Britain.
Books July to December 1991 - 1

REDWORDS
31 Cottenham Road
Walthamstow
LONDON
E17 6RP

D J REECE
4a Crete Avenue
Milford
AUCKLAND 9
NEW ZEALAND

REID-THOMPSON PUBLISHING
2 Limes Court
Limes Avenue
Mickleover
Derby
DE3 5DB.
Subjects: Local Social History.
Books July to December 1991 - 1

J REES
PO Box 115
London
SW18 1SA

REEVES TELECOMMUNICATIONS LABS LTD

John de Rivaz
West Towan House
Porthtowan Truro
Cornwall
TR4 8AX.
Subscribe to get a free sample copy. How to use home computers to draw fractal images.
PCS. Mainly a listings magazine for people living in Cornwall. Free sample and price details on request.
PICS. Worldwide publication for people interested in using science and technology to extend lifespan and who are seeking a companion for friendship or marriage. Free sample and price details on request.
HEW. A4 newsletter 20pp aimed at men and women who enjoy wrestling for fun and exercise. Free sample and price details on request.

REEVES TELECOMMUNICATIONS LABS LTD
John de Rivaz
West Towan House, Porthtowan
TRURO
Cornwall
TR4 8AX

REFLECTIONS
P O Box 70
Sunderland
SR1 1DU

REFLECTIONS OF A BYGONE AGE
15 Debdale Lane
Keyworth
Nottingham
NG12 5HT

REGIONAL PUBLICATIONS
A. Waller
5 Springfield Road
Abergavenny
Gwent
NP7 5TD. Tel 0873 85 2207
Publishers of Leisure Guides and Specialist Books connected with History and Hobbies Educational. Exploring the Brecon Beacons by Chris Barber described below is our best-seller and has been reprinted time and again over the years.
Exploring the Brecon Beacons by Chris Barber. ISBN 0 906570 19 0 first published 1990 revised 1991 £5.95.
Rails to Prosperity. The Barry Railway by Brian Miller. Paperback ISBN 0 906570 17 4 1984 £5.95. Still available.
The mapping on Monmouthshire by D.P.M. Michael. ISBN 0 906570 18 2 10.95. Full listing and all illustrated of pre-Victorian antique maps from saxton; good for study.

REID REVIEW
8 Mendip Court
Avonley Village
Avonley Road
London
SE14 5EU

RENE PUBLISHING
Witham Villa
Cosby Road
Broughton Astley

Leicester
LE9 6PA.
Subjects: Poetry.
Books July to December 1991 - 1.

RESISTER
Committee on South African
War Resistance COSAWR U K
B M Box 2190
London
WC1N 3XX

RESPONSES
Tony Rollinson
20 Teddler Road Bridgemary
Gosport
Hampshire
PO13 0XP.
'Responses' was a series of twelve pamphlet through-
out 1991 featuring new work by: Abse Armitage
Buck Chaloner Clarke Cobbing Fisher O'Sullivan
Sheppard Tabor and others. Their work was `Re-
sponded' to and they in turn received a right of reply
... original! Cheques to A. Rollinson.
Complete Responses. 142pp Feb 92 7.50. Poetry
limited edition. What's Inside the Plastic Folder by
Anthony Rollinson. Jan 92 £3.00. Poetry.
Responses Revisited. 12 issues to be published
monthly Jan 93 - Dec 93. Sae for more information.

CO-OPERATIVE RETAIL SERVICES
29 Dantzic Street
Manchester
M4 4BA

REVELATION PRESS
Hertford
Mead Lane
Hertford
SG13 7AG

REVLOC BOOKS
Y Gilros
Off Vinegar Hill
Rhosllannerchrugog
LL14 1EL.
Subjects: Sports.
Books July to December 1991 - 1

RHINOCEROS MAGAZINE
Kevin Smith
Flat 3
90 University Street
Belfast
BT7 0232 326682
Quarterly poetry journal including articles of cultural interest and literary interviews specialising in
longer sections of writer's work: long poems sequences etc. International subscribers & contributors. 100-150 pp b/w artwork £2 per issue; quarterly

THE RHINOCEROUS PRESS
24 Manor House Way
BRIGHTLINGSEA
Essex
CO7 0QN

THE RIALTO
32 Grosvenor Road
Norwich
NR2 2PZ 0603 666455
I'm not sure that you want us in SPG Yearbook. We
have only one publication.
The Rialto. Edited by John Wakeman and Michael
Mackmin. 48 pages. b & w illus. published 3 times
a year. ISSN 0268-5981. £8.00 per year (3 issues).

MR KEN RICE
24 Rye Close
Mile Cross
NORWICH
NR3 2LF

JOHN RICHARDS
934 Society St.
Lawrence College in Thanet
Ramsgate
CT11 7AE.
Subjects: Railways.
Books July to December 1991 - 1

MR ALEX RICHARDSON
14 South End
Bassingbourne
ROYSTON
Hertfordshire
SG8 5NJ

HEATHER M RICHARDSON PUBLISHING
51 Garden Walk
Cambridge
CB4 3EW

NEIL RICHARDSON
88 Ringley Lane
Stoneclough
Manchester

R RICHENS
81 Selwyn Road
Cambridge
CB3 9EA

MR A P RICHES
Evensong
Willow Wren Wharf Marina
Heys Road, Southall
TELFORD, Middlesex
UB2 5NB

JOHN RIDGWAY BOOKS
Miramar
Rowney Green Lane
Alvechurch
Birmingham
B48 7QF.
Subjects: Frank Sinatra.
Books January to June 1991 - 2.

MR PAUL RIDGWAY
No 3 The Green
Ketton
Stamford
Lincolnshire

PE9 3RA

MR PETER RIGG
150 Beaufort Street
NELSON
Lancashire
BB9 3FH

RIGHT NOW BOOKS
36c Sisters Avenue
LONDON
SW11 5SQ 071 223 8987
Travel books and journals on South East Asia,
Thailand, Burma, Laos, Vietnam, Singapore and
Indonesia.
Bound Tightly with Banana Leaves: A South East
Asian journal by Nicholas Greenwood. June 1992,
160 pages, 28 Cartoons, 32 Pages of colour photo-
graphs, 5 Maps. An amusing and lighthearted look
at life in South-East Asia ISBN: 0 951849 10 7 Price
£6.99

P. RILEY
27 Sturton Street
Cambridge
CB1 2QE.
Subjects: Poetry.
Books July to December 1991 - 5

RING O'BELLS PUBLISHING
62 Beechwood Road
SOUTH CROYDON
Surrey
CR2 0AA 081 651 6080

RINGPRESS BOOKS
Spirella Building
Bridge Road
Letchworth
SG6 4ET.
Subjects: Animals.
Books January to June 1991 - 2. Books July to
December 1991 - 8

RINGWOOD BREWERY
Christchurch Road
Ringwood
BH24 3AP

RIPLEY REGISTERS
Dormer House
Tisbury
SP3 6QQ

J. RITCHIE
40 Beansburn
Kilmarnock
KA3 1RH.
Subjects: Poetry. Religion.
Books July to December 1991 - 2

RIVELIN GRAPHEME PRESS
The Annexe, Kennet House
19 High Street
HUNGERFORD
Berkshire
RG17 0NL
0488 83480

Not just a bookshop but a major poetry imprint. Get
lists.

RIVERS ORAM PRESS
144 Hemingford Road
London
N1 1DE

ROADS
Gordon Smith
49 Meynell Heights
LEEDS
LS11 9PY

ROBDAWG
David Robinson
200 Belper Lane
Belper
Derbyshire
DE56 2UJ. Tel 0773 824527
Name the sport or leisure interest (any facet) and
hopefully before too long we will have a book out
on the subject. Similarly with quiz books and general interest on Derbyshire. Mystery thrillers the
publisher's own pet subject.

MR B THOMAS ROBERTS
26 Rectory Road
Wivenhoe
COLCHESTER
Essex
CO7 9EP 0206 226226

ROBERTS MEDALS PUBLICATIONS
6 Titan House
Calleva Park
Aldermaston
RG7 4QW.
Subjects: Military Medals.
Books July to December 1991 - 18

MR NICHOLAS ROBIN
3 Victoria Terrace
LONDON
N4 4DA

MR DAVID ROBINSON
Robdawg
200 Belper Lane
Belper
DERBY
DE5 2UJ
Anything to do with sport and leisure. Run in
conjunction with and as an aid to sport and leisure
consultancy.

MR G P ROBINSON
11 Avon Road
Tolladine
WORCESTER
WR4 9AF

MR JEFFREY ROBINSON
3 St Johns Gardens
Sunnybrow
CROOK
Co Durham

DL15 0LU

MR KENNETH ROBINSON
20 West Street
Comberton
CAMBRIDGE
CB3 7DS

MS PAMELA ROBINSON
Bookseller
124 Wilberforce Road
LONDON
N4 2SU 071 226 1354

MR R B ROBINSON
BM Square Peg
LONDON
WC1N 3XX

THE ROBINSWOOD PRESS
Christopher Marshall
30 South Avenue
STOURBRIDGE
West Midlands
DY8 3XY 0384 397475
The Robinswood Press specialises in educational
publications, particularly in remedial education,
Steiner education, etc.
TAKE TIME. 1 869981 07 3. By Mary Nash-
Wortham & Jean Hunt. 106 pages illustrated move-
ment exercises for parents, teachers, and therapists
of children with difficulties in speaking, reading,
writing and spelling. Recommended by Dyslexia
Ins titute/British Dyslexia Association (1990).
RUDOLF STEINER/WALDORF EDUCATION.
1 869981 00 6. 24 page full colour illustrated . The
foremost introduction to Steiner education, available in 6 international e ditions (1989).
THE EXTRA LESSON. By Audrey McAllen. 1
869981 06 5. 132 pages, line/colour illustrations.
Exercises for children with learning difficulties.

RESOURCE BOOKS: ROBINSWOOD PRESS
30 South Avenue
Stourbridge
CY8 3XY

ROBOOKS: ISLE OF WIGHT COUNTY PRESS
29 High Street
Newport
PO30 1ST

MR DAVID B ROBSON
59 Seabank Road
Wallasey
WIRRAL
Merseyside
L45 7PA

MR J ROBSON
99 Windermere Road
SEAHAM
Co Durham
SR7 8JH

THE ROCKET PRESS
Millcroft Stables
Berry Lane, Blewbury

DIDCOT
Oxfordshire
OX11 9QJ

ROCKINGHAM PRESS
11 Musley Lane
Ware
SG12 7EN.
Subjects: Poetry. Local History.
Books January to June 1991 - 1. Books July to
December 1991 - 1

RODMELL VILLAGE PRESS
c/o 3 Terrace Cottages
Rodmell
Lewes
BN7 3HL.
Subjects: Local Travel Guides.
Books January to June 1991 - 1

MR ALEX ROEVES
84 Grande Rue des Salines
76370 Martin Eglise
DIEPPE
France

MS MONIQUE ROFFEY
13 Ashburn Gardens
Kensington
LONDON
SW7

MR A L ROGERS
18 Brookhouse Road
WALSALL
WS5 3AD

J. ROGERS GRIMSBY
22 Windermere Avenue
Scartho
Grimsby
DN33 3DG.
Subjects: Local History.
Books July to December 1991 - 1

ROLLS-ROYCE HERITAGE TRUST
P.O Box 31
Derby
DE2 8BJ

ROMER PUBLICATIONS
Hubert de Brouwer & Harry Melkman
170 Brick Lane,
London E1 6RU
071 247 3581
Romer Publications concentrates on scientific and
educational books, childrens books included. The
main aim of the publishing house is achieving high
quality standards of the various publications. Precisely this prevents Salman Rushdie-like events and
conspiracies from the past.
Fascism down the Ages: From Caesar to Hitler; by
Frank A. Ridley; ISBN 0 951150 82 0; sec. abridged
ed. 190pp A5 pbk; £6.95
The Decline of the House of Herod; by Hubert de
Brouwer; ISBN 0 951150 83 9; 179pp A5 pbk;
£6.95. Scientifc investigation on history of Jesus. Is
sent off for Prize Draw in Roman Law.

The Children Kosher Fun Book; by L.E. Book;
ISBN 0 951150 84 7; 40pp A4, colour cover; £4.50.
First cartoons explaining dietary laws.

ROOKBOOK PUBLICATIONS
16 Angle Park Terrace
Edinburgh
EH11 2JX

MR J S ROOK
25 Selborne Road
SIDCUP
Kent
DA14 4QP

MR R C ROONEY
754b High Road
Goodmayes
ILFORD
Essex
IG3 8SX

MR PAUL ROWLANDSON
24 Springfield Road
LONDON
E6 2AH

ROBERT STEPHENSON ROPER
136 Buersil Avenue
Rochdale
OL16 4TX

ROSALBA PRESS
55 St Michael's Lane
Headingley
LS6 3BR

ROSEC PUBLICATIONS
Imprint: A Stone's Throw Away
135 Church Road
Shoeburyness
Essex
SS3 9EZ.
River by river guide to Norfolk broad pubs for those
holidaying by boat. River maps pub to a page with
photo and description cruising times distances
moorings trading and restaurant times beers available kitchen specilities cards accepted and much
more.
A Stone's Throw Away (Pubs of the Norfolk Broads
from the River Approachjes) by Rose Lewis. 64pp
1st edition/2nd edition 1991 ISBN 0 9515467 1 5
£4.95.

DOUGLAS ROSE
35 Summers Lane
London
N12 0PE

ROSEDENE PUBLISHERS
110 New Road
Hadleigh
Essex
SS7 2BP. Tel 0702 551569
For Xmas 1992! Making Something From Nothing
- an environment friendly 'green' book with over
150 projects/ideas.
The Big Search by Rose de' Rothschild Schwittau.

Hardback 220pp £12.99. Overland from Great
Britain to Katmandu - searching for father with 4
children - a diary/log full of excitement!
Time Tested Alternative Remedies - With Startling
Discoveries by Rose de' Rothschild Schwittau. Hard-
back £12.99

ROSE LANE WRITERS
Flat 2
14 Ramilies Road
LIVERPOOL 18

MALCOLM ROSE
The Workshop
English Passage
Lewes
BN7 2AP.
Subjects: Music.
Books July to December 1991 - 1

M. ROSE PRESS
4 Gate Street
London
WC2A 3HP.
Subjects: Freelance Artists Directory.
Books July to December 1991 - 1

MR D A ROSENBERG
34 Borough Road
KINGSTON UPON THAMES
Surrey
KT2 6BD

MR R ROSE
12 The Bourne
Fleet
ALDERSHOT
Hampshire
GU13 9TL

ROSE'S REPARTEE
PO Box 339
SHEFFIELD
S1 3SX

ROSS SOFTWARE SYSTEMS
7 Heathfield Avenue
Heaton Chapel
STOCKPORT
Cheshire
SK4 4QJ

ROUGE
BM Rouge
LONDON
WC1N 3XX

ROUNDOAK PUBLISHING
7 Roundoak Gardens
Nynchead
Wellington
TA21 0BX

MR DON ROUT
Flat 1, 10 Nightingale Road
Pakefield
LOWESTOFT

Suffolk
NR33 0HS
Private booklet and fanzine on theme Fire/Mountain.
Circulated within mail art network. Contacts welcomed.

H. AUBREY ROWE
26 Comforts Farm Avenue
Hurst Green
Oxted
RH8 9DH.
Subjects: Walks Books.

T.H. ROWLAND
4 De Merley Road
Morpeth
NE61 1HZ.
Subjects: Local Travel.
Books January to June 1991 - 1

NORMAN ROWLEY
Blue Gates
Weston
Lullingfields
Shrewsbury
SY4 2AA.
Subjects: Local History.
Books July to December 1991 - 1

ROXFORD BOOKS
Roxford
Hertingfordbury
SG14 2LF.
Subjects: Asian History.
Books July to December 1991 - 2

ROXIMILLION PUBLICATIONS
Bishops Park House
25 Fulham High Street
London
SW6
Subjects: Occult.
Books July to December 1991 - 2

ROYAL ACADEMY OF MUSIC
Marylebone Road
London
NW1 5HT.
Subjects: History of Musical Instruments.
Books July to December 1991 - 1

ROYAL ARTILLERY INSTITUTION
Old Royal Military Academy
London
SE18 4DN

ROYAL BOTANIC GARDENS
Kew
Richmond
TW9 3AB.
Subjects: Botany. Children's non-fiction.
Books January to June 1991 - 2. Books July to December 1991 - 5

ROYAL GREEN JACKETS
RHQ Royal Green Jackets

Peninsula Barracks
Winchester
SO23 8TS.
Subjects: Military History.
Books January to June 1991 - 2

ROYAL IRISH ACADEMY
19 Dawson Street
Dublin 2
Republic of Ireland

ROYAL MILITARY ACADEMY
Sandhurst
Camberley
GU15 4PQ.
Subjects: Art.
Books July to December 1991 - 1

ROYAL SOCIETY OF EDINBURGH
22-24 George Street
Edinburgh
EH2 2PQ.
Subjects: Mathematics.
Books July to December 1991 - 1

RPR PRESS
5 The Oval
Longfield
DARTFORD
Kent
DA3 7HD
Anthologies of new poets.

RUBBERNECK
21 Denham Drive
BASINGSTOKE
Hampshire
RG22 6LT
Free magazine, contents about non-establishment performers, writers, musicians etc.

RUBBER STEREOS (AVON) LTD
Station Road
Midsummer Norton
BATH

RUBICON PRESS
57 Cornwall Gardens
London
SW7 4BE

RUFUS STONE ASSOCIATES
12 Whitfield Park
Ringwood
BH24 2DX

MR B RUMARY
The Old Post Office
Gurney Slade
BATH
BA3 4TY

RUNNING HEAD PUBLISHING
R H Spicer
9 Frederick Place
Bristol
BS8 1AS 0272 738667

Local history publishing & supplier of indexes
'Five Men One Loaf' by Haden Spicer. 131pp Oct
1990 ISBN 0 9516344 0 2. £4.99

RUNPAST PUBLISHING
8 Gwernant Road
Cheltenham
Gl51 5ES

RUNWISE
15 Priory Road
Chichester
PO19 1NS.
Subjects: Poetry.
Books January to June 1991 - 2

RUSHMERE PUBLISHING
32 Rushmere Road
Carlton Colville
Lowestoft
NR33 8DA

PETER R.D. RUSSEK PUBLICATIONS
Little Stone House
High Street
Marlow
Buckinghamshire.
Subjects: Cars.
Books July to December 1991 - 9

MR DAVID RUSSELL
8 McGregor Road
LONDON
W11 1DE

D.S. RUSSELL
8 McGregor Road
London
W11 1DE. TEL: 071 229 3350
Specialist in poetry and experimental fiction.
'Nothing Hero'. 1984. 24pp. illustrations by the
author. £1.50. ISBN 0 9514759 0 8. Poetry.

ALAN R RUSTON
41 Hampermill Lane
Oxhey
Watford
WD1 4NS

MR WARD RUTHERFORD
76 Stanford Avenue
BRIGHTON
BN1 6FE

RYBURN PUBLISHING
Tenterfields
Luddendenfoot
Huddersfield
HX2 6EJ

RYDER PUBLISHING
Deborah Ryder
BCM Box 3406
London
WC1N 3XX
Original and exclusive stories of sado-masochism
and related erotica. catalogue missing should be

attached

MRS S M RYMELL
Lyewater Farmhouse
CREWKERNE
Somerset
TA18 8BB

SABOTAGE EDITIONS
BM Senior, London, WC1N 3XX
Aim to compromise leaders and deliver them to
contempt. Use base women to disorganise the au-
thorities and incite the young, ridicule traditions,
dislocate supplies, inflict lascivious music, spread
lechery, devalue money and be very naughty indeed. To bring all this to pass we publish 'Smile'
magazine.

MS ALEX SADGROVE
Total Public Relations Limited
6 Kale Street
Batcombe
BATH
BAS4 6AD

SAINSBURY PUBLISHING
Auldearn Main Street
Bleasby
Nottingham
NG14 7GH.
Subjects: Chemistry.
Books January to June 1991 - 1

ST. IVES PRINTING AND PUBLISHING COMP
High Street
St. Ives
TR26 1RS.
Subjects: Local History.
Books July to December 1991 - 1

ST. JOSEPH'S WORKSHOPS
190 Bag Lane
Atherton
Manchester
M29 0JZ.
Subjects: Language.
Books July to December 1991 - 1

KIRK SESSION
St Luke's Greenock
c/o The Manse
50 Ardgowan Street
GREENOCK
Renfrewshi
Subjects: Local History.
Books July to December 1991 - 1

ST JAMES PRESS (1)
PO Box 701
North Way, Walworth Industrial Estate
Andover
SP10 5YF

ST JAMES PRESS (2)
2-6 Boundary Row
London
SE1 8HP

ST JUSTIN
6E Longrock Industrial Estate
Penzance
TR20 8HX

CHURCH OF ST. MARY SCULCOATES
Parochial Church Council
c/o 16 Spring Grove Gardens
Sunnybank
Hull
HU13 1JZ.
Subjects: Local History.
Books July to December 1991 - 1

ST MICHAEL'S PAROCHIAL CHURCH COUN-
CIL
Wye Barn
The Quay
Tintern
Wye

ST. MARK'S CHURCH AMPFIELD
c/o 4 Hookwater Close
Chandler's Ford
Eastleigh
SO5 1PS.
Subjects: Story of St. Mark's Church Ampfield.
Books January to June 1991 - 1

ST. PETER'S CENTENARY COMMITTEE:
G. Wheeler
Oak Lodge
30 Delahays Drive Hale
Altrincham
WA15 8DP.
Subjects: Local History.
Books July to December 1991 - 1

PARISH OF ST. THOMAS OF CANTERBURY
Clergy House
42 Santos Road
London
SW18 1NS.
Subjects: Local History.
Books July to December 1991 - 1

UNIVERSITY OF SALFORD
Department of Politics and Contempora
Salford
M5 4WT

SALMON PUBLICATIONS
Paul Salmon
32 Park Crescent
HORNCHURCH
Essex
RM11 1BJ 0708 743811
Publishers of 'Tradition'; a quarterly publication
devoted to traditional custom and culture. Recent
features: Morris Dancing; Arthurian Legend; Green
Man; English Bagpipes; Windmills; Regimental
History. Some New Age where applicable to tradi-
tional matters. Articles welcome but no payment
possible at this stage.
Tradition: Keeping Traditions and Customs Alive.
Executive ed. Paul Salmon ; ed. Dave Van Doorn.
ISSN 0963-0791. line drawings. 75p plus 25p p&p.

sub. £3.75.

SALMON PRESS
Auburn
Upper Fairhill
.Galway
Ireland

SALOPEOT
Mr R Hoult
5 Squires Close Madeley
Telford
Salop
TF7 5AU

SALVIA BOOKS
4 Logie Green Gardens
Edinburgh
EH7 4HE

SAMARA PUBLISHING
Samara House
Tresaith
Cardigan
SA43 2JG.
Subjects: Zoology.
Books January to June 1991 - 1

SAMHAIN
John Gullidge
19 Elm Grove Road
Topsham
EXETER,Devon
EX3 0EQ

PROFESSOR A J SAMMES
Royal Military College of Science
Shrivenham
SWINDON
SN6 8LA

SAMSON BOOKS: BLACK WATCH (R.H.R.)
R.H.Q.
Balhousie Castle
Perth
PH11 5HR

SANCTUARY PRESS LTD
Nash House
Fishponds
LONDON
SW17 7LN
Monthly journal: ACTION, for a true union of
Europe

(Alan George)
SANDALL OF FROME
Sherwill
Styles Avenue
Frome
BA11 5JN.
Subjects: Local Economic History.
Books July to December 1991 - 1

MR CHRIS SANDERS
P O Box 4AS
LONDON

224

W1A 4AS 071 637 7467

T SANDERSON
9 Sovereign Close
LONDON
W5 1DE

SANDHILL PRESS: SANDERSON BOOKS
Front Street
Klondyke
Cramlington
NE23 6RF

DR J M SANDOR
9 Chasewood Corner
Bussage
STROUD
GL6 8JS

SANDPIPER BOOKS
D Bent
22a Langroy Road
LONDON
SW17 7PL

A J SANDRY
67 Mulberry Avenue
West Cross
SWANSEA
SA3 5HA

SANDHILLS PRIMARY SCHOOL
64 Merewood Avenue
Sandhills
Oxford
OX3 8EF

MR TONY SANDY
32 Haviland Close
CAMBRIDGE
CB1X 2RA

SANTA MARIA PUBLICATIONS
8 Queen's Road
Minster
Isle of Sheppey
ME12 2HD.
Subjects: Art. Archaeology.
Books January to June 1991 - 1

SARCOPHAGUS PRESS
5 Parkfield Mount
Beeston
LEEDS
LS11 7PB

SAREMA PRESS
15 Beeches Walk
Carshalton Beeches
SM5 4JS.
Subjects: Art. Biography.
Books July to December 1991 - 2

SAROS INTERNATIONAL PUBLISHERS
48 Aragon Avenue
Ewell
Epsom

KT17 2QG

SATEB
(see Worker Esperantist)

SATIS
Malcolm Rutherford
14 Greenhill Place
Edinburgh
EH10 4BR 031 447 3587
Poetry pamphlets including translations of contemporary German poetry. Format of 16pp pamphlets cardbound. Ret £1 each. Manuscripts invited. Doors of Smoke. Wolfgang Bachler. trans. Ruth & Matthew Mead. 16pp pamph let poems.
Flamingo Dance. Urs Oberlin. trans. Ruth & Matthew Mead. 16pp pamphlet. poems. £1
Songs from the Old Folks' Home. Christian Geisler. trans. Ruth & Matthew Mead. 16pp pamphlet. poems £1.00.

SATORI PRESS
149 Bower Street
Bedford
Subjects: Poetry.
Books January to June 1991 - 2. Books July to December 1991 - 1

SATURN BOOKS
Ardfallen
Green Hill, Fermoy
Co Cork
Republic of Ireland

MR DONALD SAUNDERS
30 Vatigker Park
BACK
Isle of Lewis
PA86 0JZ

GEOFFREY SAUNDERS
22 New Street
Kenilworth
CV8 2EZ.
Subjects: Education.

MR JOHN SAUNDERS
c/o Brian Howard
6 Cranedown
LEWES
East Sussex
BN7 3NA

MARK SAUNDERS PUBLICATIONS
1 Austin Close
Irchester
WELLINGBOROUGH
Northamptonshire
NN9 7AX

MR RICHARD L SAUNDERS
2a Comeraerit Road
West Kensington
LONDON
W14 9HP

SAVE BRITAIN'S HERITAGE
68 Battersea High Street

225

London
SW11 3HX

SAWD PUBLICATIONS
Plackett's Hole
Bicknor
Sittingbourne
ME9 8BA.
Subjects: Second World War.
Books July to December 1991 - 1

SAYERS AND CYMBRON
The Garden
Lissington
Lincoln
LN3 5AE.
Subjects: Travel in Europe.
Books July to December 1991 - 1

DOROTHY L. SAYERS SOCIETY
Rose Cottage
Malthouse Lane
Hurstpierpoint
Hassocks
BN6 9JY.
Subjects: Short Stories.
Books July to December 1991 - 1

SB PUBLICATIONS
5 Queen Margaret's Road
Loggerheads
Market Drayton
TF9 4EP

S.C.
Stanford Old Farm House
Leinthall
Starkes
Ludlow
SY8 2HP.
Subjects: Archaeology.
Books July to December 1991 - 1

SCARLET PRESS
5 Montague Road
London
N8 2HN

SCARTHIN BOOKS
The Promenade
Scarthin, Cromford
Matlock
DE4 3QF

SCEPTIC TANK PRESS
Anna Livia
5 Marine Road
Dun Laoghaire
Republic of Ireland.
Subjects: Humour.
Books July to December 1991 - 1

SCHIZOPHRENIA ASSN OF G B
Inter Centre for Schizophrenia
Bryn Hyfryd The Crescent
Bangor
Gwynedd

LL57 2AG

SCHOOL BOOK FAIRS
M Price
5 Airspeed Road
Priory Industrial Park
Christchurch
BH23 4HD.
Subjects: Children's Fiction.
Books January to June 1991 - 1

MR PAUL SCHULTE
7 Hamilton Road
LONDON
NW10 1NU

MR CHRIS SCHWARZ
72 Brand Street
GREENWICH
SE10

SCIAF
5 Oswald Street
Glasgow
G1 4QR.
Subjects: Travel in Central Amercia.
Books July to December 1991 - 1

SCIENCE INDEX
Middle Cottages
Boyers Orchard, Harby
Melton Mowbray
LE14 4BA

SCOPE BOOKS
62 Murray Road
Horndean
PO8 9JL

MR J W SCOPE
5 Lynton Court
Cedar Road
SUTTON
Surrey
SM2 5DL

SCORPIAN PRESS
6Admirals Walk
Portishead
BRISTOL
BS20 9LE

SCORPION PRESS
6 Admirals Walk
Portishead
Bristol
BS20 9LE.
Subjects: Mystery Fiction.
Books January to June 1991 - 1. Books July to December 1991 - 2

SCOTS INDEPENDENT (NEWSPAPERS)
51 Cowane Street
Stirling
FK8 1ER.
Subjects: Poetry.
Books July to December 1991 - 1

226

MR PETER SCOTSON
6 Sandhurst Park
TUNBRIDGE WELLS
Kent
TN2 3SZ

MR G SCOTT-CHAMBERS
4 Langton Gardens
Branton
DONCASTER
South Yorkshire
DN3 3PA

SCOTTIE ROAD '83
7 Hanbury Road
Walton
LIVERPOOL
L4 8TR

SCOTTISH ADVERTISER
Unit E
Maryhill Workspace
45 Garrioch Road
GLASGOW
G20 8RG

SCOTTISH BOOK CENTRE
137 Dundee street
EDINBURGH
EH11 1BG 031 228 6866

SCOTTISH CHILD
347A Pilton Avenue
Edinburgh
EH5 2LE.
Subjects: Crime.
Books January to June 1991 - 1

SCOTTISH CONSULTATIVE COUNCIL ON THE
GARDYNE ROAD
Broughty Ferry
Dundee
DD5 1NY.
Subjects: Education.
Books January to June 1991 - 2. Books July to December 1991 - 2

SCOTTISH CROSS COUNTRY UNION
Clifton, 8 Craigshannoch Road
Wormit
Newport-on-Tay
DD6 8ND

SCOTTISH ENTERPRISE FOUNDATION
University of Stirling
Stirling
FK9 4LA
Subjects: Education.

SCOTTISH POETRY LIBRARY
Tweeddale Court
14 High Street
Edinburgh
EH1 1TE

M.G.SCOTT LIMITED
Michael G. Scott
Blo'Norton Hall, Diss, Norfolk IP22 2JD
095 381 354
Individual letterpress printer designing and printing from all handset type. Supplier to Bookshops, Gift Shops &c. of a series (8) of 'Little Recipe Books', packets of Bookplates and Jam Labels, Writing Paper, Bewick postcards &C.
'A Little Book of Christmas Recipes'; Michael & Shirley Scott; 16pp; November 1980; ISBN 0 907396 00 3; 75p.
'A Little Book of Country Recipes'; Michael & Shirley Scott; 16pp; March 1984; ISBN 0 907396 03 8; 75p.
'A Little Book of Tea-Time Treats' Michael & Shirley Scott; 16pp; August 1989; ISBN 0 907396 08 9; 75p.

MR W SCOTT
Argyle Mansions
23 Argyle Place
ROTHESAY
Isle of Bute
PA20 0BA

SCRAM
11 Forth Street
EDINBURGH
EH1 3LE
Scottish campaign to resist atomic menace

SCRATCH
Mark Robinson
24 Nelson Street
The Groves
York
YO3 7NJ
International poetry plus an authoritative informative and wide-ranging review section. Poetry that counts to more than one or two; that laughs and rages and knows the difference. Keywords: intelligence passion and wit.
Scratch magazine; twice yearly poetry (David Crystal Tim Comming Gordon Wardman Matthew Mead David Morley et al) illustrated. ISSN 0958 2452.

SCRATCHINGS
c/o the English Dept
Taylor Bldg
Univ of Aberdeen
Old Aberdeen Scotland

SCREENTYPE:
Vevers
Nightingales
Compton
Guildford
GU3 1DT.
Subjects: Local History.
Books July to December 1991 - 1

SCRIEVINS
c/o Willie Hershaw
28 Glebe Place
Burntisland
Fife

SCRIPTMATE EDITIONS
(Ann Kritzinger)
20 Shepherds Hill
London
N6 5AH.
Subjects: Biography. Self-publishing.
Books July to December 1991 - 2

SEA DREAM MUSIC
236 Sebert Road
Forest Gate
LONDON
E7 0NP
Books about music, plays, poetry copyright, antique glass, Chrisian bias.

DENYS SEAGER CONSULTANCY
10 Jewry Street
Winchester
SO23 8RZ.
Subjects: General Fiction.
Books January to June 1991 - 1.

SEAGULL ENTERPRISES
Newton Hall
Hall Road
Walpole Highway
Wisbech
PE14 2QE.
Subjects: Parish Registers.
Books January to June 1991 - 1.

SEARCHLINE PUBLISHING
Searchline House
Bull Lane
Chislehurst
Kent
BR7 6NY

ROGER SEARLE
37 Lynmouth Road
London
N2 9LR

SEARS
8 Farm Hill Road
Waltham Abbey
EN9 1NN.
Subjects: Local History.
Books January to June 1991 - 1

SEASONS COLLECTION
PO Box 121
Deal
CT14 6SL

2ND RAPTURE
Mr Colin Mulligan
8 Tottenham Close
Ings Road
HULL
HU8 OTN
Maglet for poetry, shorts and graphics.

SECURITIES ASSOCIATION
Stock Exchange Building
London

EC2N 1EQ

MR RUFUS SEGAR & MS SHEILA SEGAR
33 Hamilton Gardens
LONDON
NW8

SELBORNE AGENCIES LIMITED
BCM Zoo Review
LONDON
WC1N 3XX

SELECT BOOKS
Rivington House
82 Great Eastern Street
London
EC2A 3JL.
Subjects: Science Fiction. Biography. Mystery Fiction. Books January to June 1991 - 1. Books July to December 1991 - 2

SELF PUBLISHING ASSOCIATION LIMITED
Tony Harold
18 High Street
Upton-upon-Severn
Worcestershire
WR8 0HW

KEITH SELKIRK
32 Moor Lane
Bunny
Nottingham
NG11 6QX

SELLY OAK COLLEGES
Central Library
Bristol Road
Birmingham
B29 6LQ

SEMPRINGHAM
11 Augustine's Road
Bedford
MK40 2NB

SENECIO PRESS
The Old Drapery
Church Street
CHARLBURY
Oxfordshire
OX7 3PP

SENTRIES
Chard Street
Axminster
EX13 5DZ.
Subjects: Travel Accommodation.
Books July to December 1991 - 1

SEPHTON ENTERPRISES
Lacy House Farm
Charlestown
HEBDON BRIDGE
West Yorkshire
HX7 6PN 0422 844335

SEPIA (KAWABATA PRESS)

Knill Cross House
Knill Cross Millbrook
near Torpoint
Cornwall
PL10 1DX

THE SEPTEMBER PRESS
42 High Street
IRCHESTER
Wellingborough
NN8 7AB

SEREN BOOKS
Nick Felton
Poetry Wales Press Limited
Andmar House Tondu Road
Bridgend
Mid Glamorgan
CF31 4LJ 0656 767834
Publisher of poetry fiction biography drama some history Lit Crit with a Welsh context. Small literary house with reps and agents worldwide Authors include RS Thomas Minhinnick Curtis Finch Abse Alun Lewis and many women poets.
Richard Burton: So Much So Little by Peter Stead. 120pp 8pp b&w plates. ISBN 1 85411 040 3. Hb. £10.95. Critical study of Burton's career back ground impact.
Alun Lewis: Collected Stories. Ed C Archard. 320pp. ISBN 1 85411 012 8. Hb £14.95. 2nd volume uniform edition of Lewis outstanding writer of World War Two.
The Chosen Ground. Ed N Corcoran. 288pp. ISBN 1 85411 024 1. Hb. £16.50. Pb ISBN 1 85411 028 5. £8.95. Collection of essays on poets of N. Ireland: Heaney Paulin Montague Muldoon etc.

MR MICHAEL SERGEANT
2 The Stables
Woolpit End, Ewhurst
CRANLEY
Surrey
GU6 7NR

SERPLAN
Broadway Buildings
50-64 Broadway
London
SW1H 0DH

MR DAVID SETTLE
10 Boyne Terrace Mews
LONDON
W11 3LR

SMITH SETTLE
Otley Mill
Ilkley Road
Otley
LS21 3JP

SEVEN ISLANDS PRESS
86 Benedict Street
GLASTONBURY
Somerset
BA6 9EZ
Exploring the ancient origins of philosophy, art and religion.

The sacred geometry of the Giza Plateau By R J Cook
107 pages. 137 illustrations. ISBN 0 9518576 0 6 £7.95
The Pyramids of Giza by R J Cook ISBN 0 9518576 14, 1992, 80 pages, 80 illustrations. £4.95

SEVEN ISLANDS
R.Y. Cook
86 Benedict Street
Glastonbury
BA6 9EZ. Tel 0458 832690
Exploring the ancient origins of philosophy art and religion. The Sacred Geometry of the Giza Plateau by R.J. Cook. 107pp 120 illustrations 1991 ISBN 0 9518576 0 6 £4.95.
The Pyramids of Giza by R.J. Cook. 80pp 80 illustrations 1992 ISBN 0 9518576 1 4 £4.95.

SEVEN MIRRORS PUBLISHING HOUSE
21 Daleside Avenue
Pudsey
LS28 8HB.
Subjects: Occult. Poetry.
Books January to June 1991 - 1. Books July to December 1991 - 7

SEVENTY PRESS
70 South Street
Reading
RG1 4RA.
Subjects: Botany.
Books January to June 1991 - 1

SEVERNSIDE PRESS
B.W. Wheeler
Severnside
Newnham
Gloucestershire
GL14 1AA.
Letterpress printing facility available up to A2 sheet size. Contact welcomed from private publishers/ similar/interests/ or others with sensible propositions. Proprietor 25 year BFMP member with extensive practical experience in letterpress field.

SEVIERS
22A Hampstead Lane
London
N6 4RT.
Subjects: Short Stories.
Books July to December 1991 - 1

MR R J SEWELL
42 Station Road
WALTHAM ABBEY
Essex
EN9 1AA

MR ANDY SEWINA
3 Beelm Villas
SALE
Cheshire
M33 2EA

SGEULAICHE PUBLICATIONS
Segeulaiche Achnahinich
Plockton

Inverness
Scotland
IV52 8TY.
Books January to June 1991 - 1

SHADOWFAX PUBLISHING
25 Drysgol Road
Radyr
Cardiff
CF4 8BT.
Subjects: Health. Psychology. Local History.
Books January to June 1991 - 3. Books July to
December 1991 - 1

IRFAN SHAH
4 Birch Close
Earl Shilton
LEICESTER
LE9 7HD

KANTA SHAH
17 Hillbury Avenue
Harrow
HA3 8EP.
Subjects: School textbooks.
Books July to December 1991 - 1

MR S B SHAH
13 Lents Way
CHESTERTON
Cambridgeshire

S SHAHID
12 Old Hall Street
BURNLEY
Lancashire

Shaman's Drum
Grim
41 Oxford Road
Southport
Merseyside

SHAPE LONDON
1 Thorpe Close
London
W10 5XL

SHAPES AND STRINGS
121 Ryelands Road
Stonehouse
GL10 2PG.
Subjects: Music.
Books July to December 1991 - 1

THE SHARKTI LAUREATE
Pamela Constantine
104 Argylke Gardens
Upminster
Essex
RM14 3EU. The founder Pamela C
English Renaissance formed the Sharkti Laureate
to proliferate the Renaissance ideal with her SL
writing group.
The Cornerstone Mystic Poems for Modern Times
by Pamela Constantine. 28pp Autumn 92 £2.00.
(NB we are not yet using ISBNs)

The New English Renaissance by the SL Writing
Group. 28pp Autumn 92 £2.00. Seven writers whose
work has appeared in seven countries provide examples of their New Renaissance writings.
Point of Destiny by Pamela Constantine. 28pp
Autumn 92 £2.00. What happens to a representa-
tive group of people on the last night of the century.

MR JOHN SHARLAND
School House
Swan Lane
Winterbourne
BRISTOL
BS17 1RL

SHARP-CUT
Spencer Hudson
5 Southwood Court
Big Wood Road
Hampstead Garden Suburb
LONDON
NW11 6SR

JOHN SHARP
'Mill Close'
Sandford Manor
Woodley
Reading
RG5 4SY.
Subjects: Technology and Manufacturing.
Books July to December 1991 - 1

MS CLARE M SHAW
10 Garforth Road
Baillieston
GLASGOW
G69 7LB

MR MARK SHAW
TM6
25 Broome House
Pembury Road
LONDON
E5 8LL

MR MICHAEL SHAW
The Quart House
99 High Street
AMERSHAM
Buckinghamshire
HP7 0DT

WERNER SHAW
Suite 34
26 Charing Cross Road
London
WC2H 0DH

SHEARSMAN BOOKS
47 Dayton Close
PLYMOUTH
PL6 5DX

SHEBA FEMINIST PUBLISHERS
10a Bradbury Street
LONDON
N16

SHEFFIELD BIRD STUDY GROUP
c/o A.J Morris
4A Raven Road
Sheffield
S7 1SB

UNIVERSITY OF SHEFFIELD
Department of Town and Regional Planning
Western Bank
Sheffield
S10 2TN

SHEFFIELD WOMEN'S PRINTING CO-OP
111a Matilda Street
Sheffield
S1 4QF

MR KEN SHELDON
Amigo Books
18 Summerhill Road
LAUNCESTON
Cornwall
PL15 7DU

MR K SHELTON
The Old Rectory
11 Bangor Road
GROOMSPORT
Co Down
BT19 2JF

MR WILLIAM SHENTON
2 Parkville Road
Swaythling
SOUTHAMPTON
SO2 2JA

MR D SHEPHERD
18 Tyersal Crescent
Tyersal
BRADFORD
West Yorkshire
BD4 8HA

G SHEPHERD PUBLISHERS
Maggs House
Bristol
BS8 1QX

SHEPHERDS BOOKBINDERS
76b Rochester Row
LONDON
SW1P 1JV
Craft binders and retailers of materials including specialties.

MS KATE SHEPPARD
4 Wyebank Road
Tutshall
CHEPSTOW
Gwent
NP6 7ER 02912 79579

WILLIAM HENRY SHERCLIFF
2 Hazel Drive
Poynton

Stockport
SK12 1PX

SHERLOCK PUBLICATIONS
Philip Weller
6 Bramham Moor
Hill Head
FAREHAM
Hampshire
PO14 3RU
This press specialises in producing journals and monographs concerned with studies of Sherlock Holmes and his times. It is connected with the world 's leading Sherlock Holmes correspondence study group 'The Franco-Midland Hardware Company'. The Dartmoor of 'The Hound of the Baskervilles' - a Practical Guide to the Sherlock Holmes locations. Philip Weller. 51pp. maps. 2nd revised edition 1992. ISBN 1 873720 04 1 £4.95 inc p&p. paperboards.
Under the Deerstalker and other Hats. Conversations with Douglas Wilmer. Edited by Philip Weller. 25pp; photos. 1990. 1 873720 01 7. £4.00 inc p&p paperboards.

SHERWOOD FOREST PUBLISHERS
PO Box 10
NOTTINGHAM
NG2 3GR
A humorous and useful look at Telecom: British Telecon? £9.99

SHERWOOD GAMES
Sherwood House
15 Annesley Road
Hucknall
NOTTINGHAM
NG15 7AD

SHETLAND LIBRARY
Lowe
Hillhead
Lewick
ZE1 0EL.
Subjects: Local Legal History (Court Books). Books July to December 1991 - 1

SHETLAND TIMES
Prince Alfred Street
Lewick
Shetland
ZE1 0EP

MR J D SHETLEY
3 The Chestnuts
Hunstor
CHICHESTER
West Sussex
PO20 6AV

SHIELD PUBLISHING
7 Verne Road
North Shields
NE29 7LP

SHIELING PUBLICATIONS
22 Nelson Street
St Andrews

231

KY16 8AJ

SHILLELAGH BOOKS
257A Ladbroke Grove
London
W10 6HF.
Subjects: Fiction General.
Books July to December 1991 - 1

SHIN BUDDHIST ASSOCIATION
of Great Britain
Wessex Hills
92B Chapmanslade
Westbury Wilts
BA13 4AN

H SHIPMAN
19 Framfield Road
London
N5 1UU

SHIP OF FOOLS
239 Lessingham Avenue
Tooting
LONDON
A press mainly dedicated to the visual work of
Patricia Farrell and the texts of Robert Sheppard,
and to their collaboratins.
Icarus - Having Fallen. Robert Sheppard and Patricia
Farrell, 10 pp. Text and images £1.50
Killing Boxes by Robert Sheppard. Poems, 4pp,
£1.00.
Miles Davis Poem and Image, 2pp, 50p.

SHIP PICTORIAL PUBLICATIONS
3 College Close
Coltishall
NR12 7DT

SHOCKING PINK
121 Railton Road
London
SE24 0LR

MR GEOFFREY SHORTER
Quadrant House
The Quadrant
SUTTON
Surry
SM2 5AS

MR R W SHORT
90 Streatham
Vale
LONDON
SW16 5TD

THE SHRINKING LAUNDERETTE
28 Howe Park
EDINBURGH
EH10 7HF

SHROPSHIRE BOOKS
Old School House
Preston Street
Shrewsbury
SY2 5NY

SHROPSHIRE LANGUAGE CENTRE
Hartsbridge Road
Oakengates
Telford
TF2 6BA

S.I.A PUBLISHING
31 Malden Way
New Malden
KT3 6EB

IGBAL SIDDIQUI
32 Warrington Avenue
SLOUGH
SL1 3BQ

MR MIKE SIGGINS
129 Ardmore Lane
BUCKHURST HILL
Essex
IG9 5SB

SIGNAL
(see The Thimble Press)

SILCONAS PUBLICATIONS
Betty Silconas
181 North Church Road,
Sparta, NJ 07871 USA
1 201 383 3828
Silconas Publications - not a market. My press
consists entirely of my own work. the poetry is
traditionalist, excluding vulgarity and suggestive-
ness. I have nature, inspirations, humor, holidays
and more. Anyone may send for a listing. If you'd
like to communicate about writing traditionalist
poetry, feel welcome to do that.
Christmas at the Silconases
A Small Swamp
A Visit to the Pumpkin Farm

SILENT BOOKS
Kate Duncan
Boxworth End
Swavesey
Cambridge
CB4 5RA Tel 0954 32199/31000
Independent publisher established six years. Pub-
lisher of high quality beautifully designed and pro-
duced books - many illustrated with wood engrav-
ing. Gift books community care range and larger
format books. Winners of several awards.
Some Like It Hot by Anne Inglis. 64pp Sept 92 ISBN
1 85183 043 X £6.95. Cookery.
The Wood Engraving of Clare Leighton Patricia
Jaffe. 160pp October 92 ISBN 1 85183 029 4
£19.95.
Sherlockian Bookplates by W.E. Butler. 64pp July
92 1 85183 031 6 £8.95.

SILENT BUT DEADLY
Martin Baxendale
4 Catherine's Close
STROUD
Gloucestershire
GL5 1PD

ANTHONY L. SILSON
22 Whitecote Gardens
Bramley
Leeds
LS13 2HZ.
Subjects: Local History.
Books July to December 1991 - 1

SILVER BIRCH PRESS
248A Telegraph Road
Heswall
Wirral
L60 7SG.
Subjects: Pictorial Local History.
Books July to December 1991 - 1

SILVER MOON BOOKS
64-68 Charing Cross Road
London
WC2H 0BB

SILVER MOON
300 Old Brimpton Road
LONDON
SW5 9JF

SILVER STAR TRANSPORT BOOKS
24 Partridge Close
Chesham
HP5 3LH

SILVEY-JEX PUBLICATIONS
14 Chaldon Road
London
SW6 7NJ

SIMANDA PRESS
1 Meriden Road
Berkswell
Coventry
CV7 7BE.
Subjects: Local History.
Books July to December 1991 - 1

R.E.G. SIMMERSON
36 Wilton Avenue
London
W4 2NY.
Subjects: Language.
Books January to June 1991 - 1.

A. & S. SIMMONDS
Maritime Books
23 Nelson Road
London
SE10 9JB.
Subjects: Bibliography.
Books July to December 1991 - 1

MR MEYRICK SIMMONDS
Beukenlaan 26
3080 Tervuren
BRUSSLES
Belgium

SIMMONS PUBLISHING

37 Lower High Street
Wednesbury
WS10 7AQ.
Subjects: Local History.
Books January to June 1991 - 1

MS JANICE SIMONS
17 Kingcup
Pandora Meadows
KING'S LYNN
PE30 3HF
Produces collections of local history material of
special interest to genealogists and local histrians.
Books currently available include collections of
marriage and obituary notices for the years 1848,
1881 & 1900 taken from the old local press for East
Anglia
Marriage & Obituary Notices 1880. Compiled by
Janice Simons. Paperback. x = 66 p ages, with front
cover illustrations. October 1990. ISBN 1 873237
00 6. £3.90 in c p & p.
Marriage & Obituary Notices 1890. Compiled by
Janice Simons. Paperback, x + 80 p ages with front
cover illustration. May 1981. ISBN 1 8723237 01 4.
Marriage & Obituary Notices 1900. Published late
summer 1991.

SIMPLE LOGIC
Paul A GLover
2 Broadway
NOTTINGHAM
NG1 1PS
Magazine and books covering all aspects of using
Atari ST Computers.

SIMPLIFIED SPELLING SOCIETY
39 Chepstow Rise
Croydon
CR0 5LX.
Subjects: Language.
Books July to December 1991 - 2

SIMPLY CREATIVE
246 London Road
Charlton Kings
Cheltenham
GL52 6HS.
Subjects: Education.
Books July to December 1991 - 1

BARRY JAMES SIMPSON
Narabo Creek
Devoran
Truro
TR3 6NF

MR N H SIMPSON
103a Woodfield Road
HARROWGATE
North Yorkshire
EH12 6DW

SIRIUS
P O Box 428
Denbigh
Clwyd
Wales
LL16 4AZ

SKEEBY PUBLISHING
Hightrees
155 Dukes Ride
Crowthorne
RG11 6DR

SKEIN
White Lodge
47 Bisley Old Road
Stroud
GL5 1LY.
Subjects: Poetry.
Books July to December 1991 - 1

SKELMERSDALE WRITERS
Library Arts Centre
Shopping Concourse
Skelmersdale
Lancashire

THE SKEPTIC
Toby Howard/Steve Donnelly
P.O. Box 475
Manchester
M60 2TH. Tel 061 748 4628
The UK's only regular magazine devoted to a
skeptical view of psedoscience and claims to the
paranormal. Articles columns reviews humour let-
ters and much much more! Now in our sixth year!
Year's subscription (6 issues) £12.00 (UK) rest of
the world £15.50 (Airmail £28).

MS JANE A SKERRETT
24 Cleveland Road
LONDON
SW13 0AB

HUGH SKILLEN
56 St. Thomas Drive
Pinner
HA5 4SS.
Subjects: Second World War History.
Books January to June 1991 - 1

MR LAWRENCE SKILLING
79 Gratton Road
LONDON
SW17 0EY

SKOOB BOOKS PUBLISHING
15 Sicilian Avenue
London
WC1A 2QH

SCOOBS OCCULT REVIEW
Mrs Caroline Wise
19 Bury Place
London
WC1A 2JH

RON SLACK
26 Glenthorne Close
Brampton
Chesterfield
S40 3AR.
Subjects: Local History.

CHRIS SLADDEN
43 Hurst Road
Hinckley
LE10 1AB

SLATERS PHOTOGRAPHIC SALES AND PUB-
LISHING
7 Malvern Close
Huntington
York
YO3 9RP.
Subjects: Entertainment.
Books January to June 1991 - 1

SLIM SMITH
BM SLIM, London WC1N 3XX
0272 246505
Yes the graphic novel about an individual voice,
including P&P or by dance of life & carpet? created
by the author on the living room is in the wrong
typeface. These ones hairdos. The identity of a nasty
fake-art.
Bab's Rhumba; 36pp; April 91; £3.00.
Doc Soap & the Burgers of Doom; 36pp; Sept 92;
£3.00.
Analogue Dreams in a Digital World; 36pp; April
93; £3.00.

SLOW DANCER
Mr John Harvey
1 Park Valley
NOTTINGHAM
NG7 1BS
Publishes New Poetry by new and established writers; Slow Dancer magazine twice a year, small
number of single author pamphlets & occasional
books. No unsolicited manuscripts, thanks.
GASH! by Tina Faulkner. Poems, 48 pages, published 23 April 92. ISBN 1 871033 14 4 £5.00
AROUND ROBINSON by Simon Armitage. Poems, 28 pages, published October 91. ISBN 1 871033
10 1 £2.50
TERRITORY by John Harvey. Poems, 28 pages,
published 23 April 92. ISBN 1 871033 15 2 £2.50

SMALL PUBLICATIONS
151 Norwich Road
Wroxham
Norwich
NR12 8RZ

MR P SMALL
17 Frances Court
24-26 Lancaster road
LONDON
SE25 4AW

SMALL PRESS WORLD
John Nicholson
11 Ashburnham Road
BEDFORD
MK40 1DX

MR PHILIP SMART
A10 Block 3
Pine Court

234

23 Sha Wan Drive
Hong Kong

MR GAVIN D SMILLIE
5 Grantley Gardens
GLASGOW
G41 3PY

SMITH/DOORSTOP BOOKS
51 Byram Arcade
Westgate
Huddersfield
HD1 1ND

MR DAVID R SMITH
9a Hillcroft Crescent
LONDON
W5 2SG

MR F R G SMITH
Sunnybank
110 Stubbington Avenue
North End
PORTSMOUTH
PO2 0JG

JOHN OWEN SMITH
Oakdene
Beech Hill
Headley
Bordon
GU35 8EG.
Subjects: Poetry. Plays.

J. SMITH'S TADCASTER BREWERY
The Brewery
Tadcaster
LS24 9SA.
Subjects: Local Military History.
Books January to June 1991 - 1

MR PETER SMITH
147 Sovereign Road
Earlsdon
COVENTRY
CV5 6JB

MR RORIE SMITH
Thai Coffee House
Dolphin House, Sutton Marine
PLYMOUTH
Devon

MS REBECCA SMITH
Sheridan
Broomers Hill Lane
PULBOROUGH
West Sussex
RH20 2DU

ROGER N SMITH
8 Canterbury Park
Didsbury
Manchester
M20 8UA

SMITHS KNOLL

46 Glebe Way
Burnham on Crouch
Essex
CM0 8QJ

MRS W E SMITH
3 Deerleap
Bretton
PETERBOROUGH
PE3 9YA

SMOKE
(The Windows Project)
40 Canning St
Liverpool
L8 7NP

PATRICK SMYTH
Marymount
3 North Circular Road
Lurgan
Craigavon
BT67 9EB.
Subjects: Handicrafts.
Books July to December 1991 - 1

SNAKE RIVER PRESS
Geoffrey Trenamen
1 Grafton Street
BRIGHTON
BN2 1AQ
Finely printed volumes of poetry illustrated with
lithographs, woodcuts, and line drawings person-
ally printed by the artist. The bindings are formally
designed and executed by selected craftsman-bind-
ers. Forthcomming titles include selected poems by
John Clare and Andrew Young. Write for a list of
books in print.

MR A G SNEDDON
46 Beechwood Road
CATERHAM
Surrey
CR3 6NA

S SNEYD
4 Nowell Place
Almonbury
HUDDERSFIELD
West Yorkshire
HD5 8PB

SOCCER BOOK PUBLISHING
72 St Peter's Avenue
Cleethorpes
DN35 8HU

SOCIAL AFFAIRS UNIT
9 Chesterfield Street
Mayfair
LONDON
W1X 7HF

INSTITUTE FOR SOCIAL INVENTIONS
Nicholas Alberry
20 Heber Road
London

(Fax 081 452 6434)
NW2 6AA 081 208 2853
'Encyclopaedia of Social Inventions' edited by
Nicholas Albery. 1990. £29.95. ISBN 0 948826 17
7. 500 best ideas (non-technological) for social
change.
'Can Civil Wars be Avoided' by David Chapman.
1991. £12.95. ISBN 0 948826 26 6. Electoral
systems for the newly-emerging democracies. 'Forest Garden' by Robert Hart. 1991. £2.95. ISBN 0
948826 23 1. Minimal labour garden of fruit and
nut trees and self-seeding vegetables and herbs .

SOCIALIST SOCIETY
29 Horsell Road
London
N5

SOCIALIST WORKERS PARTY
P O Box 82
London
E 3

SOCIAL ORG.
32 Copley Road
Stanmore
HA7 4PF.
Subjects: Political Science. Religion.
Books July to December 1991 - 2

SOCIAL AND COMMUNITY PLANNING RESEARCH
35 Northampton Square
London
EC1V 0AX

Social Science Forum
61 Richborne Terrace
London
SW8 1AT.
Subjects: Social Sciences.
Books July to December 1991 - 1

SOCIETY OF FREELANCE EDITORS AND
PROOF READERS
16 Brenthouse Road
London
E9 6QG.
Subjects: Tax.
Books July to December 1991 - 2

SOCIETY OF YOUNG PUBLISHERS
12 Dyott Street
LONDON
WC1A 1DF

SOCIETY OF SCOTTISH ARTISTS
69 Promenade
Portobello
Edinburgh
EH15 2DX.
Subjects: Art.
Books July to December 1991 - 1

SOFT PENCIL PRESS
29 Douglas Road
Acocks Green
Birmingham

B27 6HH.
Subjects: Poetry.
Books July to December 1991 - 1

SOL PUBLICATIONS
31 Chiltern
Coleman Street
SOUTHEND-ON-SEA
Essex
SS2 5AE

SOL: ADRIAN GREEN
44 Station Road
Rayleigh
Essex
SS6 7HL

MR & MRS G V SONTER
54 Hitchings Way
REIGATE
Surrey
RH2 8EW

SORCERER'S APPRENTICE
6-8 Burley Lodge Road
LEEDS
LS6 1QP
Specialist Publishers of limited edition books and
momographs on Occult Philosophies, Mysticism,
Magik and New Age. Also litature regarding Human Rights and the liberation of minorities from
cultural imprinting and philsophical/religious
supremacism.

SORREL PUBISHING
2A Randolph Place
Edinburgh
EH3 7T.
Subjects: Newcastle Menu Guide. Edinburgh Menu
Guide. Aberdeen Menu Guide. Books July to December 1991 -3

H. SOTHERAN
2-5 Sackville Street
London
W1X 2DP.
Subjects: Bibliography.
Books July to December 1991 - 2

SOTTO VOCE PRESS
Maynooth
County Kildare
Republic of Ireland.
Subjects: Plays.
Books July to December 1991 - 1

SOUND & FURY ENTERPRISES
8 College Gardens
LONDON
N18 2XR
081 803 8952
Began as a 'zine for gaming but went berserk.

SOURCE
109 Oak Tree Road
Bitterne Park
SOUTHAMPTON

SO2 4JP
Journal for Holy Wells.

MR A CARLOS DE SOUSA
R Joao Pinto Ribeiro
7-3-Esq
2700 Amadora
Portugal

SOUTH
61 Westborough
Wimborne
Dorset
BH21 1LX

SOUTH ANGLIA PRODUCTIONS
26 Rainham Way
Frinton-on-Sea
CO13 9NS

SOUTH ASIAN LITERATURE SOCIETY
9 Chenies House
43 Moscow Road
London
W2 4AH

SOUTH COAST TRANSPORT PUBLISHING
3 Morley Drive
Bishops Waltham
SO3 1RX

SOUTH FIFE ENTERPRISE TRUST LTD
6 Main Street
CROSSGATES
Fife
KY4 8AJ

SOUTHGATE PUBLISHING
Glebe House
Church Street
Crediton
EX17 2AF.
Subjects: Education.
Books July to December 1991 - 5

SOUTHOVER PRESS
2 Cockshut Road
Southover
LEWES
East Sussex
BN7 1JH
Good reprints on cookery and household managment.

SOUTHPORT WRITERS' CIRCLE
c/o 35 Codray Road
Southport
Merseyside.
Subjects: Short Stories.
Books July to December 1991 - 1.

SOUTHWELL PRESS
Mrs Jean Baker
Wilton Road
CAMBERLEY
Surrey
GU15 2QW

SOUTH YORKSHIRE WRITERS
51 Blayton Road
SHEFFIELD
S4 7DH
Publish local writers and occasional one-off selections and anthologies - plus annual magazine of new writing - THE CUTTING ROOM - submissions welcomd, but recommend purchase of sample copy for £1.57.

SOU'WESTER BOOKS
17 Crestacre Close
Newton
Swansea
SA3 4UR

MRS I SOWTER
54 Hitchins Way
REIGATE
Surrey
RH2 8EW

SPACELINK BOOKS
Lionel Beer
115 Holybush Lane,
Hampton,
Middlesex TW12 2QY
081 979 3148
Publisher of booklets on the Paranormal. No unsolicited m/s. Mainly acts as a bookseller and distributor of books, booklets and magazines, covering UFOs, crop circles, earth mysteries and wide range of paranormal topics. Several small presses handled: Ascent Publications, Phoebe Beer (Devon), Countryside Productions, Gemini (of Zimbabwe), Deryck Seymour (Devon), &c. UFOs titles are main speciality. Publisher of SPACELINK magazine: 1967-71 (back nos available) Publisher of TEMS News, 1992, earth mystery magazine.
The Moving Statue of Ballinspittle and Related (BVM Phenomena); Lionel Beer, 44pp; 1986; ISBN 0 951140 61 2; £1.75. Colour cover edition: 0 951140 60 4; £2.00.
An Anecdotal History of BUFORA; Lionel Beer; 4pp. 1983; £0.25.
The Beggining of Rayon; Edwin Beer; 210pp + Addendum 36pp. 1962; £5.00 (Biographical History).

MR SIMON SPAIN
Orange Box Editions
59 Mildenhall Road
LONDON
E5 0RT

SPAREMAN PRESS
65 Sycamore Avenue
NEWPORT
Gwent
NP9 9AJ 282235
Ranting poet.

SPARE RIB
27 Clerkenwell Close
London
EC1R 0AT

P4 SPARES
60 Woodville Road
London
NW11 9TN

MR STEPHEN A SPARKES
1 Ridgeway
Wyesham
MONMOUTH
Gwent
NP5 3JX

J SPARKS
128 Mount Street
London
W1Y 5HA

SPARTACUS PUBLICATIONS
D. Edwards
8 Shrewsbury Way
Saltney
Chester
CH4 8DY.
Subjects; Health and Hygiene.
Books January to June 1991 - 1

SPASTICS' SOCIETY
12 Park Crescent
London
W1N 4EQ.
Subjects: Newspapers on Disability.
Books July to December 1991 - 2

SPECIALIST KNOWLEDGE SERVICES
Dr Hugh Pincott
Saint Aldhelm
20 Paul Street
FROME
Somerset
BA11 1DX
0373 451777
Specialists in tailor-made computer management
systems for membership, subscript ion, distribution
and data-base administration. We don't actually
sell these but take all your chores and drudgery
away for an unbelievably small cost. We manage
membership and distribute publications for Fortean
Times, Centre for Crop Circle Studies, and the
Cerealogist, ASSAP, Strange Magazine, and the
Small Press Group.

SPECIAL SORTS PRESS
10A Dickenson Road
London
N8 9ET.
Subjects: Poetry.
Books July to December 1991 - 1

SPECIAL TWENTY
1 Fleming House
Portland Rise
LONDON
N4 2PX
Free broadsheet/zine

SPECTACULAR DISEASES
838 London Road
PETERBOROUGH

PE2 9BS
Journal and distribution of poetry.

SPECTRUM
19 Cunninghamhead Estate
by Kilmarnock
Ayrshire
Scotland
KA3 2PY

SPEL PUBLICATIONS
45 Crow Hill
BROADSTAIRS
Kent
CT10 1HT 0343 69434
Talking phrasebooks in French German and Italian.

BM SPELLBOUND
Jonathan Wood
BM Spell Bound
London
WC1N 3XX
Formerly the Vacant Hearse Press BM SPELL-
BOUND is the Contact Point for anachronistic
strange and very individual prose and poetry pub-
lished as and when it fells like it. We live in the
spaces between the lines. Approach with respect.
Nether Wood: by J. Wood. 100pp. 1990. 10. A
collectors item of decadence in its true meaning.
Fiction.
Peace of Mind: Poems for Croatia. 1991 to copies
only. Free out of print. fortune press poems about
War.
Life Poem. by J. Wood. 8pp. 1992. free. a meditative
Poem in memory of Dom Sylvester Houedard. Still
in print.

SPELLBOUND CARD CO LTD
23-25 Moss Street
Dublin 2
Ireland

MR MATTHEW SPENCER
Rosemundy Cottage
26 Shefford Road, Clifton
SHEFFORD
Bedfordshire
SG17 5RG

MR A SPENDLOW & MS J EDWARDS
23 Bright Street
YORK
YO2 4XS

SPENDTHRIFT PUBLICATIONS
31 Richmond Road
Cambridge
CB4 3PP.
Subjects: Poetry.
Books January to June 1991 - 1

SPENNITHORNE PUBLICATIONS
1 Bourton Road
Hunts Cross
LIVERPOOL
L25 0PB
Autobiography of a catholic priest who worked in

238

South Africa 1959-69.

MRS G E SPERRING-EBERT
6 Errol Road
HOVE
East Sussex
BN3 4QG

SPIDER PARK
Stanwell Street
Edinburgh
EH6 5NG

SPIKE PRESS
Avanti Books
8 Parson Green
Boulton Road
Stevenage
SG1 4QG.
Subjects: General Fiction.
Books January to June 1991 - 1. Books July to
December 1991 - 1

SPILLER FARM PUBLICATIONS
25 Liskeard Gardens
Blackheath
London
SE3 0PE

SPIRAL PUBLICATIONS
8 Kings Street
GLASTONBURY
Somerset
BA6 9JY
Books and booklets on star magik, meditation,
astral travel, higher consciousness.

SPIRAL ASCENT
37 Foxlease
BEDFORD
MK41 8AP
Spiral Ascent takes its name fron the Edward
Upward trilogy of the same name. Our origins are
a clue to our purpose. We are not 'Arty' or 'F---y'
but come to the aid of the party!

SPIRAL SCRATCH
6 Chapel Street
CAMBRIDGE
CB4 1DY

THE SPIRO INSTITUTE FOR THE STUDY
of Jewish History and Culture
Queen Mary & Westfield College
Kidderpore Avenue
LONDON
NW3 7ST

SPOKEN ENGLISH
Margaret Edwards
32 Norwood Avenue
SOUTHPORT
Merseyside
PR9 7EG

SPOKES MAGAZINE

The Orchard House
45 Clophill Road
Upper Gravenhurst
Bedford
MK45 4JH
0408 583295
Poetry

SPORTING AND LEISURE PRESS
Meadows House
Well Street
Buckingham
MK18 1EW.
Subjects: Sport.

MS EVA SPORTOLETTI
45 Via Baretti
I-10125 TORINO
ITALY

SPORTS LEISURE CONCEPTS
Portersfield Road
Cradley Heath
Warley
B64 7BX

SPORTSPRINT
138 St Stephen Street
Edinburgh
EH3 5AA

SPORTS PROGRAMMES
PO Box 74
Chapel Street
COVENTRY
CV1 4AB

SPREAD EAGLE PUBLICATIONS
3 Upper Clwyd Street
Ruthin
LL15 1HY
Subjects: Travel in Britain.
Books July to December 1991 - 1

CHRISTINE AND D. SPRINGETT
21 Hillmorton Road
Rugby
CV22 5DF.
Subjects: Handicrafts and Printmaking.
Books July to December 1991 - 1

SPRING HILL PUBLICATIONS
Spring Hill Medical Centre
Spring Hill
Arley
CV7 8FD

SPUD
38 Chaucer Road, Bedford, MK40 2AJ
The essential Society for the Prevention of
Unneccessary Directors. Sick of rotten shows? Now
you know who is to blame and why. Get the
irreplaceable SPUD Introductory History of Actor-
Managers. A subject about which you know nothing and care less? Quite. Me too. But the publication
is a treat for £5.

MR RICHARD SPURGEON
2d Wilson Grove
SOUTHSEA
Hampshire
PO5 1PD

SPURGES
22A Picket Piece
Andover
SP11 6LY.
Subjects: Handicrafts.
Books July to December 1991 - 1

SPYGLASS: RUPERT BOOKS
59 Stonefield
Bar Hill
Cambridge

SQUARE ONE PUBLICATIONS
29-31 Lowesmoor
Worcester
WR1 2RS

SQUARE PEG
BM Square Peg
LONDON
WC1N 3XX
Magazine done by a collective of gay men and
women.

MR R SQUIRES
38 Raleigh Avenue
Chelston
TORQUAY
Devon
TQ2 6DL

ST BOOKS
45 Brook Close
East Grinstead
RH19 3XZ.
Subjects: Education.
Books January to June 1991 - 2

STAFF COLLEGE
Coombe Lodge
Blagdon
Bristol
BS18 6RG.
Subjects: Education.
Books January to June 1991 - 4. Books July to
December 1991 - 1

STAG PUBLICATIONS
Thimble Farm
Green Lane, Prestwood
GREAT MISSENDEN
Buckinghamshire
HP16 0QE 6101 02406

STAG PUBLICATIONS
16 Connaught Street
London
W2 2AF.
Subjects: Humour.
Books July to December 1991 - 1

STAGECOACH
Avon Cottage
Stratford-sub-Castle
Salisbury
SP4 6AE.
Subjects: School Textbooks.
Books July to December 1991 - 2

STAGE MANAGEMENT ASSOCIATION
Southbank House
Black Prince Road
London
SE1 7SJ.
Subjects: Theatre.
Books July to December 1991 - 2

B.A STAIT
8 Mornington Drive
Cheltenham
GL53 0BH

MARTIN RICHARD STALLION
18 Cornec Chase
Leigh-on-Sea
SS9 5EW.
Subjects: Bibliography.
Books July to December 1991 - 1.

ASSOCIATION FOR STAMMERERS
St. Margaret's House
21 Old Ford Road
London
E2 9PL.
Subjects: Stammering.
Books July to December 1991 - 1

STAMP APPRECIATED POETRY MAG
(N A Keylock)
26 King's Drive Westonzoyland
Bridgwater
Somerset
TA7 0HJ

STAND MAGAZINE
179 Wingrove Road
Newcastle-upon-Tyne
NE4 9DA

STANDON AND PUCKERIDGE CRICKET
CLUB
c/o D.J Bantick
18 Britannia, Puckeridge
Ware
SG11 1TG

MR JOHN STANLEY
270 Plumstead Common Road
LONDON
SE18 2RT

MR TOM STANLEY
13 Clogrove
WELWYN GARDEN CITY
Herfordshire
AL8 6HY

STANMARC MANAGEMENT SERVICES

240

White Lodge
61 Oakley Avenue
LONDON
N20 9JG

STAPLE
Don Measham
Tor Cottage
81 Cavendish Road
Matlock
Derbyshire
DE4 3HD 0332 47181.
Staple is a well established magazine for new writing with a national rep utation which has now diversified into small press production. The first editions series can consider work which meets it published conditions. Write for details.
Lawrence and the Real England. By Donald Measham (ed). pp90. 1985 0 9510523 0 6. £2.50. illustration
ISSN 0266 4400.
Last Round (poem cycle) by David Lightfoot. Staple; first editions series 1991. p p 32. £2.50. 0 9510523 1 4. no illustrations.

STAPLEFORD HOUSE EDUCATION CENTRE
Wesley Place
Stapleford
Nottingham
NG9 8DG

STARFIRE
BM Starfire
LONDON
WC1N 3XX

STARSHINE BOOKS
PO Box 150
Chesterfield
S40 1QH.
Subjects: Children's Fiction.
Books January to June 1991 - 1

STATICS (LONDON)
41 Standard Road
London
NW10 6HF.
Subjects: Art. Humour.
Books July to December 1991 - 2

ST CUTHBERT'S, DARLINGTON
Parochial Church Council
Church Centre, Market Place
Darlington
DL1 5QG

DAVID C. STEDMAN
71A Westward Road
Stroud
Gloucestershire
GL5 4JA. Tel Stroud (0453) 750
Booklets - education economics.
The Famous Art September 1992
Other in Bread and Circuses series to follow.

ST EDWARDS PRESS
Vine Cottage
Sutton Park

Guildford
GU14 7QN

STEEL CARPET MUSIC
Peter Castle
190 Burton Road
Derby
DE1 1TQ. Tel 0332 46399
Mainly folk and traditional music/tales/lore. Books and tapes. Set up by Pete Castle a singer/storyteller to market his material but now expanding to include other artistes and related subjects. Free catalogue and news sheet (sae appreciated!)
The Cottage by the Shore by Pete Castle. August 92 ISBN 1 871391 07 5 Book and tape £6.00. Traditional songs and ballads.
A Real Good Life by 'Mum' Johnstone. 1990 ISBN 1 871391 05 9 £2.00. Autobiography of singer
Fiddles and Harps and Drums by Pete Castle. 1990 ISBN 1 871391 04 0 Book and tape £6.00. Traditional stories from around the world.

CHARMIAN STEELE
Bluebell Cottage
Upper End
Fulbrook
Oxford
OX18 4BX.
Subjects: Asian History.
Books July to December 1991 - 1

MR RODNEY STEELE
22 Eustace Road
LONDON
SW5 1JD

MR R STEER
31 Templar Road
OXFORD
OX2 3LS

RICHARD STENLAKE PUBLISHING
Richard Stenlake
1 Overdale Street
Langside
Glasgow
G42 9PZ. Tel 041 632 2304
An eccentric independent press specialising at present in Scottish interest and transport-related titles.
Caldeonian - The Monster Canal by Guthric Hutton. 52pp July 92 ISBN 1 822074 06 2 8.40.
A Forth and Clyde Canalbum by Guthric Hutton. 52pp July 91 ISBN 1 822074 10 3 £4.95.
Last Greetings From St. Kilda by Bob Charnley. Nov 89
ISBN 1 822074 02 2 5.25.

R. STENLAKE
1 Overdale Street
Langside
Glasgow
G42 9PZ.
Subjects: Local History.
Books January to June 1991 - 3. Books July to December 1991 - 3.

MS DOROTHY STEPHENS

Stapleton Cellars
West Hill Lane
BUDLEIGH SALTERTON
Devon

STEPNEY BOOKS
Jenny Smith
19 Tomlins Grove, Bow, London E3 4NX.
Community publishing group specialising in history and autobiography of London Borough of Tower Hamlets.
My Poplar East Enders; Carrie Lumsden; 77pp; 20 b/w illus; 1991; £4.95; 0 9505241 7 4; Autobiography/Social History.
Children of the Green; Doris Bailey; 128pp; 10 b/w illus; 1981; £3.95; 0 9505241 4 X; autobiography/social history.
Edith + Stepney; Bertha Sokoloff; 240pp; 6 b/w illus; 1987; £4.95; 0 9505241 6 6.

STEPPENMOLE
49 Gloucester Green
OXFORD
OX1 2DF
Fiction publishers

STEREO SCENES
22 Rutland Gardens
HOVE
East Sussex
BN3

JAN STEVENS
West Lodge
Oakfield, Mortimer Lane
Mortimer
READING
RG7 3AP

G R STEVENSON
33 Medway Gardens
RUISLIP
Middlesex
HA4 7QP

MS JANET STEVENSON
64 Mungo Park Way
ORPINGTON
Kent
BR5 4EQ

MR MARK STEWART-JONES
91 Old Woolwich Road
Greenwich
LONDON
SE10 9PP

MR KEITH STEWART
27 Leighton Avenue
Meols
WIRRAL
Merseyside
L47 0LY

STILE PUBLICATIONS
Mercury House
Otley

LS21 3HE.
Subjects: Local Walks Books.
Books January to June 1991 - 1. Books July to December 1991 - 1

UNIVERSITY OF STIRLING
Stirling
FK9 4LA
Subjects: Education.
Scottish Poetry Library

STOCKBRIDGE PRESS
16 Danube Street
Edinburgh
EH4 1NT.
Subjects: Poetry.
Books July to December 1991 - 1

STOCKBRIDGE WRITERS
49a Lynham
Whiston
MERSEYSIDE
Subjects: Poetry.
Books July to December 1991 - 1

P. STOCKHAM
at Images
4 & 6 Dam Street
Lichfield
WS13 6AA.
Subjects: Reprint of an English Civil War Letter.
Books January to June 1991 - 1.

STOCKPORT CENTRAL LIBRARY
Wellington Road South
STOCKPORT
SK1 3RS

MR GREG STOKE
126 Watsons Green Road
DUDLEY
West Midlands
DY2 7LG

STONE CREEK PRESS: INKSHED PRESS
387 Beverley Road
Hull
HU5 1LS

STONEHENGE VIEWPOINT
2821 de la Vina Street
SANTA BARBARA
CA
United States of America

MR R C STONES
Clifton Cottage
High Street
MALPAS
Cheshire
SY14 8NN

STONEWATER ROWE
Clettwr Cottage
Trer'ddol
Machynlleth
SY20 8PN.

242

Subjects: Poetry.
Books January to June 1991 - 1

STOP MESSIN ABOUT!
Carl St John
27 Brookmead Way
Orpington
Kent
BR5 2OQ 0689 833711.
The Kenneth Williams and Sid James Appreciation
Society. Classic British comedy bringing together
the fans of 'Carry On' 'Ealing' and Hancock film
shows organised in London.

STOP PRESS BOOKS
Green Gables
51 The Avenue
Healing
Grimsby
DN37 7NA.
Subjects: Humour.
Books July to December 1991 - 1

STOURTON PRESS
18 Royal Crescent
LONDON
W11 4SL

JOHN STOW
26A Tregunter Road
London
SW10 9LH.
Subjects: Biography.
Books July to December 1991 - 1

STOW'S CLASSICS
Newhaven Fort
Fort Road
Newhaven
BN9 9DL
Historical giftware

ST PETER'S NOTTINGHAM
PCC Parish Office
1/2 St Peter's Church Walk
Nottingham
NG1 2JR

STRANGE ADVENTURES PUBLISHING
Tone Lee (editor/publisher)
13 Hazeley Combe
Arreton
Isle of Wight
PO30 3AJ Tel 0983 865668
Publishing three genre magazines. All available by
mail order. Please send sae for further details.
Strange Adventures a monthly guide to 'fantastic'
media. 28pp £1.70 (inc. p&p). Genre film zine.
Fax 21 SF 'News from the future' Digest. 60pp
quarterly £2.50 (inc. p&p). Science Fiction
Premonitions bi-annual SF/Horror stories. £2.50
(inc. p&p).

STRANGE PUBLICATIONS
PO Box 66
Liverpool
L69 3PU.

Subjects: Art.
Books January to June 1991 - 1

STRANGER GAMES
318 Aldridge Road
Streetly
Sutton Coldfield
B74 2DT

STRANMILLS COLLEGE
Learning Resources Unit
Stranmills Road
Belfast
BT9 5DY.
Subjects: Children's non-fiction.
Books January to June 1991 - 6

STRATA PUBLISHING
P.O. Box 866
13 Rojack Road
London
SE23 2DB.
Subjects: Civil Engineering.
Books July to December 1991 - 1

STRATHBOGIE CHURCH OF SCOTLAND: C/
O E
Howglen
Gladstone Road
Huntly
AB5 5BW

STRATHTONGUE PRESS
Clar Innis
Strathtongue
Lairg
IV27 4XR

STRAWBERRY PRESS
Paul Nash & Helen Pipe
Stanmore
North Street, Islip
Oxford
OX5 2SQ
Fine printers

STRAWBERRY HILL RESIDENTS' ASSOCIA-
TION
44 Popes Avenue
Twickenham
TW2 5TL.
Subjects: Local History.
Books July to December 1991 - 1

STREET EDITIONS
87 St Phillips Road
CAMBRIDGE
CB1 3DA
Modern British, U.S., and European Poetry.
THE BRONTES HATS by Sarah Kirsch, translated
by Wendy Mulford & Anthony Vivas. 16.12.91
96pp Paperback £7.99 0 904225 14 3 Arts Council
Funded. DREAMING FLESH by John James.
Frontpiece Andrew Webster. 2.12.91 56pp. Paper-
back £5.99 0 904225 14 3
WRITING OUT OF CHARACTER by John
Wilkinson, Stephen Ropefer & Rod Mengham. 3
texts. 30.6.92. 48pp. Paperback. £6.50. 0 904225

MR IVAN E STREET
39 Peartee Avenue
1 Newhall
SWADLINCOTE
Derbyshire
DE11 0NB

MR ROBERT STREET
109 Oak Tree Road
Knaphill
WOKING
Surrey
GU21 2SB

STREETLY PRINTING/BEACON BROAD-
CASTING
371 Rednal Road
Kings Norton
Birmingham
B38 8EE

MR J STRIBLING
127 Lothair Road
Aylstone
LEICESTER
LE2 7QE

STRIDE
(see TAXUS)

MR P W STRIKE
72 Westmead
Princes Risborough
AYLESBURY
Buckinghamshire
HP17 9HS

STROUD PUBLISHING COMPANY
Stroud Secretarial Services Ltd
6 London Road
Stroud
GL5 2AA.
Subjects: Poetry.
Books July to December 1991 - 3

JANET STUKINS: J. BROWN
Downton Lace Studio
Borough House
101 The Borough
Downton
Salisbury
SP5 3LX.
Subjects: Downton Lace.

STYLUS PUBLICATIONS
181 Long Acre
Bolton
BL2 6EX

SUBJECT PUBLICATIONS
Beech House
31 Beech Close
Broadstone
BH18 9NJ.
Subjects: Music. School Textbooks.

Books January to June 1991 - 1. Books July to
December 1991 - 1

SUCCESS PUBLICATIONS
Robert Burgess
1 Middlefield Road
Rotherham
South Yorkshire
S60 3JH. Tel 0709 375237
A curious myriad of manuals outlining home-based
hobby related business ideas; and annual trade
directories for niche markets (currently specialist
bookdealers and personality contact addresses).
Please write for a free catalogue.
Cash From the Charts. 28pp ISBN 1 874651 01 9
3.99. A guide to selling second-hand records from
home.
Your Own Coin Dealing Business. 28pp ISBN 1
874651 04 3 3.99. The 1993 Starsearch Directory.
24pp ISBN 1 874651 05 1 2.99. Contact addresses
for top tv film and pop stars.

MR DONALD SUCKLING
2 Boyswell House
Scholes
WIGAN
Lancashire
WN1 3QG

SUFFOLK CRAFTS SOCIETY
House on the Green
Walberswick
Southwold
IP18 6TT.
Subjects: Handicrafts.
Books July to December 1991 - 1

SUFFOLK NOSTALGIA
7 Collingwood Road
Woodbridge
IP12 1JL.
Subjects: Local History.
Books July to December 1991 - 1

SUGDEN PUBLICATIONS
Libra Bookshop
West Street
Mayfield
TN20 6BA

SULIS PUBLICATIONS
5 Widcombe Parade
Bath
BA2 4JT.
Subjects: Music.
Books July to December 1991 - 1

SUMMERS PUBLISHING
22 Ribstock Gardens
Paddock Wood
Tonbridge
TN12 6BA

SUMMERSDALE PRESS
Stewart Ferris
127 Maplehurst Road
Chichester

West Sussex
PO19 4RP 0243 779327
Publish books of interest to students and young people of all ages. Nationwide distribution by Central Books. 99 Wallis Road London E9 5LN (Tel: 081 986 4854). Standard trade terms 35% S.O.R. Summersdale Press also offer a typesetting service.
The Buskers Guide to Europe (Stewart Ferris) 120 pp. A5. 16 b/w photos. April '91. ISBN 1 873475 004. £5.95. 'A trove of little gems of busking knowledge' - Making music.
The Student Grub Guide (Alastair Williams) 160pp. A5. September '91. £4.95 ISBN 1873 475 05 5. Witty Guide to Student Grub from Basic Recipes to Dinner Parties.
Europe on a Big Mac (Various) A5. £4.95. Dec. '91. ISBN 1873 475 30 6. 3 hilarious and contradicting accounts of the same crazy inter rail jour ney one summer.

MR G H SUMNER
Flat 6
12 The Paragon
Blackheath
LONDON
SE3 0NZ

SUN AND HARVEST PUBLICATIONS:
Sterling Books
43A Locking Road
Weston-super-Mare
BS23 3DG.
Subjects: Sun Dials local history of.
Books July to December 1991 - 1

SUNK ISLAND REVIEW
PO Box 74
LINCOLN
LN1 1QG
Biannual paperback anthology of new fiction, poetry, translations, articals, reviews and graphics from the UK and around the world.

SUN MOON AND STARS PRESS
Andi McGarry
Donkey Meadows
Kilmore Quay Wexford
Republic of Ireland.
Specialising in Livres d'artiste and artist's books on organic themes love life mountains sea clouds earth etc. All books are entirely handmade hard and soft coverings and in limited editions. Text and images are original ideas by the artist.
(Livres d'artist) Sea Dive by Andi McGarry. Hard cover colour illustrated - no text. 10pp 61/2' x 81/2'. Edition 30 25.00 (inc. p&p) (Livres d'artist) The Yellow Butterfly by Andi McGarry. Hard cover illustrated colour and text. 10pp 61/2' x 81/2'. Edition 30 15.00 (inc. p&p) (Livres d'artist) The Man who Lost His Sense of Humour. Hard cover illustrated colour. 10pp 61/2' x 81/2'. Edition 30 15.00 (inc. p&p)

SUNRISE PRESS LONDON
34 Churton Street
London
SWIV 2LP.
Subjects: European History.

SUNSHINE ON LEITH PUBLISHING
45 Madeira Street
Edinburgh
EH6 4AJ

SUN TAVERN FIELDS
Anthony Blampied
P.O. Box 982
London
E1 9EQ. Tel 071 790 4267
Broken Mirros/Broken Minds: The Dark Dreams of Dario Argento by Maitland McDonagh. 294pp 1991 ISBN 0 9517012 0 7 £14.99.
The Thorny Side of Love by Fran Landesman. 64pp 1992
ISBN 0 9517012 1 5 £5.95.
Doing Rude Things: The History of the British Sex Film 1957-1981 by David McGillivray. 120pp
ISBN 0 9517012 2 3 £9.95.

SUPPORTIVE LEARNING PUBLICATIONS
25 Maes-y-Waun
Chirk
Wrexham
LL14 5ND.
Subjects: Children's non-fiction.
Books July to December 1991 - 4

R.S. SURTEES SOCIETY
Tacker's Cottage
Horn Street
Nunney
Frome
BA11 4NP.
Subjects: Biography.
Books July to December 1991 - 1

SURVIVORS PRESS
33 Queensdown Road
London
E5 8NN

SUT ANUBIS
73 Kettering Road
NORTHAMPTON
NN1 4AW

TOM SUTCLIFFE
12 Parsonage Court
Bishops Hull
Taunton
TA1 5HR

MR WILLIAM SUTHERLAND
Davaar House
23 Craigendoran Avenue
HELENSBURGH
G84 7AZ

MR RICK SUTTON
Porch Cottage
Wendy
ROYSTON
Hertfordshire

SG8 0HJ

SVECIA ANTIQUA LIMITED
Mr Robert Latham
Dowding Way
TUNBRIDGE WELLS
Kent
TN2 3UY
Specialist paper supplier

S.V.P.
Central House
Southgate Street
Gloucester
GL1 2EX

SWAN BOOKS & EDUCATIONAL SERVICES
13 Henrietta Street
SWANSEA
SA1 4HW
Self-publishing of own illustrated small books, book-
marks and picture post-cards Registered with Welsh
Arts Council and West Wales Arts, etc. Illustrated
talks given: e.g 'The Ups and Downs of a Small
Press.
From Scrap to Gifts by Elizabeth Evans. Illustrated
small manual. Reprinted 1991 Special offer: £0.99
+ P&P = £1.25.
Cats Our Bosses by various authors/illustrators.
Il£lustrated, humorous. Reprinted 1991. £0.90 +
P&P £1.20
Forthcomming Title (summer 1992)
Stories of My Old Dolls by Elizabeth Evans. Will be
illustrated true anecdotes of dolls in collection.
Enquiries welcome: Swansea 0792 643685. or write
to the above address

MR DONALD SWAN
13 Albert Bridge Road
LONDON
SW11 4PX

SWAN HILL PRESS
101 Longden Road
Shrewsbury
SY3 9EB

SWANSEA REVIEW
Dept of English
University College Swansea
Singleton Park
Swansea
SA2 8PP

SHERBOURNE PUBLICATIONS: SWEENEY
MOUNT
Oswestry
SY10 9EX

MR N C SWEENEY
19 Birch Drive
Langford
BRISTOL

SWEETHAWS PRESS
Owl House
Pundgate
Uckfield

TN22 4DE

MS ISABELLE SWOLFS
Roularta Books
Tervurenlaan 153
B-1040 BRUSSEL
BELGIUM

SYCAMORE PRESS
John FUller
4 Benson Place
Oxford
OX2 6QH 0865 56154
Publishing poetry in small editions since 1968. (first
books by Fenton Hollinghurst Imlahetal). £10 to
subscribe.
Stills and Reflections by Mark Wormald. 9pp. 1988.
The Unwritten and Other Poems by Gerard Wood-
ward. 14pp. 1989. A Floribundum by members of
the John Florio Society. 12pp. 1991

MR P J SYDES
162 St Helens Road
HASTINGS
East Sussex
TN34 2EH

CENTRE FOR SYMBOLISM AND IMAGINA-
TION
IN LITERATURE (CESIL)
Portugese Department King's College
Strand
London
WC2R 2LS.
Subjects: Literature.
Books July to December 1991 - 1

SYMPHONY
(see Bemerton Press)

SYNDICATION PRODUCTION
38 Mount Pleasant
London
WC1X 0AP.
Subjects: Biography.
Books January to June 1991 - 1

SYNFINITY
Michael Law
The Chapel House
Perch Hill
WESTBURY
Somerset
BA5 1JA

SYP CHAIRMAN
12 Dyott Street
LONDON
WC1A 1DF

[T]

T.& J PUBLISHING
P.O Box 10
Totnes
TQ9 5GE

246

TABARD PRIVATE PRESS
Philip Kerrigan
White Timbers
Stokesheath Road
Oxshott
KT22 0PS
Fine printers

TABBY PUBLICATIONS
c/o 66 Nelson Gardens
Leicester.
Subjects: Art.
Books January to June 1991 - 1

TABLA MAGAZINE
11 Oulton Close
Aylesbury
Bucks
HP21 7JY

TABLET PUBLISHING COMPANY
48 Great Peter Street
London
SW1P 2HB

TABOR BOOKS
The Barn
All Saint Lane
Canterbury
CT1 2AU

TACKMARK PUBLISHING
27 Brookfield Crescent
Kenton
Harrow
HA3 0UT

MS CHRISTINE TACQ
46 Belsize Avenue
Springfield
MILTON KEYNES
MK6

TAFOL
65 Mardy Street
Grangetown
Cardiff
CF1 7QW.
Subjects: Mediaeval Welsh Erotic Poetry.
Books July to December 1991 - 1

TAG PUBLICATIONS
36 Poole Road
West Ewell
KT19 9SM

CHARLES GRIGG TAIT
6 Fambridge Road
Maldon
CM9 6AA.
Subjects: Local History.
Books July to December 1991 - 1

CHARLES TAIT PHOTOGRAPHIC
Kelton St.
Ola
Kirkwall

Orkney
KW15 1TR.
Subjects: Orkney Guide Book.
Books July to December 1991 - 1

TAK TAK TAK
Contacts: Andrew & Tim Brown
PO Box 7, Bulwell, Nottingham, NG6 OHW
Involved in several areas - publishing books (including anthologies and Polish language material)
promoting live poetry and music; and producing spoken word cassettes.
'The dangling god' by Roger Wakeling. 150 pp.
September 1991. £4.95 paperback. ISBN 1 871548 30 6. A powerful first novel.
'Mother Country/Fatherland' - an anthology; including free cassette supplement. 100 pp. September 1991. £3.00 paperback. ISBN 1871548 35 7.
Writing visuals and music on the above theme by various contributors.
'The Band Soprano'. A portrait of Lol Coxhill by Jeff Nuthall. 120 pp. Summer 1989. 6 paperback ISBN 1871548 15 2. A literary jazz duet.

MS SHEILA TALBOT
Tyclyd
Penlon
TALYBONT
Dyfed
SY24 5NP

MR GRAEME K TALBOYS
10 Greenbank
JARROW
Tyne & Wear
NE32 3NA

TALIBAH PRESS
PO Box 160
London
SE26 6NJ

TALKING STICK MAGAZINE
Suite B
2 Tunstall Road
LONDON
SW9 8DA

TALUS
c/o Dept of English
Univ of York
Haslington
York
YO1 5DD

TAMARIND LIMITED
PO Box 296
CAMBERLEY
Surrey
GU15 1QW
Childrens books

MS MARY TANGAY
Annagh House
Annagh
Tralee
Co Kerry

TAPE BOOKS
Chris Mitchell
1/L 11 Woodlands Drive
GLASGOW
G4 9EQ

TAPROBANE LIMITED
P O Box 717
LONDON
W5 3EY
First publication: The Third Sex by Gordon Wilson.
It is a book which presents new thinking covering a
number of fields: psychology, sociology, evolution
theory , 'sex equality', homosexuality, etc.

TARAGON PRESS
Mr David Summer
3 Dougalstone Avenue
Milngavie
GLASGOW
G62 6AU

TARA PRODUCTS
9 Townsend
Quainton
Aylesbury
HP22 4BP

TARTARUS PRESS
8 Hunterhouse Road
Hunters Bar
Sheffield
S11 8TW

TAURUS PRESS OF WILLOW DENE
11 Limetree Way
Danygraig
PORTHCAWL
Mid Glamorgan
CF36 5AU

L. TAVENDER
7 Mark Close
Regent's Park Road
Southampton
SO1 3RZ.
Subjects: Railways.

TAWNJAKE PUBLISHING
156 Station Road
Rainham
Gillingham
ME8 7PR.
Subjects: Health.

TAXUS
c/o Stride
37 Portland Street
Exeter
EX1 2EG
Poetry press

MR DAVID TAYLOR
9 Painswick Avenue
Stoke Lodge
BRISTOL
BS12 6DA

MR F J TAYLOR
6 Dukes Drive
Clarendon Park
LEICESTER
LE2 1TY

H TAYLOR
78 Boswell Road
Bessacar
DONCASTER
South Yorkshire
DN4 7DD

JOHN B. TAYLOR
36 Fernhill Drive
Stacksteads
Bacup
OL13 8JS.
Subjects: Local History.
Books July to December 1991 - 1

MR KENNETH J TAYLOR
Flat 1
33 Knowle Road
Totterdown Road
BRISTOL
BS4 2EB

MR LEON TAYLOR
73 Worlds End Road
Handsworth Wood
BIRMINGHAM
B20 2NS

MR M TAYLOR
97a Main Street
BANGOR ·
Co Down
BT20 4AF

ROSEMARY TAYLOR LONDON
5 Pusey House
Saracen Street
London
E14 6HG.
Subjects: Local History.
Books January to June 1991 - 1

TAYNTON PRESS
3 Taynton
Burford
Oxford
OX18 4UH.
Subjects: History of Music.
Books July to December 1991 - 1

TCL PUBLICATIONS
15 Coronation Road
East Grinstead
RH19 4AJ.
Subjects: Shipping.
Books July to December 1991 - 1

TEARS IN THE FENCE
Sarah Hopkins
Venton Manor

Dartington,
TOTNES
South Devon
TQ9 6DP 0364 73209
A bi-annual literary magazine of poetry, fiction, graphics, reviews, articles, i nterviews and fun. Concerned to promote women's writing and quality literature.

TECHNIQUE TYPESETTING
3 Broadfields Court
Broadfields
AYLESBURY
Buckinghamshire
HP19 3BG

TEENEY BOOKS
Matbro House
Garston Road
Frome
BA11 1QW.
Subjects: Children's Fiction.
Books January to June 1991 - 4. Books July to December 1991 - 10

TEESIDE POLYTECHNIC
The Library
Borough Road
Middlesbrough
TS1 3BA

TEES VALLEY WRITER
57 The Ave
Linthorpe
Middlesbrough
Cleveland
TS5 6QU

TEMPLE PRESS
PO Box 227
Brighton
BN2 3GL Tel: 0273 679129
Mr Words
The UK's leading occultural press. We publish radical texts ranging from sexuality to poetry, art and the occult. WE also distribute many independent presses internationally, and offer full typesetting services. 'The Correct Sadist' by Terence Sellers. Originally published 1990. 3rd printing Autumn 1991. 186pp. hardback. 6 illustrations. £12.50. ISBN 1 871744 05 9.
'Ratio:3 Volume 1 (Media Shamans)' by Ira Cohen Angus MacLise Gerard Malanga. 104pp. Paperback. £8.50. ISBN 1 871744 30 X. Poets from American sub-culture. First in our occultural text services.
'Ratio:3 Volume 2 (transmedia) by Z'ev Andrew McKenzie Genesis P-Orri dge. 112pp. paperback. £8.50. ISBN 1 871744 35 0. 3 inspirational writers. 3 unique visions. The transformation of language.

TEMPLE GROVE PRESS
Sevak Gulbenkian
51 Queen Caroline Street
LONDON
W6 9QL

TEMPLE LODGE PRESS
51 Queen Caroline Street
London
W6 9QL

TEMPLE ROCK PUBLICATIONS
The Farmhouse
Cuddesdon
Oxford
OX9 9ET 08677 4438
Small publisher of local books
'Oxford The American Connection' by Anne Keene 70pp 50b/w photos June 1990 0 9515963 0 6. £4.99. An account of the many links between the United States and Oxford written by an Oxford Guide who is also a grad uate

TENANT PARTICIPATION ADVISORY SERVICE
48 The Crescent
Salford
M5 4NY.
Subjects: Newsletters. Social Welfare.
Books July to December 1991 - 2

TEN GRAND MAGAZINE
Lion House Studios
Queens House
12 Queens Square
BRIGHTON
BN1
Magazine for film, tv, comics, music.

A J TENNANT
TCL Publications
15 Coronation Road
East Grinstead
RH19 4AJ
Jazz related poetry

THE TENORMEN PRESS/OSTINATO
Stephen Middleton
P.O. Box 522
London
N8 7SZ.
A jazz poetry magazine professionally designed with large review section that promotes the links between literature (in particular poetry) and improvised music. We also publish specially designed/illustrated books by creative writing about jazz.
Pitches at Silence (Dreams of Music) by Rupert M. Loydell. 36pp Dec 90 ISBN 0 9514903 1 1 £2.75 (plus 60 p&p). Poems re jazz
Living Jazz by Alexis Lykiard. 60pp Sept 91 Large format/illustrated ISBN 0 9514903 0 3 £5.95 (plus 60 p&p). Poems about jazz. The Tenormen by Stephen C. Middleton. 24pp Dec 90 Large format/illustrated ISBN 0 9514903 2 X £4.95 (plus 60 p&p). Poems about jazz.

TENTH DECADE
12 Stevenage Road
LONDON
SW6 6ES

TENTH MUSE
33 Hartington Road
Southampton

249

S02 0EW

MAGH ITHA TEORANTA
31 Elgin Heights
Bray
County Wicklow
Irish Republic

TERENCE HIGGINS TRUST
BM/AIDS
London
WC1N 3XX

TERMINUS PUBLICATIONS
592a Chatsworth Road
Chesterfield
Derbyshire
S40 3JX Chesterfield 566406
Small publishing house catering for the transport
enthusiast (train/bus) and producing A5 books
mainly pertaining to the North Midlands/Derby-
shire area.
Great Central Railway North of Nottingham - Vol
2 by A R Kaye. 84pp. 190 illus. ISBN 0 946930 12
0. £4.95 (illustrated survey)
North Midland & Peak District Railways in the
Steam Age - Vol 2 by A R Kaye. 80pp. 185 illus.
ISBN 0 946930 09 0 (illustrated survey) Riding
with Hulley's of Baslow by A R Kaye. 48pp. 90 illus.
ISBN 0 946930 13 9. Brief history of this well
known Derbyshire bus operator with illus trations
of present routes.

TERMITE TIMES
c/o Shrewsbury Youth Centre
5 Belmont
Shrewsbury
Salop
SY1 1TF

TERN PRESS
Nicholas & Mary Perry
St Mary's Cottage
Great Hales Street
Market Drayton
TF9 1JN
Fine printer

TERN PUBLICATIONS
The Old Post Cottage
Motcombe
Shaftesbury
SP7 9NT.
Subjects: History of Hospitals.
Books January to June 1991 - 1

TERROR FORCE 10
Suite 16
46-48 Osnaburgh Street
London
NW1 3ND

MR MICHAEL TERRY
Swanscomb
Coolinge Lane
FOLKSTONE
Kent
CT20 3RA

TESEO BOOKS
2 Golders Manor Drive
London
NW11 9HT.
Subjects: Biography.
Books January to June 1991 - 1

TETRAD PRESS
Hega House
Ullin Street
St Leonards Road
LONDON
E14

THAILAND WEAVING AND THE RICE CY-
CLE
Susan Conway
8 Sand's Wharf
William Morris Way
Fulham
SW6 2RZ. Tel 071 371 0006
Describes Thai Buddhist culture and the textiles
woven in traditional society. Photos of mural paint-
ings from temples showing costume styles.

THAMESLINK DTP LIMITED
Roger Cullingham
99-101 St Leonards Road
WINDSOR
Berkshire
SL4 3BZ

THARSON PRESS
Church Cottage
Morton Hall
Morton-on-the-Hill
Norwich
NR9 5JS.
Subjects: Military History.
Books July to December 1991 - 2

T.H.C.L Books
185 Lammack Road
Blackburn
BB1 8LH

THEATRE ACTION PRESS
c/o Department of Literature
University of Essex
Wivenhoe Park
COLCHESTER
CP4 3SQ
Radical theatre books and play scripts originating
in Essex University's theatre writer's residency, and
the productions of the Theatre Underground Company. COntradictory theatres. Edited by Leslie Bell.
(1984). ISBN 0 90057514 X. Hardbound £13.00;
Paperback £4.95. 295 pages.
The tragedy of Mao in the Lin piao period and other
plays by Roger Howard. 1989. ISBN 0 90057515 8.
132 pages. 132 page paperback. £5.95. Britannia
and other plays. By Roger Howard. ISBN 0
90057516 (1991) 178 pages, 6 .95.

THEATRE SCRIPTS
Upton House
Southey Green, Sible Hedingham

250

Halstead
CO9 3RN

THE CLIQUE
7 Pulleyn Drive
York
YO2 2DY

THEMATIC TRAILS
Oxford Polytechnic
Faculty of Environment Studies
Oxford
OX3 0BP

THEOSOPHICAL PUBLISHING HOUSE
12 Bury Place
London
WC1A 2LE

THE PRESS
53b All Saints Street
HASTINGS
East Sussex
TN34 3BN

THE SYNDICATE
Pettigoe Fair
22 Lansdowne Road, Frimley
Camberley
GU16 5UW

THE WORKS
St Brendans
Waterloo Road
Wexford
Republic of Ireland

THINKING EYE IDEAS
13 Fort Street
Dundee
DD2 1BS

THINLEY RINCHEN LING
Sakyapa Buddhist Centre
27 Lilymead Avenue
Knowle
Bristol
BS4 2BY

THIRD HALF
16 Fane Close
Stamford
Lincs
PE9 1HG

THIRD HOUSE
Peter Robins
35 Brighton Road
LONDON
N16 8EQ
Gay fiction in paperback

THIRD WORLD PUBLISHING COMPANY
29 Upper Camelford Walk
London
W11 1TU

THIRD WORLD QUARTERLY
c/o Shadid Qadir
188 Copse Hill
London
SW20 0SP
(tel: 081-947-1043)

THIS ENGLAND BOOKS
Alma House
73 Rodney Road
Cheltenham
GL50 1HT

THISTLE BOOKS
Chiltern Cottage
Gayton lane
Wirral
L60 3SH

THOEMMES ANTIQUARIAN BOOKS
85 Park Street
Bristol
BS1 5PJ

MR T J THOIMA
7 Sandringham Drive
Heaton Mersey
STOCKPORT
Cheshire
SK4 2DE

MR G L THOMAS
273 273 Clayhall Avenue
Clayhall
ILFORD
Essex
IG5 0TE

KELVIN S.M. THOMAS
78 Holcombe Vale
Bathampton
Bath
BA2 6UX.
Subjects: Biography.
Books January to June 1991 - 1

MR T R THOMAS
Head of Department
Mechanical Engineering/Metallurgy
Tees-side Polytechnic
MIDDLESBROUGH, Cleveland
TS1 3BA

WILLIAM GRENVILLE THOMAS
25 Romilly Crescent
Hakin
Milford Haven
SA73 3NH.
Subjects: Local History.
Books July to December 1991 - 1

MR W H THOMAS
Smithy Paddock
Croxton Road, Fulmodestone
FAKENHAM
Norfolk

NR21 0NJ

THOM PRESS EYNSHAM
66 Evans Road
Eynsham
OX8 1QS.
Subjects: Short Stories.
Books July to December 1991 - 1

MR A L THOMPSON
111 Station Road
Hampton on Thames
Middlesex
TW12 2BD

MS BETH THOMPSON
395 Broxburn Drive
South Ockendey
Essex
RM15 5PJ

HILARY THOMPSON
1 The Quay
Portscatho
Truro
TR2 5HF.
Subjects: Local History.
Books July to December 1991 - 1

MS L THOMPSON
c/o 16 Grasmere Avenue
Noctorum
BIRKENHEAD
Merseyside
L43 9SG

MR S THOMPSON
14a Grafton Road
Brigstock
KETTERING
Northamptonshire
NN14 3EY

THORMYND PRESS
PO Box 4
Church Stretton
SY6 6ZZ

THORN
M.S.C. Harding and Ed Fairclough
13 Oswald Road
Upper Tooting
London
SW17 7SS. Tel 081 767 2368
Bi-monthly 32pp pamphlet of esoterica history
features images strange tales soundbites etc. which
reflect the shift from the newtonian-Descartes para-
digm of 17th to 20th centuries to one of transforma-
tion and process as described by the increasing
understanding of the east by the west.
Thorn 1. 1.5.92 £2.00. Paganism Runes God Shape
Shifting Heresy. Thorn 2. 1.7.92. £2.00. Anglo-
Saxons Runes Cannibalism Runes Sin The Somme.
Thorn 3. 1.9.92. £2.00. Serpents Tales from the
Morgue Runes St. Anthony's Fire.

THORNGATE BOOKS
Thorngate Mill

BARNARD CASTLE
Co Durham
DL12 8QB
Herbs and So On. £3.95

PHILIP THORNTON
14 Bonnington Road
Leicester
LE2 3DB

THOTH PUBLICATIONS
BM Sothis
LONDON
WC1N 3XX
Esoteric non-fiction

THREE COUNTIES
59 Dinglewell
GLOUCESTER
GL3 3HP

THREE SPIRES PRESS
Killeen
Blackrock
Cork
Republic of Ireland.
Subjects: Poetry.
Books January to June 1991 - 2

THRESHOLDWORKS
27 Walpole Road
Tottenham
LONDON
N17 6BE

JOURNAL OF THROSSEL HOLE PRIORY
Soto Zen Monastery
Carrshield
Hexham
Northumberland
NE47 8AL

THURSDAYS
70 Poplar Road
Bearwood
Warley
West Midlands
B66 4AN

THWARTSEA BOOKS
Suite 11
23 Holland Road
Hove
BN3 1JF

BRIAN J. TILEHURST
8 Brickfield Road
Portswood
Southampton
SO2 3AE.
Subjects: Local History.
Books July to December 1991 - 1

TIME ENERGY INFORMATION
14 Railway Square
Brentwood
CM14 4LN.

252

Subjects: Health
Books January to June 1991 - 1.

MRS MONICA TIMMS
17 Baskerville Road
Lyncroft
SWINDON
SN3 5DB

TI PARKS ARTISTS BOOKS
Ti Parks
9 The Orchard,
London SE3 OQS
081 852 7246
A fully descriptive and illustrated catalogue of this
artist's very unusual artists books, book works and
anti books is available price £45. This catalogue is
a desirable book work itself. A check list is available
with SAE.

'TITANIC' SIGNALS ARCHIVE
30 Eden Vale Road
Westbury
BA13 3NY.
Subjects: 'Titanic'.
Books July to December 1991 - 1

TITCHFIELD PUBLISHING
46 High Street
Buriton
Petersfield
GU31 5RZ

TOAD HOUSE BOOKS
Mole Cottage
17 Prospect Terrace,
New Brancepeth
Durham
DH7 7EJ
Humour, travel, arts, sociology.

MR PAUL TODD
Misbourne Farmhouse
Amersham Road
CHALFONT ST GILES
Buckinghamshire
HP8 4RU

IAIN TOLHURST
West Lodge; Hardwick Estate
Whitchurch-on-Thames
Pangbourne
READING
RG8 7RA
A Gardener's Guide to Growing Strawberries Or-
ganically. 2.00 post paid

KENT LIONEL TOMLIN
21 Castle Crescent
Castle Bromwich
Birmingham
B36 9TF.
Subjects: Children's Fiction.
Books July to December 1991 - 1

JOSEPH TYE TOMLINSON
22 The Green

Elston
Newark
NG23 5PF.
Subjects: Biography.
Books July to December 1991 - 1

MR P TOMLINSON
9 Worcester Terrace
Clifton
BRISTOL
BS8 3JW

TOMPSON PUBLISHING
Oak House Moor Park
Lower Street
Chagford
Newton Abbot
TQ13 8BY.
Subject: Children's Fiction. General Knowledge.
Books July to December 1991 - 2

TOMVELIAN PUBLICATIONS
3 Scotts Drive
Hampton
TW12 2UN.
Subjects: Poetry.
Books July to December 1991 - 2

MR P TONER
6 Wharf Road
SHILLINGFORD
Oxfordshire
OX10 7EW

TONGUE IN CHEEK MUSIC
Ian Cheek
55 Albion Street
OTLEY
West Yorkshire
LS21 1BZ

MR IAN TONKS
Ashlea
Bryning Lane, Newton
Kirkham
PRESTON
PR4 3RL

MR BOB TONNER
437 Whitmore Way
BASILDON
Essex
SS14 2HL

TOPICAL PUBLISHERS
1 Elm Grove Road
CARDIFF
CF4 2BW
Your Phone Bill - Fact or Fiction? £2.50.

TOPICAL RESOURCES
4 Brookfield Drive
Fulwood
Preston
PR1 4ST

T O P S
The Old Police Station
80 Lark Lane
LIVERPOOL
L17 8UU
The Old Police Station Magazine - poetry

T.O.P.Y. HEART
P.O. Box 2055
Moseley
Birmingham
B14 7LS.
Subjects: Occult.
Books July to December 1991 - 3

TOR MARK PRESS
Subjects: Cornish Customs. Cornish Shipwrecks
Books January to June 1991 - 4. Books July to
December 1991 - 3

TOTAL
PO Box 284
Glasgow
G14 9TW

TOTTENHAM & WOOD GREEN WRITERS
55 Northumberland Park
LONDON
N17

TOUCH
13 Oswald Road
LONDON
SW17 7SS
Distributors of printed publications and records.

TOUCHSTONE
25 Albert Road
Addlestone
WEYBRIDGE
Surrey
KT15 2PX

TOLOUSE PRESS
5 South Drive
Liverpool
L15 8JJ

TOURNAMENT CHESS
8 Adelina Mews
Kings Avenue
London
SW12 0BG.
Subjects: Chess
Books January to June 1991 - 1.

TOWER BOOKS
86 South Main Street
Cork City
Ireland

TOWER HAMLETS WRITERS
178 Whitechapel Road
LONDON
E1 1BJ

MR ROGER TOWNDROW
2 Florence Place
FALMOUTH
Cornwall
TR11 3NJ

TOWN TEACHER
All Saints Church
Akenside Hill
Newcastle-upon-Tyne
NE1 2DS

TOWPATH ACTION GROUP
(Andy Screen)
23 Hague Bar Road
New Mills
Stockport
SK12 3AT.
Subjects: Canal Towpaths.
Books July to December 1991 - 1

TO YIELD PRESS
Flat Above
4 Wostenholm Road
Nether Edge
SHEFFIELD
S7 1LJ

TRADE AND TRAVEL PUBLICATIONS
6 Riverside Court
Riverside Road
Lower Bristol Road
Bath
BA2 3DZ.
Subjects: Asian Travel. Travel (South and Central
America). British Travel. Books July to December
1991 - 5

TRADE UNIONISTS FOR IRISH UNITY
& Independence
530 South Circular Road
Dublin 8
Ireland

TRADE UNION RESOURCE CENTRE (TURC)
7 Frederick Street
BIRMINGHAM
B1

TRAGARA PRESS
43 Mayburn Avenue
LOANHEAD
Mid Lothian
EH20 9EY

TRAIL PROJECT
Groundwork House
Bus Station Buildings, Castle Street
Merthyr Tydfil
CF42 8BB

TRAMBROOKS
48 Dorrington Road
Cheadle Heath
Stockport
SK3 0PZ.

Subjects: History of Trams.
Books July to December 1991 - 1

MR D S O'BRIEN
Translatum International
Saithaelwyd Ucha
Carmel, Holy well
Co Clwyd
CH8 8NU

TRANSPORT PUBLISHING COMPANY
121 Pikes lane
Glossop
SK13 8EH

TRANSVIDEO ENTERPRISES
Old School
Wormshill
SITTINGBOURNE
Kent
ME9 0TR
Teachers' resource material for environmental education. "Tree" magazine also printing of flyers etc.

TRAYLEN
Castle House
49-50 Quarry Street
Guildford
GU7 3UA

TREGATE PRESS
(Mary Hopson)
Tregate Castle
Monmouth
NP5 3QL.
Subjects: Local Religious History. Local History.
Books July to December 1991 - 2

TREGENZA STUDIOS
Mr J Ronan
Box 1004, Abbey Place, Mousehole
PENZANCE
Cornwall
TR19 6PQ

LYFROW TRELYSPEN
Roseland
Gorran
St Austell
Cornwall

TRENDRINE PRESS
Trendine
Zennor
St. Ives
TR26 3BW.
Subjects: Cornish Flora.
Books January to June 1991 - 1

TRIAD ESOTERIC PUBLICATIONS
PO Box 134
Horsham
RH13 5FG

TRIANGULAR CIRCLE COMPANY
18 Clarence Chambers
39 Corporation Street

Birmingham
B2 4LS.
Subjects: Travel.
Books January to June 1991 - 1

TRIGON PRESS
117 Kent House Road
Beckenham
BR3 1JJ.
Subjects: Architecture.
Books July to December 1991 - 6

TRINITY AND ALL SAINTS' COLLEGE
Brownberrie Lane
Horsforth
Leeds
LS18 5HD.
Subjects: Literature.
Books January to June 1991 - 1 Books July to December 1991- 1

TRINITY COLLEGE,DUBLIN
Department of Geography
Dublin 2
Republic of Ireland

TRINITY COLLEGE DUBLIN PRESS
41 Marlborough Road
Donnybrook
Dublin 4
Republic of Ireland

TRINITY COLLEGE, DUBLIN, LIBRARY
Trinity College
College Street
Dublin 2
Republic of Ireland

TRINITY HISTORY WORKSHOP
Department of Modern History
Trinity College
Dublin 2
Republic of Ireland

TRIPLE CAT PUBLISHING
3 Back Lane Cottages
Bucks Horn Oak
Farnham
GU10 4LN

MR RICHARD TROMANS
Flat above Dog's Dinner
35 High Street
HERNE BAY
Kent

K TROTMAN
Unit 11
135 Ditton Walk
Cambridge
CB5 8QD

TROUBLE & STRIFE
P O Box 8
Diss
Norfolk

IP22 3XG

TROUSER PRESS
Anthony Mann
PO Box 139, Aldershot, Hampshire, GU12 5XR
0252 314585
This 'diary of events' comments on local national
and international stories as they occurred personal
memories anecdotes and the present day life of the
author provide highly amusing observations cou-
pled with thought-provoking and controversial views
on serious matters.
'From Where I Sit' by Anthony Mann. October
1990. 282pp. paperback. £4.95 . ISBN 0 9516501
0 6. Humorous/autobiography.

MR J A TRUSSLER
18 Dartmouth Court
Dartmouth Grove
LONDON
SE10 8AS

TUBA
Charles Graham
Tunley Cottages
Tunley
CIRENCESTER
Gloucestershire
GL7 6LW
Tuba Magazine (poetry/surrealism) plus poetry
books of imaginative kind.

ROY BRIAN TUBB
13 Elmhurst Road
Thatcham
RG13 3DQ.
Subjects: Local History.
Books July to December 1991 - 2

TUBEWALKING:
World Leisure Marketing
117 The Hollow
Littleover
Derby
DE3 7BS.
Subjects: Walks in London.
Books July to December 1991 - 1

MS BRIGID J TUCKER
20 Halsmere Road
Camberwell
LONDON
SE5 9LN

MR COLIN TUCKER
24 Ecton Avenue
MACCLESFIELD
Cheshire
SK10 1QS

CRITICAL WAVE PUBLICATIONS
Mr Martin Tudor
24a Beech Road
Bowes Park
LONDON
N11 2DA

TUDOR SOVEREIGN PUBLISHING

357 Hook Rise
South Surbiton
KT6 7LW.
Books January to June 1991 - 1

MR THOMAS TUDOR
Case Postale 501
CH-1213 petit Lancy 1
Switzerland

TOUCHSTONE PRESS
12 Portland Place
Bishop's Stortford
CM23 3SH

THE TUFNELL PRESS
Robert Albury
47 Dalmeny Road
LONDON
N7 0DY 071 272 4861
Publishers of books and booklets on education
studies, gender studies; health education; sociology
and politics.
Sex Risk and Danger: AIDS education policy and
Young Womens' Sexuality. Holland et al. ISBN 1
872767 55 9. 30 pages. 1990. Paperback. £3.00.
Equal Opportunities and the New Era. Davies et al.
ISBN 1 872767 00 1. 52 pages 1991 (rev). Paper-
back. £3.95.
Learning About Sex. Young Women and the Social
Construction of Sexual Identity. Thomson & Scott.
ISBN 1 872767 70 2. 55 pages. 1991.

TULSA FIRE PROTECTION INSTALLERS
15 Ventonleague Hill
HAYLE
Cornwall
TR27 4EH 0736 752338

TUMI
8-9 New Bond Street Place
Bath
BA1 1BH

J TUNGAY
4 Fourth Avenue
Hove
BN3 2PH

PAMELA H TURBETT
17 Forest Rise
Liss Forest
Liss
GU33 7AU

TURF CLUB
The Curragh
Kildare
Republic of Ireland.
Subjects: History of the Turf Club.
Books January to June 1991 - 1

MR BARRY TURNER
Town House Publicity
45 Islington Park Street
LONDON
N1 1QB

MR DAVID W TURNER
Walden Lodge
Pean Hill
WHITSTABLE
Kent
CT5 3BG 0227 471312

TURNING POINTS
Sabine Kurjo McNeill
21a Goldhurst Terrace,
London NW6 3HB
071 625 8804. Fax 071 372 2378
Turning Points was set up in 1982 to transform consciousness through lectures, workshops and conferences. I have always published my own leaflets and programmes and eventually the book Only Connect - The Art and Technology of Networking for Personal and Global Transformation.
Only Connect; Sabine Kurjo & Jan McNeill; 110pp; 1988; ISBN 0 566034 52 2; £4.50
Networking; Communication; Information.
Energy & Medicine; Sabine Kurjo McNeill & Others; 72pp; 1991; £3.50.

TURNOUT SCOTLAND
Shealinghill
Lochfoot
Dumfries
DG2 8NJ.
Subjects: Social Welfare.
Books January to June 1991 - 1

TURTLE PUBLISHING COMPANY
2 Rosemary Avenue
Braintree
CM7 7SZ

TURTON & CHAMBERS
Unit 5
Station Road Industrial Estate
Woodchester
GL5 5EQ

THOMAS TURVES
98 Chester Road
Hazel Grove
Stockport
SK7 6HF

TV INTERNATIONAL REPARTEE
Rose's, PO Box 339,
Sheffield, S1 3SX
0742 342870
Now established as the leading British magazine for transvestites, Repartee presents a good balanced view of all aspects of cross-dressing. Repartee is fun encouraging a positive view of transvestism being something to enjoy rather than treated as a shameful problem.
TV International Repartee published quarterly in January, April, July & October. ISSN 0961-7027. 60 pages,; full colour cover; £6 each. £18 year subscription. Subject: Transvestism.

THOMAS ARTHUR TWEDDLE
M. Lancaster
Parallel Lines
1st Floor 12 Cheltenham Mount

Harrogate
HG1 1DW.
Subjects: Historical Biography.

TWEEDDALE COURT
14 High Street
Edinburgh
EH1 1TE
Scratch, Mark Robinson

TWELVEHEADS PRESS
Chy Mengleth
Twelveheads
Truro
TR4 8SN

MR JOHN A TWELVES
119 Oakdale Drive
Heald Green
CHEADLE
Cheshire
SK8 3SN

TWENTY-ONE PRESS
745 Barking Road
London
E13 9ER.
Subjects: Social Welfare.
Books July to December 1991 - 1

TWIST IN THE TALE PUBLISHING
18 Hind Street
Retford
DN22 7EN.
Subjects: Poetry.
Books January to June 1991 - 5

TWO-CAN PUBLISHING
27 Cowper Street
London
EC2A 4AP

TWO MILLIMETRE SCALE ASSOCIATION
32 Blount Avenue
East Grinstead
RH19 1JQ.
Subjects: Model Railways.
Books July to December 1991 - 1

DAVE TWYDELL
12 The Furrows
Harefield
Uxbridge
UB9 6AT.
Subjects: Sport.
Books January to June 1991 - 1

MERYL TYEN
Fitzwilliam College
CAMBRIDGE
CB3 0DG

TYNDALE & PANDA PUBLISHING
117 High Street
Lowestoft
NR32 1HN

TYNE MUSIC
11 Churchill Street
Newcastle-upon-Tyne
NE1 4HF

TYPE PUBLISHERS
Unit 367
27 Clerkenwell Close
London
EC1R 0AT.
Subjects: Education.
Books January to June 1991 - 1

TYRANNOSAURUS REX PRESS
Dr Keith Seddon
BM Box 1129
London
WC1N 3XX. Tel 0923 229784
(Note new address)
Philosophy politics religion occult wayward fiction.
We hope eventually to publish about three full-length titles each year plus several booklets - if only authors would send decent work. Inaugural list for mid-1991 held back until 1992/93 due to penury.

[U]

UFO BRIGANTIA
84 Elland Road
Brighouse
West Yorkshire
HD6 2QR

UFO DEBATE
40 Stubbing Way
Shipley
West Yorkshire
BD18 2EZ

UFO TIMES
A. West, 16 Southway,
Burgess Hill,
Sussex RH15 9ST
See BUFORA

UK CONSULTANCY SERVICES LIMITED
22 Brantwood Road
BARNEHURST
Kent
DA7 6LQ 0322 53487

UK INTERNATIONAL CERAMICS
10 Wilford Bridge
Spur Melton
Woodbridge
IP12 1RJ.
Subjects: Ceramics.
Books July to December 1991 - 1

UK RESIST MAGAZINE
Jake Lagnado
PO Box 244a
Surbiton
Surrey
KT5 9LU
UK Resist is a 'socially aware' alternative music magazine with its roots in the anarchist and punk movements of the 1980s from rap to hardcore to political debate on an almost quarterly basis.
UK Resist No.5; issued August 1991. A4 32pp £0.50 plus A4 sae /$3 ppd abroad.
UK Resist No.4. issued March 1991. A4 32pp plus free flexi-disc. £0.50 and A4 sae /$3 ppd abroad
UK Resist Nos. 1-31/2; issued between January 1990 and October 1990. All sold out.

ULSTER EDUCATION
1 Belmont Park
Belfast
BT4 3DU

ULTIMA THULE LIMITED
Stephen Billing
136 Church Parade
CANVEY ISLAND
Essex
SS8 9RD
Publishers of spiritual poetry.

ULTONIAN PRESS
48 Harberton Park Belfast
BT9 6TT

UNA DEVA
PO Box 1177
CHEDDAR
Somerset
BS27 3UQ
Publish "O" magazine - fashion, fetish, fantasies. More than 70 pages of rubber and plastics.

UNCLE JOHN PRESS
27 Cambridge Court
220 Cambridge Heath Road
Bethnal Green
LONDON
E2

UNDERSTANDING
(Dionysia Press)
20A Montgomery St
Edinburgh
EH7 5JS

UNDERTOW
(c/o University College London)

UNGAWA
PO Box 1764
London
NW6 2EQ
Look back with Europe's wildest magazine; the only publication that focuses on forgotten forbidden items from the past. Each issue covers weird films strange behaviour pin-ups pulps and bizarre personalities. Books records flicks and kicks - a veritable A-Z of depravity. Ungawa!. 0963-7540. 26 plus pages. plenty of illustrations. 2-3 times per year.

UNIBIRD
76 Iveson Drive
LEEDS
LS16 6NL

UNICHROME (BATH)
90 Locksbrook Road
Weston
Bath
BA1 3EN.
Subjects: Travel in Britain.
Books July to December 1991 - 2

(THE) UNICORN
P O Box 18
Hessle
North Humberside
HU13 0HW

UNICORN BOOKS
16 Laxton Gardens
Paddock Wood
Tonbridge
TN12 6BB

UNICORN PUBLISHING STUDIO
63 Jeddo Road
London
W12 9EE

UNIQUE BOOKS
55 Ventnor Drive
London
N20 8BU.
Subjects: Literature.
Books July to December 1991 - 2

MR CLIVE UNIT
2 Onslow Croft
Old College park
LEAMINGTON SPA
Warwickshire
CV32 6SN

UNITY THEATRE NEWS
c/o Lawrie Moore
36 Strathmore Gardens
London
N3 2HL

UNIVERSITY OF THE THIRD AGE
6 Parkside Gardens
London
SW19 5EY

UNIVERSITY OF GLASGOW FRENCH
AND GERMAN PUBLICATIONS
Geoff Woollen
Modern Languages Building
University of Glasgow
G12 8QL. Tel 041 339 8855 x459
Small academic publisher specialising in schools
and under-graduate guides to foreign literature and
civilisation
Vercors: 'Le Silence de la Mer' by W.M. Kidd.
Guides to French Literature 18 iv + 68pp ISBN 0
8561 316 4 3.50
Kafka: 'Der Prozer' by W.M.J. Bodd. Guides to
German Literature. iv + 60pp ISBN 0 8561 323 7
3.75
Feet First: Jules Valles by Walter Redfern. viii +
232pp

ISBN 0 8561 315 6 12.00.

UNIVERSITY LIBRARY OF MANCHESTER
John Rylands
Oxford Road
Manchester
M13 9PL.
Subjects: History of Local Railways.
Books January to June 1991 - 2. Books July to
December 1991 - 1

UNLIMITED DREAM COMPANY
127 Gaisford Street
Kentish Town
LONDON
NW5 2EG
071 482 0090
Not a publisher, but a service for publishers, small
presses, particularly SF.

UNPLEASANT BOOKS
Box 32
52 Call Lane
LEEDS
LS1 6DT
Curiosities by Pig Havok.

UNPOPULAR BOOKS
Box 15
136 Kingsland High Road
Dalston
LONDON
E8 2NS
Ultra Lefties, also distribute Pirate Productions.

FREDERICK THOMAS UNWIN
9 Cockloft Place
Cambridge

UPFRONT PUBLISHING
Flat 187, Samuel Lewes Trust
Amhurst Road
London
E8 2DJ

URALIA PRESS
23 Westland Road
Wolverhampton
WV3 9NZ

URBAN ANGEL PRESS
D.G. Plaiter
13 St Edward's Road
Southsea
Hants
PO5 3DH. Tel (0705) 822146
Plans to produce literature of an extreme nature
with minimum sex and violence.

URCHIN BOOKS
Suzanne Andrisson
27 May Road
Lowestoft
Suffolk
NR32 2DJ.
Urchin Books - publish work by its proprietor
Suzanne Andrisson. To date she has shown her

prolific abilities by writing one book for children consisting of a staggering 139pp. More will follow - if she pulls her finger out! The Nuts of Nook Forest by S. Andrisson. 139pp ISBN 0 9515389 0 X £4.90. Children's fantasy.

UTOPIA OR BUST
Mr Michael Hampton
9 Elham House, Pembury Estate
Pembury Road
LONDON
E5 8LT
Planet X: a poem for tomorrow, 4 pages for 75p.

[V]

VACANT HEARSE PRESS
Mr J M Wood
BM Spellbound
LONDON
WC1N 3XX
A Press deeply dedicated to strange, morbid, anach-ronistic and shamefully concupiscent fictikon and poetry; ideal for isolated garret-bound scribblers, lone wonders of the streets of London and the leafy byeways of old Merrie England. Please write with SAE for details. You will not be allowed to be disappointed.
Netherwood. Limited to 100 signed sigillised copies at £6 inc p & p, payable to J M Wood. A fantastick 97 page wonder through the morbid corridors of the tortur ed mind. Weird fiction and poetry, and occult anachronism. For lovers of decaden t despair. This has become a collector's item but some copies still available.
Sworn. Free 4 page pamphlet - morbid poetry. Forthcoming projects include 'Silverslip and Other Pieces' - on sexual and intellectual vampirism. Also work on Hay-on-Wye, Ignatius and Llanthony.

VAGUE
BCM Box 7207
LONDON
WC1N 3XX

VALIS BOOKS
52A Lascotts Road
Wood Green
London
N22 4JN.
Subjects: Biography.
Books January to June 1991 - 1

THE VAMPYRE SOCIETY
38 Westcroft
CHIPPENHAM
Wiltshire
SN14 0LY
Journal "Blood is the Life".

THE VAMPYRE SOCIETY
Ms Carole Bohanan
9 Station Approach
COULSDON
Surrey
CR5 2NR
Quarterly quality journal. Meetings and film shows.

VARIANT
73 Robertson Street
GLASGOW
Scotland
G2 8QD
A magazine of cultural cross-currrents: moving image culture, public arts, inter -media, technology, oppositional currents.

MICHAEL ARTHUR VARNEY
c/o D.C. Graphics-Printers
46 Turkey Road
Bexhill-on-Sea
TN39 5HE.
Subjects: Local History.
Books July to December 1991 - 1

MR S V VASSELL
24 Newnham Avenue
BEDFORD

VEGAN VIEWS
6 Hayes Avenue
BOURNEMOUTH
BH7

VEGETARIAN SOCIETY
Parkdale, Dunham Road
Altrincham
Cheshire
WA14 4DG

MS JILL VENMORE
5 Briarwood Road
Aigburth
LIVERPOOL
L17 6DD

VENNEL PRESS
Richard Price
9 Pankhurst Court
Caradon Close
London
E11 4TB.
Poetry from Scotland and other countries illus-trated by leading artists. In the Gairfish imprint anthologies of poetry short stories criticism and polemicon such subjects as:
Scotland and the Avant-Garde: Hugh MacDarmid; and Neil M. Gunn - foremost of European novel-ist.1:50 000 by Elizabeth James illustrated by Irene Gunston. 32pp ISBN 0 9516959 2 4 £4.99. Epi-grammatic poems. Anither Music by W.N. Herbert. 32pp ISBN 0 9516959 1 6 £4.99. Poems with a Scottish accent from our most controversial poet. Scotland and the Avant-Garde. 156pp 0 9515419 4 3 3.50. 'Behind the wit entertainment and inscru-table smile there is a transcendent intelligence at work' Poetry London Newsletter.

VENTA BOOKS
14 Keith Grove
London
W12 9EZ

VENTURE PUBLICATIONS
11 Shirley Street
HOVE

East Sussex
BN3 3WJ
Publishes a bi-monthly news magazine plus book-
lets and manuals for freelance writers.
Writers Guide Editor G Carroll. Bi-monthly news
magazine about markets and media including small
press and business journals. Usually 28-32 pages,
A5. £1.50 How to Suceed as a Writer by Avril
Harper. 39 pages, A4, manual in card covers. £6.50
Ditto, edited version of above, 40 pages, A5, in card
covers, Booklet, 3.50 (cheques made out to G
Carroll, please)

VENTUS BOOKS
Tony Breeze
70 Nottingham Road
Burton Joyce
Nottingham
NG14 5AL. Tel 0602 313356
A company formed by Tony Breeze solely for the
publication of his own work (see Playwrights Publications Company for publication of other authors)
Wasps - full length play with eight female characters - the story of a day in the life of a traffic warden.
ISBN 1 872758 06 1 £5.00 Harry's Bird - full length
play - 3F + 1M - a failed writer meets a girl from a
probation hostel in his final days in a hospice -
£5.00. The Battle of Butlers Hill - a children's novel
about the loss of the last good sledging place. ISBN
1 872758 07 X and ISBN 1 872758 08 8 £3.50

VERITY PRESS
73 Almshouse Lane
Newmillerdam
Wakefield
WF2 7ST.
Subjects: Second World War.
Books January to June 1991 - 1.

MS MONIQUE VERNHES
En Marge
94 rue Haxo
F-75020 PARIS
FRANCE

KEN VERNON
12 Court Lane Gardens
Dulwich
London
SE21 7DZ

NICK VERNON
25a Chandos Avenue
S Ealing
LONDON
W5

VER POETS
61 Chiswell Green Lane
St Albans
Herts
AL2 3AL

VERSE
Department of English
The University
St Andrews
KY16 9AL

Publishing poetry from all over the world, with
interviews and major literary criticism. Recent issues on New Formalism, Allen Curnow,
L=A=N=G=U=A=G=E poetry.

VERTICAL IMAGES
c/o Mike Diss
62 Langdon Park Road
London
N6 5QG

MR EUGENE VESEY
20 Gloucester Road
LONDON
E17 6AE

MR J VICKERS
19 Central Parade
HERNE BAY
Kent
CT6 5HX

MR SIMON G VICKERS
14 Richard Place
LONDON
SW3 2LA

VICTORIA HOUSE PUBLISHING
Selectabook
Folly Road
Roundway
Devizes
SN10 2HR.
Subjects: Children's Non-fiction.
Books July to December 1991 - 15

VICTORIA INFIRMARY CENTENARY
COMMITTE
Victoria Infirmary
Glasgow
G42 9TY

VICTORIAN COMMUNITY WRITERS
PO Box403
Carlton South 3053
AUSTRALIA

VIGIL
Suite 5 Somdor House
Station Road
Gillingham
Dorset
SP8 4QA

MR S K VIG
169 Blackstock Road
LONDON
N4 2JS

VILLAGE SQUARE PUBLISHING
County Kingsclere
Newbury
RG15 8PL.
Subjects: Short Stories.
Books July to December 1991 - 1

VILLAGE WRITERS

c/o 34 Church Road
Ballybrack
Dunlaoghaire
County Dublin
Republic o
Subjects: Fiction General.
Books July to December 1991 - 1

VILLA VIC PRESS
11 Newminster Road
Newcastle-on-Tyne
NE4 9LL

VINEYARD PRESS
Barnstaple Bookshop
59 High Street
Barnstaple
EX31 1JB.
Subjects: Local History.
Books July to December 1991 - 1

MR W J VINYARD
80 Dover Road
IPSWICH
IP3 8JQ

VIRTUE
25 Breakfield
Coulsdon
CR3 2UE

VISION SEEKER AND SHARER
Rainbow Publications
PO Box HK9
LEEDS
LS11 8JF
Quarterly defending the rights of native peoples.
Incorporating New Diggers of Albion.

VISITOR PUBLICATIONS
Surrey House
Surrey Street
Croydon
CR0 1SZ

VISUAL ARTS PUBLISHING
82 Sinclair Road
London
W14 0NJ

VISUAL ASSOCIATIONS
PECA
Station Road
Penge
LONDON
SE20 7BE

VITA PRESS
85 Landcroft Road
London
SE22 9JS.
Subjects: Health and Hygiene.
Books January to June 1991 - 1

VOLCANO PRESS
PO Box 139

Leicester
LE2 2YH.
Subjects: Religion.
Books January to June 1991 - 1

VOLTURNA & MARSLAND PRESS
52 Ormonde Road
HYTHE
Kent
CT21 6DW

VOLO EDITION
66A Ferme Park Road
London
N4 4ED

V.V.L.-POCKLINGTON
'Sunny Dene' Stain Lane
Theddlethorpe-St.-Helens
Mablethorpe
Lincolnshire.
Subjects: Poetry.

[W]

MR A L WADE
18 Arley Place
CREWWE
Cheshire
CW2 6QW

MR GRAHAM WADE
34 Holmwood Avenue
Meanwood
LEEDS
LS6 4NJ

MR MALCOLM WADE
150 Legats Way
WATFORD
WB2 2BW

MR SIMON WADE
89 South Terrace
Wales Bar
SHEFFIELD
S31 8QL

MS VICKY WADE
243 Alfreton Road
SUTTON-IN-ASHFIELD
Nottinghamshire
NG17 1JP

H.M. WADKIN
Kynance House
Hidding
Melton Mowbray
LE14 3AQ.
Subjects: Local History.
Books July to December 1991 - 1

WADSWELL PUBLICATIONS
Haythorne Common
Haton
Wimbourne
BH21 7JG.

Subjects: General Fiction.
Books January to June 1991 - 1 Books July to December 1991 - 1

MR MARTIN WAGNER
6 Effra Parade
LONDON
SW2 1PS

WAKEFIELD HISTORICAL PUBLICATIONS
19 Pinder's Grove
WAKEFIELD
West Yorkshire
WF1 4AH
Local history.

WALCOT PRESS
12 St Mary's Gardens
London
SE11 4UD

MR ANDREW WALEY
196 Muswell Hill Road
Muswell Hill
Haringey
LONDON
N10 3NG

CHARLES WALKER
Flat 1
12 Western Place
Worthing
West Sussex
BN11 3LU
Publish booklets mainly dealing with the occult paranormal UFOs and other mysteries; occasional local history and dolls.
'Race with the Devil - An Investigation into Black Magic & Satanism' by Charles Walker 48pp p/b. £2.50. ISBN 1 871362 03 2
'The Devil's Disciples' by Charles Walker. 40pp p/b. £2.50 ISBN 1 871362 05 9
'Dolls - A Guide to Collecting (1940-1980)' by Jean Walker. 24pp p/b 9 illus. £0.99. ISBN 1 871362 06 7

MR B WALKER
3 Warwick Close
Sheriff Hutton
YORK
YO6 1QW 03477 532

MISS BETTY WALKER
82 Hitchin Road
Stotfold
HITCHIN
Hertfordshire
SG5 4HT

MR J M WALKER
18 Aycliffe Road
BOREHAMWOOD
Hertfordshire
WD6 4JW

L.G. WALKER
17 Coronation Road

Burnham-on-Crouch
CM0 8HW.
Subjects: Local History.
Books July to December 1991 - 1

MR NEILL WALKER
Holywell Manor
Manor Road
OXFORD
OX1 7UH

WALKAROUND BOOKS
Gayton, Laneside Road
New Mills
Stockport
SK12 4LU

MR ROY S WALKER
107 Vale Farm Road
WOKING
Surrey
GU21 1DP

W.H. WALKER AND BROTHERS
Willow Tern
Loudwater
Rickmansworth
WD3 4LD.
Subjects: Historical Biography.
Books July to December 1991 - 1.

WALKING ROUTES CLWYD
16 Ash Court
Rhyl
LL18 4NZ.
Subjects: Walks in Wales.
Books July to December 1991 - 2

WALKWAYS
c/o J.S. Roberts
8 Hillside Close
Bartley Green
Birmingham
B32 4LT.
Subjects: Walks Books.
Books January to June 1991 - 1. Books July to December 1991 - 1

WALLACE COMMUNICATIONS
Lower Flat
Granco House Street
Dunning
Perth
PH2 05Q.
Subjects: Local History.
Books July to December 1991 - 1

WILLIAM WALLACE
49 Lamburnum Lea
Hamilton
Ml3 7LY
Scotland

MR JAMES WALLIS
8 College Gardens
LONDON
N18 2XR

STEVEN WALLSGROVE
Leycester Court
Leycester Place
Warwick
CV34 4BY.
Subjects: Local History.
Books July to December 1991 - 1

MR G E WALLWORK
46 Windmill Road
Worsley
MANCHESTER
M28 5RP

WALSALL EQUAL OPPORTUNITIES
Support Unit
Doe Bank Junior Mixed and Infants Sch
Frampton Way
Birmingham
B43 7UJ.
Subjects: Local History. Languages. Education.
Books January to June 1991 - 4. Books July to
December 1991 - 2

MRS JUNE E WALSH
Glas Fryn
Cwm Penmachno
BETWS Y COED
Gwynedd
LL24 0RN

WANDA PUBLICATIONS
43 Avenue Road
Wimborne
BH21 1BA

WANDERING MINSTREL PRODUCTIONS
3 Leah Street
Littleborough
OL15 9BS

WARATAH BLOSSOMS
PO Box 36
340 West Princess Street
GLASGOW
E4 9HF

ALWYN WARD
Flat 27, Birchcroft
17 Nether Edge Road
Sheffield
S7 1RU

WARD ENNIS PUBLISHING COMPANY
3 Earsdon Road
West Monkseaton
Whitley Bay
NE25 9SX

P G WARD
6 Lawson Close
Saltford
BRISTOL
BS18 2LB

MR WILL WARD

Apt 4
30 Ullet Road
LIVERPOOL
L8 3SR

WAREHAM BEAR PUBLICATIONS
18 Church Street
Wareham
BH20 4NT.
Subjects: Children's Fiction.
Books July to December 1991 - 6

MR ANDREW WAREN
196 Muswell Hill Road
Muswell Hill
Haringey
LONDON
N10 3N6

L WARING
7 Belmont Avenue
Ribbleton
PRESTON
PR1 6ZH

E. WARNEFORD
New Inn Farm
West End Lane
Henfield
BN5 9RF.
(See Elizabeth McDougall) Subjects: Warneford
Family History. Books July to December 1991 - 1

BERNARD WARNER
2 Whitemoor Cottages
Loxhore
Barnstaple
EX31 4SR.
Subjects: Travel in Britain.
Books July to December 1991 - 1

WARNES PUBLISHING
7 Noel Rise
BURGESS HILL
West Sussex
RH15 8BW
Titles include: "My Research into the Unknown"
and "Dogs I Have Known and Loved".

WARREN EDITIONS
28 Ifield Road
LONDON
SW10 9AA

GLYN WARREN
27 The Lakes Road
Bewdley
DY12 2QB.
Subjects: Local History.
Books January to June 1991 - 1.

WARSASH NAUTICAL BOOKSHOP
31 Newtown Road
Warsash
Southampton
SO3 6FY

MR F M WARWICK
5 Ash Grove
Cricklewood
LONDON
NW2 5LJ

WASAFIRI
P O Box 195
Canterbury
Kent
CT2 7XB

MR E S WASOSTY
Expat World
PO Box 1341
RAFFLES CITY
SINGAPORE

WATERLINE COMMUNICATIONS
Swanwick Shore Road
Swanwick
Southampton
SO3 7EU

WATERMARK PUBLICATIONS (U.K.)
P.O. Box 18
Chiddingfold
Godalming
GU8 4TP.
Subjects: Architecture.

WATERMILL PRESS: SPA BOOKS
PO Box 47
Stevenage
SG2 8UH

WATER PRESS
68 Dawes Road
London
SW6 7EJ.
Subjects: Photography.
Books January to June 1991 - 2

WATERSHED PUBLICATIONS
Brackley Farmhouse
Gollanfield
Inverness
IV1 2QT.
Subjects: Holistic Health.
Books July to December 1991 - 1

WATERSIDE PRESS
Domum Road
Winchester
SO23 9NN

PAUL WATKINS PUBLISHING
18 Adelaide Street
STAMFORD
Lincolnshire
PE9 2EN

P. WATKINS
18 Adelaide Street
Stamford
PE9 2EN.
Subjects: Regional History. Historical Biography.

Historical Architecture. Local Customs and Folklore. LocalHistory (anywhere). Mediaeval History.

WATNAY PUBLISHING
Peter J. Naylor
Ashbourne Business Centre
Shawcroft Centre Dig Street
Ashbourne Derbyshire
DE6 1GF. Tel 0335 300445.
Publishers of local history especially Derbyshire
including village histories.
Derbyshire Graves by Peter J. Naylor. 64pp 1992
ISBN 1 8724 18 01 5 £2.95.
Chaddesden - A History by H. Fearnehough. 60pp
1992
ISBN 1 8724 18 49 X 2.95.
Spondon - A History by S. Watson. 64pp 1990 ISBN
1 8724 18 00 7 £1.95.

A C WATSON
Flat 12
25 De Vere Gardens
LONDON
S8 5AN

ALICK A WATT & SON
6 Musgrave Gardens
Alton
GU34 2EQ

WAVEGUIDE TRAINING AND PUBLICATIONS
33 Carter Street
Sandown
PO36 8DQ

R WAY, BOOKSELLER
54 Friday Street
Henley-on-Thames
RG9 1AH

WEA
1 Riby Road
Keelby
Grimsby
DN37 8ER.
Subjects: Local History.

WEA: SUFFOLK FEDERATION OF WEA
BRANCH
WEA Felixstowe Branch
c/o T.A. Cox
7 Constable Road
Felixstowe
IP11 7HL.
Subjects: Local History.

WEAVERS PRESS
John T. Wilson
Tregeraint House
Zennor
TR26 3DB. Tel and fax 0736 7970
Magazine/book publisher focussing on career
change writing and business opportunity. Publishes
similar books/manuals and offers book production
service.
Escape: The Career Change Magazine edited by
John T. Wilson. 32pp bi-monthly ISSN 0951-1806.

Subscription £17.50 pa.
Freelance Writing and Photography edited by John T. Wilson. 32pp bi-monthly ISSN 0016-0385. Subscription £16.50 pa.
Great Idea - A Portfolio of Business Ideas and Opportunities edited by John T. Wilson. 24pp bimonthly ISSN 0967-098X. Subscription £75.00 pa.

WEA: WEST LANCASHIRE AND CHESHIRE DISTRICT
7-8 Bluecoat Chambers
School Lane
Liverpool
L1 3BX.
Subjects Education.

S.P. WEBB
2 Alderley Court
Berkhamsted
HP4 3AD.
Subjects: Library Science.
Books January to June 1991 - 1

MR M J WELLER
3 Queen Adelaide Court
Queen Adelaide Road
Penge
LONDON
SE20 7DZ

WELLINGTON REPROGRAPHICS
Unit 4
78-82 Nightingale Grove
LONDON
SE13 6DZ 081 463 0888

WELLSPRING
Springside
Bydown
Swimbridge
EX32 0QB

WELLSPRING PUBLICATIONS
garden Flat
150 Victoria Road
LONDON
SW4 0NW

WELLSWEEP PRESS
John Cayley
8 Duke Street, St James's
London SW1Y 6BN
Tel: (071) 839 6599
Fax: (071) 976 1832
The Wellsweep Press publishes fine, innovative literary translation from Chinese. But that's not all. We are also publishing a martial arts fantasy in three volumes and a book on human rights in China. 'Utterly desirable.' - City Limits.
18 titles in-print or forthcoming by the end of 1992.
Under-sky Underground: Chinese Writing Today, Number 1 edited by Henry Y H Zhao. 256 pp. 20x13cm. Sep. 1992. Paperback: ISBN 0948454164, £7.95.
The Lost Boat: avante-garde fiction from China edited by Henry Y H Zhao. 256 pp. 20x13cm. Aug. 1992. Paperback: ISBN 094845413X, £7.95. Hardback: ISBN 0948454830, £14.95.

After The Event: Human Rights and their Future in China. c. 200 pp. 20x13cm. Oct. 1992. Paperback: ISBN 0948454180, £7.95.
Blades From the Willows: a Chinese novel of fantasy and martial arts adventure by Huanzhulouzhu, translated by Robert Chard. 256 pp. 8 full-colour illlustrations. 20x13cm., 1991. Paperback: ISBN 0948454059, £7.95.

WELLSWEEP (DEVON)
Springside
Bydown
Swimbridge
Barnstaple
EX32 0QB.
Subjects: Children's Fiction.
Books July to December 1991 - 8

WESSEX AQUARIAN
Josephine Sellers
PO Box 1059,
Sturminster Newton,
Dorset DT10 1YA
0258 817219
Spirituality & Philosophy. New Age. Alternative Medcine.
The Return; by Josephine Sellers; 128pp pbk; published Dec 1990; ISBN 0 951696 30 0; £5.95.
Holism, Homoeopathy, Healing & The Hereafter; by Barrie Anson - Publication date Sept. 1992; ISBN 0 951596 31 9 - £7.50.

WESSEX CANCER TRUST
Royal South Hants Hospital
Brinton's Terrace
Southampton
SO2 0AJ

MISS NATHALIE Y WESSON
237 High Kingsdown
Cotham
BRISTOL
BS2 8DG

MR REG WESSON
PO Box 302
WORTHING
West Sussex
BN11 5DW

WEST COL PRODUCTIONS
H Osmaston
Goring
Reading
RG8 9AA.
Subjects: Biography.
Books July to December 1991 - 1

MS S J WESTCOTT
74 Sangley Road
Catford
LONDON
SE6 2JP

WEST DERBY PUBLISHING
279 Eaton Road
Liverpool
L12 2AG

WESTER HAILES OPPERTUNITIES TRUST
Unit 20d
Wester Hailes Shopping Centre
Wester Hailes
EDINBURGH
EH14 2SW 031 442 4252

R WESTLAKE
53 Claremont Malpas
Newport
NP9 6PL

MISS WESTON
237 High Kingsdown
Cotham
BRISTOL
BS2 8DG

(THE) WEST PRESS
48 Ellesmere Road
Benwell
Newcastle-upon-Tyne
NE4 8TS

WEST SUSSEX INSTITUTE OF HIGHER EDU-
CATION
Bishop Otter College
Chichester
PO10 4PE

MR WILLIAM WEST
1 Hawksworth Grove
Kirkstall
LEEDS
LS5 3NB
I publish practical and theoretical writings about
my work as a Reichian therapist and spiritual
healer.

WESTWOOD PRESS PUBLICATIONS
R. Hollins
44 Boldmere Road
Sutton Coldfield
West Midlands
B73 5TD. Tel 021 354 5913
Publishers of a range of local interest books by local
authors covering the Birmingham Sutton Coldfield
and West Midlands area. Also publishers of 'How to
do it' book for printers including the annual Prac-
tical Printers Handbook.
Folklore Superstitions and Legends of Birmingham
and West Midlands by Richard Brown. ISBN 0
948025 12 3 3.50.
The Book of Brum of 'Makya Selfa Tum' by Ray
Tennant. ISBN 0 948025 4 8 £2.50.
A Feast of Memories. Black Country Food and Life
at the Turn of the Century by Marjori Cashmore.
ISBN 0 948025 06 9 £5.50.

WESTWORDS
15 Trelawney Road
Peverell
PLYMOUTH
PL3 4JS

MR W T WEST

Counsel's Chambers
9 Market Street
NEW MOLTON
North Yorkshire
YO17 0LY

WEYFARERS
15 Trelawney Road
Peverell
Plymouth
Devon
PL3 4JS

WHARNCLIFFE PUBLISHING
47 Church Street
Barnsley
S70 2AH

WHARTON PRESS
74 Hilldale Road
Sutton
SM1 2JD

W.D. WHARTON
37 Sheep Street
Wellingborough
NN8 1BX.
Subjects: History of Windmills.
Books July to December 1991 - 1

WHEEL PUBLICATIONS
144 Leeming Lane South
Mansfield
NG19 9BE

A.W WHEELER
6 Church Terrace
Soth Holmwood
Dorking
RH5 4JZ

MRS E WHELAN
Westcliff House
18 Royal Crescent
WHITBY
North Yorkshire
YO21 3EJ

MR DAVID WHELDON
Flat 1
11 Holland Road
HOVE
East Sussex
BN3 1JF

MS EDNA WHELDON
Flat 6, Westcliff House
18 Royal Crescent
WHITBY
North Yorkshire
YO21 3EJ

WHITSLESTOP
Ian Gallacher
Glebelands Churchtowne
Calstock
Cornwall

PL18 9SG Tel 0822 833256
A newly launched venture rooted in the West
Country. Particularly interested in social and military. First book due out in November 1992 A Hard
Living. West Country seafraing folk in late Victorian England. 176pp Nov 1992 ISBN 0 9519778 0
6 £6.99

HENRY VICTOR JOHN WHITBY
28 Sunnydene Gardens
Bridgewater Road
Wembley
HA0 1AT

MR S A WHITBY
2 Salisbury Road
WALLASEY
Merseyside
L45 5DT

TRUSTEES OF THE WHITECHAPEL ART
GALLERY
Whitechapel High Street
London
E1 7QX.
Subjects: Art. Photography.
Books January to June 1991 - 2. Books July to
December 1991 - 1

MR ERIC WHITE
Higher Sherdon
Sandy Way
SOUTH MOLTON
North Devon
EX36 3LU

WHITE EAGLE LODGE
Bettine Pickles
New Lands
Brewells Lane
Liss
GU33 7HY.
Subjects: Biography.
Books January to June 1991 - 1

WHITE HORSE LIBRARY
Unit 3 Strattons Walk
High Street
Melksham
SN12 6LA.
Subjects: Language.
Books July to December 1991 - 1

MRS JANE WHITE
16 Oswald Road
Fetcham
LEATHERHEAD
Surrey
KT22 9TZ 0372 373750

MR J J WHITE
185 Liverpool Road
CROSBY
Merseyside
L23 0QN

P.D.E. WHITE

12 Salters Meadow
Sidmouth
EX10 9BL.
Subjects: Poetry.
Books July to December 1991 - 1

WHITE ROSE
14 Browning Road
Temple Hill
Dartford
Kent
DA1 5ET

WHITE ROW PRESS
Peter Carr
135 Cumberland Road,
Dundonald,
Belfast BT16 OBB
0232 482586
Material of (Northern) Irish interest: History, Local
History, Folklore.
Blackmouth & Dissenter; John M. Barkley; 192pp;
1991; ISBN 1 870132 45 9; £12.95 hbk. Life
(autobiography) of John M. Barkley 'one of the
most influential Irish churchmen of the second half
of the twentieth century'. Illustrated.
The Big Wind: The Extraordinary Story of the 'Big
Wind' of 1839, Ireland's Greatest Natural Disaster;
P.A. Carr; 144pp; ISBN 1 870132 50 5; £4.95 pbk.
Illustrated.
Yes Matron; a history of nurses and nursing in the
Royal Victoria Hospital, Belfast. 'An attempt to
write the nurse back into history'. 192pp; 1989;
ISBN 1 870132 20 3; £12.95 hbk. Illustrated.

MS SHEILA A WHITESIDE
76 Ash Court
RHYL
Clwyd
LL18 4NZ

WHITE TREE BOOKS
49 Park Street
Bristol
BS1 5NT

MRS V J WHITE
6 Oaklands
Guilden Sutton
CHESTER
CH3 7HE

WHITGIFT SCHOOL ARCHIVE DEPARTMENT
Haling Park
South Croydon
CR2 6YT.
Subjects: History of Whitgift School.

WHITING AND BIRCH
P.O. Box 872
90 Dartmouth Road
London
SE23 3HL.
Subjects: Social Welfare.
Books July to December 1991 - 4

MR DANIEL WHITMORE
9 Pedder Street

268

PRESTON
PR2 2QH

WHITTINGTON PRESS
Lower Marston Farm,
Risbury
Leominster
Herefordshire
HR6 0NJ
Fine Printer

WHITTINGTON PRESS
Manor Farm
Andoversford
GL54 4HP
Subjects: Ceramic Art.

WHITTLES PUBLISHING
Roseleigh House
Latheronwheel
Latheron
KW5 6DW

MR STEPHEN WHITTLE
185 Garstang Road
Fulwood
PRESTON
PR2 4JQ

ARTHUR WHITTLETON
19 Forest Way
Humberston
Grimsby
DN36 4HQ

NANCY WHYBROW
14 Browning Road
Temple Hill
DARTFORD
Kent
DA1 5ET

WHYLD PUBLISHING CO-OP
Moorland House
Kelsey Road
Caistor
Lincolnshire
LN7 6SK 0472 851374
Specialists in anti-sexist work with boys. Also producing materials on counselling-based approaches
in education and dealing with disruption violence
and aggression.
Update on anti-sexist work with boys and young
men. Ed Janie Whyld Dave Pickerill and David
Jackson. 120pp. ISBN 1 871911 04 4. 5.00 Anti-
sexist materials for boys. Sue Askew & Carol Ross.
4 packs of mater ials for use with boys. ISBN 1
871911 10 9. 5.00
Equal Opportunities - What's in it for Boys. Pack of
material for use with teachers and pupils. ISBN 1
871911 03 6. £2.50

(THE) WICCAN
PO Box BM 7097
London
WC1N 3XX

WICKED PUBLICATIONS

222 Highbury Road
Bulwell
Nottingham
NG6 9FE.
Subjects: London History.
Books January to June 1991 - 1.

C.R WICKINS
Cachette Du Valle
Ville Baudu, Yale
Guernsey
Channel Islands

MICHAEL J.L WICKES
30 One End Street
Appledore
Bideford
EX39 1PN

A.P.E. WICKHAM
Faith Farm House
Frith Lane
Wickham
Fareham
PO17 5AW.
Subjects: Arts (Ceramics)

MR C R WICKINS
Cachette du Valle
Vale
GUERNSEY
CHANNEL ISLANDS

Wide Blue Yonder
107 North Hill
Plymouth
Pl4 8JX

WIDE SKIRT PRESS
93 Blackhouse Road
Fartown
HUDDERSFIELD
West Yorkshire
HD2 1AP
Aim to publish some good work.

MR PAUL WILCOX
74 Bury Street
Mossley
ASHTON-UNDER-LYNE
Lancashire
OL5 9HN

WILD CARET PRESS
Hugh Scott
PO Box 112
Hereford
HR1 4YB 0432 840466
Wild Caret Press is the small press arm of an
independent production company active in exhibitions video tape/slide readings performances. Birth
of the Age of Woman. Paintings with poems by
seven women poetry. Susan Morland. 68 pages;
19colour plates. 1991. 0 9515048 19. £8.95.

WILDCAT CARDS

P O Box 410
Sheffield
S8 9GF

WILDLIFE PUBLISHING
Clive Herbert
67a Ridgeway Avenue
East Barnet
Hertfordshire
EN4 8TL
Tel: 081 440 6314
Publishes local titles on wildlife and the environment in and around Lond on. A new imprint launched in 1989.
'The Mammals of Barnet - a summary of the occurrence and distrbution of mammals in the London Borough of Barnet' by Clive Herbert. 1990. 44pp. £2.95. ISBN 0 95 15608 0 8.
'The Naturalist in Barnet - a focus on Barnets Wildlife' edited by Margar et Melling. 1990. 66pp. £1.95. ISBN 0 9515608 1 6. 12 feature articles by 8 authors and reviews of local literature.
'A Checklist of the birds of Barnet' by J. Colmans and Clive Herbert. 1989 . £0.50. Lists of bird species together with notes on local habitants and unusual records.

WILDLIFE GARDENING MONTHLY
55 Wyndham Road
LONDON
W13 9TE
Magazine

WILFION BOOKS
4 Townhead Terrace
Paisley
PA1 2AX.
Subjects: Poetry.
Books July to December 1991 - 1

A.M WILKINSON
26 Monckton Road
Stokes Bay
Gosport
PO12 2BQ

MR KENNETH R WILKINSON
2 Curborough Road
LITCHFIELD
Staffordshire
WS13 7NG

MR T W WILKIN
2 Romilly Street
SOUTH SHIELDS
Tyne & Wear
NE33 2SP

MRS A WILLANS
120 Reading Road
HENLEY-ON-THAMES
Oxfordshire
RG9 1DN

DR WILLIAMS' TRUST
14 Gordon Square
London
WC1H 0AG

MS ELIZABETH WILLIAMS
59 Sunningwell Road
OXFORD
OX1 4SZ

MR MIKE WILLIAMS
36 Laithwaite Close
LEICESTER
LE4 1BX

MR BRIAN WILLIAMSON
46 Wellington Road
New Brighton
Merseyside
L45 2NG
Freelance mathematician and poet from Merseyside

HENRY WILLIAMSON SOCIETY
14 Nether Grove
Longstanton
Cambridge
CB4 5EL.
Subjects: Literature.
Books January to June 1991 - 2.

MR R WILLIAMSON
13 Oakleigh Road
STRATFORD ON AVON
Warwickshire
CV37 0DW

ROY WILLIAMSON
4 Cleevemont
Evesham Road
Cheltenham
GL52 3JT.
Subjects: Music.
Books July to December 1991 - 1

MR PAUL WILLIAMS
Masion Palisses
64260 Rebenacq
France

RUNKEL-HUE-WILLIAMS
6-8 Old Bond Street
London
W1X 3TA

MR T A WILLIAMS
33 Mutley Road
Mannamead
PLYMOUTH
PL3 4SB

THOMAS TUDOR WILLIAMS
126 Haven Road
Haverfordwest
SA61 1DP

MR ALISDAIR WILLIS
39 Vere Road
BRIGHTON
BN1 4NQ

MR KEN WILLMOT
108 Bredinghurst
Orehill Road
LONDON
SE22 0PL

WILLOW PUBLISHING MAGOR
Barecroft Common
Magor Newport
NP6 3EB.
Subjects: Sport.
Books July to December 1991 - 1

EDWARD WILMOT
32 Castle Row
Canterbury
CT1 2QY.
Subjects: Historical Biography.
Books July to December 1991 - 1

PATRICE M. WILNECKER
73 Gwynne Road
Parkstone
Poole
BH12 2AR.
Subjects: Historical Fiction.
Books January to June 1991 - 1

MS C R G WILSON
35 Dale Road
Welton
BROUGH
North Humberside
HU15 1PE

DAVID A. WILSON
16 Cragside
Sedgefield
Stockton-on-Tees
TS21 2DQ.
Subjects: Horology.
Books July to December 1991 - 1

MS FRANCES WILSON
Bruiach House
Kiltarlity
BEAULY
Inverness-shire
IV4 7HG

MR RON WILSON
Karinya
12 Trinity Close
DAVENTRY
Northamptonshire
NN11 4RN

MR TOM WILSON
162 Canterbury Road
Kennington
ASHFORD
Kent
TN24 9QD

WILTON 65 PUBLISHING
Flat Top House
Bishop Wilton

York
YO4 1RY

MS ELAINE I WILTSHIRE
26 Simmil Road
Claygate
ESHER
Surrey
KT10 0RJ

WIMBLEDON BRIDGE ENTERPRISES
6 Walnut Tree Cottages
Church Road
London
SW19 5DN

WIMPOLE BOOKS
Pip's Peace
Kenton
Stowmarket
IP14 6JS

WINCHESTER GALLERY
Park Avenue
Winchester
SO23 8DL.
Subjects: Art.
Books January to June 1991 - 1.

WINDOWS PROJECT
22 Roseheath Drive
Halewood
Liverpool
L26 9UH

DR C WINDRIDGE
Four Seasons Chinese Restraunt
86a Owen Street
TIPTON
West Midlands
DY4 8EX 021 557 1592

THE WINDRUSH PRESS LTD
Windrush House
Main Street, Adlestrop
MORETON-IN-MARSH
Gloucestershire
GL56 0YN
Green fiction for children - ages 9 and up. - Used widely in schools as class readers and ideal for libraries. Distributed also through the Quill Hedgehog Club, which has sprung up and produces a quarterly newsletter for members on environmental matters.
'Quills Adventures in the Great Beyond' by John Waddington-Feather. 96 pages, 5.5 x 8.5 inches, illustrations, paperback ISBN 1 56261 015 5, published (3rd edition) 1992. £4.99
'Quills Adventures in Wasteland' by John Waddington-Feather. 132 pages, 5.5 x 8.5 inches, illustrated, paperback. ISBN 1 56261 016 3, published (2nd edition) 1991. £4.99
'Quills Adventures in Grozzieland' by John Waddington-Feather. 132 pages, 5.5 x 8.5 inches, illustrations, paperback. ISBN1 56261 017 1. Published (2nd edition) 1991. £4.99

WINDSOR PUBLICATIONS

329 St Leonards Road
Windsor
SL4 3DS

WINE SOURCE
393 Ham Green
Holt
Trowbridge
BA14 6PX.
Subjects: Wine.
Books July to December 1991 - 1

MR JOHN WINFIELD
Rm CO36 Ancaster Hall
Nottingham University
University Park
NOTTINGHAM
NG7 2RE

PETER WINGENT
10 The Dean
Alresford
SO24 9AX.
Subjects: History of Air Transport.
Books July to December 1991 - 1.

WINGHAM PRESS
Seymour Place
High Street
Wingham
CT3 1AB

WINTER PRESS
Simon Curtis
50 Rockbourne Road
Forest Hill
LONDON
SE22 2DD

H E WINTER PUBLISHING
Thorneycroft
Blindcrake
COCKERMOUTH
Cumbria
CA13 0QP
Publisher of Cumbrian and Lakeland History Booklets.
GREAT CUMBRIANS. By H E Winter. 43 pages, 1988. £2.25
A HISTORIC GUIDE TO THE LAKES. By H E Winter. 22 pages, 2 maps. 1990. £1.25 A GUIDE TO THE LAKELAND TARNS. By H E Winter. 15 pages. 1991. £1.25

WINTER PRODUCTIONS
Oak Walk
Saint Peter
Jersey.
Subjects: General Fiction.
Books July to December 1991 - 1

M.J. WINTON
5 Lynn Road
Castle Rising
King's Lynn
PE31 6AB.
Subjects: Reprints of Norfolk Directories.

Books July to December 1991 - 1

WIRE
(Poetry Society & Magazine)
21 Lidstone Close
Goldsworth Park
Woking Surrey
GU21 3BG

WISEFILE
21 Cromford Way
New Malden
KT3 3BB

WISHING WELL PUBLISHING
PO Box 176
Hull
HU9 2PQ
Witan Books
65 Audley Road
Alsager
STOKE ON TRENT
ST7 2QW
Witan Books is a vehicle for the promotion of the works of Jeff Kent, uncensored stories by real authors and anarchy, ecology and co-operation, leading towards the creation of a new society inspired by the model of Anglo-Saxon England. THE RISE AND FALL OF ROCK by Jeff Kent; 484 pages; 56 photographs; published 1983; ISBN 0 9508981 0 4; 5.75; critcal rock music history. THE LAST POET: THE STORY OF ERIC BURDON by Jeff Kent; 368 pages; 30 photographs; published 1989; ISBIN 0 9508981 2 0; 9.75; Biography of a great artist and radical thinker.
THE WARS OF THE ROACHES - King Doug, Lord of the roaches; 167 pages; 67 photographs; published 1991; ISBN 0 9508981 5 5; 9.75; Remarkable autobiography by Britain's last cave dweller.

WITMEHA PRESS
The Orchard
Wymondham
MELTON MOWBRAY
Leicestershire
LE14 2AZ

WITNEY ANTIQUES
96-100 Corn Street
Witney
OX8 7BU.
Subjects: Art.
Books July to December 1991 - 1

WITS END
27 Pheasant Close
Winnersh
Wokingham
Berks RG

WOAD PRESS WOAD
Blue Gate
Burysbank Road
Newbury
Berks.
Subjects: Social Sciences.
Books January to June 1991 - 1.

272

WOLFHOUND PRESS
S Cashman
68 Mountjoy Square
DUBLIN 1
IRISH REPUBLIC

WOLFS HEAD PRESS
PO Box 77
Sunderland
SR1 1EB
Firmly at the DIY xerox end of the scale the Wolf's Head Press corporate motto is Not only is the universe stranger than we imagine it's probabl y stranger than we can imagine. SO sit back and enjoy the ride! Wearwolf magazine (various); sporadical of diverse eclectic content. 50p+ stamp (US$3) for sample issue.
Disciples of Satan. Anon. Conclusive evidence of the satanic threat in Britain today. Not what it seems. 2 x second class stamps (US$1) Wolfs Head Press Catalogue. Everything we've got is yours for a price. One 2nd class stamp for a copy.

WOMEN AGAINST FUNDAMENTALISM
BM Box 2706
London
WC1N 3XX

WOMEN GOING PLACES
The Business Factory
15 Norfolk Place
London
W2 1QJ

WOMEN IN PUBLISHING
49 Petersham Road
RICHMOND
Surrey
TW10 6UH

WOMEN PRINT
Unit 25 Devonshire House
High Street
Digbeth
Birmingham
B12 0LP

WOMEN'S ART
Women Artists Slide Library
Fulham Palace
Bishop's Avenue
London
SW6 6EA

WOMEN'S DESIGN SERVICE
18 Ashwin Street
London
E8 3DL

WOMEN'S ENVIRONMENTAL NETWORK
Aberdeen Studios
22 Highbury Grove
London
N5 2EA

WOMEN'S NEWS
185 Donegall Street

Belfast
N Ireland
BT1 2FJ

WOMEN'S REVOLUTIONS PER MINUTE (WRPM)
62 Woodstock Road
Birmingham
B13 9BN

WOMEN'S THEATRE WORKSHOP
Interchange Studios
15 Dalby Street
London
NW5 3NQ

SOCIETY OF WOMEN WRITERS AND JOUR-NALISTS
110 Whitehall Road
Chingford
London
E4 6DW

WOMEN WRITERS NETWORK
c/o 23 Prospect Road
London
NW2 2JU

LINDA WONG
1 Purcell Avenue
Tonbridge
TN10 4DP.
Subjects: Food Decoration.
Books January to June 1991 - 1. Books July to December 1991 - 1

WOOD AND WATER
4 High Tor Close
Babbacombe Road
BROMLEY
Kent
BR1 3LQ
One of the oldest established pagan magazines. Goddess-centred.

MR R E WOODBURN
63 Highbury New Park
Highbury
LONDON
W5

WOODCRAFT PRESS
152 Hadlow Road
TONBRIGDE
TN9 1PB

WOODFIELD PUBLISHING
Woodfield House
Arundel Road
Fontwell
Arundell
BN18 0SD.
Subjects: Biography. Historical Biography. Children's Fiction. Local History(from the rest of Britain). Humour.

MR GRAHAM WOODS

273

6 Fenton Road
REDHILL
Surrey
RH1 4BN

WOOD GARTH PRESS
15 First Avenue
Bardsey
Leeds
LS17 9BE

MR THOMAS WOODHATCH
Rowlands Farm House
Newchapel Road
LINGFIELD
Surrey
RH7 6BJ

JEAN WOOD
40 Bridge Street
Poleworth
Tamworth
B78 1DT

J.E WOOD
7 Pennant Hills
Havant
PO9 3J2

WOOD LEA PRESS
Grassendale Lane
LIVERPOOL
L19 0NH

WOODMANS PRESS
(see And What of Tomorrow ?)

MS MARIA J WOOD
Flat 7, 27 Carmoor Road
Victoria Park
MANCHESTER
M13 0EA

R & J L WOOD
24 Madeleine Road
Petersfield
GU31 4AL

WOODFIELD PUB SERVICES
Ms Linda T Shepperd
Woodfield House, Arundel Road
Fontwell
West Sussex
BN18 0SD

PROFESSOR A W WOODRUFF
122 Ferndene Road
LONDON
SE24 0BA

MS SONYA WOODSEND
Tumbleweed Cottage
London Road
TETBURY
Gloucestershire
GL8 8HW

WOODSTOCK PUBLICATIONS
Spelsbury House
Spelsbury
Oxford
OX7 3JR

MS UNA WOODS
7 Balmoral Gardens
BELFAST
BT9 6PB

F W WOODWARD
South Torr
Cornwood
Ivybridge
PL21 9RB

TIM WOODWARD PUBLISHING
23 Grand Union Centre
Kensal Road
London
W10 5AX.
Subjects: Literature.
Books July to December 1991 - 1

WOOD WIND PUBLICATIONS
David Hart
42 All Saints Road
Kings Heath
Birmingham
B14 7LL Tel: 021 443 2495
Poetry-related publications, not normally publish-
ing actual poetry. Poetry listing 1-3 available at
reduced price of £1.00 + P&P
'Poetry Listing 4' compiled by David Hart. Annual
review listing of new poetry, British and other. Used
in stock-buying by public libraries etc. Review
copies of books and magazines welcome. 50 pages
ISBN 0955 9914 £3.00 'Border Country' edited by
David Hart. Documentary process book, with new
poems by national and intrnational poets, of the first
West Midlands Arts Poetry Squantum at the Hay on
Wye Festival 102 pages. ISBN 1 871320 011, £5.95
'Poetry Listing 5' due late Autumn 1992. ISBN
0955 9914 £3.00

P. WOOLLER
Walford Lodge
Walford
Craven Arms
SY7 0JT.
Subjects: Railways.
Books July to December 1991 - 1

WORD & ACTION (DORSET)
43 Avenue Road
Wimbourne
BH21 1BS

THE WORD FACTORY
17 Wathen Road
LEAMINGTON SPA
Warwickshire
CV32 5UX
Publishers poetry in booklets and on t-shirts

WORDMAKER BOOKS
Clatleigh House

Little Hyden Lane
Clanfield
Waterlooville
PO8 0RU.
Subjects: Children's Fiction.
Books July to December 1991 - 1

WORDPLAY PUBLISHING
Tony Bowerman
70 Garden Lane
Chester
CH1 4EY. Tel 0244 378927
Specialists in local guides and interpretative litera-
ture for the tourism and leisure markets
Chester Tourcards - 8 two-colour cards in a
waterproo pack. 1991 1.95. Themed walks around
Chester.
The All-In-One-Guide to Chester. A3 2 colour map
and integrated information for tourists ISBN 0
9519636 0 0 0.95.

WORDS & IMAGES
2 Charlton Cottages
Barden Road, Speldhurst
TUNBRIDGE WELLS
Kent
TN3 0LH 0892 86 2395
We provide publishing services to both professional
publishers and to those indi viduals and organisations who wish to self-publish. We offer book
design, typese tting and printing; illustration; editing and manuscript reading; commissioned w riting;
ghost writing; video scripts; computer tuition. Now
in our sixth success ful year, we offer quality work,
friendly service and reasonable cost. See Dragonfly
Press and Fern Press.

WORDS AND THE STONES
1st Floor
Scottish Life House
Glasgow
G2 5TS

WORDSHARE
Keith Ashton
3 Grainsby Close
Lincoln
LN6 7QF

WORDS MAGAZINE
23 James Collins Close
LONDON
W9 3PU
Quarterly Short Story Magazine published as
fundraising effort on behalf of the Childrens Hos-
pice Appeal (reg charity 800485) Sample Copy
Free.

WORDS PRESS
Hod House
Child Okeford
BLANDFORD FORUM
Dorset
DT11 8EH

WORDS WALKING
635 Big Ugly Creek Road
Leet

West Virginia 25536
UNITED STATES OF AMERICA

WORD TEAM
54 Borough High Street
London
SE10 1XL.
Subjects: Local History.
Books January to June 1991 - 1.

WORDWELL
P.O. Box 69
Bray
County Wicklow
Republic of Ireland.
Subjects: Irish Archaeology. Irish Prehistory.
Books July to December 1991 - 2

(THE) WORKER ESPERANTIST (SATEB)
29 Farrance Road
Romford
Essex
RM6 6EB

FEDERATION OF WORKER WRITERS
and Community Publishers
c/o 68 Grand Parade
BRIGHTON
BN2 2JY

WORKING PRESS
Stefan Szczelkun
85 St Agnes Place
Kennington Common
London
SE11 4BB. Tel 071 735 6221
An inclusive agency/imprint which promotes self-
publications on art and culture by working class
people. Sae for list for 12 plus titles. Flyposter
Frenzy edited by Mathew Fuller. 100 A4 paperback
100pp anti-copyright posters 1992 £4.95.
On Common Ground by Frank Reed. A5 paperback 96pp 2 colour cover laminated 5.80. ISBN 1
870736 27 3.
Postcards from Poland and other correspondences
by Maria Jastrzebska and Jola Scicinska. A5 landscape 160pp paperback laminated 6.95. ISBN 1
870736060.

WORKING FOR CHILDCARE
77 Hollway Road
London
N7 8JZ.
Subjects: Social Welfare.
Books January to June 1991 - 2.

WORKING KNOWLEDGE TRANSFER
Brunel Science Centre
Coopers Hill Lane
Egham
TW20 0JZ.
Subjects: School Textbooks.
Books July to December 1991 - 1

WORKING MOTHERS ASSOCIATION
77 Holloway Road
LONDON
N7 8JZ

WORKING TITLES
Garden Flat
9 Victoria Walk, Cotham
Bristol
BS6 5SR.

WORKS PUBLISHING
12 Blakestones Road
Slaithwaite
HUDDERSFIELD
West Yorkshire
HD7 5UG
Magazine for SF, imaginative fiction, graphics.

(THE) WORKS
122 Clive Street
Grangetown
Cardiff
Wales
CF1 7J

WORKSHOP & ARTISTS STUDIOS PROVISION
26 King Street
GLASGOW
G1 5QP

THE WORKSHOP PRESS
Hanna's
Bolford Street
Thaxted
Essex
CM6 2PY 0371 830366
Books on typography type design and decoration in limited editions of about 170 copies printed and bound at the press. Eight books since 1981. (all these now out of print:)
'Pages of Type' by Mark Arman 1990 pp(viii)48 ISBN 0 9509292 5 5 'Fleurons; Their Place in History & in Print' by Mark Arman 1988 pp (xii) 52 ISBN 0 9509292 4 7 'A Legacy of Metal Types' by Mark Arman 1987 pp (xii) 48 ISBN 0 9509292 3 9

WORLD PUBLISHING
Richard House
30-32 Mortimer Street
London
W1N 7RA

WORLD MUSICALS
28 Wilsford Green
Egbaston
Birmingham
B15 3UG.
Subjects: Walks Books for the whole of Britain. Books January to June 1991 - 1.

WORLDS END PRESS
Star and Garter Lane
Egerton
ASHFORD
Kent
TN27 9BE

WORLD TREE PRODUCTIONS
Umiak Mahoupe
49 Calthorpe Street,

London WC1X OHH
071 833 4463
World Tree Productions is a branch of World Tree Arts Trust which also produces theatre and art exhibitions. We publish two cassettes of Edward Lear nonsense poems set to music. Coming soon 'After-Image' by Agoshaman - a collection of short stories.
Edward Lear's Festival of Nonsense Part I; Words by Edward Lear; Music by Agoshaman; cassette published 1987; price £3.00.
Edward Lear's Festival of Nonsense Part II; by Edward Lear; music by Agoshaman; cassette published 1987; price £3.00.

WORLEY PUBLICATIONS
10 Rectory Road East
Felling
Gateshead
NE10

DR R L WORRALL
31 Braeside Avenue
SEVENOAKS
Kent
TN13 2JJ

WORTHING REFERENCE LIBRARY
Miss E Evans
Richmond Road
WORTHING
West Sussex
BN11 1HD

MR M J WORTHINGTON
Chadbury House
24 Old Worcester Road
Chadbury, EVESHAM
Worcestershire
WR11 4TD

Mr Malcolm Povey
124 Carbery Avenue
Southbourne
BOURNEMOUTH
BH6 3LH

WREKIN TRUST
Runnings Park
Croft Bank
WEST MALVERN
Worcestershire
WR14 4BP

WREN PRESS
22 St Mary's Drive
Pound Hill
Crawley
RH10 3BD

DAVID WRIGHT
71 Island Wall
Whitstable
CT5 1EL.
Subjects: 'East Kent Parishes: A Guide for Genealogists
Local Historians and Other Researchers. Books July to December 1991 - 1

276

D.C.K WRIGHT
8D West Street
Blandford Forum
DT11 7AJ

MR PAUL WRIGHT
930783
Box 5000 HC63
Clallam Bay
WA 98326
United States of America

MR W E WRIGHT
8 Princes Close
SOUTH CROYDON
Surrey
CR2 9BP

WRITEAWAY
(same address as Windows Projects)

WRITERS FORUM
89a Petherton Road
London
N5 2QT 017 226 2657
Experimental poetry and related arts - concrete
visual, performance, sound, computer, music, dance,
photography, etc. 500th publication in preparation;
£4.99 now available - send for lists.
Soleil + Chair ed. Harry Gilonis. Anthology com-
memorating the centary of Arthur Rimbaud. 42pp
1991 £3.00 ISBN 0 86162 496 3
'Cage on Cage' by John Cage. Musical visual score.
Six A4 sheets in folder third edition 1992 £1.00
ISBN 0 86162 350 9
Anthology compiled by Peggy Lefler. International
concrete and visual poetry. 3rd edition 1992 44pp
£1.00 ISBN 0 86162 436 X

WRITERS GUIDE
(G Carroll)
11 Shirley Street
Hove
E Sussex
BN3 3WJ

WRITERS NEWS LTD
P O Box 4
Nairn
IV12 4HU

WRITERS OWN MAGAZINE
121 Highbury Grove
Clapham
Bedford
MK41 6DU

WRITERS ROSTRUM
14 Ardbeg Road
Rothesay
Bute
PA20 0NJ

WRITING MAGAZINE
P O Box 4
Nairn
IV12 4HU

WRITING ULSTER
Dept of Engl Media & Theatre Stud
Univ of Ulster
Coleraine
Co Londonderry
BT52 1SA

WRITING WOMEN
7 Cavendish Place
Newcastle-upon-Tyne
NE2 2NE

MR JOSEE WUYTS
Postbus 244
6500 A E Njinegen
The Netherlands

WYRD
187 Wellington Road
Handsworth
BIRMINGHAM
B20 2ES

WYVERN
5 Polly Brooks Yard
Pedmore Road, Lye
Stourbridge
DY9 8DG

XANADU PUBLICATIONS LIMITED
19 Cornwall Road
Stroud Green
LONDON
N4 4PH

X-CALIBRE
Nemeton Publishing
P O Box 780
Bristol
BS99 5BB

XENOS
65 Abbott Crescent
Kempston
BEDFORD
MK42 7QJ
New magazine for SF, fantasy, radical departure
from the norm.

X-PRESS
Jane Colling
24 Banyard Road
LONDON
SE16 2YA 071 231 1106
Prints and Postcards
Spot the Dog , Malcom Green
Alphabet Series, Jane Colling
Print Project, Bermondsey Artists Group

MR VINCE YALLOP
59 South Park Avenue
NORWICH
Norfolk
NR4 7AY

MR GRAHAM YATES

NRAL
Jodrell Bank
MACCLESFIELD
Cheshire
SK11 9DL

INGHAM YATES
40 Woodfield Road
Rudgwick
Horsham
RH12 3EP

MR J YATES
7 Rigault Road
LONDON
SW6 4JJ

YEAR MINUS ZERO PRESS
PO Box 71
HASTINGS
East Sussex

YEOMAN PUBLISHING
32 Kingsley Road
Kingswinford
DY6 9RX

MR D S YEOMANS
Unit 12
Quay Lane
GOSPORT
Hampshire
PO12 4LJ

YES PUBLICATIONS
Holywell House
32 Shipquay Street
Londonderry
BT48 6DW.
Subjects: Military History.
Books July to December 1991 - 1

YESTERYEAR BOOKS
Daniel Young
60 Woodville lRoade
LONDON
NW11 9TN 081 455 6992
We publish/reprint period material on British classic cars. 1. Road Test Collect ions. 2. Magazine Advert Collections. 3. Owners/Buyers Guides. A4 size, perfe ct bound. Black and white illustrations. Glossy card cover. Art paper. POST-WAR ROVER by James Taylor. 168 pages. October 1990. ISBN 1 873078 01 3. £11.95. Approximately 200 pictures. MINI ANTHOLOGY: THE LAUNCH OF A LEGEND. By Daniel Young. 96 pages. January 19 90. ISBN 1 873078 00 5. £9.95.
ADVERTISING MG. By Daniel Young. 96 pages. October 1989. 0 9511760 6 4. £9.95. Approximately 130 pictures.

Y FFYNNON
c/o The Flat
Plas Llidiardau
Llanilar
DYFED
SY23 5PF

Y.I PUBLISHING
120 West Street
Bridgwater
TA6 7EU

YOFFOY PUBLICATIONS
F. Foy
7 Upper Dumpton Park Road
Ramsgate
Kent
CT11 7PE.
The publication of specialist information booklet and other in the fields of employment and curriculum vitae services music business innovations inventions specialist writing and all document preparation services available in above fields.
Releasing Your Own Records and Songwriting - Officially by Frank Foy. Paperback 1989 £2.50.
Play It Now! Paperback 1989 £8.00. Electric guitar manual by Frank Foy.
Minding the Chanses poetry anthology by Frank Foy. Paperback 1989 £9.00.

YOFFROY PUBLICATIONS
Frank Foy
7 Upper Dumpton Park Road
Ramsgate
Kent
CT11 7PE
The publication of specialist information booklets and other in the fields of employment and curriculum vitae services music business innovations inventions spcialist writing and all document preparation services available in above fields.
'Releasing Your Own Records and Songwriting - Officially' by Frank Foy 1989. £2.50 each booklet.
'Play it Now!' Electric guitar manual by Frank Foy 1989. 8.00 each paper back.
'Minding the Chanses' poetry anthology by Frank Foy 1989. 9.00 each paperback.

YORE PUBLICATIONS
Dave Twydell
12 The Furrows
Harefield
Middx
UB9 5AT Tel 0895 823404
Specialists in football books normally with an historic theme - football clubs' histories (current and defunct) reprints of pre-war football books etc. Also home video on the same subjects. Newsletters issued three times a year.
Cardiff City Official History by John Crooks. Large format cased 320pp Feb 1992 ISBN 0 9513321 8 X 16.95.
Rejected F.C. by Dave Twydell. 289pp reprint May 1992
ISBN 1 874427 00 3 12.95. Detailed histories of former league clubs. Through the Turnstile by Brian Tabner. 208pp Aug 1992
ISBN 1 874427 05 4 £13.95. History of football related to crowd figures.

YORICK BOOKS
27 Manwood Avenue
Canterbury
CT2 7AH

NORTH YORKSHIRE COUNTY LIBRARY
21 Grammer School lane
NORTHALLERTON
North Yorkshire
DL6 1DF 0609 776271

YORKSHIRE ART CIRCUS
Old School, School Lane
Glasshoughton
CASTLEFORD
West Yorkshire
WF10
Community publishers of a wide-range of titles.
Roadshow available.

YORKSHIRE DIALECT SOCIETY
Farfields
Weeton Lane
Weeton
LEEDS
LS17 0AN

YOUNG LIBRARY
Brunel House
Forde Road
Newton Abbot
TA12 4PU

R A J YOUNGSON
35 Queens Road
St George
BRISTOL
BS5 8HT

MR W J YOXALL
49 Sylvan Road
Upper Norwood
LONDON
SE19 2RU

YUDANSHA PRESS
7 Crossfields Avenue
Culcheth
WA3 5RS.
Subjects: Sport.
Books July to December 1991 - 1

[Z]

ZAMANA GALLERY
1/7 Cromwell Gardens
London
SW7 2SL

ZANZIBAR PRODUCTIONS
3 Ashfield Close
Bishops Cleve
CHELTENHAM
Gloucestershire
GL52 4LG
Offbeat surreal poetry and any oddities I find inter-
esting, also SF magazine.

ZARDOZ/ZEON BOOKS
Maurice Flanagan
20 Whitecroft Dilton Marsh
Westbury

Wilts
BA13 4DJ. Tel 0373 865371
Publishers and mail order sales of magazines and
books relating to genres of paperbacks pulps and
comics tv and film spin offs and collectables. Also
sales of vintage and collectable paperbacks and
pulps. Large sae for catalogues (34p stamp)
Paperback Pulp and Comic Collector Magazine.
100pp quarterly ISSN 0962-1520 £2.95 (plus 50p
p&p)
Lord of Atlantis by John Russell Fearn. 68pp July
1991 £4.95. Science Fantasy - Golden Amazon
adventure.
Price Guide to British Paperback Books by
Flanagan/Holland/Chibnall. 400pp Sept 1993
£12.00

ZED BOOKS LTD
57 Caledonian Road
London
N1 9BU

ZEITGENOESSISCHE
HANDPRESSENDRUCKE
H S Bartkowiak
Koernerstrasse 24
D-2000 HAMBURG 60
GERMANY
Hand Press.

ZEN ART PUBLICATIONS
Bowmore Gallery
8 Halkin Arcade
Motcombe Street
London
W1P 5DJ.
Subjects: Art.
Books January to June 1991 - 2

ZEON PUBLICATIONS
20 Whitecroft
Dilton Marsh
WESTBURY
Wiltshire
BA13 4DJ
Publishers of paperback, pulp and comic collector
magazines. Publishers and dis-tributors of paper-
back related materials, vintage cover art postcards.
Lord of Atlantis. By John Russell Fearn. £4.95
The Living World. By E C Tubb. £4.95
Fantasy Booklet - £3.00.

NEAL ZETTER
12 Kimberley Way
LONDON
E4 6DE
Books of easy-to-read poems, cynicism, humour,
satire - kids love 'em.

ZODIAC HOUSE PUBLICATIONS
Jan Roberts
7 Wells Road
Glastonbury
Somerset
BA6 9DN.
Tel 0458 835450
Our Motto: Apocalypse Now! A giant among small
presses. The flame still blazes and singes! Get our

free catalogue/magazine which not only lists our titles but tell you wny the press exists.

ZYTGLOGGE VERLAG
Eigerweg 16
CH-3073 Gumligen
Switzerland

ZZERO BOOKS
Steven Holmes
BCM Zzero
London
WC1N 3XX. tel 0985 214670
Thoughtful and lively philosophy books aiming to tell some kind of truth in an original way which is usually quite upsetting to people immersed in lie. Not affiliated to any religion political group or ideological fashion. Sae list.
The Sample. 64pp p/b with extracts from all the other books. £1.50 inc. p&p
Triumph. States of Mind. Totally original analysis of the 'topography' and functioning of what we loosely call 'ego'. 124pp p/b £3.75 inc p&p. Love and Default to Hope. Book 3 in the Series The Evolution of Decency. The most original analysis ever of the topic that most preoccupies us all; this book could change your life. Approx 60pp A4 binder £6.50 inc p&p (discount on whole series of 6 books).

ZZUB BOOKS
Box S
63 Gambier House
Mora Street
LONDON
EC1
SPG has received the sad, sad news of the death of the Rev. Nigel Brough. Plans are afoot for a memorial anthology. Details to be announced.

061
20 Russell Road
Whalley Range
Manchester
M16 8DL

3:X (Previously ION PRESS 23)
Ion D'Mentiere
95 Old Castle Road,
Cathcart, Glasgow
041 833 5984
Experimental Poetry/Prose Illust. With emphasis on good design. All desirable limited editions. Catalogue due send SAE for info.
Kaaaah (tentative title); Annemarie Cooper; 48pp; due Sept 92. Poetry/prose + illustration.
Sand Writings; David Rushmer; 24pp; in print. Poetry; £1.95.

4MATION
14 Castle Park Road
Barnstaple
EX32 8PA.
Subjects: Desk Top Publishing.

4 U
Flat 4, Dorchester Court
2 Colney Hatch Lane

Muswell Hill
LONDON
N10 1BU
Writing to order. A piece written and printed just for you. A unique service. Limited editions of one. Guaranteed. SAE for details.

Small Press Group
of Britain

Full postal address: SPG, BM BOZO, LONDON WC1N 3XX, ENGLAND

MEMBERSHIP APPLICATION

Membership of the SPG costs only £15 per annum.

Members are entitled to vote at the SPG's **Annual General Meeting** and to attend our regular open meetings.

Membership also includes a subscription to **Small Press World** (price to non-members £12 p.a. + £3 p&p), which is posted to you 4 times a year and keeps you informed on Small Press activity and provides news, opinion and much more.

Members receive substantial discounts on all SPG activities:

* 50% discount on purchase of the Small Press **Yearbook**

* 50% discount on display advertisments in the Small Press **Yearbook**

* 50% discount on display advertisements in **Small Press World**

* 50% discount on exhibiting at the SPG's **Annual Small Press Fair**

plus many more.

Send details of your Imprint with 40-word description listing your three lead titles (if any), contact name and remittance to

The Membership Secretary,

20 Paul Street, Frome, Somerset, BA11 1DX.

Enquiries and Credit Card sales 0373 451777

281

SPINE: Small Press International Network Exchange

SPINE: New backbone for International Small Press

On December 4th 1989, following the successful New York Small Press Fair, the Small Press International Network Exchange (SPINE) was formed by the Small Press Centre (New York, USA), Small Press Group (London, UK) and the Small Press Action Network (Vancouver, Canada). The Three groups agreed on the following actions:

1. Exchange of memberships, so that each group regularly receives the newsletters, press releases, and other benefits of all member organisations.

2. Cooperate on Small Press representation at international literary and publishing events. All interested groups would share costs of tables or booths at large (i.e. expensive) book fairs such as the European Book Fair in Frankfurt or the American Booksellers Association Conference in the US. Member organisations present at these events (generally those in closest geographical proximity) would undertake to represent organisations that could not be present.

3. Create a SPINE News Service to formalise the exchange of information between members. All SPINE members submit notices of events or other information of international interest to small presses to be compiled into the SPINE News Column. Each organisation prints the latest SPINE News column in their newsletter or other publications.

4. Display and promote the publishers and books of other SPINE organisations. SPINE groups will exchange books of their member publishers to be displayed at their events or in their display areas.

5. Encourage participation in SPINE by other Small Press groups and associations from unrepresented and represented countries. For more information about SPINE or to submit items to SPINEws, write to SPINEws, c/o SPAN, Box 65746, Station F, Vancouver B.C., Canada, V5N-5K7.

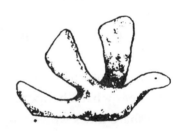

Anglo-Saxon Books

Highly recommended for dinner parties.
Monasteriales Indicia: The Anglo-Saxon Monastic Sign Language.
Learn how to order a beer or ask someone to pass the salt using 10th century sign language.

Anglo-Saxon Runes
Two books sharing the same title.
One a classic from 1840 (Kemble) and the other first published in 1992.

The Benedictine Service of Prime - Beowulf - The Battle of Maldon
All include the Old English Texts with Translations

We specialize in Old English texts and things Anglo-Saxon. New titles include *Anglo-Saxon Food: Processing and Consumption* and *An Anglo-Saxon Herbal* We welcome the submission of manuscripts for publication. In addition to books, we sell T-shirts, prints, and rune cards.

Please write for catalogue to:
25 Malpas Drive, Pinner, Middlesex, England HA5 1DQ Tel. 081-868-1564

THE NEW ENGLISH RENAISSANCE

A time when the old heroes return in new guises
and with them the values and traditions which make
human life meaningful and worthwhile

Introducing –– and written by ––

THE SHARKTI LAUREATE WRITING GROUP

Seven writers whose work has appeared in England,
America, Canada, Australia, Switzerland, India and
Korea have combined to help spearhead the concept
of a new Renaissance, originating in England.

In this unusual book, they explain individually
what this concept means to them and provide some
examples of their writings, ranging through fiction and articles, playscript and children's fantasy novel extracts, poetry, etc.

An ideal opportunity to sample the varied aspects
of the New Renaissance work of literature with
soul for which The Sharkti Laureate (a non-profit
concern) has been formed.

£2 post-free from

THE SHARKTI LAUREATE
104 Argyle Gardens, Upminster,
Essex RM14 3EU. Mail order only

Chqs/POs payable to Pamela Constantine (UK currency or IRCs)

A complete publishing field for the New Renaissance
is under preparation. Inquiries: P. Alamie Page
Send £2 for THE SOLAR COURIER, the SL's Qtly N/Letter:
articles/info on the New Renaissance plus new title
updates

SIMON KING PRESS

Publications - 1992/93

Shelley
ODE TO THE WEST WIND
Price £14

Bridges
TEN POEMS
Price £17

ORWELL - extract - Introduction to
'KEEP THE ASPIDISTRA FLYING' adapted from
CORINTHIANS XIII, together with the original version.
Price £13

SIMON KING PRESS, ASHTON HOUSE, BEETHAM, MILNTHORPE
CUMBRIA LA7 7AL

THE OLEANDER PRESS
for the eccentric and erudite traveller

The Aeolian Islands (Sicily) Philip Ward (pbk) £4.50

Albania: A Travel Guide Philip Ward £13.50 (pbk) £7.95

Annals of Oman Sirhan ibn Sirhan £14.95

Arabia in Early Maps G.R. Tibbetts £30

Arabian Gulf Intelligence (Selections from the Records of the Bombay Government, 1856) On Arabia, Bahrain, Kuwait, Oman, Qatar, UAE. 728pp. £48.75

Arabian Personalities of the 20th Century 3,700 biographies. £29.75

Bangkok: Portrait of a City Philip Ward (pbk) £4.50

Bulgaria: A Travel Guide Philip Ward (pbk) £10.95 "A beautifully written, complete account" – Newsletter, BBFS

Cam Bridges R.J. Pierpoint (pbk) £2.95 Photographic history of every bridge over the Cam in the city.

Coastal Features of England and Wales J.A. Steers £25

Come with Me to Ireland Philip Ward (pbk) £4.50

Diary of a Journey across Arabia (1819) G.F. Sadleir £13.50

A Doctor in Saudi Arabia G.E. Moloney £14.95 Travels of a New Zealander based at Riyadh 1977-82

The Emperor's Guest: Diary of a British POW of the Japanese in Indonesia D.R. Peacock £14.95

Finnish Cities Philip Ward £13.50 (pbk) £9.95 "Packed with information, particularly on art, architecture, culture and history" – Library Journal

Forgotten Games: a Novel on the Conquest of Mexico Philip Ward £7.95 "Brilliant in concept, written in prose as spare, lush and pointed as a cactus garden, as powerful and evocative as a rational nightmare, a logical daydream" – The Times

The Gold Mines of Midian Sir Richard Burton £20 First in the Midian trilogy.

Ha'il: Oasis City of Saudi Arabia Philip Ward £48.75 768pp.,107 maps and illustrations.

Hejaz before World War I D.G. Hogarth £13.50 The Arab Bureau of Cairo Handbook.

Indian Mansions Sarah Tillotson (pbk) £14.95 A social history of the haveli. Due 1992

Japanese Capitals Philip Ward £13.50 (pbk) £9.95 "The most interesting and personal guide book to appear for some time" – Japan Times

The Land of Midian Sir Richard Burton £40 the set of two completing the Midian trilogy.

Minister in Oman Neil Mcleod Innes £15.75

Motoring to Nalut Philip Ward (pbk) £2.95 Route across Western Libya

Polish Cities Philip Ward (pbk) £9.95

Rajasthan, Agra, Delhi Philip Ward (pbk) £9.95

Report on a Journey to Riyadh (1865) Lewis Pelly £13.50

Rossya: A Journey through Siberia Michael Pennington (pbk) £7.95

Sojourn with the Grand Sharif of Makkah (1854) Charles Didier £22.50 Sinai, Red Sea coast, Jiddah, Ta'if.

South India: Tamil Nadu, Kerala, Goa Philip Ward (pbk) £9.95 1991 edition

Sudan Tales: Wives, 1926-1956 Rosemary Kenrick £13.50 (pbk) £8.95

Travels in Arabia (1845 and 1848) Yrjö Aukusti Wallin £13.50

Travels in Oman Philip Ward 584pp. £27.50

Tripoli: Portrait of a City Philip Ward (pbk) £4.50 The capital of Libya before Qaddafi

Western India: Bombay, Maharashtra, Karnataka Philip Ward (pbk) £10.95 1991

Wight Magic Philip Ward (pbk) £9.95 Tales of the islanders and overners

Obtainable from charter bookshops on special order, or direct from

The Oleander Press, 17 Stansgate Avenue, Cambridge CB2 2QZ
(add £1 per paperback and £2 per hardback for delivery within the U.K.)

"Perpetual
Springtime"
a unique anthology
of thoughts, memories,
ideas, drawings, photographs,
poems, letters and essays by
Charlotte Boggis Clarke
£4.99 (+ £1 p&p)
includes a contribution to Newport
Pagnell Curch Restoration Fund

POTPOURRI PUBLICATIONS
7 Silver Street
Newport Pagnell
Buckinghamshire
MK16 0EP

WONDERFULL DEALINGS

AGNES BEAUMONT (1652-1720)was born at Edworth, Bedfordshire and baptized Ann on the 1st September 1652, the youngest of seven children (of whom three died in infancy) of John Beaumont, yeoman farmer, of Edworth and his wife Mary Pakes, of Pirton, Herts.

She is best known for a brief autobiographical account of a harrowing experience in 1674 when she was accused of poisoning her father with the help of the famous John Bunyan, a crime for which, had she been convicted, she could have been burned.

Her family was strongly nonconformist, and in 1672, having come under the spell of Bunyan's preaching, Agnes joined a congregation of his at Gamlingay. Her father had turned against Bunyan, and when he heard that she had ridden behind him to a meeting, he locked her out of the house for two days. Eventually, she promised not to attend any more meetings without his permission, and they were reconciled. That night, however, he died, probably of a heart attack, with only Agnes in the house. A former suitor, Mr Feery, the family lawyer, maliciously suggested that she had murdered him, and her brother had to summon a coroner and jury. Fortunately, Agnes was cleared of any guilt.

She died on 28 November 1720, and was buried in the Tilehouse Street Meeting yard in Hitchin. Her autobiography remained in manuscript, but copies began to circulate and in 1760 it was published in a frequently reprinted collection of conversion narratives.

Writing by women of Agnes Beaumont's social rank is rare in the seventeenth century, and her story gives valuable insight into the power of radical religious belief to inspire resistance to patriarchal authority.

WONDERFULL DEALINGS
The Narrative of the Persecution of
Mistress Agnes Beaumont in 1674
is the next title from Pythia's

Reprints of rare writing by remarkable women

Ask to be put on our mailing list
Pythia/Cecilia Press

7 Silver Street, Glastonbury, Somerset, BA6 8BS

Get Into Print

By Christopher Stevens

£6.99

Tells you:

- *How to create perfect pages using desk-top computer technology*

- *How to get the copies printed to 100% professional standards*

- *How to sell your product through the national book chains*

Paperback. Price includes postage and packing Cheques for £6.99 to: New Caxton Press, Flat Two, 11 Clifton Park, Clifton, Bristol BS8 3BX

Dealing with
Personal Problems

It seems that nothing is easy in life not even running a small press. But it's possible. The thing that has brought me into the small Press world is a deep desire to share with other people my experiences of dealing with personal problems. All our waking life we are faced with different kinds of problems. Mostly in money, health, work and relationships. I wanted to know what were the real causes of these. 6 years ago I decided to devote all the time that I could to finding out the answers. I felt I had a good start as no one knew my problems quite like me. I read all the self help books I could lay my hands on but most of them seemed too superficial and a lot of the psychology/psychiatry books were just impossible to understand. I just couldn't find an easy to follow book that helped a lay person to deal with the real deep inner personal problems, the causes of the above problems. After years of struggling trying to make sense out of my internal experiences and dealing with a lot of my problems I reached a point where I sat down one day a started to write, I was writing the book that I had looked for years before but could not find. After all this time and all the troubles I've been through I am left with a deep seated believe that all the personal problems that besiege ordinary people can be sorted out and put right before they become a person's downfall. If there are any nagging little problems in your personal life that you would be better off without then I am confident that reading my book will help you to put them right.

My book is appropriately called "How to Deal With Your Inner Personal Problems" by Martin J S Briercliffe. It is available in Paperback by mail order at £5.99 + £1.60 p&p (£7.59)

To order your copy please send with your name and address a cheque or Postal Order made payable to Interpersonal to Dept SPYB, BM Interpersonal, London WC1N 3XX.

THE EASY WAY TO ACQUIRE LITERARY MAGAZINES

As a creative writer you may have wondered about keeping up with contemporary publishing. Which are the best magazines? Who are the new poets? What are the critics saying about new verse? Who is publishing what? The advice often given to new writers is to read contemporary literary periodicals - absolutely the single best way to keep up. But there is a problem. How do you identify let alone get your hands on copies of these elusive journals? The average library doesn't stock them, high street newsagents do not have them on their shelves, bookshops are reluctant to order them. What should you do?

Oriel now provides a way forward. As a shop specialising in books for the writer, contemporary poetry and small press publications we are well placed to help. For a single payment of £35 we will mail you a different magazine each month for a year. Drawn from the full range of British literary periodicals your ORIEL MAGAZINE SUBSCRIPTION will bring you into contact with almost everything of importance being published, along with an unending list of smaller littles: AMBIT, PN REVIEW, AGENDA, POETRY REVIEW, PLANET - the list is immense.

A £35 subscription represents excellent value. for money too - many little magazines have a cover price of above £2 and we will be mailing them direct to your door. In addition your subscription will be supplemented by a number of low circulation small mags, competition entry forms, news of events and details of new publications, all at no extra cost. It is the only way to really keep in touch.

Act now. Send your £35 ORIEL MAGAZINE SUBSCRIPTION today.

Oriel
The Welsh Arts Council's Bookshop
he Friary
Cardiff CF1 4AA

I enclose my cheque for £35 payable to Oriel. Credit card payments accepted. Please charge my VISA/ACCESS (delete one) number .... Expiry date ....

From: ....

....

....
To be cost effective Oriel Magazine Subscriptions rely on bulk purchase of specific periodicals and it is therefore impossible for subscribers to select or reject individual titles.

THE SMALL PRESS CENTRE
Middlesex University
Room T202
All Saint's Site
White Hart Lane
London N17 8HR

Telephone: 081 362 5000 Ext. 6058

Hours: Noon to 5.00pm
Monday to Friday

Centre Director: John Nicholson

Send now for a prospectus and be
included on the SPC mailing list.

The Small Press Centre is
administered by the Small Press
Group of Britain Limited.

A Rudimentary Guide to Producing Your Publication

1.0 STARTING YOUR PRESS:

Choose a name for your press - an imprint you can live with, rather than one you are likely to become stuck with - and decide upon an address to use. If you don't want to use your home address, there are other options available. A **Post Office Box** (located at your local sorting office) can be obtained by filling in the relevant form and paying around £48.00 per annum. The Post Office allocates the number; you are supplied with an i.d. card and collect your mail whenever you wish. **British Monomark** (BM) numbers are more expensive. You can choose your own BM name (e.g. "BM Ken") or they will allocate you a name. Mail can either be collected at regular intervals, or posted on to your current home address - which may be useful if you are likely to be moving about a bit. British Monomarks, 27 Old Gloucester Street, London WC1N 3XX for details. You can pay for an **accommodation address**, these usually sound like a *real* address, instead of a Box Number you might be given a 'suite' or 'flat' number. **Accomodation addresses:** Angela Pike Associates, 21 Piccadilly, London W1V 9PF; Hold Everything, 162 Regent Street, London W1; Instant Office UK, 184 Temple Chambers, Temple Avenue, London EC4. And **outside London**: Elizabeth Kaspar, Little Trethigsey Cottage, Newquay, Cornwall; Simon James, 16 Preston Street, Brighton.

2.0 GETTING THE RELEVANT DATA:

If you wish to have your publication circulated outside just a circle of friends, it is a good idea to have it included in the relevant data banks that exist. Use an **ISSN** for a serial, an **ISBN** for your books and pamphlets; and get CIP data as well. What are they?

2.1 *ISBN:* International Standard Book Number. ISBNs identify publishers, imprint and book title. Single ISBNs are free, and if you are only publishing half a dozen books, there is no need to spend any money: just telephone and they will be supplied there and then. However, if you wish to select your own, you can purchase a list of 100 assigned for your use for £11.75 (1000 numbers costs £23.50). ISBNs are available only from **J.Whitaker and Sons Ltd**, 12 Dyott St, London, WC1A 1DF (tel: 071-836 8911). ISBNs get your work into bibliographic control systems, 'Books In Print', and 'The Bookseller'. Libraries and shops, which almost all have computerised accounts, use ISBNs for reference, so it is always advisable to obtain one.

2.2 *ISSN:* International Standard Serial Number. Eight figure digit used to identify periodicals and serials. Free service. Obtained from **UK National Serials Data Centre**, 2 Sheraton Street, London WIV 4BH (tel: 071-323 7166 or 7159). Send description, photocopy of contents pages, &c for their records and to get the ISSN for your serial or journal. Note that any alteration or addition to the title of the serial may require a new ISSN. (Libraries and institutions prefer users to print the ISSN on promotional literature as well.)

2.3 To have your journal or serial feature in **Current British Journals** (entries on c. 10000 journals) contact: British Library Document Supply Centre, Boston Spa, Wetherby, West Yorkshire, 1S23 7BQ (0937-843-434 x6078).

2.4 *C.I.P. data:* Cataloguing-In-Publication data. Allows subscribers to the British Library's bibliographic services to receive advance information about your publications (and to place orders). Formerly provided by the British Library, this is now supplied by **J.Whitaker and Sons Ltd**, 12 Dyott St, London, WC1A 1DF (tel: 071-836 8911; fax: 071-836 2909). There is no charge for **CIP** data. Whitaker requires advance information from you at least three months ahead of publication. Provide them with details even if you suspect that the size, pagination and publication date may change as you work on your book. **CIP** is for all books published from a UK place of publication, new and revised editions; volumes in a monographic series; the first issue of a new serial; the first issue of a serial whihc haas changed its title. Exclusions: reprints without a change of ISBN, text or imprint; non-book materials; music. Speak to Whitaker, whose handling of the **CIP** project inevitably means change in procedure. They will send you the relevant paper work, which nowadays consists of printing the following message on the verso of your publication: "British Library Cataloguing in Publication Data. A cataloguing record for this book is available from the British Library."

3.0 LEGAL DEPOSIT:
Publishers fulfill their legal obligations to the **British Library** by sending one copy of each of their publications to the **Copyright Receipt Office**, Boston Spa, Wetherby, West Yorkshire, LS23 7BQ (tel: 0937-546266) within one month of publication. Other copyright legal deposit libraries are at **Oxford, Cambridge, NL Scotland, Dublin, NL Wales.** Send 5 copies of each publication to A.T.Smail, 100 Euston St, London NW1 2HQ (071-388-5061). In practice the BL &c do not care much about the 'legality' of copyright receipt. It is of advantage to small presses to send publications in, however, with as full information as possible - for archival purposes and so on. The BL is months - years - behind in its cataloguing and is considering not including every published work in its archives: a lobby to insist on proper treatment of small press material is needed.

4.0 ADVANCE INFORMATION:
Having completed the forms for **Whitaker,** send details of your publication to some of the book retailers. **NEBS** is Blackwell's New English Book Selection department and may be of interest to small presses dealing with publications likely to be of academic interest: good-quality books primarily intended for the general reader but on subjects of academic interest should not be excluded, but there are other types of book they do not want to be informed about. For full details of their requirements, write to NEBS Dept, Blackwell's, PO Box 185, Oxford, OX1 2ED. In some cases they will order as many as 40 copies of your new titles - which is a good way to launch your publication! Send **Advance Book Information** to other library suppliers as well: the more pre- publication orders you get the better.

JMLS (formerly Menzies) have an advance information scheme: they are at JMLS, Bibliographic Services Dept, PO Box 17, 24 Gamble Street, Nottingham NG7 4FJ. Everett also have such a scheme: contact **WH Everett and Son Ltd**, Unit 8, Hurlingham Business Park, Sulivan Road, London SW6 3DU. Finally, a judiciously placed advertisement detailing your forthcoming titles will alert potential customers. Check out some of the magazines that feature in this Yearbook. (See also the section below on marketing your books.)

5.0 PAPER SIZES:

Unless you have grasped the nettle and wish to publish your work only in electronic format, you will use some sort of paper to circulate your work. Don't know what things like A4, A5 etc mean? They refer to British Standard paper sizes, as follows:

A1: 594 x 841 mm
A2: 420 x 594 mm
A3: 297 x 420 mm
A4: 210 x 297 mm
A5: 148 x 210 mm
Crown 8vo: 123 x 186 mm
Lge Crown 8vo: 129 x 198 mm
Demy 8vo: 138 x 216 mm
Royal 8vo: 156 x 234 mm
A6: 105 x 148 mm
A7: 74 x 105 mm

(You'll probably find you are using sizes A3 - A5 mostly if you are printing a magazine, book or booklet). These are the dimensions of trimmed pages. Speak to your printer before purchasing paper yourself (if there is a special paper you want to use) and check that the printer doesn't want untrimmed sheets.

6.0 MACHINERY YOU MIGHT COME ACROSS & HOW TO USE IT:

There are a few machines to which most people will have access:

most of these are so familiar and user-friendly as to require no detailed description. Here, however, follows a few hints on their use to the first-time publisher.

6.1 *Photocopiers:* Most people have access to photocopying facilities - either in your own or a friend's workplace, a high street quick printer, community centre, resource centre, library &c. Machines vary considerably: some will take virtually any paper, others are recalcitrant or produce poor quality copies. You have to find out for yourself by using the machine. The basic 'office' photocopier will reproduce your artwork in line form: the image they print is all of a piece and will reduce fine detail to blocks of black or a single colour. Some photocopiers take cartridges (blue, red, brown, &c): by passing a single sheet of paper through the copier several times, using a different colour each time, you can make fairly lavish covers for a pamphlet. Given the difficulty in registering, choose a design in which the very precise relation of shapes, text, &c on the cover is not especially important. For example, title in black, large circle in red, small circle in blue, background of yellow spots - elements that need not align precisely, though you'll want your title and name square to the edge of the paper. Your artwork in this instance should consist of four pieces of paper (all the same size - say A4), on each of which you should draw/type/paint/collage - in black - the particular elements.

6.2 *Laser Photocopiers:* State of the art laser photocopiers can screen photographic images - break the image into tiny dots, enabling clear reproduction. Some are nearly as good as photographic screening - and considerably cheaper. If you are using a printer which uses paper plates (ask them first), the image screened using a laser photocopier will produce results almost as good as if you had used a photographically-screened image, since paper plates are unpredictable when it comes to reproduction of photographs - so you can get away with a laser copy if the quality suits you. For really sharp photographic reproduction you have to use metal plates: ask your printer, who will advise you on the screening of photographs. Never paste an original photograph to your artwork: have it screened first (a photograph of the photograph is taken, using a dot-screen) and then place the screened copy in position.

6.3 *Colour Photocopiers:* Four-colour photocopiers will reproduce any colour artwork - a painting, photograph or slide. They are relatively expensive (about one pound for each A4 sheet if you are lucky to live near a **Resource Centre**; about twice this if you wander into a West End bureau). You can of course do several copies of a small design (A6 size for instance), which can then be cut out and pasted onto the front of your pamphlet. The paper most often used in colour photocopying is such that when the paper is cut a brittle edge often results (though some copiers will take textured Conqueror paper: ask - or experiment). Often, a guillotine will leave a rough edge on colour photocopies, so it is better to use a new scalpel blade to trim the images. Pasting colour photocopies of any size (A5 or bigger) often results in cracks forming on the image, especially if you need to shift it slightly. Use a wet glue or paste rather than a dry glue stick, and smooth the paper carefully from the centre; or use a hot wax roller. It is not possible to colour-photocopy onto thick card; nor to produce double-sided photocopies (since the heat from the machine melts the ink already placed on the paper): however, by fiendish and time-consuming means you can (just) photocopy a black and white text (a poem, say) onto the reverse of a colour photocopy (e.g. photo of the author fire-eating). What you have to do is carefully place an acetate over the colour copy - glue it into position at both ends with a little Pritt - before passing the sheet through the b&w photocopier. You'll make a few errors, but practice will make perfect. When the completed double-sided sheet has been printed, you'll need to trim it. Note that you should do this slowly, a single sheet at a time, and allow the photocopier to cool down between sheets: too much heat will lift the coloured ink off the paper - which can result in some aesthetically pleasing work; but which can also muck up your photocopier.

6.4 *Silkscreens:* With a silkscreen you can produce spectacular results for very little money, but it takes a fair amount of time, patience and skill. Single colour silkscreening is very simple - it gets more difficult the more colours you want to use. There is not enough room here to describe how to go about silkscreening; but there are plenty of books available on the subject (Dover Books publish at least one), and your local arts centre, adult education or resource centre will probably be able to help; or best of all, find a friend who knows something about it. Silkscreens vary in size from those you can use on the kitchen table to large units which will take A1 paper. One of the difficulties in silkscreening a card book-cover using several colours is (as with the monochrome photocopiers) registration. Only practice and patience (and plenty of mistakes along the way) will allow you to overcome this problem. A dust-jacket is an easier option (thinner material), or an image which can be cut out and stuck on the cover.

6.5 *Printing Presses:* Most small presses do not have their own printing press. If you do, you will not need any advice here as to how to use it. For those of us who must rely on commercial printers, there are a few things worth bearing in mind. The first rule is, write down in clear hand-writing exactly what you want the printer to do for you - at every stage. Your printer will have many jobs going at once and cannot be relied upon to remember the minute details of your particular job.

Always write down your instructions EVEN IF the printer says (s)he understands.

6.6 Some printers - those using metal plates rather than quick print affairs - will provide you with layout sheets (which you will usually be charged for). The quick print printers will expect you to provide artwork pasted up to the dimensions of the finished publication (i.e. don't lay out an A5 pamphlet on huge layout sheets and then expect the quick print printer to trim them). Before presenting your artwork, ask the printer you plan to use what you should do and how (s)he wants the copy presented. Ask for a mock-up - so that you can layout the sheets in the correct order for plate-making. Ask about what size grip edge (the area of paper that the printing press grasps and which therefore must be left blank) is required for covers and pages.

Don't be afraid to make an idiot of yourself, and don't wait to feel a fool until after the job is done - **always** ask beforehand if you don't know: it is your money and your publication that is at stake. This cannot be stressed enough.

7.0 MATERIALS:

Your text can be prepared at home using a quill, blunt pencil, typewriter, electronic typewriter, dot-matrix, daisy wheel, or any other instrument that will make a mark on paper. You can have your text typeset using a desktop laser printer (which uses more or less ordinary paper); or phototypeset it at a bureau (onto bromide, using a hugely expensive piece of equipment such as a Linotron). Bromide produces the best results, but it is more expensive. As always, it depends on your resources and what quality you are aiming for. Don't be put off - or, for that matter fooled - by the so-called 'new technology': word processing is quite simple to master, but it does not provide a short-cut to instant results. You (or someone you pay or whose arm you twist) still have to put in the work: the machine does not do it for you, though such things as spell-checkers do make life slightly easier. Keep copies of all your files and remember while you are word-processing to save files frequently. Don't get carried away and type all night - only to find at dawn that the ten thousand word masterpiece you wish to save is lost because of some inexplicable fault on the machine. Save as you go, stick to small files, and make a habit of taking copies of your work.

8.0 TYPESETTING:

Most people would agree nowadays that a right-justified text is better than a ragged edge (verse often doesn't need it, of course). There are still those Luddites who prefer mechanically typewritten text, as being 'uncorrupted' (e.g. numerous New Age Traveller type publications). Nowadays most word-processors and many electronic typewriters offer proportional spacing: only the recalcitrant will persist in using a typewriter, which is nevertheless still the cheapest way to produce your typescript. However, the public perception is that the work is 'unfinished' somehow, not a 'proper' publication: the content of a work is appreciated less readily than its form. This is a matter of taste, of course, but consider who your readers are going to be.

There are numerous typesetting bureaux which can give you advice: these all want you to come back another time and use them again. They may sell you typesetting software, which enables you to do most of the work at home (coding text, determining page layout, &c) or they may offer you the use of their machines. Ask about disc compatibility if you have a word processor at home. Most bureaux will give you more or less impartial advice. Laser typesetting is improving all the time and while the results are not as fine as phototypesetting, they are at least adequate. Take care of your artwork: put it in a folder or envelope to keep it clean; if you must roll it up, do so in such a way that the image of the artwork shows on the outside - this means that when you come to pasting up, the artwork does not leap away from the page.

8.1 Computer graphics and DIY typesetting are at a fairly rudimentary stage, aesthetically speaking. The technology is there, the skill to produce good results is generally lacking. The only way round this is, as ever, to use the machines and software as much as possible - which in practice means having access to the right equipment in your home, at a college or your office. The new technology means that many complex and skilled operations can now in theory be done by anybody. The reality is that crass and shoddy work is often passed off as exciting and innovative.

9.0 ILLUSTRATIONS:

For images, if you are not particularly talented and have no artistically inclined friends, go through old books lying round the house; use an enigmatic photograph or old postcard - or a detail of a picture; produce a collage or montage; get out your rotring and draw it yourself. Use a jointed metal blowpipe in a pot of ink instead of an air brush. You can buy one for a pound or so at any graphics supplier (perhaps they have a technical name for them). Collage tip: take a black felt-tip-pen with a hard, broad tip and very carefully run it across the cut edge of the scraps of paper you are using. This way the ragged edge of the collage elements will not show.

9.1 A useful resource for images is **The Dover Bookshop** at 18 Earlham St., London WC2 (tel: 071-836 2111). Dover allow you to use up to ten images from any one of their books (fat volumes of out of copyright images on a variety of subjects) in any one of your own publications. The only disadvantage lies in the fact that such images tend to be very widely used and become almost hackneyed. The trick is to select some apposite detail that can be incorporated into your own design. Distort it on a laser photocopier if you like.

9.2 Another possibility, if you've nothing lying round the house, or want special images, is to contact the **British Association of Picture Libraries**, an association of 200 picture libraries and agencies. They have a directory too. Contact them at 13 Woodberry Crescent, London N10 1PJ (tel:081-883 2531). You must pay a royalty fee for use of Picture Library images.

9.3 Note that you can also obtain images from the **British Library** in London; they will charge about £15 for the use of one of their copyright images. One problem some people find is gaining access to the B.L. Many people are successfully intimidated by the institution. You should not be put off. The thing to do is knock up some pompous looking headed note paper, type a letter explaining that the bearer of the letter is employed by (name of your press) to research some obscure subject or other (the very obscure is always a good bet); say that it will take at least two years to complete your project; mention that you cannot travel outside London because of work or financial reasons; mention your entire reliability and so forth; and have someone ('the Director of the Press' etc) sign it. Give a couple of references if necessary. Or get an SPG pal to write such a letter: one with academic qualifications is best. Such subterfuge may not be required, but it is more effective than protesting that the B.L. is public property and that it is your right to have a pass.

10.0 PASTE-UP:

Your typeset text and finished images are back on the kitchen table. You've got a plentiful supply of coffee, cigarettes, biscuits, snacks, designer drugs - whatever you need to get you through paste-up.

10.1 You'll need a few tools. A **blue pencil** for any marks on your artwork and to write in special instructions for the printer (blue doesn't show up when the printer makes the plates); a **sharp blade** (a surgical scalpel is best, scissors will do for simple jobs); some **glue** (Pritt is 'dry', quite clean; Cow Gum is wet, collects dirt, aerosol cans of spray-mount glue are poisonous - take your pick), or better still some **wax**.

10.2 A **hot wax roller** costs a fair amount - about fifty pounds - but is a worthwhile investment if you plan to do a few publications rather than a one off; or if you plan to do a fairly large job (e.g. a long magazine with plenty of photographs). Wax is clean and it allows you to reposition artwork without damaging it. When you've positioned the artwork, and given it the once over with a roller, wax also gives a smooth, flat surface (excess wax can be removed with **lighter fluid**) - which is important when it comes to the plate-making stage.

10.3 The flatter the surface of the artwork, the better: things like great chunks of typewriter correction fluid and the curling edges of badly glued paper will show up in the plate: the printer will need to erase them, which will cost you more money (often a lot of money: a 64 page magazine every page of which requires touching up, charged at the current union rate, is several times the cost of a wax roller). If you are using a photocopier, this isn't such a problem, of course: there you will want to ensure that the edges of the various pieces of artwork are not visible. Make a good copy of the finished paste-up job and use a photocopier fluid to erase any visible marks.

10.4 When trimming artwork to size and pasting up, it's a good idea to put any rubbish you might generate into a plastic bag, keeping this separate from general household waste. This way, if you find at the end of the paste-up, when you're checking everything is in order, that you have accidentally thrown away something essential - it might be something as minute as a single letter, more probably a line of text that has somehow gone astray - you can recover it without having to wade through discarded teabags, empty cans and other trash.

11.0 PRODUCING OTHER ITEMS:

Postcards, tee shirts, badges: in their own right or as promotional items linked to your publication, these can also be sold in outlets which would not take books. Record shops and comic specialists are two obvious outlets: many record shops have started to stock books as an extension of marketing badges, postcards, tee shirts, then comics, magazines and so on. Badge making machines are likely to be found at a local resource centre; or you can have badges made to your design by someone else. Tee shirts can be silkscreened - try an adult education centre or a local silkscreen printer, or one-offs can be done in high street bucket shops. Postcards can range from the very simple (a poem typed onto a sheet of card four times, the card then cut into four) to full colour jobs that you'll need to do in their thousands.

12.0 DESIGN/FORMAT:

The design of your publication is not merely a matter of indulging your artistic inclinations: it has an effect on the publication's sales and the response of its readers. By all means try to produce something that satisfies you - but bear in mind the publication's existence beyond the confines of your mind and your circle of indulgent friends - try to imagine what others, those who don't know you and won't know how much effort has gone into your publication, will make of your work.

12.1 *Basic Pamphlet design*: without a spine, your publication has limited chances in a bookshop. It will most likely be consigned to a rack, which means that only the top third of the front cover will be visible: and it is here that the essential information should be placed. It is no use having the title of an unknown story by a known author here - put the author's name instead! Likewise, don't put the author's name here if it is the issue with which the pamphlet deals which is important. You can create an artificial spine for a pamphlet by using a dust-jacket. You will still have a very thin spine, but it's better than nothing at all. A spine gives you access to that most scarce of resources: a bookshop shelf.

12.2 *Basic book jacket design*: the spine is all important. Reading top to bottom, this is where your basic information should be placed: title, author and (if there's room) name of press. On the back cover (to which every reader turns instinctively) have some explanatory blurb, the **ISBN, bar-code** (if applicable) and price. The front cover is where you can indulge yourself. Providing the basic information is repeated somewhere here, you can do just as you please. The front cover will not be on display for very long, remember: most shops will only have it on show for a few weeks after the book is published, so it may as well be as eye-catching and bright - or as enigmatic - as possible. If you are using a photograph on the cover, ask your printer about duotones and dot- for-dot printing. For a duotone, the artwork is photographed from two opposing angles: the two plates are used for printing the image, one in black and one in colour. Dot to dot printing produces a similar effect. Here the same plate is used. Having printed the image once in black, the plate is very slightly shifted and the image is reprinted in colour.

12.3 *What material do you want to have your work printed on?* The printer will provide you with samples of paper compatible with their machines. These vary from place to place. You can provide your own paper, or your own card for the cover of a pamphlet - but bear in mind the printing machinery might not take to the stock you've chosen. Ask the printer before you commit yourself to ordering vast quantities of unusable paper. Lavish papers (you can buy a few sheets and photocopy onto them) and handmade, marbled, textured papers are also generally available, as is recycled paper. Your printer should be able to provide recycled and/or acid-free paper (made from rags, acid-free does not decay as rapidly as paper made from wood pulp: think of posterity). Ask for it if you want it. For advice and further information on the quality of recycled papers, contact Earth Matters, FoE, 26-28 Underwood Street, London N1 7JQ; or Paperback (tel 081-980-2233).

Other considerations:

13.0 COPYRIGHT:
The recently revised **copyright** laws do not hugely affect small presses in any practical way. Copyright is broken every day by a vast number of people, businesses and institutions. Almost no one would pursue a claim against an obscure and impoverished outfit which remains largely out of the public eye. Those with principles will want to credit their source at least, even if they cannot pay them a substantial amount; only the despicable or lazy will reproduce without permission work by parties similarly unable to pursue their rights. In other words, don't rip off your fellow small presses and

316

others. Pay them what you can - after all, you are paying the printer, the typesetting bureau and so on. Most sympathetic parties will let you use their material, even for nothing, but if you are reproducing a substantial item, have the courtesy to ask first, if you can track them down.

13.1 Further (and precise) information about the sticky and largely incoherent state of copyright is available from **The Patent Office,** Copyright Enquiries, Room 1504, State House, 66-71 High Holborn, London WC1R 4TP (071-829-6145); and from **The British Copyright Council,** Copyright House, 29-33 Berners St, London WlP 4AA (071-580-5544). Copyright resides in any original work: you do not necessarily have to put the formal copyright sign on your work, though it is done for form's sake. Quoting from other works (a song, for instance) is allowed without payment of royalty fee, &c, if you are quoting for critical purposes or similar (but credit the copyright owner, the publisher in most cases): i.e. if you are not 'in competition' with the actual song, lyric, etc. Fair dealing is mostly a matter of common sense, but the state of the law is such as to confuse many into parting unnecessarily with money. Read up on the acts of the law at the **British Library** if in doubt.

14.0 **PAYMENT:**

If you really are in no position to provide a contract and decent royalty, pay what you can, when and if you can. Price your publication so that the writer or illustrator can expect at least a token payment. Give the author some books - not only copies of their own work, but items from your back catalogue and so on as well. If you are the author as well as the publisher, so much the better.

14.1 Paying **designers** to spice up your product is not particularly worthwhile: the cash is better spent in other ways. First, professionals charge fees even bigger than you'd expect; secondly, make your own mistakes, you will learn something useful from them. It is not necessary to overdo your design job. Let the idiosyncrasy shine through, keep it simple - just ensure that it is readable (for other people as well as for yourself: nothing is more off-putting than an illegible text: how are you meant to read the book?). Ultimately, no amount of formal flourishes will disguise a lack of content. Use a bureau or consultancy if you are ignorant of DTP &c. Find one that is reasonably priced and the staff of which you can get on with.

15.0 PRICING YOUR PUBLICATION:

Ideally, the retail price of your publication should be at least five times its cost. In practice, a small press usually ends up charging little more than three times the unit cost, allowing them to break even (bearing in mind the bookshop's cut of one third of the retail price). When pricing your book, think about who is going to sell it as well as who is going to buy it. The average bookshop will not be particularly interested in making only ten pence on one of your publications: they want to make some money and shelf-space has to be fought for! Then again, if you deal directly with mail-order purchasers, you can afford to be more generous. Think before you underprice or overprice your product. Look around and see what others are charging, ask yourself what you would pay, consider the overheads of the shops you deal with... then decide what to charge.

16.0 MARKETING:

Not just a buzz word. Rather something to bear in mind from the word go if you seriously want to shift your product (though of course your product may be deliberately unmarketable in which case skip this bit). First, does your press have an identity, a profile, some integrated sales pitch? Leaf through the Yearbook - most press names indicate an attitude, an area of concern or interest. Think about how to make some rapid sales of your book: a launch party is a good idea for a start...

17.0 PROMOTION:

A launch party needn't take place in a hotel suite or exhibition hall. Get your local bookshop to lend you some space; hire a room above a pub for a few quid; launch your book with a reading at a local festival (or downstairs in a pub); have a picnic in the park... the possibilities are endless. Try and think of some angle to launch the book: link it up to a contemporary event, a suddenly fashionable notion, go out of your way to be wacky and attract attention. You may be ignored, but people will enjoy themselves and cough up the money. Bully your family and friends into parting with cash there and then.

17.1 Annoy a few journalists. Kick up a fuss. Send out your press release a few weeks in advance and then again when the deadline approaches. Write the press release in easily digestible chunks. Mark it **"Press Release"**, mark at the top of each page in terms of how long the release is (e.g. "1 of 2" at the top of the first page, "2 of 2" at the top of the second); at the bottom of each page write "mf" ("more follows") or "ends" (marking the end of your press release). Try to put as few words as possible in each sentence: never use words of more than three syllables. The average journalist reading the release will want as far as possible to rewrite it (and not necessarily in their own words) in a format that the average reader can understand straight away. Include a sentence or two that expresses an opinion or makes a statement in quotation marks (e.g. "It is my second book," said seasoned author Ken, aged 59): the journalist will use this to give the impression that you've actually been interviewed. Your publication will be competing with hundreds of others, so don't expect instant results. It is not easy to get reviews, let alone good reviews. If you can somehow tie the book in with other newsworthy events, enabling a feature article to be written, the result may be very good (for instance, a single article in the Guardian Weekend section on one small press sold 500 copies of a book that had been in print and ignored for several years). Send review copies, dust jackets &c. as well.

18.0 Advertising:
Advertising is an additional expense and something of a gamble. You will not necessarily get results: a twenty pound ad might sell one book; a five pound ad more suitably placed may sell several hundred. Ask around, see where other small presses are advertising, use your common sense. Exchange ads with other specialist publishers. Something else to bear in mind is placing other people's ads in your publication, be it pamphlet, book or magazine. These will offset the

production costs. Remember to advertise, at the very least, your own product in the back of the book or pamphlet. With magazines, make sure that any subscription and advertising details are prominently displayed in each issue.

18.1 *Make the advert readable*. Nothing is worse than an advertisement that looks shabby: it costs very little to produce something decent, yet again and again small presses seem to opt for grotty, third-generation photocopies of ancient artwork. Black on white works best (reversed out is not as eye catching, market researchers suggest): make a clear statement, providing details of what is for sale and who is to be paid. The financial transaction is the whole point of the advertisment, after all.

19.0 MAIL ORDER:

Mail Order is labour intensive and often tedious, but you are cutting out the middle man and can establish a more personal relation with your customers if you so wish. Since book shops are increasingly rigid in their attitudes, and tend to stock only well-established work, mail-order can be especially useful for a small press (or a gang of small presses: team up with a few like minds in your locality).

19.1 When compiling a mail-order list - say you've received two dozen orders for your publication, responses from an advertisement or announcement (remember to keep the addresses) - ask each person on the list to send the names and addresses of five or six of their friends who'd like to receive news of your forthcoming publications. Put a note in your catalogue to this effect. That way, your list of contacts will gradually expand. If you receive no response after a few months from a particular person, just cross them off your list. (If you keep your list of customers on computer disc - and this applies also to journal subscription lists - you are obliged to tell them so; under the terms of the Data Protection Act 1984, anyone who objects to these details being stored in this way may ask for their particulars to be kept in a written record.)

20.0 BOOKSHOPS:

With many shops that you visit, you will find that a **Sale Or Return** policy is operational. This is a cross that every small press is obliged to bear. It is justified when applied to magazines and journals limited in their scope by a specific time (e.g. television programme details etc). However, its application has been extended to virtually every publication which the laws of fashion and economics suggest might appear redundant. Its widespread approval by bookshops up and down the country reflects the virtual abandonment of retailers' faith in the publications they sell; and the lack of information about the nature of publications to which the general public has access.

20.1 Non-bookshop outlets are also worth considering. While it is doubtful that the local supermarket will be very interested, outlets such as health shops, railway stations, garden centres &c may take some small press items.

20.2 "Are you reaching the right bookshops?" asks the **Booksellers Association,** which can provide peel-off labels of booksellers for around £10 per 100. They can also provide lists of specialised booksellers (children's; academic; libraries; religious &c). Full details from Booksellers Association Service House Limited, 154 Buckingham Palace Road, London SW1W 9TZ.

21.0 INVOICING BOOK SHOPS:

When you receive an order, send the shop an invoice with the books, marking clearly the date, your address and who the cheque should be made payable to; and the **terms of payment** (e.g. "Payment on receipt of this invoice: no statement will follow" or "Terms: 90 days"). Shops will expect a publisher's discount (33%, increasingly often more). It is up to you whether you charge postage (and how much): give maximum reduction for bulk orders (33% post-free), charge more the fewer the items ordered. If a shop orders one copy of a pamphlet costing £1.20, charge them postage as well. It is not your fault if the shop only makes five pence. Very small orders are likely to be specific requests from customers: the shop offers the service as a courtesy and does not (at least, cannot) expect to make a profit out of such marginal work. Remember to put a flyer for your other publications inside the book when you despatch it - or have some sticky labels printed that urge readers to write for your free catalogue.

21.1 Expect to wait up to several months for your invoice to be paid. Send a **statement** if you haven't received your money after four months or so. The law - a stiff letter couched in legal terms - is a last resort. You will soon establish which shops are likely to be regular customers and which are not. Spread the word about shops that don't pay at all: warn others of their attitude. A good tip that may help small presses owed money is to include the following on your invoices: "As per the advice on late payment from the Minister of State for small firms, after one month from the date of this invoice, we legally require you to add 2 per cent to the total, and a further 2 per cent for each further month's delay in payment thereafter."

22.0 REPPING:

Telephone the bookshop before you lug your suitcase of product along: ensure that the Buyer is in and will see you. It is no good speaking to the expert in the stationery department if you're trying to shift your philosophical magnum opus. Make an appointment, take along a sample of the work you're dealing with, and try and meet the requirements of the bookshop. It's a lot of work, of course - phoning up, selling the books, calling back with the right quantity, invoicing, etc, etc - but there is often no alternative. Few tasks are quite as soul-destroying - or character-building, depending on your point of view - as repping, but try and bear in mind the bookshop's requirements, not just your own wishes. If a shop thinks (or knows) it can sell a particular product, it will place an order. If the buyer knows the book will not shift, you won't get an order. The buyer is in the position he or she is in because they know - generally - what kind of customer their shop attracts. The best will in the world will not sell a volume of psychic poetry in a shop which specialises in maps or economics. Remember too that while your interest might be Literature or Philosophy or Politics, the buyer's sole interest is Cash Flow. A buyer is more likely to have risen up through the stationery departement than to have a degree in English. Try and persuade the buyer, by all means, but try not to be disillusioned if you can't sell your books straight away.

22.1 Consult other small presses, see how they sell their product. Gang together with like-minded publishers and have one of you do the repping for your area. Bookshops don't much like having to deal with two dozen small publishers when they could deal with only one central supplier: the paperwork is less, less time is used up. Which leads us onto the next point: you could become a distributor yourself, or...

23.0 DISTRIBUTORS:

You may wish to have your publication distributed by other parties. It's hard work slogging round bookshops begging them to buy your wares. So much easier if someone else would do it. Ring up and make an appointment, take a few copies along, convince the distributor that you are 'serious'. Do this before official publication, if possible, or at any rate as soon as it is feasible - the distributor will not want to be selling your old stock after you've already been to all the obvious shops. The various established distributors stick more or less to tried and tested product, items they know will sell. A distributor will require a percentage of the price of your publication (between 15 and 25 per cent); they will present you with regular sales reports; and pay you at an arranged time of year (e.g. three months in arrears). **23.1** *What is a distributor looking for?* First, something that will fit into their profile, a publication they think they can sell. You should be able to ascertain what kind of material they sell over the phone. Suppose the content of your book is apposite, what then? If the distributor is sure it will sell tolerably well, consider the design of the publication and the price. Where sales are more or less guaranteed because the subject is topical, don't ruin the book's chances by making the cover hideous or having the text set in an unsuitable font. If in doubt, have a friendly chat with the distributor and ensure you are not going to scupper the project. A laminated cover will probably be essential, general descriptive text should be readable (in a serif typeface), and the price should give adequate amounts to you as publisher, to the distributor and to the bookshop. If you've no luck, and are therefore obliged to do it yourself, again - why not get in touch with a few other small presses and see if they want stuff taken round the shops at the same time?

24.0 OVERSEAS DISTRIBUTION AND EXCHANGE:

One way of broadcasting your publication is to sell it in the American market. There are a few distributors who are worth contacting: always send a copy of your book and ask for a current catalogue in return: and pass this on to a fellow small press if the distributor does not cater for your product. 'Local' material is very hard to shift abroad, for obvious reasons, and only if it has a very strong political bias of more general application - or if it provides an interesting view of a hidden part of the world - will an overseas distributor be likely to bother with it. America is a vast market compared to Britain, let alone to your home town, but bear in mind that your book, by the time it is shipped to the States, will have to be put on sale at a relatively high price; and that books printed in the USA are anyway a lot cheaper than their equivalent here. So your product will be at a disadvantage: it will be obscure to begin with, and expensive to boot. Don't be put off by such considerations - but approach the prospect of an overseas market in a sober fashion and don't expect miracles.

25.0 FAIRS:

Fairs are another way to shift product: the **SPG Annual Book Fair** takes place every September, the **ALP** run a similar but smaller event every year as well - and there are numerous other events. It is worth trying a book fair in your locality at least once, if only to confirm your worst fears.

25.1 John Nicholson, SPG co-founder, offers these tips for small press fairs:

A. Find a suitable **venue,** one which you think is perfect. If it enthuses you then your excitement will help to persuade others.

B. Float the idea on people who you are sure will share your enthusiasm.

C. Widen the **circle of people** who know of the proposed fair. Get their feedback. That will draw them in so their enthusiasm increases the momentum.

D. All of you make a **list** (have a meeting in the pub or each other's houses) of anybody you can think of involved in similar or related activity. This will be the starting point not only of the organisers but of a **mailing list.**

E. Compile another list of **official organisations** and firms who should be interested. You will be surprised how many will be vulnerable, i.e. want to take part.

Enthusiasm is the key in John's view: small presses are at a disadvantage in that their resources are limited, so a conviction that the fair is worth doing is essential, as is the organisational ability to attract the book buying public.

There is an area in the **London Book Fair** (three days at Olympia every March) called the **Small Press Area**. This fair is the British Publishing world's beano involving libraries and bookshops. A stand costs hundreds of £s which indicates their definition of a small press. It means small publisher. In 1991 a visitor had to pay £10 - each day so no browsers! Anyhow you shouldn't sell just take orders. So it's not much use to small press as we know it.

There are **specialist fairs:** blacks, women, comics, private presses, poetry, political, anarchist etc. All have flourished for years and you can find out about them by contacting people who participate eg specialst presses or the distributors listed in the Yearbook. The National **Convention of Poets and Small Presses** is a moveable feast and a variable one as it has a dogma: no central organisation, so we can't give you a contact. There are scattered fairs of the traditional 'let's have a glorified party' sort which take over the upstairs room in a pub and invite everybody and their friends. These can buy enough to pay for the hangover. Then there are the familiar Readings fairs where poets read and then sell what they read.

From this survey you see there are huge gaps which are now filled by the **SPG's Annual Small Press Fair.** In 1992 it transcended all the fairs described, including the commercial ones. It transcended publishers because it had the back-up services (listed elsewhere in this guide) such as DTP studios, illustrators, binders, cheap printers, mailing agencies and distributors. It is this Yearbook in 3D. The complete kit in one place for one day. The potential of the small press phenomenon can be seen at this fair, which is growing annually while maintaining a low level of charges to exhibitors. It can do its annual promotion, launch new titles and catalogues, make contacts and deals, get publicity - and sell. This fair is established as a national opportunity without equal for British small presses and has become the British date in the world small press calendar.

25.2 Some book fairs to take note of: **Feminist Book Fortnight** - for details please write to FBF Group, 7 London House, Church St., London NW8 (01-402-8159); **Anarchist Book Fair**: books, pamphlets, food, accordion music. Every year, usually late October. Contact: **A Distribution** for details: 071-558-7732; SPG and ALP annual fairs: contact the organisations for full details: addresses in this Yearbook.

25.3 *International Book Fairs*: only in exceptional circumstances will a small press go to an international bookfair. For many, they are entirely irrelevant; but for others they can be useful and the **Small Press Group** as a body has determined to attend as many as possible, taking SPG titles along and offering representation for publishers who would otherwise be left out. Attendance at such Fairs costs a lot: several hundred pounds usually, which can only be met by a group of publishers co-operating and presenting their single titles together under the Small Press banner. The results are difficult to gauge, but generally must be considered positive. **The Frankfurt Fair** is the major international fair and occurs every October. **The London Book Fair**, which takes place in Spring, is increasingly an event for remainder dealers and reflects poorly on Britain's attitude to publishing. This trade event attracted only a couple of hundred ordinary citizens - so you cannot expect to sell direct many copies of your books. The **American Booksellers Association Fair**, in a different city each year, is far better in terms of organisation and response to small press product.

26.0 PRIZES, GRANTS, &C:
Remember, your publication may be eligible for an **award** or **prize**; and you may be able to get a publication financed.
Prizes:
26.1 *Guide to Literary Prizes, Grants and Awards in Britain and*

Ireland, compiled by **Book Trust** and **Society of Authors**. From Book Trust, Book House, 45 East Hill, London SW18 2QZ. Tel: 071-870 9055. This booklet, updated annually, provides addresses of regional arts associations, many of which are able to finance some small press and related activities; and details of prizes and awards available from other bodies. Prizes range from small monetary awards for books contributing to Franco-British understanding to the **Quatrefoil Award** - cash for the author of the book judged to have contributed the most towards an understanding and/or love of oriental rugs - with plenty of others in between.

26.2 *Scott Moncrieff Prize:* £1000 awarded annually for best translation of a French text into English, published in the UK by a British publisher. 20th century texts of literary merit and general interest will be considered. Boost your small press budget by contacting: **Translator's Association,** 84 Drayton Gardens, London SW10 9SB. (Three copies of the work and of the original are required).

26.3 *Arts Council Of Great Britain*: a source of grants and information (it says here). Contact Antonia Byatt, Literature Officer, Arts Council, 14 Great Peter Street, London SW1P 3NQ.

26.4 *Elephant Trust,* 1 Campden Mansions, Kensington Mall, London W8 4DU (tel:071-229 2504): was created by Roland Penrose with a view to advancing public education in all aspects of the arts and to develop and improve the knowledge, understanding and appreciation of the fine arts in the United Kingdom. Write for their guidelines if this is your area of interest.

26.5 *British Book Design and Production Exhibition*: held annually by British Printing Industries Federation and Publishers Association. Details from 11 Bedford Row, London WC1R 4DX (tel: 071-242 6904). Numerous **award categories** (General Hardback, Mass Market Paperback, Children's Book, Illustrated Book, Limited Editions, Exhibition Catalogues, &c), reasonable entrance fees, closing date early February.

27.0 USEFUL PUBLICATIONS:
There is an increasing supply of advice - guidebooks, catalogues, how-to-do-it books and all manner of sourcebooks - on th market.

If you find this guide inadequate - and it is only intended as an introduction - then check out some of these publications. There are more than we can list so ask at your library. If you are the sort of person who won't act without advice read them. Otherwise save you time and money. Make your own mistakes, you'll pay attention then. If you are greedy for advice there are loads of courses, costing hundreds of £s and we haven't bothered to note their addresses (call yourself a small press?) but your library may know. If you want a qualification: **London College of Printing**, London Schools of - Writing, Publishing, Computer Studies, Computer Technology. See the details of the new Small Press Centre in Part 1 of this Yearbook - the SPG plans seminars and other educational interventions in the coming year.

27.1 *Alan Armstrong's Top 3000 Directories and Annuals 1990/91*. Published by **Dawsons**, Alan Armstrong Ltd, 2 Arkwright Road, Reading, Berkshire RG2 0SQ.

27.2 *Alembic Guide for Private Presses*. Covers the world for private presses: services and contacts. Invaluable. (see Alembic).

27.3 *Alternative Printing Handbook* (Penguin £3.95) is recommended by Last Ditch. Published 1983 so it may be out of print, but well worth tracking down'.

27.4 *Artists Newsletter,* PO Box 23, Sunderland SR4 6DG (tel: 091 567 3589) are interested in small press matters and publish a bi-annual supplement on Contemporary British Artists' Books. They also do a list of handbooks, directories &c for artists, craftspeople and photographers.

27.5 *ALP* publish a very useful newsletter, PALPI and an annual catalogue (see below: 'Other Organisations' and Section 2 for details).

27.6 *The Book Exchange*, 9 Elizabeth Gardens, Sunbury-on-Thames, Middlesex TW16 5LG (tel: 09327 84855) is 'the international journal appraising new books in English'. Send them your catalogue and ABIs.

27.7 *Book Marketing News*, Book Marketing Council, The Publishers Association, 19 Bedford Square, London WC1B 3HJ. ISSN 0264-3219 is a trade paper with useful news items and some symptomatically interesting insights into the workings of the trade.

27.8 *"Booknews"* listings: write to Book Trust, 45 East Hill, London SW18 2QZ to be featured.

27.9 *The Bookseller*, the trade's magazine, is published by Whitaker, 12 Dyott Street, London WC1A 1DF.

27.10 *Bookwatch,* 7-up Sycamore Place, Hill Avenue, Amersham, Bucks HP6 5BG (tel: 0494 728232) are national bestseller list compilers for the Sunday Times, Daily Express, Daily Telegraph, The Bookseller, &c. They publish 'Books in the Media', weekly listing of around 1,000 titles linked to tv, radio, films &c. Free helpline service for subscribers. Market research for publishers including weekly retail sales tracking in national sample with option of tv regional breakdown.

27.11 *British Book News*, the British Council's monthly journal for bookbuyers, is at 65 Davies Street, London W1Y 2AA (tel: 071-930 8466). Advance book information forms must reach them three months before publication. Call Nigel Cross on 071-389 7865 for further information. He is the Forthcoming Books Editor. Subscription to BBN (ISSN 0007-0343) is £24.75 p.a. (UK individuals); single copies are £2.25.

27.12 *Directory of Specialist Bookdealers* in the UK, listing 740 bookshops, is available from Peter Marcan Publications, 31 Rowliff Road, High Wycombe, Bucks HP12 3LD. Price £20.00.

27.13 A new directory of children's writers from Scotland 'will help anyone arranging a children's book event to find authors, poets or illustrators willing to take part. £2.50 from **Book Trust Scotland**, 15a Lynedoch Street, Glasgow.

27.14 *'Edinburgh Review'*: one of this journal's many good features is its interest in small press activity of all sorts and from all countries. Always of interest to small press enthusiasts. Contact: The Editor, Edinburgh Review, Polygon Books, 22 George Square, EH8 9LF Scotland.

27.15 *The European Bookseller*, Tranley House, Tranley Mews, 144-145 Fleet Road, London NW3 2QZ. Tel: 071 485 5994. "The magazine for Europe's English language book trade".

27.16 Freelance News: quarterly update about freelance scene for publishers. £6.50 subscription from Elvendon Press, Freepost, Goring-on-Thames, Reading RG8 9BR

27.17 *Freelance Writing & Photography*, a quarterly magazine 'which aims to provide stimulating ideas, inspiration and encouragement to all freelance writers and photographers'. Sub is £7.50 p.a. Tel: 061-928-5588 for further details.

27.18 *A Guide To Independent & Privately Published Periodicals* (2nd edition) is available from G.Carroll, 11 Shirely Street, Hove, East Sussex. Check it out if periodicals are your area of interest.

27.19 *How To Publish Your Poetry*, Peter Finch (Alison and Busby, 126pp, £6.99) is written by a widely published poet and bookshop manager. Packed with useful advice, remarks and wise saws from many poets, practical hints, plus a thorough bibliography. For the would-be poet, this is an invaluable handbook.

27.24 *Independent Media*, £15 p.a. sub from Freepost Independent Media, c/o DVA, 7 Campbell Court, Branley, Basingstoke, Hants RG26 5BR.

27.21 *Inky Parrot Press*: publishing outlet of the Graphics Section of Oxford Polytechnic Design Dept. The catalogue of **Fine Press Printing** was compiled by Inky Parrot as part of the Second Conference of Fine Printing and is the most comprehensive listing of private printing presses currently available, with details of 185 in the UK plus the most recent Fine Printed publications of 81 of them; plus 23 specialist suppliers of materials and services. It costs £9.50 post free from Inky Parrot Press, Design Dept, Oxford Polytechnic, Headington, Oxford OX3 OBP.

27.22 *Independent Publishers Guild* 'Bulletin': a publication from the IPG, 147-149 Gloucester Terrace, London W2 6DX. Occasionally features items concerning small press activity.

27.23 *'Private Press Books'* is published by the **Private Libraries Association,** Ravelston, South View road, Pinner, Middlesex. Worldwide compilation of fine print works. Write for more details.

27.24 *Publishers Handbook*, published by Grosvenor Press International, is worth looking at in your local library if you want more information. This is a 'trade' publication, 468 pages long, with information on Agents, Design, Marketing Services, Distribution,

330

Sales, &c.

27.25 *Publishing News,* Gradegate Ltd, 43 Museum Street, London WC1A 1LY (tel: 01-404-0304). Bombard them with your press releases!

Writers News, Brunel House, Newton Abbot, Devon TQ12 4YG. Tel: 0626 61121. A new magazine for writers.

27.26 *The Writer's Guide to Self Publishing,* Charlie Bell (Dragonfly Press, 24pp, £2.25). A little booklet aimed at the amateur writer who wishes to see his or her work in print, containing the usual solid advice, clearly laid out for the beginner.

27.27 *The Writer's Handbook* (Macmillan/PEN), edited by Barry Turner, is described as 'the complete reference for all writers and those involved in the media'. Contributors include Peter Finch.

27.28 *Writers News,* Brunel House, Newton Abbot, Devon TQ12 4YG. 0626 61121. A new magazine for writers.

27.29 Writers and Artists Yearbook: details from 35 Bedford Row, London WC1R 4JH. Available in your local library.

27.38 Look through this Yearbook and you will find lots more: Dragonfly, Hi-Resolution, Antony North, Quartos, Weavers - who offer advice of different sorts.

27.30 *Small Press World,* 11 Ashburnham Road, Bedford, Bedfordshire MK40 1DX. A new magazine that has grown out of *Small Press Monthly* under the editorship of John Nicholson. Quarterly, covering all subjects of interest to the autonomous publisher, with plenty of news, networking, letters, new publications listings and much more. Essential, a supplement to this *Yearbook* and an indispensable tool.

27.31 *Getting Into Poetry* is a readers' and writers' guide to the poetry scen by Paul Hyland, published by Bloodaxe Books, PO Box 1SN, Newcastle upon Tyne, NE99 1SN. Price £5.95, ISBN 1 852241 18 7, it is to designed to help the reader in "the jungle of contemporary poetry".

28.0 OTHER ORGANISATIONS:

The SPG does not exist in a vacuum or work in isolation. Far from it. Here follows details of other, related organisations, which may be of more benefit to you or which may better suit the profile of your press. Kennedy said, "Ask not what the SPG can do for you, but what you can do for the SPG" - and this should be your attitude when approaching mutual-help groups!

28.1 *The Association of Little Presses*, 89a Petherton Road, London N5 2QT. See entry in Section 2.

28.2 *Independent Publishers' Group*: a new group formed by a wide range of independent newspaper and magazine publishers who wish to draw attention to the rich diversity of independent publication and to safeguard their future in the face of an increasing concentration of media ownership. Titles affiliated include "British Bike", "Marxism Today", "New Statesman and Society", "Outlook" and "Everywoman". Tel: 071 359 5496.

28.3 *Homing-In* is an organisation catering for anyone working from home, including publishers. Newsletter published 6 times a year, meetings, &c: 656 London Road, Milborne Port, Sherborne, Dorset DT9 5DW (0963-250764).

28.4 *Women In Publishing*: was founded in 1979 and now has a worldwide membership of over 500. They welcome all women working in publishing and related trades. Monthly meetings are held on the second Wednesday of each month, at 6.30 for 7.00 pm, at the Publishers Association, Bedford Square, London WC1. All women are welcome. Membership is £15 p.a. (unwaged £10). Entrance charge for non-members is £1.00 (unwaged £0.50). They also run about a dozen **training programmes** each year. Speakers and course leaders for all **Women in Publishing** courses are senior professional women from within and outside the book trade. The courses are administered by a small group of volunteers. If you would like to help organise and plan courses, contact the Training Officer. The courses are open to all women. All one day courses are held on Saturdays at convenient London venues, and lunch, coffee and tea are included in the price. All meals plus two nights' accommodation are included in the price of the residential weekend. WiP aims to promote the status of women within publishing; to provide a forum for the discussion of subjects of interest and the sharing of information and expertise; to encourage networking and mutual support among women; to offer practical training for career and personal development. Contact:

WiP, 12 Dyott Street, London WC1A 1DF.

28.5 *Hands Off Reading Campaign*: opposed to introducing VAT on publications. At 1 Dean's Yard, Westminster, London SW1P 3NT (01- 799-9811).

28.6 *BAPA:* British Amateur Press Association. Founded 1890: membership composed mainly of people concerned "with receiving and reading the various amateur publications which BAPA sends out on behalf of the members who produce them". Few members produce magazines: circulation is mainly confined to BAPA members, the publishers not seeking the general public readership. Contact: 78 Tennyson Road, Stratford, London E15 4DR (01-555-2052).

28.7 *Independent Publishers Guild,* 147-149 Gloucester Terrace, London W2 6DX.

28.8 *The Publishers Association* is "an association run by and for its publisher members, and to be eligible for membership you must be a bona fide publisher of books and/or learned journals operating in the UK. The association is primarily concerned with representing the interests of publishers to the UK and foreign governments, the European Commission, and other bodies in the book trade to ensure that publisher's interests are safeguarded, and that the government gives us all possible assistance." Full details if you think they'll have you from 19 Bedford Square, London WC1B 3HJ (071-580-6321).

28.9 *Federation of Radical Booksellers*, c/o Lifespan, Townhead, Dunford Bridge, Sheffield S30 6TG.

28.10 *Campaign for Press and Broadcasting Freedom.* Tel: 071-923-3671.

29.0 TOOLS AND SERVICES: CONTACT ADDRESS:

29.1 Electric 'handy' **wax rollers** and wax to use in them are available from Caslon Ltd. Wax is £4.10 + VAT a box, a roller is £54.50 + VAT. Caslon is at 15 Bakers Row, London EC1. Tel: 071-837 3131. Both rollers and wax are light enough to be posted.

29.2 Interesting **paper and card** (suitable for instant print style printers) and envelopes, &c: from G.F.Smith & Son, 2 Leathermarket, Weston Street, London SE1 3ET (tel: 071-407 6174). They will accept fairly small orders (i.e. 500 sheets of A4) and can emboss certain types of card with curious textures. Ask them for a brochure. **29.3** Universal **Filters** for PCs are available from Polaroid. Protects your eyes from low frequency radiation. Widely available. For your stockist, contact CW Cave & Tab Ltd, 5 Tenter Road, Moulton Park, Northampton NN3 1PZ. Tel: 0604 643677. Fax: 0604 648542.

29.4 *Community Copy Art*: friendly, cheap, pleasant. Macintosh **DTP, Laser Photocopying** including reasonably priced **colour** photocopies, design facilities (wax, paste-up materials, &c). In our opinion, the best place in London to use if you haven't got your own 'studio'. Community Copy Art, Culross Buildings, Battle Bridge Road, King's Cross, London NW1. Phone 071 833 4417.

29.5 *Words & Images:* a partnership consisting of a freelance graphic designer and an editor/writer; a complete in-house writing and design service. Reasonably priced **electronic publishing, editing, proof-reading,** reviewing, design for print, book production - the works. For further information see entry and advertisement in this Yearbook.

29.6 *Icon Graphics*, PO Box 69, Aberystwyth, Dyfed SY23 2EU (tel: 0970 625 205): **DTP, design and layout,** direct mail services, promotional services, typesetting, fax services &c.

29.7 *Northern Writers Advisory Services*, 77 Marford Crescent, Sale, Cheshire M33 4DN (tel: 061 969 1573). See advertisement in this Yearbook. They aim to provide good copy-editing, proof-reading, word-processing and DTP at prices small presses can afford. Copy-editing and proofreading and DTP at £5.00 per hour. A word of advice from NWAS: "A plea for copy editors - they only add slightly to the cost of production; they can save your eyes and spot that one silly typo before the readers do!"

29.8 *Link Up,* 51 Northwick Business Centre, Blockley, Glos GL56 9RF, is a small **desktop publishing** team based in the Cotswolds. 'We are concerned with Green and environmental issues, focussing on what is working in the world, instead of always emphasising what is not. We support Natural Healing methods and Complementary Medicine - realising that they have a part to play in maintaining health. These ideas of welcoming change as a creative opportunity are promoted through our quarterly magazine, also called Liñk Up. Although this publication comprises the main part of our work we also carry out personal and comprehensive typesetting and general office services.' Tel: 0386 701091

29.9 *'Gamecock'*, Peter Lloyd, 11 Park Road, Rugby, Warwick (tel: 0788 76913): **typography,** graphic design, printing.

29.10 *Hi Resolution,* 4 Smallbridge Cottages, Horsmonden, Kent TN12 8EP, are a **DTP** service offering typesetting, consultancy and troubleshooting services. 'People use Hi Resolution because we're fast, friendly and intelligent. For a job with no specification we'll make sensible decisions or if you know what you want that's what you'll get'. Phone 0580 211194.

29.11 *Peter Stockham Associates,* Staffordshire, 'offer a comprehensive **consultancy** service to satisfy all publishing needs': see entry under "Images" in main directory for phone details &c.

29.12 *Roger Booth Associates,* 18 - 20 Dean Street, Newcastle upon Tyne NE1 1PG (tel: 091-232 8301) will give a quotation for **typesetting** (and printing if required) of your publications. Output at 300 dots per inch on laser printer. Recommended by ALP.

29.13 Typesetting undertaken by Counter Productions. Tel: 071-274 9009 now. Numerous fonts available, advice - we've assembled this DIY guide - and if we can't do it we'll tell you who can.

29.14 *Top Floor Design,* Lion House, Muspole Street, Norwich NR3 1DJ (tel:0603 660237) 'is an innovative graphic **design** consultancy that offers a complete service from concept to print, specialising in publishing and editorial design.'

29.15 *Opas Ltd,* Suite 11, Kinetic Centre, Theobald Street, Borehamwood, Herts WD6 4PJ (tel:01-207 2462) provides engineering and maintenance service to the typesetting industry. They can supply and service a wide range of **office equipment.**

29.16 *Cygnus Media Services,* 45 Woodlands Road, Earlswood, Redhill, Surrey RH1 6HB (tel: 0737 768812) offer **typesetting, sub-editing, disk conversion** and printing.

29.17 *Ennisfield Print & Design* will quote for long and **short run books** and also offer typesetting and design services. Tel: 071-729 0515.

29.18 *David Green Printers Ltd*, Kettering, Northamptonshire, offer a complete **in-house service** from disk to distribution. Tel: 0536 522458.

29.19 *Greater Manchester Council* for Voluntary Service advises on **DTP** to non-profit groups. Tel: 061 2737451.

29.20 *HA Office Supplies*, Unit 2, 9 Long Street, London E2 (tel: 01-739 8765) specialises in new and reconditioned **office machinery**, paper, ribbons, &c, &c. Recommended by Bob Cobbing of ALP.

29.21 Freelance **graphics** from SPG member Geoffrey McAllen: "Based upon 18 years in the colour field and an ONC in printing research and sciences, I have decided to offer my services to a general sphere of small publishers and printers, specializing in quality design and reproduction". Contact: Mr. G.McAllen, Glanrhyd, Llanfair Clydogau Lampeter, Dyfed, Mid-Wales.

29.22 *Preston Editions*: Peter Preston in one weekend **typeset and prepared for printing** the entire MS of 336 page book. Not bad. Want to know more? Contact 5 Creek Road, East Molesley, Surrey

29.23 Antony Rowe Ltd: the market leader in **short run book printing**. Highly recommended by very many SPG members. Contact: Antony Rowe Ltd, Bumper's Farm, Chippenham, Wiltshire, SN14 6QA. Tel: 0249 659705; fax: 0249 443103.

29.24 *SRP:* also highly spoken of, the **Short Run Press** similarly specialises in an area likely to be of interest to small presses. Phone: 0296-631075

29.25 *Union Place Resource Centre*, 122 Vassall Road, London SW9 6JB (071-735-6123). All your **printing** requirements met. Cheap **DTP**.

29.26 *The Printing Centre*, Store Street, London WC1, offers cheap use of **typesetting equipment** (at very reasonable prices). Recommended by many small presses.

29.27 *Instant Print West One*, 12 Heddon Street W1 (01-434-2813). Very reasonable **Printing of booklets**. Recommended by numerous small presses.

29.28 *Leulex*, Unit 5, 203-213 Mare Street, London E5 (tel: 071 533 4446) is a cheap **printer** recommended by Romer Publications. Also a cheap source of stationery &c - ALP recommended.

29.29 *PDC Copyright,* 33 Lower Bridge Street, Chester CH1 1RD, is a **printer** recommended by SPG North. Tel: 0244 311073.
29.30 *Dot Press:* as used by WiP. Dot **prints** stationery and magazines through to four-colour books. Tel: 0865-326611.
29.31 *BPCC Wheatons Ltd* (tel: 0892 544366) **print runs of 1000 or more.** They provide a Book Plan Diary, free layout sheets &c. The Sales and Marketing Director at head office has written to us pointing out, however, that they are "now tending to deal with larger publishers than [sic] smaller ones." So take note!
29.32 *Ormond Road Workshops,* 25 Ormond Road, London N19 (tel: 081 203 3865). Excellent **screenprinting** facilities, dirt cheap, with a very helpful staff, creche facilities, &c.
29.33 Barcodes are available from **Symbol Services,** The Baltic Centre, Great West Road, Brentford, Middlesex TW8 9BU (081-847- 4121). Shipments are made within 24 hours. They can provide codes in film form; or on sticky labels - if you suddenly find that, after all, you need a bar code for a book that you have already had printed.
29.34 *Numeric Arts* is another supplier of **bar codes.** They are at Gardner Road, Maidenhead, Berks, SL6 7PP (0628-39753) and, in the North of England, at PO Box 39, Congleton, Cheshire CW12 3LY (0260-278853).
29.35 Barcodes Limited is at Vale Road, Portsdale, E.Sussex BN4 1GD: 0273 422093.
29.36 Craft Bookbinding undertaken by John Westwood, The Malt House, Church Lane, Streatley, Reading RG8 9HT (tel: 0491 873001). Fine Bindery, Unit One, Bridge Approach, Mill Road, Wellingborough WN8 1QN. (0933/276689.) Panther Press, Duckmill Lane, Bedford MK42 0AX. (0234/60176) Shepherds Bookbinders also make papers and have a shop at 76b Rochester Row, London SW1P 1JU. If you want more binding information contact The Society of Bookbinders, 49 Albion Road, Reigate, Surrey RH2 7SY.
29.37 *W. MacCarthy & Sons,* 310 - 326 St James Road, London SE1 (tel: 071-237 1946), make **cardboard boxes and containers** in short runs - 'any design you want, well and reasonably priced and in as short a run as you want - which makes them unique', writes Liver and

Lights.

29.38 Bubble Wrap Packing is available in bulk from Peter Hunter, 21 Cooperative St, Coventry CV2 1PT (tel:0203 682576); and try your local Yellow Pages.

29.39 Labels - for price changes, distribution stickers, &c - are available from Able Label, Steepleprint Ltd, Earls Barton, Northampton NN6 OLS. Tel: 0604 810781 for details.

29.40 Fly Weight **envelope stiffener:** from Challoner Mktg Ltd, Amersham, Bucks: 0494 721270. Lightweight stiffener to stop your artwork and publications from being destroyed in the post.

29.41 Sentinel Foam Ltd, Hart Street, Maidstone, Kent ME16 8RQ (0622 677151): supplier of padded **envelopes.**

29.42 Cheap **professional typesetting** from BB Books, Spring Bank, Longsight Road, Copster Green, Blackburn, Lancs BB1 9EY (0254 49128). IBM electronic composition.

29.43 *Emjay Reprographics*, 17 Langbank Avenue, Rise Park, Nottingham NG5 5BU. Tel: 0602 751753. "A reliable and experienced mail-order, printing and distribution facility".

29.44 T shirts printed by Jen Tait, 2 Baggrave View, Narsby, Leicestershire LE7 8RB UK. Write for details.

29.45 T shirts printed by Calm Down Puppy, 332 Commercial Way, London SE15 1QN. TEl: 071 639 7603. As used by the SPG!

29.46 *Wellington Reprographics*: specialist **printing** company, which also offers **typesetting** and studio service. Tel: 081 463 0888.

29.47 *Typedone*, 404 Solent Business Centre, Millrook Road West, Southampton SO1 0HW. Tel: 0703 702681. **DTP** Bureau, offering massive typeface range.

29.48 Paper suppliers: **Paperpoint, Wiggins Teape Fine Papers Ltd,** 130 Long Acre, London WC2 9AL. Vast range of exciting **papers,** from poster paper through to thick card. Tel: 071 379 6850. Falkiner Fine Papers in Southampton Row, London are a helpful shop. John Purcell, 15 Romsey Road, SW9 0TR. 071/737/5199. If you want real parchment contact The Parchment Works, Willen Road, Newport Pagnell, Bucks MK16 0DB.

29.49 *Kadocourt Ltd*, Unit 11 Faraday Road, Rabans Lane, Aylesbury, Bucks HP19 3RY, are **binders and finishers** offering a range of services to publishers, including shrinkwrapping, re-covering, slip cases, &c &c. Tel: 0296 86192.

29.50 Printed reel to reel **label** specialists: Essex Labels, 44k Leyton Industrial Village, Argall Avenue, London E10 7QP.

29.51 Ever wondered where to get that cold seal sticky **corrugated cardboard** for packing books? It's called Cushionwrap and it's from the low profile British Sisalkraft Ltd, Commissioners Road, Strood, Kent ME2 4ED. tel: 0634 290505 and they'll put you in touch with a local supplier. This is invaluable for those presses doing mail order who have awkward-sizes books to pack. And it is cheaper than many padded envelopes.

29.52 Recycled products available from **Millway Stationery Ltd,** Chapel Hill, Stansted, Essex CM24 8AP. Tel: 0279 812009. According to the ALP Newsletter, the cheapest source for stationery etc.

29.53 *Neal's Yard Desktop Publishing Studio,* 'the launderette of DTP' is at 2 Neals Yard, WC2 (tel: 071-379 5113). Now well-established, they offer all kinds of facilities. **DIY DTP** from £6.00 an hour. They write: "We try to provide highest quality machines and expertise to individuals and small organizations who would not otherwise have access to such resources."

29.54 *Outset Mailing Centre,* Cannon Wharf, 35 Evelyn Street, London SE8 5RT (tel: 071-23\ 9923, fax: 071-237 0159) offer direct mail services.

29.55 *BMS LTD,* Merlin Way, North Weald Ind Estate, North Weald, Epping, Essex CM16 6HR (tel: 037882-4343, fax: 037882-4552) offer mailing services for publishers and the direct marketing industry.

29.56 *John Morin Graphics,* 82a Gaffer's Row, Victoria Street, Crewe, Cheshire CW1 2JH (tel & fax: 0270-211455): typesetting and page make-up on Macintosh computer, scanning and or available. Free sample settings short run printing for magazines and booklets at very reasonable rates. Free information pack and advice freely given.

29.57 *High View,* Bernard Harrison, Moorland Way, Gunnislake, Cornwall PL18 9EX. Tel: 0822 833500. Fax: 0822 832500. "High

View undertakes complete in-house design, typesetting, printing, binding and distribution services. The advantages of dealing with a single professional contact in all these fields are obvious and are greatly appreciated by our clients."

29.58 *Intype*, Jennie Clark & Eric Shields, Input Typesetting Ltd, Woodman Works, Durnsford Road, Wimbledon Park, London SW19 8DR (tel: 081-947 7863). "Low cost short run book service. Books, book proofs, reprints, manuals, catalogues, price lists, in-house magazines, fanzines, programmes, on-demand publishing. Runs of 25 up to 1000 copies. Fast delivery, comptetitive pricing, help and advice, price scale on request."

29.59 *Chris Hicks, Bookbinder*, 64 Merewood Avenue, Sandhills, Oxford OX3 8EF (tel: 0865-69346). "We undertake binding, repair and restoration work on books of all types and periods. We can also execute short-run work, solander and slip cases, presentation and fine bindings."

29.60 *InterMedia Graphic Systems Ltd*, Brian Howard, Lewes Business Centre, North St, Lewes, East Sussex BN7 2PE. Tel: 0273-478725. "Supplier of DTP software, hardware, training and consultancy. Bureau service supplies disk copying facilities, tapes and data cartridges. PC & Apple computers, monitors, scanners, laserprinters &c."

29.61 *56a Info-Bookshop*, is at 56 Crampton Street, London SE17, near the Elephant and Castle, in South East London. "We specialise in worldwide anti-capitalist and anti-authoritarian goodies but we encourage small presses to send us catalgoues or check the store out. We open Monday, Thursday and Friday from 3 to 7pm."

30.0 **PROMOTION & DISTRIBUTION:**

Beware. Many of these distributors take only a few clients. Self help is the first and last resort of small press. Do it yourself. Cooperative mailings are a common practice of American small presses. They can lead to joint catalogues and joint distribution schemes. Obviously this makes sense if the presses involved share a profile. eg they all produce quality paperbacks or hand-made books. The same applies the other way to zines, cheapo oddities or little poetry magazines. Shared enthusiasms - science fiction, occult, locals, deviance - cut across formats. The idea won't work if too many take part or the range is too diverse. That is why the SPG can't do it as a group. But a perfect use of this Yearbook would be to form 'sections' for mutual cooperation under the SPG's aegis. Distribution is the final hurdle. But then small presses sell somehow so it never stopped us before.

30.1 *A Distribution,* anarchist and related material, 84b Whitechapel High Street. London E1 (tel: 071-558 7782). SPG member.

30.2 *Airlift Book Company,* 26-28 Eden Grove, London N7 8EF (01-607 5792): deal in Literature, Women's titles, Mind/Body/ Spirit, General: much of it American. Some small press distribution.

30.3 *AK,* 3 Balmoral Place, Stirling, Scotland FK8 2RD: Stockists of 'the complete range of anarchist and related literature in print in Britain today, from all the publishers big and small, as well as loads of out of print and difficult to find stuff'; including matter from overseas, titles concerning feminism, squatting, punk, animal rights, ecology, situationism, etc. Write for a full list of titles. SPG member.

30.4 *A Mail* offer labels: see entry elsewhere.

30.5 *Anticopyright Poster Distribution Service,* 30 Piercefield Place, Adamsdown, Cardiff, South Glamorgan, Wales.

30.6 Annual Touring **'Grey Literature' Exhibition**: Alan Armstrong Ltd, Specialist Booksellers, 2 Arkwright Road, Reading RG2 0SQ (Fax: 0 734 755164).

30.7 *Bookspeed,* independent wholesaler, 48a Hamilton Place, Edinburgh EH3 5AX (tel: 031 225 4950).

30.8 *Central Books,* 99 Wallis Rd, E9 5LN (081 986 4854).

30.9 *Collets Library Supply Service,* international book suppliers, library suppliers, subscription agents. Tel: 0933 224351.

30.10 *Counter Productions,* PO Box 556, London SE5 0RL (tel: 071-274 9009): select mail order of small press material (including SPG members), North American anarchist and post-modernist publications, books, magazines, journals and much more. Write for free catalogue. SPG member.

30.11 *Cromwell Books Services,* Jubilee House, Chapel Road, Hounslow, Middlesex.

30.12 *Element Books Distribution:* Longmead, Shaftesbury, Dorset SP7 8PL (0747-51339). Distributors of books concerned with spirituality, mysticism, psychology, and related 'alternative' matters. Few small press items.

30.13 *Gazelle* describe themselves as a distributor for small publishers and a 'complete marketing service for the UK and Europe'. Gazelle Book Services Ltd, Falcon House, Queen Square, Lancaster LA1 IRN (tel: 0524-68765).

30.14 *Haigh & Hochland,* journal subscription services, international university booksellers, The Precinct Centre, Oxford Road, Manchester M13 9QA (tel: 061 273 4156).

30.15 *Momenta Publishing Ltd,* Broadway House, The Broadway, Wimbledon SW19 IRH are publishers' representatives specialising in academic, technical and medical works. Yearly fee up front required. Slide package taken round to potential buyers.

30.16 *Monolith Distribution,* John Harrison, 2 Baggrave View, Barsby, Leicestershire, LE7 8RB. A mail order book and magazine service, dealing in prehistory, stone circles, Stonehenge, earth mysteries, ley lines, UFOs, paganism, New Age travellers, festivals, alternative living. Send SAE for free catalogue.

30.17 *The Morley Book Co.Ltd,* Elmfield Road, Morley, Leeds LS27 ONN (tel:0532-538811).

30.18 *Password* specialises in distribution of poetry to the booktrade. Before three million shower them with effusions they expect a very high standard of production values from clients. They have Arts Council backing. 23 New Mount Street, Manchester M4 4DE.

30.19 *Paul Green,* 83(b) London Road, Peterborough, Cambs PE2 9BS UK. Distributor of imported poetry and poetry related material. Many titles from Canada and USA; some remaindered stock. Also British poetry presses Northern Lights and Micro-brigade. Send off for lists and regular updates.

30.20 *Publisher's Databank* (for marketing research purposes &c): The Ultimate Database Company, 97 Valence Road, Lewes, East Sussex BN17 1SJ (tel: 0273 473135).

30.21 *QED Books* specialise in materials for schools. Shared mailings, distribution and exhibitions. 1 Straylands Grove, York YO3 0EB.

0904 424381.

30.22 *Scriptomatic Ltd*, 'mailings made easy', Scriptomatic House, Torrington Park, London N12 9SU.

30.23 *Shelwing*: is a mailing house created especially to assist publishers. They offer high-quality shared mailings to library suppliers and booksellers regularly. For further information, please write to Shelwing Ltd, Warner House, Bowles Well Gardens, Off Wear Bay Road, Folkestone, Kent CT19 6PH; or telephone 0303 56501. They might solve your publicity problems.

30.24 *Spacelink Distribution*: specialists in paranormal and UFO phenomena: see Section 2 for details.

30.25 *Specialist Knowledge Services,* Saint Aldhelm, 20 Paul Street, Frome, Somerset: subscription agent, consultancy & mail-order book-service providing a wide catalogue of psychic, mystical and alternative titles (tel: 0373-51777).

30.26 *Turnaround*, 27 Horsell Road, London N5 1XL: distributors of material, including small press, mostly relating to social issues and issue-politics. They distribute this Yearbook.

30.27 *Universal Subscription Service Ltd*, subscription agents and booksellers, Universal House, 3 Hurst Road, Sidcup, Kent DA15 9BA.

30.28 *The Unlimited Dream Company:* representation of small press, especially science fiction, and budding authors. Signings and promotions organised. SPG approved! Contact Mr Paul Gamble, 127 Gaisford Street, Kentish Town, London (tel: 071-482-0090). SPG member.

30.29 *Vine House*, distributors - contact Richard Quibb, Waldenbury, North Common, Chailey, East Sussex BN8 4DR (082572-3398).

30.30 *BEBC* is The Bournemouth English Book Centre Ltd, 9 Albion Close, Parkstone, Poole, Dorset BH12 3LL. Tel: 0202-71555, fax: 0202-715556. Described as "a complete distribution service for small publishers".

30.31 *BRAD* is Book Representation and Distribution Ltd, at 244a London Road, Hadleigh, Essex SS7 2DE. Tel: 0702-552912, fax: 0702-556095.

30.32 *DS4A Distributors* is c/o Greenleaf Bookshop, 52 Colston

Street, Bristol.

31.0 OTHER RESOURCES:
* The **Poetry Library** is located at the Royal Festival Hall, South Bank Centre, London. Tel: 071-921 0943. Free membership, about 45,000 titles in stock - and information service on bookshops, magazines, workshops &c, &c.
* Centre for Alternative Technology at Llwyngwem Quarry, Machynlleth, Powys, Wales SY20 9AZ (0654-2400): mail order books, pamphlets, information on **alternative technology** - 'technology as if tomorrow mattered'. The Alternative Technology Association (same address) publishes an annual report and newsletters. osh format).
* Small Press **Archive**, University College London, Gower St., is an archive administered by Geoffrey Soar (tel: 387 7050 x 2617).
* **Miniature Book Society**, Ian MacDonald, 11 Low Road, Castlehead, Paisley, Scotland PA2 6AD.
* Provincial Booksellers Fairs Association run lots of fairs all over Britain. Old Coach House, 16 Melbourn Street, Royston, SG8 7BZ. 0763/348400.
* Booksellers Association Directory, 154 Buckingham Palace Road, SW1W 9TZ.
* **REFER**, the journal of the ISG (reference libraries) Charles A Toase, Wimbledon Reference Library, Wimbledon SW19 7NB.

32.0 MEDIA CONTACT ADDRESSES:
See what they will carry, then bombard them!
32.1 UK trade publications:
Books, 43 Museum Street, London WC1 (tel: 071-404 0304)
Bookcase, W.H. Smith & Son, Greenbridge Road, Swindon (tel: 0793 616161)
Bookselling News, 154 Buckingham Palace Road, London SW1 (tel: 071-730 8214)
Library Association Record, 7 Ridgmount Street, London WC1 (tel: 071-636 7543)
Books For Your Children, 34 Hardorne Road, Edgbaston, Birming-

ham B15 3AA (tel: 021 454 5453)

Book Marketing News, 13 Bedford Square, London WC2 (tel: 071-580 6321)

Printing World, Benn Publications, Sovereign Way, Tonbridge TN9 1RW (tel: 0732 364422)

New Library World, Seaton House, Kings Ripton, Huntingdon (tel: 04873 238)

Bookdealer, Suite 34, 26 Charing Cross Road, London WC2 (tel: 071-240 5890)

32.2 UK consumer publications:

City Limits, 3rd Floor, 115 Shaftesbury Avenue, London WC2H 8AD (tel: 071-379 1010)

The Daily Express, 121 Fleet Street, London EC4P 4JT (tel: 071-353 8000)

The Daily Mail, Northcliffe House, Tudor Street, London EC4Y OJA (tel: 071-353 6000)

The Daily Telegraph, Peterborough Court, South Quay, 181 March Wall, London E14 9SR (tel: 071-538 5000)

Evening Standard, Northcliffe House, 2 Derry St, N8 5TT (tel: 071-938 6000)

The Financial Times, Bracken House, 10 Cannon Street, London EC4P 4BY (tel: 071-248 8000)

The Guardian, 119 Farringdon Street, London EC1R 3ER (tel: 071-278 2332)

The Independent, 40 City Road, London EC1U 2DB (tel: 071-253 1222)

The Listener, 199 Old Marylebone Road, London NW1 5QS (tel: 071-258 3581)

Literary Review, 51 Beak Street, London W1R 3LF (tel: 071-437 9392)

London Review of Books, Tavistock House South, Tavistock Square, London WC1H 9JZ tel: (071-388 6751)

The Mail on Sunday, Northcliffe House, London EC4 (tel: 071-353 6000)

The Observer, Chelsea Bridge House, Queenstown Road, London SW8 4NN (tel: 071-236 0202)

The Spectator, 56 Doughty Street, London WC1N 2LL (tel: 071-405 1706)

The Sunday Express, 121 Fleet Street, London EC4P 4JT (tel: 071-353 8000)

The Sunday Telegraph, Peterborough Court, South Quay, 181 Marsh Wall, London E14 9SR (tel: 071-538 5000)

The Sunday Times, 1 Virginia Street, London (tel: 071-782 5000)

Time Out, Tower House, Southampton Street, London WC2 (tel: 071-836 4411)

The Times, 1 Virginia Street, London (tel: 071-782 5000)

The Times Literary Supplement, Priory House, St John's Lane, London EC1M 4BX (tel: 071-253 3000)

Today, 70 Vauxhall Bridge Road, London SW1V 2BP (tel: 071-630 1333)

32.3 *TV & radio:*

LBC, Communications House, Gough Square, London EC4 (tel: 071-353 1010)

GLR, 35a Marylebone High Street, London W1 (tel:071-486 7611)

'Bookmark', BBC TV Centre, Wood Lane, London W12 7RJ (tel: 081-743 1272)

The Media Show, 4th floor, 24 Scala Street, London W1P 1LU (tel: 071-323 3270)

Capital Radio, Euston Tower, London NW1 (tel: 071-388 1288)

Daytime Live, BBC TV, Pebble Mill Road, Birmingham B5 7QQ (tel: 021 414 8888)

Kaleidoscope, BBC Radio 4, Room 8057, Broadcasting House, London W1A 1AA (tel: 071-580 4468)

BBC Breakfast Time, BBC TV Centre, Wood Lane, London W12 7RJ (tel: 071-743 8000)

TV AM, Breakfast TV Centre, Hawley Crescent, London NW1 8EF (tel: 071-267 4300)

Today, BBC Radio 4, Broadcasting House, London W1A 1AA (tel: 071- 927 5566)

Outlook, BBC World Service, Bush House, Aldwych, London WC2 (tel: 071-240 3456)

Bookshelf, BBC Radio 4, Broadcasting House, London W1A 1AA

(tel: 071-927 4634)

World of Books, BBC World Service, Bush House, Aldwych, London
WC2 (tel: 071-240 3456)

33.0 *Use this Yearbook.*
Go through it and note down anything interesting, useful or daft.
Highlight it in day-glo so you can find it quickly. Contact people who
you like the sound of. Ask them for advice. They may ask you how
you cope. You can soon build up a mailing list of potential sympa-
thisers or, hopefully, friends. Always put your name, imprint and
return address on the mail you send to each other. You may build up
a network of people who agree to mutual publicity if only at the level
of exchanging free adverts or listings in each others publications. Use
the directory as a huge publicity resource just as the **Small Press
Group** does. We send members batches of posters to distribute for
their group's fair. Think of the vast and varied audiences. Through
its membership the **SPG** reaches thousands who other groups don't
reach. Steer your own course. But use your common sense. You
waste your time and money, and upset others, if you do blanket
mailings. Not everybody is sympathetic. And tell us how you get on
- next year your tip will be in this guide.

33.1 *Buy from this book.*
There must be something in here you want - and can't get anywhere
else. Send the cash (and p&p).If you don't buy from each other why
should others buy from you? **And please mention this Yearbook.**

Index
to the DIY Guide

Introducing **THE BOOK FACTORY-**

Bringing real economy, adaptability and service to book production.

We are specialised Perfect Bound Book & Manual printers and finishers and this specialization enables us to offer you runs from as low as 100 copies!

Now you can now have professionally printed and finished books, ideal as short-run reprints or First-Time printings, really economically and really fast.

If you need longer runs, we're still the best around! Runs up to 5000 copies can be printed, bound and delivered in two weeks (or even faster if required) and at prices that you'll find really attractive.

We control the entire operation from platemaking to delivery because we have all the necessary equipment in-house, so we are not dependent on outside suppliers. This also allows us to control the quality of your job, from start to finish.

We're sure that you'll see just how important a service like ours could be to your publishing operations, so please call us for a quote or more information on how the Book Factory can save you both money & time and solve your short and medium-run book printing problems.

The Book Factory
PERFECT-BOUND BOOK AND MANUAL PRINTERS & FINISHERS

35/37 Queensland Road, London N7 7AH
Telephone: 071 - 700 1000
Fax: 071 - 700 3569